THE OXFORD HANDBOOK OF

PHILOSOPHY OF DEATH

THE OXFORD HANDBOOK OF

PHILOSOPHY
OF DEATH

Edited by

BEN BRADLEY

FRED FELDMAN

JENS JOHANSSON

OXFORD
UNIVERSITY PRESS

OXFORD
UNIVERSITY PRESS

Oxford University Press is a department of the University of Oxford.
It furthers the University's objective of excellence in research, scholarship,
and education by publishing worldwide.

Oxford   New York
Auckland   Cape Town   Dar es Salaam   Hong Kong   Karachi
Kuala Lumpur   Madrid   Melbourne   Mexico City   Nairobi
New Delhi   Shanghai   Taipei   Toronto

With offices in
Argentina   Austria   Brazil   Chile   Czech Republic   France   Greece
Guatemala   Hungary   Italy   Japan   Poland   Portugal   Singapore
South Korea   Switzerland   Thailand   Turkey   Ukraine   Vietnam

Oxford is a registered trademark of Oxford University Press
in the UK and certain other countries.

Published in the United States of America by
Oxford University Press
198 Madison Avenue, New York, NY 10016

Library of Congress Cataloging-in-Publication Data
The Oxford handbook of philosophy of death / edited by Ben Bradley,
Fred Feldman, and Jens Johansson.
p. cm.
Includes index.
ISBN 978–0–19–538892–3 (alk. paper)
1. Death.   I. Bradley, Ben, 1971–   II. Feldman, Fred, 1941–   III. Johansson, Jens.
BD444.O94 2012
128′.5—dc23
2012009021

ISBN 978–0–19–538892–3

1 3 5 7 9 8 6 4 2
Printed in the United States of America
on acid-free paper

Contents

PREFACE

....

PETER OHLIN, the philosophy editor at Oxford University Press in New York, had been thinking about the idea of putting together a collection of essays on topics connected with the metaphysics and ethics of death. Oxford had already published several books on these topics. Peter was aware that they were also being addressed in a large and growing body of new work—journal articles, books, book proposals, conferences, and so on. He thought it would be good to put together a collection of the best of these.

The idea was discussed with the editors of the current volume. We were all enthusiastic about working together on the project. We had high hopes, but at the same time, some concerns. We agreed that there would not be much point in reprinting some previously published (and in many cases *republished*) old papers from the 1970s and 1980s. There are already several very useful collections of that work. Indeed, there is already a fair amount of overlap among those anthologies. We did not have much enthusiasm for creating yet another reshuffling of those papers, however impressive and important they may be. We were much more excited about the idea of putting together a collection of all new papers on these topics.

In recent years it has become increasingly clear that serious philosophical reflection on the nature and value of death essentially involves a number of subtle and sometimes complex topics in metaphysics, axiology, and the philosophy of mind. In addition, there are quite a few concepts that have resisted straightforward analysis. We agreed that we wanted to have papers written by philosophers with the requisite expertise; we wanted authors whose views about death had firm foundations in metaphysics, ethics, conceptual analysis, and philosophy of mind.

Since the publication of some important work several decades ago, critics have pointed out a wide variety of previously unnoticed difficulties and confusions. New puzzles have come to light. We hoped to have original papers in which contributors would deal creatively with these difficulties. We hoped to be able to offer papers that would reflect and advance the current state of the debates about death. We wanted work that would not just report on the history of the debates; we wanted things that would move the debate forward. We recognized that we would not succeed unless we could get papers from truly outstanding philosophers.

Accordingly, we spent a fair amount of time trying to construct a list of possible contributors. We hoped to find people who would be able to produce sophisticated, knowledgeable, creative, new papers. After some discussion, we finally agreed on a list of people to invite. Most invitees had already made significant contributions to the philosophical literature on death, but some were better known for their work in other areas. We were confident that they would make especially valuable contributions even if they had not previously written specifically about death. We sent out our invitations; we explained the sort of collection we were trying to construct. We were thrilled when just about everyone on our list shared our enthusiasm and agreed to participate.

We are very grateful to Peter Ohlin. The idea for this handbook originated with him. We have benefited from his generosity, insight, and steady support throughout the production of the book. He fully understood and appreciated our concerns at every stage. We are also grateful to all the others at Oxford University Press who played a role in bringing the book to fruition. We also benefited from the careful editorial work of Aaron Wolf.

We are especially grateful to the outstanding philosophers who have contributed papers for this collection. These are busy people. They have plenty of projects of their own to pursue. Some of them would otherwise have not thought of writing a paper about philosophical problems about death. But each of them agreed to spend some extra time working on a paper that would fit naturally into our scheme.

One of our contributors deserves special mention. Gary Matthews contributed an interesting and original paper to this volume; of course we are grateful to him for that. But we are grateful to him for far more in addition. Gary was Fred's colleague at the University of Massachusetts for more than forty years; throughout that time Gary was a steadfast friend and generous commentator. Ben had the good fortune to be able to study with Gary during his (Ben's) student days at UMass. And Jens also briefly knew Gary during a semester when he (Jens) was visiting Amherst. Though we all came at these questions from different perspectives, Gary's influence can be seen in all of our work, and indeed in the work of several others who have contributed to this volume. We all benefited from his insight, patience, broad knowledge of the history of philosophy, and tremendously agreeable manner. Gary died before this book was completed; he is sorely missed.

With respect, affection, and gratitude—all still tinged with grief—we dedicate this book to our teacher and colleague, Gary Matthews.

CONTRIBUTORS

Christopher Belshaw is a Senior Lecturer in Philosophy at the Open University. His other work on death includes *10 Good Questions about Life and Death* (Blackwell 2005) and *Annihilation: The Sense and Significance of Death* (Acumen 2009), as well as a number of book chapters and journal articles. He has also written on environmental philosophy and is working now on a book on animals.

Lars Bergström is Emeritus Professor of Practical Philosophy at Stockholm University, where he also defended his doctoral dissertation *The Alternatives and Consequences of Actions* in 1966. Between 1974 and 1987 he was Professor of Practical Philosophy at Uppsala University and he is a member of the Royal Swedish Academy of Sciences. His main areas of interest are moral philosophy, philosophy of science, and the philosophy of W. V. Quine.

Ben Bradley is Associate Professor of Philosophy at Syracuse University. He is the author of *Well-Being and Death* (Oxford University Press 2009), "When Is Death Bad for the One Who Dies?" (*Nous* 2004), "How Bad Is Death?" (*Canadian Journal of Philosophy* 2006), "The Worst Time to Die" (*Ethics* 2008), "Fischer on Death and Unexperienced Evils" (*Philosophical Studies*, forthcoming), and "Death and Desires" (with Kris McDaniel, to appear in *The Metaphysics and Ethics of Death*, Oxford University Press, forthcoming).

John Broome is White's Professor of Moral Philosophy at the University of Oxford, and a Fellow of Corpus Christi College, Oxford. His books include *Weighing Goods: Equality, Uncertainty and Time* (Blackwell 1991), *Weighing Lives* (Oxford University Press 2004), and *Ethics Out of Economics* (Cambridge University Press, 1999). He now works on rationality and reasoning, and also on the morality of climate change.

Kai Draper is Professor of Philosophy at the University of Delaware. He is author of "Rights and the Doctrine of Doing and Allowing" (*Philosophy and Public Affairs* 2004), "Disappointment, Sadness, and Death" (*Philosophical Review* 1999), and a variety of other articles in moral philosophy and epistemology.

Fred Feldman is Professor of Philosophy at the University of Massachusetts Amherst, where he has been teaching since 1969. He has long been fascinated by philosophical problems about the nature and value of death. He is author of *Confrontations with the Reaper: A Philosophical Study of the Nature and Value of Death* (Oxford University Press, 1992), *Pleasure and the Good Life: On the Nature,*

Varieties, and Plausibility of Hedonism (Oxford University Press, 2004), *What Is This Thing Called Happiness?* (Oxford University Press, 2010), several other books, and more than seventy-five papers in professional journals.

John Martin Fischer is Distinguished Professor and Chair of the Department of Philosophy at the University of California, Riverside, where he has held a University of California President's Chair (2006–2010). He has written on various topics in philosophy, including free will and moral responsibility. He has published papers on the metaphysical and ethical dimensions of death, and he is the editor of *The Metaphysics of Death* (Stanford University Press, 1993). His collection *Our Stories* (Oxford University Press, 2007) includes papers on death, immortality, and the meaning of life.

Cody Gilmore is Associate Professor of Philosophy at the University of California, Davis. He is the author of "Time Travel, Coinciding Objects, and Persistence" (*Oxford Studies in Metaphysics*, vol. 3, 2007), "Defining 'Dead' in terms of 'Lives' and 'Dies'" (*Philosophia* 2007), "Parts of Propositions" (in Shieva Kleinschmidt, ed., *Mereology and Location* (Oxford University Press, forthcoming), "Slots in Universals" (*Oxford Studies in Metaphysics*, vol. 8, forthcoming), and other papers in metaphysics.

Matthew Hanser is Professor of Philosophy at the University of California, Santa Barbara. His papers on killing and harm include "Harming Future People" (*Philosophy and Public Affairs*, 1990), "Why Are Killing and Letting Die Wrong?" (*Philosophy and Public Affairs*, 1995), "The Metaphysics of Harm" (*Philosophy and Phenomenological Research*, 2008), and "Harming and Procreating" (M. Roberts and D. Wasserman, eds., *Harming Future Persons*, Springer 2009).

Jens Johansson is Associate Professor of Philosophy at Uppsala University, Sweden. He is the author of several journal articles about the philosophy of death and related issues, including "Non-Reductionism and Special Concern" (*Australasian Journal of Philosophy* 2007), "Kaufman's Response to Lucretius" (*Pacific Philosophical Quarterly* 2008), "Parfit on Fission" (*Philosophical Studies* 2010), and "Past and Future Non-Existence" (forthcoming in *The Journal of Ethics*).

F. M. Kamm is Littauer Professor of Philosophy and Public Policy, Harvard Kennedy School, and Professor of Philosophy, Department of Philosophy, Harvard University. She is the author of *Creation and Abortion* (Oxford University Press, 1992), *Morality, Mortality*, vols. 1 and 2 (Oxford University Press, 1993, 1996), *Intricate Ethics* (Oxford University Press, 2007), *Ethics for Enemies: Terror, Torture, and War* (Oxford University Press, 2011), and numerous articles on normative ethical theory and on practical ethics.

Steven Luper chairs the philosophy department at Trinity University in San Antonio, Texas. His books include *The Philosophy of Death* (Cambridge University Press 2009) and *Invulnerability: On Securing Happiness* (Open Court 1996), and he is presently editing the *Cambridge Companion to Life and Death* (Cambridge University Press, forthcoming). Among his essays are "Annihilation" (*Philosophical*

Quarterly 1985), "The Absurdity of Life" (*Philosophy and Phenomenological Research* 1992), "Exhausting Life" (*Journal of Ethics: An International Philosophical Review*, forthcoming), and "Adaptation," to appear in *The Metaphysics and Ethics of Death* (Oxford University Press, forthcoming).

Don Marquis is Professor of Philosophy at the University of Kansas. He is the author of a widely reprinted and widely discussed essay on the ethics of abortion that was published in 1989. He has written a number of essays on the ethics of abortion since that time.

Gareth B. Matthews was Professor of Philosophy Emeritus at the University of Massachusetts. He wrote books and articles on ancient and medieval philosophy, philosophy of religion, philosophy of mind, and philosophy of childhood, including *Socratic Perplexity and the Nature of Philosophy* (Oxford University Press 1999) and *The Philosophy of Childhood* (Harvard University Press 1994).

Phillip Mitsis is A. S. Onassis Professor of Hellenic Culture and Civilization at New York University and Academic Director of the American Institute of Verdi Studies. He has published on Greek epic and tragedy, and on the history of ancient and early modern philosophy. His writings on Epicurus include *The Pleasures of Invulnerability: Epicurus' Ethical Theory* (1988).

Alastair Norcross is Associate Professor of Philosophy at the University of Colorado. He has written many articles on consequentialist moral theory and various topics in applied ethics, including "Puppies, Pigs, and People: Eating Meat and Marginal Cases" (*Philosophical Perspectives* 2004), "Animal Experimentation" (*Oxford Handbook of Bioethics* 2007), and "Good and Bad Actions" (*Philosophical Review* 1997).

Eric T. Olson is Professor of Philosophy at the University of Sheffield. He is the author of *The Human Animal: Personal Identity without Psychology* (Oxford University Press 1997) and *What Are We? A Study in Personal Ontology* (Oxford University Press 2007) as well as many articles on the nature and persistence of human people.

Connie S. Rosati is Associate Professor of Philosophy at the University of Arizona. Her research mainly addresses issues about personal good, moral motivation, and the nature and objectivity of law. She is the author of "Persons, Perspectives, and Full Information Accounts of the Good" (*Ethics* 1995), "Personal Good" (*Metaethics after Moore*, edited by Terry Horgan and Mark Timmons, 2006), "Objectivism and Relational Good" (*Social Philosophy and Policy* 2008), and "Some Puzzles about the Objectivity of Law" (*Law and Philosophy* 2004). She is currently working on a book about personal good.

Theodore Sider is Frederick J. Whiton Chair of Philosophy at Cornell University. He is the author of *Four-Dimensionalism*, *Riddles of Existence* (with Earl Conee), *Logic for Philosophy*, and *Writing the Book of the World*.

Roy Sorensen continues to cheat Death as Professor of Philosophy at Washington University in St. Louis. Professor Sorensen is the author of six books: *Blindspots*

(Oxford University Press/Clarendon Press, 1988), *Thought Experiments* (Oxford University Press, 1992) and *Pseudo-Problems* (Routledge, 1993), *Vagueness and Contradiction*, (Oxford University Press, 2001), *A Brief History of the Paradox* (Oxford University Press, 2003), and *Seeing Dark Things* (Oxford, 2008). He is currently taking his time completing a short book entitled *A Brief History of Nothing*.

Torbjörn Tännsjö is Kristian Claëson Professor of Practical Philosophy at Stockholm University. He has published extensively in moral philosophy, political philosophy, and bioethics. He is presently working on a book with the preliminary title: *Thou Shalt Sometimes Murder: An Inquiry into the Ethics of Killing*.

Dean Zimmerman is Professor of Philosophy at Rutgers University. He is editor or coeditor of several books, including an ongoing series, *Oxford Studies in Metaphysics* and *The Oxford Handbook of Metaphysics*, to which he contributed a chapter on materialism and persons. Zimmerman is author of "The Compatibility of Materialism and Survival: The 'Jumping Elevator' Model" (*Faith and Philosophy* 1999), along with numerous other articles in metaphysics and philosophy of religion.

THE OXFORD HANDBOOK OF

PHILOSOPHY OF DEATH

INTRODUCTION

PHILOSOPHY OF DEATH

BEN BRADLEY, FRED FELDMAN, AND JENS JOHANSSON

THE philosophy of death spans many subdisciplines of philosophy. It is "inter-subdisciplinary." Perhaps in part for that reason, philosophy of death is not typically recognized as a distinct subfield of philosophy. If you look at Brian Leiter's *Philosophical Gourmet Report* specialty rankings in philosophy, you will not find a specialty ranking for philosophy of death. If you are on a search committee in a philosophy department, you might have no applicants who list philosophy of death as an area of specialization or competence. Yet many philosophers are working on the philosophy of death even if they don't think of their work in that way. As we will see, what we say about many well-known questions of philosophy will have implications for what we think about death.

The first philosophical question to ask about any X is "what is X?" Thus our handbook begins with the question "what is death?"—or, as Cody Gilmore puts it, "when does a thing die?" (chapter 1). It is natural to say that to die is to cease to be alive. But there seem to be cases in which a thing ceases to be alive without dying. These include cases of suspended animation, where life processes stop but could be restarted, and fission, where a living being divides into two new living beings. One of the main challenges in understanding death is to understand the difference between cases where fission involves death and cases where it does not. Gilmore provides a novel account of this difference; he suggests that fission entails death unless it involves what he calls "generative division."

Among the oldest philosophical questions are questions about personal identity. What is a person? What are the persistence conditions for people? The answers to these questions bear on the question of what happens to us when we die. Most nonphilosophers seem to believe that each person has a nonphysical soul that continues to exist after the death of the body, perhaps in heaven, hell, or purgatory. But this view is not widely held by philosophers, because the existence of a nonphysical soul is usually thought to be problematic. The most popular views about what we are include the view that we are, fundamentally and essentially, animals—the biological view—and the view that we are essentially psychological entities—the psychological view. If the biological view is true, then what we say about our persistence conditions should mirror what we say about the persistence conditions of other biological organisms such as trees. If we are essentially psychological entities, and our persistence conditions are determined by relations of psychological connectedness over time, it would seem we go out of existence at or before biological death (unless, perhaps, another organism stands in the appropriate psychological relations). Fred Feldman defends the view that we continue to exist after death, either as dead people or as dead things that were once people (chapter 2). Eric Olson gives objections to this view, but concludes that all views about what happens to us when we die are beset with problems (chapter 3). In chapter 4, Dean Zimmerman argues that the view that it is possible to survive one's death is defensible on a variety of metaphysical views (which is not to say that we in fact do survive our deaths).

Philosophical questions about time have been thought to be relevant to questions about death. In various ways, it has been thought to matter whether the past and future are real. If the future is not real, perhaps we should not be afraid of our future deaths, since they are not real. If the past is not real, perhaps death cannot be bad for us, since once we die and are purely past, we will in no way exist to be the subject of harm. Ted Sider argues that we need not adopt any particular view about the metaphysics of time in order to hold that death is bad (chapter 5). According to Sider, we must be careful to distinguish whether we are making ordinary claims, such as that the table is hard, or claims about fundamental reality, such as that there are no tables but only simples arranged tablewise. The claim that death is bad is an ordinary claim, while views about the reality of the past and future are views about the underlying nature of reality; the ordinary claim about death could be underwritten by a variety of metaphysical views but might not be undermined by any of them. Lars Bergström suggests another way in which facts about time might affect how we should think about our deaths (chapter 6). If time is not linear but circular, then we will, in some sense, live again one day. Perhaps accepting this view about time should to some degree temper our sadness about our deaths.

As Gareth Matthews and Phillip Mitsis explain in chapters 7 and 8, the great Ancient Greek philosophers (Socrates, Plato, Aristotle, Epicurus) typically argued that we should not fear death, because it is not bad for us. Most of these arguments do not strike contemporary philosophers as compelling. For example, Socrates's suggestion that death is like a dreamless sleep (how refreshing!) seems hard to take seriously. But Epicurus's arguments, and those of his Roman admirer Lucretius, have continued to engage us; a few are convinced by them, and even those who think them unsound have different views about where they go wrong. Two arguments have received the most attention. The timing argument goes like this: there is no time at which death could harm me, since, as I go out of existence at the moment of my death, I do not overlap in time with my own death; thus death cannot be bad for me. The symmetry argument goes like this: there is no reason to be afraid of my own future nonexistence, because future nonexistence is no more to be feared than past nonexistence, and I neither fear nor have any reason to fear (or have any negative attitude toward) my own past nonexistence. Roy Sorensen and Jens Johansson address these arguments at length in chapters 10 and 11, and they are also addressed in several other chapters.

Epicurus seemed to think that since a person goes out of existence when she dies, death cannot be bad because the dead person can have no painful experiences. But those who think death is bad are not moved by this line of reasoning. The standard way to account for the badness of death is to endorse some sort of deprivation account. According to the deprivation account, death is bad for someone if, and to the extent that, it deprives that individual of a more valuable life. Thus it is possible for death to be bad without involving any painful postmortem experiences. Deprivation accounts are defended in the two papers that did the most to restart the contemporary philosophical discussions of death: Thomas Nagel's "Death" (1970) and Bernard Williams's "The Makropulos Case" (1973). John Broome provides a careful statement of the deprivation account in chapter 9.

Some have wondered whether the fact that death deprives its victim of the goods of life is sufficient for death to be a genuine misfortune for its victim. Kai Draper has argued that other mere deprivations, such as failing to find Aladdin's lamp, do not seem like genuine misfortunes, because it is inappropriate to feel bad about them. In chapter 13 he takes up the question of what attitude it is appropriate to take toward one's death. Christopher Belshaw also argues that mere deprivation is insufficient for death to be a misfortune. Rather, he says (chapter 12), the victim must also have had a desire to live.

There is another desire-based view of the badness of death that has found a number of adherents. Joel Feinberg and George Pitcher claimed that death is bad in virtue of the fact that it frustrates the interests, that is, the desires, of the deceased (Feinberg, 1984; Pitcher, 1984). When death frustrates an interest, it is bad for the individual who had that interest, and moreover, it is bad for her at the time she had the interest. Thus we would seem to have an answer to the timing problem: death is bad for its victim at times before she died. This view enables us to account for posthumous harm in the same way we account for the harm of death: events occurring after one's death can frustrate interests one had while alive. Steven Luper defends a version of this view of posthumous harm in chapter 14.

Williams's 1973 paper sparked much interesting discussion of immortality: would it be a good thing to live forever? Williams claimed that one would eventually run out of reasons to live, and then death would cease to be a misfortune. His arguments for these claims were suggestive but cryptic. John Fischer and Connie Rosati criticize those arguments in chapters 15 and 16. Fischer argues that a certain sort of immortal life might well be worth having, while Rosati appeals to facts about agency to explain why we want to extend our existence.

One reason we might care about these questions about the badness of death is that we care about justifying the claim that killing is wrong, and the wrongness of killing seems to have something to do with how bad death is for the victim. If death weren't bad, we might think our attitudes toward murder were unjustified. But it seems wrong to say that the degree of wrongness of killing someone depends on how bad it is for that person to die, because even if death would not be very bad for its victim (perhaps because he is very old and does not have long to live anyway), it would still be seriously wrong to murder that person. Matthew Hanser attempts to explain this in chapter 17 by appeal to a respect-based view of the wrongness of killing.

While killing another person is normally seriously wrong, there are some cases of killing about which it is not so obvious what to say. What, if anything, might make it permissible to kill fetuses, nonhuman animals, combatants, murderers, or the terminally ill? Some of these topics are taken up in the final four chapters.

Sometimes there is controversy over the wrongness of killing certain individuals at least in part in virtue of controversy over whether death is bad for those individuals. For example, it is sometimes argued that death is not bad for nonhuman animals or human fetuses in virtue of the fact that they lack relevant desires, or have insufficient psychological connectedness over time. Don Marquis and Alastair Norcross criticize these arguments concerning animals (Norcross, chapter 20) and fetuses (Marquis, chapter 18).

Sometimes there is little controversy that death is bad for an individual, but there are reasons to think that killing that individual might be justified in any case. Frances Kamm takes up the case of killing in war (chapter 19), while Torbjörn Tännsjö considers the case of killing convicted murderers (chapter 21).

In various ways, and from different perspectives, all these essays might be thought to answer one or both of the following questions: what is death, and why does death matter? These are the questions that define the growing intersubdisciplinary field of philosophy of death.

REFERENCES

Feinberg, Joel. 1984. *Harm to Others*. Oxford: Oxford University Press.

Nagel, Thomas. 1970. "Death." *Noûs* 4: 73–80.

Pitcher, George. 1984. "The Misfortunes of the Dead." *American Philosophical Quarterly* 21: 183–188.

Williams, Bernard. 1973. "The Makropulos Case: Reflections on the Tedium of Immortality." In his *Problems of the Self*, pp. 82–100. Cambridge: Cambridge University Press.

CHAPTER 1

....

WHEN DO THINGS
DIE?

....

CODY GILMORE

Many different projects have been pursued under the heading "the definition of death." Those who pursue these projects differ in what they are trying to define and in what sense they are trying to define it. Some take their target to be a notion of death that applies only to human beings or only to persons.[1] Some try to "define" their target merely in the epistemic sense of specifying a reliable and easily detectable mark or indicator of it.[2]

This chapter pursues a more general and metaphysical project. My central target will be *dying*, the concept (or property or relation) expressed by the verb "to die" as it occurs in sentences in the perfective aspect, such as "Mary died at midnight." I assume that this is a general biological concept that applies univocally across a wide range of entities, including human beings, cats, trees, bacteria, and individual cells (e.g., human skin cells) that are not organisms. These things all die, in the same sense of "die." My main concern in the chapter is not to define the word "die" or to analyze the concept it expresses. Rather, it's the project of giving informative, metaphysically necessary and sufficient conditions for a thing to die at a time. In particular, it's the attempt to formulate a true and informative instance of the following schema:

> S   Necessarily, for any x and any t, if t is an instant, then x dies at t if and only
> if _____.[3]

Each instance of S can be thought of as an answer to the question "when does a thing die?"[4] One natural answer is, "when it stops being alive." This corresponds to an instance of S that I dub the Cessation Thesis (CT):

> CT   Necessarily, for any x and any t, if t is an instant, then x dies at t if and only
> if x ceases to be alive at t.[5]

CT does not purport to specify the meaning of the word "dies" or to be an analysis of the concept expressed by that word. One can endorse CT even if one holds that (i) the given concept is simple and unanalyzable or that (ii) the concept does have an analysis but not one that involves the concept of being alive. Likewise, one can endorse CT even if one holds that the sentence "if John died at noon, then he ceased to be alive at noon" is not analytic. What the Cessation Thesis says is merely that there is a metaphysically necessary connection of a certain sort between dying and ceasing to be alive.[6] Whether any of the relevant concepts have analyses is a separate question.

Here is an analogy noted in a similar context by Ned Markosian (1998, pp. 214–215). One can give an answer to Peter van Inwagen's Special Composition Question ("Under what conditions do some things compose something?") without thinking that one's answer constitutes an analysis of the concept of the composition or a definition of the word "compose." For example, van Inwagen himself endorses the following answer to the Special Composition Question: (VIPA) necessarily, for any xx, there is something that xx compose if and only if the activities of xx constitutes a life. (Here "xx" is used as a plural variable.) But VIPA is not an analysis of the concept of composition. That concept can be analyzed as follows:

xx compose y at t = df. (i) no two of xx overlap at t, (ii) each of xx is a part of y at t, and (iii) each part-at-t of y overlaps-at-t at least one of xx,

where "x overlaps y at t" is defined as "$\exists z[z$ is a part of x at t & z is a part of y at t]." Composition is a purely mereological concept, one whose analysis involves only logical and mereological notions. Rather than analyzing the concept of composition, VIPA aims to specify certain metaphysically necessary connections between that concept and other concepts that are not involved in its analysis. One might take a parallel view about CT and dying. One might think that while CT is true, the analysis of the concept of dying does not involve the concept of being alive, but rather, runs something like this:

x dies at t = df. x becomes dead at t,

where the concept of being dead is unanalyzable. I want to leave this analysis open. (For more on this, see note 24.)

Enough about CT for now. The plan for the chapter is as follows. In sections 2 and 3, I discuss a pair of problems for CT—one arising from suspended animation, the other arising from fission—and I consider a series of repairs. Unsurprisingly, none of the repairs is completely satisfactory. We shouldn't assume that informative, individually necessary, jointly sufficient conditions for dying at a time (or for any ordinary concept) are likely to be had. On the other hand, we shouldn't assume from the outset that this is an unattainable or unworthy goal, or that there is nothing interesting to learn by pursuing it. Though it may be predictable *that* our attempts to formulate such an account will fail, I doubt that anyone will pretend to know in advance exactly *what* the most plausible accounts are or exactly *why* they fail, if they do. Succeed or fail, the project ought yield a clearer picture of the distinctive "modal profile" of dying.

With an (imperfect) account of dying in place, section 4 takes up a different question: When are things *dead*? The question is harder than one might think, but it's easier than "when do things die?" and can be dealt with more quickly.

1. Preliminaries

Before we get started, it will be convenient to introduce some of the expressions, concepts, and doctrines that will be in play.

1.1 Presentism and Eternalism

These are rival views about the ontology of time. Presentism is the view that the only things that exist or are real are the present time and its contents, and eternalism is the view that past, present, and future times and their contents all exist equally.[7] Just as Neptune exists despite being far away in space, eternalists say, Pangaea and the 2086 NBA scoring champion both exist despite being "far away in time." (Presentists, by contrast, say that Neptune exists, but Pangaea and the 2086 NBA scoring champion do not.)[8] Given eternalism, we will need to draw a distinction between the ontological notion of *existing*, on the one hand, and the locational notion of *existing at* or, as I will say, *being present at*, a time, on the other. Pangaea exists, according to eternalists, but it is not present at any instant in the year 2012; rather, it is present only at pre-Cenozoic instants. Intuitively, a thing is present at a time just in case part of its career occurs at that time.

Presentists and eternalists both agree that Neptune is *present at* the current time and that Pangaea is not, and they both agree that Neptune *exists*. They disagree about whether Pangaea exists: eternalists say that it does, and presentists say that it does not. Throughout the chapter, I assume that eternalism is true, though most of what I say can probably be reframed in presentist terms, at the cost of some awkwardness. I also assume that there are such things as instants, and that time is a continuum of them.[9]

1.2 The Termination Thesis

The Termination Thesis (TT) is the view that

> TT   for any x and any instant t, if x dies at t, then x ceases to be present at t.[10]

Those who endorse TT—*Terminators*—will say that when Lenin died, he ceased to be present and, hence, is presumably not contained in his display case in Red

Square now.[11] What does that display case contain, according to Terminators? The two most natural options are (i) a human-shaped object that began to be present when Lenin died and that is composed of (mostly) the same particles that composed Lenin at the end of his life, or (ii) some particles that are "arranged corpse-wise" but that do not compose anything at all. We might call the former *Lenin's corpse* and the latter *Lenin's remains*.

Some friends of TT may wish to say that the things that *die* (people, organisms, what have you) are *constituted by* but not *identical to* certain other material objects (bodies, portions of matter, what have you). Further, they may wish to say that, typically, when a person or an organism dies, the thing that constitutes it in the final moments of its life typically does not cease to be present. On this view, when Lenin died, he ceased to be present, but the thing that constituted him in the final moments of his life did not cease to be present. Perhaps, then, Lenin's display case contains something that once constituted Lenin but was never identical with him, namely, his body. Together with TT as stated, this view entails that

L   Lenin's body did not die when Lenin died.

L may seem surprising, since one would think that Lenin's body was character-ized by the same distribution of intrinsic physical properties as was Lenin over those final moments, and that it stood in the same spatial and causal relations to other things as Lenin did. And it is tempting to think that when two things are alike in these ways, they are also alike in whether they die at the given time. But for Terminators who are willing to reject the relevant "supervenience-of-dying" principle, L is available.

However, anyone who thinks that Lenin's display case contains something that died in 1924 (Lenin, a body, an organism) will want to reject TT as I have framed it.[12] Likewise for those who think that trees often remain standing for several years after they die. Most of what I will say in this chapter should in principle be accept-able both to friends and foes of TT, though, for what it's worth, I tend to sympa-thize with its foes.

One final point about TT before we move on. I have stated it in terms of dying and presence. But it is typically stated in terms of dying and existence, as follows:

TT*   Things cease to exist when they die.

TT* might be read just as a more colloquial formulation of TT, in which case I have no complaints about it. But it might instead be given a second reading that puts it in tension with eternalism. On the second reading, TT* entails that if Socrates has died (and has not somehow begun to exist again in the interim), then *there is no such entity as Socrates*, where this is not merely a matter of Socrates's temporal location but is a matter of ontology. Eternalists want to say that, like all past, pres-ent, and future things, Socrates *exists* (at least in a tenseless sense) and has never *ceased* to exist, though, of course, they will add that he does not bear the *being present at* relation to any instant in the year 2012. Eternalists also want to say that Socrates died. So they will need to reject TT*, on its second reading.

But it seems to me that the intuitive idea philosophers have in mind when they use the label "the Termination Thesis" is one that can be accepted by presentists and eternalists alike. It is a view about things that live and die, and about their relationship to time. Informally, it is the view that a thing "ends" when it dies; it does not keep persisting as a dead thing after it dies. This view is neutral with respect to debates about the ontology of time, as is TT, my formulation of the Termination Thesis. By contrast, TT*, on its second reading, is not neutral in this way, which makes me think that it shouldn't be identified with the Termination Thesis.

The interaction between the dispute over TT and the dispute between presentism and eternalism is summarized in table 1.1.[13] The diagram adopts the simplifying assumption that opponents of TT ("anti-Terminators") will say that *people* typically remain present for a while after they die. But not all anti-Terminators will really want to say this. Some of them will say that Lenin and his body both died at the same time, and that Lenin ceased to be present then, but his body did not.

Having introduced a pair of metaphysical controversies relevant to philosophical questions about death, I turn now to six expressions that will play a role in subsequent discussion (or that are easily confused with those that will).

1.3 "Is Alive"

I won't try to define the adjective "alive," analyze the concept it expresses, or give informative necessary and sufficient conditions for being alive. These tasks are too much for a single chapter, not to mention one whose main focus is on death. Instead, I'll assume that, as with most ordinary concepts, we grasp the concept of being alive even in the absence of anything like an analysis of it. My project here is not to shed new light on being alive, but rather to *use* this concept to shed light on death. I think the reader will agree (at least by the end of the chapter) that even if the concept of being alive were crystal clear and perfectly understood, either as a primitive or via one's favorite analysis, there would still be hard and interesting questions about the *connections* between being alive and dying. Those connections are among the topics to be explored here.

As with "dies," my default assumption is that "alive" is not context sensitive. To see the significance of this assumption, suppose that a biologist is giving a lecture about the flora of California to a group of tourists. She points to a bristlecone pine and utters the sentence, "Surprisingly, that tree is alive." Now suppose that two paramedics arrive at the scene of a car accident. One of them rushes to a victim lying motionless in a ditch, checks the victim's pulse, and shouts, "He's alive!" According to the "no context sensitivity" assumption, "alive" expresses the same concept (or property or relation) in both contexts.

I take this concept, like the one expressed by "dies," to apply to a wide range of biological entities, including not just organisms (particular human beings, trees, amoebas) but also individual cells that are not organisms. Being alive, on this view, does not by itself entail having a properly functioning brain or a properly functioning heart. Bacteria

Table 1.1 Death and Time

	Presentists say: Things cease to exist when they cease to be present.	**Eternalists** say: Things do not cease to exist when they cease to be present.
Terminators say: Things cease to be present when they die.	Things cease to exist when they die. Reality (i.e., reality now) (No Lenin) Putin Corpse? Remains?	Things cease to be present but don't cease to exist when they die. Reality 2010 … Putin Lenin 1870
Anti-Terminators say: Things at least sometimes remain present for a while after they die.	Things at least sometimes remain present, and hence keep existing, for a while after they die, but as soon as they cease to be present, they cease to exist. Reality (i.e., reality now) Lenin Putin	Things at least sometimes remain present for a while after they die, and they don't cease to exist when they cease to be present. Reality 2010 … Putin Lenin 1870

are alive but don't have hearts or brains.[14] Whether the concept applies to biological entities that are neither organisms nor cells—such as organs, organelles, and viruses—I leave open. (The same goes for "dead" and "a death": my default assumption is that none of these is context sensitive and that each expresses a general biological concept that can apply equally to human beings, blood cells, and many things in between.)

Presumably, whether a thing is alive at a given time is a matter of what sorts of physical and chemical processes its parts are engaged in at that time.[15] I take it, in other words, that a thing is alive at a given time just in case it is performing the right sorts of "life-functions" at that time. This much seems relatively uncontroversial, but as soon as one tries to say anything more precise about what the *right sorts* of life-functions are, one encounters difficulties.[16] So I will leave this task to others.

I noted earlier that there is controversy about whether things cease to be present when they die. One assumption I take to be shared by all participants in this controversy is that

> P1   necessarily, for any x and any t, if t is an instant and x is alive at t, then x is present at t.

P1 may seem too obvious to be worth mentioning, but in fact it captures an important respect in which being alive differs from being dead (and being famous). A thing can be dead at an instant at which it is not present; it cannot be alive at such an instant.

Finally, it will be convenient to speak of a dyadic relation "associated" with being alive: *being alive at*. A thing can bear this relation to certain times and fail to bear it to others. Lenin bears it to each of the instants in 1923 but to none of the instants in 1925. I assume that, necessarily, a thing x bears *being alive at* to an instant t just in case x is alive at t. So much for "alive."

1.4 "Dies"

To die at an instant is to undergo a certain sort of *transition* then. Can we specify the nature of this transition in a more informative way? It is natural to think that, at least *typically*, a thing x dies at an instant t

- if and only if x ceases to be alive at t,
- if and only if x becomes dead at t, and
- if and only if a death of x culminates[17] at t.

Whether each of these biconditionals holds in full generality is a difficult question. We will have much more to say about the first of these in sections 2 and 3.

A number of further questions naturally arise concerning the connections between the concept expressed by "dies" and the concepts expressed by "alive" and "present": Can a thing be alive at an instant at which it dies?[18] Can it *fail* to be alive at such an instant?[19] Can a thing be *present* at an instant at which it dies?[20] Can a thing *fail* to be present at such an instant?[21] For reasons given in the notes, I think our default answer to each of these questions should be yes.

Some may balk at the claim that things die at *instants*. It is hard to know *precisely* when a thing dies, and not merely because we lack detailed information about a thing's physiological processes. Consider Nixon's death. No matter how complete our knowledge of the biochemical details in this case, we would still be unable to *know*, of any independently identified instant t, that Nixon died at t (and not a femtosecond earlier or later). One might be tempted to infer from this that, strictly speaking, Nixon didn't die at any instant, but only at some extended interval. (Such a doctrine might seem to harmonize with the slogan that "death is a process, not an event.")

I think this would be a mistake. In the first place, such a view wouldn't make it any easier to know the facts about when Nixon died. It would be just as hard to know which precisely demarcated *interval* or *intervals* were the ones at which Nixon died as it would be to know which *instant* was the one at which he died. Second, the most we can confidently infer from our observations about Nixon is that whether a thing dies at a given instant t (as opposed to some nearby instant) is often a *vague* matter. And there is no easy argument from the claim that

(a) each instance of the schema "The unique instant at which Nixon died is the one that is exactly ___ seconds earlier than midnight EST, January 1, 2000" is either vague or false,

to the claim that

(b) the sentence "there is exactly one instant at which Nixon died" is either vague or false.

For even if (a) is true, one might think that the reason *why* it's true is just that there is vagueness as to *which* instant was the unique instant at which Nixon died. In that case, many will say that it is still true and nonvague that Nixon died at *some*— indeed, exactly one—instant, and hence that (b) is false.[22]

Granted, there may be better arguments for (b), and presumably there is a coherent view according to which things die only at extended intervals, rather than at instants. But to keep things simple, I will assume for the remainder of the chapter that things die at instants. I take no stand on whether they *also* die at intervals.

1.5 "Is Dying"

Consider the concept expressed by the verb "to die" as it occurs in sentences in the *progressive* aspect, such as "Mary was dying at midnight." To a very crude first approximation, a thing x is dying at an instant t if and only if x is alive at t but is involved in some process at t that, if allowed to continue without interference, would soon cause x to die.[23] A thing cannot *die* at an instant unless it becomes dead then, but it can *be dying* at an instant without becoming dead then. Indeed, a thing can be dying for a while but then fully recover and go on to live for many years. (Presumably, it is *metaphysically possible* for a thing to be dying for a while and then go on to live for infinitely many years thereafter, and never die.)

1.6 "Is Dead"

Typically, a thing is dead at an instant if and only if the thing died at some earlier instant (or perhaps at t itself, depending upon x's condition then).[24] I assume that *being dead at* and *being alive at* are *incompatible* in the sense that nothing can bear both of these relations to the same instant. Nothing can be both dead and alive at the same time.

Many things, however, are neither alive nor dead at a given time: Pangaea, for example, is neither alive nor dead at this time. It's not even present now. Further, there are many things that are neither alive nor dead at instants at which they are present:

my wallet was present at each instant in the year 2009 but was neither dead nor alive at any of them. (Later, I'll give arguments that support similar claims about organisms.) In sum, *being alive at* and *being dead at* are *contraries*: they exclude each other but, unlike *contradictories*, the absence of one does not entail the presence of the other.

Finally, I assume that *being dead at* is quite different from relations such as *being bent at* or *being 2 kg in mass at*. Instead, it is more like *being an ex-convict at*, *being ten miles from the North Pole at*, and *being famous at*. Roughly, whether a thing x bears *being bent at* to an instant t depends only on what x is like in itself at t and is independent of how x is related to things outside itself at t, as well as being independent of how things are at other instants. By contrast, whether a thing x bears *being ten miles from the North Pole at* to an instant t depends upon how x is related to something outside itself (the North Pole) at t, and whether x bears *being an ex-convict at* to t depends upon how things are at other times: it depends upon whether x was a convict at a time earlier than t. This is all very loose, but it points toward an intuitive distinction among dyadic relations to instants. Call those that are like *being bent at, intrinsic**; call the others *nonintrinsic**.

As an aid to grasping this distinction, some may find it helpful to think in terms of the following rough-and-ready test. To determine whether R is intrinsic*, ask the following questions:

- Is R a dyadic relation that a thing can bear to an instant?
- Must a thing be *present* at an instant in order to bear R to that instant?
- Is it metaphysically possible that (i) there is a thing x that bears R to an instant t, even though (ii) t is the only instant that exists; (iii) there is nothing before or after t; and (iv) x and its parts are the only things (other than t itself, perhaps) that are present at t?

If the answer to any of these questions is no, then R is probably not intrinsic*. If the answer to each of them is yes, then R is probably intrinsic*. So much for the notion of an intrinsic* relation in general. How does this notion apply to the specific relations that interest us here?

Being alive at might be intrinsic*; this is a hard question.[25] Likewise for *being (in the process of) dying at*. But *being dead at* is clearly nonintrinsic*. A thing cannot be dead at an instant t unless it died at some earlier instant (or perhaps at t itself). Whether a thing is dead at a given instant, then, is a partly *historical* matter; it is partly a matter of how things are at earlier times. Moreover, *being dead at*, like *being famous at*, is a relation that a thing can bear to an instant at which the thing is not present. Let t be some instant in the year 2012. Then Socrates is dead at t. (He's also famous then.) But even if he remains present for a while after he dies, he is almost[26] certainly not present at t.

Both friends and foes of TT ought to agree on all of this. However, if we drop TT and assume that some things remain present for a period of time as dead things after they die, we can provide an especially vivid illustration of the fact that *being dead at* is not intrinsic*:

> **Lenin and His Body Double**. Lenin is dead but still present at t, an instant in the year 2012. To keep museum visitors happy while Lenin is taken off display for maintenance, curators have constructed a copy of him. The copy is so well-made

that, at t, Lenin and his copy are "molecule-for-molecule duplicates." In the terminology introduced above, they are both *present* at t, and they bear exactly the same *intrinsic* relations* to t. And yet, since the copy was never alive and never died, it is not dead at t. Lenin and his copy bear all the same intrinsic* relations to t, but only Lenin bears *being dead at* to t. Hence that relation is not intrinsic*.

Strictly speaking, this case is overkill. Regardless of whether TT is true, the points made in the previous paragraph suffice to show that *being dead at* is not intrinsic*. So much for the adjective "dead."

1.7 "Is a Death"

The word "death" is used as a count noun in sentences such as "the executioner oversaw seven deaths last year." I take it that, so used, it is a predicate of events. In particular, I assume that an entity is a death only if (i) it is an event and (ii) its subject (or "theme") dies at the instant at which it occurs (or "culminates").

1.8 The Singular Term "Death"

The word "death" is used as a singular term in sentences such as "this chapter is about death" and "death is something that we all think about from time to time." I assume that it refers to an abstract entity on such uses, but it is no easy matter to identify this entity in an independent way.[27] None of the following statements is obviously correct:

(a) Death = the property *being dead* (or the relation *being dead at*)
(b) Death = the property *dying* (or the relation *dies at*)
(c) Death = the property *being in the process of dying* (or the relation *being in the process of dying at*)
(d) Death = the property *being a death*

It seems that a novel, for example, can be about *death* without being about the property *being dead*. Likewise for each of the other properties and relations mentioned above. These considerations might drive us to postulate yet another abstract entity, the referent of "death," to put alongside those that we've already recognized. On the other hand, it might be suggested that the given considerations turn on some ambiguity or context-sensitivity in the term "death." Perhaps some occurrences of that term refer to *being dead*, other occurrences of it refer to *being a death*, and so on. In that case, we might not need to add to our stock of abstracta. I won't pursue this issue here.

2. Cryptobiosis

CT says that necessarily, a thing dies at a given instant if and only if the thing ceases to be alive then. In this section and the next, I discuss a pair of problems for CT.[28]

A first problem for CT is that it conflicts with a plausible claim about suspended animation, or *cryptobiosis*—namely, that some organisms become frozen or desiccated in such a way that they temporarily cease to be alive but do not then die. The term "cryptobiosis" was introduced by the entomologist and biochemist David Keilin "for the state of an organism when it shows no visible signs of life and when its metabolic activity becomes hardly measurable, or comes reversibly to a standstill" (1959, p. 166). Keilin contrasts cryptobiosis with *dormancy*: dormant organisms retain a detectable metabolism; cryptobiotic organisms do not. A wide variety of unicellular and multicellular organisms undergo cryptobiosis in nature. Especially noteworthy are tardigrades—small (between 1.5 and .1 mm long) insectlike animals with eight legs and a multilobed brain (Garey et al., 2007). Tardigrades are famous for their ability to undergo anhydrobiosis, a form of cryptobiosis involving desiccation, and to remain viable in such a state for years.

Some of the most interesting cases of cryptobiosis are ones that have been induced experimentally. Keilin describes experiments carried out by Paul Becquerel in the early 1950s in which already desiccated, anhydrobiotic tardigrades (among other things) were cooled to temperatures of between 0.008 and 0.047 degrees above absolute zero and successfully revived after about two hours (Keilin, 1959, pp. 178–179). One pressing question that arises here is whether the life-processes (e.g., metabolism) of such organisms have completely *stopped* or rather are merely *slowed but still-ongoing*.[29] Keilin forcefully argues that, at least in the case of cryptobiotic organisms at very low temperatures, their metabolism and other life processes have stopped. James S. Clegg argues that this conclusion applies not just to organisms at very low temperatures but also to anhydrobiotic organisms in nature:

> I have previously...given reasons why one is compelled to conclude that the removal of all but, say, 0.1 g H_2O/g dry weight (easily achieved by anhydrobionts), will inevitably result in the cessation of metabolism. For example, one can calculate that this amount of water is insufficient to hydrate intracellular proteins, without which a metabolism is obviously not possible...Central to these matters is the definition of "metabolism." It should be appreciated...that metabolism is not merely the presence of chemical reactions in anhydrobionts, indeed, those are inevitable at ordinary biological temperatures. It seems reasonable to require that a metabolism must consist of systematically controlled pathways of enzymatic reactions, governed in rate and direction, integrated and under the control of the cells in which they are found. An additional requirement concerns the transduction of free energy from the environment and its coupling to endergonic processes such as biosynthesis and ionic homeostasis. (2001, p. 615)

Now, to see how all this bears on CT, consider a cryptobiotic tardigrade, o, that is frozen at a temperature just a fraction of a degree above absolute zero, and suppose that it is ametabolic. Everyone agrees that it is alive before it is frozen and after it is thawed and hydrated. But its status while frozen (at time t) is more controversial. One might claim that (i) o is still alive at t, that (ii) o is dead at t, or that (iii) o is neither alive nor dead at t. As I mentioned above, I am assuming that *being alive at* and *being dead at* are incompatible, so I will ignore the view that such an organism is *both* alive *and* dead. Finally, one might think that the tardigrade's status is a vague or indeterminate matter. In particular, one might think that (iv) the tardigrade is a borderline case of being alive, a borderline case of being dead, but a clear case of not being both-alive-and-dead.[30] (It will be a matter of debate, however, whether and in what sense (iv) is a *rival* to each of (i) through (iii). More on this below.)

Start with (ii), the claim that the tardigrade is dead (defended by Wilson, 1999, pp. 101). This is implausible, mainly because of facts about the tardigrade's internal structure: in some sense, the organism is still *structurally intact* and relatively *undamaged*. It still has eight legs, a head, a brain, and other internal organs, all of which are intact. It still has cells, and they presumably still have intact membranes, nuclei, mitochondria, and most of the same macromolecules they contained before they were frozen, a sufficient proportion of which remain undamaged. Indeed, so far as its parts and their arrangement go, the organism is in good shape. The main change that occurs when it becomes cryptobiotic is that the physical and biochemical activity in the organism largely shuts down. When the tardigrade is eventually thawed and exposed to water, this activity resumes.

These facts about the tardigrade's internal structure and behavior make it over-whelmingly natural to say that the organism is still *viable*, that it *can* be alive in the future (whether or not it is alive while cryptobiotic), and that it has the *capacity* and the *disposition* to be alive (under appropriate conditions). Indeed, it can be revived rel-atively easily, merely by being thawed at room temperature and then hydrated, without first being repaired. (To be sure, some damage may be sustained during cryptobiosis and some of this damage may eventually need to be repaired. But the organism must return to a more active metabolic state *before* it repairs itself.) All of this supports the claim that the cryptobiotic tardigrade is not dead and, relatedly, that it did not die when it became cryptobiotic. Note that this is intended as an argument for the negation of (ii), namely,

   (v)   ¬o is dead at t.

It is not intended merely as an argument for the claim that o is not a clear case of being dead.[31] Indeed, the given considerations strike me as a *persuasive* argument for (v). Organisms that are intact and undamaged in the relevant ways, and that have relevant capacity to resume metabolic activity, are flat-out *not dead*, just as a red shirt is flat-out *not green*.

So let us turn to (i), the claim that the organism is *alive* (defended by Kolb and Liesch, 2008; Luper, 2009, p. 44).[32] This also faces problems. Earlier, I sug-gested that a thing is alive at a time just in case it is performing "the right sorts of life-functions" at that time. *Whatever* those life-functions may be, it seems unlikely that they are being performed by a frozen or thoroughly desiccated cell or multicellular organism. Such an entity is not moving, growing, reproducing, repairing itself, or absorbing matter from its environment. If Keilin and Clegg are right, it is completely ametabolic. Assuming that being metabolic at a given time is necessary for being alive at that time,[33] we have a prima facie case for the conclu-sion that our frozen tardigrade is not alive. This is an argument for the negation of (i), namely,

(vi) ¬o is alive at t,

not merely for the claim that o is not a clear case of being alive.[34]

Taken together, the arguments for (v) and (vi) yield an apparently stable argument for (iii), the claim that the frozen tardigrade is neither alive nor dead. It is not alive because it is not performing the relevant life-functions; in particular, it is not metabolizing. It is not dead because it is structurally intact and undamaged in a way that makes it relatively easy for it to be alive in the future: no prior repair is needed. Having offered a positive argument for (iii), we need not give any separate consideration to (iv), the claim that our organism is a borderline case of being alive and a borderline case of being dead. Either (iv) is rival to (iii), in which case our argument for (iii) gives us a reason to refrain from accepting (iv), or (iv) is not a rival to (iii), in which case we are free to accept them both if we like. The important thing is the argument for (iii).

Some may be tempted to attack (iii) by appeal to the claim that "alive" and "dead" are contradictories. (I expect to hear the words, "if a thing isn't alive, then *by definition* it's dead!") But we already have independent reason to reject this claim. My wallet is not alive, but it's also not dead. In response, one might attack (iii) by appeal to a weaker principle: for any x, if there is an instant at which x is alive, then for any instant t, either x is alive at t or x is dead at t. But we have independent reason to reject this as well: I am alive at this instant, but there are plenty of instants before my conception at which I'm neither alive nor dead. Finally, the critic of (iii) might appeal to a third, still weaker principle: for any x and any instant t, if x is alive at some instant earlier than t, then either x is alive at t or x is dead at t. This is starting to seem ad hoc, but that aside, we will see in section 2.2 that there are independent reasons (arising from "deathless fission") to reject even this third principle.[35] For now, let me just say that I find the case for (v) and (vi) far more compelling than any of the increasingly ad hoc principles just mentioned. Thus *being alive at* and *being dead at* still appear to be contraries, not contradictories. The relationship between them is like that between *being red at* and *being green at*; it is not like the relationship between *being red at* and *being non-red at*.

Among philosophers, Michael Wreen (1987), Fred Feldman (1992, pp. 60–62, 170–171), Ingmar Persson (1995, p. 500), and Christopher Belshaw (2009, p. 9) have all endorsed the view that cryptobiotic organisms are neither alive nor dead, and on roughly the grounds given here. This view has been advocated by biologists too. Here is Clegg:

> Consider that an organism in anhydrobiosis lacks all the dynamic features characteristic of living organisms, notably due to the lack of an ongoing metabolism to transduce energy and carry out biosynthesis. In that sense it is not "alive," yet neither it is it "dead" since suitable rehydration produces an obviously living organism... [T]he severely desiccated anhydrobiont is indeed reversibly ametabolic and we may conclude that there are three states of biological organization: alive; dead; and cryptobiotic. (2001, p. 615)

Anyone who accepts such a view about cryptobiosis will be forced to reject CT. To see this, consider a typical cryptobiotic tardigrade, and suppose being cryptobiotic is incompatible both with being alive and with being dead. Then when the tardigrade became cryptobiotic, it *did* cease to be alive (since it was alive throughout some interval that immediately preceded the instant at which it became cryptobiotic), but it did *not* die (since a thing cannot die at an instant unless it becomes dead at that instant). Call this the *cryptobiosis argument*.

To be sure, the argument is not airtight. Not everyone will find it plausible that metabolism is necessary for being alive, or that being viable (in the relevant sense) is incompatible with being dead. Future research might undermine the Keilin-Clegg view that cryptobiotic organisms are ametabolic. As things stand, however, the argument strikes me as being forceful. It deserves to be taken seriously.

So, for those who are persuaded by it, let us consider some alternatives to CT. If merely *ceasing to be alive* is not sufficient for dying, what is? What more is needed? Feldman's treatment of these questions is very helpful. I end up rejecting his positive view (in section 2.4) and putting forward an alternative (in section 2.6), but his critical discussion of a trio of preliminary accounts merits a summary, so I'll start there.

2.1 Permanence

An initial thought is that the difference between entering cryptobiosis and dying is that when an organism does the former, it ceases to be alive only *temporarily*, whereas when an organism does the latter, it ceases to be alive *permanently*. This suggests:

> Permanence   Necessarily, for any x and any t, if t is an instant, then x dies at t if and only if "x ceases permanently to be alive at t." (Feldman, 1992, p. 63)

But anyone who is convinced by the cryptobiosis argument will want to reject Permanence as well, as the following case brings out:

> **Shattering**.   At t1, Alpha makes the transition from being "actively alive" to being cryptobiotic. It remains in this condition until t2, at which time it is dropped and shatters. At no time after t2 is Alpha alive or even present again.

If the cryptobiosis argument is correct, then things cease to be alive when they go directly from being "actively alive" to being cryptobiotic. In that case Alpha ceases to be alive at t1. Moreover, since it turns out that Alpha never becomes actively alive thereafter, friends of the cryptobiosis argument will say that Alpha ceases *permanently* to be alive at t1. So, if they were to accept Permanence, they would be forced to say that Alpha *dies* at t1. But they won't want to say that, since they think that things do *not* die when they go from being actively alive to being cryptobiotic, which is what Alpha does at t1. So they will want to reject Permanence.[36]

2.2 Permanence and Irreversibility

The same example also generates problems for the suggestion that permanently and *irreversibly* ceasing to be alive is necessary and sufficient for dying. This suggestion can be stated as

> P&I Necessarily, for any x and any t, if t is an instant, then x dies at t if and only if "x ceases permanently and irreversibly to be alive at t" (Feldman, 1992, p. 64).

Friends of the cryptobiosis argument will say that in the Shattering case, there is no instant at which Alpha ceases permanently and irreversibly to be alive. They will say that it ceases permanently to be alive at t1, when it enters cryptobiosis. If there is any instant at which Alpha becomes "*irreversibly nonliving,*" that is plausibly t2, when it is shattered. But it does not *cease* to be alive then, according to supporters of the cryptobiosis argument. By t2, they will say, Alpha had already been in a nonliving condition for some time. So at neither instant does it *cease permanently and irreversibly to be alive.* Accordingly, friends of the cryptobiosis argument will see P&I as yielding the bizarre verdict that Alpha does not die at either t1 or t2, or indeed, at any instant. I take it that they will judge this principle to be unacceptable as a result.[37]

2.3 Irreversibility$_1$: The Physical Impossibility of Living Again

A natural fix is to remove the requirement that the time at which the thing ceases to be alive must be the same as the time at which its status as nonliving becomes irreversible, and to say that the thing dies at the latter time. Feldman formulates a version of this proposal that entails the following principle:

> IR$_1$ Necessarily, for any x and any t, if t is an instant, then x dies at t if and only if "(i) x ceases permanently to be alive at or before t, and (ii) at t, it becomes physically impossible for x ever to live again" (1992, p. 64).

How should the relevant notion of physical impossibility be understood here? I offer the following rough suggestion. Start with a notion of *time-indexed physical necessity.* Say that it is physically necessary at t that so-and-so just in case the conjunction of (i) the laws of nature and (ii) a complete intrinsic description of the past and present relative to t entails that so-and-so.[38] Then say that it is physically impossible at t that so-and-so just in case it is physically necessary at t that *not* so-and-so.

Understood in this way, IR$_1$ may help with the Shattering case. The organism Alpha did cease permanently to be alive at or before t2, and there may be some plausibility to the thought that at t2, it became physically impossible for Alpha ever to be alive again.[39] Moreover, t2 is apparently the only time in the Shattering case that meets these conditions. So IR$_1$ may yield the desired verdict here—namely, that Alpha dies at t2 and at no other instant.

However, there are two potential problems for IR$_1$. First, it will be rejected by those who endorse the possibility of things that die and later return to life (of which more later). Second, it may be vulnerable to counterexamples of a different sort. One might think that there could be a once-living, cryptobiotic organism that, purely as the result of some change in its environment, and without undergoing any significant *intrinsic* change at all, becomes such that it is physically impossible for it ever to live again. In such a case, IR$_1$ would yield the implausible verdict that the organism dies at the relevant instant, even though the organism undergoes no significant intrinsic change at that instant and apparently remains cryptobiotic for some time thereafter. Consider the following case:

> **Deep Space**. A desiccated tardigrade, Delta, rides through deep space on a chunk of rock, when suddenly the stars surrounding it in all directions explode into supernovas. Though the laws of nature are not deterministic, there is a certain instant t such that: (i) Delta is intuitively still cryptobiotic at t and will remain so for some time thereafter, but (ii) at t, it begins to be physically necessary that radiation from the supernovas will permanently destroy Delta before any potentially life-restoring processes reach it. Later, at t*, radiation from the supernovas finally reaches Delta and causes intrinsic changes in it that render it nonviable. Delta remains present for some time thereafter.[40]

As applied to this case, IR_1 says that the tardigrade Delta dies at t. But, to supporters of the cryptobiosis argument at least, this ought to seem incorrect. They will want to say that Delta does not die until the later instant t*.

It is worth noting that IR_1 does not even get off the ground unless one assumes that the laws of nature are not deterministic. For suppose that the laws are deterministic, and let o be an organism that ceases to be alive at t1 by entering cryptobiosis. Further, suppose that o never returns to life thereafter. Then I take it that at t1, it becomes physically necessary that o will never be alive again.[41] After all, in a world with deterministic laws, *everything* about the future is physically necessary (in the sense of being entailed by the past and present together with the laws). So, in such a world, as soon as it becomes *true* that a given thing will never live again, it also becomes *physically necessary*. In such a context, IR_1 does no better than Permanence in dealing with problems about cryptobiosis.

2.4 Irreversibility₂: The *Internally Grounded* Physical Impossibility of Living Again

To cope with cases like Deep Space, Feldman proposes a repair that, he thinks, "comes pretty close to solving the problem of suspended animation" (1992, p. 65). The repair entails

> IR_2 Necessarily, for any x and any t, if t is an instant, then x dies at t if and only if "(i) x ceases to be alive at or before t, and (ii) at t, internal changes occur in x that make it physically impossible for x ever to live again" (1992, p. 65).[42]

How might IR_2 help in the Deep Space case? At t, the thought goes, Delta became such that it was physically impossible for it ever to live again, but this was not because of any *internal changes* that occurred in Delta at t; rather, it was because of external changes that occurred at t. The tardigrade didn't undergo any significant internal changes then at all. So IR_2 apparently does not say that Delta died at

t. This gives it an advantage over IR_1. (Does IR_2 say that Delta *does* die at t*, the instant at which it is made nonviable by radiation? Perhaps. We will return to this question.)

2.4.1 *Clarifying Irreversibility$_2$*

Now let's look at IR_2 a bit more closely. Clause (ii) says "at t, internal changes occur in x that make it physically impossible for x ever to live again." Here is a proposal about how this clause should be understood (or what it should be replaced with).

We can start by defining a *distribution* as a (total or partial) function from real numbers to (perhaps empty) sets of intrinsic* relations. And we can say that a thing x *instantiates* a given distribution f *over* a given interval I just in case: (i) f is a distribution; (ii) I is a continuous interval of time; and (iii) for each real number n and set s, f(n) = s iff s is the set of intrinsic* relations that x bears to the instant in I that is located n minutes prior to the end of I. Loosely speaking, if x instantiates f over I, then when you feed a number n into the function f, that function will spit out the set whose members are all and only the intrinsic properties that x had n minutes before the end of I. If x was not present at the given instant, then the set in question will be empty, since things cannot bear intrinsic* relations to ("have intrinsic properties at") instants at which they are not present.

We can now use these notions to define one further technical term: "intrinsically biologically hopeless," or just "hopeless$_{ib}$":

> D1 x is hopeless$_{ib}$ at t = df. (i) t is an instant and (ii) there is some proposition
> p that states the laws of nature,[43] some interval I leading up to t, and some
> distribution f such that:
> (a) x instantiates f over I, and
> (b) necessarily, for any instant t_1, any interval I_1 that leads up to t_1, and any later
>   instant t_2 if (p is true and x instantiates f over I_1), then x is not alive at t_2.

Intuitively, to say that x is hopeless$_{ib}$ at t is to say that x has an intrinsic history leading up to t that, given the laws of nature, guarantees that x is not alive thereafter. In other words, the distribution of x's intrinsic properties (or lack thereof) over some period leading up to t makes it physically impossible for x to be alive after t. Thus, whether or not a thing x is hopeless$_{ib}$ at a given instant t need not be purely a matter of x's intrinsic condition at t itself; it can also depend upon x's intrinsic *history*, prior to t.

It is worth pointing out that D1 does not require that a thing be present at an instant in order for it to be hopeless$_{ib}$ at that instant. To see this, suppose that it's metaphysically impossible for a thing to cease to be present at one time and then become present again later on; that is, suppose that "intermittent presence" is impossible. Further, suppose that Socrates ceased to be present at t1, and let t2 be some later instant. Then Socrates is hopeless$_{ib}$ at t2.

For there will be some interval leading up to t2 that includes t1 and, say, just the final few minutes of Socrates's career. Call that interval I_s. Now consider the distribution f_s that Socrates instantiates over I_s, and suppose that t_1 is m minutes earlier than t_2. Then for any n less than m, $f_s(n)$ will be the empty set, since Socrates wasn't present at the instant that occurred n minutes before t_2 and hence did not bear any intrinsic* relations to that instant. But for any n* greater than m, $f(n^*)$ will be a nonempty set, since Socrates was present at the instant that occurred n* minutes before t_2 and hence[44] did bear some intrinsic* relations to that instant. Thus the distribution f_s that Socrates instantiates over I_s entails ceasing to be present during the interval over which it is instantiated. Given the impossibility of intermittent presence, nothing can instantiate this distribution over a given interval and then be present (or alive) after that interval. Therefore it is not even metaphysically possible, much less physically possible, for *Socrates* to instantiate that distribution over a given interval and then be alive (hence present) at some later instant.

With the notion of hopelessness$_{ib}$ in hand, we can formulate a new instance of the schema S:

> IR$_2$* Necessarily, for any x and any t, if t is an instant, then x dies at t if and only if: (i) x ceases to be alive at or before t, and (ii) x becomes hopeless$_{ib}$ at t.

This, I suggest, is the best way to capture the intuitive idea underlying Irreversibility$_2$ in explicit terms. At least I am not aware of any formulation that clearly does better on this score.[45]

To get a feel for the principle, let's return to the Deep Space case. Suppose that the tardigrade was alive at t1, that it became cryptobiotic and ceased to be alive at the later time t2, that (due to extrinsic factors) it became physically impossible for the tardigrade to live again at t, and that the tardigrade was badly damaged by radiation at t*. The tardigrade does not become hopeless$_{ib}$ until t* at the earliest. Nothing about its pre-t* intrinsic history guarantees (given the laws) that it won't be alive later. There are possible worlds governed by the same laws in which that tardigrade goes through qualitatively the same intrinsic history but, because of its more favorable surroundings, manages to return to life again later. Hence IR$_2$* avoids the result that the tardigrade dies at t.

Does IR$_2$* say that the tardigrade dies at t*, when it is damaged by radiation? That depends upon whether the tardigrade then becomes hopeless$_{ib}$—that is, on whether it then becomes such that its intrinsic history makes it physically impossible for it to live again. And that is not a question that we can usefully pursue here, although we will soon address some related questions.

One small point about IR$_2$* is worth making before we move on: this principle leaves open the possibility that a thing dies at an instant at which it is not hopeless$_{ib}$. To see this, suppose that Bob is alive at t1, at the later instant t2, and at each instant in between, but not at any instant after t2. Further, suppose that Bob is hopeless$_{ib}$ at each instant after t2, but not at t2 itself or at any earlier instant. Then I take it that Bob ceases to be alive at t2 and that he *becomes* hopeless$_{ib}$ at t2, even though he is not hopeless$_{ib}$ *at* that time. If so, then IR$_2$* tells us that Bob dies at t2.

2.4.2 Is Postmortem Revitalization Physically Impossible? Necessarily So?

So far I have been trying to get clear about what Irreversibility$_2$ says. I think it is best formulated as IR$_2$*. Now I want to argue that Irreversibility$_2$ is false.

Dead things tend not to return to life. But must it in every case be *physically impossible* for a dead thing to live again? This is doubtful. To begin to see why, consider the following story:[46]

> **Restoration**. Beta is an ordinary organism. It begins to be alive at t1, lives a typical life, and at t2, as a result of old age and standard wear and tear, it ceases to engage in metabolism or any other life-functions. The portion of matter that constituted Beta[47] in the moments leading up to t2 then begins to decompose slightly. (Call this portion of matter p_B.) At t3, before much further decay has had a chance to set in, p_B is frozen and preserved. At t4, scientists begin the delicate process of causing p_B to constitute something viable once again. Without introducing any new matter or removing any of the original matter, the scientists gradually and nondisruptively reverse the damage that has recently occurred. At t5, p_B constitutes something that is a perfect intrinsic duplicate of *Gamma*, a frozen organism that entered cryptobiosis in the normal way. The scientists then thaw p_B. At t6, p_B constitutes something that is alive and has an active metabolism.
>
> Moreover, at no point in this sequence of events is any law of nature violated. On the contrary, there are laws of nature (perhaps different from ours), there is a proposition that states them, and they are "obeyed" throughout the entire process.

Note that there are certain issues on which Restoration is careful not to take an explicit stand. It takes no stand on whether Beta dies at any point in the story, and it takes no stand on whether the thing that becomes actively metabolic between t5 and t6 is Beta. More generally, it takes no stand on whether there is someone that both ceases to engage in metabolism at t2 and begins to engage in metabolism between t5 and t6.

We can ask a number of questions about the case. First, is it, or something relevantly like it, physically possible? That is, do the *actual* laws of nature permit it? Second, is it, or something relevantly like it, metaphysically possible? Third, if we further specify the story by stipulating that it involves something that dies and then comes to be alive again later, is the resulting story physically and/or metaphysically possible?

We can start with the first question. Is Restoration physically possible? I doubt that anyone *has in fact* reanimated the remains of bacteria or insects (not to mention humans) that have been rendered nonviable by old age and structural damage. Indeed, the case may be technologically impossible, by present-day earthly standards. Perhaps the technology that would be required to carry out such a procedure is unlikely ever to be developed by creatures with brains like ours. Moreover, the likelihood that such processes of repair will occur *spontaneously*, without intervention by intentional agents, may for all practical purposes be zero.

Still, it would come as a surprise to learn that *the laws of nature* somehow bar the occurrence of such processes. One would think that, in principle, those processes ought to be physically possible, even if humans will never develop the technology needed to make them happen. After all, a thing that has been partially disassembled and rendered nonfunctional can typically be reassembled and made functional again, without violating any laws of nature. I can see no antecedent reason to think that organisms are different from cars in this regard.[48] Organisms are just more intricate and harder for us to manipulate.

Admittedly, this is all speculative. Whether the laws of nature permit the relevant "reanimation procedures" is an empirical question, and nature is full of surprises. I don't know whether these processes are physically possible. But for all I know—and, I suspect, for all *anyone* knows—they are.

Even if Restoration is *not* physically possible, the second question arises: is it metaphysically possible? Is there a metaphysically possible world in which a story relevantly like Restoration is true? Some may think not, on the grounds that the story violates a law of nature and that these laws are all metaphysically necessary (Bird, 2007). Others, however, ought to take the story to be metaphysically possible. It is, after all, consistent, conceivable, and intuitively possible. It involves nothing more exotic than some matter, and an associated object or two, possessing different intrinsic properties at different times, and standing in the right sorts of causal relations. Even if the laws of nature in the *actual* world rule out the given story (which I doubt), surely there are possible worlds governed by different laws in which something like that story is true.

So let us turn to the third question. Is it physically and/or metaphysically possible that the given processes occur *and in such a way that they involve something that dies and then becomes alive again later*? Suppose that we further specify the story by adding the following:

> Organism Beta dies at t2 or shortly thereafter and is alive at t6, after the "repaired matter" that composes it is thawed.

Call the resulting story *Restoration+*. In Restoration+, we have one and the same organism first dying, then having its remains restored (whether or not it is present during that process), then returning to life later. Restoration does not take an explicit stand one way or the other on the question of whether something dies and later returns to life; Restoration+ does. Are there metaphysically possible worlds at which Restoration+, or something relevantly like it, is true?

For those who admit the metaphysical possibility of Restoration itself, I can think of two main reasons for denying the possibility of Restoration+. First, one might think that

    (a)   Restoration entails that the organism Beta does not really *die* at t2 (or shortly thereafter), when it ceases to engage in metabolism.

Second, one might think that

> (b) Restoration entails that it is a mere *copy* of Beta, not Beta itself, that is alive and constituted by p_B at t6.[49]

I don't find either reason compelling.

According to (a), Restoration is not a case in which an organism lives, dies, and is subsequently revitalized; rather it is a case in which an organism is actively metabolic, then becomes cryptobiotic, and then subsequently becomes actively metabolic again, all without dying or becoming dead in the process.

This strikes me as strained. By any ordinary standard, Beta is dead at t3 and has been for some time. I doubt that any biologist who considered the case would say that Beta has merely entered a phase of dormancy or cryptobiosis. It did not cease to engage in the relevant life-functions as the result of any of the standard causes of cryptobiosis—desiccation, freezing, and so on. Rather, it ceased to engage in those life-functions as the result of a standard cause of *death*—namely, old age and structural damage. Its trajectory thereafter was common to things that have *died*: it continued to sustain further damage and was decomposing—if it even remained present at all! This is quite unlike the typical trajectory of things in cryptobiosis: they remain approximately static. Moreover, by t3, Beta is no longer *disposed* to live (or metabolize), even in circumstances that are favorable to life for things of its kind. It is no longer *viable*. It manages to metabolize again only with the help of advanced technology. Thus the natural thing to say is that, in the story, Beta is dead at t3 and died at some earlier time, probably t2 or very shortly thereafter.[50]

Next consider (b), which says that Restoration entails that Beta is neither alive nor constituted by p_B at t6. According to (b), the organism that is constituted by p_B at t6 is merely a copy of Beta, not Beta itself. Is this plausible? If one (i) holds that Beta dies at t2, (ii) takes TT to be a necessary truth, and (iii) denies the possibility of intermittent presence, then one will accept (b). But as far as I can tell, the rest of us will want to reject it.

Opponents of the TT will presumably want to say that the organism Beta continues to be present throughout the entire story. After all, it's not as if Beta's death is especially violent. Its remains don't get scattered or radically altered in shape or superficial appearance. Throughout the entire case, there is what might be described as "the body of an organism." Thus, if it *ever* happens that a thing continues to be present for a while after it dies, this would seem to be just such a case. In particular, if one rejects the TT, then the overwhelmingly natural thing for one to say will be that, in the story, Beta is alive from t1 to t2, that Beta dies at t2 or shortly thereafter, that Beta continues to be present as a dead thing, that it gets frozen at t3, that it gets repaired from t4 to t5, that it is then thawed and revived, and that it is alive again at t6. This conflicts with (b).

But even those who *accept* TT will presumably want to say that Beta dies and lives again later (or at least that Restoration doesn't rule this out), unless they take a hard line against the metaphysical possibility of intermittent presence.[51] For suppose that Beta dies and ceases to be present at t2. Then if it's so much as *possible* for a material substance to become present again after it has ceased to present, it ought to be possible that Beta does this at some point during the process of repair and revitalization.[52] After all, the "postrepair organism" is made of the same matter, in roughly the same arrangement, as was the original organism (Beta) just before its death, and no *other* organism was composed of that matter in the interim. Moreover, the final predeath phases in Beta's life presumably stand in a rather intimate causal relation to the initial postrepair phases in the life of the repaired organism: the repaired organism has the intrinsic properties that it has at t6 largely because the original organism had the intrinsic properties that it had just prior to t2.[53] If Beta had been different in any of various ways prior to t2, the repaired organism would also have been different in those same ways at t6. Finally, it's plausible that, if the given organisms are (or constitute) *people,* then those people could be psychologically continuous with each other and could stand in any other mental relations that might be required to support the intermittent presence of a person. In sum, even Terminators should reject (b), unless they are foes of intermittent presence.[54]

The issues here are complex and subtle, and they allow for a wide variety of internally consistent, stable positions. We shouldn't expect any decisive refutations. On the whole, however, neither (a) nor (b) looks very promising to me. If one admits, as I think one should, the metaphysical possibility of Restoration, then one ought to admit the metaphysical possibility of the more specific story Restoration+, in which Beta dies and later returns to life.

And in that case one ought to reject Irreversibility$_2$. Even if it is *true* that things die only when they become hopeless$_{ib}$ (which I doubt), this is not *metaphysically necessary*: there are possible worlds in which a thing dies and later comes to be alive again, all in conformity with the laws of nature governing the given world. Hence there are possible worlds in which a thing dies without then becoming such that its intrinsic history, together with the laws governing the given world, guarantee that the thing won't be alive again later. Contrary to Irreversibility$_2$, becoming hopeless$_{ib}$ is not necessary for dying.

As I said earlier, I suspect that for all anyone knows, Restoration is physically possible. But it's plausible that if Restoration is physically possible, then so is Restoration+. This makes me suspect that for all anyone knows, (i) Restoration+ is physically possible and hence (ii) there are physically possible counterexamples to Irreversibility$_2$.

2.5 Irreversibility$_3$: The *Technological* Impossibility of Living Again

Because it invokes the notion of physical impossibility, Irreversibility$_2$ makes it "too hard" to die. Contrary to Irreversibility$_2$, a thing can die at a time even if it continues to be physically possible for the thing to live again.

One likely suggestion at this point is that we should understand irreversibility not in terms of physical impossibility but rather in terms of technological impossibility. Roughly, the idea is that a thing dies when its having ceased to be alive becomes "technologically" irreversible. This might lower the bar for dying. Even if it is still physically possible for a given organism to return to life, it might not be technologically possible.

Regardless of how this "technological irreversibility thesis," Irreversibility$_3$, is spelled out, it faces three problems. The first and most fundamental problem is that it entails that whether a thing dies at a given time can depend upon extrinsic factors that intuitively should have no bearing on the thing's vital status. To see this, consider:

> **Alpha and Omega**. Alpha and Omega are duplicate organisms of the same species that live at different times. At t1, as a result of damage, Alpha ceases to be alive and starts to decay. No technology that is available to Alpha could reverse the situation. Omega's career is an intrinsic duplicate of Alpha's career (and is governed by the same laws of nature) but occurs later. Thus Omega, as it is when it is n years old, is a duplicate of Alpha, as *it* is when *it* was n years old. At t2, Omega ceases to be alive and starts to decay just as Alpha did. However, at t2, new technology is available to Omega. This technology could be used to revitalize Omega, but is not so used. Omega continues to decay in just the same manner as did Alpha.

Irreversibility$_3$ entails that Alpha dies at t1 but that Omega does not die at t2. This is extremely implausible. Intuitively, whether or not a given organism o dies at a given instant t should be fixed by facts about the laws of nature governing o, together with facts about what o is like intrinsically at certain times—times such as t itself, any earlier instants at which o is present, and perhaps some fairly brief period of time following t. The point is well put by David Hershenov: "death is best thought of as a nonrelational alteration in an individual's body or organs. "Death" is a biological concept (and a nonrelational one) and thus should be determined solely by biological factors rather than technological features." (2003a, p. 93).

Regardless of how one articulates this "intrinsicality of dying" principle in detail, it will entail that whether or not an organism dies at a time cannot depend upon *wildly* extrinsic factors, such as facts about what sorts of technologies are available to the organism at the given time. Hence, on any remotely adequate way of formulating the intrinsicality principle, it will tell us, when applied to the case above, that Alpha and Omega don't differ in whether they die (at t1 and t2, respectively). Thus the intrinsicality principle will rule out Irreversibility$_3$.

Here is a second problem for that thesis. It does not state a *sufficient* condition for a thing to die. Suppose that Gamma has ceased to live by going into cryptobiosis. Further, suppose that, at time t, it becomes technologically impossible for Gamma to live again, not because of any intrinsic change in Gamma, but because the only existing technology that could have been used to revive Gamma ceases to be available to it, and indeed ceases to be present altogether. (Perhaps the civilization that developed the technology is destroyed in a nuclear war.) As applied to such a case, Irreversibility$_3$ will tell us, incorrectly, that Gamma dies at t.

Third, that thesis fails to state a *necessary* condition for a thing to die. In the Restoration case, I claimed, Beta dies at t2. But technology is then available to Beta that could be—and indeed *will* be—successfully used to revive Beta, and such technology continues to be available to Beta throughout the rest of the story. So Beta's ceasing to be alive does not then become "technologically irreversible" in either of the relevant senses. Thus Irreversibility$_3$ tells us, incorrectly, that Beta does not die at t2.

2.6 Incapacitation

In effect, we have so far been asking, "What's the difference between dying and becoming cryptobiotic?" I think the difference is best captured in terms of dispositions or capacities, roughly as follows: when a living thing becomes cryptobiotic, it retains a sufficiently robust, intrinsically grounded *disposition* or *capacity* to be alive (under an appropriate range of conditions). In short, it remains viable. But when it dies, it loses the relevant capacity; it ceases to be viable. Neither dead things nor cryptobiotic things are alive. But cryptobiotic things are viable, whereas dead things are not.

This doesn't entail that it's physically or technologically impossible for dead things to return to life. What it does entail is that it's "harder" for dead things to return to life than it is for cryptobiotic ones. Cryptobiotic things often do it "on their own," "without external intervention" and without first being repaired.[55] Dead things need help, or else a lot of luck.

Ingmar Persson has suggested a definition of "dies" that harmonizes with these thoughts. Persson's definition entails the following instance of schema S:

> Incapacity Necessarily, for any x and any t, if t is an instant, then x dies at t if and only if "at t, x loses the capacity to live" (1995, p. 501).[56]

In my view, this account has two important virtues. (Persson himself, however, invokes only one of these, and he seems to deny that the account has the other virtue). Indeed, as far as the problems about cryptobiosis go, the account is approximately right. But I also think that it has a drawback worth noting. I'll start with the virtues.

2.6.1 *Virtues*

First, as Persson notes, Incapacity plausibly makes dying an intrinsic matter (or at least a *not-radically-extrinsic* matter). Whether or not a thing x has, at a time t, the capacity to φ depends only on the intrinsic properties that x has at t, together with the laws of nature—at least when the property *φ-ing* itself is intrinsic.[57] Suppose that two chameleons are intrinsic duplicates and are governed by the same laws of nature. Then, if one of them has the capacity to turn brown, so does the other. If two people are duplicates and one of them is lactose intolerant (lacks the capacity to digest lactose), then so is the other. So, since *being alive* is intrinsic (or almost intrinsic[58]), we get the result that whether or not a given thing has, at t, the *capacity* to be alive will depend only on the thing's intrinsic properties at t, together with the laws. Organisms that are intrinsic duplicates and governed by the same laws will never differ with respect to the capacity to be alive. And two duplicate organisms that undergo duplicate "internal processes" over a given interval (and are governed by the same laws) will never differ with respect to whether they *lose* the capacity to be alive during that interval.

Thus, unlike Irreversibility₁ and Irreversibility₃ (but like Irreversibility₂), Incapacity avoids the bizarre result that whether or not a thing dies at a time can depend on "wildly extrinsic" factors. At time t, when distant events make it physically impossible for the frozen, intrinsically unchanging tardigrade ever to live, that organism doesn't lose the *capacity* to live and so, according to Incapacity, doesn't die. The tardigrade does, however, plausibly lose that capacity at t*, when it's damaged by radiation. So Incapacity again yields the desired verdict—namely that the tardigrade *does* die at t*. Incapacity also helps with the case of Alpha and Omega. These organisms have duplicate careers, and they both cease to perform any life-functions and begin to decay at an age of n years old. Since Omega has access to "revitalization technology" at the relevant age but Alpha does not, Irreversibility₃ says that Alpha dies at an age of n years but that Omega does not, despite their intrinsic similarity at those ages. Incapacity does better. In view of their intrinsic similarity and the fact that they are governed by the same laws, either they both lose the capacity to live at age n years, or neither of them does. So, according to Incapacity, either they both die at that age, or neither does. This seems right.

Incapacity also has a second virtue. One can lose the capacity to do something without its then becoming physically impossible for one ever to do it again. Broken watches get fixed, athletes make comebacks, and so on. If one stops exercising for a while, one might lose the capacity to bench press 150 lbs. Then, after lifting weights for a few months, one might regain that capacity. One thus loses the capacity to bench press 150 lbs without then undergoing some internal change that makes it physically impossible for one ever to bench press 150 lbs again. Or some engine component in one's car might break, causing the car to lose the capacity to run, without its then becoming physically impossible for the car to ever run again.

Thus, unlike Irreversibility₁ and Irreversibility₂ (but like Irreversibility₃), Incapacity allows for the possibility of a thing—such as the organism Beta in the Restoration+ case—that dies at a time without its then becoming *physically impossible* for the thing ever to be alive again. In that case, it seems plausible to say that Beta *loses* the capacity to be alive at t2, when it stops metabolizing and starts to decompose, and that it *regains* that capacity later on, at some point during the process of repair. (Still later, it goes on to *manifest* or *exercise* that capacity.) According to Incapacity, therefore, Beta does die at t2, even though it continues to be physically possible for Beta to live again.

Interestingly, Persson himself does not see the matter this way (1995, p. 501). Instead, he says that his proposal is equivalent to Feldman's (which we have labeled Irreversibility₂). Accordingly, Persson does not argue, as I have, that Feldman's account faces a problem that Incapacity avoids. If I'm right, Incapacity deserves more credit than Persson gives it.

In sum, Incapacity has two major virtues: (i) it doesn't entail that dying is a "wildly extrinsic" matter, and (ii) it doesn't entail that, as a matter of metaphysical necessity, postmortem revitalization is physically impossible. Indeed, I'm not aware of *any* plausible counterexamples to Incapacity stemming from cryptobiosis, revitalization, or any similar phenomenon.

2.6.2 A Vice

The word "capacity" probably introduces some context-sensitivity into "at t, x loses the capacity to live" that is lacking in "x dies at t."[59] This in itself is no problem for Incapacity, provided that the relation expressed (relative to the present context) by the former expression is necessarily coextensive with the relation expressed by "x dies at t."

But I wonder how likely it is that those relations are necessarily—or even actually—coextensive. After all, I doubt that there is some uniquely natural or "reference-eligible" relation in the vicinity that both expressions can just "lock onto." Rather, I suspect that there is a huge range of more-or-less equally natural relations in the vicinity that differ just a little from one another. Consider, for example, the relations expressed (relative to the present context) by "at t, x loses a robust capacity to live", "at t, x loses a very robust capacity to live", "at t, x ceases to be very capable of living", "at t, x ceases to be disposed to live in normal conditions", "at t, x ceases to be viable", "at t, x ceases to be robustly viable", and "at t, x ceases to be even remotely viable".

Some of these relations may have the same extension in the actual world but different extensions in other possible worlds. Others may have different (but probably largely overlapping) extensions even in the actual world. None of them seems any more likely than any of the others to be necessarily coextensive with *dies at*, and each seems to be roughly as good a candidate as the relation expressed by "at t, x loses the capacity to live." So I'm not confident that "x dies at t" and "at t, x loses the capacity to live" express necessarily (or even actually) coextensive relations. Accordingly, I'm not confident that Incapacity is true. But there probably isn't much we can do to improve on it. Things die when they cease to have a *sufficiently robust* capacity to live. How robust is sufficiently robust? I see no way to give an informative answer to this question. The best we can do is to point to examples.

After so many false starts, this may seem a bit anticlimactic and underwhelming as a positive view. Admittedly, Incapacity is less informative and less precise than one might have hoped. But as far as the problem of cryptobiosis goes, I doubt we can do better. In my view, all the other accounts we've considered do worse.

Before we turn to a different puzzle about death, one final point about Incapacity: it leaves open the possibility of a thing that dies without ever having been alive. We can imagine an organism popping into existence fully formed but in a state of cryptobiosis. If it shattered and ceased to be viable soon thereafter, Incapacity would yield the result that it died, even though it never lived. This is in the spirit of the "intrinsicality of dying" principle that we gestured toward earlier. If two cryptobiotic things undergo the same sequence of intrinsic changes over a given interval (and are governed by the same laws of nature), they shouldn't differ with respect to whether they die during that interval, even if only one of them was ever alive previously. Incapacity respects this claim.

3. FISSION

To die is not merely to cease to be alive. For one thing, an organism that goes directly from being alive to being cryptobiotic does cease to be alive but doesn't die—at least not then! For another, if an amoeba divides into two new amoebas, it does cease to be alive[60]—indeed, it ceases to be present at all. But, as Jay Rosenberg has pointed out, it doesn't die then.[61] (Or *ever*, unless the case is rather bizarre. See the "Annie" case at the end of section 4.) The passage from Rosenberg is worth quoting:

> Some amoebae, to be sure, do die. Sometimes an amoeba cannot get sufficient food or oxygen or moisture to sustain its life, and that kills it. But some amoebae do not get an opportunity to die…let us consider a well-fed, healthy amoeba alone in a drop of well-oxygenated pond water. I shall call it "Alvin." Alvin, let us suppose, lives happily through Tuesday and then, precisely at the stroke of midnight, Alvin divides, producing two offspring whom I shall call "Amos" and "Ambrose." On Wednesday, we find two amoebae—Amos and Ambrose—swimming happily about in our drop of pond water. But what has become of Alvin? One thing is quite clear: Alvin is not an inhabitant of our drop of pond water on Wednesday…His life, therefore, must have come to an end. But it is equally clear that Alvin did not die. (1983, pp. 21–22; 1998, pp. 34–35)

Fred Feldman accepts Rosenberg's point and draws parallel conclusions about certain cases of biological fusion. His main example involves chlamydomonas, single-celled plants that sometimes engage in a process of fusion in which two haploid individuals combine to form a new, diploid individual. Feldman claims that when a haploid chlamydomona engages in fusion, it ceases to be alive but doesn't die. (As Feldman notes, one might take certain cases of metamorphosis to have a similar structure. Perhaps caterpillars cease to be alive but don't die when they metamorphose into butterflies.)

These cases are threats to Incapacity no less than to CT. Not only did Amos cease to be alive at midnight; he also ceased to have the capacity to live at that time. (I assume that, necessarily, if a thing has, at t, the capacity to live, then it is present at t.) So even if Incapacity solves the problem of cryptobiosis, it's still false. It offers no help with Rosenberg's case.

3.1 Three Extant Attempts at a Repair

The new puzzle cases all involve biological entities that go directly from being alive to being nonpresent—and hence not alive—without dying. Why is it that the entities in question do not die in these cases? Presumably, there are cases in which a biological entity *does* die when it goes directly from being alive to being nonpresent. If a healthy, active bacterium is sliced in half and its remains quickly disperse and decompose, maybe it dies and ceases to be present at the same time. Thus a puzzle arises: what's the difference? Say that a case in which a biological entity goes directly from being alive to being nonpresent is a *termination*, and that it is *deadly* if the thing dies when it ceases to be present, but *deathless* otherwise. In virtue of what are the deadly terminations deadly? In virtue of what are the deathless terminations deathless?

Not everyone will be gripped by these questions. Some will lack firm intuitions about the cases. Some will doubt that anything significant is at stake here. I won't try to argue that the facts about the modal profile of dying have instrumental value. I don't know what use they are for ethics, biology, or other parts of metaphysics. But for those who find the questions of some intrinsic interest and who would like to press on, there is progress to be made. (Others are free to skip ahead to section 4, which stands on its own.)

3.1.1 First Try: Deathless Division as Division into Living Things

One thing that all these cases have in common is this. We have a living thing and its constituent matter (or some living things and their constituent matter). Then, at a certain instant, the living thing ceases to be present, while the matter continues to be present. Immediately after the thing ceases to be present, the given matter makes up some other thing or things. The original thing "turns into" the other things.

So what's the difference between the deadly and the deathless cases? One natural thought is that the deathless terminations involve a living thing or things that turn into some other *living* thing or things. The reason why an amoeba doesn't die when it divides is that it turns into two other *living* things; and the reason why two chlamydomonas don't die when they fuse is that they turn into another living thing. Correspondingly, the reason the bacterium does die when it gets sliced in half is that none of the pluralities of things it turns into—*two halves of a bacterium,* or *some organelles and miscellaneous cell parts,* or *some fundamental particles*—is such that each of its members is alive.

As for the notion of *turning into* invoked here, I doubt that it can be rigorously defined, but here is a rough characterization that should be good enough for present purposes:

TI   xx *turn into* yy at t if and only if there is a portion of matter m such
      that (i) xx are made up of[62] m throughout some interval leading up to t;

(ii) each of xx ceases to be present at t; and (iii) throughout some interval that immediately follows t, yy are made up of m, plus or minus a little.

The predicate "___turns into…at ****" is nondistributive. From "a turned into b and c at t," one cannot validly infer "a turned into b at t" or "a turned into c at t." The relation expressed by this predicate has two slots for pluralities of things (corresponding to the two plural variables, "xx" and "yy" in TI) and one slot for a time (corresponding to the singular variable "t"). That relation can hold in various patterns: between one thing, many things, and a time (as in the case of amoebic fission); between many things, one thing, and a time (as in fusion); perhaps between one thing, one thing, and a time (in metamorphosis); and between many things, many things, and a time (as when two amoebas divide at the same time, thus turning into four amoebas). The vague phrase "plus or minus a little" in clause (iii) is needed to allow for cases in which, say, a little matter is lost at the moment of division. Without this phrase, we wouldn't be able to say that the original amoeba turns into the two new amoebas, since the portion of matter that they're made up of at the beginning of their lives *mostly overlaps*, but is not *strictly identical to*, the portion of matter that made up the original amoeba at the end of its life.

With this notion in hand, we can state a new instance of schema S based on the "natural thought" proposed above. The idea is that a necessary condition for dying is *not turning into some other living thing or things*. Borrowing from Feldman, we can formulate it thus:

A₁ Necessarily, for any x and any t, if t is an instant, then x dies at t if and only if (i) at t, x loses the capacity to live; (ii) "it's not the case that x turns into a living thing, or bunch of living things, at t; and [iii] it is not the case that x is a member of a set of living things whose members fuse and turn into a living thing at t" (1992, p. 68).

Since Rosenberg's dividing amoeba does turn into some living things when it divides, it does not satisfy clause (ii), and as a result A₁ does not tell us that the amoeba dies. Since Feldman's fusing chlamydomonas do turn into a living thing when they fuse, they do not satisfy clause (iii); and as a result A₁ does not tell us that they die. So far, so good.

But as Feldman notes, A₁ is vulnerable to counterexamples too. Suppose that we put a mouse into a "cell-separator" that "grinds up mice and emits a puree of mouse cells…in such a way that all the mouse cells come out alive" (1992, p. 69). In this case, Feldman claims, the mouse turns into a bunch of other living things (namely, its cells) and hence it fails to satisfy clause (ii).[63] A₁ thus yields the intuitively incorrect verdict that the mouse does not die when put into the cell separator.

We can extract a lesson. Sometimes, when a living thing turns into some other living things, the original thing dies. Sometimes it doesn't. What's the difference? What makes the mouse's termination deadly? What makes the amoeba's termination deathless?

3.1.2 Second Try: Deathless Division as Division into Living Organisms

Here is a tempting thought. What makes the amoebic fission deathless is the fact that it involves an amoeba that turns into two amoebas, where both of these result- ing amoebas are *organisms* in their own right; and what makes the mouse fission deadly is the fact that it involves a mouse that turns into mere living cells, where these cells are *not* organisms. The suggestion, then, is this: necessarily, a case of biological fission is deathless if and only if it involves a thing that turns into some living organisms. This suggestion, generalized so as to apply to cases of fusion as well, can be incorporated into a new instance of schema S:

> A$_2$ Necessarily, for any x and any t, if t is an instant, then x dies at t if and only if (i) at t, x loses the capacity to live; (ii) "it is not the case that x turns into a living organism or a bunch of living organisms at t; and [iii] it is not the case that x is a member of a set of living organisms that fuse to form a living organism at t" (Feldman, 1992, p. 70).

But A$_2$ is vulnerable to the following counterexample, also due to Feldman. An isolated frog cell, C, is kept alive in a laboratory. Eventually, C undergoes fission: it ceases to be present and turns into two daughter cells. Since neither of these is an *organism* (they're both mere living cells), C satisfies clause (ii) of A$_2$. And since the other clauses are obviously satisfied as well, A$_2$ yields the verdict that C died when it divided. But this verdict seems wrong. Neither an amoeba nor an isolated frog cell dies when it divides into two new cells. So A$_2$ is false as well. At this point Feldman draws his discussion to a pessimistic close: "Fission and fusion are puz- zling. I find that I cannot explain the difference between their deathless forms and their deadly forms" (1992, p. 71).

3.1.3 Third Try: Deathless Division as Division into Living Things without Downgrading

Edward Wierenga is more optimistic. He suggests that the reason the mouse died when it turned into living cells is that the mouse was an organism but the cells weren't. The mouse, we might say, was "biologically downgraded." When the frog cell divided into two frog cells, however, it was not biologically downgraded, since, although the daughter cells were not organisms, neither was the original parent cell. According to this proposal, then, a case of biological fission is deathless if and only if it involves (i) an organism that turns into some organisms or (ii) a living nonorganism that turns into some living things (organisms or not). When this idea is generalized in such a way as to apply to fusion as well as fission, it can be grafted on to Incapacity to yield:

> A$_3$ Necessarily, for any x and any t, if t is an instant, then x dies at t if and only if (i) at t, x loses the capacity to live; (ii) "if x is an organism then it is not the case that x turns directly into a living organism or a bunch of living organisms at t, and it is not the case that x is a member of a set of

living organisms whose members fuse and turn into a living organism at t, and [iii] if x is not an organism then it is not the case that x turns into a living thing, or a bunch of living things, at t, and it is not the case that x is a member of a set of living things whose members fuse and turn into a living thing at t" (Wierenga, 1994, p. 81).

A$_3$ handles all the cases so far considered. It tells us that the amoeba doesn't die when it divides into two new amoebas; *mutatis mutandis* for the frog cell. And it tells us that the mouse does die when it is sent through the cell separator.

Does A$_3$ succeed? It depends on what we should say about cases in which a multicellular organism is composed of cells each of which is an organism in its own right. If such cases are possible, then there are counterexamples to A$_3$. For, suppose that such a multicellular organism is sent through a cell separator. This strikes me as a way of *killing* that organism and hence that the organism *dies*. But the organism does turn into some living things—its cells—that are themselves organisms, hence it doesn't satisfy clause (ii) of A$_3$. So A$_3$ tells us, incorrectly, that the organism does not die.

Could there be a multicellular organism each of whose cells is itself an organism? It's easy to image a creature that we'd be tempted to describe that way. But we can focus on an actual case. Consider the slime mold slug (or "grex"), described here by Jack Wilson:

> At one point in the life cycle of certain species of cellular slime molds, a number of independent, amoebalike single cells aggregate together into a grex. The grex is a cylindrical mass of these cells that behaves much like a slug. It has a front and back, responds as a unit to light, and can move as a cohesive body. The cells that compose a grex are not always genetically identical or even related. They begin their lives as free-living single-cell organisms. The grex has some properties of an individual and behaves very much like one. (1999, p. 8)

Wilson seems to be taking care not to assert that the slug is an *organism*, but, for what it's worth, it's easy to find biologists making this assertion in journal articles. ("The cellular slime mold *Dictyostelium discoideum* undergoes a transition from single-celled amoebae to a multicellular organism as a natural part of its life cycle" (Devreotes, 1989, p. 1054). "During the life cycle, solitary amoebae collect to form a multicellular organism" (Siegert and Weijer, 1992, p. 6433).)[64]

So my best guess is that the Wierenga-inspired proposal, A$_3$, is false. Whether or not a slime-mold slug and its constituent cells are all organisms, I suspect that it's at least metaphysically possible for there to be a multicellular organism each of whose cells is an organism too. Such a thing could be sent through a cell separator, and if it were, it would turn into a bunch of organisms, but it would die nonetheless.

3.2 Three New Attempts at a Repair

Three new proposals are worth floating at this point. Call them (i) the *teleological* approach, (ii) the *causal* approach, and (iii) the *generative* approach.

3.2.1 *Fourth Try: Deathless Division as Biologically Normal Division*

The teleological approach says—roughly—that a biological fission is deathless if and only if its occurrence is *biologically normal* and/or has some *biological purpose* or *function*. The thought here is that mice and slime mold slugs die when they go through the cell separator because the divisions in question are not biologically normal. Those divisions do not conform to the normal life cycle of the entities in question. Amoebas and frog cells divide deathlessly because these divisions are biologically normal. As programmatic as it may be, the idea is already clear enough to generate at least three worries.

First, one might think that facts about biological teleology are grounded in facts about evolutionary history and hence are extrinsic, historical facts. In particular, one might claim that intrinsic duplicates could undergo duplicate processes but differ in whether those processes are biologically normal. Ordinary amoebas evolved; many of their structures and behaviors were selected for. This is why the given behaviors and structures count as biologically normal or have biological purposes. But a "swamp amoeba" is metaphysically possible. Such a thing is an intrinsic duplicate of an ordinary amoeba, but it has no evolutionary history: it comes into existence via "cosmic coincidence." A swamp amoeba might undergo a division that is intrinsically just like the division of an ordinary amoeba. If it did, one might think that its division is just as deathless as the ordinary amoeba's. But since the swamp amoeba has no evolutionary history, many will want to say that its division is not biologically normal and has no biological purpose or function, and hence that the teleological approach wrongly counts the swamp amoeba as dying when it divides.

A second potential objection to the teleological approach concerns actual cases of abnormal cell division. Many cells in multicellular organisms undergo *programmed cell death* (apoptosis) as the normal conclusion of their life cycle. But sometimes, a cell malfunctions and divides into two daughter cells instead of undergoing the programmed cell death that would have been biologically normal for it. In such a case, one might find it plausible that (i) the division is not biologically normal and has no biological purpose or function and that (ii) the cell does not die when it divides (although it does cease to be present and hence does cease to have the capacity to live). If so, then one will see the teleological approach as yielding an incorrect verdict in this case.

The first two objections to the teleological approach argue that a division can be deathless without being biologically normal; hence, normality is not necessary for deathless fission. A third objection argues that normality is not sufficient for deathlessness. Suppose that mice or slime mold slugs had a different evolutionary history. Suppose that they evolved in world in which cell separators were common. Perhaps a certain dramatic end-of-life behavior enhanced the fitness of genetically related individuals and was selected for: the aged organism climbs onto the rim of the churning cell separator, says its final good-byes, and dives straight in. The organism ceases to be present, and a bunch of living cells emerge from the opposite end, preserved in a nutrient bath, waiting to be harvested by the kin of the recently departed organism.

(I assume that more realistic examples are not hard to formulate.) In such a case, one might find it plausible that (i) the division is biologically normal and does have a biological purpose or function and that (ii) the multicellular organism nevertheless kills itself, and hence dies, in the process. Moreover, such a conclusion shouldn't seem surprising. In cases that don't involve fission or fusion, death is often biologically programmed. In those cases, the fact that a given organism or cell is doing something that it is biologically programmed to do doesn't stop it from being true that the organism or cell dies. Why should fission cases be any different?

3.2.2 *Fifth Try: Deathless Division as Internally Caused Division*

The causal approach says—roughly—that a biological division is deathless just in case its proximal causes (or the bulk of them, anyway) are internal to the entity that divides. (A proximal cause is a *direct* cause: c is a proximal cause of e if and only if c is a cause of e, and there is no c* such that c is a cause of c* and c* is a cause of e.) According to the causal approach, a mouse (or a slime mold slug) dies when it goes through a cell separator because the proximal causes of its division are outside events—namely, the actions of the cell separator machine. The mouse does not divide on its own; some external thing divides it. (This is true even if the mouse is biologically programmed to throw itself into the cell separator.) By contrast, when an amoeba or frog cell divides, it does this on its own. The causes are internal. Likewise for the malfunctioning cell that divides instead of dying as it was programmed to do.

It would be nice to be able to say what it is for a given thing or event to be an *internal cause* of a given division, but this is not the place to attempt it. So set this aside, and just give the friends of the causal approach the notions they need to formulate their proposal. Even then, the proposal faces two problems.

First, one might think that when a planarian is cut in half in a science class and turns into two planarians, the division is deathless but not internally caused. This is a common view among those with whom I've discussed the case, though I find myself without a firm opinion on it.

Second, one might think that, under special circumstances at least, a multicellular organism might die when, as a result of internal causes, it divides into its constituent cells. Suppose that I drink a strange poison that becomes incorporated into each of my cells. I feel fine for a few hours. Then, at a certain moment, the poison triggers "separation behavior" in my cells, so that each cell separates itself from its neighbors while remaining alive. I dissolve into a puree of living human cells. On its face, this is a deadly but internally caused division. The proximal cause of my division is internal, but I die nonetheless.

3.2.3 *Sixth Try: Deathless Division as Division into Newly Living Things*

The generative approach says—roughly—that a given division is deathless just in case it involves a living thing that turns into a plurality of living things no member of which was alive before the division.

Thus the mouse dies when it goes through the cell separator because the living things that it turns into—its cells—were all alive before the division. Likewise, I die when I drink the "separation triggering" poison because the living things that I turn into—my cells—were alive before the division. But the amoeba and frog cell do not die when they divide, because the living things that they turn into—the daughter cells—were presumably not even *present*, much less *alive*, before the division.

In the case of the planarian that gets cut in half, there seem to be three plausible options. First, one could say that (a) when it divides, it turns into two living things—two new planarians—that were not present before the division. Hence, according to the generative approach, the planarian does not die. This seems to be a popular verdict.

Second, one could say that (b) when it divides, it turns into two living things—two planarians—that *were* present before the division but that were not then planarians, or organisms, or even alive. Rather than being living things themselves before the division, they were mere "arbitrary undetached parts" of a living thing: the right and left halves of the original planarian. So again, the planarian turns into living things that were not alive before the division, and hence the generative approach yields the popular verdict that it does not die.

Third, one could say that (c) when the planarian divides, the two large things that it turns into are not alive. They are mere masses of living cells but are not living things in their own right, at least not yet. Two living things (two new planarians) will eventually develop from those masses of cells, but those new planarians are not present immediately after the division. Thus, when the planarian divides, it turns into *its cells* (each of which is living but not newly living), and it turns into *two cell masses* (neither of which is alive at all), but it does not turn into any plurality of things each of whose members is newly living. In the context of these claims, the generative approach yields the apparently unpopular verdict that the planarian *does* die when it gets cut in half. Is this a problem?

For what it's worth, when I'm in the frame of mind to accept (a) or (b) above, I also find it natural to say that the planarian doesn't die when it gets cut in half; but when I'm in the frame of mind to accept (c), I find it natural to say that the original planarian *does* die when it is cut in half. Thus my intuitions about whether the planarian dies vary as certain metaphysical assumptions about the case vary. But they vary in such a way that they always match the verdict of generative approach. And yet all is not well.

Counterexample 1. Consider a case of cellular fission in which the two daughter cells enter cryptobiosis at the very moment at which they begin to exist. In such a case, the original cell ceases to be alive, it ceases to be present, and—on the assumption that cryptobiotic things are not alive—it fails to turn into a plurality of newly *living* things. Hence the generative approach tells us, incorrectly, that such a fission is deadly. (Thanks to Stephen Crowley for this case.)

A Repair. A suitably modified version of the generative approach would say that a division is deathless if and only if it involves a living-*or-cryptobiotic* thing that turns into a plurality of living-*or-cryptobiotic* things no member of which was alive or cryptobiotic before the division. (And if we like, we can define "cryptobiotic" as "not alive but having the capacity to live.")

Counterexample 2. Suppose that we decide to kill a rat by putting it through the cell separator. However, at the very moment the rat goes through the separator and ceases to be present, each of its constituent cells undergoes fission and turns into two new cells. The result, as before, is a puree of living cells, but this time each of the resulting cells is a *newly created* living thing. This means that the generative approach will say that the rat didn't die when it went through the cell separator. But that's clearly false. The rat does die. The fact that each of its constituent cells just happens to divide at the given moment is entirely irrelevant to whether or not the cell separator kills the rat.

A Repair. Granted, the rat turns into some new living things—the daughter cells of the cells that composed the rat in final moments of its life. But, informally, these new living things are not the result of the *rat's* division; rather, they are the result of *its cells'* divisions. Perhaps this explains why our rat dies (despite turning into a bunch of new living things). To capture this suggestion more precisely, it will help to introduce a technical term, "generative division," defined as follows:

> GD x undergoes **generative division** at t = df. there are some yy such that: (i) each of yy begins to be alive-or-cryptobiotic at t, (ii) x turns into yy at t, and (ii) there is some y such that:
> (a) y is one of yy;
> (b) y is not a **fission**-product of something (e.g., a cell) that was a living-or-cryptobiotic proper part[65] of x throughout the final moments of x's life;[66]
> (c) y is not a **fusion**-product of some things (e.g., some cells) that were living-or-cryptobiotic proper parts of x throughout the final moments of x's life;[67] and
> (d) y is not a **metamorphosis**-product of something (e.g., a cell) that was a living-or-cryptobiotic proper part of x throughout the final moments of x's life.[68]

The modified version of the generative approach, then, says this: if a living-or-cryptobiotic thing turns into two or more living-or-cryptobiotic things at a time t, then it *dies* at t if and only if it does not undergo *generative division* at t. Generative divisions are deathless; the others are deadly.

This proposal yields the intuitively correct verdicts on all of the fission cases we've considered so far: it tells us that the amoeba and the frog cell do not die when they divide, and it tells us that the mouse, the rat, and the drinker of "separation-triggering" poison do die when they divide.

With this in mind, we can return to our overarching question, "When do things die?" If we extend the "generative approach" in such a way that it applies to fusion and metamorphosis, we can graft it onto Incapacity. The result is a new instance of schema S:

Terminus Necessarily, for any x and any t, if t is an instant, then x dies at t if and only if:
(i) at t, x loses the capacity to live;
(ii) x does not undergo generative division at t;
(iii) x does not undergo generative fusion or generative metamorphosis at t.[69]

Terminus says that things die when they lose the capacity to live, provided that they don't simultaneously undergo certain specified forms of fission, fusion, or metamorphosis. Is Terminus a success? I doubt it. But I think it's more likely to be true, or approximately true, than anything else on the table.

Before we leave the topic of fission, I want to point out a potential counterexample to Terminus. Suppose that, for whatever reason, the cells in a slime mold slug start to crawl away from one another and eventually all go their separate ways. By the end of the process, the slug itself is no longer present. Thus the slug ceases to be present, loses the capacity to live, and "turns into" its constituent cells, which remain alive. Such a division would not count as a *generative* division; no newly living things result from it. So Terminus yields the verdict that the slug dies. Some might find this implausible: would a slime mold slug really *die* if its cells merely crawled apart from each other and resumed their independent way of life?

I lack strong intuitions about the case. I'm inclined to look to Terminus for guidance here and defer to its verdict. Those with stronger intuitions may end up rejecting Terminus on the basis of this case.[70]

4. WHEN ARE THINGS DEAD?

Enough about dying. Let's turn to being dead. A final task before we conclude is to formulate a true and informative instance of the following schema:

> S*   Necessarily, for any x and any t, if t is an instant, then x is dead at t if and only if _____.

In this vein, Rosenberg writes:

> "Aunt Ethel is dead"...seems to say just what "Aunt Ethel has died" says...To say that a person is dead, then, seems...to report on a past event rather than a present condition. "Being dead," as we customarily speak, picks out only the "nominal condition" of having died. (1998, pp. 42–43)

This passage suggests the following principle:

> Dead$_R$ Necessarily, for any x and any t, if t is an instant, then x is dead at t if and only if there is some instant t* such that: (i) t* is earlier than t and (ii) x dies at t*.

According to Dead$_R$, a thing is dead at a time just in case it died at an earlier time. As Feldman has noted, anyone who accepts the metaphysical possibility of revitalization cases (e.g., Restoration+) will face pressure to reject Rosenberg's proposal.

Suppose that Beta dies at t2 and is alive later, at t6. Then Dead$_R$ counts Beta as being dead at t6. But since Beta is alive at t6 and since being alive and being dead are incompatible with each other, this verdict seems incorrect. If a thing were to die and later be revitalized, it would become dead when it died, but—contrary to Rosenberg—it wouldn't continue to be dead forever after. By the time it returns to life, it will have stopped being dead.

Thus being dead is not a purely historical property. Whether a thing has that property at a given time is partly a matter of the thing's history (the thing must have died, or perhaps die just then) but it is also partly a matter of the thing's present intrinsic condition. If the thing is currently alive, it is not dead, regardless of what happened to it in the past.

To handle these observations, Feldman (1992, p. 108) offers a definition of "dead" that entails the following principle:

> Dead$_F$ Necessarily, for any x and any t, if t is an instant, then x is dead at t if and only if there is some instant t* such that: (i) t* is earlier than t, (ii) x dies at t*, and (iii) x is not alive at t or at any instant between t* and t.

Informally, Dead$_F$ says that to be dead at a time is to have died at some earlier time and not to have returned to life since then. This solves the problem about revitalization. Since Beta is alive at t6, clause (iii) is not satisfied, and so Dead$_F$ says, correctly, that Beta is not dead at that time.

Dead$_F$ does face a different problem, however (Gilmore, 2007). Return to the Restoration+ case. At t5, after the repair work is complete, but while Beta is still frozen, Beta is an intrinsic duplicate of Gamma, a frozen organism that entered cryptobiosis in the normal way. As I noted, this makes it plausible to say that Beta, like Gamma, is cryptobiotic at t5. But if Feldman, Clegg, and their allies are right, this should lead us to say that Beta is neither alive nor dead at t5. Thus Beta's history is as follows: it is alive at t1, it dies at t2, it is dead for a period of time thereafter, it gets frozen (while dead) and then gets repaired, and by t5 it has become cryptobiotic and has ceased to be dead, though without yet returning to life.

Dead$_F$ yields the wrong verdict here. Since Beta died at t2 and is not alive at t5 or at any instant between t2 and t5, Dead$_F$ tells us that Beta is dead at t5. But—given plausible views about cryptobiosis—Beta is cryptobiotic and hence *not* dead at t5. Contrary to Dead$_R$, having died and having not returned to life since then is not a sufficient condition for being dead. That proposed condition is compatible with being cryptobiotic, which is incompatible with being dead.

In light of our discussion of cryptobiosis in section 2, the natural fix is to say that a thing is now dead just in case it died (and hence lost the capacity to live) at some earlier time (or perhaps just now) and has not regained that capacity since it died. Although Beta has not returned to life as of t5, it has regained the capacity to live by then, and for that reason it is no longer dead. Put more formally, the suggestion is this:

> Dead$_G$ Necessarily, for any x and any t, if t is an instant, then x is dead at t if and only if there is an instant t* such that: (i) either t* = t or t* is earlier than t; (ii) x dies at t*; (iii) it's not the case that: *at t*, x has the capacity to live; and (iv) for each instant t_b between t* and t, it's not the case that: *at t_b*, x has the capacity to live.[71]

Four comments about Dead$_G$ are in order.[72]

(1) Unlike Rosenberg's proposal, but like Feldman's, Dead$_G$ allows for the possibility of "undead" things, things that are not dead but once were. The dead and the undead are alike in that they've all died. The difference between them, according to Dead$_G$, is that a dead thing lacks the capacity to live and has lacked it ever since some moment at which it died. Not so for an undead thing.

(2) Unlike either Rosenberg's proposal or Feldman's, Dead$_G$ allows for the possibility of things that go directly from being dead to being neither alive nor dead. This was what happened to the organism Beta (in the Restoration+ case) sometime between t2 and t5. At t2, Beta lost the capacity to live and hence died and became dead. It remained dead for some time. Then, at some point during the process of repair, and before it actually returned to life, it regained the capacity to live and hence ceased to be dead.

(3) Unlike either Rosenberg's proposal or Feldman's, Dead$_G$ allows for the possibility of (a) a thing that is *alive* at the instant at which it dies; (b) a thing that is *dead* at the instant at which it dies; and (c) a thing that is *neither alive nor dead* at the instant at which it dies.

Start with (a). Suppose that Mary is alive at t1, at the later instant t2, and at every instant in between, but at no other instants. Further, suppose that she has the capacity to live at each of these instants, but not at any others. Thus, not only does she cease to be alive at t2, she also loses the *capacity* to live at that time. Finally, suppose that Mary doesn't undergo fission, fusion, or metamorphosis at t2; rather, she stops living as the result of illness. Then—given Terminus—she dies at t2, an instant at which she is still alive. Moreover, given that Mary has the capacity to live at t2, Dead$_G$ tells us that she is not dead then, though she is dead at each instant thereafter.

Next consider (b). Let John's case be just like Mary's, with the exception that John is not alive at t2, nor does he have the capacity to live then. But he is alive, and does have the capacity to live, at t1 and at each instant between t1 and t2. Here again we should say that John loses the capacity to live at t2, and hence—given Terminus—that he dies then. And given that he does not have the capacity to live at t2, Dead$_G$ yields the result that he is dead then, as well as at each instant thereafter.

Finally consider (c), and let Margaret's case be just like John's, with the exception that Margaret is cryptobiotic at t2: she is not alive then, but she does then have the capacity to live. Like John and Mary, Margaret is alive, and has the capacity to live, at t1 and at each instant between t1 and t2. As in the previous cases, we should say that Margaret loses the capacity to live at t2 and hence that she dies then. Given that she does have the capacity to live at t2, however, Dead$_G$ yields the verdict that she is not dead then. Thus Mary is neither alive nor dead at t2, when she dies. According to Dead$_G$, therefore, whether a thing is alive, dead, or neither at an instant at which it dies depends upon the thing's intrinsic condition at that instant. This strikes me as a virtue.

(4) Dead$_G$ is compatible with both answers to the question, "Do amoebas die when they divide?" Suppose that Amos divided at t1, at which point he ceased permanently to be present and ceased permanently to have the capacity to live. Is Amos dead now, at the later time t2? According to Dead$_G$, that depends on whether Amos died at t1. If he did, then he's dead now (since he does not now have the capacity to live, and has lacked that capacity since some moment when he died, namely t1). If he didn't die then, he's neither alive nor dead now, but merely nonpresent, like Pangaea and the Colossus of Rhodes.

It's worth noting that Dead$_G$ yields plausible results when applied to more complicated fission cases as well. Let Annie be an amoeba that lives, dies at t1 (of oxygen deprivation, say), is dead for a period of time thereafter, gets repaired and regains the capacity to live, returns to life at t2, and finally divides into two new amoebas at t3. Annie is not present (and hence is not alive and does not have the capacity to be alive) at any time thereafter. Is Annie dead now, at t4? Again, this will depend on whether amoebas die when they divide, as it should.

If Annie did die at t3, when she divided, then Dead$_G$ yields the result that she is dead now. For she doesn't have the capacity to live, and this has been true ever since some moment at which she died, namely t3.

But suppose that Rosenberg is right, and Annie did *not* die when she divided. Then Dead$_G$ will tell us that Annie is *not* dead now. Although she doesn't now have the capacity to live, and although she did die at some earlier time (namely, t1), it's *not* true that *she has lacked the capacity to live ever since some instant at which she died*. The only instant at which she died, given Rosenberg's view about fission, is t1. And we *can't* say that Annie has lacked the capacity to live ever since t1. After all, she regained that capacity between t1 and t2 and indeed was *alive* from t2 to t3.

This complicated fission case gives us a reason to prefer Dead$_G$ to certain other tempting repairs to Dead$_F$. Consider, for example,

Dead$_{G^*}$ Necessarily, for any x and any t, if t is an instant, then x is dead at t if and only if there is some instant t* such that: (i) t* = t or t* is earlier than t, (ii) x dies at t*, and (iii) x does not have the capacity to live at t.

This handles standard revitalization cases (unlike Dead$_R$), and it handles the case in which a thing goes directly from being dead to being neither dead nor alive (unlike Dead$_F$), but given Rosenberg's view about fission, Dead$_{G^*}$ doesn't handle the complicated case involving Annie. In that case, Dead$_{G^*}$ tells us that Annie is dead at t4. But given Rosenberg's view, what we *should* say, and what Dead$_G$ *does* say, is that Annie is neither alive nor dead at t4.

So it seems that regardless of whether one accepts Rosenberg's view about fission, one will see Dead$_G$ as delivering the right conclusions about all of the relevant cases.

5. Conclusion

When is a thing dead? Dead$_G$ gives an answer in terms of dying and having the capacity to live: roughly, being dead is a matter of having died and having not regained the capacity to live since then. And when does a thing die? Terminus gives an answer in terms of being alive and having the capacity to live. A thing dies, it says, when the thing loses the capacity to live—perhaps temporarily, perhaps reversibly—without undergoing "generative" fission, fusion, or metamorphosis.

Under what conditions is a thing *alive*? Under what conditions does a thing have the *capacity* to do something or to be a certain way? We would know more about when things die if we had answers to these questions. But Terminus and Dead$_G$ cannot be faulted for remaining mostly silent on them, any more than an account of knowledge in terms of belief, truth, and so on, can be faulted for failing to provide a theory of truth. Terminus and Dead$_G$ don't answer every question one might have about death, but this doesn't make them uninformative. They make nonobvious claims about how dying and being dead are related to other notions in the vicinity, and in my view, they constitute a significant improvement upon existing proposals.

Neither principle puts itself forward as an analysis or definition of any word or concept. Dead$_G$ gives an account of being dead in terms of dying (inter alia), and Terminus gives an account of dying in terms of being alive. But one can accept these principles without thinking that the concept (or property or relation) of dying is somehow prior to or more basic than the concept of being dead; one might even think that it's the other way around—for example, that dying is to be analyzed as becoming dead. Terminus and Dead$_G$ take no stand on this. But they do impose *constraints* on attempts to analyze the relevant concepts and to define the relevant words. For example, on the assumption that a thing can cease to be alive without losing the capacity to live, those who accept Terminus should deny that dying can be analyzed as ceasing to be alive.

In this chapter I have sidestepped what some may take to be the most interesting philosophical dispute about death: namely, the dispute between "brain death" accounts and "cardiopulmonary" accounts of human death.[73] One reason for this, as I've mentioned, is that I have tried to give an account of death (or, strictly, *dying*) in general, and most things that die don't have hearts, lungs, or brains.

But there is also a second reason. A human person or human organism, like anything else, dies at an instant t if and only if it loses the capacity to live at t (and doesn't undergo the specified sort of fission, etc.). If this fails to settle the dispute between the brain death account and the cardiopulmonary account, that's only because each side can still argue that it gives the correct answer to the question "when does a human person lose the capacity to live?" Perhaps the brain-death theorist can argue that a human person loses the capacity to live at the moment of "brain death" and the cardiopulmonary theorist can argue that a human person loses the capacity to live when it loses the capacity for "cardiopulmonary function." If so, then this a dispute worth having, but it is not in the first instance a dispute about death, any more than the dispute between, say, deflationists and correspondence theorists about truth is a dispute about knowledge.[74]

NOTES

1. See DeGrazia, 2005; DeGrazia, 2008; and Lizza, 2006 for discussion and many further references.
2. This epistemic project is often called "giving *criteria* of death." For helpful discussion of the different things that have been meant by "defining" in the so-called "definition of death" literature, see Feldman, 1992, pp. 12–18; Fischer, 1993, pp. 3–8; and Belshaw, 2009, pp. 16–28.
3. Instances of S try to spell out the conditions for dying *at an instant*. The restriction to instants is important, since things may die also at entities that are not instants, and the conditions for dying at a noninstant may be quite different from those for dying at an instant. For example, it may be that if a thing dies at an instant t, then it also dies at any extended interval of time that includes that instant. And it may be that things die at places ("he died at the top of Mt. Shasta") and at space-time regions that are not instants. If so, this would make it extremely difficult to formulate a true and informative instance of the unrestricted schema "necessarily, for any x and any y, x dies at y iff ____." The only way to make the project even remotely manageable is to focus on S instead of the unrestricted schema.
4. Those philosophers who take themselves to be asking a question framed in terms of a notion of death that applies only to people or to humans (DeGrazia, 2008) might instead be construed as trying to formulate a true and informative instance of a different schema, namely:

   S_H Necessarily, for any x and any t, if t is an instant and x is a human being [*simpliciter* or, alternatively, *at some time*], then x dies at t if and only if _____.

   So construed, their question is framed in terms of the very same (general, biological) concept of death as is my question, but their question is *narrower*: not "when do *things* die?" but "when do *humans* die?" Perhaps this narrower question admits of a more informative, more precise answer than does the broad question that I ask here. See the final two paragraphs of section 5 for more on this.

5. In response the question, "when does a thing die?" one might say "it depends on what kind of thing it is." One could fill in the details by formulating an instance of the following schema:

Series$_D$ Necessarily, for any x and any t, if t is an instant, then x dies at t if and only if either: x is a K1, and φ1, or x is a K2, and φ2, or…, or x is a Kn, and φn.

Here is a silly example of an instance of Series$_D$:

Series$_1$ Necessarily, for any x and any t, if t is an instant, then x dies at t if and only if: either (i) x is a human being and x's heart and lungs cease irreversibly to function at t, or (ii) x is a tree, and x falls down at t.

The example is silly because it's obviously false. I had a cat that died at a certain instant, but since it was neither a human being nor a tree, it generates a counterexample to Series$_1$. Less silly instances would need to have enough clauses so that everything that can die falls under at least one of those clauses. I have no objection to such principles, but I wouldn't know how to begin formulating one (in which the separate clauses for different kinds of things did real work). See Markosian, 2008, pp. 354–355, for a discussion of "series-style" answers to the "special composition question": under what conditions do some things compose something? I take the "series" terminology from him.

6. Strictly speaking, it doesn't even say this. A proponent of CT could consistently deny the existence of concepts, properties, and relations.

7. These are not the only alternatives. There is also, for example, the Growing Block view, according to which the past and present exist but the future does not, and reality grows as time passes. See Dainton, 2010, for a detailed discussion of all these views.

8. Presentists invoke primitive tense operators such as "it was the case that" and "it will be the case that" to capture facts about how things were and will be. Thus they can say "Pangaea does not exist" and "it was the case that Pangaea exists."

9. This is standard but not uncontroversial; there are a number of alternatives. First, one might think that time is "gunky," so that there are temporally extended intervals (each of which is composed of briefer but still temporally extended subintervals) but no temporally unextended instants (Arntzenius, 2008). Second, one might think that time is "grainy" and so composed of minimal units that do not subdivide further, but each of which is temporally extended (Braddon-Mitchell and Miller, 2006). Third, one might be a relationist about time and deny the existence of temporal locations of any sort, be they intervals, instants, or extended "grains." (See Hawthorne and Sider, 2006, for discussion.) Finally, one might doubt the existence of instants on the grounds that space-time, rather than space and time, is the fundamental "spatiotemporal arena." One might think that instants exist only if they are parts of space-time, and one might think that something about the geometric structure of space-time prevents any of its parts from counting as instants (Gibson and Pooley, 2006, p. 160; Lockwood, 2005, p. 152).

10. Without using "ceases to," we might try: for any x and any instant t, if x dies at t, then there are continuous intervals I and I* such that: (i) I immediately precedes t, (ii) x is present at each instant in I, (iii) I* immediately follows t, and (iv) x is not present at any instant in I*. (A continuous interval I *immediately precedes* an instant t iff t is the *end point* of I, that is, iff no instant in I is later than t, and there is no instant t* that is later than each instant in I but earlier than t. A continuous interval I *immediately follows* an

instant t iff t is the *starting point* of I, that is, iff no instant in I is earlier than t, and there is no instant t* that is earlier than each instant in I but later than t. Closed intervals include their starting points and end points. Open intervals include neither. Partially open intervals include one but not the other.) However, if John is present throughout the first half hour following 11:00 a.m., then nonpresent throughout the next 15 minutes, then present throughout the next 7.5 minutes, then nonpresent throughout the next 3.75 minutes, and so on, and if John is not present at any instant after noon, one might be tempted to say that John *ceases to be present* at noon, even though he is not present throughout any continuous interval that immediately precedes noon.

11. The Termination Thesis is accepted by Hershenov (2005); Johansson (2005, p. 45); Luper (2009, pp. 46–47); Merricks (2001, p. 151); Olson (2004); Rosenberg (1998, p. 50); and Yourgrau (2000, p. 49). It is rejected by Belshaw (2009, pp. 10–12); Carter (1999); Feldman (1992, pp. 89–105) and (2000); Mackie (1999); and Thomson (1997). See Johansson, 2005, p. 45 for further names and citations.

12. There is a different, weaker thesis in the neighborhood that may have some claim to the title "The Termination Thesis," namely,

TT$_r$ For any x and any instant t, if x is a *person* [alternatively, *human person*; alternatively, *one of us*, whatever we are] and x dies at t, then x ceases to be present at t.

Whereas TT says that for any entity x whatsoever, if x dies at t, then x ceases to be present at t, TT$_r$ says merely that *people* cease to be present when they die. Accordingly, the friend of TT$_r$ is free to say that Lenin's body died but did not cease to be present in 1924, provided that she holds that Lenin's body is not person. Baker (2000, p. 120) defends essentially this view.

13. Table 1.1, and indeed the entire chapter, should be understood as being neutral on the dispute between endurantism and perdurantism. Endurantism, roughly, is the view that if x is a material object, then x is (i) temporally unextended and (ii) "wholly present" at each instant at which it is present. Perdurantism, roughly, is the view that if x is a material object, then x has a different temporal part at each different instant at which it is present. See Balashov, 2011; Hawley, 2010; and Sider, 2001a for more careful formulations of these and other views about persistence.

14. Likewise, one should deny that being alive entails having a soul unless one is prepared to say that plants and red blood cells have souls.

15. Though see note 25 on maximality constraints.

16. See van Inwagen (1990), Feldman (1992), Hoffman and Rosenkrantz (1997), Boden (1999), Cleland and Chyba (2002), and Luper (2009) for sophisticated discussions and a path into a very large literature.

17. Parsons, 1990, ch. 9, gives an account of the perfective aspect according to which the logical form of

(1a) Mary died

is given by

(1b) $\exists e \exists t$ [IS A DYING(e) & THEME(e, Mary) & CULMINATES(e, t) & t<now].Informally, (1b) says: there is an event e such that: (i) e is a dying event, (ii) Mary plays the "theme" role in e, (iii) e culminates at some instant t that is earlier than now. "Culminates" does not just mean "ends," since a dying event might occur, and end, without ever culminating. According to Parsons, this happens when a thing is in the process of dying for a while but then recovers: there is a dying event that goes on for a while and comes to an end without culminating.

18. Suppose that the interval occupied by John's life is continuous and topologically closed at its later end, so that there is a *last* instant at which John is alive—call it t_1—but no *first* instant at which is no longer alive. Suppose also that John goes *directly* from being alive to being dead, so that for some instant t_2 after t_1, he is dead at each instant between t_1 and t_2 (and presumably at t_2 and thereafter as well). Then he dies at t_1, an instant at which he is alive. After all, I take it that the only other candidates (for being instants at which John dies) are later instants, but for each such instant t, John is dead at t and throughout some temporally extended interval leading up to t, which is a sufficient condition for not dying at t. (If you're dead at t and have been for awhile, you don't die at t.)

19. Suppose that Mary is alive at each instant in some interval leading up to t but that she is dead, not alive, at t and at each instant thereafter. Then presumably she dies at t, an instant at which she is not alive.

20. In the case described in note 18 above, John dies at t_1, an instant at which he is alive and (given P1) present. Moreover, even friends of the Termination Thesis can accept the possibility of this case, provided that they think that a thing can be present at an instant at which it ceases to be present.

21. We might augment the case described in note 19 above by stipulating that Mary is present only at those instants at which she is alive. This will yield the result that she is not present when she dies.

22. Epistemicists about vagueness can say this, as can supervaluationists, though this fact is often treated as a vice of the latter theory. Moreover, it would seem that those who see some form of ontic indeterminacy at work here could say the same. See Williamson (1994) for more on these views.

23. Feldman defines "x is dying at t" as follows:

process P is terminal for organism x = df. x is of some kind, K, such that (1) P is a causal process; (2) P can be broken down into a number of stages, each of which (other than the last) is the loss or decrease of a property that is vital for K; (3) P's last stage is the death of x; and (4) P contains no covert external linkages....

x is dying2 at t = df. at t, x is engaged in a process that would be terminal for x, if it were allowed to reach its conclusion without interference. (1992, p. 84)

Parsons, 1990, ch. 9, gives an account of the progressive aspect according to which the logical form of

(2a) Mary was dying

is given by

(2b)   ∃e∃t[IS A DYING(e) & THEME(e, Mary) & HOLDS(e, t) & t<now].

Informally, (2b) says: there is an event e such that: (i) e is a dying, (ii) Mary plays the "theme" role in e, (iii) e occupies a stretch of time that includes some instant t that is earlier than now. Thus, the difference between

(1a)   Mary died and its "progressive correlate," (2a), is explained in terms of the difference between *culmination* and *holding*. See note 17.

Parsons (1990, ch. 9) and Szabó (2004) discuss various attempts to analyze progressive sentences in terms of their perfective correlates. Both express pessimism about such attempts. Szabó proposes a "reverse analysis," which explains the truth conditions of simple perfective sentences such as (1a) in terms of their progressive correlates, such as (2a). See also Szabó (2008).

24. Parsons (1990, ch. 10) gives an account of adjectives according to which the logical form of

   (3a)   Mary was dead

   is given by

   (3b) $\exists s \exists t[$IS A BEING-DEAD(s) & THEME$(e,$ Mary$)$ & HOLD(s, t) & $t<$now$]$

   Informally, (3b) says: there is a token state s such that (i) s is a token of the type *being dead*, (ii) Mary plays the "theme" role in s, (iii) s occupies a stretch of time that includes some instant t that is earlier than now.
   As Parsons (1990, p. 111) notes, the verb "to die" is typically classified as an *inchoative* (an intransitive verb that has the meaning "become adj," for some associated adjective) whose associated adjective is "dead." On this view, "die" means "become dead." When this view is combined with Parsons's account of inchoatives, we get the result that the logical form of

   (1a)   Mary died

   is given by

   (1c) $\exists e \exists t[$CULMINATES(e, t) & THEME$(e,$ Mary$)$ & $\exists s[$IS A BEING-DEAD(s) & THEME$(s,$ Mary$)$ & HOLD(s, t) & BECOME(e, s) & $t<$now$]]$

   (1c) purports to be a *more refined* account of the logical form of (1a) than is (1b). Informally, (1c) says that there is an event e, an instant t, and a token state s such that: (i) e culminates at t, (ii) Mary plays the "theme" role in e, (iii) s is a token of being dead, (iv) Mary plays the "theme" role in s, (v) s occupies a stretch of time that includes t, (vi) e is an event of something's *coming to be in* token state s, and (vi) t is earlier than now.

25. There are two main reasons one might have for thinking that it is not strictly intrinsic*. First, one might think that it is governed by a maximality constraint, according to which a thing x is alive at a given time t only if x is not a proper part (or a "large, arbitrary" proper part) of some larger thing that is alive at t. If it is governed by such a constraint, then it might be possible for me to be alive now but to have some duplicate that is not alive now because it is embedded in a larger thing (e.g., the mereological sum of the duplicate and one extra skin cell) that is alive now. See Sider (2001b). Second, one might think that whether x is alive at t depends on facts about the accelerations and relative velocities of its constituent particles at that time, and one might think these facts depend upon facts about the positions of these particles at earlier and later times. (Still, these facts will presumably supervene on facts about what's going on in an arbitrarily brief interval encompassing t, and so they are not "radically extrinsic.")

26. Perhaps he is an immaterial soul. Perhaps his body was preserved and has remained hidden in some sheltered place all these years (Luper, 2009, p. 47) or is lying in a museum identified only as "Athenian 35a." Perhaps the persistence-and-assimilation conditions for dead things are "mereological essentialist," so that a thing, once it becomes dead and so long as it remains dead, behaves as if it were a mere portion of matter: it continues to be present just in case all of the relevant matter continues to be present, and it never gains or loses any of its matter. In that case, if the matter that composed Socrates at the moment of his death is still present but widely scattered, and if Socrates has not returned to life since his death, then Socrates himself is still present but widely scattered.

27. That is, other than as *the referent of the singular term "death."*

28. There are two more exotic groups of potential counterexamples to CT (and indeed to each of the instances of S to be considered here) that I won't discuss. The first group involves time travel. If a time traveler disappears at instant t in 2010 and reappears at instant t* in 1776 or 2076, one might think that he ceases to be alive, but does not die, at t. (Also see the rather different scenarios discussed in Sorensen, 2005.) The second group of cases involve living things that simply "pop out of existence" spontaneously, without undergoing any deterioration beforehand. Such a thing might seem to cease to be alive without dying. (Thanks to Ted Sider for this.) I suspect that examples in the first group could be handled by carefully reframing certain parts of our proposals in terms of "personal time" (Lewis, 1986, p. 69; Sorensen, 2005). I offer no suggestions regarding the second group.

29. Keilin offers a detailed survey of scientific work on related questions, running from Anton van Leeuwenhoek's observations on cryptobiotic rotifers in 1702 up through the mid-twentieth century. He reports that "between 1858 and 1859 members of learned societies and the lay press of Paris were, according to Broca, divided into two hostile groups: the resurrectionists and the anti-resurrectionists," with the former holding that the processes had stopped, and the latter holding that the processes had merely slowed (1959, p. 159).

30. Framed in terms of a sentence operator, "def," for definiteness, this comes to (iv*)

(a) ¬def (o is alive at t) & ¬def¬(o is alive at t) &
(b) ¬def (o is dead at t) & ¬def¬(o is dead at t) &
(c) def¬(o is alive at t & o is dead at t)

The friend of (iv*) may or may not also want to accept

(d) def (o is alive at t ∨ o is dead at t),

which, intuitively put, says that o is a clear case of being either-alive-or-dead.

31. In terms of "def," this comes to: ¬def (o is dead at t).

32. Peter van Inwagen seems to lean in this direction as well. He writes:

I find it attractive to suppose that the cat's life persists even when the cat is frozen...Perhaps this description will strike some readers as contrived and tendentious. It is not really essential to my position to suppose that our frozen cat is alive. If someone insists that the frozen cat is not alive, I do not think that he is misusing the word "alive." I would say that he was proposing a stipulative sharpening of the meaning of "alive," which is just what I was doing in the previous paragraph. (1990, pp. 146–147)

I suspect that van Inwagen has a higher credence in (iv) than in (i) and a higher credence in (i) than in (ii) or (iii).

33. For a defense of this claim, see Boden (1999). The biologist John Maynard Smith writes that

[t]he maintenance of a living state requires a constant flow of energy through the system. A freeze-dried insect is not alive: it was alive, and may be alive again in the future. Energy must be supplied in either the form of suitable chemical compounds or as sunlight, and in either case atoms are continuously entering and leaving the structure of the organism. (1986, p. 2)

Hoffman and Rosenkrantz (1997, pp. 158, 208), who also quote this passage, agree with Smith. As far as I am aware, neither Smith, nor Hoffman and Rosenkrantz, nor Boden takes a stance on whether cryptobiotic organisms are *dead*. Interestingly, Hoffman and Rosenkrantz hold that living entities cease to be present when they enter suspended animation and that they begin to be present again when they are revived, thus undergoing "intermittent existence" or what I would prefer to call "intermittent presence" (1997, p. 159).

34. In terms of "def," this comes to: ¬def(o is alive at t).

35. To anticipate: when an ordinary amoeba divides, it ceases to be present and hence ceases to be alive, but it does not then *die*, and hence is not *dead* at the times thereafter. In an otherwise convincing paper, David Hershenov responds to this view about fission in much the same way as my imagined critic responds to (iii):

> If the living one-celled amoeba didn't die when it divided, then that entails that it is either still alive, or at best, in an indeterminate state of being neither determinately alive nor determinately dead. Since it is admitted that amoebas cease to exist when they divide, it sounds absurd to say that they are not also dead. (2006, p. 113)

As I see it, however, there is nothing "indeterminate" about the state of cryptobiosis or about the state of being a (nonpresent) amoeba that divided without dying. Entities in these states are simply neither alive nor dead, just as a yellow shirt is simply neither green nor red: it is not hovering in some indeterminate condition. I don't detect anything absurd about this position.

36. Feldman, 1992, pp. 63–64, offers a somewhat different criticism of Permanence.

37. Though if one were willing to say that Alpha dies at a certain time that is not an instant—say, the *fusion* of t1, t2, and the instants between them—this might make P&I seem tenable. Thanks to Jens Johansson for this point.

38. cf. the formulation of determinism in van Inwagen, 1983, pp. 58–64.

39. If determinism is false. See below.

40. One might also imagine a case that involves a permanently expanding universe in which, at an instant t, it becomes physically necessary that a certain cryptobiotic tardigrade will be in roughly its then-current intrinsic condition at all times thereafter (presumably for an infinitely long period of time).

41. This can be put more carefully as follows: t1 is an initial boundary point of some interval each instant in which has the property *being an instant t such that it is physically necessary at t that o not be alive at any instant later than t*.

42. Feldman's doubts about IR_2 arise from what he takes to be "the obscurity of the concepts of *internality, physical impossibility,* and *life*" (1992, pp. 65–66). I don't find these concepts obscure. I am more troubled by certain other features of IR_2—namely, the fact that it quantifies over such entities as *changes* and the fact that it invokes the notions of *occurring in* and *making.* I will restate Irreversibility$_2$ in a way that avoids these latter notions.

43. This is short for "p is a minimal, complete statement of the laws of nature"—that is, p leaves no laws out, and p contains no extraneous material. I assume that any such proposition is *true.*

44. Presumably *being present at* is itself an intrinsic* relation, but even if not, it seems plausible that necessarily, if a thing is present at an instant, then that thing bears some intrinsic* relation to that instant.

45. There are a number of closely related principles in the vicinity, and it is not entirely clear to me which of them best serves the purposes of the defender of the intuitive idea of Irreversibility$_2$.

For one thing, in D1, one could rewrite clause (b) as "necessarily, for any instant t1, any interval I1 that leads up to t1, any later instant t2, and *any y,* if (p is true and y bears R to t1), then y is not alive at t2." This shifts from *de re* talk of the physical impossibility of *x*'s living again after undergoing such-and-such an intrinsic history to *de dicto* talk of the physical impossibility that *there be something* that lives again after undergoing such a history.

For another, instead of requiring, for x to be hopeless$_{ib}$ at t, that x's intrinsic history over some interval leading up to t guarantee the physical impossibility of x's living again (given the laws), one could adopt one of the following requirements:

– that x's intrinsic condition at t itself guarantee the relevant impossibility (given the laws), or
– that the distribution of x's intrinsic conditions over an *arbitrarily brief* interval surrounding [alternatively: leading up to] t guarantee the relevant impossibility (given the laws).

46. This is essentially the same case discussed in Gilmore (2007, p. 225). Luper (2009, pp. 46–49) discusses a similar case.
47. The expression "x constitutes y at t" can for present purposes be defined as " ∃z[z overlaps x at t if and only if z overlaps y at t]."
48.   Perhaps a typical death involves a complex sequence of chemical reactions that, once under way, are physically impossible to reverse. One might think, however, that under unusual circumstances, certain organisms (especially multicellular ones) can die in a way that involves no significant or irreversible *chemical* changes at all. One might think that if a living organism is frozen and becomes cryptobiotic, it can be killed merely by being split into pieces. Once broken apart, the organism is no longer *disposed* to be alive again in the future (even after it thaws), and it is natural to say that it is no longer *viable*; hence there are grounds for saying that it has stopped being cryptobiotic and has died. But since the entire process is carried out at a very low temperature, no major changes need occur at the chemical level. Perhaps the organism breaks apart in such a way as to leave each of its constituent cells intact and still cryptobiotic. In that case, it becomes much harder to argue that the organism's death involved a sequence of chemical reactions that is physically impossible to reverse. If there is anything physically impossible about revitalizing the organism, it would have to be the process of putting its pieces back together in such a way as to restore the organism's disposition to live when thawed. For what it's worth, I find it prima facie unlikely that *no* such process is physically possible.
49. Third, one might think that (c) Restoration is not detailed or specific enough for (a) or (b) to be true, but that Restoration does entail the proposition that if Beta dies at t2 then it's not the case that Beta is alive at t6. I will assume that (c) does not require separate discussion. In particular, I will assume that the considerations I mount against (a) combine with the considerations I mount against (b) to yield a case against (c).
50. It's worth considering how far the friend of (a) would be willing to generalize on the claim. Suppose that most of the apparently dead people whose bodies (or remains) are in the morgue have not yet become hopeless$_{ib}$. Should we say that they haven't yet died? Suppose that Lenin hasn't yet become hopeless$_{ib}$. Has he not yet died? I think we should say no in both cases. To the extent that I have any grip at all on the *dies at* relation, I know that it's a relation that Lenin bears to some time in the year 1924. Lenin has died, even if it turns out to be physically possible for him to live again. Similar points are made by Hershenov, 2003a, and are discussed by Belshaw, 2009, pp. 35–37.

51. Wiggins (1980) and Lowe (1983) deny the possibility of material objects that undergo intermittent presence. This possibility is embraced by Hershenov (2002 and 2003b); Hoffman and Rosenkrantz (1997, p. 159); Baker (2005); Merricks (2009), and nearly all friends of temporal parts—for example, Hudson (2001).

52. Among friends of intermittent presence, there is controversy about what it takes for a thing to "jump a temporal gap" in its career. Some say that a certain causal relation, immanent causation, must hold between the thing's final pre-gap phases and its initial post-gap phases (Zimmerman, 1999). Some say that the matter that composes the thing in its final pre-gap phases must be identical with, or mostly overlap, the matter that composes the thing in its initial post-gap phases, and that this matter must be arranged in the same way at both times (Hershenov, 2002, 2003b). Some say that if the thing is a person, then some sort of connectedness or continuity must hold between its pre-gap and post-gap psychological states, or that the pre- and post-gap persons must "have the same first-person perspective" (Baker, 2000, 2005). For further discussion, see Merricks, 2009, whose defense of intermittent presence is bound up with his claim that there are no true and informative critieria of personal identity over time, and Johnston, 2010, pp. 90–125.

53. Might some *even more intimate* causal relation be required, if the given phases are to be phases in the career of single material substance? (After all, in light of the processes of repair that occur during the gap, some of the particles that compose the repaired organism have the relative positions they have, not purely because of the operations of the organism's own internal life processes, but also because of the processes of repair that were imposed from the outside.) Perhaps. But I take it the momentary condition of complex object is always (in the actual world) partly caused by external forces and events. Moreover, I don't see what's to stop us from simply considering a different case, in which the requisite immanent causal relations do obtain, but which is otherwise as much like Restoration as possible—perhaps a case in which the reversal of damage occurs "by chance" and involves a relatively minor changes.

54. Henceforth I will leave this qualification implicit.

55. Developing certain ideas from Lawrence Becker, 1975 and David Cole, 1992, Hershenov writes that:

Given all the problems canvassed above, I suggest that whatever account of death one ends up defending, that a provision be included which maintains that human beings are dead when they cannot revive themselves, i.e., the pertinent organs cannot resume their functioning without external intervention. (2003a, p. 99)

If *external interventions* are restricted to *the intentional acts of sentient beings*, then I suspect that in some cases it is physically possible (even if highly unlikely) for a dead thing to return to life without external intervention.

56. Persson takes his proposal to solve the problem about cryptobiosis. He adds a further clause to deal with the problem about fission.

57. The facts about a thing's dispositions and capacities might not be fixed by its intrinsic properties alone, for two reasons. First, one might think that there could be intrinsic duplicates in different possible worlds governed by different laws of nature; these duplicates might have different dispositions and capacities. In our world, where it's a law that opposite charges attract, a given electron e might have the disposition or capacity to attract positively charged things. In a world governed by the law that opposite charges repulse, there might be a duplicate of e, e*, that lacks the disposition or capacity to attract positively charged things.

Second, even within a single world (with unchanging laws), intrinsic duplicates might not always have the same dispositions or capacities. I might lose the capacity to lift Frank without changing intrinsically, if Frank gains weight. I might lose the disposition to cry when struck by Frank without changing intrinsically if Frank becomes weaker. See McKitrick, 2003, and Fara, 2009.

58. See note 25. Whether a thing is alive at a given instant might depend upon facts about what it is a part of, and on facts about what is going on in an arbitrarily brief interval encompassing the given instant. These are not "radically extrinsic" facts, so they do not, I assume, introduce any "radical extrinsicness" into the facts about whether a thing has the capacity to be alive.

59. A predicate is *context-sensitive* iff its content (the property or relation it expresses) depends upon some feature of context. It seems to me that "loses the capacity to live" is a better candidate for being context-sensitive than is "dies." After all, phrases of the form "is capable of φ-ing" and "has the capacity to φ" are plausible candidates for being context-sensitive more generally. If a historian discovers a 200-year-old collection of guns, most of them badly corroded, she might find one that's in especially good condition and say truly, "This one's capable of firing. It's in perfect condition." If the same gun, in the same intrinsic condition, is used in a sniper training session, the instructor might say truly, "This one's not capable of firing. It's not cocked." If "has the capacity to live" is context-sensitive, it's natural to think that "loses the capacity to live" is too. I see no similar reason to think that "dies" is context-sensitive.

Manley and Wasserman, 2007 suggest that many *disposition* terms such as "fragile" are context-sensitive and point out that this is perfectly consistent with the claim that each of the properties that the predicate expresses (relative to one or another context) is *intrinsic*. I suspect that parallel remarks go for "is capable of φ-ing," "has the capacity to φ," and "loses the capacity to φ."

60. There are, of course, various ways of resisting the claim that amoebas typically cease to be alive when they divide. One might take the original amoeba to be identical to one of its fission products but not the other, despite the apparent symmetry of the fission. One might embrace "temporally relativized identity" and say that the original amoeba is identical to each of its fission products, while denying that those products are identical to each other after the fission (Gallois, 1998). One might follow David Lewis's treatment of personal fission (1983, pp. 55–76) and claim that, despite appearances, there are actually two amoebas in the vicinity even before the division; it's just that they both have the same spatial location until after the division. One might hold that the situation involves just a single amoeba that is singly located prior to the fission but bi-located thereafter (Dainton, 2008). And one might take it that, definitely, the original amoeba is identical to exactly one of its two fission products but that, for any x, if x is one of the original amoeba's fission products, then it is not the case that, definitely, the original amoeba is identical to x (Johansson, 2010).

61. Rosenberg (1983, pp. 21–22) makes the point that amoebas do cease to exist but don't die when they divide. Rosenberg's point is endorsed by Feldman (1992, p. 66); Wierenga (1994); Persson (1995); Kass (1997, p. 22); Wilson (1999, p. 101); McMahan (2002, p. 425); and Luper (2009, p. 47); Belshaw (2009, p. 228, n. 10) expresses agnosticism but indicates that he leans toward the claim. Hershenov (2006, p. 113) rejects the claim. Rosenberg doesn't explicitly address the question of whether amoebas *cease to be alive* when they divide. Feldman claims that they do, and he

concludes that the case of amoebic fission is a counterexample to the claim (endorsed by Rosenberg) that to die is to cease to be alive.

62. We can define "yy are made up of m at t" as "x [x overlaps m at t if and only if x overlaps at least one of yy at t]."

63. Note that none of the mouse's cells is a *new* entity that comes into existence when the mouse ceases to exist. Rather, each of these cells was present throughout the final moments of the mouse's life. Therefore, the mouse will count as *turning into* its cells in this case only if we understand the notion of "turning into" in such a way as to allow for the possibility that a thing x, at a time t, turns into the yy even though none of the yy is *new*, that is, even though each of them was present prior to t.

64. Also see Luper, 2009, p. 47, who mentions slime molds in connection with deathless fission (but not as a counterexample to Wierenga's proposal), and who holds that "organisms may have component organisms" (2009, p. 18). For a survey of debates about the concept of an *organism* in philosophy and biology, see Pepper and Herron, 2008.

65. Typically, "proper part" is defined as follows: x is a proper part of y at t = df. x is a part of y at t and x≠y. In the present context, however, it will be convenient to define it as follows: x is a proper part of y at t = df. x is a part of y at t, and there is a z such that z is a part of y at t, and nothing is a part of both x and z at at t. The idea here is that a proper part of a thing must "leave out" some part of the thing.

66. That is, it is not the case that there is some z, interval I, and some zz such that: (i) I leads up to t, (ii) z is a proper part of x at each instant in I, (iii) z is alive at each instant in I, (iv) z turns into zz at t, (v) each of zz begins to be alive at t, and (vi) y is one of zz.

67. That is, it is not the case that there is an interval I and things, zz, such that: (i) I leads up to t, (ii) each of zz is a proper part of x at each instant in I, (iii) each of zz is alive at each instant in I, and (iv) zz turn into y at t.

68. That is, it is not the case that there is some z and interval I such that: (i) I leads up to t, (ii) z is a proper part of x at each instant in I, (iii) z is alive at each instant in I, and (iv) z turns into y at t.

69. Define "x undergoes generative fusion or metamorphosis at t" as "there are xx and a y such that: (a) x is one of xx, (b) for some interval leading up to t, each of xx is alive-or-cryptobiotic at each instant in that interval, (c) y begins to be alive-or-cryptobiotic at t, (d) xx turn into y at t." Unfortunately, this definition is not precisely parallel to the definition of "generative division," and in fact I don't know *how* to construct a parallel definition. Fortunately, there don't seem to be any counterexamples to Terminus involving fusion or metamorphosis.

70. Indeed, some will lack strong intuitions about any of the odd cases considered in this chapter and will be willing to defer to the Cessation Thesis on all of them.

71. I will ignore time-travel-based counterexamples to Dead$_G$. See note 28.

72. Dead$_G$ is similar in some ways to the definition of "dead at"—labeled *D3*—proposed in my (2007); these four comments apply, *mutatis mutandis*, to both. But Dead$_G$ does not purport to be a definition or analysis of any word or concept. And Dead$_G$ bypasses the notion of a "toxic2 property" that gets defined and employed in D3. As far as I can tell, Dead$_G$ avoids the objection to D3 raised by Seahwa Kim (2010).

73. These two types of account are not exhaustive. See Belshaw, 2009, pp. 39–63 for an insightful overview that harmonizes with much of this chapter.

74. I am grateful to Andrew Cortens, Stephen Crowley, Scotty Dixon, Michael Glanzberg, Alex Jackson, Jens Johansson, Brian Kierland, Seahwa Kim, Matt Leonard, Adam Sennet, and an audience at Boise State University for helpful feedback on the material in this chapter.

REFERENCES

Arntzenius, Frank. 2008. "Gunk, Topology, and Measure." In Dean W. Zimmerman, ed.,
    Oxford Studies in Metaphysics. Vol. 4, pp. 225–247. Oxford: Oxford University Press.
Baker, Lynne R. 2000. *Persons and Bodies: A Constitution View.* Cambridge:
    Cambridge University Press.
Baker, Lynne R. 2005. "Death and the Afterlife." In William J. Wainwright, ed., *The
    Oxford Handbook for the Philosophy of Religion,* pp. 366–391. Oxford: Oxford
    University Press.
Balashov, Yuri. 2011. "Persistence." In Craig Callender, ed., *Oxford Handbook of the
    Philosophy of Time,* pp. 13–40. Oxford: Oxford University Press.
Becker, Lawrence C. 1975. "Human Being: The Boundaries of a Concept." *Philosophy
    and Public Affairs* 4: 334–359.
Belshaw, Christopher. 2009. *Annihilation: The Sense and Significance of Death.*
    Montreal: McGill-Queen's.
Bird, Alexander. 2007. *Nature's Metaphysics: Laws and Properties.* Oxford: Oxford
    University Press.
Boden, Margaret A. 1999. "Is Metabolism Necessary?" *British Journal for the
    Philosophy of Science* 50 (2): 231–248.
Braddon-Mitchell, D., and K. Miller. 2006. "The Physics of Extended Simples."
    Analysis 66 (3): 222–226.
Carter, W. R. 1999. "Will I Be a Dead Person?". *Philosophy and Phenomenological
    Research* 59:167–172.
Clegg, James S. 2001. "Cryptobiosis: A Peculiar State of Biological Organization."
    Comparative Biochemistry and Physiology Part B 128: 613–624.
Cleland, Carol E., and C. F. Chyba. 2002. "Defining 'Life.'" *Origins of Life and
    Evolution of the Biosphere* 32: 387–393.
Cole, David. 1992. "The Reversibility of Death." *Journal of Medical Ethics* 18:
    26–30.
Dainton, Barry. 2008. *The Phenomenal Self.* Oxford: Oxford University Press.
Dainton, Barry. 2010. *Time and Space.* 2nd ed. Montreal: McGill-Queen's.
DeGrazia, David. 2005. *Human Identity and Bioethics.* Cambridge: Cambridge
    University Press.
DeGrazia, David. 2008. "The Definition of Death." *The Stanford Encyclopedia
    of Philosophy.* (Fall 2008 edition). Edward N. Zalta (ed.). URL = <http://plato.
    stanford.edu/archives/fall2008/entries/death-definition/>.
Devreotes, P. 1989. "Dictyostelium discoideum: A Model for Cell-Cell Interactions in
    Development." *Science* 245: 1054–1058.
Fara, Michael. 2009. "Dispositions." In *The Stanford Encyclopedia of Philosophy*
    (Summer 2009 edition). Edward N. Zalta (ed.). URL = <http://plato.stanford.edu/
    archives/sum2009/entries/dispositions/>.
Feldman, Fred. 1992. *Confrontations with the Reaper: A Philosophical Study of the
    Nature and Value of Death.* Oxford: Oxford University Press.
Feldman, Fred. 2000. "The Termination Thesis." *Midwest Studies in Philosophy* 24:
    98–115.
Fischer, John Martin. 1993. "Introduction: Death, Metaphysics, and Morality." In
    John Martin Fischer, ed., *The Metaphysics of Death,* pp. 3–30. Palo Alto, CA:
    Stanford University Press.

Gallois, André. 1998. *Occasions of Identity*. Oxford: Oxford University Press.

Garey, James R., Sandra J. McInnes, and P. Brent Nichols. 2007. "Global Diversity of Tardigrades (Tardigrada) in Freshwater." *Hydrobiologia* 595: 101–106.

Gibson, Ian, and Oliver Pooley. 2006. "Relativistic Persistence." *Philosophical Perspectives, 20, Metaphysics*: 157–198.

Gilmore, C. 2007. "Defining 'Dead' in Terms of 'Lives' and 'Dies'." *Philosophia* 35: 219–231.

Hawthorne, John, and Theodore Sider. 2006. "Locations." In John Hawthorne, *Metaphysical Essays*, pp. 31–52. Oxford: Oxford University Press.

Hawley, Katherine. 2010. "Temporal Parts." In *The Stanford Encyclopedia of Philosophy* (Winter 2010 edition), Edward N. Zalta, ed. URL = <http://plato.stanford.edu/archives/win2010/entries/temporal-parts/>.

Hershenov, David. 2002. "Van Inwagen, Zimmerman and the Materialist Conception of Resurrection." *Religious Studies: An International Journal for the Philosophy of Religion* 38: 11–19.

Hershenov, David. 2003a. "The Problematic Role of 'Irreversibility' in the Definition of Death." *Bioethics* 17: 89–100.

Hershenov, David. 2003b. "The Metaphysical Problem of Intermittent Existence and Possibility of Resurrection." *Faith and Philosophy* 20: 24–36.

Hershenov, David 2005. "Do Dead Bodies Pose a Problem for Biological Approaches to Personal Identity?" *Mind* 114: 31–59.

Hershenov, David. 2006. "The Death of a Person." *Journal of Medicine and Philosophy* 31 (2): 107–120.

Hoffman, Joshua, and Gary Rosenkrantz. 1997. *Substance: Its Nature and Existence*. London: Routledge.

Hudson, Hud. 2001. *A Materialist Metaphysics of the Human Person*. Ithaca, NY: Cornell University Press.

Johansson, Jens. 2005. *Mortal Beings*. Stockholm: Almquist & Wiksell.

Johansson, Jens. 2010. "Parfit on Fission." *Philosophical Studies* 150: 21–35.

Johnston, Mark. 2010. *Surviving Death*. Princeton: Princeton University Press.

Kass, Leon. 1997. "The Wisdom of Repugnance." *New Republic*, June 2, 1997, pp. 17–26.

Keilin, David. 1959. "The Problem of Anabiosis or Latent Life: History and Current Concept." *Proceedings B of the Royal Society of London* 150: 149–191.

Kim, Seahwa. 2010. "On Gilmore's Definition of 'Dead'." *Philosophia* 39: 105–110.

Kolb, Vera M. and P. J. Liesch. 2008. "Abiotic, biotic, and in-between." In R. B. Hoover, G. V. Levin, A. Y. Rozanov, and P. C. W. Davis, eds., *Instruments, Methods, and Missions for Astrobiology XI* (*Proceedings of SPIE* vol. 7097) p. 70970A (1–6).

Lewis, David. 1983. *Philosophical Papers*. Vol.1. Oxford: Oxford University Press.

Lewis, David. 1986. *Philosophical Papers*. Vol. 2. Oxford: Oxford University Press.

Lizza, John P. 2006. *Persons, Humanity, and the Definition of Death*. Baltimore: Johns Hopkins University Press.

Lockwood, Michael. 2005. *The Labyrinth of Time*. Oxford: Oxford University Press.

Lowe, E. J. 1983. "On the Identity of Artifacts." *Journal of Philosophy* 80: 220–232.

Luper, Steven. 2009. *The Philosophy of Death*. Cambridge: Cambridge University Press.

Mackie, David. 1999. "Personal Identity and Dead People." *Philosophical Studies* 95: 219–242.

Manley, David, and Ryan Wasserman. 2007. "A Gradable Approach to Dispositions." *Philosophical Quarterly* 57: 68–75.

Markosian, Ned. 1998. "Simples." *Australasian Journal of Philosophy* 76: 213–226.

Markosian, Ned. 2008. "Restricted Composition." In Theodore Sider, John Hawthorne, and Dead Zimmerman, eds., *Contemporary Debates in Metaphysics*, pp. 341–363. Oxford: Blackwell.

McKitrick, Jennifer. 2003. "A Case for Extrinsic Dispositions." *Australasian Journal of Philosophy* 81: 155–174.

McMahan, Jeff. 2002. *The Ethics of Killing: Problems at the Margins of Life*. Oxford: Oxford University Press.

Merricks, Trenton. 2001. *Objects and Persons*. Oxford: Oxford University Press.

Merricks, Trenton. 2009. "The Resurrection of the Body." In Thomas P. Flint and Michael Rea, eds., *The Oxford Handbook of Philosophical Theology*, pp. 476–490. Oxford: Oxford University Press.

Olson, Eric. 2004. "Animalism and the Corpse Problem." *Australasian Journal of Philosophy* 82: 265–274.

Parsons, Terence. 1990. *Events in the Semantics of English*. Cambridge, MA: MIT Press.

Pepper, John W., and Matthew D. Herron. 2008. "Does Biology Need an Organism Concept?" *Biological Reviews* 83: 621–627.

Persson, I. 1995. "What Is Mysterious about Death?" *Southern Journal of Philosophy* 33: 499–508.

Rosenberg, Jay F. 1983. *Thinking Clearly about Death*. Englewood Cliffs, NJ: Prentice-Hall.

Rosenberg, Jay F. 1998. *Thinking Clearly about Death*, 2nd ed. Indianapolis, IN: Hackett.

Sider, Theodore. 2001a. *Four Dimensionalism: An Ontology of Persistence and Time*. Oxford: Oxford University Press.

Sider, Theodore. 2001b. "Maximality and Intrinsic Properties." *Philosophy and Phenomenological Research* 63: 357–364.

Siegert, Florian and Cornelius Weijer. 1992. "Three-Dimensional Scroll Waves Organize *Dictyostelium* Slugs." *Proceedings of the National Academy of Sciences* 89: 6433–6437.

Smith, John Maynard. 1986. *The Problems of Biology*. Oxford: Oxford University Press.

Sorensen, Roy. 2005. "The Cheated God: Death and Personal Time." *Analysis* 65 (2): 119–125.

Szabó, Zoltan Gendler. 2004. "On the Progressive and the Perfective." *Noûs* 38 (1): 29–59.

Szabó, Zoltan Gendler. 2008. "Things in Progress." *Philosophical Perspectives* 22: 499–525.

Thomson, Judith Jarvis. 1997. "People and Their Bodies." In Jonathan Dancy, ed., *Reading Parfit*, pp. 202–229. Oxford, Blackwell.

van Inwagen, Peter. 1983. *An Essay on Free Will*. Oxford: Oxford University Press.

van Inwagen, Peter. 1990. *Material Beings*. Ithaca, NY: Cornell University Press.

Wierenga, Edward. 1994. "Review of Fred Feldman, *Confrontations with the Reaper*." *Teaching Philosophy* 17: 78–81.

Wiggins, David 1980. *Sameness and Substance*. Cambridge, MA: Harvard University Press.

Williamson, Timothy. 1994. *Vagueness*. London: Routledge.

Wilson, Jack 1999. *Biological Individuality*. Cambridge: Cambridge University Press.

Wreen, Michael J. 1987. "The Definition of Death." *Public Affairs Quarterly* 1 (4): 87–99.

Yourgrau, Palle. 2000. "Can the Dead Really Be Buried?" *Midwest Studies in Philosophy* 24: 46–68.

Zimmerman, Dean. 1999. "Materialism and Survival." In Eleonore Stump and Michael Murray, eds., *Philosophy of Religion: The Big Questions,* pp. 379–386. Oxford: Blackwell.

....

CHAPTER 2

DEATH AND THE DISINTEGRATION OF PERSONALITY

FRED FELDMAN

....

1. INTRODUCTION

....

Quite a few years ago, in another context and while thinking about other things, I said that I thought that there are some dead people. Not ghosts. Not restless specters. Just corpses. I said that I thought that in typical cases people go on existing as corpses for a while after they die. I mentioned that a mummy might go on existing for quite a long time. A mummy would be a dead person, right?

Some of my friends thought this was a totally crazy notion. They insisted that no mummy could be a person! No moldering corpse could be a person! A corpse might be the left-over remains of a person, but it could not actually be a person.

To avoid pointless conflict, I retreated to what I assumed would be a less provocative position. Instead of saying that there are dead people, I maintained merely that there are some dead things that formerly were people. In effect, I said that something could be a person for a while and then (around the time of its death) it could stop being a person but could go on existing as a corpse for a while. Or, if in ancient Egypt, for a long time.

My friends then thought they had me cornered. My view was untenable. For I had admitted that when something that has been a person dies, it stops being a person. Surely I would have to agree that if a thing that has been a person stops being a person, it must go out of existence. No one can survive the loss of personality. Thus, I would have to admit that when a person dies, he or she goes out of existence.

So, in effect, my friends had presented an argument. The argument purports to establish the conclusion that people go out of existence when they die. Elsewhere, I have dubbed this the "Termination Thesis" (Feldman, 1992, p. 89). The argument makes use of just two main premises:

1. When a person dies, he or she loses the property of being a person.
2. But when a person loses the property of being a person, he or she ceases to exist.
3. Therefore, when a person dies, he or she ceases to exist.

I will refer to this as the "Personality Argument for the Termination Thesis." My central claim in this paper is that the Personality Argument is not sound.

Note that the argument is based on two central claims about personality. The first is the claim that death deprives us of our personalities. The second is that no one can survive the loss of personality—when we are deprived of our personalities, we go out of existence. Clearly, to evaluate the argument, we need to understand personality. What is the property we ascribe to a thing when we say that it is a person?

I began to think about the property of being a person. I have now come to some conclusions. Perhaps first among these is that although the word "person" (and "people" and "persons") is used unproblematically in ordinary conversation, very few who use the word can give any coherent account of what they mean by it.[1] I asked a lot of people to explain what they meant when they said that something is "a person." Some got angry; some said it was a stupid question; a few made some vague remarks before giving up. We talk about persons; we don't know what we mean.

Philosophers and others with axes to grind do have views about the nature of personality. I think these views fall into several main categories: there are biological theories of personality. According to one variant of this thought, when we say that something is a person, we are saying something about the biological species to which it belongs. On this view, to say that something is a person is to say that it is a member of the species *Homo sapiens*.

Quite a large collection of theories fall into the category of psychological theories of personality. According to these views, there is some psychological trait or ability, P, such that to say that something is a person is to say that it has P. A typical psychological theory finds its roots in some of the things Locke said about personality. On this approach, the property of personality is to be identified with the property a thing has when it conceives of itself as persisting as one and the same thing through time.

Another large collection of theories can be classified as moral theories of personality. One of the most well-known moral theories of personality was defended by Michael Tooley in his 1972 paper "Abortion and Infanticide." Tooley said that, as he used the term "X is a person," it is synonymous with "X has a (serious) right to life" (p. 40).

Here's how I am going to proceed: I am going to discuss each of the main families of concepts of personality—biological, psychological, and moral.[2] In each case, I will first say something about some of the main variants of the view. Then, for each of these families, I will select what I take to be a paradigm instance of that family.

For each of the paradigm concepts of personality, I will go on to discuss several metaphysical, semantical, and semilogical questions as they pertain to that concept. My hope is that what I say about these paradigm concepts will carry over to other concepts from the same family. Then, having identified and clarified the paradigm concept, I will turn to the main questions: if we understand personality in the specified way, what happens to the Argument from Personality for the Termination Thesis? Does the proposed concept of personality support the view that people must lose their personalities when they die? Does it support the view that people must go out of existence when they lose their personalities?

I start with a discussion of the biological conception of personality.

2. BIOLOGICAL CONCEPTIONS
OF PERSONALITY

Many philosophers have noted that in ordinary usage, "person" often just means "human being," whereas "human being" refers to a member of the species *Homo sapiens*.[3] But it is interesting to note that there is a certain amount of controversy about who is to count as a human being. Apparently, the dominant current view is that there have been two distinct subspecies of *Homo sapiens*. "Our" subspecies is *Homo sapiens sapiens*. This subspecies has instances all over the earth, and instances have been documented as far back as 200,000 years ago. The other subspecies is *Homo sapiens idaltu*. Individuals of that subspecies lived around 160,000 years ago in Africa. That subspecies is now extinct. Some taxonomists include several other varieties of archaic humans in the species *Homo sapiens*. But a lot of this is controversial. It's not clear precisely how the concept of "human being" is supposed to connect to these groupings.

While philosophers have proposed other biological conceptions of personality,[4] let us agree to use the term "person(b)" to express the concept of personality based on the idea that a person is a member of "our" subspecies.[5] Thus, we may define the term as follows:

> D1: x is a person(b) at t = df. x is a member of the subspecies *Homo sapiens sapiens* at t.

If we adopt this concept of personality we will have to accept a certain collection of metaphysical and conceptual implications.

a. The Intrinsicality of Personality(b). It has often been noted that species membership is not a purely intrinsic feature.[6] It would be possible for there to be two individuals that are intrinsically alike but not of the same species. Imagine, for example, that there are two populations of microbes, M1 and M2. Imagine that the members of M1 are earthly microbes with a certain genetic structure and history. Imagine that the members of M2 are intrinsically just like the members of M1, but that M1 and M2 are utterly unrelated. There is no common ancestor for M1 and M2. They arose independently on different planets. In this case, though a member of M1 might be intrinsically indiscernible from a member of M2, those two members would not be conspecific. In order to be conspecific, they would have to have a common ancestor.

Thus, since personality(b) is entirely a matter of biological subspecies membership, it, too, would not be an intrinsic feature of the things that have it. It would be possible for there to be a nonpersonal(b) individual who is nevertheless an intrinsic duplicate of a person(b). Such a creature would be nonpersonal(b) because it is not a member of *Homo sapiens sapiens*. It would be impossible to tell whether something is a person(b) merely by inspecting its intrinsic properties. A complete unraveling of the individual's genetic code would not be sufficient— unless we assume that it's impossible for the same genetic code to arise independently elsewhere.

b. A Matter of Degree. There is an inclination to think that each organism belongs to precisely one species—either it is a robin or it's a blue jay. But the facts are not quite so simple. There are of course hybrids. Some creatures are the offspring of individuals of two different species. And in some other cases, there seems to be a continuum of individuals starting with ones on either end who are clearly in different species, but with a multitude of intermediate individuals. The intermediate individuals are more or less closely related to the "pure" species exemplars. A good example of this can be found in the case of arctic sea gulls. They form a "ring" consisting of numerous individuals falling into several main species and a variety of intermediate groups that are not clearly in any of the main species. In certain areas, the intermediate gulls can breed with their purebred neighbors both to the east and the west. This suggests that species membership is really a matter of degree. One gull may be fully and entirely a member of a certain species while other gulls may be "to a certain extent" members of that species while at the same time being "to a certain extent" members of another species.[7]

If we reflect on the evolution of a species, we see that this phenomenon of partial membership is not restricted to some rare instances up at the North Pole. If we assume that every species gradually evolved from some preceding species, then we have to grant that in every case there was a transition starting with individuals that were clearly in one species and involving many intermediate individuals and ending with individuals that are clearly in another species. The intermediate individuals would be to some extent members of the earlier species but at the same time to some extent members of the later species. This would give us even more reason to think that species membership is a matter of degree.

If this is right, and it holds for the subspecies *Homo sapiens sapiens*, then we would have to say that for every individual who is a member of *Homo sapiens sapiens*, he or she is a member of that subspecies to some degree. Perhaps most of us nowadays are full-fledged members—that would make us "pure people(b)." But that would not be true of all of our ancestors, and it might not be true of some of our very distant current cousins.

If we look at this phenomenon in a slightly different way, we may choose to say that the concept of personality is vague, or indeterminate, in such a way that there would be groups of individuals who fall into a gray area in which it is neither determinately true nor determinately false that they are people(b).

c. The Conventionality of Personality(b). Taxonomists debate the merits of competing taxonomies. One may point out certain advantages of viewing things in one way; another may argue for a different system. This has happened, for example, in the case of bluebirds. Some claim that there are many subspecies; others prefer to list a smaller number. In the end, it seems to be something of a political debate— one taxonomy is declared to be the "winner" largely because it has been adopted by more ornithologists. If a different taxonomy had been more popular, it would have been the winner. Perhaps when we say that a certain taxonomy is "correct" or "true," all we mean is that it is the winner in this conventional competition.

If we accept the biological concept of personality, then we will have to allow that there is something conventional about personality, too. We'd have to grant that it is somehow "up to us" to decide whether to view things in such a way that the concept of personality(b) would apply to a certain thing. All competing taxonomies might agree about the current extension of *Homo sapiens sapiens*. But they might disagree about our distant ancestors. One taxonomy might declare an ancient ancestor to have been an early member of our subspecies; another taxonomy might declare that ancestor to have been a late member of an earlier subspecies. The decision about where to place that ancestor might be a matter of political debate. It might be "up to us"—or perhaps, up to the paleoanthropologists.

d. The Persistence of Personality(b). Some properties come and go. I formerly had the property of being a graduate student. I no longer have it. Other properties are persistent. They stick with the things that have them. It seems to me that personality(b) is a persistent property. If a thing ever is a person(b), then it will always be a person(b) so long as it exists. I have no argument for this. I realize that taxonomists could decide to adopt a new taxonomy according to which some things that formerly were counted as members of a species are no longer so counted. But it seems to me that in such cases the taxonomists have really just decided to adopt a new species concept. Everything that fell into the former species still falls into it. Everything that now falls into the new species has always done so.

e. Personality(b) does not determine a Natural Kind. According to a traditional view, the domain of natural objects is divided into a bunch of sets;[8] each natural object falls into precisely one of these sets; within each set, the members share some important intrinsic property—the "essence" of the kind; nothing outside one of these sets has the essence associated with a given set; there is nothing conventional or artificial about the division of things into these sets. The borders between these sets may be seen as the "joints," where Nature has been carved not by us, but by the way things are in themselves.[9] Ideally, there should be no individuals in gray areas between these sets. Each of these sets would be a natural kind.

If God had created a fixed array of species; if there were an intrinsic natural essence associated with each species; if all and only members of a species had the essence associated with that species; if each organism were a permanent member of precisely one species; if there were nothing conventional about species membership, then the division of organisms into species would have been a division into natural kinds. Since actual biological species lack all of these features, they are not natural kinds. And as a result of that, *Homo sapiens sapiens* is not a natural kind. Therefore, personality(b) does not determine a natural kind.[10]

f. The Biologicalness of Personality(b). If we take personality to be the property of being a member of *Homo sapiens sapiens*, then we will have to say that every person is a biological organism. After all, every member of our subspecies is an animal.[11] Personality in that case becomes entirely a matter of biology.

g. The Psychologicalness of Personality(b). It should be clear that it is possible for there to be people(b) without psychology. Surely there are comatose members of the subspecies *Homo sapiens sapiens*. So there are comatose persons(b). I assume that it would be possible for a person(b) to come into existence, to grow and develop, and eventually to die without ever having been conscious. Going further, it seems clear that such an individual could have permanently lacked even the capacity for consciousness. If such an individual had the right sort of DNA, and the right sort of ancestry, he or she would be a permanently and unalterably nonpsychological member of our subspecies. Psychology is no more than a happy accident for the rest of us. Thank your lucky stars.

h. The Humanity of Personality(b). There is debate and confusion about the personality of such things as gods, corporations, humanoid-looking creatures like the Na'vi in *Avatar*, chimps, and dolphins. Some want to say that these things are people; others want to say that they are not. Others are perplexed. But if we accept personality(b) as our concept of personality, these questions are settled. Clearly, God is not a member of *Homo sapiens sapiens*. Therefore, God is definitely not a person(b). Nor are corporations, chimps, or dolphins. Science-fiction creatures such as the Na'vi and Mr. Spock are also not members of our subspecies and so are not persons(b). If we accept personality(b) as our concept of personality, we will have to say that none of these is a person. Not even a little bit.

i. The Vitality of Personality(b). In typical cases if an organism is a member of a certain species (or subspecies), then it continues to be a member of that species (or subspecies) when it dies. A familiar thought experiment should confirm this.[12] Suppose a butterfly collector goes out in the morning and catches and kills a bunch of butterflies. Suppose he comes home at the end of the day. He spreads out the day's catch on a table. He consults authoritative guidebooks to identify the specimens. "Aha. This one is a monarch; this one is a viceroy; and this one is an eastern tiger swallowtail." He then pins the butterflies to a board, each with its appropriate label. The butterflies on his display board still exist and still are members of their respective species—dead ones. Why shouldn't the same be true of other biological species and subspecies—even *Homo sapiens sapiens*?[13]

Suppose suspended animation is possible. An organism can cease to be alive for a while and then come back to life. Suppose an organism is a member of a certain species; suppose the organism goes into suspended animation and then revives. Surely no one would want to say that the organism stopped being a member of its species while it was in suspended animation. I conclude that if personality is understood in the biological way as personality(b), then personality does not entail life. Something can be a person(b) at a time even though it is not alive at that time.

j. Personality(b) and the Termination Thesis. Earlier, I mentioned my friends' argument in favor of the Termination Thesis. The argument looked like this:

1. When a person dies, he or she loses the property of being a person.
2. When a person loses the property of being a person, he or she ceases to exist.
3. Therefore, when a person dies, he or she ceases to exist.

Now suppose we interpret the concept of being a person according to the paradigm biological view. Then the argument as a whole looks like this:

1. When a person(b) dies, he or she loses the property of being a person(b).
2. When a person(b) loses the property of being a person(b), he or she ceases to exist.
3. Therefore, when a person(b) dies, he or she ceases to exist.

I cannot see any reason to suppose that premise (1) is true. I think that in typical cases, if an organism is a member of a certain species (or subspecies), then it continues to be a member of that species (or subspecies) when it dies.[14]

I conclude that if we accept the biological concept of personality, then we must reject the little argument that I attributed to my friends.[15] That's because a person(b) can die without losing his or her personality(b). My own view is that if we accept the biological conception of personality, we should reject the Termination Thesis.

3. PSYCHOLOGICAL CONCEPTIONS OF PERSONALITY

Many philosophers have endorsed psychological theories of personality. According to these views, there is some psychological trait or ability, P, such that to say that something is a person is to say that it has P. A typical psychological theory is the one according to which the property of personality is to be identified with the property a thing has when it conceives of itself as persisting as one and the same thing through time. Thus, if I think that there was a time in the past when I was a child who did so-and-so, and that there will be time a time in the future when I will be an old man who will do such-and-such, then I am a person. If I cannot conceive of myself in this way as a persisting object, I am not a person.

Locke seems to be endorsing a complex view that contains a variant of this idea as a component in the passage where he says:

> We must consider what Person stands for; which, I think, is a thinking intelligent Being, that has reason and reflection, and can consider it self as it self, the same thinking thing in different times and places; which it does only by that consciousness, which is inseparable from thinking, and as it seems to me essential to it: It being impossible for any one to perceive, without perceiving, that he does perceive. (1979, 2.27.9, p. 335)

But there are many other versions of the view.

The other classic source for the psychological conception of personality is Boethius, who says that a person is "an individual substance of a rational nature" (1918, p. 93). Many modern philosophers accept Boethius's suggestion that rationality is a fundamental feature of personality, but they typically go on to say that other psychological features are as well.[16] Peter Singer, for instance, defines "person" as "a rational and self-conscious being" (1993, p. 87). Daniel Dennett claims that in addition to (1) being rational, persons must also be (2) beings to which states of consciousness are attributed, (3) beings whose personality is stance dependent, (4) capable of reciprocation, (5) capable of verbal communication, and (6) conscious in a special way (self-conscious, for instance) (1976, pp. 177–178).[17,18] Thus, both Singer and Dennett think that consciousness, or some variety thereof, is a fundamental feature of personality. This thought is also shared by many other philosophers. Lynne Baker, for instance, says that a person is "a being with a first-person perspective" (in other words, roughly, a being that can conceive of itself as itself) (2000, p. 6). And Harry Frankfurt famously says that for something to be a person, it must be able to have second-order volitions, by which he means that it must be able to want a desire for something to be its will (1971, p. 10).[19] Other philosophers have proposed psychological conceptions of personality that focus on some psychological trait not yet mentioned. John Harris, for instance, says that the concept of a person is the concept of a being that is capable of valuing its own existence (1985, p. 18; 1999, p. 307). Robert Joyce, on the other hand, says that "person" can be defined as a being that has the natural potential to self-reflectively know, love, desire, and relate to oneself and others (1988, p. 200). It is clear, then, that psychological conceptions of personality are many and extremely varied.

For purposes of discussion, let us focus on a simplified Lockean version of the psychological concept of personality. It may be defined as follows:

> D2: x is a person(p) at t = df. x is able at t to conceive of itself as itself existing before t, and x is able at t to conceive of itself as itself existing after t.

A number of commentators have pointed out that this concept of personality is certainly not equivalent to the biological concept of personality(b).[20] Clearly, there are members of our subspecies who are unfortunately unable to conceive of themselves as existing at other times—little babies, the comatose, the profoundly mentally disabled, and others. And equally clearly, there is no reason to suppose that the specified psychological ability is restricted to persons(b). Perhaps members of *Homo sapiens idaltu* were like us in this respect. Maybe even some chimps and dolphins are like this. Fictional characters like the Na'vi and Mr. Spock are described as being like this. Surely, if the God of the Old Testament exists, He is like this. All these things would be people(p) but not people(b).

But this psychological concept of personality is different in even deeper ways from the biological concept of personality.

a. The Intrinsicality of Personality(p). I find it difficult to see how there could be two things that are intrinsically indiscernible and yet one of them is a person(p) and the other is not. If the first thing can conceive of itself as itself, and the second thing is just like it intrinsically, it seems to me that the second one can think of itself as itself, too. If this is right, then personality(p) is an intrinsic property of the things that have it. In this respect, personality(p) differs from personality(b).

b. A Matter of Degree. It might be very easy for you to conceive of yourself as yourself at different times. It might be harder for me to do it. You might do it several times a day. I might do it just once a month. But if you can do it, and I can do it, then each of us is a person(p). It does not seem to me that the ease or frequency with which you can do it makes you "more of a person(p)" than I am. So I am inclined to think that personality(p) is not a matter of degree. If my inclination is correct, then this is another respect in which personality(p) is different from personality(b).

c. The Conventionality of Personality(p). Earlier, I pointed out that there is something conventional about personality(b). As with all such matters of biological taxonomy, it seems to be possible for an agreement among the taxonomists to determine precisely where one subspecies ends and another one begins. If they had come to a different agreement, the borderline would have been elsewhere. Elegance, simplicity, fruitfulness and other pragmatic factors may favor one taxonomy over another.

Convention seems to play a much smaller role in the case of personality(p). We may be inclined to say that no one and no group has the power to decide that certain individuals can conceive of themselves as themselves at different times. Either they can do it or they can't. The fact of the matter may be somewhat less stark. Perhaps there is some vagueness in the expression "can conceive of himself as himself." There could be borderline cases where it's not clear whether we want to say that the expression applies to a certain individual; in this case there would be indeterminacy about whether an individual is a person(p). Maybe on one precisification of the concept it will turn out that the individual is a person(p) whereas on another he is not. We have the power to adopt one precisification rather than another. To that extent, personality(p) might be slightly "up to us."

d. The Persistence of Personality(p). It is pretty clear that personality(p) is not a persistent property. Someone who suffers a sufficiently severe brain injury may lose the property of being a person(p). This seems to me to be a respect in which personality(p) is different from personality(b). For it seems to me that while a blow to the head may make you lose your personality(p), it cannot make you lose your personality(b).

e. Natural Kinds. Personality(p) does not carve nature at its joints. It gathers together a motley collection of gods, dolphins, chimps, people(b), and computers. The individuals in this collection are not alike in any metaphysically interesting way. They are gathered together into this unnatural kind in virtue of the fact that each of them has a certain contingent psychological capacity. I claimed earlier that personality(b) does not determine a natural kind. I stand by that claim, but I recognize that there is a historical tradition according to which biological species are supposed to count as natural kinds. On the other hand, no one would claim that personality(p) determines a natural kind.

f. The Biologicalness of Personality(p). Whereas the biological concept of personality makes personality a matter of biology, the psychological concept of personality does not. I think we can imagine something that is a person(p) even though it is not a biological organism at all. God, pretty obviously, would be such a thing. Some think they can imagine a nonbiological computer that has been set up in such a way as to be able to conceive of itself as itself at different times. The computer HAL 9000 in *2001: A Space Odyssey* seems to have this ability. If so, it would be a person(p) though not a biological organism. (This gives us even more reason to believe that personality(p) does not determine a natural kind.)

g. The Psychologicalness of Personality(p). Biological personality clearly does not entail psychology. There are unconscious people(b). Nor does biological personality entail even the capacity for psychology. There are people(b) who cannot become conscious. The irreversibly comatose are examples. This is another respect in which psychological personality differs from biological personality. For, while there might be unconscious people(p), it is impossible for there to be a person(p) who utterly lacks the capacity to become aware of himself as himself at another time. This is an immediate implication of the definition of personality(p).

h. The Humanity of Personality(p). No matter how smart they may be, dolphins, chimps, Na'vi, gods, and other such things are not members of *Homo sapiens sapiens*. So they are not persons(b). But if we assume that these things can conceive of themselves as themselves at different times, then they are persons(p). Some empirical evidence suggests that chimps do have the relevant sort of self-awareness.[21] If that's right, then they are persons(p). The same would be true of other self-conscious beings, real or fictional. Welcome to the club. Personality(p) does not entail humanity.

i. The Vitality of Personality(p). Where biological organisms are concerned, psychology requires life. Dead men are not conscious. This suggests that personality(p) entails life. But if a computer like HAL 9000 could be aware of itself as itself, and if such a computer is not alive, then there are some people(p) who are not alive. The connection between personality(p) and life is, at best, merely contingent.

j. Personality(p) and the Termination Thesis. Now let us see how the Argument from Personality fares under this second interpretation. The argument looks like this:

1. When a person(p) dies, he or she loses the property of being a person(p).
2. When a person(p) loses the property of being a person(p), he or she ceases to exist.
3. Therefore, when a person(p) dies, he or she ceases to exist.

I think the first premise of this argument is true. I think that when a thing that has been a psychological person dies, its brain "shuts down." It stops functioning. It loses all of its psychological capacities, and so it loses the capacity to conceive of itself as itself at other times. So I think that when people(p) die, they stop being people(p).

On the other hand, I see no reason to accept premise (2). For it seems clear to me that personality(p) is a property that a thing can have for a while and then lose; indeed, in a perfectly familiar sort of case, an individual might start off without personality(p), and then he might come to have personality(p), and then he might lose his personality(p) while continuing to exist. Imagine an individual who is for a while just an embryo whose brain is not sufficiently developed for any sort of con-sciousness, and then who is a walking-around sort of regular person(p), and then who is irreversibly comatose. He goes through a phase during which he is a person(p), but this is preceded and succeeded by phases during which he is not a person(p).

In light of this feature of personality(p), it seems that there is no good rea-son to suppose that things would have to go out of existence when they lose their personalities(p). So if we accept the psychological conception of persons(p), then we should reject the Argument from Personality for the Termination Thesis.

I think it's interesting to note that on the biological interpretation, the first premise of the argument is false, whereas on the psychological interpretation, the second premise of the argument is false. Perhaps a failure to appreciate the differ-ences between these two concepts of personality has led some to think there is a valid version of the argument in which both premises are true.

4. MORAL CONCEPTIONS OF PERSONALITY

Another large collection of theories can be classified as moral theories of person-ality. One of the most well-known moral theories of personality was defended by Michael Tooley in his 1972 paper "Abortion and Infanticide." In the passage I men-tioned earlier, Tooley said:

> How is the term "person" to be interpreted? I shall treat the concept of a person as a purely moral concept, free of all descriptive content. Specifically, in my usage the sentence "X is a person" will be synonymous with the sentence "X has a (serious) moral right to life." (p. 40)

Several years later, after further reflection, Tooley modified this definition. He then defined a person by saying that a person is a being that has at least one of the nonpotential properties whose possession is sufficient for having a right to life (1983, p. 35). Later in the same work, Tooley proposed a somewhat different account of the nature of personality. He then defined a person by

> asking what relatively permanent, non-potential properties, possibly in conjunction with other, less permanent features of an entity, make it intrinsically wrong to destroy an entity, and do so independently of its intrinsic value. A person can then be defined as an entity that possesses at least one of these enduring properties. (1983, p. 57)

This last account seems to me to be deeply problematic. For it implies that something can be a moral person only if it is intrinsically wrong to destroy it. But many familiar normative views imply that when it's wrong to destroy a thing, it's wrong because the destruction of that thing has bad consequences—worse than the consequences of leaving it alone. On any such view, there is nothing that is intrinsically wrong to destroy. And the immediate consequence of this is that there are no moral people.

Many other philosophers have endorsed moral conceptions of personality much like Tooley's early one. Joel Feinberg, for instance, thinks that "person" has a normative sense according to which a person just is the sort of being that can have rights and duties (1980, p. 186); H. Tristam Engelhardt says essentially the same thing (1988, p. 175).[22] While Tooley, Feinberg, and Engelhardt all give definitions of personality in order to make claims about the morality of abortion, moral conceptions have also been proposed by philosophers outside the abortion debate. In fact, moral conceptions of personality, like psychological conceptions, have a long and venerable history. Kant, for instance, suggests in *Groundwork of the Metaphysics of Morals* that "rational beings are called persons because their nature already marks them out as an end in itself, that is, as something that may not be used merely as a means, and hence so far limits all choice (and is an object of respect)" (1997, p. 37 [4:428]). Later, in *The Metaphysics of Morals*, he says that "a person is a subject whose actions can be imputed to him," and he goes on to say that "[m]oral personality is therefore nothing other than the freedom of a rational being under moral laws" (1996, p. 16 [6:223]).[23] Outside the Kantian tradition, myriad other moral concepts have been thought to be fundamental to personality. Roland Puccetti claims that to say that something is a person just is to say that it is a moral agent (1968, pp. 12–13).[24] Richard Rorty says that persons are things that possess moral dignity (1979, p. 127). Steve Sapontzis claims that for something to be a person is for it to be a thing whose interests must be respected (1981, p. 609).[25] And Eugene Schlossberger says that persons are things with full moral standing (1992, p. 32).[26] The list goes on and on.

For purposes of our present inquiry, let us make use of the first of Tooley's concepts of moral personality:

D3: x is a person(m) at t = df. x has a serious moral right to life at t.

The determination of which things are people(b) is a somewhat straightforward matter of biological classification, and the determination of which things are people(p) is a fairly straightforward matter of psychology, but the determination of which things are people(m) is profoundly *un*straightforward. Those who think that chickens, pigs, and cows have a serious moral right to life will insist that such creatures are people(m). Those who think that such creatures do not have any moral right to life will say that they are not people(m). It is not clear how this dispute is to be adjudicated.

Some, perhaps following Bentham, are dubious about the notion of moral rights in general. They may think that nothing has any such right. They would then have to say that there are no people(m). This might sound silly, but when we recall precisely what the statement means, it should seem much less silly.

But for purposes of discussion, let us assume that ordinary healthy human beings, while in the prime of life, have a serious moral right to remain alive. Then they are persons(m). And let us agree that it's an open question whether other creatures (chimps, dolphins, dogs, fetuses, trees, etc.) have a serious right to life. If we accept these assumptions provisionally, we can go on to consider some features of the concept of personality(m).

a. The Intrinsicality of Personality(m). It seems to me that it is at least conceivable that something could gain or lose the right to life as a result of another person's actions. For example, suppose God looks down on us and observes our behavior. Suppose He sees that some of us have been good and others have been bad. Suppose He then gives the good ones a serious moral right to life, and withdraws that right from those who have been bad. Or suppose He grants that right to the Chosen People, but withholds it from others. Or suppose He grants or withholds this right on a mere whim. In this case, there might be two things that are intrinsically indiscernible, but one of them is a person(m) and the other is not. These things seem possible. So it's not clear that personality(m) is an intrinsic property. It's at least conceivable that things sometimes have it in virtue of the fact that they stand in certain relations to others.

b. A Matter of Degree. The question whether personality(m) comes in various degrees may be understood to be the question whether some people(m) have a greater moral right to life than others. If we understand the question in this way, then it seems reasonable to answer it in the affirmative. We may think that all members of *Homo sapiens sapiens* come into existence with a fairly serious moral right to life. But we may also think that someone may behave so badly that his right to life is diminished. Going beyond this, we may even say that if someone has committed a sufficiently horrific and unjustifiable series of crimes, he may lose his right to life altogether—at least according to one time-honored view.

A number of commentators have endorsed the idea that different sorts of creatures have the right to life to different degrees. Thus, for example, Mary Anne Warren suggests that while adult human beings have a full right to life, lower animals and mere fetuses have some right to life, but not a full right to life (2002, pp. 78–79). If any such view is correct, then the right to life is a matter of degree. And in that case, personality(m) is a matter of degree.

c. The Conventionality of Personality(m). We may all agree that the legal right to life is a matter of convention. It's up to the legislature or the Supreme Court to determine who has this right. But we are not here considering the question of whether we have a legal right to life. We are considering the question of whether we have a moral right to life. I have no settled view on this. I am inclined to think, however, that if there is a moral right to life, then it would not be up to us to decide who has it.

d. The Persistence of Personality(m). I should acknowledge that I don't have a very firm grasp on the concept of moral rights. Perhaps when we say that a person has a moral right to something, we mean that he deserves to have access to that thing; he deserves to have no one stand in his way of possessing it. Others have a corresponding obligation to help him get it; or, at least to keep out of his way as he tries to get it for himself. If this is what we mean when we say that a person has a right to something, then it appears that rights are transitory. Suppose someone has a serious right to life; suppose he then goes on a completely unjustified killing spree. Just for kicks, he brutally murders dozens of innocents. Some would say then that this fellow's right to life has been seriously diminished, if not erased altogether. If such a thing is possible, it shows that the right to life is not a permanent property. It's possible for something to be a person(m) at one time, and then become much less a person(m), or maybe not a person(m) at all, at another time.

Some apparently think that we have a serious right to life because we have the capacity to suffer, or because we have the power of autonomous moral action.[27] It's clear that a person(m) could lose his capacity to suffer, or could lose his power of autonomous moral action. In such a case, the person(m) would lose his serious right to life. Thus, in such cases as well, a person(m) could lose his personality(m). Since such cases are obviously possible, we should acknowledge that if there is a serious moral right to life, it is something that can be lost. If so, personality(m) is impermanent.

e. Natural Kinds. If we assume any of the plausible views about the extent of the serious right to life, we will conclude that the class of persons(m) does not constitute a natural kind. For on any such view, this class would be a scattered collection of individuals chosen from a variety of distinct categories. Aside from the fact that they all have a serious moral right to life, they seem to have not much in common.

f. The Biologicalness of Personality(m). It seems reasonable to suppose that a thing could not have a serious moral right to life if it were impossible for that thing ever to live. Thus, if we assume that HAL 9000 is not a living thing, and could not live, then we might want to conclude that it has no serious moral right to life. In that case HAL 9000 would not be a person(m) in spite of the fact that it is a person(p). (Maybe he has a serious right not to be turned off.)

g. Personality(m) and Psychologicalness. It may seem that personality(m) does not entail psychology. For if we assume that a comatose person still has a right to life, then we must conclude that something can be a person(m) even though it is not conscious. If we think that trees have the right to life, then the conclusion is even more obvious. For in that case something could be a person(m) even though it does not have, and never could have had, any psychological states at all.

On the other hand, if we assume that the moral right to life depends essentially on the presence of some psychological state such as the ability to value life, then nothing could be a person(m) unless it had that psychological ability. So the psychologicalness of personality(m) depends upon what we take to be the source, or foundation, of the right to life.

h. The Humanity of Personality(m). From the fact that something has a serious right to life, we may not infer that it is a human being. Dolphins, chimps, Na'vi, humanlike creatures from other planets (if there are any such things), all would have a reasonable claim on personality(m). Yet none of them is a member of *Homo sapiens sapiens*.

i. The Vitality of Personality(m). Suppose a morally upstanding young man has a currently incurable disease. He decides to try cryopreservation. He enters into an agreement with the cryopreservationists: he will give them a lot of money; they will keep him safely frozen until a cure is found for his disease; then they will reanimate him and he will then get the treatment he needs. Everyone signs the contract and they shake hands. Accordingly, he is frozen. He goes into suspended animation. Later, a cure for his disease is found. The cryopreservationists say "[t]he hell with him. Let him remain an ice cube. Anyway, he has no right to life." If we assume that the young man had a serious right to life before he was frozen, we will presumably want to say that he still has the right to life. If so, personality(m) does not entail life.

j. Personality(m) and the Termination Thesis. The present version of the Argument from Personality looks like this:

1. When a person(m) dies, he or she loses the property of being a person(m).
2. When a person(m) loses the property of being a person(m), he or she ceases to exist.
3. Therefore, when a person(m) dies, he or she ceases to exist.

In this form, the Argument is completely unpersuasive. Premise (1) says (in effect) that when you die, you lose your right to life. I cannot see why that would have to be true. It would depend upon the feature that grounds this right. If we come to have this right simply in virtue of our being members of *Homo sapiens sapiens*, then we would go on having it even while dead. If we come to have it as a result of something that's lost at death (such as the ability to suffer) then we would lose it at death. Since I don't know why we have the right to life (assuming that we have it in the first place) I am in no position to judge whether we would necessarily lose it at death.

But several popular views about the right to life imply that (2) is false. Consider the idea that you have the right to life in virtue of the fact that you have the capacity to value your own life. That's what makes you be a person(m). Suppose that as the result of a blow to the head, you become unconscious and lose the capacity to value your own life. It surely does not follow that you would then go out of existence.

Suppose you have the right to life in virtue of being a morally decent person. Suppose you then commit a series of horrific crimes. Suppose that as a result of this you lose your right to life. Then you no longer have a serious right to life and so you are no longer a person(m). But you still exist. You might be sitting there in your cell on death row.

If the serious right to life depends upon any property that can be lost while its former bearer continues to exist, then the serious right to life can be lost in the same way. In that case, something that has been a person(m) could cease being a person(m) without ceasing to exist. (2) would in that case be false and the Argument from Personality would again fail.

5. CONCLUSION

I have no clear conception of what personality is. Some of the conceptions I have discussed here seem to me to be decidedly implausible.[28] Nevertheless, some conclusions can be drawn: if personality is a matter of species membership, then people can continue to exist even after death. The Argument from Personality would then fail at premise (1). If personality is a matter of psychology, then people stop being people when they die, but this gives us no reason to suppose that they must go out of existence when they lose their personality(p). So, again, the Argument from Personality would fail, but this time at premise (2). If personality is a moral concept, then it might be reasonable to say that people stop being people when they die; but there would be no reason to say that people go out of existence when they lose their personalities(m). The details would depend, in this case, on what we take to be the basis for our moral right to life. But in any case, the Argument from Personality would fail.[29]

NOTES

1. I use "persons" and "people" interchangeably as the plural of "person." I use "personality" to refer to the property of being a person. "Personhood" and "person-ness" might do as well, but they seem a bit weird.
2. In addition to definitions falling into these three main categories, there are a number of outlier definitions. For example, there is the legal concept of a person according to which something (including a corporation, or a union, or a town) is a person in some jurisdiction iff the laws of that jurisdiction give the thing some of the rights and obligations of natural persons; for example, the right to sue or be sued; the obligation to pay taxes, the right to "speak" freely, the right to own property. In the interest of keeping things simple, I will not discuss these outlier concepts of personality.

    Furthermore, some philosophers apparently want to construct concepts of personality that involve combinations of elements selected from these different main strands. Thus, someone might say that a person is a human being (biological) that has self-awareness (psychological). I leave it to the interested reader to determine the implications of such theories.

3. See for example Goodman, 1988, p. 7; DeGrazia, 1997, pp. 307–308; and Snowdon, 1996, pp. 39–40.

4. For example, David Wiggins's view about persons is often seen as a biological view. According to his view, which he calls the Animal Attribute View, a person is an animal that has whatever features a typical human has. Since a typical human has many features, his analysis of personality is quite long. He says that his view "sees person as a concept whose defining marks are to be given in terms of a natural kind determinable, say animal, plus what may be called a functional or (as I shall prefer to say) systemic component. Perhaps x is a person if and only if x is an animal falling under the extension of a kind whose typical members perceive, feel, remember, imagine, desire, make projects, move themselves at will, speak, carry out projects, acquire a character as they age, are happy or miserable, are susceptible to concern for members of their own or like species... [note carefully these and subsequent dots], conceive of themselves as perceiving, feeling, remembering, imagining, desiring, making projects, speaking..., have, and conceive of themselves as having, a past accessible in experience-memory and a future accessible in intention..., etc." (1980, p. 171). Wiggins acknowledges that according to his view, some nonhumans might be classified as persons. So, while his view is often seen as a biological view, it might be better classified as a hybrid view that has both biological and psychological elements. Wollheim proposes a view that is somewhat similar to Wiggins' (1984).

5. I assume that you, dear reader, are like me a member of *Homo sapiens sapiens*.

6. For a nice discussion of whether species membership is an intrinsic feature, see Okasha, 2002. He argues that "on all modern species concepts (except the phenetic), the property in virtue of which a particular organism belongs to one species rather than another is a relational rather than an intrinsic property of that organism" (p. 201).

7. For an interesting recent discussion of ring species, see Irwin, Irwin, and Price, 2001.

8. I am suppressing the proviso "at a given level of abstraction."

9. The idea that the division into natural kinds "carves nature at its joints" seems to have its roots in something Plato said. See Phaedrus 266.

10. For an excellent discussion of this point, see Bird and Tobin.

11. Perhaps this helps to explain some of the motivation behind animalism.

12. I appealed to this example in Feldman, 1992, p. 97.

13. Suppose a researcher discovers a completely intact frozen body in a glacier. He brings it back to the laboratory for analysis. After studying the DNA, he announces that he has discovered an early member of *Homo sapiens sapiens*. Surely it would be wrong for a critic to say that it can't be a member of *Homo sapiens sapiens* simply because it is dead.

14. Some animalists might disagree with me here. Eric Olson, for example, probably would want to say that when an animal dies, it loses its species membership. Perhaps he would say this because he thinks that when an animal dies, it goes out of existence. In the present context, that would be question-begging. He claims that organisms go out of existence when they die in Olson, 2004, pp. 269–270.

15. As I mentioned at the outset, there are other biological concepts of personality. I believe that what I have said here carries over to all of them, but I acknowledge that I have not argued for this larger point.

16. It appears, however, that John Pollock does not. He claims that "the concept of a person must simply be the concept of a thing having states that can be mapped onto

our own in such a way that if we suppose the corresponding states to be the same, then the thing is for the most part rational" (1989, p. 111).

17. Dennett accepts conditions (1)-(3) because he thinks that persons are what he calls Intentional Systems (that is, beings whose behavior can be explained and predicted by attributing to them beliefs and desires [and other intentional states, such as hopes and fears]). He accepts (4) because he thinks that persons are not only Intentional Systems, but also second-order Intentional Systems (that is, beings whose behavior can be explained and predicted by ascribing to them second-order intentional states). He accepts (6) because he thinks that persons necessarily have second-order volitions.

18. Kathleen Wilkes accepts Dennett's six conditions of personality but is tempted to add a seventh: the ability to use tools (1988, p. 23). She goes on to add that "few, I hope, would wish to challenge any of these conditions; as yet they are too broadly stated to merit dispute" (p. 24). It's hard to see how some of these conditions could possibly be beyond dispute, even when broadly stated.

19. In the course of his paper, Frankfurt also suggests that a number of other features are necessary for something to be a person, including rationality, first-order desires, and the capability of having and lacking freedom of the will. Frankfurt also says that, in addition to the concept of personality he addresses in his paper, there is a biological concept of personality according to which "person" connotes "no more than membership in a certain biological species" (p. 6).

20. See, for example, Snowdon, 1996, pp. 39-40; and Frankfurt, 1971, p. 6.

21. David Chalmers and David Bourget have compiled a useful annotated bibliography of recent papers on the topic of animal consciousness at Mind Papers: A Bibliography of the Philosophy of Mind and the Science of Consciousness, section 8.4c. http://consc. net/mindpapers/8.4c.

22. Both Feinberg and Engelhardt acknowledge that there are conceptions of personality in addition to the moral one.

23. Kant goes on to define psychological personality as "the ability to be conscious of one's identity in different conditions of one's existence" (p. 16 [6:223]).

24. Carol Rovane has a similar understanding of persons. She gives what she calls an "ethical criterion of personhood" according to which "persons are agents who can engage in agency-regarding relations" (1998, p. 72).

25. Sapontzis, however, claims that "person" not only has a moral sense, but it also has a "metaphysical" sense.

26. Schlossberger, too, suggests that there are multiple conceptions of personality.

27. A variety of ideas like this are discussed in Regan, 1975, pp. 205-206.

28. I should clarify this. When I say that I find many of these views to be implausible, what I mean is that if they are offered as accounts of, or analyses of, or precisifications of, or explications of any concept ordinary people have in mind when they speak of "persons," then I cannot imagine why anyone would believe them. If they are mere stipulations—if the cited philosophers are just telling us that they have chosen to use the word "person" to mean the same as "second-order intentional system" or whatever—then of course I would not say that the stipulation is implausible. I would just say that the philosophers in question have chosen a tremendously misleading way of expressing themselves.

29. Thanks to Ben Bradley, Jens Johansson, and Melinda Roberts for helpful comments on earlier drafts of this chapter. Special thanks to Kristian Olsen for careful and insightful technical and philosophical assistance throughout the production of this chapter.

References

Baker, Lynne Rudder. 2000. *Persons and Bodies: A Constitution View*. Cambridge: Cambridge University Press.

Bird, Alexander, and Emma Tobin. 2010. "Natural Kinds." In *The Stanford Encyclopedia of Philosophy* (Summer 2010 edition), Edward N. Zalta, editor. URL = http://plato.stanford.edu/entries/natural-kinds/.

Boethius. 1918. *The Theological Tractates*. Translated by H. F. Stewart and E. K. Rand. New York: G. P. Putnam's Sons.

DeGrazia, David. 1997. "Great Apes, Dolphins, and the Concept of Personhood." *Southern Journal of Philosophy* 35: 301–320.

Dennett, Daniel. 1976. "Conditions of Personhood." In *Identities of Persons*, edited by Amélie Oksenberg Rorty, pp. 175–196. Berkeley: University of California Press.

Engelhardt, H. Tristam. 1988. "Medicine and the Concept of the Person." In *What Is a Person?* edited by Michael F. Goodman, pp. 169–184. Clifton, NJ: Humana Press.

Feinberg, Joel. 1980. "Abortion." In *Matters of Life and Death*, edited by Tom Regan, 183–217. Philadelphia: Temple University Press.

Feldman, Fred. 1992. *Confrontations with the Reaper: A Philosophical Study of the Nature and Value of Death*. Oxford: Oxford University Press.

Frankfurt, Harry G. 1971. "Freedom of the Will and the Concept of a Person." *Journal of Philosophy* 68: 5–20.

Goodman, Michael F. 1988. *What Is a Person?* Clifton, NJ: Humana Press.

Harris, John. 1985. *The Value of Life*. London: Routledge and Kegan Paul.

Harris, John. 1999. "The Concept of the Person and the Value of Life." *Kennedy Institute of Ethics Journal* 9: 293–308.

Irwin, Darren E., Jessica H. Irwin, and Trevor D. Price. 2001. "Ring Species as Bridges between Microevolution and Speciation." *Genetica* 112–113: 223–243.

Joyce, Robert. 1988. "Personhood and the Conception Event." In *What Is a Person?* edited by Michael F. Goodman, 199–211. Clifton, NJ: Humana Press.

Kant, Immanuel. [1797–1798]. 1996. *The Metaphysics of Morals*. Translated by Mary Gregor. Cambridge: Cambridge University Press.

Kant, Immanuel. [1785]. 1997. *Groundwork of the Metaphysics of Morals*. Translated by Mary Gregor. Cambridge: Cambridge University Press.

Locke, John. [1690]. 1979. *An Essay Concerning Human Understanding*. Peter. H. Nidditch, editor. Oxford: Clarendon Press.

Okasha, Samir. 2002. "Darwinian Metaphysics: Species and the Question of Essentialism." *Synthese* 131: 191–213.

Olson, Eric T. 2004. "Animalism and the Corpse Problem." *Australasian Journal of Philosophy* 82: 265–274.

Pollock, John L. 1989. *How to Build a Person: A Prolegomena*. Cambridge, MA: MIT Press.

Puccetti, Roland. 1968. *Persons: A Study of Possible Moral Agents in the Universe*. London: Macmillan.

Regan, Tom. 1975. "The Moral Basis of Vegetarianism." *Canadian Journal of Philosophy* 5: 181–214.

Rorty, Richard. 1979. *Philosophy and the Mirror of Nature*. Princeton, NJ: Princeton University Press.

Rovane, Carol. 1998. *The Bounds of Agency: An Essay in Revisionary Metaphysics*.
   Princeton, NJ: Princeton University Press.
Sapontzis, S. F. 1981. "A Critique of Personhood." *Ethics* 91: 607–618.
Schlossberger, Eugene. 1992. *Moral Responsibility and Persons*. Philadelphia: Temple
   University Press.
Singer, Peter. 1993. *Practical Ethics*. 2nd ed. Cambridge: Cambridge University Press.
Snowdon, P. F. 1996. "Persons and Personal Identity." In *Essays for David Wiggins:
   Identity, Truth and Value*, edited by Sabina Lovibond and S. G. Williams,
   pp. 33–48. Oxford: Blackwell.
Tooley, Michael. 1972. "Abortion and Infanticide." *Philosophy and Public Affairs* 2:
   37–65.
Tooley, Michael. 1983. *Abortion and Infanticide*. Oxford: Clarendon Press.
Warren, Mary Anne. 2002. "The Moral and Legal Status of Abortion." Revised
   version. In *Ethics in Practice: An Anthology*, edited by Hugh LaFollette, pp. 72–82.
   Malden, MA: Blackwell.
Wiggins, David. 1980. *Sameness and Substance*. Oxford: Blackwell.
Wilkes, Kathleen V. 1988. *Real People: Personal Identity without Thought
   Experiments*. Oxford: Clarendon Press.
Wollheim, Richard. 1984. *The Thread of Life*. Cambridge, MA: Harvard University
   Press.

CHAPTER 3

THE PERSON AND THE CORPSE

ERIC T. OLSON

1. THE REALLY BIG QUESTION

The really big question about death is what happens to us when we die. If we had an oracle willing to answer just one philosophical question about death, this is the one most of us would ask. It may be that there is some sort of afterlife, and we continue existing after death in a conscious state. But what if there isn't? Then what?

We might simply cease to exist. Death is annihilation. But there is a third possibility, less dramatic and yet more unsettling: each of us continues existing as a corpse. Unless it is unusually violent, death is simply the transition from a living state to a nonliving state. So what awaits us at the end of our lives is not annihilation, but decay and dissolution, and only when this process is far advanced do we cease to exist. Until then we are literally food for worms. If you don't like the sound of that, you can at least take comfort in the fact that you will be completely unconscious when it happens. Based on what we observe, this may seem the most likely answer to the really big question.

These alternatives—afterlife, annihilation, and persistence as a corpse—may not be exclusive. Perhaps we could cease to exist at death yet somehow return to being later on. It may even be possible to become a corpse, rot away to nothing, and *then* be resurrected. I won't explore these suggestions here.

This chapter is about whether the alternative to life after death is annihilation or the worms (one part of the really big question). Suppose for the sake of argument that there is no afterlife, or at least none immediately following death.

Suppose also that there really are such things as corpses: that the particles composing a human person normally continue to make up something after one's
death. I mention this because some metaphysicians deny it: they say that when a
person or any other organism dies peacefully, her particles cease to make up any
larger thing, so that strictly speaking there are no corpses, but merely particles
"arranged corporeally."[1] This would rule out our becoming corpses. I will set it
aside for now.

Assuming that there are corpses but no afterlife, our question is how the living person relates to her corpse. Are they one thing or two? Shall I one day be a
corpse, just as I was once a child? Is the corpse that will issue from my death me,
the author of these words? If death is annihilation, the answer is No: my corpse is
something other than me. Nothing is ever first a living person and then a corpse.
If death is the transition from a state of being alive to a state of being dead, on the
other hand, the answer is yes: my corpse is me. The very thing that is first a living
person is later a lifeless corpse.

For practical purposes it may hardly matter which of these is the case. Few
of us will have any real preference either way. But it makes a big difference to
our nature and place in the world. If we did become corpses, it would mean that
our fundamental nature is the same as that of brute material objects. Though
we differ from sticks and stones in our mental and biological properties, these
differences would be only temporary, and not woven into our inmost being.
A human person would be nothing but a lump of matter that happens briefly
to have some special abilities. Most of the great figures in the Western tradition, from Plato and Aristotle to Kant and Wittgenstein, would have found
this absurd. It is also incompatible with the most popular contemporary views
of personal identity, as we shall see. What if death were annihilation? Then it
would be absolutely impossible for us to pass from a living to a nonliving state:
we could not exist without being in some sense alive. This would be a sort of
metaphysical vitalism. It would mean either that we are not material at all, or
that we are material things of a radically different metaphysical nature from
sticks and stones. This gives "annihilationism" something in common with the
doctrine of life after death.

2. NO FACT OF THE MATTER?

You might think that my question is somehow empty. It hasn't got a unique right
answer, like the question of whether the square root of 4489 is 63. The dispute
between annihilationists and "corpse survivalists" is merely verbal. Both views are
equally correct, and merely describe the same facts differently. The idea is not that
the person and the corpse are neither definitely one nor definitely two—a case of
vague identity. That would make both annihilationism and survivalism wrong: the

only correct description would be that the corpse is "sort of" identical to the person and "sort of" not. The thought is that you can say either. There is, to use a dangerous phrase, no fact of the matter here.

The simplest way to make sense of this view, if not the only way, is something like this:

> Whether your corpse is you depends on what we mean by the word "you." There is a being that has the physical and mental properties we attribute to you in life and which goes on existing as a corpse afterward. There is another such being that comes to an end when you die. We might call the first the corporeal person and the second the psychological person. The corporeal person becomes a corpse at death; the psychological person is annihilated. If by "you" we mean the corporeal person, then you are the corpse; if we mean the psychological person, then you're not. But it's pointless to ask which of these beings is "really" you. Both are equally good candidates for the reference of the second-person pronoun. And that's all there is to say about how you relate to your corpse. If the question seems difficult, it's because we're unsure whether it asks about the corporeal person or the psychological person. Make the question determinate and the answer is obvious.

Call this *pluralism* (Sider, 2001, is a good example). It implies that those who appear to disagree about whether people become corpses are simply talking about different things: some about corporeal people, others about psychological people. The only real disagreement is about words—about which beings the word "person," and personal pronouns and proper names, typically refer to.

Pluralism will strike some as nothing but good healthy common sense. But the assumption that there are two good candidates for being you—two conscious, intelligent beings now sitting in your chair and reading—is a contentious piece of metaphysics, and it is reasonable to ask why we should accept it. For that matter, the pluralist will need to say whether *all* questions about our identity over time are indeterminate in this way. Suppose we ask whether you will survive the act of reading this chapter. Does pluralism imply that one reader will perish on finishing the chapter and another will survive, and that it's pointless to ask which is really you? If so, there are far more than two intelligent beings sitting there. If not, we'll want to know what makes the two cases different.

The most familiar version of pluralism is the ontology of temporal parts or "four-dimensionalism," which in its usual form implies that every matter-filled region of space-time, no matter how arbitrary, contains a material thing. This (assuming that we ourselves are material) gives us a corporeal person, a psychological person, a being that comes to an end when it finishes this chapter, and a vast number of further intelligent beings, all now sitting in your chair and reading. On this view, our question about the person and the corpse would have a determinate answer only in the unlikely event that our personal pronouns and associated expressions always refer to corporeal people and never to psychological people, or vice versa. I will set aside pluralism until section 13.

3. SPEAKING OF THE DEAD

I turn now to proposals for answering our question.

Some say that ordinary thought and talk about death presuppose that people exist as corpses after they die (Feldman, 2000, pp. 101–103). For instance, we call a human corpse a dead person. And what is a dead person, if not something that was once a living person? This is not to say that a dead person is a person who is dead—that to be a dead person at a given time is to be at once a person and dead. The phrase "dead person" may be like the phrase "former student." But nothing can be a dead person without at least having *been* a person. It follows that the person comes to be a corpse.

Or consider this children's riddle: Who's buried in Grant's Tomb? The answer, of course, is Grant. (It's funny if you're eight years old.) The answer is not Grant's corpse. And the riddle asks not *what*, but *who* is buried there. Or again, we say things like "I want to be buried next to my parents," not "I want my corpse to be buried next to my parents' corpses." We say that many famous people are buried in Highgate Cemetery. All this seems to presuppose that when we bury someone's corpse, we bury him or her. But to bury the person and to bury his corpse is not to bury two things: we don't say that Grant and his corpse are both buried in Grant's Tomb. Once more, it follows that the corpse is the person.

The claim is that annihilationism conflicts with something we are all committed to, and thus implies that nearly everyone is mistaken about one of the most elementary facts concerning death. Such mistakes are of course possible, but a charge like this would require strong evidence. So much the worse, the argument concludes, for annihilationism.

This reasoning seems to me to have no force at all. For one thing, if the ordinary saying that many people are buried in cemeteries implied that people become corpses, it would also imply that there is no afterlife (or at least none beginning at death): you can't be both lying in the grave and at the same time enjoying the life of the world to come. But our willingness to say such things is hardly reason for doubt about the afterlife. It would be absurd to argue: "The belief in life after death conflicts with the ordinary statement that many people are buried in cemeteries, thus implying that nearly everyone is mistaken about death, a charge we ought not to make without strong evidence. So much the worse for life after death." For that matter, those who actually believe in the afterlife are no less inclined than the rest of us to say that people are buried in cemeteries.

A second point is that if our ordinary sayings about death implied that people become corpses, they would imply things that no one believes. Suppose Grant had been dead so long that his tomb contained only dust. It would be no less proper to say that he is buried there. If this statement implied that Grant really is there in the tomb, it would imply that some beings who were once living people are now literally piles of dust. Yet no one (well, almost no one) accepts that.

These points might show that people simply have inconsistent beliefs about death. I would prefer to be cautious about drawing metaphysical conclusions from ordinary talk: I doubt whether the saying that Grant is buried where his remains are presupposes that those remains *are* Grant, rather than simply his remains. But either way, the burial argument is undermined.

What about the saying that a dead person is something that was once a living person? I think it implies only that a dead person is the immediate result of a living person's death. It is like the saying that a demolished house is something that was once an intact house. Someone staring disconsolately at a smoldering pile of rubble might say, "That was once my house." This statement hardly implies that some one thing is first a house and later a pile of rubble. For all ordinary language tells us, the person may relate to the corpse in the same way.

4. THE PERSON/BODY ARGUMENT

Here is another argument based on ordinary thought and talk, this time for the opposite conclusion: A corpse is a dead body. More specifically, Ben's corpse is Ben's dead body. What makes it his dead body is that it was once his living body. So a person's corpse is the thing that is his body when he is alive. It follows that we become corpses only if we are the things that are our bodies when we are alive. But clearly we're not the same thing as our bodies. Ben's body does not read the *Guardian*. You can't have a conversation with Ben's body. (Not literally, anyway.) If people became corpses, it would follow that people's bodies really do read newspapers and have conversations, that Aristotle's body was the greatest philosopher of antiquity, and so on, which is absurd. Therefore people are not their corpses.

The argument has three main premises: (1) When a person is alive, there is a thing that is his body; (2) the thing that is a person's body when he is alive is the thing that is his corpse when he is dead; and (3) people are not their bodies. For present purposes I am willing to concede the first premise, and I will discuss something like the second later. Let's consider the third.

That Ben is one thing and his body is another is supposed to follow from the fact that there are expressions we can properly attach to the term "Ben" but not to the term "Ben's body" (or vice versa), such as "reads the *Guardian*." This is taken to imply that there is something true of Ben that is not true of his body, or that Ben has a property that his body lacks (or vice versa), in which case they can't be the same thing. The inference assumes that we can derive many of the properties of people and their bodies from the sorts of expressions we can attach to the terms "Ben" and "Ben's body" in ordinary language.

Can we? Well, here are some things we can say in ordinary circumstances:

> Ben reads the *Guardian*.
> Ben is six feet tall.

Ben weighs 170 pounds.
Ben's body is healthy/diseased.
Ben's body is made up primarily of water and proteins.
Ben's body has a surface area of 1.7 square meters.

And here are some things we cannot ordinarily say:

*Ben's body reads the *Guardian*.
*Ben's body is six feet tall.
*Ben's body weighs 170 pounds.
*Ben's body has the flu.
*Ben is made up primarily of water and proteins.
*Ben has a surface area of 1.7 square meters.

Whatever interest these patterns of usage may have for linguists, it's doubtful whether they offer any metaphysical insight. Otherwise, we should have to take seriously the idea that people have height and weight but no surface area, while our bodies have the opposite pattern of properties, and that human bodies can be healthy or diseased but cannot have any specific illness such as flu.

If the absurdity of saying that Ben's body reads the *Guardian* is not due to the fact that Ben's body is something that doesn't read, where does it come from? Maybe we use the phrase "Ben's body" to refer to Ben when we want to ascribe properties of a certain "brute physical" sort to him, difficult though it is to characterize this sort. To say that Ben's body is reading, then, would be to say that Ben is reading, with the implicature that reading is a brute physical property. In that case the statement may be strictly true, but defective owing to a false implicature. In any event, the difference in the way we use the terms "Ben" and "Ben's body" is unlikely to tell us whether people become corpses.

5. THE ESSENTIALISM ARGUMENT

The arguments we have considered so far are based on ordinary thought and talk. Let us turn now to arguments with metaphysical premises. First, an argument for annihilationism.

Each of us is essentially a person: nothing that is in fact a human person could exist without being a person. And a person is by definition something with certain mental properties—that is, to be a person at a time is to have those properties at that time. (This is not meant to be tendentious. If you like, consider it a stipulative definition of the technical term "psychological person.") These mental properties might be rationality and self-consciousness, or what have you. But whatever they are, a corpse hasn't got them. So nothing can be at once a corpse and a person. It follows that if you were to become a corpse, you would exist for a time without being a person—which, as you are a person essentially, is impossible. Therefore we don't become corpses.[2]

The claim that each of us is essentially a (psychological) person—*person essentialism*—is no truism or deliverance of common sense, and its implications go far beyond the claim that we don't become corpses. It entails, for instance, that I was never a fetus: a fetus, early in its gestation at least, is no more a psychological person than a corpse is. Person essentialism is a claim in need of an argument. But it's hard to find any such argument that amounts to more than an invitation to find it intuitively compelling (see, for instance, Baker, 2000, p. 220).

6. The Psychological-Continuity Argument

A similar argument turns on the claim that some sort of psychological continuity is necessary for us to persist through time. Suppose there is a being existing in the past or future: a child, an old woman, a fetus, a corpse, or what have you. How would that being have to relate to you, as you are now, for it to *be* you? Many answer that it would have to be in some way psychologically continuous with you. That is, it would be you only if its mental states then were causally related in a special way to the mental states you are in now. For instance, you remember reading the previous sentence. The reading causes the memory, presumably by laying down traces in your brain, making you psychologically continuous, now, with one who did the reading a moment ago. And you now relate to yourself as you are at more distant times by chains of such direct psychological connections. If no past or future being could be you without then being psychologically related in this way to you as you are now, then you could not become a corpse. Because a corpse, when it is a corpse, has no mental properties at all, it cannot then be psychologically continuous with you, and so cannot *be* you.

Is the psychological-continuity requirement true? The literature abounds with arguments for the claim that some sort of psychological continuity is *sufficient* for us to persist (Shoemaker 1984 is particularly clear example). For instance, if we imagine your brain transplanted into my head, it is easy to conclude that the resulting being would be you because he would be psychologically continuous with you. (I don't say that this is right, only that it's easy.) But this cannot show that psychological continuity is *necessary* for us to persist, which is what the argument for annihilationism needs. And that claim is far less attractive. If Fred lapses into an irreversible vegetative state, where his mentality is completely destroyed but his life-sustaining functions continue so that the resulting being can breathe on its own and remain biologically alive for many years, his loved ones don't automatically conclude that he has ceased to exist, and that the living being in the hospital bed was never a person. Nor does lack of psychological continuity lead many of us to deny that we were ever fetuses.

7. THE DEAD-ANIMAL ARGUMENT

Here is a popular argument in support of corpse survivalism (Ayers, 1991, pp. 216–228, 278–292; Mackie, 1999; see also Williams, 1973, p. 74; and Thomson, 1997, p. 202): We are animals—organisms of the animal kingdom. And when an animal dies peacefully, it comes to be a dead animal—a corpse. It follows that we come to be corpses.

If an animal really does become a corpse when it dies, then the question for us is whether we are animals. If so, we become corpses. If not, presumably we don't: I don't suppose anyone believes that we are *non*animals that persist through death as corpses.

Are we animals? The psychological-continuity argument (as well as the essentialism argument) would imply that we're not. You can't move an animal from one head to another by transplanting its brain. If we could move *you* from one head to another by transplanting your brain, you cannot be an animal. You would have a property that no animal has, namely, being such that you would go with your transplanted brain.

Here is an argument for our being animals (Olson, 2003): There is a human animal located where you are. Because it has a working brain and is otherwise physically identical to you, with the same behavioral dispositions and the right sort of history, we should expect that animal to be conscious and intelligent. In fact it ought to be psychologically just like you. How, then, could it be anything other than you? That would mean that there were *two* conscious, intelligent beings sitting there and reading this, you and the animal. Worse still, it would be hard to see how you could ever know which of those two beings you are. If you think you're the one that isn't the animal, then the animal too would seem to believe, mistakenly, that *it* is the nonanimal; and it would be in the same epistemic situation with respect to its belief as you are with respect to yours. So even if you really were something other than the animal you see when you look in the mirror, you could never have any conclusive grounds for believing it. The obvious way to avoid these awkward consequences is to accept that we are animals.

8. ANIMALS AND CORPSES

Rather than argue about whether we are animals, I will devote the remainder of this chapter to the question of whether animals become corpses when they die, and hence whether we become corpses if we are animals. (Again, it's clear enough that we don't become corpses if we're not animals.) But some of my arguments will be of interest even if we're not animals.

Why suppose that an animal becomes a corpse when it dies? One might appeal once more to ordinary language (Feldman, 1992, p. 34, pp. 93–95). For instance, we call a corpse a dead animal, and a dead animal, surely, is something that was once a live animal. Fishmongers boast that their herring were caught that very morning—when, of course, those herring were alive. And so on.

But ordinary talk about dead animals is no more metaphysically transparent than ordinary talk about dead people. Suppose a museum exhibits a dinosaur skeleton dug up in the Gobi desert. In any ordinary context, the claim that *it* was never alive, or wasn't a real dinosaur, would mean that what appear to be fossil bones are in fact artificial reproductions. Yet it is unlikely that the museum piece itself was ever literally alive. Even if an animal still exists when only its dry bones remain (making up less than a tenth of its original matter), little if any of the matter making up the dinosaur when it died is left in its mineralized skeleton. We can, of course, point to the skeleton and say truly, "That animal lived 100 million years ago." But then we can do the same by pointing to a footprint or a drawing. These statements do not imply that the thing we point to *is* an animal that lived in the distant past, but only that it is a sort of relic or trace or representation of such an animal. (They are cases of deferred ostension.) And the same may be true of the fishmongers' boast.

Of course, the dead fish in the market relate to the live ones in the sea in a more intimate way than the fossil skeleton does to the dinosaur, and this might be a reason to think that the dead fish were once alive even if the skeleton wasn't. That would support the claim that human animals become corpses when they die. But this is a different argument, based not on ordinary talk but on metaphysics.

9. THE ANNIHILATIONIST'S DILEMMA

The metaphysical argument can be put in the form of a dilemma. If you watch an animal die, the appearance is that something starts out in a living state and ends up in a nonliving state. It doesn't look as if the dying thing goes out of existence and something else takes its place. (This may be why we so naturally call the corpse an animal and say that it was once alive.) Now think about what it would mean if the corpse were something numerically different from the live animal. Where could the corpse have come from? How did it *get* there? There seem to be just two possibilities.

The corpse might have existed before the animal's death, somehow composed of the same matter as the animal. This would mean that the atoms composing a living animal always compose something else as well, namely, the thing that will one day be the animal's corpse. The "corpse-to-be" would be physically identical to the animal, yet not an animal itself. And somehow it would be able to survive the event that annihilates the animal. This would be an odd sort of biological dualism. We might call it *corpse concurrentism*.

Or the animal's death might bring the corpse into being. So nothing persists through an animal's peaceful death other than its small parts, such as individual atoms. Killing an animal would be a way of bringing a new object into being.

Peaceful death would be an essentially creative event, like conception. Call this *corpse creationism.*

If animals don't become corpses, then either corpse concurrentism or corpse creationism must be true. And both look like views best avoided.[3] The obvious remedy is to accept that the corpse *is* the animal that died, just as it appears to be. For that matter, all those who say that animals cease to exist at death face this dilemma, whether they take us to be animals or not.

Note, however, that our becoming corpses would not by itself solve the problem. At some point a corpse will itself cease to exist. If its particles then continue to compose something—a "postcorpse," we might say—this object will be something other than the corpse. We can then ask where *it* came from, and we shall be forced to choose between "postcorpse concurrentism" and "postcorpse creationism," which look no more comfortable than the horns of the original dilemma. The solution would seem to be that the corpse continues to exist until its particles cease to compose anything at all[4]—fairly late, presumably, in the process of decomposition. In other words, there are no postcorpses. But if we have to deny the existence of postcorpses, why not say the same about corpses, avoiding the original dilemma? I will return to this thought in the final section.

10. ANIMAL IDENTITY

The annihilationist's dilemma is the primary case for corpse survivalism. The case against is that it's hard to find a good account of animal identity that is consistent with it.

Whether animals come to be corpses turns on what it takes for an animal, or an organism generally, to persist through time. The best-known answer, and the one endorsed by most of those who have thought most deeply about it, is that an organism persists just as long as its biological life continues. (This was the view of Aristotle and Locke; see also van Inwagen, 1990, p. 145; and Wilson, 1999, pp. 89–99.) It is characteristic of living organisms that they take in matter and impose on it a complex and delicate form. The organism maintains this form despite wholesale material turnover. The process of imposing and maintaining this dynamic stability is the organism's life. That an organism begins to exist when its life begins is fairly uncontroversial (even if there is disagreement about when this occurs in human beings—whether at fertilization or at gastrulation some sixteen days later). The proposal is that an organism comes to an end when its life ends. More generally, an organism existing at one time is identical to something that exists at another if and only if the event that is the organism's life at the one time is the event that is the other thing's life at the other. Call this the *life account* of organism identity.

The life account rules out an animal's becoming a corpse: a thing has no biological life when it's dead. Survivalists need a different account of animal identity. They will presumably accept that every organism must have a life at *some* time—what else could make it an organism? And perhaps they can agree that while an organism is alive, it goes where its life goes. The reason I am the animal that sat in this chair last week (if indeed I am an animal) is not that I am now composed of the same matter that composed it then, or even most of the same matter: few atoms remain parts of me for long. Nor is it that I am the result of a process of gradual material turnover starting with that animal then, or that I am spatiotemporally continuous with it. This is true of many things besides me: for instance, my left foot is the result of a process of gradual material turnover starting with the animal that sat in this chair last week, and it is spatiotemporally continuous with that animal; yet my left foot isn't me. What makes me the animal that sat here last week seems to be that that animal's biological life is my life: the activities of the atoms composing it then constituted a grand self-organizing event that continues to this day, when it is constituted by the activities of my current atoms. But perhaps this needn't rule out an organism's existing after its life has come to an end. What survivalists need is an account of what it takes for an animal to persist after it has died. What determines which future corpse is me? How does a corpse have to relate to me, as I am now, in order to *be* me?

A natural thought is that a certain corpse is me because of its historical links to my biological life (Ayers, 1991, pp. 216–228). While an organism is alive, it goes where its life goes; afterward it persists, composed of matter that its life last animated, for as long as that matter retains enough of the arrangement its life imposed on it. When that is no longer the case, the organism comes to an end.

The *historic-dependence account* of organism identity, as we might call this, fits nicely with an attractive account of what makes something a part of an organism at a given time, or what determines it spatial boundaries (Ayers, 1991, p. 224f.). An organism appears to extend beyond the spatial boundaries of its life. The extremities of a sheep's horns, for instance, are "dead": they are not served by its blood supply or caught up in its metabolic processes. Yet they seem to be parts of the organism. What makes them parts of it ought to be something to do with their historical connection to its life: it is the earlier activities of this life that originally made them. And if the earlier activities of an organism's life enable it to extend beyond that life's spatial boundaries, they might enable it to extend beyond that life's temporal boundaries too. So the reason why the sheep's horns are parts of it is the reason why the sheep's corpse is the sheep.

11. THE HISTORIC-DEPENDENCE ACCOUNT

The historic-dependence account allows that animals come to be corpses when they die; the life account implies that they don't. I am not aware of any other account of animal identity. Which is right?

Sensible though it may sound, the historic-dependence account is hard to state in any detail. The original thought was that a dead thing existing at a later time is an organism that was alive at an earlier time just in the case that the dead thing is composed, at the later time, of some of the matter that composed the organism when it was last alive, and this matter retains enough of that life-caused arrangement. But suppose our sheep dies and its remains are burnt to ashes—apart from an ear, which remains intact. Then the ear is composed of some of the matter that composed the sheep when it was last alive, and that matter continues to be arranged more or less as it was then. According to our original thought, the ear must therefore *be* the sheep: the sheep has become a detached ear. In fact, the formulation is compatible with the sheep's becoming an ear even if the rest of its remains are preserved as well—it could become an "undetached" ear—for in that case, too, the ear would be composed of some of the matter that composed the sheep when it was alive, with its arrangement preserved. I take that to be absurd.

We might avoid the detached-ear problem by saying that after its death, an organism must continue to be composed of *enough* of the matter composing it when it died. It won't be easy to say how much is enough, but I suppose an ear's worth is too little. And we might solve the undetached-ear problem by specifying that after its death, an organism cannot be a part of a larger object composed of matter appropriately related to the organism's life. That would give us something like this:

If x is an organism at t and y exists at a later time t^*, $x = y$ if and only if either

i. y is alive at t^* and the event that is y's life at t^* = the event that is x's life at t, or

ii. y is not alive at t^*, y is composed at t^* of a sufficient proportion of the particles that compose x when x dies, y's particles at t^* are arranged at every time between x's death and t^* more or less as they are when x dies, and at t^* y is not a part of any other thing whose particles relate to x's in these ways.

(Devising a time-symmetric version would be a straightforward but tedious exercise.)

But we can easily see that this is inadequate. For one thing, it doesn't allow for a corpse to acquire any new particles. If the corpse absorbs moisture in damp weather, the absorbed molecules would not become parts of it; they would be foreign bodies, like pebbles embedded in a tree trunk. The same would go for ambient oxygen atoms caught up in the chemistry of decomposition. That conflicts with the usual natural histories of the dead.

Nor does the account appear to allow for a corpse to be revived. The trajectories of a dying animal's particles could be reversed—a process that would look like a film of an animal's death and subsequent decay running backward, resulting in a living animal. If the corpse *is* the animal that was once alive, then the result of reviving it ought to be the original animal too: no one would suppose that an animal can live, die, and become a corpse, but would necessarily cease to exist if brought back to life. The proposed account allows this only if the revived animal would have the same biological life as the original. Because the persistence of the organism while it lives is supposed to depend on the sameness of its life, however, and not vice versa, there is no guarantee that this would be so.

12. Troubles for Historic Dependence

These defects could perhaps be remedied at the cost of some added complexity. To my mind, the real trouble with the historic-dependence account lies not in the fine detail, but in its broad structure. For one thing, it is irreducibly disjunctive: it says that what it takes for an organism to persist is one thing while it is alive and something else entirely when it's dead. The sort of continuity that its identity over time consists in changes dramatically at death. That is inevitable, for a living organism and a corpse are, in a way, radically different sorts of thing: living organisms have a dynamic stability involving constant renewal of their matter, like a fountain, whereas the stability of a corpse, like that of a stone, is due entirely to the intrinsic stability of its materials (van Inwagen, 1990, pp. 83–94).

Might the account's disjunctive form be only apparent? Could its disjuncts be species of a single sort of "continuity of form"—some unified condition broad enough to cover the persistence of both living things and corpses? It seems unlikely. Suppose we neatly divide a higher animal—a sheep, say—into "upper" and "lower" sections, where the upper part contains the brainstem and other parts that coordinate its life-sustaining functions, but is only half the size of the lower part. And suppose we undertake all possible measures to prevent any further damage to these parts, providing life-support machinery, and so on. What would happen to the animal? The account implies that if this occurred while the animal was alive, it would survive, for a while at least, as the upper part, since that is where its biological life would now be going on. (The lower bit would have no life at all: it would be only a mass of individual cells.) And that seems right. But what if we divide the animal when it's dead? The account doesn't say what would happen, but it suggests that the animal would be either the lower bit, or else a disconnected object composed of both. That it would be the upper bit seems all but ruled out. Continuity of life and continuity of the arrangement brought about by a life are completely different conditions. If there is any unified condition encompassing both that is more than a vague gesture, no one has ever proposed it.

There is of course nothing wrong with irreducibly disjunctive conditions as such. Being an uncle is one: an uncle is either a brother of a parent or a husband of a parent's sibling. But such concepts, as Plato said, don't carve nature at the joints. They are artificial, gathering up disparate phenomena to suit our interests. *Organism*, on the other hand, is a natural-kind concept if anything is. That there is a science devoted to the study of organisms as such is no mere reflection of contingent human interests. *Organism* could hardly be an irreducibly disjunctive concept. Admittedly, it doesn't follow from this that the conditions under which organisms persist are not disjunctive. But it would certainly be surprising if they were.

A second worry for the historic-dependence account is that it tells us so little about what it takes for an organism to persist when it's dead. The problem is not merely that it appeals to conditions whose obtaining is a matter of degree without specifying that degree: that it doesn't say, even vaguely, what proportion of the original particles suffices, or how similar their arrangement must remain to the original one. More serious is that it gives no information about what happens to a corpse in a range of important cases. Suppose a hand falls off (or a hoof, or a paw). With a bit of good will, the account might just about imply that the corpse is not thereby reduced to a detached hand or annihilated; but beyond that we're on our own. Does the corpse get smaller by a hand? Or does it become disconnected, composed of detached hand and "hand complement"? Does it matter whether the hand remains intact, or whether it remains in contact with the rest of the corpse? To take another case, what happens if the corpse is cut precisely in half? Does it go with one of the halves? If so, which one? Does it matter where the cut is made? Or suppose the corpse is sliced neatly into a dozen equal sections. Does it survive? If so, in what form? Does it make a difference if the sections get put back together? Does it matter what sort of organism it is? The account is entirely silent on these questions.

Perhaps this is because the account as I have described it is radically incomplete. Maybe it's right as far as it goes, but tells us only a fraction of what there is to know about the conditions of organism persistence. The full version, with all the detail filled in, would answer the troublesome questions (even if in some cases the answer is that it would be indeterminate whether the resulting being was the original organism: they would not be definitely one, but not definitely two either). But I have no idea how to fill in the missing detail. I don't even know where to begin. There are many different and incompatible ways of proceeding, and I see no principled way of deciding among them. The reason is that I have no idea what happens to a corpse if a hand falls off, or it is cut in half, or the like. Nor, to my knowledge, does anyone else.

It may be that we are just irredeemably ignorant about these cases: the questions have answers, but for some reason we can't know them. (Merricks, 1998, offers such a reason.) But that would not address the disjunctiveness problem. What's more, it looks doubtful whether the questions actually have answers. Is there really a fact, laid up in heaven, about what happens to a corpse if it's cut in half?

13. Pluralism and Corpse Eliminativism

How could these questions about organism identity—or, more precisely, corpse identity—fail to have answers? We have already seen two views that would account for this. One was pluralism: the view that, for any possible candidate for being the history of an organism, there is an object—a candidate for being the organism—with precisely that history. This implies that if the corpse loses a hand, there is a being that begins with the organism and coincides with it till death, then becomes a corpse, and finally gets smaller by a hand. Another being does the same, but retains the detached hand as a part and becomes disconnected. And insofar as nothing about the way we use the term "animal" or "corpse" or "human being" (or the relevant pronouns and proper names) determines which of these candidates the term applies to, the question of what happens to the corpse has no definite answer. However, pluralism makes it unlikely that the question of whether we become corpses at death has any definite answer either; so whatever its merits, it's no help in defending survivalism.

The other view was that strictly speaking there are no corpses, but only particles arranged corporeally: "corpse eliminativism." Talk of corpses is no more than a convenient fiction. Talk of corpses persisting through time is a fiction too. We can say that a corpse gets smaller when a hand falls off, or we can say that it becomes disconnected; but if there are no corpses, neither statement will be strictly true. They will be merely useful but loose ways of describing a situation that contains only particles. And it would be no surprise if the rules governing this loose talk gave only scant guidance on what statements about corpses are appropriate, especially in hard cases like the ones I've mentioned (Olson, 1997, pp. 149–151).

Eliminativism implies that we don't become corpses when we die (even if it permits us to speak loosely as if we did). It also answers the awkward question of where the corpse comes from if it's not the person or organism that died, avoiding the annihilationist's dilemma. As a way of defending annihilationism, though, it seems a drastic measure. Worse, it looks self-defeating. Our cluelessness about whether a corpse continues to exist through various transformations is hardly unique. We are no better off when it comes to the persistence of sticks, shoes, or any other ordinary nonliving objects: they too raise questions that seem to have no right answers. If that supports eliminativism, it's a reason to deny the existence of these things as well. Shall we end up having to say that there are no living organisms or people—that we ourselves do not exist? That would be a strange way of saying what happens to us when we die!

But the argument for corpse eliminativism is not so easily generalized to *living* organisms. The life account of organism identity (section 10) avoids the objections facing the historic-dependence account. It is not disjunctive. Nor does it raise questions that seem to have no answers, even vague ones. If a live animal has a hand fall off, or is cut in half or what have you, there will be at most one resulting object with a life, and the life account suggests that that object is the original animal. Living organisms are metaphysically better behaved than nonliving things. That's why Aristotle and others combine something like the life account with the view that the only real composite objects are living organisms. (Van Inwagen, 1990, is a detailed defense of this view.) So we might say that we cease to exist at death because the only nonliving objects are noncomposite objects—that is, things without parts. Though perhaps not very comforting, that would at least be theoretically elegant.

For all its initial attraction, then, the view that we become corpses at death is hard to defend. If we ask what it would take for us to persist through time if it were true, the answer seems to be some sort of historic-dependence account. But the artificiality and radical incompleteness of such an account suggests that it could be true only given pluralism, which would make it indeterminate whether we become corpses. Yet the alternative, that death is annihilation, is beset with problems so severe that the best solution may be to deny the existence of corpses, and many other ordinary objects too. An easy and satisfying metaphysics of death is elusive.[5]

NOTES

1. Van Inwagen, 1990; Merricks, 2001. Some things, the xs, *compose* something y if and only if each of the xs is a part of y, no two of the xs share a part, and every part of y shares a part with one or more of the xs.
2. That each of us is a person essentially appears to play a central role in an argument of Rosenberg's against our becoming corpses (1998, pp. 47–51).
3. Though I have defended corpse creationism in the past; see Olson, 2004. p. 272.
4. More carefully: Consider the particles that compose a corpse at the last moment when it exists (or if there is no such moment, at a moment preceding the first time when it no longer exists and arbitrarily close to it). Now consider the first moment when the corpse no longer exists (or a moment following the last time when it does still exist and arbitrarily close to it). Those particles compose nothing at that moment.
5. I thank Chris Belshaw, Jens Johansson, Dave Robb, and Jim Stone for comments on earlier versions of this chapter.

REFERENCES

Ayers, M. 1991. Locke. Vol. 2. *Ontology*. London: Routledge.

Baker, L. R. 2000. *Persons and Bodies: A Constitution View*. Cambridge: Cambridge University Press.

Feldman, F. 1992. *Confrontations with the Reaper*. New York: Oxford University Press.

Feldman, F. 2000. "The Termination Thesis." *Midwest Studies in Philosophy* 24: 98–115.

Mackie, D. 1999. "Personal Identity and Dead People." *Philosophical Studies* 95: 219–242.

Merricks, T. 1998. "There Are No Criteria of Identity over Time." *Noûs* 32: 106–124.

Merricks, T. 2001. *Objects and Persons*. Oxford: Oxford University Press.

Olson, E. 1997. "Relativism and Persistence." *Philosophical Studies* 88: 141–162.

Olson, E. 2003. "An Argument for Animalism." In *Personal Identity*, R. Martin and J. Barresi, eds., pp. 318–334. Oxford: Blackwell.

Olson, E. 2004. "Animalism and the Corpse Problem." *Australasian Journal of Philosophy* 82: 265–274.

Rosenberg, J. 1998. *Thinking Clearly about Death*. 2nd ed. Indianapolis: Hackett.

Shoemaker, S. 1984. "Personal Identity: A Materialist's Account." In *Personal Identity*, S. Shoemaker and R. Swinburne, eds., pp. 67–132. Oxford: Blackwell.

Sider, T. 2001. "Criteria of Personal Identity and the Limits of Conceptual Analysis." *Philosophical Perspectives* 15: 189–209.

Thomson, J. J. 1997. "People and Their Bodies." In *Reading Parfit*, J. Dancy, ed., pp. 202–229. Oxford: Blackwell.

van Inwagen, P. 1990. *Material Beings*. Ithaca: Cornell University Press.

Williams, B. 1973. *Problems of the Self*. Cambridge: Cambridge University Press.

Wilson, J. 1999. *Biological Individuality*. Cambridge: Cambridge University Press.

....

CHAPTER 4

PERSONAL IDENTITY AND THE SURVIVAL OF DEATH

....

DEAN ZIMMERMAN

…If by any means I might attain unto the resurrection of the dead.

St. Paul, Philippians 3: 11, King James Version

1. INTRODUCTION

....

1.1 "Surviving Death," Criteria of Personal Identity, and Two Metaphysical Debates

Physical bodies belonging to the kind *Homo sapiens* appear, one and all, to be headed for disaster. Each body's ongoing existence depends upon the activities of cells, organs, and larger biological systems. There comes a time when, for one reason or another, the parcels of matter that constitute these structures stop doing their jobs. At one moment, a bunch of atoms are caught up in the life of an organism: oxygen is being transported by red blood cells, sodium and potassium ions are being shuttled around in nerve cells, and so on. Suddenly, the self-same atoms cease to perform these biological functions—they come to constitute a corpse, in which all the living cells are rapidly dying. Let us call this sort of failure, in which the matter making up one's entire body abruptly stops sustaining crucial biological processes like respiration and circulation, "the death of the body" (for the difficulties of providing a *real* definition of "death," see chapter 1, this volume).

It is conceivable that bodily death, as I have described it, is an illusion. Although it *looks* as though the matter making up our bodies becomes a corpse, in fact it does not do so. How could this be? Perhaps, unbeknownst to the rest of us, the atoms and molecules in question continue to support the same biological life— somewhere else! Peter van Inwagen once told a "just-so story" according to which God secretly steals each human body, just as a person is about to die, by whisking away all of its matter (or at least some large crucial portion thereof), replacing it with the corpse-simulacrum we bury or cremate (van Inwagen, 1998, pp. 45–51). The story shows that there is at least one strategy God could use to secure our ongoing existence—though it would require perpetration of a vast hoax, and it is a little hard to believe that God actually conducts business in this fashion. (For the record, it should be noted that van Inwagen does not take his story to be the literal *truth* about how God effects our survival.)[1]

In this chapter, I shall assume that nothing peculiar happens to the particular atoms and molecules making up our bodies when we die (they stay right here on earth, usually constituting a corpse); and I ask the question whether, nevertheless, human persons might somehow be able to survive the kind of event I am calling "the death of the body." I shall not address the momentous question whether any of us *actually* survives bodily death, but a slightly different question: whether survival is even *possible* for creatures such as ourselves.

But what kinds of creatures *are* we? Philosophers offer radically different theories about the nature of human persons. Since Locke's famous chapter on identity in his *Essay Concerning Human Understanding*, philosophical discussions about our nature have been dominated by questions about the conditions under which a person will or will not persist through time: If a certain cobbler were to awaken with all the memories and character traits that had formerly belonged to the prince, and vice versa, would that mean that a person had switched bodies? Does a person continue to exist after brain death, so long as his or her body remains alive? Answers to such questions can be given in a systematic way by formulating "criteria of personal identity"—general statements about the persistence conditions of persons. Different philosophers have argued for radically different criteria of personal identity; and their criteria have different implications for the question whether survival of death is possible, and, if it is, what would be required for it to occur. Some criteria of personal identity imply that the persistence of human persons depends entirely upon psychological continuities, others claim that only ongoing biological continuities are relevant, and still others fall between these positions. (A few philosophers deny that any informative criteria of personal identity can be given.)

One burden of this essay is to explain why it has proven so difficult to reach agreement about the correct criterion of identity for persons. Questions about criteria of identity cannot be sharply separated from two other deep disagreements about the metaphysical nature of persons: (1) whether dualism or materialism is true, and (2) whether the doctrine of temporal parts is true. I shall argue that believers in temporal parts should draw quite different conclusions about the criteria of personal identity than those who reject temporal parts, and that—for those who reject temporal parts—it matters a great deal whether dualism or materialism is true.

In section 2, after briefly characterizing the nature of the question—What kind of thing am I?—I describe several (partial) answers: dualism, materialism, the doctrine that persons have temporal parts, and the rejection of this doctrine. Then, in section 3, I sketch some criteria of personal identity on either end of a spectrum running from the purely psychological to the purely biological. Among philosophers with a view about these matters, the largest proportion is probably constituted by those who combine materialism with the doctrine of temporal parts. Section 4 is addressed to such philosophers, and contains an argument for the conclusion that they should take our persistence conditions to be partly a function of our own attitudes. Persons are (what Mark Johnston has called) "Protean" in nature. I argue that Proteanism, rightly construed, should make it quite easy for us to survive death, even on materialistic assumptions about our constitution—so long as there is a deity who wants us to survive.

But Proteanism is only plausible if the doctrine of temporal parts is true. If it is false, there is no reason to think we are Protean, and every reason to think that our persistence conditions depend upon the natural kind to which we belong, not upon how we think about ourselves. At this point in my argument, the question whether dualism or materialism is true becomes crucial. Section 5 makes the unsurprising point that dualism presents no obstacle to the possibility of our surviving death. In section 6, I contend that, although materialism (without temporal parts) makes survival of death trickier, a resourceful God would have little trouble bringing it off.

1.2 Who Will Be Interested in This Chapter?

The argument for a Protean criterion of identity (section 4), shall, I hope, be of interest to anyone who takes seriously the idea that we might persist by means of temporal parts. But, beyond the argument for Proteanism, the conclusions of the chapter will be of greatest interest to those who think there is, or may well be, a God. Most of today's atheists are materialists; and the forms of survival-for-materialists that shall emerge require miraculous events. Furthermore, my conclusions about the prospects of survival-for-dualists provide little comfort for (that rare bird!) the dualist atheist. A person's mental life evidently depends upon her possession of a living, healthy brain; so, even if she is an immaterial thinking thing, it seems unlikely that she could go on thinking after the destruction of that organ—barring, once again, some miracle. Without God in the picture, dualism by itself would not lead us to expect any very meaningful kind of survival of death.

Some philosophers have taken materialism to be obviously true, and to be incompatible with our enjoying any kind of life after death—thus providing a knock-down argument against the existence of a good God who will right wrongs and explain the meaning of our earthly circumstances in the afterlife.[2] If I am right, these arguments would fail, even if materialism were as obvious as many take it to be. So the chapter should interest atheists who make use of such arguments—however quaint they may find the supernatural machinery that I frequently wheel in.

1.3 Forms of "Survival" I Shall Ignore

Whatever consolation there may be in the thought that one will "live on, in the memories of loved ones," it is not a kind of survival I shall consider here. Nor shall I be satisfied to be told, as Einstein told the relatives of his deceased friend Besso, that nothing really goes out of existence: the universe is a four-dimensional whole, and "the distinction between past, present, and future is only an illusion, however persistent" (Prigogine, 1980, pp. 203–204). Perhaps there is solace to be found in such thoughts, but they do not offer the personal survival promised by many religions. My friends may remember me, and my earthly life may take up a certain portion of a four-dimensional space-time manifold, but neither fact will make it the case that, after my death, there will be someone around of whom I can now truly say: "I will be he!"

Some religions hold out the prospect for something that sounds a bit like survival but that also seems to preclude survival—at least, survival as a person. The Buddha described a kind of deliverance to be found in Nirvana; but, according to many interpreters, the deliverance consists in annihilation—permanent freedom from the wheel of death and rebirth. On the other hand, for much of Hinduism, to be united with Brahma after death is not to be annihilated, although it is to cease to be a person. I do not know whether merging with an impersonal One should count as "surviving death"; but it is not *personal* survival, and I will not explore the idea here.

Another proposal for surviving death that I shall set to one side depends upon the following intriguing analogy: "a brain is like a computer, and a person is like a program being run on that computer." Since a program is a set of instructions that can be run on many different computers, the analogy suggests a way for a person to survive the destruction of his or her present brain. All that is required is a new brain (or a supercomputer of sufficient complexity) to "run the program" with which the person is identical. Frank Tippler claims that *we shall be emulated in the computers of the far future*; this is "the physical mechanism of individual resurrection" (Tippler, 1994, p. 220). I am immortal because I am a program that will run endlessly in computers or other devices designed by "a God Who exists mainly at the end of time"—at something Tippler calls the "Omega Point" (Tippler, 1994, p. 5).

If I were a program, then God certainly could "resurrect" me by such means. But the most straightforward interpretation of the idea that *I am a program* has bizarre consequences. One and the same program can run, simultaneously, on many different computers; and it can also exist as a mere code, unimplemented. What kind of thing can be present in many places and times (in virtue of being instantiated or exemplified by many things in different places and times), and can exist although it is unexemplified? It is what metaphysicians call a "universal." A universal does not change, *in itself.* The pattern of fifty stars and thirteen stripes exemplified by Old Glory, and the melody of "Twinkle, Twinkle, Little Star" are examples of universals. The individual flags and musical performances that *exemplify* such patterns are changing things, but the patterns themselves do not change. The pattern of a melody requires that certain changes occur, *if* it is exemplified; but that does not mean that the melody, considered as an abstract thing that can be in many places and times, changes at all. It is an immutable pattern. A computer program is similar to a melody; both include rules governing the kinds of changes a thing must undergo if it is to play the melody or run the program. But the program itself is not the brain or computer that is changing, any more than the melody to "Twinkle, Twinkle…" is identical to my whistling of it; the program is something that is present in anything running the program at every time it is running the program, just as the song is present whenever anyone whistles it. But if "I am a program" implies that I am an unchanging universal, the view has got to be wrong.[3]

On a more plausible reading of the proposed analogy between persons and software, the point is that a *personality* is like a program. But it seems quite wrong to say that, whenever and wherever there is an example of someone with the same personality, one has the very same *person.* Gradually altering someone else's mind until he is psychologically similar to me would not cause either of us to become located in two places! It is far from clear that merely simulating my personality using different hardware in the future would be enough to insure *my* survival, rather than the existence of a mere doppelganger.

John Leslie, in discussing several varieties of immortality, suggests a similar but less mechanistic form of survival. Each of us might well, he thinks, be something like an idea in the mind of God—a character in a story God tells "himself" or "herself." (Neither gender is literally applicable to Leslie's pantheistic deity—nor, for that matter, to the God of Judaism, Christianity, or Islam; however, when talking about the deity of the Western religious traditions in this chapter, I shall follow their usual conventions and use masculine pronouns.) If God bothered to think of us at all, Leslie argues, we should expect that the deity would go on thinking about us, telling stories according to which we live on after bodily death (Leslie, 2007, pp. 61–65). As in the person-as-program proposal, I fear there is a kind of "category mistake" here; a person cannot be an idea in anyone's mind, even in a mind capable of telling itself an infinitely complex story. So I will neglect this form of survival as well.[4]

2. Materialism, Dualism, and the Doctrine of Temporal Parts

2.1 What Kind of Thing Am I?

It is a question of great moment to me whether *I* can continue to exist after the death of *my* body; and the same question can be asked by anyone, using the same form of words. As shall appear, the philosophical debates most relevant to this question tend to begin with a slightly different question: under what conditions is a person who exists at one time identical to a person who exists at another? But an answer to this question might not provide me with an answer to *my* question, for a couple of reasons.

Following John Locke, philosophers sometimes use "person" to mean something like: "a thinking thing capable of self-consciousness." On the face of it, this sounds like a capacity that a thing could gain or lose. I happen to believe that I existed before I had the capacity for full-blown self-consciousness; I acquired it only when my nervous system reached a certain complexity, and I may perhaps lose it again, due to irreversible brain damage, even though I might continue to live for some time. On Locke's understanding of "person," and given these assumptions about my origin and possible fate, *being a person* would be a contingent property of me, something that can be gained or lost.

I am happy to allow that there may be a perfectly respectable use of "person" that works like this—a meaning according to which I might once have been a non-person and could become one again. But, with "person" understood in this way, it would be one thing to find out the conditions under which I would or would not survive *while remaining a person*; and it would be another to find out what *my* persistence conditions are. After all, on this interpretation of "person," I can continue to exist without being a person.

Eric Olson has suggested that there is at least one perfectly good meaning for the phrase "is the same person as" that does not entail absolute identity (1997, pp. 65–70). He considers the idea that to be the same person as someone is to play a kind of role—it can be compared to being the same cabinet minister as someone, when the latter phrase is used in a sentence like: "The Earl of Tunisia was, from 1952 to 1954, the same cabinet minister as Winston Churchill had been during World War II—namely, Minister of Defense." And I believe Olson is right: we can certainly make some sense of the idea of using "being the same person as Dean Zimmerman" to refer to a title or role that could be passed on to someone other than me. One can cook up fanciful (and creepy) science fiction scenarios in which I deliberately cause some other human being to gradually acquire my memories, personality, and feelings of obligation, in order that I might live on *in someone else*—someone who is obviously not identical with me, but who can be relied upon to take my place after I have died. I suppose if that sort of thing were a common occurrence, a phrase like "being the same person as Dean Zimmerman" could come to mean something similar to "being the Minister of Defense." But when I wonder whether there are any conditions under which I could survive death, I am not wondering whether there are any conditions under which *someone else* might come to resemble me in the future, playing a role similar to mine in future social circles. So, if "the same person as Zimmerman" refers to a kind of *role* adoptable by someone other than me, then answering questions about the conditions under which the same person would exist will not necessarily tell me what would happen to *me* under those conditions.

A further complication that must be taken into account is the possibility that persons might come in several different kinds; and that some might be able to survive changes that others cannot. Why think that everything having a certain capacity—in this case, the capacity for thought and self-consciousness—must have similar persistence conditions? A wall of brick and a wall of ice may have similar capacities for resisting pressure, but the one can persist through increases of temperature that will melt the other. So suppose there *are* different kinds of persons with different persistence conditions. My greatest concern is not with personal identity *in general* but rather with the identity over time of the kind of person *I* happen to be.

In order to sidestep these issues, I shall give "person" a somewhat artificial gloss when formulating criteria of identity. I belong to a natural kind of entity that, at least in its mature, healthy form, has the abilities Locke associated with personhood—namely, the abilities to think and to be self-conscious. I also have certain persistence conditions essentially—that is, there are certain kinds of change I can undergo, and others that I could not possibly survive. In my discussion of criteria of personal identity (including the psychological and biological theories formulated as (PC) and (BC), below), "person" will mean "person like me": that is, a kind of thing that shares my persistence conditions and that, at least *normally*, satisfies Locke's definition of a person as a thinking, self-conscious being. The many similarities among the human minds that express their thoughts using first-person pronouns, and the similarities among the human bodies with which we speak or write words like "I," "ich," and so on, strongly suggest that each of our uses of first-person pronouns manages to refer to a thing of the same natural kind; and I shall assume that is the case.

2.2 Semantic Ascent: To What Sort of Thing Does My Use of "I" Refer?

I frequently shift from the question, What kind of thing am I? to the question, To what kind of thing did I refer by means of the word "I" just now? A substantive answer to the second question would not merely tell us something about words; it would answer the first question as well. This is an instance of what Quine called "semantic ascent." As he pointed out, where there are great differences of opinion about some subject matter, for example, the nature of persons, it is often useful to speak, for a little while at least, about a closely related but less tendentious subject matter: namely, the *words* that are used to talk about the subject matter (Quine, 1960, p. 272).[5] Semantic ascent would not be so innocuous if "I," when I speak the word out loud or write it down, refers to something very different from the subject of my thought when I silently ask myself, What kind of thing am I? But I do not expect that thought and expression are so loosely related as that.[6]

"I" is what David Kaplan called an "indexical"; so the natural place to start, when looking for its referent, is the best accounts of how this particular indexical works. I shall assume a roughly Kaplanesque account of the meanings of indexical terms, though I should hope the morals to be drawn would apply within other plausible theories.

Like "now," "here," and demonstrative uses of "that," there are two components to the meaning of a particular use of "I": one is a rule that governs everyone's use of the word, and another is the thing that gets designated by the word on this particular occasion, something that can vary from one use to another. The common meaning, the rule upon which all users are relying, is what Kaplan calls the indexical's "character." Sentences containing the word "I" are not, in general, about *speaking* or *using words*, they are about *people*. What I said, when I said I was hungry, was not that someone is talking and using the word "I" to refer to a hungry person; I was saying that a particular individual, namely, Zimmerman, was hungry. Kaplan would put the point by saying that "I" is "directly referential," contributing the thing "I" designates, in the context of use, to the "content" of what is said (i.e., to the proposition expressed), rather than contributing the character of "I" (i.e., *the speaker of this sentence*).

The "I"-rule appears to be quite simple: *in the context of a particular use of the word, it refers to the agent (typically the speaker or the writer) who is using it.* Speaking (or otherwise using a word) is an intentional action; so "the speaker" must refer to an agent, a thinking being. And, if the world were politely cooperative, serving up exactly one agent, one conscious being who is *the* speaker on any occasion when "I" is used, the rule would be easy enough to apply—once we figure out what these singular agents are.

Because the rule governing the reference of "I" does not advert to any description beyond "the user of the word," one can see how it might successfully refer to someone who uses the word despite the fact that she has many false beliefs about her own nature. Thomas Nagel compares our ability to refer to ourselves in the first person, even if we are confused about our persistence conditions, with our use of natural kind terms, like "gold":

> The essence of what a term refers to depends on what the world is actually like, and not just on what we have to know in order to use and understand the term. I may understand and be able to apply the term "gold" without knowing what gold really is—what physical and chemical conditions anything must meet to be gold. My prescientific idea of gold, including my knowledge of the perceptible features by which I identify samples of it, includes a blank space to be filled in by empirical

discoveries about its intrinsic nature. Similarly I may understand and be able to apply the term "I" to myself without knowing what I really am. In Kripke's phrase, what I use to *fix the reference* of the term does not tell me everything about the nature of the referent.

...Various accounts of my real nature, and therefore various conditions of my identity over time, are compatible with my concept of myself as a self, for that concept leaves open the real nature of what it refers to. (Nagel, 1986, pp. 41–42)

To sum up: whatever "I" refers to when I intentionally use the word, the refer-ent is a conscious agent, and so a thing with mental states. Beyond that, however, there is controversy about its nature. I shall focus on two of the most general con-troversies about the kinds to which human persons belong. One is the relatively familiar debate between dualists and materialists. The other is a more recondite metaphysical debate about whether, whenever an object lasts for some period of time, there must also be many other shorter-lived objects coinciding with it—that is, the debate over whether or not things have *temporal parts*. The two debates are orthogonal: adopting a certain position with respect to one of them does not fore-close one's options with respect to the other.

2.3 Dualism and Materialism

For present purposes, I take dualism to be a metaphysical thesis about human beings: namely, the doctrine that, for every person who thinks or has experi-ences, there is something—a soul or spiritual substance—that lacks many or most of the physical properties characteristic of nonthinking material objects like rocks and trees; and that this soul is essential to the person, and in one way or another responsible for the person's mental life. Materialism is the denial of this; each of us is composed entirely of stuff that can be found in lifeless, uncon-scious forms.[7]

Dualism comes in two principal varieties. Many dualists believe that each per-son simply *is* the soul—that extra, unusual component, the one that is present only in things with a mind. When I am conscious, that is because *it* is conscious, and I am identical with it. I shall call this view "simple dualism." Compound dualists, on the other hand, take the person to be a composite entity, consisting of soul and body. Compound dualists, in turn, may be divided into two classes. Aristotelian and Thomistic forms of dualism deny that each of us is identical to a soul; we are, rather, body-soul composites. And, at least in living human beings, it is not the soul itself that thinks; instead, it is the whole composed of body and soul that does whatever thinking is going on.[8] Some other compound dualists, however, want to have it both ways: Although I am, myself, a compound of soul and body, never-theless my soul has my mental properties—it is, itself, a thinking, feeling entity; indeed, one that has all the same thoughts and feelings as myself (Swinburne, 1986, pp. 145–146).[9] I shall set this version of compound dualism to one side, since it leads to a strange conclusion: that there are two thinkers, thinking exactly the same thoughts as myself, only one of which is identical with *me*.[10]

2.4 The Doctrine of Temporal Parts

I imagine that most people reading this chapter will already think of themselves as either dualists or materialists. Fewer will already have a view about whether they persist through time by means of temporal parts; so the doctrine and its denial deserve a little more attention.

The doctrine of temporal parts is the result of taking the temporal dimension of a thing to be rather like its spatial dimensions; in a slogan, things take up time in the same way they take up space. There are at least three respects in which temporal and spatial extension are supposed to resemble one another, according to the friends of temporal parts. The first involves the sheer number of parts; I will call the doctrine "Momentary Parts." The second involves the way extended things inherit properties from their parts; I will call the doctrine "Property Inheritance." The third involves the way smaller parts go together to make up larger parts; I will call it "Arbitrary Sums."

Taking up space is a matter of occupying many different locations; and the normal way to do that is by having different parts located *just* in those different locations. Similarly, according to the friends of temporal parts, things "take up time"—that is, things exist at more than one time—by having different parts located *just* at the different times at which they exist. So, if I exist at noon and also at midnight, there is an instantaneous part of me that exists just at noon, and another one that exists just at midnight—each with exactly the shape and size I have at the moment it exists. *Momentary Parts* is the doctrine that, at each instant a person exists, there is an instantaneous entity occupying the same location as the person—what one might call a "person-stage"—and that every part that the person has at that time (e.g., the person's hands, heart, and hairs) shares an instantaneous part in common with that brief, person-like thing.

Another common assumption about a thing that occupies many places is that its character at those different places is due to the nature of the parts it has at those places. A flag is red with white polka dots in virtue of having round parts that are purely white and another part that is purely red (but with many holes in it). A flag is solid red in virtue of having many different parts in many different places, each the same red color as the others. The doctrine of *Property Inheritance* says that something similar is true with respect to time: the color and other intrinsic properties of a temporally extended object are due to the nature of its shorter-lived temporal parts. A flag that starts out bright red and gradually fades to a light pink hue changes its color in virtue of having many very brief parts with slightly different colors; a flag that keeps its color has many different temporal parts with exactly the same color.

A metaphysician could, in principle, accept Momentary Parts while rejecting Property Inheritance. Where I am, at each moment, there is an instantaneous thing located exactly there; but I am not pale or skinny or tall in virtue of its color, shape, and size—rather, the reverse. How could this be? Perhaps because the short-lived thing is a second-class, derivative entity—less fundamental than the longer-lived person with whom it coincides.[11] In any case, the doctrine of temporal parts, as I shall understand it, includes both views.

Metaphysicians who accept these two doctrines typically also allow that there are many shorter- and longer-lived wholes made out of the temporal parts of any given persisting thing—that is, more or less arbitrary sums of temporal parts. Again, an analogous spatial principle seems appealing. If an object can be divided into thirds, any two contiguous thirds should constitute another part of the object, one that is two-thirds as large as the whole. More generally, for any connected subregion of an object's location, the parts of the object within that subregion constitute a further part of the object, located within just that subregion. Similarly, if a number of my temporal parts occupy a continuous subinterval of the period during which I exist, there ought to be a temporal part of me consisting of just those parts, existing just during that period. For example, the temporal parts of me that exist at each instant of a certain day should compose a twenty-four-hour-long person-like entity that is also a part of me.

The first two doctrines do not dictate exactly what sort of summation principles the friends of temporal parts should accept. Should every collection of temporal parts—however arbitrary and gerrymandered—be allowed to have a sum, an object composed of just them, existing at no other times? There is room for disagreement here; but there is also great pressure, backed by further spatial analogies, to recognize many objects sharing most of my temporal parts with me.

The spatially analogous cases are objects with vague boundaries. Clouds, mountains, and even (when one looks closely enough) living bodies, are "fuzzy around the edges." There are many parts that are not definitely "inside" and not definitely "outside"—for example, a water molecule on the edge of a cloud, an outcropping of rock in the high foothills of a mountain, or some carbon dioxide about to be expelled from the lungs of an animal. The most natural ways to understand this sort of vagueness take it for granted that, when we refer to clouds, mountains, and animals, there are many candidates for our terms, differing slightly in their boundaries—some including, others excluding, various borderline parts. We could choose to *draw* boundaries more precisely, thereby referring to a narrower range of these candidates; we could "lay it down" that the mountain ends exactly *here*; but, in order for such a procedure even to make sense, the candidates must already exist, awaiting our choice to focus on some rather than others.

Many persisting objects exhibit a similar vagueness along the temporal dimension—indeterminacy in the times at which they come into being and cease to exist. When does some water vapor become sufficiently dense to count as a cloud? When does a massive hunk of granite become so worn down that it is no longer a mountain? At what precise instant does an animal begin its life, or cease to exist? These questions about temporal boundaries seem as vague as corresponding questions about spatial ones; and, as in the spatial case, they seem to admit of stipulation—we can choose to draw more precise boundaries around the beginnings and endings of vague persisting things. But, again, since we do not bring things into existence simply by stipulation, the persisting objects with different beginnings and endings must already exist in order for us to be able to choose among them. The doctrine of temporal parts can make sense of the existence of many candidate objects of reference, usually in the same place at the same time, but differing slightly in their origins and ends; but that requires Arbitrary Sums—there must be sums of temporal parts that include or exclude parts for relatively trivial reasons. In other words, for any changes we could conceivably select in an attempt to become more precise when talking about the histories of ordinary objects, there must already exist sums of temporal parts with temporal boundaries marked by such changes.[12]

2.5 Leaving the Options Open

A chapter in a handbook about death is probably not the place to address, head on, the question which combination of metaphysical views is true. Many philosophers regard the contest between dualism and materialism as having been decisively settled, long ago, in favor of the latter. I would argue that they are wrong,[13] but in the present context it will suffice to consider our prospects for survival of death on both dualistic and materialistic hypotheses. (I shall give short shrift to dualism— its friendliness to the possibility of survival is obvious.) The size of the opposing camps in the philosophical dispute over temporal parts are, I suspect, roughly equal; so it is well worth exploring what should be said on both alternatives. What I try to show is that survival of death is a real possibility, no matter how the cards fall—whether or not we have temporal parts, and whether or not we have (or are) souls.

In the next section, I set forth a representative sample of the competing criteria of personal identity over time that have been offered by philosophers, focusing on popular ones that appeal to psychological and biological continuities. In section 4, I argue that, assuming the doctrine of temporal parts, both dualist and materialist should agree that the best account of our persistence conditions is Proteanism: a subtle hybrid criterion of identity that takes our self-conception into account. In section 5, I consider what one should think about the competing criteria if the doctrine of temporal parts is false. Here, the difference between dualism and materialism becomes more significant.

3. COMPETING CRITERIA OF PERSONAL IDENTITY OVER TIME

3.1 A Schematic Criterion

Locke's discussion of personal identity focused philosophical attention upon the question: Under what conditions is a person who exists at one place and time identical with some person existing in a certain place at a certain subsequent time? Many philosophers have taken up Locke's search for what is often called a "criterion of identity over time" for persons—that is, a way to fill in the blank on the right hand side of the following schematic statement:

    (SC)   A person x who exists at a time t is the same person as a person y who exists at a later time t^* if, and only if:_____.

In my discussion of various ways to fill out (SC), I shall assume that, if something is a person, it could not fail to be a person. I shall also assume that, if x at t is the same person as y at t^*, then x and y are one and the same thing—numerically identical; one, not two. These assumptions should not be too controversial, since I am using "person" as a term for the kind of thing that has persistence conditions *like mine*, whatever they might be. I assume that you—the readers of this book— and I are sufficiently similar in nature for there to be an interesting way of filling in (SC) that applies to us all.

Some ways of filling in (SC) may fail to be profound philosophical theories about the nature of persons, even if the resulting version of (SC) is true; because some fillings are almost completely uninformative. For example, one might fill in the blank with: "x is a person, y is a person, and x is identical with y." This would tell us only that personal identity is a species of numerical identity (ruling out the sameness-of-person-as-sameness-of-role thesis described in the preceding subsection). It would tell us nothing about the kinds of episodes persons can survive, and the kinds of episodes they cannot survive—that is, nothing about the *persistence conditions* of persons. So philosophers have tried to do a little better than that, formulating criteria using concepts that do not, at least on first blush, entail anything about the identities of x and y.

The most popular proposals include criteria that yield very different pictures of the persistence conditions for persons. Some put more emphasis upon psychological connections between the person at the earlier time and the person at the later time, while others emphasize biological connections.[14]

3.2 Psychological Criteria

Locke himself seems to have wanted to fill in (SC) with something about *memory*, putting him far to the psychological side of this disagreement. Although his actual views may have been subtler than this, his 18th century readers generally took him to be saying that the person y at the later time t^* is the same as the earlier individual, x, if, and only if, the former has a memory of something x did at t. Butler, Reid, and others raised some serious objections to the criterion.[15]

For one thing, memory seems to require analysis in terms of personal identity, rendering the proposal less philosophically interesting than it might at first have seemed; so latter-day Neo-Lockeans, like Sydney Shoemaker, have replaced "memory," in their statements of psychological criteria, with "quasi-memory"— a quasi-memory being an apparent memory of a type of event that happened to

the earlier person, and that is caused by the earlier event (important qualifications must be added, specifying the *right kind* of causal path between the event and
the seeming-memory; and there are worries about whether the appropriate causal
dependence can be described without bringing in the identity of the experiencing
person with the remembering person).[16]

Locke's theory also seems in trouble because of cases like Reid's brave officer: in
middle-age, he remembers events in his childhood, which are forgotten in old-age;
but in old-age he nevertheless recalls heroic deeds from his adulthood. Locke's criterion, read straightforwardly, implies that the old man is the same person as the
adult hero, who is the same person as the child, though the old man is not the same
person as the child. One popular response is to require, not direct quasi-memory
connections between the person at the one time and the person at the other, but
only that they be connectable indirectly, by a chain of direct quasi-memories holding among persons who exist at times between the t and t^* of (SC).

Locke's reliance upon episodic memory has also fallen out of favor. If someone
had amnesia about particular episodes in her past, while nevertheless retaining the
very same character traits and skills, the same likes and dislikes, the same general
beliefs, and so on, we should hardly hesitate to identify the pre-amnesiac with the
post-amnesiac. So Neo-Lockeans like Shoemaker and Parfit extend the range of
psychological connections relevant to personal identity, so as to include the carrying out of intentions formed at an earlier time, the continued belief in a conviction
formed at an earlier time, and so on; and they offer criteria of personal identity in
terms of indirect chains of persons and times among which a sufficient number of
these direct psychological connections hold.[17]

In principle, a psychological version of (SC) should make allowances for the
possibility that such chains of direct psychological connections might split, as would
happen if some kind of "fission" occurred: for example, if the hemispheres of a single person were to survive transplantation into two bodies, or if a teletransportation
device were to generate two people instead of one—assuming that teletransportation is able to preserve the right kind of quasi-memory and other direct psychological connections between pre- and post-teleportee. Although one could allow, with
David Lewis (1976), that in cases of fission there were two people all along; it is at
least as common for defenders of psychological theories of personal identity to add
a "no branching" clause.

Taking all these qualifications on board, defenders of a psychological criterion
wind up with something along these lines:

> (PC)   A person x who exists at a time t is the same person as a person y who exists
> at a later time t^* if, and only if: (1) either x at t is directly psychologically
> connected to y at t^*; or x at t is directly psychologically connected to a
> person u at an intermediate time t^1, and u at t^1 is directly psychologically
> connected to y at t^*; or…; and (2) however long this chain might be, it
> never divides in either temporal direction, i.e., there is no person z and
> time t^2 in the series such that z at t^2 is directly psychologically connected
> to *two* people, v and w, at another time.

This statement of a psychological criterion is a very rough approximation of the accounts given by, for example, Shoemaker and Parfit.[18] The second clause is supposed to rule out both the "fusion" of two persons into a single person; and the "fission" of one person into two. Contemporary Neo-Lockeans are not all committed to this precise proposal, of course; but they all have their ways of adding epicycles to Locke's account in order to deal with problems of forgetfulness, fission, fusion, and so forth. (PC) is simply a sketch of one of the more plausible attempts to provide a psychological criterion of identity; for present purposes, it can stand in for all of them.

Like many other psychologically based criteria, (PC) certainly implies that a person goes where his or her brain goes—at least so long as the removal of the brain does not interfere with its ability to support an ongoing psychological life. It is not so obvious what verdict (PC) would give in the case of a Star-Trek style teletransporter; nor in the case of the fabled device that effects a "brain state transfer" (BST). The BST machine is said to "read off" the psychological states subserved by one person's brain, while it simultaneously (i) causes another brain to support the same individual psychology and (ii) "scrambles" the original brain so that it no longer does so. Should the Neo-Lockean say that the causal connections between the experiences of the person who goes into the teletransporter, or who undergoes BST, are *directly connected* by, say, quasi-memory to the seeming-memories of those experiences enjoyed by the person who appears at the receiving end of the teletransporter, or who sits on the other side of the BST device? Plenty of Neo-Lockeans (e.g., David Lewis and Derek Parfit) are willing to count these processes, and other ways of preserving a person's psychological characteristics, as sufficiently direct to qualify as person-preserving. Call these "liberal Neo-Lockeans." Others—"conservative Neo-Lockeans"—disagree, requiring that the causal path by which psychological connections are secured may never pass entirely outside the boundaries of something that itself qualifies as a person who exemplifies the psychological states involved in the process—anything less is not a sufficiently direct connection.[19] Liberals and conservatives agree that, when a brain is transferred from one head to another, there is a person who exists during the interim while the brain is kept alive (in the traditional "vat of nutrients"). Until it is transplanted, the person is no larger than a detached brain.[20] By contrast, when the teletransportation or BST devices are imagined to operate, the causal process preserving a person's individual psychology is generally supposed to be entirely carried, at least briefly, by the information states of a computer that is not—or not obviously—a person. The conservative Neo-Lockeans deny that a person can survive this sort of process.

3.3 Biological Criteria

Far to the other side of the psychological–biological spectrum are "animalists," such as Peter van Inwagen and Eric Olson, who describe the identity conditions of a person in entirely nonpsychological terms.[21] Human persons are, they say, human animals. Animals are living things, organisms; and their persistence conditions coincide with what biologists tell us about the lives of organisms—in our case, organisms belonging to mammalian species, such as *Homo sapiens*. The life of an organism is a homeostatic event, a process whereby a relatively unified and independent material object perpetuates itself, maintaining the integrity of its boundaries and inner structure despite considerable gain and loss of parts. A human person just *is* an organism; so the beginning of a life marks the origin of a person, and the ending of a life represents the end of the person. A biological criterion of personal identity takes roughly this form:

> (BC)   A person *x* who exists at a time *t* is the same person as a person *y* who exists at a later time *t** if, and only if: the matter making up the person *x* at *t* comprises all of the matter caught up in the homeostatic biological event known as the life of an organism; and the matter of *y* at the later time *t** also comprises all the matter that is then caught up in the very same life.

An uncompromising animalist (of whom there may well be none!) would admit that the same biological life can go on, at least for a time, after brain death; indeed, even after the liquefaction of the brain stem;[22] and that an organism can die even though a single organ—liver, heart, kidney, or, most relevantly, brain—should be removed and kept alive, perhaps surviving transplantation into a different organism. It might seem, to the recipient of the brain transplant, that she once inhabited a different body; but in fact she would be wrong, according to the uncompromising animalists—a victim of false memories. And what about severed heads? It is doubtful whether any biologist would be willing to say that the head of an animal is an organism in itself, even if it were detached from its body and kept alive by artificial means. A truly uncompromising animalist will follow where biology seems to lead, concluding that a severed, still-living human head is not the same person as the organism from which it was removed, even if the head is kept alive and remains (seemingly) alert for a couple of days—a medical possibility proven by distressing experiments on monkeys and dogs.

The uncompromising animalist faces difficult questions about whether a brain in a vat or a severed head can think. One should have supposed that thoughts could be occurring in virtue of the ongoing functioning of the brain, whether it is alive in a vat or a severed head. Are they thoughts without a thinker, or thoughts in the mind of a quite different *kind* of thinker, one who is not an animal? Neither alternative is a happy one.

More moderate animalists, although they accept the letter of (BC), cannot bring themselves to go quite so far. Peter van Inwagen and Eric Olson are moderate animalists. They affirm (BC), but deny that a person would survive complete brain (including brain stem) death; and they affirm that I would go wherever my living, complete brain goes. They reconcile this with (BC) by arguing that, since the life of an organism is monitored and controlled by signals to and from the brain stem, the continued functioning of the brain stem is necessary for the life of the organism to continue; and a living head or whole brain (perhaps even just a living brain stem itself, though I am not so sure of their views about this case), is sufficient for a human being's life to continue.[23]

3.4 Ongoing Disagreement about Criteria of Identity

Locke and defenders of Neo-Lockean views, like Parfit and Lewis, typically proceed by what Mark Johnston calls "the method of cases": they tell stories about magical, science-fictional, or at least technologically impossible scenarios in which one person's memories and other psychological characteristics are imposed upon the body and brain of another, or one brain is successfully transplanted into another's body; and they coax their audience into sharing their judgments about whether, in that case, the resulting person would be the same person as the source of the memories and mental traits. But as Bernard Williams (1970) emphasized long ago, our reactions to such stories can be made to shift around. It is easy for defenders of (BC) to describe the same cases in ways that elicit reactions incompatible with (PC). How would you like to have your brain scrambled, until it is rendered incapable of thought? Would you feel any better if you learned that someone, in another room, was having his brain scrambled as well? How about if you learned that, after the scrambling, he would be given memories of things he never did, character traits he never had? Would it make you any happier to be told that they resemble the memories and character traits you have right now?

The extent of the philosophical disagreement about how to complete (SC) goes far beyond debates among defenders of the four criteria so far considered: liberal and conservative psychological criteria, and uncompromising and moderate biological criteria. Many competing criteria of identity can be supported by cases that these two versions of (PC) and two versions of (BC) seem to get wrong. In their contributions to this volume, Fred Feldman and Eric Olson weigh the pros and cons of (what Feldman calls) the "Termination Thesis," as opposed to (what Olson calls) "Corpse-Survivalism." (BC) and (PC) imply the Termination Thesis: "people go out of existence when they die" (Feldman, chapter 2 this volume). More carefully, (BC) and (PC) imply that, in the ordinary course of things, if a living human body and brain die (with no deity or machinery to produce the person's psychological characteristics elsewhere), a person ceases to exist. But, as Feldman and Olson show, there is much to be said for a contrary view, Corpse-Survivalism: "one continues existing as a corpse after death."

> Unless it is unusually violent, death is simply the change from a living to a nonliving state. So what awaits us at the end of our lives is not annihilation, but decay and dissolution, and only when this process is far advanced do we cease to exist. (Olson, chapter 3, this volume)

Alternatives to (BC) and (PC) can be formulated that respect the pull of Corpse-Survivalism by adding epicycles to these criteria: one sort of continuity is required for the ongoing existence of a person, while alive; and another, less stringent sort of physical continuity is sufficient, by itself, from death onward.

The beginnings of a human life present the defender of (PC) with a similar choice. Only things with psychological states can be indirectly psychologically connected to me. So, according to (PC), I am not the same person as the very early fetus, a living organism that nevertheless "grew into me." An alternative to (PC) could be developed that allowed biological continuity to determine the persistence conditions of a thing until psychological states first make their appearance; whereupon psychological continuity takes over.

Some cases (both imaginary and actual) pull us in one direction, some in another; and radically different theories about how to fill in (SC) have won significant numbers of defenders, with no convergence in sight. The galling stalemate has elicited two main reactions: (1) the apparent disagreement is not a deep one; it is due to some kind of ambiguity or conceptual confusion which, once it has been cleared up, allows apparently opposing theories to be equally valid ways of describing the world; and (2) the apparent disagreement is very real, and many of us are simply wrong about our own persistence conditions; but this should not surprise us, since the method of cases is a frail reed, not to be trusted.

Reaction (1) makes sense only if our ways of talking about ourselves and others, and our identities over time, already contain (or could easily come to include) significant ambiguities or indeterminacies, ones that can be resolved in equally good ways. Either we mean one of them, but could just as well have meant one of the others (and those who defend the wrong criteria of identity are feeling the pull of these equally good meanings); or our usage is in fact already ambiguous or indeterminate, requiring only resolution to clear up the apparent disagreement. Olson calls this strategy "Pluralism," and notes that its most common form assumes the doctrine of temporal parts, described in section 2, above. In the next section, I explore the implications of a temporal parts metaphysics for personal identity, arguing against the idea that disagreement about persistence conditions is a sign of failure to choose between equally good psychological and biological criteria for persons. If the temporal parts metaphysics accurately describes our mode of persistence through time, we should conclude, with Johnston, that we are Protean in nature. In the final section, I consider the implications of supposing that we do not persist by means of temporal parts. In that case, whether dualism or materialism is true, we should conclude that (2) is the right diagnosis of ongoing disagreement over how to complete (SC): There is a fact of the matter, and many of us are wrong.

4. TEMPORAL PARTS AND PROTEAN PERSONS

4.1 So Many Speakers!

The "I"-rule, "refers to the speaker," appears simple enough. And, if the world were politely cooperative, serving up exactly one conscious being who is *the* speaker on

any occasion when "I" is used, it would obviously refer to that being; and knowledge of which thing was conscious would tell us who the referent is. But if the
doctrine of temporal parts is true, things are not nearly so simple. There are hordes
of objects sharing my current temporal part, some with pasts that go back to temporal parts of Elvis, or Napoleon, or some ancient mastodon, and futures that
include temporal parts of twenty-second-century US presidents, or alligators yet
unborn; still others have pasts and futures much shorter than mine, such as the
twenty-four-hour temporal part of me that will cease to be exactly twenty-four
hours from now, and the ten-minute-long temporal part that began five minutes
ago, and so on. When I am using the first person, in thought or speech, each member of the horde is intrinsically just like me. Each of us has exactly similar mental
states and is making the same noises; and so each of us would seem to be a speaker.
Does each, then, refer to itself by the word "I"?

Full knowledge of the Kaplanian character of "I," plus knowledge of all the
relevant facts about the physical and mental world (including facts about everyone's dispositions to use certain words in certain contexts), ought to be enough
to enable a sufficiently intelligent being—that is, a god—to figure out the referent
of the word in our mouths (or to figure out whether and to what extent it has a
determinate referent). But that is a lot of knowledge! Could we figure it out with a
humanly attainable amount of information concerning the rule governing "I," and
the circumstances in which we are using it?

Kaplan points out that the rule for determining the referent of an indexical, its
character, may remain quite opaque to competent speakers:

> Many users of the so-called directly referential expressions lack a real
> understanding of the exact mechanism or rule of reference by which the referent
> is determined. Though we act *in conformity* with some such rule, we do not
> invariably know the rule in the sense of being able to articulate it....
>
>   So long as we were able to cling to the illusion that words like "I" and
> "Aristotle" abbreviate simple descriptions that are immediately available to
> introspection, we could think that anyone who used such an expression knew
> how it secured its reference and might express this knowledge in using the word.
> But who still thinks that nowadays? (1989, pp. 577–578)

Those who reject temporal parts may suppose that, because there is only one
thinker and speaker for every meaningful use of the first person, the rough and
ready statement of the rule governing "I" is sufficiently detailed to select exactly
one referent; but since, "nowadays," temporal parts theorists abound, many philosophers can no longer think it is so easy as all that.

The metaphysics of temporal parts implies that, in exactly the location where I
am now, there are many other person-like things which share my current temporal
part, but that differ in their pasts and futures, some having utterly bizarre histories.
Could "I" be radically ambiguous in my mouth, or vacuous due to a presupposition
of uniqueness, because each of these person-like things is trying to refer to itself by
means of the same "token" or use of the word?[24] Many of them can, presumably, be
dismissed as ineligible to be the referent of "I." As a general policy, we ignore objects

with highly unnatural boundaries. When we count things, or make claims about "everything," we tacitly restrict the "domain of discourse" in ways that rule out uninteresting things or objects with gerrymandered borders. When asked, "How many things are in the fridge?" one does not count the top and bottom half of a can of soda as two things. (In a sufficiently odd context, one might count the can as one thing and the liquid inside it as another—if one were counting portions of liquid and solid objects separately for some reason.) Generally speaking, we restrict our attention to objects that "stand out" from their surroundings and can be kept under observation: in other words, sums of temporal parts that have natural spatial boundaries (at their surfaces, there is a significant difference between the thing and its surroundings) and natural temporal boundaries (their origins and endings represent relatively sharp discontinuities in the persisting sums of temporal parts in the vicinity).

Most members of the horde coinciding with me would be disqualified, if available referents for "I" are culled by elimination of things with highly unnatural boundaries; these things may be "speaking" in some sense, but they are not referring to themselves. However the search for criteria of personal identity (described in section 3) has turned up numerous competing and relatively natural ways to gather together person-stages into interesting groups, such as (PC) and (BC). Can the friends of temporal parts expect that, by looking closely at the fine details of the rule for determining what "I" designates on any occasion of its use, they might thereby settle whether my usage refers to a psychological continuer, a biological continuer, or some other person-like thing that (they think) shares my current thoughts? It might be part of the character of "I" that it refers to the user of the word (in speech or thought) who has the *most* natural boundaries. But I doubt that will get us very far.

Our judgments about real and imaginary cases—brain death, teletransportation, and so on—are not just random responses; they fall into a number of self-consistent patterns. (PC), (BC), and variants represent several of these patterns. On the temporal parts metaphysics, there is a candidate for being me for each combination of origin and ending boundaries, and a corresponding criterion of identity that could be formulated so as to pick out things with just those kinds of boundaries. None of these candidates seems radically ineligible, due to gerrymandering, for being the referent of "I" in my current person-stage's mouth. After all, none of these relatively natural joints is perfectly natural, or anything close to it. There is much vagueness and arbitrariness in the temporal boundaries of a human life. Did my life begin at conception, or at the point when twinning was no longer possible, or upon my first acquiring the most rudimentary of psychological dispositions, or at the beginning of the third trimester (if that is a different point from the previous boundary), or at "viability," or at birth, or when I first began to think of myself from a first-person point of view? Will my life end with the last beat of my heart, or the last breath I exhale, or the last firing of neurons; or might *my* life end much earlier than the biological life of my body; that is, might I cease to exist long before my body dies, due to irreversible "brain-death"? Each of these claims about when

I come into and go out of existence is at least somewhat defensible; each boundary is somewhat natural (though each, of course, remains quite vague). The doctrine of temporal parts guarantees that there are objects beginning and ending at every combination of these boundaries.

Is each of these largely overlapping, relatively natural objects a speaker, referring to itself? The resulting ambiguity of "I" would be more than just a kind of harmless indeterminacy of reference amongst objects that differ in such tiny ways that we could never come to care about their differences. Some of them came into existence months before others; some may well cease to exist long before my last breath; the objects favored by corpse-survivalists will continue to exist long after that.

To simplify matters, I shall focus on just two of the many relatively natural ways to build person-like sums out of collections of human person-stages: an uncompromising version of (BC) that assigns radically biological boundaries, and a liberal version of (PC) that assigns radically psychological boundaries. A *biological continuer* will consist of stages that are bounded by the biological generation and death of a member of the species *Homo sapiens*. Biological continuers include embryo-stages, and occasionally the stages of living human bodies in which the cerebellum has been destroyed or surgically removed. A *psychological continuer* consists of stages bound together by psychological connections: later stages have seeming-memories of events that correspond to experiences had by earlier stages, and they have these seeming-memories because of those earlier experiences; later stages have intentions caused by decisions made by earlier stages; later stages display virtues or vices due to disciplined or undisciplined behavior on the part of earlier stages; and so on. Let the causal dependencies involved in these connections be those due to "any reliable cause," so that teletransporters work, but the chance appearance of a much later duplicate, with an erratic causal history leading back to some person, will not count as survival. To find the psychological continuer of which a given person-stage is a part, trace such connections backward and forward as far as they go, without branching. Psychological continuers will not include some of the early embryonic stages that are parts of biological continuers. If teletransportation technology or brain transplants were to become possible, psychological continuers could include person-stages of a different biological continuer altogether. If any human organisms come into existence with some kind of psychological states, and go out of existence at the same time that their thinking ceases, then there could be some biological continuers that are also psychological continuers. But probably, as a matter of empirical fact, none exactly coincide: all the organisms that will have minds (at least, all the ones with which we are familiar) begin to exist long before they have mental states; and many utterly lose the ability to think long before they die.

Under the pretense that only the biological and psychological continuers coincident with me are viable candidates for "the speaker" who is using "I" while writing this paper and thinking these thoughts, many questions remain: Does the rule governing use of the first-person select just one of these as referent; and if so, which one? Does "I" fail to refer to either (like "the tallest man on earth" when there is a tie)? Is "I" ambiguous; or, what is nearly the same thing, does the one sound really count as two instances or tokens of the word, one referring to the biological continuer, the other to the psychological continuer? And how should one even begin to try to answer these questions? There is no handbook filled with detailed rules for the uses of indexicals that will answer them. The best we can do is to grope for plausible-seeming principles about the way the word "I," as we use it, would find its referent, given the doctrine of temporal parts.[25]

4.2 Deference to Authority and to Others

Nagel suggested that "I," like "gold," might refer to something with an essence quite unknown to the user. The same sort of deference to unknown "external" factors can occur in our use of proper names. Sometimes I use a name, say, "Bob," with very little knowledge about the person referred to other than the fact that somebody else was talking about somebody or something they were calling "Bob." ("Did you happen to overhear her conversation? Who was she talking about?" "Don't worry, she wasn't talking about you, she was talking about Bob." "Oh, good. But who is Bob?" "I don't know; just some guy she was talking about.") I can successfully refer to someone while relying entirely upon someone else's knowledge about the person (Bob might turn out to be a monkey). If the rule by means of which "I" refers were sufficiently deferential to the usage of others, my own self-conception would be irrelevant to the question what sort of thing I am. A crude thesis about deference to others would go like this: Although I am convinced that "I," in my mouth, refers to an animal, a biological continuer with the persistence conditions of (BC); nevertheless, due to the fact that most others who speak my language think very differently, "I" in my mouth refers to a psychological continuer.

Another crudely stated doctrine of deference to other users would result in an easy way for God to insure my survival: Suppose that, in the presence of competing candidates for being the referent of "I," the *highest authority* (whoever that might be) can simply stipulate that I mean just *one* of them; and, whether or not I am aware of the stipulation, that is the thing to which "I" would refer. If God desires to resurrect each of us by decreeing, as we die, "Let there be a duplicate of *that* person, rapidly healing, at such-and-such location in the heavenly realms," then all God need do is lay it down that what we refer to by "I" is a psychological continuer.[26]

I will not say that the character of "I" is *not* deeply deferential to authority or widespread usage. Plenty of English words display similar kinds of deference. Suppose the word did work in such a way that, though I am as deeply convinced that I am a mere animal as anyone could be, God's decree could result in my referring to a psychological continuer (with psychological connections preserved by any reliable cause). Then it would be easy to resurrect each of us: God need only create one psychological continuer for each person who ever lives, each one deliberately duplicating exactly one person who died (so that even if two people died in exactly similar states, each would have his or her own psychological continuer). Or suppose instead that the usage of others is enough to make it true that my use of "I" refers to a psychological continuer, whatever my own attitudes might be. What would happen if the psychological continuers God creates for each of us are made to think and use words in ways that insure *they* all refer to psychological continuers using the first person? If deference to others includes a sufficient amount of deference to future English-speakers as well, we could *now* be referring to psychological continuers in virtue of the usage of these future person-stages.

The argument to follow presupposes that the rule for "I" does *not* display much, if any, deference to others; but it appeals to a principle that could be used, together with a doctrine of deference to others, to derive the conclusion that the usage of these divinely created psychological continuers would be relevant to whether we, now, refer to sums of temporal parts that include these distant person-stages.[27]

4.3 Supposing "I" Is Not So Deferential to Others

I doubt whether the reference of "I" in my mouth should be sensitive to the decisions of God—someone with whom most of us do not have conversations (at least, not in English).[28] And, although it would not much matter for my purposes, I doubt we should posit a great deal of deference to others in the rules for determination of the referent of "I."[29]

Comparison to other indexicals and demonstratives suggests that—assuming the doctrine of temporal parts—the speaker's intentions can play a highly significant role, one that trumps what others may think I mean, or may themselves mean by the word. Consider "now," "here," and demonstrative uses of "that" or "this" (accompanied by pointing or some other way of presenting something to someone). Like "I," they are used to refer to different things upon different occasions; and there are systematic rules about their use—for example, "now" can only refer to a time, and it must be one that at least overlaps the time at which it is used; "here" can only refer to a place, and (unless the speaker is pointing at something) it must be a place that includes the location of the speaker's body; "that," accompanied by gestures, can only refer to something that can be seen in the direction indicated by the user of the term. But, in most contexts, these simple rules alone will not be enough to select just one thing to be the referent of the word; and a precise referent can only be determined by various additional factors in the context of use.

"Now" might be used to refer to a split second (as in, "Let the race begin...now!"); but there are many periods of time, of varying length, overlapping the moment when a given person uses the word—for example, a day or night or hour or century that includes that moment—and "now" can be used to refer to one of these longer periods of time. Imagine a worker who is given a set of instructions each morning by a contractor. If the contractor says, "Now you should dig a hole for the foundation so we can begin pouring cement tomorrow," "now" (arguably) refers to that whole day. Shorter and longer periods are available to be meant by "now"; and the context of use determines which period is selected. Although other features of a context might be able to trump the speakers' intentions with respect to the length of time indicated, they must surely be highly salient features of the contexts in which "now" is used.

"Here" can obviously refer to larger or smaller regions, depending upon context; "I'm here" can mean "I'm in this room," but it can also mean "I'm in this town" or "I'm in this country," depending upon the situation. Many regions exist that include the relatively small place occupied by the speaker's body; and very many of them are potential meanings of the word "here" in a speaker's mouth. And, again, the speaker's intentions must often be the crucial factor in determining the size of the region picked out—though, again, I am not saying that these intentions could never be trumped by any other contextual features.

Similarly, when many things appear in the direction someone is pointing, further features of the context of use must rule some of them out in order for "that" to achieve even a moderately determinate reference. When pointing to a body of water and saying "that is salty," one might be referring to a tiny inlet, or a much larger bay of which it is a part, or an entire ocean. They are all *there*, in the world, as candidates for the attempted demonstration; the actual referent of "that" depends upon additional facts about the context.

What facts? Kaplan's considered opinion is that an attempted demonstration is "directed by the speaker's intention to point at a perceived individual on whom he has focused" and that it is "the directing intention" that determines the referent of the demonstration; the pointing is a "mere *externalization* of this inner intention" (p. 582). If I am focusing my attention upon the *bay* and intend to point to it when I point toward the inlet *and* the bay *and* the ocean (all at once, as I must), then the referent of "that," in "that is salty," is the bay and not the inlet or ocean. The directing intention may include descriptive elements that, although they *could* be relevant in some circumstances, are trumped by other factors. If I point to some water and say "that is salty," intending thereby to be pointing to the ocean of which this bay is a part…but it is really a lake, not a bay; then one should probably say that I succeeded in pointing to the lake; and that, if it is salty, what I said was true, despite my misconception. If I point to what I take to be some liquid in a small inlet, intending thereby to demonstrate only the liquid here; but in fact there is just one, giant, partless blob filling the inlet, the bay, and the ocean; again, my directing intention, though a relevant factor in the context, is trumped (try to forget, for the moment, that the idea of a partless, space-filling blob may be incoherent!). But when many candidates are there to be meant, and I intend to point to one of them, it should take some doing to wrench my demonstration away from it!

"I" seems to me to be a sort of internal demonstration, a mental act of pointing. So I shall assume that the kind of thing some person-stages take persons to be— the sort of spatial and temporal boundaries they take persons to have—are highly relevant contextual factors when determining the agent behind a given use of "I" by those stages. Again, the intention the stages have to point to a thing of a certain kind may be trumped by other relevant contextual factors. Suppose van Inwagen is right about the following doctrines: besides subatomic particles, there is nothing smaller than an entire animal in the vicinity of my body; I am a physical thing;

and particles cannot think. In that case, whether or not I think of myself as a soul or a brain, my intention to point, using the first person, to a thinker that is immaterial, or a thinker that is a brain, will succeed only in pointing toward a whole animal. But if van Inwagen is wrong, and there are many physical objects here, equally well-qualified, intrinsically, to be thinkers; then my intention to point, in the first-person way, to just the thinking *brain* might well succeed—even if other person-stages refer to animals using the first-person. Now consider the temporal case: Suppose I am a soul, though I believe with all my heart that I am an animal, and I intend my first-personal internal pointing to pick out a thing with biological persistence conditions. Since nothing with biological persistence conditions is thinking this thought, but a soul is the *real* thinker, some aspects of the directing intention become irrelevant or are overridden, and "I" simply refers to a thing with…whatever the (naturally nonbiological) persistence conditions are for souls. And if souls do not have temporal parts, then even tacit views on my part about how souls *would* persist, *were* there such things, become irrelevant to the reference of "I" when used by this soul. But the doctrine of temporal parts implies that there are many thinking things, of varying temporal length, toward which any such internal pointing could be directed. Assuming materialism, there are many physical objects with different origins and endings. In the absence of sharp, natural boundaries, and the presence of multiple somewhat natural candidates, the intention to point, internally, to a thing satisfying certain physical conditions could hardly be irrelevant to the determination of reference. Or so it seems to me.

This much is, I hope, fairly secure, and compatible with significant deference to the usage of others: Imagine a world in which all speakers, everywhere and at all times, used an English-like language with a word having the character of our "I"; and suppose they always, quite explicitly, self-consciously, and consistently thought of themselves as having the persistence conditions articulated in (BC) and that nothing about their articulated self-conception is undermined by unarticulated dispositions to react in one way or another to the continuation or cessation of their psychological or biological lives. Under the assumption that they are physical objects with temporal parts, they really ought to succeed in referring to biological continuers by their uses of "I"; and to fail to also, on those occasions, refer to psychological continuers. Likewise, mutatis mutandis, for a world of convinced believers in (PC). The two kinds of thinking things are "there to be meant." When *everyone* is trying hard to mean one of them—whatever exactly such "trying" consists in, whether it involves explicit beliefs or mere dispositions to behave in certain ways, or, more likely, some weighted combination of the two—, they ought to succeed. With suitable changes, the argument to follow could be run using whole communities. However, I suspect that "I" is much more like an internal demonstrative, sensitive to the attitudes of the user.

I am not sure to what extent the use of "I" should be tethered to explicit beliefs held by the person-stages using the word, as opposed to unconscious beliefs, or dispositions the stages have to generate further person-stages that would act in relevant ways—dispositions which may be psychologically inaccessible to the current and upcoming stages. Some who hold similar views emphasize explicit beliefs of the "I" user.[30] Although, for my purposes, not much hangs upon it, I shall assume that attitudes about the referent of "I" need not be made fully explicit in order to be relevant factors in the context of a given act of internal, first-personal pointing.

The Protean criterion of identity for persons for which I shall argue is heavily indebted to Mark Johnston's work; and I shall follow Johnston in assuming that there is a family of "*person-directed attitudes*" that are especially relevant to determination of the kinds of events one could or could not survive, in the near future; and that one did or did not survive in the near past (what I shall call a person's "local persistence conditions"). These attitudes comprise:

> (i) [O]ne's future-oriented and retrospective concerns for oneself and others;
> (ii) one's expectations about experiences and memories of those experiences;
> (iii) one's expectations about the relations between action and desert. (Johnston, 1989, p. 448)

An adult person, at any given time, will have a host of person-directed attitudes, and, to the extent that the person has a coherent body of attitudes, the three kinds that Johnston mentions will converge upon a certain relation R that these attitudes are tracking. To be a good candidate for R, a relation must be the sort of thing around which one could organize one's life; it must be at least somewhat natural and important, so that short-lived things could come to care (in the special person-directed way) about other short-lived things to which they stand in R.

Let "R organizes x's person-directed attitudes at t" (or "R organizes x's life at t") mean that, at t, x's attitudes are tracking R—x tends to hold himself responsible for what R-related past person-stages did, looks forward to or fears what R-related future person-stages experience, and so on. (I remain neutral, here, about the extent to which a criterion of personal identity that appeals to these distinctive person-directed attitudes could be deeply informative. One might naturally worry that these attitudes can only be characterized in ways that immediately involve the notion of *being the same person.* However, even if they do, the Protean account of our persistence conditions would still tell us something extremely interesting about our nature.) My argument for a Protean theory of persons will make the simplifying assumption that there are really only two good candidates for the role of R-relation—one biological, the other psychological.

A person's specifically egoistic concerns, expectations about memories, and expectations about personal responsibility, might definitively favor a relation of biological continuity like the one at the heart of (BC). Such a person—an "organism-identifier"—would not expect to remember the things the recipient of a BST would *seem* to remember, she would not dread the evils she thinks will befall the recipient, or look forward to her joys. Likewise, she will not expect to arrive at the receiving end of the teletransporter. She knows that *someone* will have experiences after these events, and that someone will *seem* to remember things she has done; but her attitudes and the actions they would motivate reveal that she honestly does not expect it will be her. A "psychology-identifier," on the other hand, would have person-directed attitudes that definitively track a relation of psychological continuity like that used in (PC). She would be inclined to use a BST in order to prolong her life, regard teletransportation as a new way to travel, and so on.

I offer an argument from the doctrine of temporal parts (something, incidentally, Johnston rejects) for the conclusion that persons are, as Johnston says, "Protean" in their persistence conditions: we may be able to survive a certain kind of episode at one time but not at another time due entirely to changes in our ways of thinking about ourselves. This sort of change need not be thought of as violating the principle that a thing's persistence conditions are essential to it. In the sense in which persistence conditions are essential, survival of the BST procedure or teletransportation, after one has changed from organism-identifier to psychology-identifier, is something that happens in different conditions—the statement of the persistence conditions of a thing turns out, on this view, to require that we mention facts about the person-directed attitudes that person-stages display at various times. The change is much like other changes in our capacities to survive this or that exigency. Right now, for example, most of us are disposed to die upon ingestion of a small amount of arsenic. But, by following a regimen of gradually increasing doses, most of us could lose this disposition and acquire another. Nothing paradoxical about that!

4.4 The Argument from Temporal Parts to Protean Persons

One might think that the referent of "I" in a person-stage's mouth should simply be a function of *that stage*'s person-directed attitudes; the current attitudes determine, once-and-for-all, the temporal boundaries of the referent of this particular use of "I."

> *Once-for-All Determination of Persistence Conditions*: If a brief series of candidate person-stages are organizing their person-directed concerns and expectations around psychological continuity at t, then their first-person thoughts are about a psychological continuer; and if they are organizing their person-directed concerns and expectations around biological continuity at t, then their first-person thoughts are about a biological continuer.

Accepting this doctrine, however, leads to odd results in the case of a series of person-stages that change in their person-directed attitudes, first organizing their concerns around biological continuity, say, and then around psychological continuity. So long as biological continuity is retained through the change of attitude, Once-for-All Determination of Persistence Conditions requires that someone who at first succeeded in referring to herself has lost the ability to do so—at least, by means of the word "I." When she now uses the word, she refers to something that came into existence much later than her, and may cease to be much sooner or even (should BST, teletransportation, or brain transplantation become available) live much longer. It is strange to imagine that, because of a change of attitude, someone could lose the ability to refer to herself using the first person, coming instead to refer to someone else.

Indeed, it seems to me to be more than odd; it is a violation of a feature of repeated use of "I" by a single person, a feature it shares with repeated uses of proper names. Suppose I have met someone named Hortense Baltazaar; and I have acquired quite a bit of information about her: she is a champion fencer, a whiz at chess, and a gourmet chef. It never occurs to me for a moment that there might be two living people with such an odd name. I tell all my friends about her. Unbeknownst to me, there *is* another person with this name. And one day, I am told that someone named Hortense Baltazaar has passed away—but it is the other Hortense. I might learn further things about this other Hortense, and report them to my friends; but, so far, it seems clear that the word "Hortense" in my mouth means only the first one. It is as though names are "file folders" that one updates by adding information to them; and I have only one file with the name "Hortense" on it; so everything has to go in there. Now, one might tell stories in which, although I believe there to be one Hortense, there are actually two; and my use of the name is ambiguous—for instance, if I see them both very often, and have an equal amount of information and misinformation about each one, yet believe them to be the same person. Such circumstances require some rigging up; it is not enough simply to come to have many false beliefs about *my* Hortense that happen to be true of the other Hortense. I still just have one name in my vocabulary, and I should be interpreted as talking about just one or the other of the two, if at all possible.

"I" seems sufficiently close to a proper name to require similar treatment. If a person uses "I," and then uses it again, she may have acquired false beliefs about herself on the second occasion, or have learned that she was wrong about herself on the first occasion; but we should only attribute a change in referent if there is no way it can be helped. I call this idea

> *Intended Constancy of First-Person Reference*: When a person-stage is speaking English, and uses the word "I" to refer to some longer sum of person-stages, each of which also speaks English, and some of which also use the word "I," one should interpret them all to be referring to the same sum of person-stages, if at all possible.

Intended Constancy represents a kind of deference to one's own past and future use. When I believe that there is "just one Hortense" among my acquaintances, my repeated uses of the name "Hortense" are meant to be co-referential; and this intention can "trump" false beliefs I have about the bearer of the name, even when they single out someone else. Similarly, for repeated uses of "I."

Intended Constancy is in tension with the Once-for-All principle in the case of a series of person-stages that change from being organism-identifiers to psychology-identifiers. If at all possible, they should be taken to be referring to the same thing both before and after; so, if there is an alternative to supposing they have begun to refer to something else using "I," Intended Constancy puts pressure on us to take that alternative.

Johnston's Protean conception of persons provides such an alternative. I offer an argument for it by appealing to Intended Constancy of First-Person Reference and a principle somewhat weaker than the Once-for-All principle:

> *Local Determination of Local Persistence Conditions*: If a series of candidate person-stages organize themselves around R throughout a period T; then, so long as there is no discontinuity or branching of R during T, those stages constitute a persisting person throughout T.

The argument will make use of Sydney Shoemaker's by-now familiar story about a BST procedure, in which a machine "records the state of one brain and imposes that state on a second brain by restructuring it so that it has exactly the state the first brain had at the beginning of the operation." The process destroys or scrambles the original brain. Shoemaker grants that most of us would think "that it would amount to killing the original person and at the same time creating (or converting someone into) a psychological duplicate of him" (Shoemaker and Swinburne, 1984, p. 108). Imagine a community of stubborn organism-identifiers who persist in taking this view of the matter, a community including Orville, the most stubborn of them all. Orville and his people regard the BST procedure as execution, and the clones as imposters—as do the clones, once they realize what has happened, since they emerge psychologically similar to Orville and his friends, and therefore equally stubborn. In Shoemaker's story, radiation has drastically reduced the life-span of a human organism, and a society of psychology-identifiers deals with the problem by cloning new bodies and using the BST procedure to (as they see it) prolong their lives. Suppose Psyche is a convinced psychology-identifier. She and her friends regard the BST device as a lifesaver, providing something that approximates immortality.

Shoemaker claims that a good case can be made for saying that "what *they* mean by 'person' is such that the BST-procedure *is* person-preserving (using 'person' in *their* sense)." But there is also, he thinks, good reason to think that "what they mean by 'person' is what we mean by it; they call the same things persons, offer the same sorts of characterizations of what sorts of things persons are, and attach the same kinds of social consequences to judgments of personal identity." Shoemaker concludes that, if both are true, then we, too, should regard the BST procedure as "person-preserving"; as should, presumably, Orville and his friends. But a different conclusion is possible: we mean the same thing by "person"; but, because of differences in their person-directed attitudes, Psyche can survive a BST while Orville cannot. Shoemaker himself rejects the doctrine of temporal parts; but one who accepts it should draw exactly this conclusion. After all, the person-stages in both communities are parts of both biological-continuers and psychological-continuers. If Orville and his people clearly think of themselves as the kinds of things that could not survive a BST, why would their first-person thoughts refer to a thing that *does* survive such an episode? After all, there is, ready to hand, a person-like thing who does not survive it. The only obstacle to success in referring to the latter sort of person, so far as I can see, would be a concomitant intention to refer to something with natural boundaries: if the psychological-continuers had much more natural boundaries than the biological-continuers, the greater naturalness might trump their explicit self-conception. But neither (PC) nor (BC) marks perfectly natural boundaries; a mere "other-things-being-equal" default to a more natural meaning should not override the organism-identifiers' own expectations about the events they could or could not survive.

The same could be said, mutatis mutandis, about Psyche and her fellow psychology-identifiers. Putting these thoughts together, one has the first stage of an argument for Proteanism:

1. The only thing that could make Orville's first-person thoughts refer to something that could survive BST is for him to intend to pick out a thing belonging to a certain natural kind, and for psychological continuity to represent a deeper "natural joint" than biological continuity.
2. The only thing that could make Psyche's first-person thoughts refer to something that could *not* survive BST is for her to intend to pick out a thing belonging to a natural kind and for organic continuity to represent a deeper "natural joint" in the realm of objects.
3. Neither joint is deep enough to override the boundaries privileged by their own person-directed attitudes.
4. So Orville's first-person thoughts refer to something that could not survive the BST; and Psyche's refer to something that could.

Now imagine a third character, Charlie, who moves from the one community to the other, gradually undergoing a change from being an organism-identifier to being a psychology-identifier. Charlie can be just like Orville while he is living in that community; and just like Psyche, once he becomes habituated to her way of looking at things. *Local Determination of Local Persistence Conditions* implies the following conditional:

5. If Orville's first-person thoughts refer to something that cannot survive BST and Psyche's refer to something that could; then Charlie's first-person thoughts initially refer to something that cannot survive BST, and later on refer to something that can.

Since 4 is the conclusion that Orville and Psyche do differ in this way, the further conclusion can be drawn:

6. So Charlie's first-person thoughts at first refer to something that cannot survive BST, although later on they refer to something that can.

According to the principle, *Intended Constancy of First-Person Reference*, if Charlie's organism-identifying and psychology-identifying person-stages were all speaking English, they should all be interpreted as referring to the same sum of person-stages by means of "I," if at all possible. So:

7. Charlie's first-person thoughts, both before and after the change, should be interpreted as referring to the same sum of person-stages, if at all possible.

Putting 6 and 7 together:

8. So, if at all possible, Charlie's first-person thoughts should be interpreted as referring to a single sum of person-stages that at first lacks the ability to survive BST and then acquires this ability.

Again, the doctrine of temporal parts makes a huge difference: why think that Charlie's pre- and postconversion uses of "I" and his corresponding first-person thoughts should fail to succeed in referring to the same sum of temporal parts? Suppose Charlie, while an organism-identifier, suffered a complete breakdown in psychological-connectedness (e.g., he suffered a brain injury that rendered him infantile; he had to learn everything again); and also that, after years among the psychology-identifiers, he finally tries that BST procedure. There *is* a sum of temporal parts that includes the early person-stages (bridging the gap in psychological continuity) and also the later person-stages (bridging the gap in biological continuity). The combination of Charlie's repeated use of the first person, together with his first-person attitudes during these episodes, together converge upon this particular sum of temporal parts. It is arguably less natural, in its boundaries, than a psychological continuer or a biological continuer; but it has its own kind of integrity, in virtue of satisfying the Local Determination principle. The difference in naturalness is a matter of degree, and should be overcome by Charlie's contribution to what he means by "I." Since it is quite possible to interpret Charlie in this way, the qualification on 8 can be removed:

9. Charlie's first-person thoughts should be interpreted as referring to a single sum of person-stages that at first lacks the ability to survive BST and then acquires this ability.

The doctrine of temporal parts thus supports the idea that a person can change from having the persistence conditions associated with things that are essentially organisms to having the persistence conditions of psychological continuers in virtue of changes in the way he or she (and perhaps the relevant community) thinks and talks.[31]

4.5 Proteanism and Survival of Death

Resurrecting Protean persons *while they are psychology-identifiers* is an easy matter for God; God need only play the part of the BST device or a teletransporter. All that is required for survival is one reliably-caused psychological continuer for each psychology-identifier who dies—for each one, God initiates a new series of person-stages, at some unspecified time and place, with mental states that are the natural continuation of the original person's psychology. The cause is a reliable one, so long as God resolves to pick up the pieces of our mental lives more or less where we left off. This resolution underwrites counterfactuals, such as "Had Jones been thinking about Vienna as he died, the series of person-stages commencing in this particular quadrant of the New Earth would have had a recollection of having just thought about Vienna." Suppose there were, in some bizarre cosmic coincidence, two exactly similar dying people who would then need to be resurrected by means of exactly similar new person-stages. So long as God initiates one sequence of afterlife stages because of the one person, and another because of the other person, the causal dependencies link the dying stages of each person with exactly one series in the hereafter; and there is a definite fact of the matter concerning who's who.

But what of Protean persons who remain stubborn organism-identifiers until death—resolutely thinking of themselves as entirely biological, as destined to pass away with their bodies no matter how much psychological continuity might hold between them and any subsequent person-stages? Can they foil God's plans to resurrect everyone? With her dying breath (or breaths…it's a long speech), the organism-identifier might say:

> I don't care whether or not God generates a psychological continuer for me, since I could not be such a thing. When I say "I," I'm referring to a thing that cannot survive my body's impending biological breakdown. All of my current inclinations to make plans, feel regret, and so on point to *biology* as setting the boundaries of my history, not *psychology*. For example, I have no expectation to continue on so long as my brain is preserved alive, nor would I accept the offer of a BST procedure even in the face of almost certain death; and I would regard anything that carries on my biological life as me, even if I now knew that it would be devoid of psychological connections with me. Granted, God can create someone who will use "I" to refer to a psychological continuer with whom I now share stages; but my persistence conditions now are determined by my person-directed attitudes now. So God's post-mortem trickery may succeed in resurrecting *somebody* who is here with me, but it will not be *me*.

Is there anything God could do about a recalcitrant resurrection-resister like this? A strategy for ensuring the survival of mere organisms will be described below. But, if Proteanism is correct, the would-be organism-identifier is not a mere organism; and careful thought about the persistence conditions of Protean persons seems to me to show that resolute organism-identification until death is not enough to block a simple divine strategy for resurrection.

My argument for Proteanism about persons was built upon *Local Determination of Local Persistence Conditions*. This is a principle about the kinds of episodes a person could survive during periods of time throughout which person-directed attitudes remain unchanged. It implies nothing, one way or the other, about what happens during episodes that *coincide with* changes in person-directed attitudes. What should one say about a series of person-stages that organize their common life around R, and then switch to organizing their life around R*, if the switch occurs at the same time as a breakage in the R-relatedness of the person-stages? If R* holds between the earlier and the later person-stages, do the later stages get their way, dragging the earlier stages with them into their post-R-organizing life?

Or do the earlier stages get their way, preventing the later stages from grabbing them?

Mark Johnston's version of Proteanism takes a stand on this question; but I think it is the wrong stand—at least, assuming the doctrine of temporal parts.[32] His "Teletransporters" correspond to my community of psychology-identifiers; his "Human Beings" can stand in for my organism-identifiers (though their persistence conditions are slightly different; they go where their brains go); and Teletransportation functions much like a BST device. Human Beings undergo "reculturation" when they come to organize their person-directed attitudes around the relations of psychological continuity favored by Teletransporters. Reculturation might take place as a gradual process, through classes or prolonged contact with Teletransporters. But for those who cannot make the switch so easily, the Teletransporters offer an alternative:

> [S]uppose that the Teletransporters believe in baptisms under fire. They only offer reculturation by means of an initial Teletransportation which produces as near a duplicate human body as is compatible with its having the Teletransporters' concept of personal identity. (Johnston, 1989, p. 460)

God might try to resurrect Protean persons by a similar "baptism under fire." God need only fiddle slightly with the psychological states of the resurrected person-stages, so that they all have the sorts of dispositions that would underwrite reference to psychological continuers by means of their use of the first person. Presumably, such a change is consistent with enough psychological continuities of *other* sorts to preserve sameness of Protean person. Each of us, whatever our current ways of thinking about ourselves, could, in this life, undergo sudden psychological-identifier conversion—as a bizarre side effect of drugs, say, or a blow to the head. Each of us could be turned into someone who expects to go wherever her thoughts are reliably continued, absent branching; who holds herself responsible for things done so long as she seems to remember doing them and she believes that the memory is caused by the doing of them; and so on. If God needs to bring about such a conversion, wholesale, in order to get us all over to the other side, so be it.

Johnston, however, does not believe in baptisms under fire.

> What is an insignificant difference at the level of timing makes for a crucial difference at the level of personal identity. Only if Teletransportation follows reculturation can our Human Being correctly see the whole process as one which provides *him* with access to superfast travel and practical freedom from disease. (Johnston, 1989, p. 460)

By Johnston's lights, then, when there is a gap in the R-relatedness of stages, but continuity of R*-relatedness, switching from organizing one's life around R to R* will only carry a Protean person across the gap if the switch occurs before the gap. But why are first thoughts necessarily better thoughts? Friends of temporal parts are generally fans of spatial–temporal analogies. Here, a spatial analogy suggests exactly the opposite conclusion.

Suppose I lead an expedition up an uncharted river, which I call "The Amazon." Clearly, I intend to keep using the name in the same way, so that if I explore a stream connected with this one and call it "The Amazon," I intend to be referring to the same thing. Now suppose also that, as I start out, I have definite views about which way I ought to go at any juncture in order to stay on the same river: always take the *widest* stream at any point where streams converge, treating the narrower stream as a mere tributary. Suppose that, at nightfall, my party arrives at a fork, and the right-hand stream is much wider than the left-hand stream, though it looks as though it may be shallower and may soon end in a swamp. I tell my fellow explorers that tomorrow we shall set off on the rightmost stream. While I am pitching my tent, some of the others speak with the natives, learning that the right-hand stream soon becomes unnavigable, and does indeed end in what they call "Alligator Swamp"; while the left-hand stream goes on and on, perhaps all the way to the edge of the earth. Knowing how stubborn I am, my comrades fear that I will stick to my "widest stream" principle and that our exploration will come to a quick, uninteresting conclusion in a nearby swamp. So, instead of trying to convince me to take the leftmost stream, they slip me an Ambien, and, while I sleep, bundle me into a canoe and set off—all the time whispering in my ear that widest isn't always best; depth and distance matter; and so on. When I awaken, they say: "Look at how far this stream goes, how deep the channel is! The other stream was shallow, and it petered out quickly. Surely there is more to sameness of river than width of stream; why not allow other factors to play a role in the principle for choosing a fork—things like navigability and the length of the stream?" The suggestibility engendered by the drug, together with their whispered advice, have done their work in the night, and I respond: "Of course you're right; I don't know what I was thinking!" Instead of ordering them to turn us around, I say: "Let us continue up the Amazon." At least for the time being, I acquiesce in their modification of my principle for choosing between the mainstream and a mere tributary. Perhaps, a hundred miles further on, I might go back to my old way of thinking, and allow width to trump all other factors. Doing so would not, however, cause the Amazon suddenly to shrink; it would not cause it to "snap back" to this early fork, with Alligator Swamp as its headwaters.

(To make the analogy perfectly parallel to the case of Charlie, one should get rid of the branching. Suppose that I put a precise limit on the width required for something to be the Amazon river; and that the first "juncture" was simply a spot where the river became narrower than that. My fellow explorers would then have to convince me that navigability was more important than width.)

The friends of temporal parts will, I hope, find the analogy compelling—so long as they have accepted the argument for Proteanism. I conclude that, if the doctrine of temporal parts were true, it would be easy for God to cause each of us to survive the deaths of our bodies. But of course that is a big "if"! Those of us who doubt that we persist by means of temporal parts will doubt that survival could be effected so easily.

5. Dualism without Temporal Parts

5.1 Setting Temporal Parts to One Side

If the doctrine of temporal parts were true, the dualist, like the materialist, would be obliged to admit that there are many beings, each thinking exactly the same things I am thinking right now—for there would be the current stage of my soul, and all the other longer sums of soul stages that have this one as a part, in addition to whichever sum of soul stages lasts for my entire life. With a host of sums of temporal parts on the scene, dualism is likely to lead to a Protean theory about our persistence conditions for the same reasons materialism led to a Protean theory. Different degrees and kinds of psychological continuity could be used to draw rather different temporal boundaries around sums of soul stages (on simple dualism) or soul-plus-body stages (on compound dualism), each of which is itself a thinking thing; and the boundaries around the sum of stages that *I* am ought to be sensitive to my self-conception just as they were on a materialist metaphysics of temporal parts.

For the remainder of this chapter, I shall explore the prospects for surviving death on the assumption that the doctrine of temporal parts is false. First, a question with a fairly simple answer: should dualists who are hostile to temporal parts think survival is possible? In the next section, I pose the more difficult question for the relevant materialists.

5.2 Simple Dualism

Two forms of dualism were described above: simple dualism and compound dualism. I begin with the first (and by my lights less problematic) version.

I can speak in propria persona at long last, since I take simple dualism to provide the most plausible theory about my own nature, and I see no reason to suppose that fundamental things, including souls, must be constantly gaining and losing temporal parts. I conclude that I have no reason to suppose that there are many things thinking exactly the same thing as myself right now. There is my soul, it is the thing that has my mental properties, so it is I—end of story. What does God have to do to insure that I survive the destruction of this body? Simple: keep my soul in existence after my body dies.

I have argued elsewhere that a certain form of simple dualism is not as easy to dismiss as most philosophers seem to think; indeed, that it is better off than its most popular materialist rivals.[33] But I admit that some forms of dualism are not so plausible. Traditionally, dualists have tended to argue that souls must, for one reason or another, exist forever once they have come into existence. Few today find these arguments compelling; but, if they were right, it would take a miracle for me *not* to survive the death of this body. The sort of dualism I find more appealing does not imply the natural immortality of the soul—quite the contrary. The view is a version of simple dualism developed by William Hasker under the label "emergent dualism" (though "naturalistic dualism" might be a better name, given the other uses to which the word "emergence" is put) (Hasker, 1999, pp. 188–203).[34] Emergent dualists regard human persons as distinct from, but natural by-products of, a functioning nervous system; once a brain is sufficiently complex to generate conscious experiences, it also generates a new subject to have them. On this conception of the soul, it would be natural to suppose that the soul fades away as soon as its brain ceases to function. However, even though emergent dualists insist that souls are causally dependent upon brains, soul and brain would nevertheless be what Hume would have called "distinct existences." The soul, so conceived, would not, strictly speaking, be identical with any part of the brain; and this would leave open at least the possibility that the subject of experience could be miraculously preserved after the death of the brain that generated it. A future "resurrection of the body" would, then, simply be God's uniting each soul with an appropriate animal body—one that includes the sort of organ needed by that particular soul in order for it to persist and function. (Dualists who are also keen to identify the pre- and postresurrection bodies can adapt one of the methods proposed in the next section for materialist-friendly survival: a reassembly theory, or the Falling Elevator Model.)

Emergent dualists accept the radical dependence of persons upon functioning brains. When brain function is impaired, so is the soul's ability to think. If memories and character traits are lost or altered when the right (or wrong!) parts of the brain are damaged, the more radical case of a soul preserved without any brain at all would presumably lack all psychological continuity with its pre-mortem self. Critics of dualistic forms of survival are apt to say that, in such a case, everything that we find important about our ongoing existence would be lost—so of what value would the afterlife be?

Granted, if God merely preserved our souls without restoring any of our cognitive faculties, we would be no better off than someone in a permanent vegetative state. Similarly, our lives would lose much of their meaning were God to preserve us, as bare souls, and then bring us into union with brains that gave us alien, unappealing character traits and completely illusory memories. But these mere possibilities do not show that the ongoing existence of a soul is insufficient for a person's continued existence—merely that a person could continue to exist without most of the things that matter to us (but who ever doubted that?). The emergent dualist supposes that there is one and only one thinker of my current thoughts, that the thinker of these thoughts is identical to an immaterial substance, and that this substance can exist after suddenly losing all my current memories and character traits. It follows that I can exist, despite such psychological losses, and that whatever happens to my soul happens to me. In any case, the only real hope for us, if the emergent dualist is right, requires God's miraculous intervention; and we should trust a benevolent deity to "re-clothe" us with appropriate bodies and brains, if we believe in an afterlife at all.

5.3 Compound Dualism

Emergent dualism is a form of simple dualism: a premortem human person *is* a soul, and this makes survival a simple matter of preserving the soul (i.e., the person) without the original body. But if a person is a *compound* of soul and body, survival of bodily death is more complicated. According to Aquinas and other compound dualists, the thinker of my current thoughts is a unified entity consisting of both matter and soul; and the soul is the "substantial form" of my body, something that makes it a human person, and in virtue of which I am able to do distinctively human things, like thinking. I am not identical to this form; and, although I am able to think in virtue of it, still, strictly speaking, the human being is the one who thinks, not the form.[35] Contemporary Thomists disagree about whether, on their view, God's preserving my soul apart from my body should be thought to preserve *me*.[36] Either the soul alone would have to come to constitute all of me; or I would go out of existence, reappearing only when the soul is once again united with a body. On the first alternative, two things—me and my soul, after my death—could be intrinsically exactly alike, each of us having the soul as its one and only part; and yet we would somehow differ in kind. Some philosophers are comfortable with views according to which a pair of things can have all the same parts, arranged in the same ways, and yet differ radically from one another.[37] They are free to take this route; but I am skeptical about these kinds of coincident entities. Were I a compound dualist, I should take the second alternative: preserving my soul alone does not insure that I survive; if an afterlife is possible, I must be able to go out of existence and then come back into existence, once my soul is again properly related to a parcel of matter so that the two form a human being.

This second proposal is rather like the kind of reassembly materialism described below, according to which the ongoing existence of the right kind of parts insures that the person can come back into existence when they are properly reassembled. Unlike normal, materialistic forms of a reassembly theory of survival, it simply posits an extra, immaterial part, which—like the mysterious luz bone—can only ever be part of one person. Around this special part, the original body-soul compound can be reconstructed.

> [S]ince the soul was what made matter this human being, presumably in the resurrection of the body it will again make the matter it informs this human being. Preservation of identity will not have to be guaranteed by recomposing the human being of the identical atoms as before, and puzzles about what happens when the same atoms have been part of more than one human being are avoided.[38]

The metaphysics of compound dualism strikes me as more problematic than that of simple dualism; but, if one can wrap one's mind round a Thomistic metaphysics with a separable substantial form for each person, its story about the mechanics of resurrection will doubtless come to seem a reasonable one.

6. Materialism without Temporal Parts

6.1 Three Proposed Necessary Conditions for Materialist Survival

I conclude with what might seem to be the hypothesis hardest to reconcile with survival of bodily death: namely, materialism under the assumption that there are *not* many thinking things here (all sharing a common temporal part), but only one. I ignore esoteric materialistic theories (for example, Chisholm (1978) once took seriously the idea that each of us might be a tiny physical particle lodged somewhere in the brain), considering only the hypothesis that I am an entirely physical thing, having the size and shape of a human body.[39] Like bushes, birds, and baboons, the physical thing in question is a living thing, an organism. Most materialists draw the natural conclusion: our persistence conditions ought to be somewhat similar to those of other organisms—that is, human persons should survive or fail to survive in roughly the same kinds of circumstances as other living material objects, with the case of the higher mammals being the most instructive. There is controversy over exactly what these persistence conditions *are*; but most materialists in this camp hold views about criteria of personal identity far to the biological side of the spectrum. I concentrate on them because they represent the hardest case: the death of the body, as I have described it, can easily seem to be an event no organism could survive; and so philosophers who believe we are, essentially, organisms have naturally concluded that survival is impossible.[40] Some opponents of temporal parts suppose that, although we may *look* like mere animals, we are in fact physical objects with psychological persistence conditions.[41] I shall largely ignore them here, because the materialist theory of resurrection I most favor—the Falling Elevator Model—will satisfy versions of (PC) if it can satisfy versions of (BC). On the Falling Elevator Model, the same organic life continues, despite the death of the body; and that continued life includes the continued functioning of the same bodily organs. If God can transport my brain, in good working order, past the death of my body and into some sort of afterlife, then any reasonable psychological criterion of identity will declare the resulting person to be me.[42]

Some philosophers have despaired of finding any informative persistence conditions for human organisms; and Trenton Merricks has argued that, once we have given up the quixotic quest for such conditions, materialism should not seem obviously incompatible with bodily death. After all, if we cannot even say what our persistence conditions are, why should we worry that life after death would violate them (Merricks, 2001)? I am convinced that there *must* be informative necessary and sufficient conditions for the persistence of organisms and other complex objects, however difficult they may be to state with precision (due in part, no doubt, to the fact that they are genuinely vague) (Zimmerman, 1998). So I cannot avail myself of Merricks's strategy.

Here are three popular (and rather plausible) proposals for necessary conditions upon the ongoing existence of material objects. Together, they militate against the possibility of survival, assuming the kind of materialism under discussion. The first principle may be called "gradual replacement":

(GR)   A living body cannot, all at once, come to be constituted by a parcel of matter that, at the smallest scale, is entirely new; whenever a material particle becomes a part of a body, there must be many other particles of the same size that have been and continue to be parts of the body.[43]

The second may be called "essentially alive":

(EA)   A living material object cannot continue to exist as a dead heap of matter; when a living thing ceases to be alive, it ceases to be.[44]

The third is "no causal gaps":

(NG)   Every stage in the history of a material object, other than the first, must be directly causally linked to prior stages in the history of that object. (van Inwagen, 1998, p. 47; Olson, 2010, pp. 56–60)

The incompatibility of survival and materialism seems to follow from the principles. What happens when the matter of which I am composed rapidly ceases to subserve biological functions? There are really only four possibilities: Either (i) I continue to exist as a nonliving hunk of matter (in chapter 3 in this volume, Olson calls this thesis "Corpse-Survivalism") or (ii) I suddenly come to be constituted by entirely new stuff (all new matter, or some kind of matter-substitute), or (iii) I continue to exist without any material parts at all, or (iv) I cease to exist. We can rule out (i) by (EA); (ii) and (iii), by (GR). Obviously, (ii) is incompatible with (GR); but so is (iii), since it requires that I—by hypothesis, a purely material object—could lose every single part at once and yet continue to exist.[45] That leaves only (iv): the death of my body means I no longer exist. And if there are no direct causal links between my final earthly stages and some future life, (NG) says I must be gone forever.

This line of argument can be resisted in several ways, however. Two of the more popular are a reassembly account of survival that violates (NG), and a view about the nature of biological lives that allows a single life to contain discontinuities that violate (GR). Consideration of these alternatives reveals that the prospects for survival are not so bad, even on purely materialistic assumptions about persons, and even without the help provided by a metaphysics of temporal parts. I prefer the Falling Elevator Model, which rejects (GR); but reassembly theories are not so bad off as many seem to think, and I begin by defending them against recent criticisms.

6.2 Resurrection by Reassembly

At one time, it was common to explain the resurrection of all who have died in terms of the reassembly of every human body: God searches the cosmos for the exact matter that constituted each one of our bodies at the moment of death, and puts each body back together again. A materialist about persons could develop a reassembly theory along these lines, accepting (GR) and, perhaps, (EA) as well. On this reassembly picture, a purely material person either ceases to exist when her body dies, or—assuming Corpse-Survivalism, instead of Essentially Alive—becomes a corpse that gradually ceases to exist when sufficiently dispersed. Eventually, this very same material object comes back into existence when her scattered matter is retrieved and reassembled. (NG) is thereby violated: a material object can enjoy a second-period existence, even though the final stages of its first period of existence do not directly bring about the earliest stages in the second.

(Reassembly accounts might fit more naturally with Corpse-Survivalism than with Essentially Alive. Would reassembling the scattered parts of an inert object, like a boulder, bring that very object—that very boulder—back into existence? This strikes me as more plausible than the claim that reassembling a living thing would bring the living thing back. But accepting the former, while denying the latter, is an unstable position for the Corpse-Survivalist. If I can become an inert object, a mere corpse, I should be as easy to reassemble as the boulder. And once my corpse exists, I exist, according to Corpse-Survivalism; so what could prevent my resuscitation?)

Peter van Inwagen argues that, if *God* were directly responsible for bringing the parts of a body back together, and giving them the form of a living human being, the result could only be a new person. The life that results from God's creative act would not be the continuation of one that ended in a death, since later stages of a single life must be *directly* causally dependent upon earlier stages, linked by biological forms of "immanent causation"—that is, the normal kinds of causal dependence that remain within a single organism.

In his defense of a reassembly account of resurrection, David Hershenov compares the persistence of living things to the persistence of artifacts, such as sculptures. When a statue has been broken into pieces, and then reassembled much later by archeologists, the result is something that the original sculptor made, despite the absence of direct "immanent causal connections" between the restored statue and its original.

> God could be understood as the "original artist" who created the world and arranged its matter and laws so that there would be organisms. Such background assumptions would make it plausible to think that God could resurrect people if He were faithful to His original blueprint that formed and maintained the human beings in question. (Hershenov, 2002, p. 458)

Just as reassembly of a once-destroyed statue, by *whomever*, results in a work attributable to the original sculptor; so reassembly by God of the parts I had at death can result in the recreation of God's original "work," namely, the organism that died—so long as they are reassembled in a way that resembles the organization they had in life. If materialism is true, bringing back all the human organisms that ever died should be enough, on Hershenov's principles, to insure that we all survive death.

Even dualists have made use of reassembly in their conjectures about the machinery of resurrection. Christians have traditionally believed that, after death, a person continues to exist in a completely immaterial form; but that, eventually, the soul shall be reunited with *the very same body* that had died. The puzzling aspects of this doctrine were not lost on the early Christian fathers and medieval doctors of the church; the objections they considered apply directly to purely materialist accounts of the survival of persons by means of reassembly. The ancient worries about the resurrection of cannibals and their victims pose troubling questions for the reassembly account. Here is the problem in its most acute form: however unlikely, it seems not absolutely impossible that all the material in a dying person's body should, one day—perhaps after generations of eating and being eaten—wind up constituting the body of another person precisely at the moment of that person's death. There seems no obstacle, at least in principle, to that dying person's being exactly like the original person, in size, shape, genetic makeup, and so on. To use Mark Johnston's terminology, the "peri-mortem states" of the original victim and the descendent of the cannibals could be, by the strangest of coincidences, exactly the same, materially and structurally—they were, as Johnston puts it, "peri-mortem duplicates." What happens when God reassembles the matter that constituted both dying persons? Which one, if either, would be ushered into the New Creation by a policy of divine reassembly?

Johnston turns these questions into an argument against the traditional picture of resurrection-by-reassembly. According to Johnston, any sensible reassembly theory implies the truth of the following duplication principle: necessarily, if a body dies in a certain peri-mortem state, and if, at a later time, the very matter that formerly constituted that body were caused by God to return to that very state—arranged just as it was in the dying person's body—then the original body would be brought back to life. The cannibal story is in tension with this duplication principle; for the principle, together with the mere *possibility* of the cannibal scenario, requires that, in some possible world (however outré and macabre), two bodies become one body. Whether that means that two bodies could come to be in the same place at the same time, or that nonidentical things could become identical, it is not a happy result—Johnston thinks neither should be regarded as a genuine possibility, and any theory that implies such possibilities must be rejected (Johnston, 2010, pp. 29–40).

But the advocate of reassembly need not accept Johnston's duplication principle. As I have argued elsewhere, materialists who reject temporal parts will be hard-pressed to avoid a "closest continuer" clause in their criteria of personal identity (Zimmerman, 1998, pp. 198–201; and Zimmerman, 2010b, pp. 38–44); that is to say, such materialists will have to admit that the continued existence of a person can depend upon the absence of equally good candidates for being that person. Johnston as much as admits that such a clause will be required in the statement of criteria of identity for *some* physical objects, namely, organisms. He allows that, in a case of the perfect fission of an organism, the original organism ceases to exist, and two new organisms come into existence; and he does not deny that a closest continuer clause is needed to state persistence conditions for organisms (Johnston, 2010, pp. 364–368). He elsewhere insists that an adequate theory of personal identity must allow for at least the conceptual possibility of symmetrical organisms able to survive the destruction of half their organs and systems (Johnston, 1989, pp. 376–377). So there seems no escape from the conclusion that, in the perfect fission of a strangely symmetrical human-like organism, there is an individual (an organism) that does not survive, but that could have survived a process intrinsically just like the ones going on within the original organism and just one of the fission-products—*in the absence of the other.* A closest continuer clause would, then, be needed in order for Johnston to describe the persistence conditions of organisms.[46] Closest continuer theorists should have no qualms about drawing the temporal mirror-image of this moral, which applies to cases of fusion[47]: if, at present, there exists a certain person who has existed in the past, there must have been a closest predecessor of that person; the presence of two equally good prior candidates for being the same later person can make a difference as to whether a new person has come into existence, rather than a formerly existing person having merely continued to exist.[48]

Once alerted to the need for a "no closest predecessor" clause in criteria of personal identity, the advocate of resurrection-by-reassembly will naturally look with skepticism upon Johnston's duplication principle. God's reassembly of a peri-mortem duplicate of some earlier person might be sufficient to bring the earlier person back, in the "normal" case; but *not* when there is an equally close predecessor of that person—someone whose peri-mortem state is just as similar to the initial state of the divinely reconstructed being, and who is equally similar in other respects that matter. A "no closest predecessor" clause could be added to Johnston's duplication principle in a number of different ways—that is to say, there are different metaphysical theories one could hold about the conditions that are necessary and sufficient for bringing back a living thing by means of reassembly. One respect in which a pair of potential predecessors (or ancestors) could differ in closeness, relative to a certain person existing at a certain time, is *temporal proximity.* Latching onto this kind of closeness, the proponent of reassembly could insist that, in the case of peri-mortem duplicates, a reassembled body would belong to the temporally closer predecessor, blocking resurrection of the original person. This sort of reassembly theorist would qualify Johnston's duplication principle: necessarily, if a body dies in a certain peri-mortem state, and, at a later time, the very matter that formerly constituted that body were caused by God to return to that very state, then the result would be the original body brought back to life, *so long as that matter did not constitute someone else's peri-mortem state at any time during the intervening period.*

This is not the only tempting way to modify the duplication principle, in light of the need for a no-closest-predecessor clause. A materialist might think temporal proximity irrelevant, or at any rate something that could be trumped by other kinds of closeness. One intriguing possibility is that, when God miraculously returns some matter to a form resembling duplicate peri-mortem states, one candidate could be much closer than the other due entirely to differences in the nature of God's activity. The view can be motivated by considering an analogous sort of case that would arise for defenders of a liberal psychological criterion. The case is fanciful, but no more so than a scenario in which peri-mortem duplicates appear: On a planet of cannibalistic time travelers, there are two men, John and Jack, whose births are many generations apart, and who happen to be made out of the same matter arranged in the same way just as they enter their respective time machines in their respective "home eras." Their time machines function rather like teletransportation devices; they demolish a body as they "read off" its structure, and then somehow use this information to generate one "elsewhen"—in this case, much later than either departure. Liberal versions of (PC) imply that such adventures are survivable; but, when a time traveler appears many years after the functioning of both time machines, he will be equally similar, intrinsically, to each man as he entered his machine. What should a liberal psychological criterion say? Plausible attempts to articulate (PC) in detail will impose causal constraints upon a series of stages in the life of a single person; and the question, Is this man John or Jack? would be answered by finding out whose time travel device caused this particular appearance of a man. Suppose the explanation for the time traveler's appearance goes back to John's entry into his time machine, and not to Jack's. Then the traveler is John and not Jack—at least, that is the verdict of a liberal psychological criterion.

Setting (PC) to one side, I return to the attempt to articulate a criterion of bodily identity that is consistent with reassembly. The proposed solution to the puzzle about John and Jack has an analog for a pair of peri-mortem duplicates, Jane and Jill. Suppose that God eventually assembles a body made of the materials common to Jane and Jill at their deaths, arranging the same physical stuff just as it was at the last instant of both lives. The resulting body is revived, healed, and improved. Could God's miraculous assembling of a Jane-and-Jill-like body be causally connected to Jane and not Jill, in something like the way the appearance of the time traveler was causally connected to John's time machine and not to Jack's? Well, why not? I suppose one might object that, since God knows the reassembled body is just like both Jane and Jill, the act of reassembling it could not be done with the intention of duplicating one but not the other. It does not, however, seem difficult to imagine a way for God to act that would make Jane, and not Jill, the causal explanation of a particular body's appearance. God could effect the reassembly simply by issuing a very general decree: "Let there be a body just like Jane's was when she went out of existence, consisting of the same matter in the same arrangement, but rapidly coming back to life rather than decaying." The resulting body would be intrinsically the same as would be the result of a similar command aimed at resurrecting Jill; but if a particular body is reassembled at a particular time because of the decree about *Jane*, then Jane is a closer predecessor along a dimension that a reassembly theorist may take to be decisive.

Borrowing a suggestion from David Hershenov, the reassembly advocate could point out that, in the wildly improbable case of exact peri-mortem duplication, God could still resurrect both Jane and Jill; though, with Jane resurrected first, Jill would have to wait long enough for her old material parts to become available—and more miracles might be called for, to speed up Jane's metabolism. Once the matter originally in Jane's resurrected body has been freed up, God can reassemble Jill, as well; he simply issues a new decree that causes a peri-mortem duplicate of Jill to appear.[49]

Opponents of closest continuer theories will balk at these moves. But, if I am right, a sensible materialism requires them; and, as noted earlier, Johnston seems to agree that the persistence of *organisms*, at any rate, can depend upon the absence of competitors. He is hardly in a position, then, to dismiss the reassembly theorist's modification of the duplication principle.

6.3 The "Falling Elevator Model"

A quite different response to the argument for the incompatibility of death and survival would question (GR), the doctrine of gradual replacement, and grasp alternative (ii): a living thing could suddenly come to be constituted by a completely different set of fundamental particles or a new batch of whatever sort of stuff ultimately makes up human bodies.

Trenton Merricks's (2001) anti-criterialist strategy might be regarded as a species of this approach: there is no particular kind of continuity—of parts or of anything else—that is required to hold between the dying body and the resurrected one, if the person is to survive death by resurrection. I am inclined to believe that van Inwagen is right, however: There are certain kinds of causal dependencies that must hold throughout the life of a single organism, ones that would not hold between a dying body and a resurrected one, if the latter were simply the result of God's reassembling the old matter along similar lines.

> The atoms of which I am composed occupy at each instant the positions they do because of the operations of certain processes within me (those processes that, taken collectively, constitute my being alive)....[I]f a man does not simply die but is totally destroyed (as in the case of cremation) then *he* can never be reconstituted, for the causal chain has been irrevocably broken. If God collects the atoms that used to constitute that man and "reassembles" them, they will occupy the positions relative to one another they occupy because of God's miracle and not because of the operation of the natural processes that, taken collectively, were the life of that man. (van Inwagen, 1998, p. 47)

In response to van Inwagen's worries about the possibility of resurrection, I developed a "just-so story" that I called "the Falling Elevator Model" of resurrection.[50] The model was supposed to respect van Inwagen's requirement that chains of causation between dying body and resurrected one be suitably direct, unbroken. I described a mechanism by which God could cause these very organisms to appear, elsewhere and perhaps elsewhen. But it was a story that violated (GR); since *all* the matter constituting my body at death remains right where it is, to be buried or scattered, never to constitute me again (in all likelihood).

The Falling Elevator Model is so-called because it involves a last-second jump that saves us from what looks like certain death—a strategy sometimes used by cartoon characters when an elevator cable breaks and they are hurtling toward the subbasement. Reaction to the proposal was mixed. Hud Hudson, Kevin Corcoran, Tim O'Connor, and Jonathan Jacobs said: "That's so crazy, it just might work!" They made good use of it in their versions of Christian materialism. Others (e.g., William Hasker, David Hershenov, and Eric Olson) thought it was merely crazy, and have criticized it from various perspectives.[51]

Here are the bare bones of the Model. Van Inwagen accepts a biological criterion along the lines of (BC): an organism begins to exist when some matter first gets caught up in a biological life, and the same organism goes on existing until that life ends. As noted above, Van Inwagen is a moderate: he holds that, in the case of a whole brain transfer, the person goes with the brain (not because the brain insures psychological continuity, but because he thinks the brainstem is essential to the life of an organism, and could constitute a maimed human animal all by itself). An essential feature of the life of an organism is that it displays a kind of "self-maintenance," earlier stages tending naturally to cause later stages that closely resemble the earlier ones in crucial ways. The resulting causal dependence of later stages in the life of an organism upon earlier ones is a kind of "immanent causation." If a BST device scrambles the brain of one organism and imposes that organism's human psychology upon the brain of another organism, it would be absurd to say that an organism had switched bodies. Perhaps a little less obviously, an organism could not be torn to bits by a teletransporter, and then reappear elsewhere when the device assembles a living body using new materials but based on the same pattern. Proponents of biological criteria naturally conclude from these reflections that the distinctive causal dependencies within an organism could not pass through the computer banks of a teleportation device or a blueprint in God's mind. On this reading of (BC), I could not show up somewhere else, after the event I have been calling "the death of my body," simply by God's using what He knows about the state of my body at death as a blueprint for assembling one that exactly resembles it. Such a body would not continue the life of this one; it would be a new organism, a mere duplicate.

The Falling Elevator Model is a way to allow the life of a dying organism to go one way, while the dead matter goes another way. The trick is to posit immanent-causal connections that "jump" from the matter as it is dying, connecting the life to some other location, where the crucial organic structures within the organism are preserved. Immanent causation is not peculiar to organisms; all ordinary physical objects in which we take an interest are the kinds of things that exhibit causal dependencies of later stages upon earlier stages. This includes boring objects, like hunks of dead matter. If a pile of matter persists throughout a period of time, the existence and properties of the later stages of the matter must be partly causally dependent upon the existence and nature of the earlier stages. Since each bit of matter in my body is supposed to stay behind when I die, to be buried (or devoured or...), there must also be immanent-causal connections between the matter in the dying body and the dead material left behind—on pain of making God a body-snatcher. So every portion of the matter in my body must undergo something like fission at the time of my death. Consider just the atoms in my body; and pretend that my body consists entirely of atoms (and the parts of atoms). The Falling Elevator Model affirms that, at the moment of my death, God allows each atom to continue to immanently-cause later stages in the "life" or history of an atom, right where it is then located, as it normally would do; but that God *also* gives each atom the miraculous power to produce an exact duplicate at a certain distance in space or time (or both), at an unspecified location I shall call "the next world." The local, normal, immanent-causal processes linking each atom to an atom within the corpse are sufficient to secure their identities; no atom need cease to exist merely because it exercises this miraculous "budding" power—a power to produce *new* matter in a distant location.[52] Still, the arrangement of atoms that appears at a distance is directly immanent-causally connected to my body at the time of my death; and there are no other arrangements of living matter produced by my dying body that are candidates for continuing my life. So, even though the atoms do something that resembles fission, what they really do is bud: producing exactly similar offspring in the next world, while remaining in this one. The organism itself does *not* fission; my body's life does not divide, but goes in one direction only, carrying my body with it to a new location.

Resurrection by reassembly required a closest predecessor clause in its account of the persistence conditions of persons; and, on widely held assumptions, the Falling Elevator Model will require a closest continuer clause. Imagine a world $w1$, just like the actual world except that, many years ago, God secretly caused my atoms to bud, generating duplicates in the next world in just the way the Falling Elevator Model recommends that God do at my death—but in $w1$, I am *not* about to die, and the atoms in my body carry on with their terrestrial biological activities in the same way they did in the actual world. Since this budding happened during the middle of my childhood, in $w1$ a child appeared in the next world who remembers—or seems to remember—my childhood. On the face of it, the mere occurrence of this budding event should not have killed me as a child; I should have been able to survive having my atoms cause duplicates to appear far away in this manner, so long as the atoms in my body did not themselves do anything unusual, then and there. If I would *not* have survived this unnoticed childhood budding of my atoms, it could only have been because my survival is incompatible with one stage in my life producing competing stages (even when one of the competitors is far away in space-time). But, in that case, appeal to a closest continuer is required straightaway: for in $w1$ there is a history involving hunks of matter undergoing events that are intrinsically just like the events in my actual history; but in $w1$ I am replaced by a duplicate at the undetectable point of budding merely because of something that happens outside the region in which that history occurs.

Suppose, then, that in $w1$ I survive this childhood budding of my atoms. Now imagine a world $w2$ in which the budding occurs simultaneously with the destruction of my earthly atoms. The Falling Elevator Model implies that Zimmerman himself would thereby have leapt to the next world. But the same history that, in *w2*, constitutes a single person—childhood me and then the resurrected me—occurs in *w1* and *fails* to constitute a single person. So, on this supposition, too, the presence or absence of close continuers makes a difference. Whatever one says about what happens in a childhood "budding," the Falling Elevator defender winds up affirming a closest continuer account of my persistence conditions: whether certain intrinsically similar events constitute the life of a single person can depend upon events that happen outside of the places where the events in that life *actually* occur.

The argument is not airtight; some materialists can embrace the Falling Elevator Model without commitment to a closest continuer theory. Hud Hudson, in his ingenious use of the Falling Elevator story, shows how to avoid the closest continuer account of personal identity by tearing a page from David Lewis's book: cases of fission can be regarded as cases in which there were two things *all along*, sharing temporal parts prior to, but not after, the fission event (Hudson, 2001, ch. 7). In the case of the childhood budding followed by my normal life and eventual resurrection, the child and I shared our childhood temporal parts; but then, in the next world, we ceased to overlap. However, whether or not a person had been allowed to continue in the time and place at which budding occurred, pre-budding stages plus childlike stages that appear in the next world would have constituted a single person; and the presence or absence of additional close continuers would not interfere with that fact.

Van Inwagen and many other Christian materialists—for example, Trenton Merricks, Kevin Corcoran, Lynne Rudder Baker, and Timothy O'Connor—reject the metaphysics of temporal parts that allows Hudson to avoid a closest continuer theory. Elsewhere, I have argued that van Inwagen (along with other advocates of (BC)) will be forced to accept a closest continuer account of personal identity in order to make allowance for the fact that organisms can undergo fission.[53] If I am right about this, the fact that the Falling Elevator Model requires a closest continuer theory should not count as an extra cost—at least, not for those who reject temporal parts, while maintaining that persons are organisms.

6.4 Giving Up the Gradual Replacement Principle

How bad is it to have to deny (GR), when it comes to living bodies? Not so bad, I think. Hershenov claims that, for new parts to be assimilated by a body, many of its old parts must remain; and so my envisioned "jump" is impossible (Hershenov, 2002, pp. 460–563). But (GR) is not just *obviously* true, for living things; and there is reason to suspect that it is at least not *definitely* true for any material objects in our world. Atoms and molecules persist through time in reasonable ways; there are definite answers to the question whether a certain atom or molecule in a living body is the same as one found later on in a corpse. However, at sufficiently small scales, the particles composing the atoms in our bodies start to behave oddly. Electrons, protons, and neutrons obey surprising statistical laws that ought to undermine our confidence in the persistence through time of the particles constituting the atoms in our bodies. Electrons, protons, and neutrons are all fermions; and indistinguishable fermions—for example, all the protons in my body—caught up in the same quantum–mechanical system do not seem "trackable" over time. When plotting the probability of such a system evolving in various ways throughout a period, one must ignore potential differences in its future states that involve nothing more than the permutation of indistinguishable particles—for example, permutations in which two electrons, protons, or neutrons switch places. Why do nature's laws fail to distinguish between circumstance A, in which *this* proton shows up *there* and *that* proton shows up *here*, and circumstance B, in which *that* proton shows up *there* and *this* proton shows up *here*? Many theoretical physicists and philosophers of physics have argued that the best explanation is that the imagined difference between A and B does not exist—these are not two distinct states of the system. If the two protons really persisted over time, A and B *would* be distinct states; and so the protons do not really persist.[54]

Since our bodies are interacting with other systems consisting of further indistinguishable electrons, protons, and neutrons, one cannot accept this conclusion and straightforwardly affirm that most of the neutrons, protons, and electrons in my body right now were also present in my body moments ago—at least, not if that means they were definitely *not* present in the *other* physical objects surrounding me moments ago. At this subatomic level, there seems to be a set of particles that constitutes all of my body, without remainder; despite the fact that no members of it are identical with previous parts of my body—at least, no members of it are *determinately* identical with indistinguishable particles in my body at earlier times. Given indeterminacy of identity over time for indistinguishable particles, gradual replacement seems to be at least not determinately true.

The moral I have drawn from quantum statistics is not inevitable. There are alternative explanations of the strange statistics of subatomic particles. Bohm's version of quantum theory, for example, renders identity of particles through time unproblematic but unknowable. And even without Bohmianism, it has been argued that the statistics do not rule out the possibility of undetectable facts about fermion identity-through-time.[55] Still, I should not want to gamble on an assimilation principle that requires the falsehood of an attractive explanation of this strange feature of quantum statistics. One quite plausible moral to draw from quantum theory is that atoms and other distinguishable objects made of atoms can persist through time, despite the fact that, at each time, they are decomposable without remainder into a set of particles that do not, strictly speaking, persist through time. If such objects can gain new parts, then they can do so despite the fact that, at some level of smallness, they are wholly constituted by sub–atomic particles none of which existed earlier or even (so far as we know) had parts that existed earlier.

6.5 Plenty of Available Just-So Stories

I have surveyed two possible methods by which God might resurrect persons—methods consistent with supposing that we are entirely physical beings. Reassembly accounts may not be open to the kinds of criticisms leveled against them by

Johnston and others; but they still require giving up (NG). The Falling Elevator Model rejects (GR); but this does not seem too costly. It may in fact be indeterminate whether our material parts are, at the smallest level, only replaced gradually. Contemplation of this seeming possibility leads me to conclude that (GR) is not a necessary truth. But I find (NG) much harder to deny. So I prefer the second account of materialist-friendly survival.

Were I a materialist arguing for the possibility of survival using either reassembly or a last minute leap, I would want to conclude the telling of such tales with van Inwagen's qualifications:

> My method was to tell a story, a story I hoped my readers would grant was a metaphysically possible story, in which God accomplished the Resurrection of the Dead.... [T]here may well be other ways in which an omnipotent being could accomplish the Resurrection of the Dead than the way that was described in the story I told, ways I am unable even to form an idea of because I lack the conceptual resources to do so. (van Inwagen, 1998, p. 50)

These are, after all, "just-so stories."

7. CONCLUSION

Is it possible for me to survive the death of my body? The question should be answered affirmatively on almost every account of the nature of human persons that has any plausibility.

If the doctrine of temporal parts is true, "I," in my mouth, should be taken to refer to a Protean person; and a Protean person could make it into the afterlife by a very simple expedient: God need only create a psychological-continuer for me, and insure that he organizes his life around reliably produced, nonbranching psychological continuity. (Although only materialist versions of a temporal parts metaphysics were considered, I claimed that the same conclusion should be drawn for a dualism with temporal parts.)

Among philosophers who reject the doctrine of temporal parts, one finds both dualists and materialists. At least one kind of dualism—simple dualism—is obviously compatible with the possibility of my surviving the death of my body; although, in all likelihood, survival would require a miracle. Compound dualism faces some puzzling questions about what happens to me at death (and the whole idea of souls-as-forms is hard to grasp). But it seemed to have a coherent reassembly story to tell about the resurrection of the very same body, in virtue of the persistence of the original soul. It serves as the form of a body-soul union with a fair claim to be the original human being.

Other philosophers who reject temporal parts also reject immaterial souls; they believe that we are physical bodies made entirely of stuff that can be found in inanimate objects. Traditionally, Christian theologians have held that such bodies can be brought back into existence by reassembly. Although this idea turned out to be less problematic than some have thought, it still flies in the face of a plausible principle about living things—namely, that their lives cannot display causal gaps. So, for materialists who reject temporal parts, I developed the Falling Elevator Model as a picture of at least *one* way for God to allow a dying animal to "jump" into another location, sloughing off all the atoms and molecules that constituted it at the crucial moment. Whether the materialists for whom I built the Falling Elevator Model happen to favor psychological or biological criteria of identity for their material persons, such a trip should remain possible.

As I noted at the outset, all the means I have considered for surviving death depend upon divine intervention. Readers interested in the even more pressing question, Will I in fact survive the death of my body? had best inquire into the existence of God.[56] For myself, I think that God exists; and, as a consequence, I believe that this life cannot be the end of (or even a fraction of) the whole story. Eventually, we shall all find out... or, if I am wrong, not.[57]

Notes

1. See van Inwagen, 1998, pp. 49–51.
2. See, e.g., Paul Edwards's introduction in Edwards, 1997, esp. pp. 69–70; and Flew, 2000, pp. 99–100.
3. For trenchant criticism of (what he calls) "The Program View," see Olson, 2007, pp. 145–149.
4. Derek Parfit's work on personal identity may well be the most influential since Locke's. Parfit focused upon "what matters in survival," arguing that it is the holding of a certain kind of psychological continuity between a person at one time and a person at another—a relation that can hold between two different persons. Sometimes the word "survival" is now used in a special philosophical sense, to refer to the holding of this relation: the fact that a person "survives" some event would not, then, mean that the original person continues to exist; it would only mean that everything that should matter to us about our continued existence still holds between the original person and a (possibly distinct) person who exists after the event (see, e.g., Rey, 1976). I will not be using "survival" in this technical, Parfit-inspired sense in this paper.
5. For a creative (and no doubt controversial) use of semantic ascent in the literature on personal identity, see Parfit, 1984, p. 290.
6. Though here I have been given pause by a suggestion of Pavel Davydov's. "I" is obviously context-sensitive; in the context of my use, it refers to me, while in the context of your use it refers to you. But there may be much more to its context-sensitivity. Perhaps the difference between occasions when "I" is used for interpersonal communication and occasions when one is alone or addressing oneself *also* represents a change in context to which "I" is sensitive. This is a possibility that should not be lightly dismissed—although that is what I must do here.
7. This characterization of dualism is somewhat stipulative. For a more careful discussion of the difficulties of defining dualism and materialism, see Zimmerman, 2006.
8. St. Thomas's dualism is notoriously difficult to interpret. Contemporary dualists inspired by St. Thomas attribute thought to the whole human being, a union of soul

(an individual, substantial form) and matter; but, as shall appear, they differ over whether, after death, the soul comes to constitute the person or is simply a former part of the person around which he or she will be reconstructed.

9. For criticism of compound dualism, see Olson, 2001.

10. See Olson, 2001.

11. For a thorough exploration of the metaphysical options in this vicinity, see Hawthorne, 2006, ch. 5.

12. An argument for temporal parts along similar lines may be found in Sider, 2001a, pp. 120–139.

13. For my reasons, see Zimmerman, 2010a; and for a dualist manifesto, see Baker and Goetz, 2011.

14. Most proposed accounts of personal identity fall pretty far to one side or the other along the physical–psychological spectrum; but there are important intermediate positions, like that of Unger, 1990.

15. For discussion of Locke's theory of personal identity, and its early interpreters and critics, see Martin and Barresi, 2000.

16. See Shoemaker and Swinburne, 1984, pp. 80–91

17. Shoemaker and Swinburne, 1984, pp. 87–101; and Parfit, 1986, pp. 219–228.

18. There are deep differences between their views, once one begins to ask what counts as a "direct psychological connection"; compare the theories developed in Shoemaker and Swinburne, 1984, pp. 87–101; and Parfit, 1986, pp. 219–28.

19. Conservative Neo-Lockeans may be motivated by the thought that persons are substances, and substances must possess powers of self-perpetuation. For discussion, see Shoemaker, 1997.

20. Assuming materialism, that is. If compound dualism is true, the person would be the brain-plus-soul-as-form—arguably "larger," in a nonspatial sense, than the brain alone.

21. See van Inwagen, 1990 and Olson, 1997.

22. The remarkable abilities of human bodies to survive brain stem death are described in Mackie, 1998.

23. See van Inwagen, 1990, pp. 169–212; and Olson, 1997, pp. 131–142.

24. As Pavel Davydov has reminded me, some ways of distinguishing "tokens" of a word might identify one token for each subject which is making the sound "I" by means of my vocal cords—thereby multiplying tokens of "I," one for every sum of temporal parts that includes my current vocalizing stages. But, as he also points out, all these tokens might nevertheless be co-referential. I should think a good rule for determining the referent of a token of "I" in a given context would, in fact, give the same result for each. A spatial comparison may help motivate this conclusion: On a radically fine-grained view of how tokens should be individuated, "The treasure is here," scrawled on the dessert sand, would contain an indefinite number of tokens of "here," one for each part of the dessert roughly centered upon the word (each of which *could* have been meant by someone who wrote those words); but the (no doubt vague) location that *each* such token indicates, in the particular circumstances, ought to be the same.

25. A metaphysics of temporal parts is not the only view that will open up space for ambiguity in our talk about the persistence of persons. In Olson, 1995, and Sider, 2001b, alternatives to temporal parts are explored which would lead to similar conclusions: (1) nihilism (Olson, 1995, pp. 149–152; Sider, 2001b, p. 194) or mereological essentialism (Sider, 2001b, p. 194), with many equally good "loose" ways of talking

about persistence of persons; (2) relativity of identity, with several equally good candidate kinds to which my identity might be relative (Olson, 1995, pp. 153–156); (3) stage-theory, with many equally good candidates for the kind of temporal-counterpart-relation relevant to determining what I did or will do (Sider, 2001b, pp. 192–193); and (4) a "'promiscuous' endurance theory" with many coincident objects corresponding to equally good candidates for being me, some satisfying versions of (PC), others versions of (BC) (Sider, 2001b, pp. 193–194). On at least some of these metaphysical views, one could give an analog of the argument I shall give for Proteanism. I shall, however, ignore them. Each is much less popular than the two views I consider here: namely, the doctrine of temporal parts, and a nonpromiscuous endurance theory.

26. José Benardete once suggested to me that Timothy Williamson's defense of epistemicism looks like an argument for the existence of God: only God could establish precise boundaries for the English words "bald," "heap," etc. Jonathan Edwards, himself a temporal parts theorist, held an extreme sort of divine command theory of personal identity that would have allowed God to decide whether "I," in my current stage's mouth, refers to a psychological continuer or a biological continuer—or, for that matter, a radically discontinuous thing that included some temporal parts from Adam himself among its parts. For discussion of Edwards's views, see Rea, 2007, pp. 332–345; and Johnston, 2010, pp. 121–125.

27. The principle is called "Constancy of First-Person Reference." In effect, the whole argument could still be run, replacing an individual and the relation around which she "organizes her life" with a community of language-users and the relation their overall usage and dispositions select as relevant to a single life. God simply has to do for everyone what I, in the argument, imagine him doing for me.

28. Suppose Berkeley were right when he says (in the Fourth Dialogue of his *Alciphron*) that the data of vision (and other senses) represent a kind of divine language by means of which God speaks to us. Could God's communication with us by means of, for example, a "Visual Language" somehow help to make divine stipulations more relevant to the interpretation of words in English and other natural languages?

29. Compare Nozick, 1981, p. 69.

30. My approach is in contrast to, or at least in tension with, Marya Schechtman's "narrative self-constitution theory," according to which the boundaries of a person are determined primarily by a narrative self-conception that can be made fully articulate, as opposed to psychological attitudes of which one may not be fully aware; see Schechtman, 1996, pp. 114–119.

31. It may be helpful to relate the position taken here to the discussion of personal identity in Sider, 2001b. I regard Intended Constancy of First-Person Reference and Local Determination of Local Persistence Conditions as, in Sider's terms, constraints on "eligibility" that come from our "usage" (Sider, 2001b, pp. 190–191). There is an available "candidate meaning" for our reference to human persons (namely, things belonging to the kind: Protean person) that is more eligible than the things Sider calls "psychological-persons" and the things he calls "body-persons." So one should conclude that we refer to Protean persons using the first person (and other names assumed to be co-referential with first person pronouns). The argument for Proteanism would be a case of "ongoing philosophical investigation" establishing "a superior theory" among competing criteria of personal identity (Sider, 2001b, p. 201).

32. Although, officially, Johnston rejects the doctrine of temporal parts, his hylomorphism introduces a plenitude of overlapping persisting objects that will do

just as well for the purposes of my argument for Proteanism. Johnston's most recent arguments for Proteanism can be found in chapter 4 of Johnston, 2010, and are summed up on pp. 293–295. They crucially involve the notion of a disagreement's being "investigation transcendent." Johnston's argument is complex, and I am not sure how closely our arguments for Proteanism correspond to one another.

33. In Zimmerman, 2010, I argue that the most intuitively plausible forms of materialism can be ruled out; whereupon dualism becomes just one more speculative hypothesis about what kind of thing we are, alongside a range of unlikely and no less speculative materialist options. The contributors to Baker and Goetz, 2011 explore the potential empirical fruitfulness of (what they call) *The Soul Hypothesis*.

34. Karl Popper's dualism also seems to be of the emergent kind (Popper and Eccles, 1977; for discussion, see Hasker, 1999, pp. 185–158). Robin Collins is sympathetic to the view, and briefly sketches a proposal for the mechanism of emergence (Collins, 2011, 244–245). Richard Swinburne does not quite fit the profile. He is skeptical about the extent to which any mind-brain correlations can receive scientific explanations, and this leads him to the conclusion that God takes a more active role in generating and sustaining souls than Hasker supposes (Swinburne, 1986, 198–199).

35. For contemporary attempts to explain a metaphysics of substantial forms that has these results, see Stump, 1995; Leftow, 2001; and Oderberg, 2005.

36. On Stump's reading of Aquinas, the separated soul constitutes the person during the unnatural period between death and resurrection. A particular can "exist when it is constituted only by one of its main metaphysical parts, namely, the soul. And so although a person is not identical to his soul, the existence of the soul is sufficient for the existence of a person" (Stump, 2003, p. 53) (For contemporary defense of a Thomistic dualism that takes this line, see also Oderberg, 2005.) According to other interpreters, St. Thomas denies that the separated soul of a person is that person. For discussion of the controversy, and a Thomistic account of the resurrection in which persons enjoy "gappy existence" and the persisting soul secures something like immanent-causal connections between dead and resurrected bodies, see Christina Van Dyke, 2007.

37. For materialists who make use of coincident entities in their explanations of the resurrection, see Baker, 2007, and Corcoran, 2001b.

38. Stump, 1995, p. 516; see also Stump, 2006.

39. A few materialists identify persons with just the *brains* in our bodies—a difference that will not be relevant to questions about survival of death.

40. E.g., Olson, 1997, p. 71.

41. See Shoemaker, 1997 and 1999.

42. I here gloss over an important distinction among materialists who reject temporal parts: namely, the difference between those who affirm and those who deny that there can be more than one entirely physical object existing in the same place at the same time, made out of the same matter. Those who affirm the existence of such coincident objects will typically suppose that, where I am, there is a human body that is not a human person, and also a human person (namely, me) that is not a (mere) human body. The close relation between me and my body is one of "constitution"— the body constitutes the person. The differences between coincident objects related by constitution come out primarily in their persistence conditions. The *mere* body, for example, can "survive death" in a Pickwickian sense, continuing to exist but *as a corpse*; while the human person would cease to be, were its life utterly snuffed out. I shall not give the views of constitution theorists (e.g., Shoemaker, 1999, Baker, 2007,

Corcoran, 2001b) separate treatment. In general, they agree that there is a human *animal* where each person is; and that, if God could preserve the animal through the death of the body (without losing important psychological connections in the process), God could certainly preserve the person as well. So my Falling Elevator Model, below, will work for them. The reassembly proposals to be discussed first, however, will be of less value to most constitution theorists. (Corcoran, for example, would not be able to make use of reassembly, since his persons satisfy a biological criterion along the lines of (BC); while Baker has no use for either proposal—her persons are not tethered to either body *or* animal; they need not even display the Neo-Lockean's psychological continuities, but can freely go whither God wilt.)

43. See Hershenov, 2002 for defense of the principle; and Zimmerman, 2010b for criticism.

44. Fred Feldman, in this volume, calls this widely held principle "the termination thesis" (though he argues against it).

45. Jens Johansson has pointed out that (iii) would not be ruled out by (GR) if enough of my parts to constitute me could *become immaterial*. But this alternative does not provide much hope of escape for the materialist who wants survival of death (without body snatching) and a strong assimilation requirement. If all the atoms in my body, say, became immaterial at my (apparent) death, then the matter left behind would not be the matter formerly making up my body (at least, so long as we deny that there were two atoms all along, sharing temporal parts). If only larger structures (like the brain, bones, and blood vessels) become immaterial, then again there will be a violation of an assimilation requirement with respect to these larger parts.

46. Johnston's attitude toward closest continuer theories is complicated by the fact that he rejects them for "higher-order individuals" such as species (e.g., the Tiger), which survive fission by coming to be "multiply-embodied"; and that he regards persons as similar to species in this regard. When a person seems to undergo fission, what happens is that the original human organism ceases to be, replaced by two new ones; and there is, in addition to the three organisms, a single person who survives twice over. The person is a higher-order individual, constituted by each of the three organisms (Johnston, 2010, pp. 364–368). Admitting the need for a closest continuer clause in the identity conditions for *any* individuals undermines criticisms of materialist accounts of resurrection, if those criticisms depend crucially on the supposed implausibility of an appeal to the absence of closest continuers (or, in the case of Johnston's argument against reassembly, closest predecessors).

47. I believe most of those who accept the need for a closest continuer clause in criteria of personal identity would agree that fusion cases should be treated similarly. But I note that Hawley, 2005 contains an interesting argument for treating the cases differently.

48. Some materialists suppose that facts about identity over time, for human persons, do not supervene upon the facts about the behavior of our parts and their causal relations. They can reject a closest continuer account of our persistence conditions; and they will have their own reasons to reject Johnston's duplication principle. Merricks's defense of the compatibility of survival and materialism appeals to the idea that our persistence through time is not determined by the behavior of the matter of which we are made; and O'Connor and Jacobs explicitly use this sort of failure of supervenience to defend a materialist theory of resurrection that does

not commit them to a closest-continuer criterion of identity (their view is not a reassembly theory of resurrection, but a variant of the Falling Elevator Model).

49. See Hershenov, 2003, p. 34. The context of Hershenov's suggestion is the question: what happens if many human beings overlap in the atoms constituting their bodies at death?—something much more likely than precise peri-mortem duplication. So long as not everyone is resurrected at once, he says, there is nothing to worry about. The newly resurrected can ingest, inhale, and in other ways absorb "fresh" matter, gradually freeing up the shared bits of their bodies; soon enough, everyone's peri-mortem state would be reproducible.

50. See Zimmerman, 1999.

51. See Hudson, 2001, ch. 7; Corcoran, 2001b, pp. 201–217; O'Connor and Jacobs, 2010; Hasker, 1999, pp. 224–231; Hershenov, 2002; and Olson, 2010.

52. Johnston's criticisms of the Falling Elevator Model (Johnston, 2010, pp. 106–107) turn upon a misunderstanding at this point. He thinks that the fissionlike process undergone by each atom can only have two interpretations: either every original atom ceases to be, replaced by two duplicates, one in the corpse and one in the hereafter; or else a new atom is left behind on earth, while the original atom jumps away as part of the living body that appears in "the next world." But then of course the corpse really *is* a simulacrum, just as on van Inwagen's "body-snatching" model. My alternative was developed precisely to avoid this result.

53. Zimmerman, 1999, pp. 197–201. For criticism of my argument, see Hasker, 1999, pp. 229–230; for my reply, see Zimmerman, 2010b, pp. 38–44.

54. For discussion, see Redhead and Teller, 1992; and Huggett, 1997.

55. See Saunders, 2006.

56. For the opinions of some well-known contemporary philosophers on the question of God's existence, see Clark, 1993, Morris, 1994, and Antony, 2007.

57. I tried out a version of the argument for Proteanism in 2004, in one of two talks I gave as the Dasturzada Dr. Jal Pavry Memorial Lectures, at Oxford. Later versions were aired at: St. Louis University; a conference on "Persons: Human and Divine," supported by the Pew Christian Scholars Program and hosted by Syracuse University; a conference sponsored by the Institut für Christliche Philosophie, at the University of Innsbruck; The Faraday Institute for Science and Religion, St. Edmond's College, Cambridge; and the 2010 Metaphysical Mayhem at Rutgers. I am grateful for all the discussions that ensued; they greatly influenced the current version, though in ways I can no longer recall with much precision. I am sure I owe debts to the late (great) Bill Alston, Tamar Gendler, Eric Olson, David Hershenov, Ted Sider, and numerous participants in Metaphysical Mayhem, including: Andrew Bailey, Janelle Derstine, Bradley Rettler, and Jeff Russell. One thing I remember clearly is John Hawthorne suggesting to me, when I was first thinking about these issues, that deference to future stages might trump all; and I know that he sharpened my thinking about many parts of the Pro-Proteanism argument. Jens Johansson provided an excellent set of comments that enabled me to catch many mistakes. Pavel Davydov helped me immensely at the eleventh hour, showing me—among other things—the naïveté of my original discussion of indexicals. Although I think that the Pro-Proteanism argument was greatly improved by Davydov's generous advice, I am certain that I have not addressed all of the legitimate concerns he raised. Consequently, (much as I would like to) I cannot hold him responsible for the results.

REFERENCES

Antony, L., ed. 2007. *Philosophers without Gods.* Oxford: Oxford University Press.

Baker, L. 2007. "Persons and the Metaphysics of Resurrection." *Religious Studies* 43: 333–348.

Baker, M., and Goetz, S., eds. 2011. *The Soul Hypothesis.* New York and London: Continuum.

Chisholm, R. 1978. "Is There a Mind-Body Problem?" *Philosophical Exchange* 2: 25–34.

Clark, K., ed. 1993. *Philosophers Who Believe.* Downers Grove, IL: InterVarsity Press.

Collins, R. 2011. "A Scientific Case for the Soul." In Baker, M. and Goetz, S., eds. 2011, pp. 222–246.

Corcoran, K., ed. 2001a. *Soul, Body, and Survival: Essays on the Metaphysics of Human Persons.* Ithaca, NY: Cornell University Press.

Corcoran, K. 2001b. "Physical Persons and Postmortem Survival without Temporal Gaps." In Corcoran, K., ed. 2001a, pp. 201–217.

Edwards, P., ed. 1997. *Immortality.* Amherst, NY: Prometheus.

Flew, A., 2000. *Merely Mortal?* Amherst, NY: Prometheus.

Gasser, G., ed. 2010. *Personal Identity and Resurrection.* Farnham, UK: Ashgate.

Hasker, W. 1999. *The Emergent Self.* Ithaca, NY: Cornell University Press.

Hawley, K. 2005. "Fission, Fusion and Intrinsic Facts." *Philosophy and Phenomenological Research* 71: 602–621.

Hawthorne, J. 2006. *Metaphysical Essays.* Oxford: Clarendon Press.

Hershenov, D. 2002. "Van Inwagen, Zimmerman, and the Materialist Conception of Resurrection." *Religious Studies* 38: 451–469.

Hershenov, D. 2003. "The Metaphysical Problem of Intermittent Existence and the Possibility of Resurrection." *Faith and Philosophy* 20: 24–36.

Hudson, H. 2001. *A Materialist Metaphysics of the Human Person.* Ithaca, NY: Cornell University Press

Huggett, N. 1997. "Identity, Quantum Mechanics and Common Sense." *Monist* 80: 118–130.

Johnston, M. 1989. "Relativism and the Self." In *Relativism: Interpretation and Confrontation,* ed. M. Krausz, pp. 441–472. Notre Dame, IN: University of Notre Dame Press.

Johnston, M. 2010. *Surviving Death.* Princeton, NJ: Princeton University Press.

Kaplan, D. 1989. "Demonstratives" and "Afterthoughts." In *Themes from Kaplan,* ed. Almog, Perry, and Wettstein, pp. 481–614. Oxford: Oxford University Press.

Leftow, B. 2001. "Souls Dipped in Dust." In Corcoran, K., ed. 2001a, pp. 120–138.

Leslie, J. 2007. *Immortality Defended.* Malden, MA: Blackwell.

Lewis, D. 1976. "Survival and Identity." In Rorty, A., ed. 1976, pp. 17–40.

Mackie, D. 1998. "Going Topless." *Ratio* 11: 125–140.

Martin, R. and Barresi, J. 2000. *Naturalization of the Soul.* London: Routledge.

Merricks, T. 2001. "How to Live Forever without Saving Your Soul." In Corcoran, K., ed. 2001a, pp. 183–200.

Morris, T., ed. 1994. *God and the Philosophers.* New York: Oxford University Press.

Nagel, T. 1986. *The View from Nowhere.* New York: Oxford University Press.

Nozick, R. 1981. *Philosophical Explanations.* Cambridge, MA: Harvard University Press.

O'Connor, T., and Jacobs, J. 2010. "Emergent Individuals and the Resurrection." *European Journal for Philosophy of Religion* 2: 69–88.

Oderberg, D. 2005. "Hylemorphic Dualism." In *Personal Identity*, ed. Paul, Miller, and Paul, pp. 70–99. Cambridge: Cambridge University Press.

Olson, E. 1995. "Relativism and Persistence." *Philosophical Studies* 88: 141–162.

Olson, E. 1997. *The Human Animal*. New York: Oxford University Press.

Olson, E. 2001. "A Compound of Two Substances." In Corcoran, K., ed. 2001a, pp. 73–88.

Olson, E. 2007. *What Are We?* New York: Oxford University Press.

Olson, E. 2010. "Immanent Causation and Life after Death." In Gasser, G., ed. 2010, pp. 51–66.

Parfit, D. 1986. *Reasons and Persons*. Oxford: Oxford University Press.

Popper, K., and Eccles, J. 1977. *The Self and Its Brain*. New York: Springer-Verlag.

Prigogine, I. 1980. *From Being to Becoming*. New York: W. H. Freeman and Co.

Quine, W. 1960. *Word and Object*. Cambridge, MA: M.I.T Press.

Redhead, M. and Teller, P. 1992. "Particle Labels and the Theory of Indistinguishable Particles in Quantum Mechanics." *British Journal for the Philosophy of Science* 43: 201–218.

Rey, G. 1976. "Survival." In Rorty, A., ed. 1976, pp. 41–66.

Rorty, A., ed. 1976. *The Identities of Persons*. Berkeley: University of California Press.

Saunders, S. 2006. "Are Quantum Particles Objects?" *Analysis* 66: 52–63

Schechtman, M. 1996. *The Constitution of Selves*. Ithaca, NY: Cornell University Press.

Shoemaker, S. 1997. "Self and Substance." *Philosophical Perspectives, 11 (Mind, Causation, and World)*: 173–184.

Shoemaker, S. 1999. "Self, Body, and Coincidence." *Proceedings of the Aristotelian Society*, supplementary vol. 73: 287–306.

Shoemaker, S. and Swinburne, R. 1984. *Personal Identity*. Oxford: Blackwell.

Sider, T. 2001a. *Four-Dimensionalism*. Oxford: Clarendon Press.

Sider, T. 2001b. "Criteria of Personal Identity and the Limits of Conceptual Analysis." *Philosophical Perspectives* 15 (Metaphysics): 189–209.

Stump, E. 1995. "Non-Cartesian Substance Dualism and Materialism Without Reductionism." *Faith and Philosophy* 12: 503–531.

Stump, E. 2003. *Aquinas*. New York: Routledge.

Stump, E. 2006. "Resurrection, Reassembly, and Reconstitution: Aquinas on the Soul." In *Die menschliche Seele: Brauchen wir den Dualismus?*, ed. Niederberger and Runggaldier, pp. 151–172. Frankfurt: Ontos Verlag.

Swinburne, R. 1986. *The Evolution of the Soul*. Oxford: Clarendon Press.

Tippler, F. 1994. *The Physics of Immortality*. New York: Doubleday.

Unger, P. 1990. *Identity, Consciousness and Value*. New York: Oxford University Press.

Van Dyke, C. 2007. "Human Identity, Immanent Causal Relations, and the Principle of Non-Repeatability: Thomas Aquinas on the Bodily Resurrection." *Religious Studies* 43: 373–394.

van Inwagen, P. 1990. *Material Beings*. Ithaca, NY: Cornell University Press.

van Inwagen, P. 1998. *The Possibility of Resurrection*. Boulder, CO: Westview Press.

Williams, B. 1970. "The Self and the Future." *Philosophical Review* 79: 161–180.

Zimmerman, D. 1998. "Criteria of Identity and the 'Identity Mystics.'" *Erkenntnis* 48: 281–301.

Zimmerman, D. 1999 "The Compatibility of Materialism and Survival: The 'Falling Elevator' Model." *Faith and Philosophy* 16: 194–212.

Zimmerman, D. 2010a. "From Property Dualism to Substance Dualism." *Proceedings of the Aristotelian Society*, supplementary vol. 84: 119–150.

Zimmerman, D. 2010b. "Bodily Resurrection: The Falling Elevator Model Revisited." In Gasser, G., ed. 2010, pp. 33–50.

Zimmerman, D. 2006. "Dualism in the Philosophy of Mind." In *Encyclopedia of Philosophy*, 2nd ed., ed. Borchert, D., pp. 113–122. NY: Macmillan.

CHAPTER 5

THE EVIL OF DEATH

WHAT CAN METAPHYSICS CONTRIBUTE?

THEODORE SIDER

WILL a clear view of what death *is* help us decide whether it is bad? Not necessarily. The discovery that death = X might instead affect our appraisal of X, leaving our appraisal of death untouched.

Learning which quantum theory correctly describes human bodies would not affect anyone's attitude toward his or her loved ones. On the other hand, a child's discovery of the nature of meat (or an adult's discovery of the nature of soylent green) can have a great effect. In still other cases, it is hard to say how one would, or should, react to new information about the underlying nature of what we value—think of how mixed our reactions are to evidence of cultural determinism or atheism, or of how mixed our reactions would be to learning that we all live in the Matrix. (Maybe there is no objective fact about how we should react. Derek Parfit's (1984, section 95) fear of death diminished when he became convinced of certain theses about the metaphysics of personal identity. Perhaps there is no objective fact of the matter as to whether this was rational; perhaps it was rational for him but would not be for others.)

What can metaphysics contribute to the question of the evil of death? It cannot, on its own, settle the question, since there is no simple rule telling us how to adjust value in light of new information about underlying nature. Given a clear view of the nature of death, there will remain the question of its disvalue. However, metaphysics can help us attain this clear view. Moreover, a clear conception of what metaphysical positions do and don't say, and a clear conception of how metaphysics works in general, can remove impediments to a rational appraisal of the evil of death.

1. How Metaphysics Works

One of the tasks of metaphysics, as traditionally conceived, is to investigate Ultimate Reality, what "lies behind the appearances." When a certain apple is red, what is the underlying nature of this fact? Does a certain particular, the apple, instantiate a universal of redness; or does a certain bundle of universals (or tropes) contain the universal (trope) redness; or does the fact not involve a universal at all, as a nominalist would have it? Should we think of the apple, ultimately, as being an aggregate of temporal parts, the current among which is red? Or perhaps the ultimate description of reality should not mention the apple at all; perhaps all that ultimately exist are subatomic particles, some of which are "arranged applewise," as Peter van Inwagen (1990) would say.

How to think about this traditional task of metaphysics is itself a metaphysical question.[1] But it's hard to make any sense at all out of metaphysics unless one makes *something* like this distinction: a distinction between the way the world ordinarily (manifestly, apparently) is, and the way the world ultimately (fundamentally, really) is.

There is a vexed question about how to describe the first side of this distinction: the notion of the world *ordinarily* being a certain way. I want to count the existence of the apple, and its being red, as part of the way the world ordinarily is. But suppose the ultimate description of reality makes no reference to apples, and instead makes reference only to subatomic particles. What, then, is the status of the English sentence, "there is a red apple"? Certain hard-liners would say that it is false. Their attitude is like Eddington's (1928) toward his table: since, as physics tells us, matter is mostly empty space, the ordinary English sentence "the table is solid" is false. Liberals about Eddington's table say instead that the English sentence "the table is solid" is true even though matter is mostly empty space. Common sense is mistaken about what it takes to be solid, but not about whether tables are solid. Similarly, liberals would say, the English sentence "there is an apple that is red" is true even though *ultimately* there are no apples. Though my sympathies are with the liberals, I don't want to take a stand on who is correct. So let's understand the notion of the world "ordinarily" being a certain way neutrally; "There is a red apple" is part of the ordinary description of the world whether or not it is true in English.[2]

There is another vexed question, about how to understand "underlying." In what sense do the fundamental facts underlie the ordinary facts? Some metaphysicians say that the ordinary facts hold *in virtue of* the fundamental facts, others speak of *supervenience*, and still others speak of *truthmaking*. I don't want to take a stand on any of this; but I do want to mention one thing that "underlying" does *not* mean: it has nothing to do with "paraphrase" or conceptual analysis. An old tradition, tracing at least back to Russell (1905), holds that a principal task of philosophy is to clarify the structure of our thoughts and sentences by analyzing, in a more perspicuous form, what we mean by them. But a metaphysical account of the underlying nature of X is not intended as an account of what we mean by our talk about X, any more than a quantum theory of the underlying nature of apples, persons, and other physical objects is intended as a theory of what we mean by our talk of those objects.

So, fundamental metaphysics gives an account of the ultimate reality that underlies ordinary facts. These ordinary facts are the ones we're familiar with in everyday life, the facts that we commonly take ourselves to be truly reporting using ordinary sentences such as "the table is solid" and "the apple is red." Liberals and hard-liners may disagree over whether these sentences really are true, but it's undeniable that there are *some* facts *in the vicinity*; these are what I'm calling the "ordinary facts"; and the task of fundamental metaphysics is to discover what underlies them.

Ignoring the distinction between ordinary and underlying facts can lead to distortions of the ethical significance of metaphysical views. To take an example, return again to the metaphysical position according to which all that exists, ultimately, is subatomic particles. It would be too quick to say that given this metaphysics death never occurs (since there exist no people to die) and is therefore not an evil. To say that the metaphysics implies that "death never occurs" would be to assimilate the bearing of this metaphysics on death to the bearing on death of an afterlife. Intuitively, the two are quite different. Discovering that there is an afterlife is the kind of discovery about death's nature that would lead us to reevaluate its evil; it would be like discovering the nature of meat or soylent green. Discovering that death is, ultimately, a change in the arrangement of particles rather than, ultimately, the disappearance from fundamental reality of the object that is the deceased, would also be a discovery about the nature of death, but it would seem to be more like discovering the quantum nature of our bodies, and need not lead us to reevaluate death's evil. Thus a bald statement of a metaphysical position—"no persons exist, only subatomic particles!"—without attention to its intended status, as a description of ultimate reality rather than ordinary facts, is apt to distort its significance.

Of course, even when metaphysical views are understood in this way, one might hold that they nevertheless have ethical significance. It's open to argue that the thesis that the world consists, ultimately, of subatomic particles implies moral nihilism, just as it's open to argue that certain physical theories imply moral nihilism. (Consider, for example, the version of quantum mechanics according to which the world consists ultimately of a single particle moving through configuration space (Albert, 1996).) My point is just that if these ethical conclusions are to be drawn, they must be drawn with the distinction between ordinary facts and their underlying reality clearly in view.

2. THE METAPHYSICS OF TIME

The metaphysics of time, in particular, has been thought to bear on the evil of death. The issues are easiest to approach by contrasting two polar opposite conceptions of time.[3]

According to the first, time is like space, on a variety of fronts. First, in terms of existence: past and future objects are equally real. Second, in terms of parts: objects have temporal in addition to spatial parts. Third, in terms of "perspective": just as the fundamental spatial facts are as described from an aspatial perspective—"x is five feet from y" rather than "x is here" or "y is far away"—so the fundamental temporal facts are as described from an atemporal perspective: "x occurred before y" rather than "y is occurring now" or "x occurred in the past."

According to the second, time is unlike space, and should rather be thought of as being analogous to modality (at least, analogous to the way most people think of modality; David Lewis [1986] is a notable exception). In terms of existence: merely past and future objects do not exist, just as merely possible objects do not exist. Just as there simply do not exist any golden mountains (although there could have), there simply do not exist any dinosaurs or human outposts on Mars, (although there did and perhaps will, respectively). In terms of parts: objects do not have temporal parts. Objects are not spread out over time, just as objects are not spread out across possible worlds. In terms of perspective: just as the fundamental facts are those that hold from the perspective of the actual world (Lewis, of course, denies this), so, the fundamental facts are those that hold from the perspective of the present time.

The labels of "four-dimensionalism" (or "the B-theory") and "presentism" (or "the A-theory") go along with these two pictures, although terminology is inconsistent.[4] Now, the components of these perspectives are, to some degree, independent. Thus one can hold, with the four-dimensionalist, that past and future objects exist and that the atemporal perspective is fundamental, while holding with the presentist that objects lack temporal parts; or one can hold with the presentist that the present perspective is the fundamental one and that objects lack temporal parts, while admitting the existence of past and future objects. Further, there are additional contrasts beyond those of existence, parts, and perspective.[5] Further, there are many hybrid views, for example those that treat the past differently from the future. But for present purposes, just the two polar conceptions will suffice.

Let me clarify these conceptions by looking carefully at their fundamental descriptions of temporal reality. The four-dimensionalist's description uses the conceptual resources of predicate logic. She takes the domain of her most unrestricted quantifiers to include objects drawn from the past, present, and future (just as we all take the domain of our most unrestricted quantifiers to include spatially distant objects). Thus the four-dimensionalist accepts, in her fundamental theory, sentences like "there are dinosaurs" and "there are human outposts on Mars," as well as "there are computers." And she feels free to introduce a proper name, in her fundamental language, to stand for any member of that domain, regardless of its location in time. Thus she might introduce a name s for Socrates, in addition to a name b for Barack Obama (provided she did not hold the view mentioned earlier, that only subatomic particles are ultimately real). Further, she takes her domain of entities to include temporal parts. For instance, she will accept the existence of a certain temporal part s_h of Socrates when he is drinking hemlock, as well as the existence of a certain temporal part b_i of Obama while he is being inaugurated as president of the United States. Further, the sentences that she accepts are those that are true "from the atemporal perspective." For example:

(H) s_h drinks Hemlock
(I) b_i is inaugurated

Three points about (H) and (I): first, note the symmetry between them, even though Socrates is in the distant past and Obama is in the present. Each consists of a simple attribution of a property to an entity. Second, these sentences are intended to lack tense—to be tenseless descriptions of four-dimensional reality.[6] Third, notice that even though drinking hemlock and being inaugurated are temporary properties of persisting entities (such as people), they can nevertheless be attributed simpliciter (rather than relative to a time) to the temporal parts s_h and b_i, since those temporal parts are instantaneous.[7] Continuing with our overview of the four-dimensionalist's fundamental description of the world: descriptions of temporal facts (such as the fact that Socrates is in the past) call for no new logical resources beyond those of predicate logic, nor do they require privileging the perspective of any one time. Rather, they require describing the locations of objects within the four-dimensional space-time manifold. For example, the four-dimensionalist might introduce a two-place predicate, *is temporally before*, and say: s_h is before b_i. To indicate that both s_h and b_i are in the past, a four-dimensionalist might introduce a name, c, for her current temporal part, and say: s_h is before c and b_i is before c. And to express the fundamental fact that underlies the ordinary claim "there no longer exist dinosaurs," she might say: "No dinosaurs are simultaneous with c; all dinosaurs are located before c."

The presentist's fundamental description of reality is quite different. This is not to say that there is no overlap. The presentist does accept the logical apparatus of first-order logic, and will therefore quantify over, name, and ascribe features to objects in a domain. But even when his quantifiers are wholly unrestricted, he will deny that the domain of those quantifiers includes any merely past or future objects. So although he will accept "there exist computers," he will *not* accept "there exist dinosaurs" or "there exist human outposts on Mars." Relatedly, he will not include, in his fundamental language, proper names of merely past or future entities (such as Socrates), since no such entities exist according to him.[8] (This is not to say that he objects to proper names like "Socrates" *in descriptions of ordinary facts*; see below.) Further, he does not admit temporal parts. Further— and this is crucial—in order to express temporal claims (such as the fact that there once existed dinosaurs), he introduces tense operators. These are new logical expressions, in addition to those from predicate logic. Grammatically, they are like modal operators in that they form grammatical sentences when prefixed to grammatical sentences. One tense operator is P, read as "it was the case in the past that"; another is F, read "it will be the case in the future that." The presentist describes the past and future using these and other tense operators. For example, he would describe the ordinary fact that there once existed dinosaurs by saying, in his fundamental language:

(D)   P (there exists a dinosaur)

Intuitively, this means that the embedded sentence "there exists a dinosaur" is true with respect to some time in the past. However, the presentist denies that this intuitive gloss is any kind of metaphysical reduction. Rather, the tense operators are metaphysically unanalyzeable; the fact expressed by (D) is rock-bottom, metaphysically speaking. (Compare: many of Lewis's opponents say that the fact that ◊ (there exists a golden mountain) is metaphysically rock-bottom; the modal operators □ and ◊ are metaphysically unanalyzeable.) Notice how the idea that "the present perspective is fundamental" emerges here: there is an asymmetry between how the presentist describes facts about the past and future, on the one hand, and facts about the present on the other. The past and future must be described using sentences prefixed with tense operators, such as (D) and "F(there exist human outposts on Mars)," whereas the present is described using sentences without tense operators, such as "Ted is typing." Each sentence describes reality from the point of view of the present; when a sentence is prefixed with a tense operator, it describes the past or future from the point of view of the present, so to speak.

3. TIME AND DEATH

One of the traditional puzzles about the evil of death is: how can death be bad for those who have died, given that they no longer exist? A natural reply, given by Thomas Nagel (1970) and many others, is that dying is bad because it *deprives* the deceased of the goods of life. But this reply is sometimes argued to fail on metaphysical grounds, or else to require further metaphysics if it is to succeed. For, it is said, the proposed answer leaves the central puzzle unresolved. Perhaps it has resolved one puzzle, namely, that of how death can be bad when dead people have no "positive" states; its answer is that the evil of death isn't a positive state but rather a deprivation. But the central puzzle is, allegedly, that of how death can be bad when dead people have *no properties at all*. The dead do not exist, it is said, and so do not have any properties at all, not even the property of being deprived of the goods of life. The proposed solution simply presupposes that the dead do have the property of being deprived of the goods of life, and hence is no solution at all, at least not without the introduction of some further metaphysics.

That further metaphysics could be provided in different ways. According to Harry S. Silverstein (1980, 2000), it is provided by four-dimensionalist metaphysics. For the four-dimensionalist, the dead exist atemporally, in the sense of being included in the domain of the unrestricted quantifier in the four-dimensionalist's fundamental language. The dead have the same ontological status as spatially distant planets, according to the four-dimensionalist, and so it is unproblematic to ascribe properties to them. According to Palle Yourgrau (1987, 2000), it is provided by a distinction between being and existence.[9] Yourgrau's view is, in essence, the result of beginning with the presentist position I sketched earlier, but then adding that even though there do not *exist* past and future entities, there *are* past and future entities. Even though the dead do not exist, they nevertheless *are*, and hence are capable of having properties.

Silverstein and Yourgrau have, I believe, metaphysically coherent views about death; but I don't think that either of these views *needs* to be adopted if one is to say that death is an evil for the dead. To bring this out, it will help to consider a precise version of the deprivation thesis. According to Fred Feldman (1991), a state of affairs in general (whether concerning death or something else) is bad for a person if and only if that person's entire life would have been better for her if the state of affairs had not occurred than if it had occurred. Death is no different: death is bad (when it is bad) because the deceased's entire life would have been better if she hadn't died. For example, Princess Diana's untimely death was bad for her because:

(F) Princess Diana's entire life would have been better for her, had she not died when she did, than it in fact was.

What I want to argue is that Feldman's account of the evil of death does not depend on four-dimensionalist or Yourgrauian metaphysics (though it is consistent with each). In particular, Feldman's account could be combined with (non-Yourgrauian) presentist metaphysics.

Presentism is a claim about the ultimate nature of time. Thus it provides an account of the ultimate reality that underlies ordinary claims about time. For example, what underlies the ordinary claim that there once existed dinosaurs is the tensed claim: P(there exist dinosaurs). Now, when Feldman proposes that (F) is the ground of the evil of Diana's death, I do not take this as being intended in a metaphysical spirit, as assuming any particular stance on the ultimate nature of the underlying facts. I rather read his claim (F) as being neutral on fundamental metaphysics. (Similarly, I read him as being neutral on the underlying physics of (F).) Read in this spirit, Feldman's proposal is simply that (F), understood as a claim of *ordinary fact*, is what explains the evil of Diana's death. Assuming that presentism is compatible with (F) thus understood, presentism is compatible with Feldman's proposal.

But is presentism compatible with ordinary facts such as (F)? It has been alleged that presentism is incompatible with the truth of *any* sentence containing a proper name of a merely past (or future) entity, in which case presentism would preclude (F). The argument is simple: since proper names are "directly referential," as Kaplan (1989) and Kripke (1972) have argued, any proposition expressed by a sentence containing a proper names is a "singular" proposition, which contains the referent of the proper name as a constituent; thus sentences containing proper names for past entities do not express propositions, given presentism, and so cannot be true.[10]

This argument ignores the distinction between ordinary and underlying facts. The direct reference theory of proper names is best taken, by the metaphysician, in the same spirit as *all* claims of ordinary fact: as the appearances whose underlying reality is up for metaphysical investigation. Recall the metaphysician who thinks that all that ultimately exists are subatomic particles. Still, this metaphysician does not deny the ordinary fact that there are apples, tables, and chairs; she just holds that the ultimate reality that underlies this ordinary fact does not involve apples, tables, and chairs. Think, next, about what such a metaphysician would say to the direct reference theorist's claim "the sentence 'Alfie the apple is red' expresses a singular proposition containing Alfie as a constituent." Her attitude toward this sentence will be parallel to her attitude toward the simpler sentence "Alfie is red." Each corresponds to an ordinary fact, and each of these ordinary facts is made true by an ultimate reality that does not involve any such object as Alfie.

Similarly, the presentist is not committed to denying ordinary facts about merely past entities, such as the fact that Socrates drank hemlock or the fact expressed by (F); nor is she committed to denying the ordinary fact (assuming, with Kaplan and Kripke, that it is a fact) that (F) expresses a singular proposition about Diana. What she is committed to is the claim that these ordinary facts are made true by an ultimate reality that does not include Socrates or any other merely past objects.

This ultimate reality includes a multitude of tensed truths, truths expressed by sentences prefixed by tense operators, which describe—in this distinctive, tensed, way—in full detail the entire past. Let F be the fundamental fact—expressible by a long or perhaps even infinite conjunction of tensed sentences—that underlies (F). F is not a singular fact about Diana. (A sentence expressing F, in the presentist's fundamental language, would not contain a proper name for Diana, since this language contains no names for merely past individuals.) Now, one could try to argue that for this reason, F cannot ground the evil of Diana's death. But on the face of it, this would be like arguing that Diana's death can't be bad for her if all that exist ultimately are subatomic particles. It would be like drawing conclusions about the value of loved ones on the basis of a quantum theory of their bodies. On the face of it, although we are indeed entitled to assume that whatever grounds the evil of Diana's death must *in the ordinary sense* concern Diana herself, we are not entitled to assume that whatever grounds the evil of death must *fundamentally* concern the entity Diana herself.

To reiterate this point: there is a sense in which the underlying presentist meta-physics of (F) is "purely general" (at least with respect to Diana): the conjunctive sentence in the presentist's fundamental language that expresses *F* does not men-tion Diana by name. But this should not be equated—at least not without further argument—with (F) being purely general in the ordinary sense. Presentism is fully compatible with there being a big difference between singular ordinary facts, like the ordinary fact expressed by (F), and general ordinary facts, like the ordinary fact expressed by sentences like "there existed some person, with such-and-such characteristics, whose entire life would have been better had she not died than it was in fact." All that presentism implies is that there is a broad similarity between their underlying metaphysics; the underlying metaphysics of each is, fundamen-tally, purely general (except with respect to presently existing entities).

I have been arguing that we must keep in mind the distinction between ordinary facts and underlying reality, when we evaluate the ethical implications of metaphysical theses. We must also keep this distinction in mind when we decide which fundamen-tal metaphysics to accept. Yourgrau argues against four-dimensionalism by saying:

> I find it exceedingly difficult to give up my intuition that dead people simply do not exist...And I do not mean merely that the dead do not now exist; for objects in time, what does not exist now does not exist at all. (Yourgrau, 1987, pp. 87–88)

Now, this may be a persuasive argument; but it must be properly understood. Remember that sentences in the four-dimensionalist's fundamental language are understood as describing reality atemporally; thus the mapping between four-dimensionalist talk and tensed ordinary talk is not straightforward. In par-ticular, although it is true that the four-dimensionalist accepts "dead people exist" (and "dinosaurs exist," and so on) in her fundamental language, these claims can-not be equated with similar-sounding ordinary claims. The ordinary claim that "Socrates exists" (for example), is present-tensed, and equivalent to "Socrates *still* exists." And the underlying four-dimensionalist metaphysics of this sentence is that Socrates has temporal parts that are simultaneous with our current temporal parts, which is of course not true.[11] Now, Yourgrau is aware of this, as is evidenced by his use of "*simply* does not exist" and "does not exist *at all*" to mark his disagreement with the four-dimensionalist; and it is open to him to claim that "intuition" informs him that fundamental reality does not contain existing dead people. All I ask is that the content of this alleged intuition be made clear, and that it not be conflated with the ordinary belief that dead people no longer exist.

4. CONCLUSION

I have argued that fundamental metaphysics is a search for the fundamental real-ity that underlies ordinary facts; I have argued that the relationship between the-ses of fundamental metaphysics and questions of value is not a straightforward or mechanical one; I have described two metaphysical views about the nature of time, presentism and four-dimensionalism; and I have argued that, properly under-stood, presentism is consistent with the idea that death is bad because it deprives the deceased of the goods of life.

Nothing I have said addresses the deep and difficult questions about the evil of death. Philosophers like Nagel and Feldman say that death is bad because of what it costs us, that facts of the form *a certain person's entire life would have been better, had she not died* ground the evil of death. All I have done is clarify what the metaphysician has to say about the "metaphysical structure" of such facts. The real questions are about the structure of our values, and they remain to be answered: do such facts explain why it is so bad to die?[12]

NOTES

1. See, for example, Schaffer, 2009; Sider, 2011; and especially Fine, 2001.
2. My own view is that the dispute between hard-liners and liberals is irrelevant to our present concern, and indeed, to nearly all questions aside from those of metasemantics. See Sider Forthcoming.
3. The first view is prominently associated with J. J. C. Smart (1963, chapter 7, 1972) and W. V. O. Quine (1950, 1960, section 36), and the latter with Arthur Prior (1967, 1968, 1970, 1976, 1996). For more on these issues, see Sider, 2001, and Sider, 2011, chapter 11.
4. For example, in my 2001 I used "four-dimensionalism" to stand for the mere acceptance of temporal parts, rather than for the whole first conception; and "the A-theory" is sometimes used just for the view that the present perspective is fundamental.
5. See, for instance, Hawthorne, 2006; Fine, 2006.
6. It may be that under a full syntactic analysis, all English sentences are tensed; in that case, the four-dimensionalist might prefer to replace the English sentences (H) and (I) with sentences of predicate logic: Hs_h, Ib_i.
7. See Lewis, 1986, pp. 202–204.
8. And since he regards his fundamental language as obeying classical logic, according to which the sentence $\exists x\, x = a$ is a logical truth, for each proper name a.
9. The distinction is in the tradition of Meinong and Parsons (1980), but differs importantly since Yourgrau rejects incomplete and impossible objects, and argues for his view on metaphysical, not semantic, grounds.
10. For more on this and related issues, see Sider, 1999.
11. Compare Silverstein, 2000, pp. 124–127.
12. Thanks to Ben Bradley, Fred Feldman, and Palle Yourgrau for comments and guidance.

REFERENCES

Albert, David Z. 1996. "Elementary Quantum Metaphysics." In J. T. Cushing, A. Fine and S. Goldstein (eds.), *Bohmian Mechanics and Quantum Theory: An Appraisal*, pp. 277–284. Dordrecht: Kluwer Academic Publishers.

Eddington, Arthur Stanley. 1928. *The Nature of the Physical World*. New York: Macmillan.

Feldman, Fred. 1991. "Some Puzzles about the Evil of Death." *Philosophical Review* 100: 205–227.

Fine, Kit. 2001. "The Question of Realism." *Philosopher's Imprint* 1: 1–30.

Fine, Kit. 2006. "In Defense of Three-Dimensionalism." *Journal of Philosophy* 103: 699–714.

Haslanger, Sally and Roxanne Marie Kurtz (eds.). 2006. *Persistence: Contemporary Readings*. Cambridge, MA: MIT Press.

Hawthorne, John. 2006. "Three-Dimensionalism." In his *Metaphysical Essays*, pp. 85–110. Oxford: Oxford University Press.

Kaplan, David. 1989. "Demonstratives." In Joseph Almog, John Perry and Howard Wettstein (eds.), *Themes from Kaplan*, pp. 481–563. New York: Oxford University Press.

Kripke, Saul. 1972. "Naming and Necessity." In Donald Davidson and Gilbert Harman (eds.), *Semantics of Natural Language*, pp. 253–355, 763–769. Dordrecht: D. Reidel. Revised edition published in 1980 as *Naming and Necessity* (Cambridge, MA: Harvard University Press).

Lewis, David. 1986. *On the Plurality of Worlds*. Oxford: Basil Blackwell.

Nagel, Thomas. 1970. "Death." *Noûs* 4: 73–80.

Parfit, Derek. 1984. *Reasons and Persons*. Oxford: Clarendon.

Parsons, Terence. 1980. *Nonexistent Objects*. New Haven: Yale University Press.

Prior, A. N. 1967. *Past, Present, and Future*. Oxford: Oxford University Press.

Prior, A. N. 1968. *Papers on Time and Tense*. Oxford: Oxford University Press.

Prior, A. N. 1970. "The Notion of the Present." *Studium Generale* 23: 245–248.

Prior, A. N. 1976. "Thank Goodness That's Over." In his *Papers in Logic and Ethics*, pp. 78–84. London: Duckworth.

Prior, A. N. 1996. "Some Free Thinking about Time." In Jack Copeland (ed.), *Logic and Reality: Essays on the Legacy of Arthur Prior*, pp. 47–51. Oxford: Clarendon Press.

Quine, W. V. O. 1950. "Identity, Ostension, and Hypostasis." *Journal of Philosophy* 47: 621–633. Reprinted in Quine 1953: 65–79.

Quine, W. V. O. 1953. *From a Logical Point of View*. Cambridge, MA: Harvard University Press.

Quine, W. V. O. 1960. *Word and Object*. Cambridge, MA: MIT Press.

Russell, Bertrand. 1905. "On Denoting." *Mind* 14: 479–493.

Schaffer, Jonathan. 2009. "On What Grounds What." In David Chalmers, David Manley and Ryan Wasserman (eds.), *Metametaphysics*, pp. 347–383. Oxford: Oxford University Press.

Sider, Theodore. 1999. "Presentism and Ontological Commitment." *Journal of Philosophy* 96: 325–347. Reprinted in Haslanger and Kurtz 2006: 367–391.

Sider, Theodore. 2001. *Four-Dimensionalism*. Oxford: Clarendon Press.

Sider, Theodore. 2011. *Writing the Book of the World*. Oxford: Clarendon Press.

Sider, Theodore. Forthcoming. "Against Parthood." In Karen Bennett and Dean W. Zimmerman (eds.), *Oxford Studies in Metaphysics, volume 8*.

Silverstein, Harry S. 1980. "The Evil of Death." *Journal of Philosophy* 77: 401–424.

Silverstein, Harry S. 2000. "The Evil of Death Revisited." *Midwest Studies in Philosophy* 24: 116–134.

Smart, J. J. C. 1963. *Philosophy and Scientific Realism*. London: Routledge & Kegan Paul.

Smart, J. J. C. 1972. "Space-Time and Individuals." In Richard Rudner and Israel Scheffler (eds.), *Logic and Art: Essays in Honor of Nelson Goodman*, pp. 3–20. New York: Macmillan.

van Inwagen, Peter. 1990. *Material Beings*. Ithaca, NY: Cornell University Press.

Yourgrau, Palle. 1987. "The Dead." *Journal of Philosophy* 84: 84–101.

Yourgrau, Palle. 2000. "Can the Dead Really Be Buried? " *Midwest Studies in Philosophy* 24: 46–68.

CHAPTER 6

DEATH AND ETERNAL RECURRENCE

LARS BERGSTRÖM

MANY people—perhaps the vast majority of mankind—seem to believe that there is some kind of life after death. This is remarkable, if only because corpses appear to be so completely dead. Some people believe that each person has an immaterial soul that somehow lives on when the body is transformed into a corpse, but this is unlikely in view of the fact that a person's mental life appears to be intimately connected with what happens in his or her brain. Even so, there is perhaps some other way in which we might survive death.

The belief in some kind of afterlife may of course be an instance of wishful thinking, but it is unclear to what extent a life after death is something to be wished for. To wish for good things—at least if one believes that they are at all possible—is perhaps not irrational, but it is not so obvious that life after death would be a good thing. It is very unclear what kind of life it could be. In this chapter I shall explore the idea that life after death is exactly the same as life before death. This follows from the theory of *eternal recurrence*. Eternal recurrence—or "eternal return," as it is sometimes called—can be described in different ways; roughly, the basic idea is that the whole history of the universe has happened before and will happen again; cosmic history is cyclic, with no beginning and no end. In particular, whenever someone dies, he or she will be born again in the next cycle of cosmic history. So even if all of us die, our death is never definitive. There is always an afterlife, and this afterlife is just like the life we live before death. In one sense, we are certainly mortal—but, in another sense, we are also immortal.

The idea that everything has happened before and will happen again may seem very implausible, but many philosophers have been attracted to it, and it used to be held by many people in earlier times. For traditional man, time was cyclical in the sense that life consisted in the repetition of archetypes; for example, each year (often in the spring) men abandoned the past and started all over again, thereby achieving purification and recreation.[1] The distinguished historian of religions Mircea Eliade, in his book *The Myth of the Eternal Return*, writes as follows:

> This cyclical conception of the disappearance and reappearance of humanity is also preserved in the historical cultures. In the third century B. C., Berossus popularized the Chaldean doctrine of the "Great Year" in a form that spread through the entire Hellenic world (whence it later passed to the Romans and the Byzantines). According to this doctrine, the universe is eternal but it is periodically destroyed and reconstituted every Great Year (the corresponding number of millennia varies from school to school). (Eliade, 1955, p. 87)

Eliade approvingly quotes another author as follows:

> According to the celebrated Platonic definition, time, which determines and measures the revolution of the celestial spheres, is the moving image of unmoving eternity, which it imitates by revolving in a circle. [...] No event is unique, occurs once and for all (for example the condemnation and death of Socrates), but it has occurred, occurs, and will occur, perpetually; the same individuals have appeared, appear, and reappear at every return of the cycle upon itself. Cosmic duration is repetition and *anakuklosis*, eternal return.[2] (Eliade, 1955, p. 89)

Eliade also says that "the eternal return—the periodic resumption, by all beings, of their former lives [...] is one of the few dogmas of which we know with some certainty that they formed a part of primitive Pythagoreanism" (Eliade, 1955, p. 120); and "the Greek theory of eternal return is the final variant undergone by the myth of the repetition of an archetypal gesture, just as the Platonic doctrine of Ideas was the final version of the archetype concept, and the most fully elaborated" (Eliade, 1955, p. 123).[3]

In later years, the belief in eternal recurrence appears to have become much less widespread. This is probably because of the overwhelming influence of Jewish and Christian conceptions of cosmic history as linear and bounded by two unique events: Creation and Last Judgment.[4] But some philosophers, notably Nietzsche,[5] have been attracted to the idea, and it seems to have been accepted by C. S. Peirce.[6] In one place, Nietzsche sketches an argument for eternal recurrence as follows:

> If the world may be thought of as a certain definite quantity of force and as a certain definite number of centers of force—and every other representation remains indefinite and therefore useless—it follows that, in the great dice game of existence, it must pass through a calculable number of combinations. In infinite time, every possible combination would at some time or another be realized; more: it would be realized an infinite number of times. And since between every combination and its next recurrence all other possible combinations would have to take place, and each of these combinations conditions the entire sequence of combinations in the same series, a circular movement of absolutely identical series is thus demonstrated: the world as a circular movement that has already repeated itself infinitely often and plays its game in infinitum. (Nietzsche, 1968, p. 549)

Peirce seems to have reasoned in a similar way.[7] Anders Wedberg claims that paragraph 1066 of *Der Wille zur Macht*—from which the above quotation is taken—can be interpreted to contain five postulates from which the eternal recurrence can be strictly derived. The five postulates are (in my translation):

P1. Time is the infinite and unbounded sequence of discrete moments T $= \ldots, t_{-2}, t_{-1}, t_0, t_1, t_2, \ldots$ (where a "moment" may be a point or a certain short interval of time).

P2. At each moment in T, there occurs exactly one of the states in the set Σ, where Σ is the finite set of all the possible total states of affairs.

P3. Each state in Σ occurs as some moment in T.

P4. Σ is a finite set $\{s_1, s_2, s_3, \ldots, s_p\}$.

P5. If the same state occurs at t_i and t_j, then there is a state in Σ that occurs at both t_{i+1} and t_{j+1}.

Wedberg shows in detail that, if P1, P2, and P3 are satisfied, then the conjunction of P4 and P5 is equivalent to eternal recurrence, that is, the thesis that there exists a specific sequence S of the states in Σ, such that the history of the world has the form…SSSSSS…But Wedberg also notes that, while Nietzsche himself regarded P4 as the most problematic of the postulates, each of P1, P2, P4, and P5 can very well be questioned (Wedberg, 1968, pp. 69–74).

Most people today may be inclined to dismiss the doctrine of eternal recurrence as pure fantasy. However, one may wonder if it can be refuted by rational arguments. To some extent, this depends upon the exact version of the doctrine, and it also depends upon the nature of time and other cosmological facts—and these are matters upon which there appears to be no solid and convincing consensus among the experts.

1. RECURRENCE IN LINEAR TIME

We ordinarily think of time as linear; that is, we believe it can be represented by a line, where the points on the line represent moments or instants of time.[8] The line may or may not be bounded, in one end or in both. Eternal recurrence in linear time would mean that time is infinite, and that the history of the universe is finite, but occurs over and over again, without beginning and/or without end. Each occurrence of cosmic history[9] is qualitatively exactly like every other, the only difference is that they occur at different times.[10]

Given what we currently believe about the universe, it appears that eternal recurrence in linear time is not to be expected. In particular, physicists seem to hold that the world is not completely deterministic. If it is not, it seems very unlikely that the whole cosmic history would be qualitatively the same whenever it occurs. Besides, even if it were true that whenever it comes to an "end" it always "begins" all over again, we have no reason to believe that it will always begin in exactly the same way as before.

This talk of a beginning and an end of cosmic history may be bewildering. In one sense, eternal recurrence means that there is no beginning and no end. Clearly, however, the idea is that there is a *sequence* of cosmic histories, where every element in the sequence has a beginning and an end, but where there is perhaps no beginning and no end to the sequence itself. We might imagine that each instance of cosmic history begins with a Big Bang and ends with a Big Crunch or Heat Death (maximum entropy). But there seems to be no particular reason why one should expect there to be more than one instance of cosmic history—unless one finds it hard to believe that there is simply no time, or just empty (but infinite) time, before and after a single (finite) cosmic history.

2. CLOSED TIME

A completely different idea is that time is not linear, but closed (or "circular" or "cyclic"). If so, it can be represented by a circle, or some other closed curve, rather than by a straight line.[11] The idea is that if we move from one instant or moment of time to a later moment, and so on, and so on, we will ultimately arrive at the very same moment that we started from. Someone might express this latter thought by saying that time itself recurs or repeats itself.

However, some philosophers say that a time cannot recur or repeat itself, since this would mean that one and the same time occurs at different times—while in fact each time can occur only once.[12] This objection is not very strong. We may be inclined to agree that a time does not occur at different times, but this is perhaps mainly because a time does not "occur" (at some time) at all. Rather, the idea that a time, t, recurs must be taken to mean that there is some sequence of times, $<x_1, x_2, \ldots, x_n>$, where each x_{i+1} is later than x_i, such that $t = x_1 = x_n$.[13]

The relation *later than* is usually taken to be irreflexive, asymmetric, and transitive. But if time is closed, these assumptions are problematic. For irreflexivity as well as asymmetry implies that, for every time t, t is not later than t, whereas if times "recur" in the sense just indicated, transitivity would imply that t is later than t. We would have a contradiction on our hands. So it might seem that, if time is closed, either irreflexivity and asymmetry or transitivity must be given up.

We can hardly stay away from the relation *later than* altogether, for this relation (or something equivalent) seems to be absolutely essential for our notion of time. However, W. H. Newton-Smith claims that "no two-term relation will be adequate for characterizing order in a closed structure" (Newton-Smith, 1980, p. 59). As a matter of fact, he seems to think that if time is closed, it has no direction—since each time is later than every other time, and each time is even later than itself.[14] This is strange in view of the fact that he himself points out that positing closed time would require a distinction between *locally before*, which is an asymmetric but not transitive relation, and *globally before*, which is reflexive, symmetric, and transitive (Newton-Smith, 1980, pp. 58–59). Surely, this is on the right track, but Newton-Smith seems to forget about this possibility as soon as he has mentioned it.

Let us stick to the relation *later than*, and let us retain the usual characterization of this relation as irreflexive, asymmetric, and transitive. Let us notice, however, that these properties have to be relativized, explicitly or implicitly, to some set in which the relation in question holds; for a relation may be, for example, transitive in one set but not in another. Now, if time is closed, it is quite reasonable to assume that *later than* is not connected in the set T of all times. For, as we have seen, this would lead to contradictions; for example, a time would be later than itself (because of transitivity) and not later than itself (because of irreflexivity). But in "local" subsets of T, that is, subsets whose elements are comparatively close to one another, we can still uphold the connectedness of the relation. In view of common usage, *later than* should always be taken as irreflexive, asymmetric, and transitive—but if time is closed, it should only be applied in local subsets of T.[15]

Suppose time is really closed. Suppose, for example, that the history of the universe starts with a Big Bang and ends with a Big Crunch, which immediately (or after a while) takes us back to the time of the Big Bang and then further to the Big Crunch, and so on forever. Of course, we would never notice, since we only exist for a very small interval of time in the cosmic history. So we would naturally, but falsely, believe that *later than* is transitive without any restriction (and that time is linear). For the times at which we exist constitute a very local subset of the set T of all times.

If, for every time *t*, there is some sequence of times, $<x_1, x_2, \ldots, x_n>$, such that $t = x_1 = x_n$ and each x_{i+1} is later than x_i, then time certainly has a direction. The direction is determined by the asymmetric relation *later than*. And even if, in this sense, every instant in closed time will "recur," it will not follow that every time is later than itself. Nor will it follow that for every pair of times, each member is later than the other.

But is there any reason to believe that time is closed? Perhaps not. But neither, it seems, is there any reason to believe that time is linear. For all we know, both alternatives seem equally possible.[16] Both are equally compatible with all possible empirical evidence. Furthermore, it seems unlikely that simplicity could break the tie. In some respect, a straight line may be simpler that a circle, but with the straight line there is also the problem of how, and why, it begins and ends—unless it is of infinite length, which is also problematic and not very simple. Linear time may be simpler in the sense that it appears more "natural" to ordinary people—at least in modern times—but, given the manifest "unnaturalness" of modern cosmology, this is surely not a very relevant consideration. Besides, the fact that people *nowadays* tend to think of time as linear may be primarily due to the overwhelming influence over many centuries of Christian dogma.

We may conclude, then, that closed time is a realistic possibility, which in turn appears to imply a plausible version of eternal recurrence.

3. Objective and Subjective Perspectives

Some philosophers would still insist that eternal recurrence in closed time is incoherent: if time were closed, they would argue, it would *not* be the case that every time will recur. For example, J. R. Lucas says: "If time really were cyclic, there would not be a recurrence of events [...] not the same sort of event all over again, but the very same event just once" (1973, p. 58). Lucas claims that recurrence presupposes precisely that time is *not* cyclic (closed). Adolf Grünbaum seems to have the same view; he says that "cyclic recurrence affirms the openness of time" (1973, p. 198).

It might be replied that this is just a matter of words. Lucas and Grünbaum may be right as long as "recurrence" is taken in its normal sense, but this normal sense probably reflects our normal, unreflecting belief that time is linear. If we believed that time is closed, the normal sense of "recurrence," in contexts like this, would probably be the one indicated above.

However, there may still be some doubt as to whether this reply has any philosophical substance. Is there any real difference between recurrence in closed time—from now on, unless otherwise indicated, "recurrence" will always mean recurrence of this kind—and no recurrence at all? In particular, if there is a difference, is this difference of any interest to those of us who do not want to die (or, for that matter, to those who want to die)?

We need to distinguish here between objective and subjective differences.[17] From an objective point of view, there is a theoretical difference between linear and cyclical time, but this difference is never noticed by anyone. It is not noticed from any subjective point of view. Still, the *prospect* of death may appear quite different to those who believe in closed time than to those who do not. In other words, the *belief* in closed time—or the belief that closed time is at least a realistic possibility— may make a great difference from a subjective perspective.

When the prospect of death is terrifying it is, I suggest, the prospect of not having any future, of never again having any experiences. But the very idea of a "future" is only intelligible from within a subjective perspective. From an external perspective, eternal recurrence in closed time may be just the same as no recurrence at all, but from a subjective point of view it might be a great comfort, since it would remove the prospect of never again having a subjective point of view.

According to Thomas Nagel, "if death is an evil, it is the *loss of life*, rather than the state of being dead, or nonexistent, or unconscious, that is objectionable" (1979, p. 3). This seems to me to be only partly correct. I should not really object to the loss of life, if it were not followed by the permanent state of being dead.[18] The loss of life seems quite tolerable if time is closed, for in that case death is followed by life.

But is that really what happens in closed time? Philosophers like Lucas and Grünbaum may insist that death is *not* followed by life in closed time, since in closed time a person's life occurs only once. From a subjective point of view, it may appear that death will be followed by life in closed time—since the subject will never experience the time between death and life—but this, it might be argued, is an illusion. From an objective or external point of view, this illusion is dissolved; objectively, life is not later than death, since *later than* is only applicable in local subsets of the set of all times. However, as Nagel has argued, the subjective perspective is not (always) illusory and it is not inferior to the objective perspective; "our objective understanding of things [...] is in essence only partial," and "objective reality cannot be analyzed or shut out of existence any more than subjective reality can" (1979, p. 212). From a subjective perspective it certainly seems that death *is* followed by life in closed time.

It may be noticed that eternal recurrence in this sense appears to be subjectively equivalent to a kind of time travel between death and birth: from a subjective perspective, they would feel the same, and both prospects would (therefore) be equally desirable. It would not be time travel performed intentionally or even consciously, but it would be time travel in the sense that the person in question moves from one location in time to another.[19] If this were possible in linear time, it is hard to see why it should be impossible in closed time.

It may be objected that we cannot move in time at all. Some philosophers believe that time's passage is a myth, an illusion, and that it is also an illusion—more or less the same illusion—that we advance through time.[20] Nevertheless, we certainly experience a passage of time. We often express this by saying that time moves or flows, but on second thoughts we would probably be more inclined to say that time does not move any more than space does. It is rather *we* who move; more exactly, our subjective points of view move from one position in space and in time to another, and so on. There is a difference, though. In space, we move around in many different ways and we have the impression that most of the time we move voluntarily, but in time we seem to move along automatically in one direction whether we like it or not. There is nothing we can do about it. We cannot control our movement in time (except, perhaps, by committing suicide). Our impression that time moves (while we do not) can perhaps be explained by the fact that we cannot affect our own movement in time.[21]

But *do* we move in time?

4. MOVEMENT IN TIME

From an objective point of view, it may be quite correct to say that we do not move in time. In particular, if the world is a four-dimensional manifold of events, ordinary objects and human bodies are a kind of perduring solids or "worms" that are composed of temporal parts, or stages, located at various times and places. Neither the worm itself, nor any of its stages, move in time. They just have some location in time. But from a subjective point of view, we certainly advance through time.[22]

The subjective perspective, the point of view of a person—the *subject*, for short—moves along from one stage of a human body to the next, and so on.[23] This is the perspective from which the person refers to times and places by words like "now" and "here"; these words have no place in an objective perspective, they can only be used by a subject.

Nevertheless, J. J. C. Smart and others claim that movement in time is just an illusion. They point out that movement is movement with respect to time, and they ask (Smart, 1967, p. 126): if motion in space is feet per second, at what speed is motion in time? Seconds per what? That is a good question, but it seems clear that the answer must involve two kinds of time, subjective and objective.[24] Objectively, there is no movement in time, but subjectively we certainly move forward in (objective) time. This is nicely expressed by Hermann Weyl as follows:

> The objective world simply *is*, it does not *happen*. Only to the gaze of my consciousness, crawling upward along the life line of my body, does a section of this world come to life as a fleeting image in space which continuously changes in time. (Weyl, 1949, p. 116)

Everyone knows that subjectively some days, weeks, and years appear much longer or shorter than others. So our answer to Smart's question should be something like this: in many cases our movement in time is just one objective second per subjective second, but sometimes we move at considerably more or less than one objective second per subjective second. We may not currently have access to any good objective instruments to measure subjective time—to construct such instruments, might be a task for psychologists—but it can hardly be doubted that there is such a thing as subjective time.

However, it has been held, more specifically, that passage of time, or "a moving present," is incompatible with closed time. For example, Robin Le Poidevin says that

> once we introduce the idea of a moving present into the picture of cyclic time, we cannot but imagine the present going around the circle repeatedly, and if the circle represents time itself, then we have to say, thus contradicting ourselves, that each event happens both once and an infinite number of times. We are in fact importing *two* representations of time into the picture: the circle itself, and the motion of the present around it. But we cannot, it seems have both. So there appears to be a tension between the idea of cyclic time on the one hand and the passage of time on the other.[25]

Le Poidevin claims that there is a contradiction here and that time is represented in two incompatible ways. By contrast, I suggest that two different systems of time of time are involved, one objective and the other subjective. As far as I can see, this does not yield any contradiction. The circle represents objective time, but the movement around the circle is movement in subjective time. It is misleading to say that "the present" moves around the circle, for "the present" must surely be taken to refer to some time, and times do not move. But as I argued above, we, or our subjective points of view, move from one position in objective time to the next, and so on. Of course, for most of the (objective) time we are dead (or, not alive), so nothing happens subjectively; given closed time, we may assume that in subjective time we move directly from death to birth—or to some (objective) time after birth where we begin to have a subjective point of view.

Another point in Le Poidevin's argument is that, if there is a moving present in cyclic time, then we would have to say that "each event happens both once and an infinite number of times." This does not follow. Objectively, as we have repeatedly noted, everything happens just once in closed time. But, from a subjective perspective, since we move forward in objective time, the same events can be expected to occur over and over again in subjective time, if objective time is closed. It can also be expected that this repetition will never be experienced or remembered. But since there is also a kind of eternal repetition in subjective time, we should perhaps think of subjective time as linear rather than closed.

It might be asked how a subject can return to a time where it has already been. Is such time travel at all possible? Well, this is just what must be the case if objective time is closed. But, a skeptic may wonder, in the interval between death and birth, the subject does not exist at all, so how does it move over this interval? This question also seems to involve the problem of personal identity. So let us move on to that.

5. Personal Identity

It is sometimes said that a person who reappears in a different cycle of cosmic history could not be numerically the same as before. Identity is usually taken to presuppose some kind of continuity, physical or psychological. According to Milic Capek, the Stoics believed, like Aristotle, that even though Socrates could reappear again and again, the Socrateses would be numerically different (since numerical identity presupposes uninterrupted existence). And St. Thomas rejected eternal recurrence on the ground that re-creation of numerically identical individuals would be contradictory.[26]

Similarly, Lucas says: "Even if in another cycle there was, or will be, some one qualitatively identical with me, he will not be me unless either I can remember being him or he will be able to remember being me" (1973, p. 59). Clearly, this rules out intercycle personal identity under eternal recurrence. If a person has memories from one cycle to another, then there is indeed a kind of psychological continuity, but, on the other hand, this requirement can hardly be satisfied if the cycles are qualitatively exactly similar. One cycle cannot be qualitatively identical with another if it contains memories from the other. Besides, there cannot be memories from one cycle to another in closed time, since there is in fact only one cycle. A person has certain memories at any given time; the moving subject does not acquire any memories *in addition* to that.

In any case, it seems that the problems of combining personal identity with eternal recurrence seem to arise only for the linear time case—and we have argued that linear time is in any case not very promising for eternal recurrence.[27] In cyclical time, on the other hand, it seems that a person simply has to be the same in every instance of the person's life, since there is after all only one instance of this life.

Someone might say that in closed time there is presumably a very long period of time from the death of a person until he or she is born, and it may be asked how the person can retain his or her identity during all that time. This could be seen as a problem, even if it is granted that the person will not subjectively notice the long period between death and birth. (From a subjective point of view, it does not matter whether the interval between death and birth is long or short.)

However, it could be argued that in closed time, there is in fact both physical and psychological continuity between the person who dies and the (same) person who is born, even though this continuity works backward in time rather than forward. One may of course question the assumption that the dying person has the same subjective point of view as the newborn baby, but we can hardly doubt that the subject, at any given time in his or her life, is the same as the subject at that time. This should be enough for anyone who wants to be born again to the same life as before.

But is it at all reasonable to want such a thing? This may be doubted. So let us now turn to that question.

6. Different Attitudes toward Eternal Recurrence

It has been said that eternal recurrence is "a sorry counterfeit of immortality," and that "[w]hat we really long for after death is to go on living this life, this same mortal life, but without its evils, without its tedium—and without death."[28] Similarly, Schopenhauer said that "at the end of his life, no man, if he be sincere and at the same time in possession of his faculties, will ever wish to go through it again. Rather than this, he will much prefer to choose complete non-existence."[29] More recently, Paul Davies says that "the literal reappearance of the same people and events in cycle after cycle, [is] an idea that strikes most people today as utterly sterile and repugnant" (1995, p. 29).

It may be true that what many people want is a prolonged and perfectly happy life, or perhaps just an ordinary human life, but without misfortunes and without end. On the other hand, a life without end would not be an ordinary human life, and it would probably be unbearably boring. Bernard Williams cites the case of a woman in a play who takes an elixir of life until, at the age of 342, she reaches a state of "boredom, indifference and coldness" and refuses to take the elixir, whereupon she dies.[30]

Williams argues that "an endless life would be a meaningless one" (1973, p. 89). He does not discuss eternal recurrence, as a possible version of "an endless life," but he considers the possibility that death would be followed by an indefinite or infinite series of psychologically disjoint lives, some kind of reincarnation or metempsychosis, where a person may take on very different personality traits and other characteristics in subsequent lives. He says that "out of the alternatives it is the only one that for me would, if it made sense, have any attraction—no doubt because it is the only [way of avoiding permanent death] which has the feature that what one is living at any given point is actually a *life*" (Williams, 1973, pp. 93–94). But there are still problems with this: is it really *oneself* that survives in all those different lives, and can one really want to live lives that are so different from one's own? Williams also notes that those who believe in reincarnation usually see it as something negative, something that one hopes to be released from as soon as possible.

Eternal recurrence avoids the problematic aspects of reincarnation, but it also retains its desirable features. It provides a way to avoid permanent death, without running the risk of eternal boredom. It satisfies the consideration that "death gives the meaning to life," as Williams puts it (1973, p. 82). So we can have our cake and eat it too.

Or is there perhaps also something frightening or repugnant in the idea of eternal recurrence? As we have just seen, several people seem to take exception to this idea, but as far as I can see, they seldom give any grounds for this—except perhaps the general ground that life is evil, but this does not seem to apply in the case of those who fear the loss of life.

It appears that Nietzsche tended to oscillate between different attitudes toward eternal recurrence. In one well-known passage, he says the following:

> What if some day or night a demon were to sneak after you in your loneliness and say to you: "This life as you now live it and have lived it, you will have to live once more and innumerable times more; and there will be nothing new in it, but every pain and every joy and every thought and sigh and everything immeasurably small or great in your life must return to you, all in the same succession and sequence—even this spider and this moonlight between the trees, and even this moment and I myself. The eternal hourglass of existence is turned over and over, and you with it, a speck of dust!"
>
> Would you not throw yourself down and gnash your teeth and curse the demon who spoke thus? Or did you once experience a tremendous moment when you would have answered him: "You are a god, and never did I hear anything more godly." If this thought were to gain possession of you, it would change you, as you are, or perhaps crush you. The question in each and every thing, "Do you want this again and innumerable times again?" would weigh upon your actions as the greatest weight. Or how well disposed would you have to become to yourself and to life to desire nothing more than this ultimate eternal confirmation and seal?[31]

Nietzsche seems to have thought of eternal recurrence, partly at least, as a thought experiment or test. Hatab says: "Nietzsche is putting the perennial question of the meaning of life in the most dramatic and acute form imaginable. It poses the meaning question in terms of whether one will say Yes or No to life as actually lived, with no alternative."[32] In one place, Nietzsche states his position as follows: "My teaching says: Live in such a way that you must *desire* to live again; this is the task—you will live again *in any case*."[33]

7. CONSEQUENCES

In order to form an opinion of the desirability of eternal recurrence, we need to ask what its consequences would be for human life. However, we should distinguish here between consequences of eternal recurrence itself and consequences of the belief in eternal recurrence. It is mainly the latter that are of importance. Let me give some examples.

Belief in eternal recurrence may affect our attitudes to time. It has been noted that most of us have a bias toward the near and toward the future, at least with regard to pleasure and pain.[34] This bias might be greatly diminished if we believed in eternal recurrence, for presumably, in that perspective different stages of our lives would tend to become of more equal importance to us. From a subjective point of view, they may all seem to lie in the future. Consequently, we might even acquire an attitude of temporal neutrality and this, according to Derek Parfit, would be good for us; we would lose in some ways, but we would also gain, and the gains "would outweigh the losses" (1984, p. 174).

Again, our attitudes to death and dying can be expected to change if we came to believe in eternal recurrence. Not only would there be less fear of death; it also seems quite likely that people would become less eager to prolong their lives when the prospects for a good life are bad. And people may be more prepared to commit suicide. Under normal circumstances, if the future looks bad, we may nevertheless want to live on because we think that a bad life can be preferable to death. But if we come to believe in eternal recurrence, we may see things differently. Death seems less bad, if it is followed by life, and we may wish to avoid the repetition of a bad future.

Belief in eternal recurrence may also result in a sense of meaningfulness. The way we live will matter more to us, if we believe that our lives will recur. We need no longer have the feeling that our life ends absurdly, that it has no purpose, that it is a preparation for nothing. For example, at the very end of his *Reveries over Childhood and Youth*, W. B. Yeats writes:

> It is not that I have accomplished too few of my plans, for I am not ambitious; but when I think of all the books I have read, and of the wise words I have heard spoken, and of the anxiety I have given to parents and grandparents, and of the hopes that I have had, all life weighed in the scales of my own life seems to me a preparation for something that never happens. (1955, p. 106)

By contrast, with eternal recurrence life is a preparation for something, namely, for lives that will happen again and again in the future. Nietzsche seems to have had a similar thought when he claimed that belief in eternal recurrence would counteract "the paralyzing sense of general disintegration and incompleteness" (1968, p. 224).

Just as a single life can appear to be a preparation for nothing, so the whole history of humanity can seem to be futile since it plays such a small role from the point of view of the universe as a whole. In the words of Bertrand Russell,

> Man is the product of causes which had no prevision of the end they were achieving [...and] all the labours of the ages, all the devotion, all the inspiration, all the noonday brightness of human genius, are destined to extinction in the vast death of the solar system, and [...] the whole temple of Man's achievement must inevitably be buried beneath the débris of a universe in ruins. (1919, pp. 47–48)

This picture of humanity is chilling, but it may seem rather less chilling to people who believe that time is closed. However, such a reaction is perhaps not very rational, for it is still true that the history of humanity happens only once in closed time. Nevertheless, the reaction may occur. From the point of view of humanity, and endless future with "a universe in ruins" is certainly bleak, but if we believe that this future is not endless, but is instead followed by the past history of the universe, many of us may feel less depressed. If someone finds it more rational to focus on the horror of a "universe in ruins," we need not let that affect us.

So far I have only considered consequences of the *belief* in eternal recurrence, and I am not sure that eternal recurrence itself has any consequences for human life that are worth mentioning. However, it might appear to be a consequence of eternal recurrence that we have no free will. For example, Hatab considers the thought that, "the repetition scheme seems to imply a rigid determinism [...]. Whatever I do next has happened an infinite number of times in the same way, and so there is only one possible future" (2005, p. 127). It is true that eternal recurrence in linear time sits best with determinism and, therefore, absence of free will. But in closed time the situation is different. Here, there is no objective repetition, and no determinism has to be assumed.

8. JUSTICE

Even if eternal recurrence is an attractive notion for privileged people, it might seem unfair to those who are less privileged. This is one important respect in which eternal recurrence is different from various doctrines of reincarnation that are adhered to in certain religious traditions. Reincarnation—where some part of a living being survives death by being reborn in a new body, with a new personality—allows for compensation of the underprivileged in subsequent lives. But in eternal recurrence, the underprivileged are always underprivileged. Can eternal recurrence be desirable if this is so?

It is perhaps *possible* for this kind of injustice to be explained away. For example, just as someone may lead a great many different lives at different times, if reincarnation occurs, so one might lead many different lives at the *same* time—as long as one is completely unaware of this. This could even amount to a kind of solipsism: there is only one subject, but this subject is incarnated in many different bodies, some of which live at the same time while others live at different times. In other words, without knowing it, the subject plays many different roles—in fact, all the roles there are in all of history. If this were the case, there would be no serious form of injustice. The one and only subject would simply be privileged in some of its roles and underprivileged in others. Under such circumstances, eternal recurrence would not be morally repugnant. But, of course, we do not have much ground for assuming that such circumstances actually obtain.[35]

In any case, eternal recurrence does not seem to make injustices any worse if time is closed. But recurrence would indeed be morally repugnant, if it occurs in linear time. For injustice would be worse if it is repeated endlessly. In closed time, on the other hand, all injustices in cosmic history occur only once.

9. LIVES NOT WORTH LIVING

Injustices might be tolerable as long as everyone lives a good life, but in a world, such as ours, that contains an overwhelming amount of suffering, it may seem morally impossible to wish for eternal recurrence. How can one wish for the recurrence of the Holocaust, for example?

In defense of Nietzsche's position, Hatab seems to think that there is a solution to this problem: "The crucial point is that affirmation does not mean *approving* of everything, but rather affirming the necessity of otherness for the emergence of one's values, which means that affirmation retains opposition to countervalues, retains the space of one's Yes and No" (2005, p. 139). There may be some truth in this, but it does not seem to remove the problem.

However, the problem is neither suffering as such nor the total balance of pleasure over pain in the universe. For a life may be worth living—from the point of view of the person living it—even if it contains a lot of suffering and even if it contains more pain than pleasure. And, since other things are equal in eternal recurrence, as long as a person's life is worth living it is worth living each time it is lived. So, eternal recurrence would be desirable if everyone's life is worth living.

But is everyone's life worth living? Some people seem to think so. For example, Thomas Nagel says: "All of us, I believe, are fortunate to have been born."[36] Of course, one can be fortunate to have been born even if one's life, at a certain moment in time, is no longer worth living. Again, a person's life may be worth living even if it would have been better, all things considered, if he had never lived. For example, Hitler's life was perhaps worth living even if the world would have been much better without him. But I take it that someone is fortunate to have been born only if his or her life is worth living. Therefore, if Nagel is right, it seems that everyone's life is worth living and that eternal recurrence is desirable from each individual point of view. I myself find it hard to believe that everyone is fortunate to have been born, but I shall make no attempt to settle that question here.

Eternal recurrence may perhaps be objectively desirable even if many lives are not worth living—provided that *most* people are fortunate to have been born.

In any case, the desire for eternal recurrence can hardly be morally repugnant if time is closed, for in that case everything happens just once. Even if some lives are not worth living, eternal recurrence cannot make things objectively worse.

10. CONCLUSION

The arguments that have been sketched above are perhaps not conclusive, but I believe they give at least some support to the view that eternal recurrence is both possible and desirable. The acceptance of this view may in turn reduce or exterminate the fear of death that many of us feel at least some of the time. Eternal recurrence gives a pretty attractive answer to the question of "what dreams may come, when we have shuffled off this mortal coil." It is perhaps the only intelligible and attractive version of eternal life that we can think of, and even if it presupposes a rather nonstandard conception of time, it seems to be fairly compatible with what is known about the world we live in.[37]

NOTES

1. See Eliade, 1955, p. 85.
2. The quotation is from Henri-Charles Puech.
3. See also Sorabji, 1983, pp. 182 ff.
4. See Capek, 1967, pp. 61–62. But also Eliade, pp. 129–130. Eliade also says: "From the seventeenth century on, linearism and the progressivistic conception of history assert themselves more and more" (p. 145).
5. See, for example, Hatab, 2005; and Nietzsche, 1968, pp. 544–550.
6. See Capek, 1960. For more contemporary proponents or sympathizers of the doctrine, Eliade points out that "the work of two of the most significant writers of our day— T. S. Eliot and James Joyce—is saturated with nostalgia for the myth of eternal repetition and, in the last analysis, for the abolition of time" (p. 153).
7. See Capek, 1960, pp. 291–292. Capek notes that this reasoning is related to a certain theorem proved by Henri Poincaré, but that Nietzsche grasped this intuitively a few years before it was proved by Poincaré (see p. 291). However, Capek claims that eternal recurrence "is incompatible with our present physical knowledge" (1960, p. 294); for example, he cites "the lack of constancy and the lack of persistence through time of the alleged "particles" of contemporary physics" and the fact that relativity theory forces

us "to deny the existence of events simultaneous in an absolute sense" (p. 293). Capek's reasoning is criticized by Bas van Fraassen, 1962.

8. People disagree about whether time is continuous, dense, or discrete, but this seems to be irrelevant for problems concerning eternal recurrence, so it will not be discussed here.

9. One may wonder if the notion of a cosmic history makes sense at all, if "time is relative" as in relativity theory. Different reference frames split space-time differently into space and time. But some physicists seem to believe that there is nevertheless a kind of "universal" or "cosmic" time in the universe, namely, the time that is relative to a frame of reference from which the background heat radiation that fills space appears exactly uniform in all directions (see Davies, 1995, pp. 127–129). Besides, even if clocks are affected by motion and by gravity, as in relativity theory, it may perhaps be doubted that time is therefore likewise affected. This seems to presuppose that time is not absolute. There is no consensus on this. For example, J. R. Lucas says: "Time is not the same as change or motion, it is not just what the clocks say. For we are aware of the passage of time, even when we are not aware of any changes in the external world" (1973, p. 8).

10. If time is absolute, this is perhaps a qualitative difference. Otherwise, it can be regarded as merely numerical.

11. Some philosophers may even argue that if there is eternal recurrence, then, in virtue of the Principle of the Identity of Indiscernibles, time must be closed. For, according to that Principle, there can be no numerical difference where there is no qualitative difference. Susan Weir, e.g., argues in this way (Weir, 1988, p. 204). But this, again, seems to presuppose that time is not absolute—for if time is absolute and linear, there is a qualitative difference between different cycles of cosmic history, namely, that they occur at different times.

12. See, for example, Lucas, 1973, p. 58, and Newton-Smith, 1980, p. 57. I will come back to the problem of repetition below.

13. Indeed, there is some indication that Peirce might have believed in closed time. Capek quotes what he calls a "peculiar argument" from Peirce (Collected Works, I, pp. 498–450) as follows: "since every portion of time is bounded by two instants, there must be a connection of time ring-wise. Events may be limited to a portion of this ring, but the time itself must extend round or else there will be a portion of time, say future time and also past time, not bounded by two instants" (Capek, 1960, pp. 295–256). Wedberg points out that there are formulations in Nietzsche's work that suggests that he sometimes thought of time as closed, even though this is incompatible with his assumption that time is infinite and discrete. Wedberg suggests that Nietzsche might have started with this assumption and then, after having used it to support eternal recurrence, changed his mind about time under the influence of Leibniz's principle of the Identity of Indicernables (see Wedberg, 1968, pp. 80–83).

14. The same point is evidenced by the fact that, when he illustrates closed time with a circle, he does not indicate direction with an arrow, as he does in the case of open, linear time (see p. 58). Lucas has a similar view. He says that "there are difficulties about the order of events in cyclic time. If we take "before" and "after" in their usual sense, every event will be both before and after every other event; and it will become impossible [...] to identify them by reference to their temporal ordering. [...] Moreover, even if we could introduce an order into cyclic time, we cannot import a direction" (1973, pp. 59–60).

15. Notice, that this is somewhat different from Newton-Smith's suggestion. He recognizes two relations, two senses of "before," while I stick to one well-known relation—which may, however, not be connected in the set of all times (depending upon whether time is closed). His suggestion, as well as mine, removes contradictions, but it seems to me that mine is more natural in view of common usage.

16. According to Lawrence Hatab, Nietzsche did not try to decide between linear and cyclical time for eternal recurrence. This was partly because Nietzsche's immanent naturalism is incompatible with an external, "God's eye" standpoint from which one can survey all of reality and make the relevant decision (see Hatab, 2005, pp. 71–73).

17. Thomas Nagel has made important contributions to our understanding of this distinction; see, for example, Nagel, 1979, in particular the chapter entitled "Subjective and Objective," pp. 196–213. Most of us believe that the ambition to achieve objectivity, especially evident in the natural sciences, leads to an increased and more correct understanding of reality, but Nagel forcefully argues that a purely objective conception of the world can never be complete. The objective facts are not all the facts there are. Many truths are only accessible from a subjective perspective. For example, a complete and objective description of every person in the building where I am now writing this paper does not include the fact that I am one of these persons—even though this is clearly a fact. Similarly, there may be facts about time that are only evident from a subjective perspective—for example the facts that it is now 10 a.m. and that time now moves very slowly.

18. Nagel says in a footnote: "It is sometimes suggested that what we really mind is the process of dying. But I should not really object to dying if it were not followed by death" (1979, p. 3). By contrast, I should not object to death, if it were followed by life, as in closed time. However, in fairness to Nagel, it should be added that in the paper discussed here he uses "death" and its cognates to mean permanent death; see p. 1.

19. Notice that this kind of time travel is not like the kind that occurs in science fiction stories. It does not involve the movement of a body of a certain age to an earlier time; rather, it is the movement of a person from one time, and from one body with a certain age, to another time, and to a rather different and much younger body. The time traveler is transformed into an earlier version of himself (or herself). So there is no room for any of the usual paradoxes here; for example, the time traveler will not be in a position to kill himself or his parents or grandparents, thereby preventing himself from being born or from being in a position to travel backward in time. Moreover, in time travel of the science fiction kind, there is a problem of how departure and arrival can be separated by two unequal intervals of time, as for example, when I travel from the year 2009 back to the year 1954 in a couple of hours (see e.g., Lewis, 1976, p. 145). This is not a problem for eternal recurrence in closed time, since there is then only one sequence of times, and one direction of movement in time.

20. See, for example, Smart, 1967, p. 127.

21. Suppose we always moved uniformly in space, without any control at all over the movement, as if we were looking out the window of a moving train. If so, we might be inclined to say that space, or "the landscape," moved or passed by outside the window.

22. Physicists may not care about this. For example, Davies says: "We can envisage the time dimension stretched out as a line of fate, and a particular instant—'now'—being singled out as a little glowing point. As 'time goes on,' so the light moves steadily up

the time line toward the future. Needless to say, physicists can find nothing of this in the objective world" (1995, p. 258). On the other hand, if human beings are enduring, three-dimensional objects, it is hard to see how one can deny that they move in time.

23. Periods of unconsciousness and multiple personalities are disregarded here.

24. The distinction between objective and subjective time is not the same as the distinction between external and personal time proposed by David Lewis, 1976, p. 146. For Lewis, personal time is primarily tied to bodily processes and the normal order of the stages of a human body; it has no essential connection to a subjective perspective.

25. Le Poidevin, 2003, pp. 86–87. Let us disregard the strange idea that time—or moments of time—can move; this would seem to involve us in the absurdity that one and the same moment of time can be located at different times. Instead, let us ask whether something like Le Poidevin's argument may be applied to the position outlined above, namely, that a subject (i.e., a person's subjective perspective) advances through time.

26. See Capek, 1967, p. 62.

27. Besides, the problems may not be overwhelming for linear time either. For the mental in general, and the subjective point of view in particular, might be expected to supervene upon physical traits, and these are the same in different cycles even in linear time (given eternal recurrence). But perhaps we cannot dismiss the possibility that the mere numerical difference in linear time entails that subjective points of view must be different.

28. Unamuno, 1972, pp. 57 and 252. Unamuno goes on to say: "And what else is the meaning of that comical notion of eternal recurrence which issued from the tragic inner voice of poor Nietzsche, in his hunger for a concrete, temporal immortality?" (p. 252). As far as I can see, however, Unamuno does not tell us why eternal recurrence is a "comical notion" and a "sorry counterfeit of immortality."

29. *The World as Will and Representation* (I, 324), quoted here from Hatab, 2005, p. 87.

30. See Williams, 1973, pp. 82–100. The woman, Elina Makropulos, is forty-two years old for three hundred years. Richard Sorabji has suggested that her life would have been better if she had grown older for ever, or if she had become a Christian mystic with a sense of timelessness; see Sorabji, 1983, p. 181.

31. *The Gay Science*, section 341, here quoted from Hatab, 2005, p. 66.

32. Hatab, 2005, p. 2. But Hatab also says that "Nietzsche always regarded eternal recurrence as more than simply a hypothetical thought experiment pertaining only to human psychology; he always took it to express something about life and the world as such" (p. 9).

33. Quoted from Hatab, 2005, p. 117.

34. See, for example, Parfit, 1984, p. 158 ff.

35. Conversely, we may not have much ground for assuming that they do not obtain either.

36. Nagel, 1979, p. 7. Nagel adds: "unless good and ill can be assigned to an embryo, or even to an unconnected pair of gametes, it cannot be said that not to be born is a misfortune."—According to Nagel, "life is worth living even when the bad elements of experience are plentiful, and the good ones too meager to outweigh the bad ones on their own" (p. 2), but he also says that "a sufficient quantity of more particular evils can perhaps outweigh" the goods that life contains (p. 2; italics mine).

37. I am grateful to Björn Eriksson and Jens Johansson for helpful comments on an earlier version of this chapter.

REFERENCES

Capek, Milic. 1960. "The Theory of Eternal Recurrence in Modern Philosophy of Science, with Special Reference to S. C. Peirce." *Journal of Philosophy* 57: 289–296.

Capek, Milic. 1967. "Eternal Return." In *The Encyclopedia of Philosophy*, volume 3, P. Edwards ed., pp. 61–63. New York and London: Macmillan.

Davies, Paul. 1995. *About Time: Einstein's Unfinished Revolution*. London: Penguin Books.

Eliade, Mircea. 1955. *The Myth of the Eternal Return*. London: Routledge & Kegan Paul.

Grünbaum, Adolf. 1973. *Philosophical Problems of Space and Time*. 2nd ed. Boston: Reidel.

Hatab, Lawrence J. 2005. *Nietzsche's Life Sentence: Coming to Terms with Eternal Recurrence*. New York and London: Routledge.

Le Poidevin, Robin. 2003. *Travels in Four Dimensions: The Enigmas of Space and Time*. Oxford: Oxford University Press.

Lewis, David. 1976. "The Paradoxes of Time Travel." *American Philosophical Quarterly* 13: 145–152.

Lucas, J. R. 1973. *A Treatise of Time and Space*. London: Methuen.

Nagel, Thomas. 1979. *Mortal Questions*. Cambridge: Cambridge University Press.

Newton-Smith, W. H. 1980. *The Structure of Time*. London: Routledge & Kegan Paul.

Nietzsche, Friedrich. 1968. *The Will to Power*. Translated by W. Kaufman and R. J. Hollingdale. New York: Random House.

Parfit, Derek. 1984. *Reasons and Persons*. Oxford: Clarendon Press.

Russell, Bertrand. 1919. "A Free Man's Worship." In *Mysticism and Logic and Other Essays*. London: Longmans Green and Co.

Smart, J. J. C. 1967. "Time." In vol. 8, *The Encyclopedia of Philosophy*, P. Edwards, ed., pp. 126–134. New York and London: Macmillan.

Sorabji, Richard. 1983. *Time, Creation and the Continuum*. London: Duckworth.

Unamuno, Miguel de. 1972. *The Tragic Sense of Life*. Princeton: Princeton University Press.

van Fraassen, Bas C. 1962. "Capek on Eternal Recurrence." *Journal of Philosophy* 59: 371–375.

Wedberg, Anders. 1968. "Die Ewige Wiederkunft: Ett Filosofihistoriskt Tidsfördriv." in *Nio Filosofiska Studier*, H. Wennerberg ed., pp. 67–86. Uppsala: Filosofiska Föreningen.

Weir, Susan. 1988. "Closed Time and Causal Loops: A Defence Against Mellor." *Analysis* 48: 203–209.

Weyl, Hermann. 1949. *Philosophy of Mathematics and Natural Science*. Princeton: Princeton University Press.

Williams, Bernard. 1973. "The Makropulos Case: Reflections on the Tedium of Immortality." In his *Problems of the Self*, pp. 81–100. Cambridge: Cambridge University Press.

Yeats, W. B. 1955. *Autobiographies*. London: Macmillan & Co.

CHAPTER 7

DEATH IN SOCRATES, PLATO, AND ARISTOTLE

GARETH B. MATTHEWS

1. SOCRATES

Anyone who undertakes to say anything at all about the views of Socrates has a problem. Socrates himself left no writings. Our main source for determining his views is, of course, his most famous pupil, Plato. But extracting the views of Socrates from the writings of Plato presents a considerable challenge.

Not very long after the death of Socrates, Plato wrote the Apology, an account of the trial at which Socrates was convicted of the charges against him and then sentenced to death. Plato also wrote many dialogs in which Socrates is the lead figure. The figure of Socrates in those dialogs, especially in the early ones, yields the most memorable portrait we have of any ancient philosopher. But Plato was not a philosophical journalist. He was a great writer and an original thinker, without superior in the whole history of Western philosophy. In consequence, we have no very good basis for deciding exactly how much we think we know about Socrates is really Socrates and how much is Platonic invention and elaboration.

This problem is further complicated by the fact that the figure of Socrates in Plato's dialogs changes over time. The mischievously questioning figure of the early dialogs, who insists that he does not know the answers to his most important questions, morphs, in the middle and later dialogs of Plato, into a rather solemn instructor who seems to have answers to almost all his questions, and arguments to back up his answers to those questions, some of them quite complex and challenging arguments. Socrates the gadfly of the early dialogs thus becomes, in the middle and later dialogs, Socrates the tireless lecturer.

The simplest way of trying to deal with the morphing problem is to say that, while the portrait Plato draws of Socrates and the views he ascribes to him in the early dialogs are probably reasonably true to the historical person, the Socrates figure of Plato's middle and late period is much more Plato than it is Socrates. There are, of course, various difficulties with this strategy, but I won't go into them here.

Many readers have thought that Plato's record of the trial of Socrates, the Apology, is the most accurate account we have of things that the historical Socrates actually said. They have reasoned that, since the Apology was circulated soon after the death of Socrates, many Athenians who had actually attended the trial were then still alive. Under these circumstances, the reasoning goes, Plato would not have taken great liberties in what he reported. That reasoning, though hardly unimpeachable, gives us some basis for taking the Apology as a reasonably faithful guide to the thinking of the historical Socrates. I shall therefore take the Apology as my guide to the views of Socrates on death.

1.1 Socratic Wisdom

One of the most famous passages in the Apology is the one in which Socrates recounts how the oracle at Delphi had said that no one is wiser than Socrates. Socrates himself claims to have been at first perplexed by this pronouncement, since, in his own view, he knows nothing worthwhile (literally, nothing "noble and good"; Apology, 21d). But he comes to see a way to reconcile the oracle's attribution of wisdom to him with his own disavowal of significant knowledge. By a nice twist of irony he interprets the judgment of the oracle that no one is wiser than he as a recognition that he, perhaps alone among Athenians, has at least the wisdom of not thinking that he knows things he does not know.

It is the admission that he has at least this modest wisdom that motivates Socrates's thoughts on death at the end of the Apology. In the first phase of the trial, Socrates had said this:

> T1. To fear death, gentlemen, is no other than to think oneself wise when one is not, to think one knows what one does not know. No one knows whether death may not be the greatest of blessings for a man, yet men fear it as if they knew it is the greatest of evils. And surely it is the most blameworthy ignorance to believe that one knows what one does not know. It is perhaps on this point and in this respect, gentlemen, that I differ from the majority of men, and if I were to claim that I am wiser than anyone in anything, it would be in this, that, as I have no knowledge of things in the underworld, so I do not think I have. (Apology, 29ab)[1]

After Socrates is first convicted of, among other things, corrupting the youth, and then sentenced to death, he returns to the question of what we can know about death:

> T2. What has happened to me may well be a good thing, and those of us who believe death to be an evil are certainly mistaken. I have convincing proof of this.

For it is certainly impossible that my customary sign did not oppose me if I was not about to do what was right. (40bc)

Socrates had just explained that his divine sign had opposed him whenever he was about to do something wrong. His reasoning in T2 seems to be that, if those of his activities that had resulted in his death sentence had been a bad thing, his divine sign would have warned him of this fact. But, since it did not, the things that he did that resulted in his receiving the death sentence must not have been a bad thing. By implication, death itself would not be a bad thing. It might even be a good thing.

Socrates does not leave matters there, however. That is, he does not surmise that death is not a bad thing simply because his divine sign had not warned him that his actions might lead to death. Instead, he offers independent reasoning to justify that conclusion. Thus Socrates continues:

T3. Let us reflect in this way, too, that there is good hope that death is a blessing. For it is one of two things: either the dead are nothing and have no perception of anything. Or it is, as we are told, a change and a relocating of the soul from here to another place. (40c)

1.2 Death as a Dreamless Sleep

So far, the disjoint possibilities Socrates offers may well seem to be exhaustive: either the dead are nothing or else death is a change of location for one's soul. But we should be suspicious of the way Socrates fills out these two, supposedly exhaustive, possibilities. He begins with the possibility that death is "no perception of anything." This he compares to having a dreamless sleep:

T4. If it is a complete lack of perception, like a dreamless sleep, then death would be a great advantage. For I think if one had to pick out that night during which a man slept soundly and did not dream, put it beside other nights and days of his life, and then see how many days and nights had been better and more pleasant than that night, not only a private person but a great king would find them easy to count compared with the other days and nights. (40cd)

As Socrates surely realizes, there is an important respect in which death as the final cessation of conscious experience is not at all like a mere night of dreamless sleep. Simply put, death is apparently not something one wakes up from. So the analogy is defective and should not give us any comfort.

Socrates might respond that, when we go to sleep, we cannot be completely certain whether we will wake up or not, which is no doubt true. Still, when he asks the jurors to compare nights of dreamless sleep with nights of sleep interrupted by dreams, perhaps some of them nightmares, he is asking them to compare finite periods of time, each of which is succeeded eventually by a wakeful state, with an everlasting period of no consciousness at all. A "night" of eternal sleep would be radically different from an ordinary night of dreamless sleep in at least one important respect: there would be no return to consciousness. That important difference is enough to render the analogy less than fully comforting.

Socrates does add:

> T5....all eternity would then seem to be no more than a single night. (40d)

But this comment does not offer much comfort either. A patient in a coma for some extended period of time, perhaps, for many years, might say, "It seemed to be only a single night." Still, the prospect of becoming comatose for an extended period of time might be itself frightening. However, more to the point, facing the prospect of an extended coma from which one eventually recovers would still be less frightening than going "to sleep" forever.

1.3 Death as a Change of Location

The other possibility Socrates considers, death as a relocation of the soul, is presumably less threatening than extinction. Socrates develops his ideas about this possibility as follows:

> T6. If, on the other hand, death is a change from here to another place, and what we are told is true and all who have died are there, what greater blessing would there be, gentlemen of the jury? If anyone arriving in Hades will have escaped from those who call themselves judges here, and will find those true judges who are said to sit in judgment there, Minos and Radamanthus and Aeacus and Triptolemus and the other demi-gods who have been upright in their own life, would that be a poor kind of change? Again, what would one of you give to keep company with Orpheus and Musaeus, Hesiod and Homer? I am willing to die many times if that is true. (40e–41a)

The possibility that death is the relocation of the soul to another place is thus filled out by appeal to Greek mythology. This is the way it would be "if what we are told is true." But suppose "what we are told" is not true. Suppose the relocation is a trip to a fiery hell, or to a place of endless desolation. What then?

Socrates speculates that, in his new location, he might meet Ajax and other war heroes. Then he adds this comment:

> T7. Most important, I could spend my time testing and examining people there, as I do here, as to who among them is wise, and who thinks he is, but is not. (41b)

But again, just the possibility that death is the soul's relocation to another place is not guaranteed to bring with it the possibility, let alone the certainty, that that relocation might include an opportunity to do what one most likes to do in this life, which for Socrates is to examine other people philosophically.

1.4 Conclusion

The final words of Socrates at his trial, according to Plato's Apology, are these:

> T8. Now the hour to part has come, I go to die, you go to live. Which of us goes to the better lot is known to no one, except the god. (42a)

So what may we conclude from the Apology about Socrates's views concerning death?

According to this work, Socrates thinks, first, that we do not know whether death is a good thing for the one who dies, or a bad thing. Second, it is the most blameworthy ignorance to think we know what we do not know. Since we do not know what, if anything, awaits us after death, it is therefore blamefully ignorant to think we know whether death is good or bad for the one who dies.

Third, there is some reason for Socrates to think that death might be a good thing for him, and perhaps, by extension, for others. The reason is that his divine sign never told him not to engage in the activities that led to his trial, conviction, and death sentence.

Fourth, Socrates argues that death is either oblivion for the one who dies or it is the soul's relocation to another place. Socrates fills out the first alternative in such a way that, according to him, we should welcome death just as we welcome the rest of a night of dreamless sleep. I have argued that that the disanalogy between eternal oblivion and a night of dreamless sleep makes Socrates's supposedly comforting analogy ring hollow. The particular way Socrates fills out the second alternative, relocation to another pace, does make it appealing to him. For, as he elaborates what it would mean to be relocated to another place, this relocation would be an opportunity to meet military heroes and continue to do philosophy. The trouble is that filling out the second alternative in that way renders the disjunction we began with inexhaustive. There are, unfortunately, many other ways in which death could be construed as the soul's relocation to another place; some of them would not include the opportunity to meet one's heroes or engage in endless philosophy. (I have not considered whether meeting with one's heroes might eventually become boring, or whether endless philosophy might one day lose its attraction, even to Socrates.)

2. PLATO

The dramatic setting for Plato's dialog, Phaedo, is the jail where Socrates has been kept, pending his execution. We are told that no execution could be carried out while a ceremonial ship was making its yearly voyage. But now, at the time of the discussion in the Phaedo, the ship had returned and this was to be the day that Socrates would drink the hemlock. The words of Socrates in this discussion are thus presented as the last words of Socrates before his death. It is soon obvious, however, that the figure of Socrates in this middle dialog of Plato's is very different from the figure of Socrates in the Apology. The simplest way to understand this transformation is to suppose that, whereas the ideas and reasoning of the Apology offer a fairly accurate presentation of the ideas and reasoning of the historical Socrates, the Socrates in Plato's Phaedo is pretty much a mouthpiece for Plato himself.

In fact, it is much too simple to say that the Socrates of the Apology is the historical figure, whereas the Socrates of the Phaedo is a stand-in for Plato himself. To mention just what is most obvious, the Phaedo is not a treatise, but a dialog. Even if the ideas and arguments discussed in this work are Plato's rather than those of the historical Socrates, the dialog form gives Plato the freedom to discuss them without committing himself to the viability of any of them.

This is not, however, the place to develop a more nuanced interpretation of the relationship between the figure of Socrates in the Phaedo and the views we may plausibly ascribe to Plato at the time he wrote this dialog. So, in this context, let's just suppose that the Socrates of the Phaedo is indeed a stand-in for Plato himself.

2.1 The Phaedo

In the Phaedo Socrates presents no fewer than four distinct arguments for the immortality of the soul. We might be tempted to think that Plato's aim in this dialog is to prove that we should accept the second possibility Socrates had presented in the Apology, in T3, namely, that death is the soul's relocation to another place. But this is not really so. The arguments in the Phaedo lead to the conclusion that the soul is something akin to the Platonic Forms, which are, if not exactly abstract objects, still completely unchanging realities. Take this passage, in which Socrates is speaking, we are assuming, on Plato's behalf:

> T9. Consider then, Cebes, whether it follows from all that has been said that the soul is most like the divine, deathless, intelligible, uniform, indissoluble, always the same as itself, whereas the body is most like that which is human, mortal, multiform, unintelligible, soluble and never consistently the same. (Phaedo, 80ab)

Whatever exactly this suggestion comes to, it does not suggest that one's soul in the afterlife would enjoy hanging out with military heroes or examining, philosophically, one's fellow citizens to see if they know what courage is, or what justice is. So, it seems, Plato in the Phaedo is not filling out the second possibility enunciated in the Apology at all. Rather, he is arguing for the persistence, indeed the immortality, of a rather austere entity that is much more like an abstract object than it is like a human companion or philosophical conversation partner.

Should we, or anyone on death row, be comforted by the thought that death is the release from the body of our most intellectual self, something that is immortal by being uniform, indissoluble, always the same as itself and, in its nature, akin to the Form of the Good, the Just, and the Beautiful? What would (or what will?) it be like to survive death as a separated Platonic soul—something akin to the Platonic Forms? And is this prospect comforting or alarming?

Surprisingly, Plato has Socrates in the Phaedo say quite a bit about what the afterlife will be like. It is, however, a challenge to fit together this picture of the afterlife he paints with what Plato had Socrates tell us about the nature of the surviving soul.

To be sure, Socrates does not claim to have any real knowledge of what exist-ence will be like in the afterlife. Instead, Plato has Socrates claim only to be repeat-ing the tales he has heard from others. (This reminds us of what Socrates had said in the Apology, in T6.) Nevertheless, the Socrates of the Phaedo clearly takes those tales and fables very seriously. He introduces his account this way:

> T10. Indeed, to speak about this from hearsay, but I do not mind telling you what I have heard, for it is perhaps most appropriate for one who is about to depart yonder to tell and examine tales about what we believe that journey to be like. (61d)

2.1.1 Suicide

Socrates's interlocutor at this point in the dialog, Cebes, is puzzled about what he takes to be Socrates's belief, that death is to be welcomed, even though suicide is wrong. How could that be? Here is part of what Socrates say in response:

> T11. There is the explanation that is put in the language of the mysteries, that we human beings are in a kind of prison, and that one must not free oneself or run away. That seems to me an impressive doctrine and one not easy to understand fully. However, Cebes, this seems to be well expressed, that the gods are our guardians and that human beings are one of their possessions. (62b)

Cebes has difficulty reconciling the idea that we human beings belong to the gods, yet, as Socrates has also suggested, should welcome the escape of their souls from imprisonment in their bodies:

> T12.As for what you were saying, that philosophers should be willing and ready to die, that seems strange, Socrates, if what we said just now is reasonable, namely, that a god is our protector and that we are his possessions. It is not logical that the wisest of men should not resent leaving this service in which they are governed by the best of masters, the gods, for a wise man cannot believe that he will look after himself better when he is free. (62de)

Immodestly Socrates says he would be worried if he were not confident of his own goodness:

> T13. Be assured that, as it is, I expect to join the company of good human beings. This last I would not altogether insist on, but if I insist on anything at all in these matters, it is that I shall come to gods who are very good masters. That is why I am not so resentful, because I have good hope that some future awaits human beings after death, as we have been told for years, a much better future for the good than for the wicked. (63bc)

There follows a picture of the last judgment and the ways in which those who have lived good lives will be rewarded and those who have not will be punished. The details of this picture are not important for my purposes here. What I want to emphasize is the puzzle of how this picture of reward and punishment in the after-life can be fitted together with the metaphysics of soul survival, where that is taken to mean the persistence of something akin to the Forms.

2.2 Philosophy as Practice in Dying

Admittedly, Plato has Socrates put forward this picture of the last judgment as a sort of fable. But what could be the literal meaning of this fable? Our best hint comes from passages like this one:

> T14. I want to make my argument before you, my judges, as to why I think that a man who has truly spent his life in philosophy is probably right to be of good cheer in the face of death and to be very hopeful that after death he will attain the greatest blessings yonder…I am afraid that other people do not realize that the one aim of those who practice philosophy in the proper manner is to practice for dying and death. (64a)

Not many of us philosophers today will know what to make of the suggestion that their one aim is to "practice for dying and death." The most I can make of this suggestion myself is to take Plato to mean that philosophy is aimed at coming to know the Forms, such as Justice, Beauty, Piety, and preeminently, the Form of the Good. Perhaps, then, the soul of the good philosopher will be able to contemplate the Forms eternally, and especially the Form of the Good. But what it would it be like to contemplate eternally the Form of the Good? Is there even anything it would be like to do that? Unfortunately, Plato does not give us any help in trying to answer those questions.

2.3 Conclusion

If, then, we take Plato's Phaedo to be an expression of Plato's own views about death and we take the Apology to present Socrates's views about death, we can make this comparison. First, whereas Socrates thinks death might mean eternal oblivion for the human individual, Plato has a number of arguments for the immortality of the human soul. Socrates thinks that, if death is eternal oblivion, it may be like the blessing of a dreamless sleep; but Plato, having a number of arguments for the soul's immortality, does not take seriously the possibility of death as eternal oblivion for the person who dies.

Second, whereas Socrates suggests that the afterlife may be almost an extension of the present life, only better. Plato allows that such stories of the afterlife are only mythological. However, Plato's suggestions about the literal metaphysics of the soul's afterlife leave us with very little understanding of what it would be like to actually be a separated soul. His optimism about his postmortem fate needs, I think, to stand on two legs. Concerning the first leg, his confidence in there being an afterlife at all rests, for its justification, on the cogency of his arguments for the immortality of the soul. (I have not even stated any of those arguments here, let alone tried to assess their cogency.) As for the second leg, his confidence that the prospect of eternal life is something to be welcomed needs an account of what it might be like to live as a separated soul. Saying that it will be actually doing what philosophy is practice for doing is not of much help.

Third, although Socrates seems to take the mythological stories about the afterlife quite literally, Plato seems to distance himself somewhat from any commitment to their literal truth, What is lacking in Plato's approach to these stories, however, is a serious attempt to, first, identify the literal truth behind the traditional metaphors, and, second, to fit this literal truth together with his metaphysical story about soul survival as the eternal existence of something akin to the Forms. Without those additional elements, Plato has not made clear why the Socrates of the Phaedo should be more optimistic about his postmortem prospects than Socrates is in the Apology.

3. ARISTOTLE

Whereas Plato offers specific, and sometimes very detailed, arguments for the immortality of the soul, nothing comparable is to be found in Aristotle. This should not be surprising. Plato is a soul-body dualist. For him a human being is the temporary union of two distinct substances. By contrast, Aristotle thinks of the human soul, not as a distinct substance, but rather as the functional form of a living human body. When a human body ceases to perform any life functions, such as metabolism, perception, or movement, its functional form, its soul, no longer exists. The corpse, he thinks, is not a human being, except in an extended sense of the term.

3.1 Soul Separation

What we do find in Aristotle, however, is the idea that at least part of the soul, namely, the intellect, is separable from the body and is immortal. Here in Book I of Aristotle's De anima, is reasoning to that effect:

> T15. The intellect seems to be born in us as a kind of substance and not to be destroyed. For it would be destroyed, if at all, by the feebleness of old age, while as things are what happens is similar to what happens in the case of the sense organs. For if an old man acquired an eye of a certain kind, he would see even as well as a young man. Hence old age is not due to the soul's being affected in a certain way, but to this happening to that which the soul is in, as in the case of drunkenness and disease. (408b18–24)[2]

Aristotle does not spell out what it would be for the intellect to survive a person's death, let alone never be destroyed. But the passage is nevertheless tantalizing. Here is another suggestive passage from the end of De anima I:

> T16. That, therefore, the soul or certain parts of it, if it is divisible, cannot be separated from the body is quite clear; for in some cases the actuality is [the actuality]of the parts themselves. Not that anything prevents at any rate some parts from being separable, because of their being actualities of no body. (413a3–7)

The reasoning behind these pregnant sentences seems to go along the following lines. To think of something is, in a way, to take on the form of the thing one is thinking of (413a13ff). But the intellect can think of all sorts of things, including all sorts of materials. If the intellect were the actuality of, that is, the form of, say, the brain, then the brain itself would be able to take on the form of any material that one can think of. But that would be impossible. Organic matter, such as the stuff that makes up the brain, cannot take on the form of gold or lead. But one can use one's intellect to think of both gold and lead. Therefore the intellect is something distinct from, and therefore separable from, the body.

The great medieval Aristotelian, St. Thomas Aquinas, took Aristotle's idea that the human intellect is not the form of anything bodily as the basis for his argument that the human soul survives death as a "subsisting thing," although not as a full substance in its own right.[3] According to Aquinas, the soul of an individual human person is immortal. After one's death, the separated soul awaits reunion with its body (more exactly, union with a spiritualized version of its very own body) in the resurrection. Needless to say, this reasoning of St. Thomas goes well beyond anything to be found in Aristotle. In fact, as I shall try to show, it contradicts Aristotle.

In Book 3 of the De anima Aristotle distinguishes between two kinds of intellect: the passive (or potential) intellect, and the agent (or active) intellect. In chapter 5 of that book he says that the agent intellect, but not the passive intellect, is "immortal and eternal" (430a22). What exactly it might mean for the agent intellect, alone and without the passive intellect, to be immortal and eternal has been the subject of speculation over the centuries. It seems that the agent intellect, without the aid of the passive intellect, might contemplate something eternally; but it could not have episodic thoughts. That is, without the passive intellect it could not think first this, and then that. Thus it would not be anything like a human mind, with its stream of consciousness. And thus it seems that no individual human mind could survive as an agent intellect.

3.2 Immortality as an Impossibility

Lest there be any doubt about whether Aristotle considered that he, or we, might enjoy, or suffer, eternal life, it is well to consider this passage from Aristotle's Nicomachean Ethics:

> T17. For there is no such thing as choosing impossible things, and, if one said he chose such things, he would be thought to be silly; but there is wishing even for impossible things, e.g. immortality.[4] (1111b20–23)

In T17 Aristotle makes clear that, in his view, immortal life for a human being is simply an impossibility, no matter how much we may wish for it. In other passages Aristotle rules out there being an afterlife of any sort, even, by transmigration, a second life. Consider this passage from his discussion of courage in the Nicomachean Ethics:

> T18. Now death is the most fearful of all things; for it is the end, and nothing is thought to be any longer either good or bad for the dead.[5] (1115a26–28)

Admittedly, there is in the last book of the Nicomachean Ethics this rather strange admonition:

> T19. But we must not follow those who advise us, being human beings, to think [only] of human things, and, being mortal, [only] of mortal things, but we must, so far as we can, make ourselves immortal, and strain every nerve to live in accordance with the best thing in us; for even if it be small in bulk, much more does its power and worth surpass everything. (1177b31–78a2)

It may be at least initially puzzling what it could mean to, "so far as we can, make ourselves immortal." But there is no evidence, either in this chapter or elsewhere in Aristotle's corpus, that Aristotle thinks we can actually succeed in "making ourselves immortal." His idea is rather that, so far as we can, we should lead a contemplative life that emulates the contemplative life of immortal beings, that is, of the gods.

3.3 Suicide Again

It may also be puzzling how Aristotle could think that, whereas suicide is wrong, being courageous is virtuous, even if being courageous means making it likely, or even certain, that one will die as a result of one's virtuous action. Part of the puzzle is rather easily resolved. Aristotle does not, like Plato, suggest that our souls are imprisoned in our bodies by an act of the gods, so that it would be impious to arrogate to ourselves the right to release ourselves from this divinely instituted imprisonment. Much more simply, Aristotle thinks that committing suicide would be an act of cowardice:

> T20. But to die to escape from poverty or love or anything painful is not the mark of a brave man, but rather of a coward; for it is softness to fly from what is troublesome, and such a man endures death not because it is noble but to fly from evil. (1116a12–15)

That judgment about suicide and cowardice, however, raises a fundamental question for Aristotelian ethics.

3.4 Eudaimonia

According to Aristotle, the unqualified good for a human person is eudaimonia.[6] Notoriously, it is difficult to translate "eudaimonia." The standard English translation is "happiness." But "happiness" in modern usage seems too shallow for what Aristotle has in mind. "Flourishing" has been suggested as an alternative. But it is not obvious that "flourishing" is specific enough to do the job. I am going to try to finesse this problem by translating "eudaimonia" as happiness*, and "eudaimôn" as happy*. I understand happiness* to be, certainly not a state of mere amusement, or even contentment, or satisfaction, but rather an ideal state of human well-being. What exactly that state of well-being might consist in, or what Aristotle thought it would consist in, I shall not try to determine here. I shall point out simply that

Aristotle says we all desire happiness*, and desire it for itself, not just as the means for getting something else.[7]

Aristotle is both a psychological eudaimonist and an ethical eudaimonist. That is, he supposes not only that the desire to be happy* is what motivates our actions, but also that success at actually being happy* is what makes a person ethically virtuous.

Let us focus for a moment on psychological eudaimonism and the thought that performing a virtuous act may lead to one's own death and one may even realize that performing this act will have such a consequence. How can Aristotle think that the desire to be happy* may motivate a right-thinking person, no matter how courageous, to perform an action that that person realizes will probably lead to her or his own death? If one believed in an afterlife, his answer might be that that a sufficiently courageous person might choose death in the expectation of a reward in the hereafter. But, as T18 makes clear, Aristotle thinks that death is, for each of us, eternal oblivion. So a right-thinking person, according to Aristotle, will not be motivated to choose death in the expectation of reward in the afterlife.

Alternatively, Aristotle might think that performing an action that one thinks might well lead to one's death would be irrational and so not anything a right-thinking person would do. But, to the contrary, he clearly thinks that such an action might be supremely virtuous, and, therefore, it might be something completely rational, indeed, ideally rational. But how could it be?

In fact, there is a double puzzle here: (i) how could I rationally suppose that doing something that will bring about my death will contribute positively to my own happiness*? And (ii) how could I be right about this? That is, how could it be the case that there are circumstances in which doing something that will bring about my death will actually contribute positively to my own happiness*, and not just contribute to my reputation or renown?

3.5 Virtuous Acts and Virtuous Persons

Aristotle draws a very important distinction between being a virtuous person and performing a virtuous act, and so, for example, between being a brave person and performing a brave act. Aristotle thinks we become virtuous persons, if at all, by habituation through practice. To begin with, we need to have a good upbringing to become a virtuous person. We then learn to perform virtuous actions by having them modeled for us. To become a virtuous person we need to have performed virtuous acts until we do so from a firm and unchangeable character (or disposition; 1105a32–33).

Thus Aristotle's notion of a brave soldier is not that of a soldier who performs a single brave act, no matter how brave that act was. Rather, on his view, a brave soldier is someone who performs brave acts from a firm and unchangeable character or disposition. To ask what motivates an already brave soldier to perform an act that leads to a noble death should not, therefore, be to ask simply what goes through the soldier's mind at the moment he made the decision to perform the action Aristotle would honor him for. It is rather to ask what developed the soldier's character in such a way that, when the appropriate moment arrived, he acted bravely from a firm and unchangeable character or disposition. And so we have a solution to the double puzzle.

We may find Aristotle's preoccupation with battlefield courage disturbing. I do. But his distinction between the virtuous act and the virtuous person is, I think, profound. Moreover, it is helpful, not only in trying to understand what motivates people to perform acts of great courage or generosity, but also in thinking about our own choices and the implications those choices have for the sort people we will become, or have already become.

3.6 A Complete Life

The double puzzle above may remind us of a perplexity Aristotle discusses early on in the Nicomachean Ethics. Having concluded in chapter 7 of Book 1 that eudaimonia is "activity of the soul in accordance with virtue, and if there are several, with the best and most complete [virtue]." Aristotle adds "in a complete life." Two chapters later he tries to make clear why he added "in a complete life":

> T21. For there is required [for eudaimonia], as we said, not only complete virtue but also a complete life, since many changes occur in life, and all manner of changes, and the most prosperous may fall into great misfortunes in old age, as is told of Priam in the Trojan cycle; and one who has experienced such chances and has ended wretchedly no one calls happy*. (1100a4–9)

Aristotle then asks whether adding the restriction, "in a complete life" means that no one is truly happy* until dead, when it would be too late to be happy? Aristotle spends the next chapter, chapter 10, trying to deal with this perplexity.

Priam is Aristotle's favored example of someone with a life that seems to be happy* until near the end, but then ends wretchedly. According to legend, King Priam of Troy lost thirteen sons in the last year of his life and was himself butchered at the very end. Aristotle's point is that we do not know whether someone who has been happy* throughout a very long life might not suffer a reversal of fortune and meet with a calamity that would undermine the claim of happiness* that had seemed so secure up until that point. From this we may conclude that the ascription of happiness* to a life is always defeasible, up until death.

Is the claim to happiness* defeasible even after death? That is, can the ascription of happiness* to someone be defeated by what happens even after that person's death? In a way this thought seems to Aristotle to be absurd. After all, he has told us that happiness* is an activity of soul in accordance with virtue and he thinks there is no activity of soul after one's death. Yet he thinks that what happens to one's children and to one's reputation after death may appropriately alter, even if only slightly, the assessment of one's happiness*. I don't think he means this may happen by backward causation! I think his idea is that being virtuous, or failing to be virtuous, has natural consequences, including natural consequences for one's children and one's reputation. Of course, those natural consequences may be thwarted or subverted by chance circumstances. Yet, ceteris paribus, one's virtue, and therefore one's happiness*, is naturally reflected in the well-being of one's children and in the nobility of one's reputation. Conversely, ceteris paribus, unhappiness in one's children and a sullied reputation means that one's life was not really as happy* as it had seemed to be.

3.7 Conclusion

Aristotle displays none of the cheerful optimism that radiates from Socrates's last words in the Apology. Nor does he present any of the arguments for the soul's immortality that we find in Plato's Phaedo. Instead he tries to help us face up to our mortality in a way that will enhance our chances of living worthy lives. But he admits that, whether our lives actually turn out to be happy*, is not entirely up to us.

NOTES

1. Translations from Plato are taken, with occasional modifications, from Plato, 1997. Citations are given as Setphanus pages and page sections.
2. Translations from Aristotle's De anima are taken from Aristotle, 1968.
3. Summa theologiae 1a q75 a2.
4. Translation mine.
5. Except for T17, translations from the Nicomachean Ethics are taken from Aristotole, 1999.
6. Nicomachean Ethics 1.7.
7. *Ibid.* 1.4.

REFERENCES

Aristotle. 1968. *De Anima.* Translated by D. W. Hamlyn. Oxford: Clarendon Press.
Aristotle. 1999. *The Nicomachean Ethics.* Translated by David Ross. Oxford: Oxford University Press.
Plato. 1997. *Plato: Complete Works.* John M. Cooper, editor. Indianapolis, IN: Hackett.

CHAPTER 8

WHEN DEATH IS THERE, WE ARE NOT

EPICURUS ON PLEASURE AND DEATH

PHILLIP MITSIS

AMONG ancient Greek philosophers, the Epicureans were not alone in thinking that a significant variety of benefits, both moral and otherwise, would accrue to agents who could free themselves from the fear of death. In their own way, Socrates, Plato, and the Stoics all offered arguments that were aimed to soothe death's sting by reducing or eliminating our attachments to life in the light of such overriding commitments as philosophy, eternal psychic perfection, moral virtue, and so on. But it was the Epicureans who insisted most vociferously that a thanatology must serve as the crucial lynchpin of any compelling ethical theory. Moreover, it is their particular formulations of ancient arguments that, for a variety of historical reasons, have largely captured the attention of subsequent philosophers, especially their attempt to mount a systematic defense of their most striking and grandiloquent claim, one succinctly encapsulated by Lucretius, the Roman Epicurean poet, in the lines "death is nothing to us, and concerns us not a jot, since the nature of the mind is understood to be mortal" (*DRN* 3.830; trans. Rouse). It is this claim in particular that has garnered by far the most recent attention, in part, no doubt, because of the Epicureans' insistence that death can do us no harm despite the fact that it means our utter personal extinction or annihilation—a claim that in its basic assumptions, at least, frees the discussion from any untoward theological constraints and, accordingly, is more amenable to the analyses of most contemporary professional philosophers. At the same time, so little of any actual sustained argument for Epicurus's claim survives, much less any record of the ancient philosophical parrying between Epicureans and their opponents over it, that inevitably, at least from the perspective of the historian, the ancient Epicureans are typically given either too much or too little credit for their views. Understandably, many contemporary philosophers find it sufficient for their purposes to use what have become some standard Epicurean jumping off points in the literature—for example, the symmetry argument, the subject argument, the timing question, the tedium of mortality problem, and so on—to develop their own arguments both for and against "Epicurean" positions using logical and metaphysical machinery of which the ancient Epicureans could have had little inkling. At the same time, however, it is perhaps worth remembering that Epicurus offered his arguments in a particular historical context and from within a particular vision of a good life that is often remote from contemporary preoccupations, with the result that all too often the Epicureans are casually charged with having some rather obvious philosophical blind spots that in point of fact bear little relation to any of their actual views. By the same token, they are just as often charitably credited with having insights that they are unlikely to have welcomed. Thus, it might be of some use, if only as historical background for the rest of this volume, to try to set the record straight about the philosophical origins of those of Epicurus's claims that still provoke fruitful controversy, even if his developed arguments in defense of them are mostly irrecoverable.

I begin by offering a brief sketch of the general context of Epicurus's views about death and their place in his overall ethical theory. On the one hand, this can perhaps serve to illustrate why the Epicureans did not think that they were in the business of merely trying to cleverly defend a perversely counterintuitive, albeit isolated, view—a sneaking suspicion that often lurks just below the surface of many contemporary attacks on the "Epicurean" position. Indeed, to the contrary, Epicurus believed that his strong claims about death's inability to affect the quality of a pleasurable life follow naturally from a particular conception of the good. Among philosophers in Greco-Roman antiquity, this was by no means a minority position, and it is probably no exaggeration to claim that such deeply contrasting attitudes to the harm of death represent one of the most characteristic divides between most ancient and modern philosophers. By the same token, the fact that Epicurus was a hedonist and yet held that death in no way harms a pleasant life often occasions particular puzzlement along with the conclusion that either he was deeply confused or could not have really meant his claims about death in a strict sense. Again, however, there is often a deep historical disconnect between Epicurus's guiding assumptions about a pleasurable life and the kinds of intuitions about meaningful lives and possible pleasant lives that many contemporary philosophers rely on to undercut so-called Epicurean positions. Thus, in order to avoid confusions from the outset, it might be worth offering a few very rough initial characterizations about how ancient Epicureans conceived of a pleasurable life within the wider context of their ethical thinking.

As in much of ancient philosophy, the Epicureans offer a normative account of happiness and the good life that is embodied in the thoughts, arguments, and actions of the exemplary wise man. Thus, the primary focus of their thanatology is to show that the pleasures and lives of the wise can in no way be harmed by death. Their attitude toward the rest of us benighted souls and the kinds of lives that we are living can perhaps be best summarized by a passage in Lucretius that anticipates the following old Catskill joke by a couple thousand years. Two elderly women are complaining to each other about their stay at a resort and the first says, "The food was really horrible," to which the second replies, "Yes, I know, absolutely terrible. And the portions were so small." Lucretius claims that the lives of all but wise Epicureans are so miserable that they would be much better off wishing for death to relieve them of their misery; perversely, however, they continue to wish for more of the same, all the while complaining about the shortness of lives that are themselves only sources of pain and disturbance (*DRN* 3.940–44).

Thus, for most of us, he claims, death mercifully comes in the form of beneficent natural euthanasia, and the sooner the better. As we shall see, since Epicureans believe that they have good reason for thinking that death causes no harm to those leading the best kind of life, Lucretius's rather rhetorical and dark-humored sally helps to reinforce the standard school line that death brings no harm to anyone, wise or not. Of course, this is not the kind of argument that is anywhere near the high end of their technical arsenal, but it does offer a glimpse into a certain attitude and style of argument prevalent in ancient philosophical contexts where philosophers are far less reticent to pronounce negatively on the values of every so-called life plan other than their own. It also shows where they are more inclined to expend their argumentative energies and why they are less likely to devote their time to the kinds of hard cases and grayish counterexamples that typically populate today's more ecumenical discussions about lives and their possibilities. It is worth remembering in this context, for instance, that for their rivals the Stoics, the world was divided into fools and wise men, the latter of which were as rare as the Ethiopian Phoenix; and the Stoics illustrated this rigid divide by noting that someone who is drowning near the surface is drowning just as much as someone who has sunk to the bottom. Such an attitude is pervasive among the Epicureans as well, with perhaps one passing exception. As opposed to the typically harsh, aggressive view that finds expression in Lucretius, there are some slight traces of a second, slightly more nuanced response by Philodemus, his Greek near contemporary. Philodemus seems to concede that death might be a harm to those, at least, who have a certain amount of philosophical ability and are striving toward a life of Epicurean wisdom, but who have not yet achieved it; that is, they are still drowning, but with some hope of coming up for air. Unfortunately, it is hard to know exactly what more can be made of this possible exception to the strict Epicurean line about death's inability to harm lives prematurely, especially since, for purely rhetorical reasons, Philodemus at times seems to sympathetically make concessions to opposing objections that he doesn't really endorse (Armstrong, 2004). If an

Epicurean were to actually take this kind of amendment on board more generally, of course, it would open up a Pandora's Box involving all kinds of claims about thwarted potentialities and the consequent harm caused by death to those who are thus thwarted—claims that elsewhere seem to be either ignored or rejected in surviving Epicurean texts. Thus, it seems more likely that, rather than setting out some technically defensible rider to the standard Epicurean claim, this one stray concession by Philodemus had a pastoral rhetorical purpose, say, for instance, to hasten people to philosophy and the good life before it is too late. Nonetheless, we can perhaps discern some faint traces of what has since become a common line of objection to the Epicurean claim about the harm of death. We can also infer, perhaps, that such objections may have elicited a more detailed debate among Epicureans and their ancient opponents; but, unfortunately, as is so often the case, at this point the trail quickly goes cold and we are left only with speculations. It is revealing, though, that the only kind of thwarted possibility that seems to have occasioned any sort of special notice on their part is one connected with the possibility of achieving the state of an Epicurean philosopher. This seems to be entirely in keeping with their typical preoccupation with the normative case of the wise man, to which we can now turn.

There is a pithy description of the wise man's life in another fragmentary passage from Philodemus:

> But a sensible person, one that has learned that it is possible to acquire everything sufficient for a happy life, from that point on walks about as one already laid out for burial and enjoys each single day as if it were an eternity. When it is taken from him, he neither <considers the things taken from him> surprising nor goes along with them as if he were thereby missing out on some aspect of the best possible life. But if he extends his life, he accepts any added time, as he reasonably should, as though having happened on an unexpected piece of good fortune and gives thanks according to the way things are. (Henry, 2009, col 38.14–25)

Before filling in the details of this account, a few quick clarifications might be in order. Like the Stoics, the Epicureans view a good life as consisting in the achievement of a particular state of an agent with a range of properties that can be justified objectively by a direct appeal to nature. They also tend to view that state as the only one having any real value. There are some complexities here, and the Epicureans do not offer the kind of schematic distinctions the Stoics do with their doctrine of preferred indifferents—that is, things that do not have moral value but among which we can still show preferences—but it seems fairly clear that they would be equally unlikely to be moved by contemporary arguments that, say, stress the significance of completing various stages of a life (Striker, 1989) or of being able to tell certain kinds of overarching narratives about the course of one's life as a whole and its various possible trajectories (Velleman, 2000). A better parallel would be to the kind of autobiography told by the seventeenth-century Spanish mystic, Teresa of Avila. She spends a few perfunctory chapters describing her earlier sinfulness and unworthiness and then focuses the bulk of her narrative on trying to capture for her reader the only moments she finds valuable in her life, her mystical unions with the divine. The shape of a normative Stoic or Epicurean life is similar, except that upon achieving the ultimately valuable state the wise man can no longer fail to hold on to it nor need worry, like Teresa, whether similar episodes will be granted in the future by someone or something not under one's control. Once one has achieved the state of Epicurean happiness, which is a purely autonomous achievement, one is in possession of what is ultimately valuable and sufficient for a life as a whole—a bit like a hedonic double first. There are no other stages in a life that are valuable for us to experience per se, nor are there any other competing narratives or life-plans of any comparable value. Moreover, if one were to become worried about losing such a perfect state, one would violate one of its main conceptual requirements and could not really be said to have achieved it. That is, if one were to worry about the continuation of one's perfected state or fear its loss, one could not have satisfied all the requirements for the achievement of Epicurean *ataraxia* or freedom from psychic disturbance in the first place. So, too, although it is reasonable to take prudential steps to ensure that one's perfected state continues—the pursuit of pleasure is a perfectly natural goal, after all—one can do so only without the sort of attachment that would occasion any regret or disturbance if the state were being cut short. Nor, more strikingly, does Epicurus think that a longer or shorter period of being in such a state is any better from the point of view of one's happiness or of the overall value of one's life.

To be sure, we may find much of this rather obscure. It is easy to think of all kinds of individual pleasurable states, for instance, that do not necessarily get better by being prolonged, or that in fact might be ruined by being extended for too long. But, at first blush, it is hard to see how the criteria we use for making judgments about the appropriate duration of individual episodes of pleasure can be smoothly transferred to judgments about some pleasurable condition of a life taken as a whole, especially since the Epicurean is committed to the somewhat different and stronger claim that longer and shorter periods of a perfected life have the exact same value in terms of their overall pleasure. Thus, it obviously would be foolhardy to claim that it is easy to make philosophical sense of any of these general Epicurean views or to fit them coherently into a plausible account of hedonism (see Rosenbaum, 1990, for an heroic attempt). But at the same time, I hope to have given some preliminary indications of why, say, such contemporary philosophical practices as engaging in thought experiments about death and hedonism that rely on our commonplace attitudes and intuitions are likely to misfire in an Epicurean context. Would, for instance, the Epicurean wise man prefer a painful operation, of the sort conceived by Parfit, to be done in the future or to have been done in the past? And are his attitudes about death in any way parallel to his attitudes to these sorts of pains? The Epicurean would insist first of all that there are no compelling reasons for us to trust our own so-called ordinary intuitions about pleasant experiences when facing questions about death. All but the wise are confused about their assessments of pleasures since their beliefs and experiences have become corrupted. At the same time, I think, this very style of argument that proceeds by fictional examples would fall with a dull thud in the argumentative contexts of ancient Epicureanism. Apart from the standard ancient Epicurean worry about the intelligibility of making any inferences from our experiences, however conscious, to a state of death which is not experienced, the Epicurean wise man in such cases would have no hedonic basis in Epicurean terms for making a judgment, nor would Epicureans allow any inferences except from the point of view of the wise man's normative experience of pleasure. Any suggestions that there might be reasons for preferring a later to an earlier death are immediately ruled out by their account of the particular features of the wise man's experience of pleasure which, for an Epicurean at least, trumps the kinds of unreconstructed intuitions that such fictional examples might elicit from us. We will need to return to some further features of Epicurus's hedonism for a final assessment of the kind of support that it can lend his arguments about death, but for the moment we can now turn to those arguments themselves.

1. THE DEATH ARGUMENTS

Several claims about death's inability to harm us survive in ancient Epicurean texts or are attributed to Epicureans, but we can only speculate about how Epicurus himself might have thought that these various arguments are related. Moreover, although he was famous in antiquity both for the amount and variety of his writings, we do not have even one secure title for a work of his devoted exclusively to death, though it seems unlikely that such a central and characteristic concern of his philosophy could have gone thus neglected. We do have evidence, though, that his followers wrote works focused on death, so it is fairly plausible to conclude that in doing so they were following in the footsteps of their founder. Even so, what survives from what was no doubt a long history of extensive and fairly developed discussions are mostly a few scattered assertions by Epicurus himself, Lucretius's poetic summary in *De Rerum Natura*, and some scraps from the badly fragmented Herculaneum papyrus text of the fourth book of Philodemus's *De Morte*, which only recently has been edited and translated (Henry, 2009). Nonetheless, these claims, even in summary form, on their own harbor a sufficiently difficult set of philosophical challenges to have given rise to a sophisticated array of arguments from contemporary philosophers attempting to contend with what, ironically, the ancient Epicureans themselves took to be a rather commonplace set of considerations in support their arguments. So, too, most contemporary arguments take the form of what the Epicureans themselves would have regarded in the first instance as a distinctly rearguard action, in the sense that few contemporary ethical theorists have taken seriously to heart Epicurus's primary concern that a proper recognition of our mortality needs to be at the very heart of any systematic ethical and political theory. Although the past few decades have seen some significant changes from the days when philosophers barely gave a nod to the fact that we must confront death and that our attitudes toward this prospect might have a significant impact on our overall prudential and moral deliberations, it is still only fairly recently that philosophers have started to seriously link their analyses of the metaphysical puzzles generated by Epicurus's claims about death with broader ethical and political concerns, for the most part still focusing on questions about individual welfare and happiness (e.g., Feldman, 1992 and 2004). The verdict is far from in, of course, whether this key aspect of Epicurus's ethical project will continue to gain further traction in many wider arenas of contemporary ethical and political argument, but for the Epicureans, this was the most significant element of their thanatology.

Although we have little in the way of supporting argument, it is fairly clear that the Epicureans traced a host of personal and societal evils to the fear of death. Indeed, they single it out as the most pervasive and corrosive harm afflicting both individuals and societies. One might object, of course, that the fear of death is an unavoidable feature of our psychologies or that it necessarily figures in deep-seated evolutionary explanations of animals in general; but the Epicureans disagree and claim that such fear can be eradicated since it arises solely from mistaken beliefs and corrupting social practices. Actual arguments are few and hard to come by, but we do have Lucretius's account of the origins of human societies—an account that was to prove hugely influential for Rousseau and other Enlightenment thinkers—in which he tries to show that the fear of death is merely a lamentable human construct (*DRN* 5.925–1457). Animals and early, presocial humans avoid pain and as a consequence death, he argues, but they have no conscious conception of death itself and hence, by nature, no fear of it per se. He denies, moreover, the kind of claim that Hobbes makes in arguing that we not only have ample reason to fear death, but also that such fear actually benefits us since it makes us both more inclined to look after our own self-interest and to be more tractable in our dealings with our neighbors. For Hobbes, if we did not fear death, we could not properly cultivate our own best interests nor could we form political communities that protect us from harm generally. Lucretius strongly disagrees and argues that a war of all against all arises only after agents have come to think that they must heap up material goods in order to insulate and protect themselves from death—a tactic that not only is futile and self-defeating, but that creates the very scarcity of goods that drives agents into a Hobbesian competition in the first place. This competition is further exacerbated by religious ignorance and the stories of priests about dire punishments in an afterlife. It is a primitive ignorance of celestial phenomena that first gives rise to men's fear of death (*DRN* 5.1204 ff), since they attribute to gods the ability to control natural phenomena, and their misplaced fear of divine power is then easily manipulated by priests for their own ends. Fortunately, once we understand the principles of Epicurean atomism, Lucretius insists, we can easily free ourselves from the fear of the gods and the fear of an afterlife. But it this unholy nexus of scientific ignorance and religious superstition that, in a phrase much quoted in the Enlightenment, was "so potent in persuading to evil deeds" (*DRN* 1.101).

It is hard to know exactly what kinds of psychological evidence and arguments the Epicureans might have hoped to use in defense of these claims about the pervasive influence of the fear of death and its deleterious effects on individuals and societies (Konstan, 2008 for a suggestive reading). But from the perspective of the later history of philosophy, it is perhaps ironic that in the long tradition of thinkers from Rousseau to Marx who have been influenced by many central Epicurean claims about the origins of societies, religion, alienation, etc. and their psychological mechanisms, it is the fear of death that seems to have dropped out from their accounts as the crucial originating source of our troubles. The Epicureans, no doubt, would have viewed this as a lamentable omission, but we unfortunately have few clues about how they might have tried to go about demonstrating it.

However keen the Epicureans themselves were to show how the fear of death, in its own right, has bad systemic effects on our lives, what has captured the attention of contemporary philosophers is their claim that the fear of death is based entirely on a simple conceptual mistake. A succinct statement of this claim can be found in Epicurus's *Letter to Menoeceus*:

> Therefore that most frightful of evils, death, is nothing to us, seeing that when we exist, death is not present, and when death is present, we do not exist. Thus it is nothing either to the living or the dead, seeing that the former do not have it, and the latter no longer exist. (Long and Sedley, 1987, 24 A5, *Ad Men.* 125)

The Epicureans offer an impressive battery of empirical observations in defense of their materialist contention that we are strictly material entities whose matter is dispersed upon death and, along with it, the relevant atomic structures upon which both our existence and identities as persons are grounded (cf. *DRN* 3, 1–857). To be sure, there were other available views about our postmortem prospects and the Epicureans also cast doubt on the possibility and desirability of many of those as well. They deny, for instance, that any kind of postmortem survival could elicit our proper concern, since our personal identity critically depends not only on our being enmattered in our bodies, but also on our being in continuous possession of an unbroken chain of memories (*DRN* 3.843–862). It is the question of annihilation itself, however, that has provoked most contemporary interest. In a short paper in 1970, Thomas Nagel defended the claim that even though, or perhaps just because, we are annihilated at death, we have reason to regard it as being harmful to us. Nagel's paper was important for bringing the question of death a new philosophical prominence and much of the subsequent philosophical work done on this question has followed Nagel's particular emphases on this question. At the same time, Nagel's paper had the effect of raising Epicurus's profile among historians as well, many of whom were clearly surprised to learn that a figure long dismissed as a shallow purveyor of tepid self-help bromides, could have provoked counterarguments of such sophistication. There has since arisen a small industry of classically trained scholars taking up one or another of Epicurus's assertions and trying to flesh them out (see Warren, 2004 for a thorough and even-handed recent survey). Even the most charitable of these scholars, however, has to admit that reconstructions of Epicurus's individual arguments tend to fall in line with contemporary philosophical preoccupations, as do any attempts to forge any systematic connections between them.

For Nagel, Epicurus's argument raises three initial important challenges for anyone who claims that death harms us and is thus to be feared. One must show when death harms us; how it does so; and that it actually harms us, either in the sense of our being subjects whose existence can be located in particular categorical spatiotemporal states or in some other relational sense. There is no historical evidence that Epicurus himself ever organized his arguments along these three categorical axes, but I will do so, if only for the sake of exegetical convenience.

Surviving Epicurean texts suggest that we typically make mistakes on all three counts because of a common conceptual error. We fail to apprehend the nature of our extinction and continually project ourselves into our deaths as if we were still alive and experiencing a series of continued harms at death's hands. We often do this even while claiming to understand that we will be annihilated at death. The point is made in the following way by Lucretius:

> For if there is going to be unhappiness and suffering, the person must also himself exist at that same time, for the evil to be able to befall him. Since death robs him of this, preventing the existence of the person for the evils to be heaped upon, you can tell that there is nothing for us to fear in death, that he who does not exist cannot be unhappy, and that when immortal death snatches away mortal life it is no different from never having been born. So when you see a man resent the prospect of his body being burned and rotting after death, or being destroyed by fire or by the jaws of wild beasts, you may be sure that his words do not ring true, and that there lurks in his heart some hidden sting, however much he may deny the belief that he will have any sensation in death. For he does not, I think, grant either the substance or ground of what he professes. Instead of completely stripping himself of life, unawares he is making some bit of himself survive. (Long and Sedley, 1987, 24 E, *DRN* 3.861–78 trans. modified).

Epicurus often moves easily between the claim that death cannot harm someone who does not exist and the claim that death cannot harm someone who does not perceive it as being painful. The latter claim derives from his hedonism: something that causes us no pain does not harm us. Since our death is a state without any sensation, it is painless, hence harmless. It has recently been argued, however, that there is perhaps some slight evidence in Philodemus that Epicureans saw an important difference between these two claims and perhaps even tried to move between them for purposes of their argument (Armstrong, 2004). This is highly speculative, I think, since Epicureans seem to treat the two claims as interchangeable in all the other texts we have (cf. *Ad Men*.124–6). Of course, it is impossible to know for sure how Epicurus might have reacted to the kinds of moves that Nagel makes between unperceived harms and death, or attempts to show that since we can be harmed by things we are not aware of, we can be harmed by death. On the one hand, Epicureans clearly might be willing to accept objective claims about harms that individuals do not perceive, that is, they think that most people are wrong about their pleasures and are unwittingly suffering harm because of the mistaken choices they are making (cf. *DRN* 3.1053–1075). This might lead us to suspect that they would concur with Nagel in thinking that existing agents can be harmed by things of which they are not aware. Of course, one might be willing to ascribe this kind of unperceived harm to agents without accepting Nagel's further claim that the harm of death is somehow analogous. It seems fairly likely that the Epicureans would have held fast to their claim that there is a categorical difference between ascribing harm to those who exist and to those who do not. Thus, I will assume on the Epicureans's behalf that their arguments are more effective when couched in language about nonexistent subjects as opposed to existing subjects who are merely unaware of a harm that they are suffering. We have no secure evidence, however, that they themselves were ever pushed on this distinction or felt the need to retreat to this stronger claim about nonexistence.

Epicureans repeatedly make the following kind of claim about our annihilation. In trying to conceive of our own deaths we find it difficult—Freud would later say impossible—to extract ourselves from the imagined scene of our death. As a consequence, we tend to project ourselves into our own and others' deaths in a way that makes us view death "not as the annihilation of consciousness, but as the consciousness of annihilation"—to quote the nice Epicurean-like jingle of Silverstein (1980). Instead, they argue, we should come to understand that we really cannot intelligibly imagine what it would be like to be nothing.

Whether we find this claim particularly profound or not—most contemporary philosophers actually find it rather banal—for the Epicureans, this kind of conceptual error regularly colors one of our most important worries about death, that is, that it deprives us of the *praemia vitae* or the rewards of life:

> No more for you the welcome of a joyful home and a good wife. No more will your children run to snatch the first kiss… "Unhappy man," they say, "unhappily robbed by a single hateful day of all those rewards of life." What they fail to add is this: "Nor does any yearning for those things remain in you." If they properly saw this with their mind, and followed it up in their words, they would unshackle themselves of great mental anguish and fear. (Long and Sedley, 1987, 24 E, *DRN* 3.894–903)

The notion that death robs us of the goods of life, or even just some further moments of life itself, may be one of our most common intuitions, but it quickly runs up against the Epicurean's demands for further clarification (see Rosenbaum, 1986 and 1989a, for defenses of Epicurean positions). For instance, exactly when does death rob us of life or life's goods? It certainly cannot rob us of anything when we are dead, the Epicurean replies, since we are not there to be robbed. By the same token, to claim that our future death is currently harming us by robbing us of something while we are now alive would seem to assume some form of backward causation, otherwise how could a posthumous event do us any harm now? We have no evidence that the Epicureans themselves ever relied on any claims about backward causation in this context, but their views of causation in general lend themselves to this kind of charitable construal. In any case, even without openly rejecting backward causation, the Epicureans still conclude that since death can harm us neither when we are dead nor when we are alive, it never harms us.

One might object, of course, that it is possible to locate the harm of death in that very moment of transition between life and death (cf. Luper, 2009). It has recently been argued that such a view may underlie Philodemus's apparent concession that a budding Epicurean philosopher might be harmed by premature death. For the person harmed by not having achieved a philosophical life, it is argued, such harm must occur at the instant of death (Sanders, 2009). Such an account is not impossible, but it is hard to see how, from a wider Epicurean perspective, it can escape from difficulties of its own. This is because there is a long tradition in Greek atomism in chipping away at the notion of a transition between units of time. The Epicureans, for instance, hold that any perceptible instant of time can be broken down into smaller discrete units of time, in the way that objects can be reduced into atoms (*DRN* 4.794–98). So the first question the Epicurean might ask is how do we understand the corresponding subject who is supposed to be making the transition between life and death? If I am not alive at that particular moment of transition between the last unit of life (T1) and the first unit death (T2), how is it that I can be harmed? Or if I am in some sense still alive, worries again arise about backward causation, since how is it that I am now being harmed by my future state of being dead at T2 and beyond? It seems open to the Epicurean, that is, to continue asking for clarification about the nature of the subject meant to be undergoing this instant of transition. If there is a subject persisting through the moment of transition, then there is not yet really a case of death—a case of dying perhaps, but not of death. If there is no persisting subject after T1, however, then it is hard to see how something that no longer exists can be said to be undergoing a transition. In Aristotelian terms, we might say that the notion of a moment of transition between life and death needs to be disambiguated between mere alteration and substantial change. Neither of these options by itself, however, directly conflicts with the Epicurean claim that death can harm us neither when we exist nor after we have been annihilated.

In the light of such difficulties in fixing the harm of death in a temporal sequence, many have thought to cash out Nagel's suggestion that the harm of death occurs at no particular fixed time. This claim is part of his larger argument that the harm of death is "irreducibly relational" and that "most good and ill fortune has as its subject a person identified by his history and his possibilities, rather than by his categorical state of the moment…" (1970, p.77). One common way of illustrating this claim is by appealing to judgments about the relative worth of lives based on comparative counterfactual judgments. So, for example, Mozart, Bellini, and Schubert all had intensely creative, but relatively short lives. Wouldn't their lives have been better and the world of music much richer, if they had not been cut off by death so early? Nagel argues that our common intuitions suggest that we can recognize the harm that death caused in each of these cases, even if we cannot exactly place it temporally. It lies precisely in the enormous range of possibilities lost to these extraordinary lives because of their early deaths.

In attempting to give more precision to such intuitions, a large literature relying on possible world semantics has recently arisen (Bradley, 2009). We can only
speculate how Epicureans might have responded to such arguments (cf. Warren,
chapter 2), however, it is fairly clear that they would have been suspicious of comparisons based on modal properties of persons and so-called possible world coun-
terparts. Given their deeply rooted empiricism, they would insist on conclusions
cashed out in categorical states of agents. There is a brief bit of evidence to this
effect from Cicero (Tusc. i. 9–11), where it is suggested that Epicureans think that
comparisons involving the dead rest on simple mistakes of logic because one cannot coherently predicate properties such as "happy" or "miserable" of something
that no longer exists. The Epicurean holds that the benefits and harms that I experience today and will experience tomorrow can be compared coherently only if it
turns out that I am there at both those times as an existing subject so that their
effects on me can be gauged. Comparisons between times when I do and do not
exist can appear to be of the same form, but they are crucially different and fail
to go through because there is no persisting subject to ground both sides of the
comparison.

Such considerations are not likely to move most possible worlds theorists, of
course, but they do point to some importantly different background assumptions.
The Epicureans are worried about the practical effect of theories and expect that
metaphysical and ethical beliefs will be mutually reinforcing. So, for instance,
the Epicurean would register a general worry about how modal accounts of individual identity might affect our ethical beliefs because of their likely indifference
to capturing any meaningful sense of our mortality. Grant, for instance, that
there are possible worlds in which I may live forever. How should that affect my
attitudes toward death? Nagel, for instance, concludes his paper with the claim
that "if there is no limit to the amount of life it would be good to have, it may
be that a bad end is in store for us all." (Nagel, 79) For the Epicurean, the idea
that we should base our judgments about death in accordance with a theoretical
framework that allows for the possibility of our continuing on forever makes
two fundamental mistakes. First, it is likely to engender irrational and unsatisfi-
able yearnings for immortality that will turn out to be the source of troubling
anxiety:

> Hence a correct understanding that death is nothing to us makes the mortality
> of life enjoyable, not by adding infinite time, but by ridding us of the desire for
> immortality. (Long and Sedley, 1987, 24 A, Ad Men. 124)

Second, by failing to be bound by the actual natural limits of human desires
and lives, such an account conjures up a view of a possible life that is itself unnatural and undesirable. An unending life, Epicureans argue, would become unen-
durable because of its repetitiveness and tediousness. Most people who think they
would like to live forever have given little thought to what such a life actually
would entail. Engaging in the same tasks again and again for an eternity would,
the Epicurean insists, make us like Sisyphus and it would empty our tasks of all

interest and meaning. Accordingly, Lucretius puts the following reproach in the voice of a personified Nature:

> For there is nothing else that I can devise and invent to please you: everything is always the same. If your body is not already withering with years and your limbs worn out and languid, yet everything remains the same, even if you shall outlive all generations, and even more if you should be destined never to die. (*DRN* 944–49, trans. Rouse)

To the objection that, despite the tedium of immortality (Williams, 1973), at least we would not need to fear death if we were immortal, the Epicurean claims that everyone would naturally prefer a shorter happy life to a painful one of unending tedium. More important, the notion of an unending life is nothing but an irrational fantasy in the first place. Given our nature and the fact of our inevitable annihilation, speculations about unending possible lives can only lead us to be fearful of death by engendering desires for something that is neither actual nor desirable. If we want to usefully think about ourselves in terms of modal properties, we might do so not, as it were, horizontally, but vertically, in the sense of realizing in the here and now our potential understanding of both the natural world and ourselves, and as a consequence, learning to lead the happy lives that are at this very instant within our grasp. We are not immortal gods, but we can come to live finite lives worthy of the gods.

One might agree with the Epicurean that counterfactual speculations about what it would be like to live forever are of limited practical use when confronting the prospect of our actual annihilation. Yet, even if one agrees that an unending life is neither possible nor desirable, one might still want just a little extra time, say, either to give one's life the kind of overall shape one expects for it or to finish the narrative one would like to tell about oneself. If death can interrupt these potential goals of mine, don't I have reason to fear it? Again, the Epicurean thinks that such worries are based on a series of mistaken assumptions.

Let us take first the question of life's duration and the notion that, even if we have rid ourselves of the desire for immortality, we still might reasonably wish for some extra time and, as a consequence, have reason to fear death's premature arrival. As we have seen, the Epicureans think that the wise man, although taking steps to continue in his perfect condition, will not desire to do so in a way that would make him fearful of its interruption. There is nothing that his perfect state lacks or needs further time to achieve. Warren raises the objection that the budding Epicurean philosopher, however, has every reason to fear premature death, and he argues that such fear will make it impossible for anyone not yet in a perfected state of *ataraxia* to ever achieve it, since the only way to eradicate that fear is to already be in the actual state of *ataraxia* (Warren, 2004 153–59). I think the Epicureans would find this a rather toothless objection, however, since for them it turns out to be merely another version of the sophistic paradox of knowledge—that is, how can one come to know something without already knowing it—which they reject. Moreover, in terms of the relation of reason and emotion it gets the cart before the horse. The Epicureans are thorough rationalists and believe that once someone comes to understand the truth of a proposition such as "death does no harm," one's emotional states will follow suit and one's fear of death will disappear. As a consequence, one's rational arguments and knowledge are not the prisoners of one's occurrent emotional states. Thus, as soon as the budding Epicurean thoroughly understands the truths of Epicureanism, as we saw in Philodemus's description above, he "from that point on walks about as one already laid out for burial and enjoys each single day as if it were an eternity." One does not ascend the ladder to Epicurean perfection by means of one's emotional states, but by rational arguments.

The Epicureans, moreover, may have offered another kind of argument to help us come to the realization that we are not really concerned about the mere duration of our lives per se. The argument I am referring to has come to be known as "the symmetry argument," though, again, we have no direct evidence that the Epicureans put their symmetry argument to this particular use. Indeed, several scholars doubt that the Epicureans ever formulated, in the first place, the symmetry argument in the form in which it has commonly come to be understood.

The text in Lucretius is the following:

> Look back again to see how the unending expanse of past time, before we are born, has been nothing to us. For Nature holds this forth to us as a mirror image of the time to come after our death. Is there anything terrible there, does anything seem gloomy? Is it not more peaceful than any sleep? (*DRN* 3.972–77)

The passage occurs as the capping argument in a stretch of Lucretius's poem where he is mocking various kinds of complaints about the shortness of life. It therefore seems plausible to conclude that the Epicureans see some kind of connection between our general attitudes to life's duration and those toward our prevital and postmortem nonexistence. Lucretius's poetic metaphor suggests, moreover, that he is talking about an asymmetry between our prospective and retrospective attitudes to periods of our nonexistence, since Nature is holding up prevital nonexistence for us to look at as a mirror image of death. However, a number of scholars have doubted that this passage is about our attitudes to these periods at all, as opposed to just a claim about the nature of these two periods in their own right (Aronoff, 1997; Warren, 2004). Much of the dispute depends on how much weight we want to put on the poetic image, the tenses of the verbs, and the fact that we have no other unambiguous examples of this kind of symmetry argument surviving from antiquity. This is not the place to go into the philological problems that this passage presents, but I think it is fair to say that at the moment, there is no scholarly consensus about the exact status of Lucretius's argument. Moreover, even if we charitably attribute the usual symmetry argument to Epicureans on the basis of Lucretius's imagery, we have no surviving arguments in further defense of it. We only know that an argument whose form and goal is ambiguous on its own is embedded in an account that questions many common attitudes about the duration of lives. I will offer one possible connection here, but mostly in the spirit of illustrating how classical scholars attempt to flesh out arguments on the basis of the thinnest wisps of evidence.

So let's assume for the sake of argument that Lucretius is actually trying to point out a commonly held, but what he takes to be irrational, asymmetry in our attitudes toward the two periods of nonexistence that encompass our lives. We typically live our lives without being bothered by the thought that there was a time in the past when we did not exist, yet we may find the thought of our future nonexistence both terrible and gloomy. The passage would then seem to suggest that it is irrational to hold asymmetric attitudes toward two states that are the relevantly the same and that we should revise our negative attitudes to death accordingly. Recognition of the symmetry between prevital and postmortem nonexistence might also enable us, perhaps, to stop projecting ourselves into our future nonexistence, a common Epicurean complaint, and hence to come to understand that we are not really worried by the duration of our lives per se. If we were so worried, we might wish that we had been born earlier so that our lives would be longer, or we might bemoan the lost possibilities of our earlier nonexistence. Lucretius elsewhere argues that our exact same material constituents may have come together many times in the past (DRN 3.847–861), but we betray no concern for any of our past doubles. By the same token, we typically display a similar lack of concern for any other prevital possibilities, since they also lack the proper connection to our selves (cf. DRN 3.845–51); nor, presumably, would we show much concern for any possibilities of our lives extending further into the past because we actually understand their true purchase. Thus, if it seems merely irrational to lament lost possibilities of the time before we were born, it is equally irrational to lament the loss of our possibilities in death, since they are both equivalent states of our nonexistence. In a sense, the Epicureans suggest that the kinds of considerations we use for establishing the metaphysics of personal identity at the beginning of lives—one that does not allow for different possible beginnings—holds for the end of our lives as well, in the sense that possible postmortem trajectories are similarly not to be factored in as plausible constituents of our actual identities; nor can they be treated as possible loci for attributing harm.

Clearly, most of these claims go beyond anything that can be straightforwardly extracted from this one particular passage in its own right, though they all represent possible inferences from one or another of scattered claims that can be found, at least in embryonic form, in Epicurean texts. Did Epicureans see systematic connections between their arguments here? It is plausible to assume that they must have. Did they or should they have seen any of the connections suggested here? On the one hand, this particular reconstruction can obviously be attacked on many fronts. We can first question, as many have, whether the alleged symmetry is in fact strong enough to warrant regarding both periods of our nonexistence in the exact same manner. Our prevital nonexistence is followed by life, whereas our postmortem nonexistence is followed by nothing, so we might appeal to that difference to justify holding an asymmetric attitude. Worrying, as well, for the Epicurean is the prospect that the general strategy of getting us to revise our attitudes might

backfire. An alternative way of keeping my attitudes symmetrical is to begin viewing my prevital nonexistence with the same dread and gloom that I view my death.
Of course, the Epicurean might argue that such a strategy is mistaken both because
it increases anxiety and because it makes mistakes about the nature of our pre-vital
nonexistence. (Rosenbaum, 1989a). But the mere demand for consistency that this
argument seems to make may be insufficient on its own to block its strategy from
backfiring and to avoid alerting me to the fact that I should begin regretting that
my life did not extend further into the past. Finally, the particular connection to
views about duration per se can come in for attack as well, for we may think that it
fails to account for the ways in which we tend to think of our projects and our lives
as extending into the future and, moreover, that our control over our future, to the
extent that we have control, seems relevantly different from our lack of control over
our past.

On the other hand, however, there are reasons for thinking that the Epicureans
believe that they can defuse such objections. Even though in some ways we may
have more control over our death than our birth, the deepest and most relevant
similarity between prevital and postmortem nonexistence, the Epicureans suggest, is our ultimate lack of control over both. We all live, when facing the prospect of death, in an unguarded castle and cannot hope to cheat death. Moreover,
they believe that such objections assume a mistaken bias toward the future. A wise
man's state of pleasure consists in a mix of pleasurable memories and future expectations that generates no anxiety about future control and that derives just as much
pleasure from one's past experience as from the future. Such a life has no particular bias toward the future, though it can include any added future pleasures as "an
unexpected gift of fortune." Thus, if I am leading a pleasurable life in the right way,
Epicurus claims, I have no need to be anxious about whether death might rob me
of time I would need for living a completely happy life. I can therefore live each single day as if it were an eternity and I can mentally traverse both the course of my
life and the two periods of nonexistence that limit it with equal equanimity.

In making their argument, the Epicureans offer a vision of the pleasant life as
an ongoing state of consciousness that is invulnerable to outside interference, in
the sense that it cannot be harmed by factors outside of an agent's control. Such a
claim might strike many contemporary hedonists as weirdly optimistic in the way
that Stoic claims about the invulnerability of moral character to external events
may appear either melodramatic or unappealing to contemporary moral theorists.
Both think as well that once one achieves the perfected state of a sage, one's happiness is not increased or made more worthwhile by being prolonged. Such claims
might strike many, no doubt, as being on a rational par with St. Teresa's mystical visions. But it was from such a view of a perfected life that many of the death
arguments still exercising today's most accomplished philosophers found their
origins. Moreover, it is perhaps worth remembering that at its deepest stratum,
Epicurus's argument, along with that of the Stoics, is one more ancient variation
of Socrates's claim that the good man cannot be harmed by death. When viewed
from the perspective of the long history of these arguments, it may be that the

intuitions supporting such claims from the origins of Western philosophy could do with the occasional airing in today's discussions. Of course, this is not to suggest that philosophers should endorse mere bravado; but it is perhaps noteworthy that at a time when philosophers' lives were still supposed to exemplify their arguments, most philosophers followed the siren call of Socrates's claim. While it is true that we no longer expect our philosophers to publicly proclaim either their moral perfection or fearlessness in the face of death—indeed, such proclamations would no doubt be met with general derision—it is hard not to notice how arguments about the harm of death are likely to come to different conclusions given these two different intellectual contexts. Most contemporary discussions test our intuitions on morally indifferent agents and attempt to clarify why we think that death harms them—so, for example, Nagel's suggestion that a bad end may be in store for all of us. Most ancient discussions begin with the morally perfect, happy wise man and develop with the expectation that nothing can harm his perfection. This latter view may be well on its way to becoming incomprehensible in its own right, but it is perhaps suggestive that a cluster of arguments derived from it have endured as one of the very few legacies from ancient philosophy that still provokes more than purely scholastic interest. It is hard to explain why that might be the case, but permit me the following historical observation. It may be that some echoes of Socrates's claim, however muted, continue to somehow still resonate in our conceptions of what makes for a good life and with it, the notion, however quaint, that there are some characteristics of the best lived human lives that, in order to retain their value, must remain immune to death's harm or, at the very least, are incompatible with a fear of death. If it turns out that no rational basis can be found for such claims, then perhaps they should be offered up as yet another gift to death, although as the Greek poets used to say, death neither expects nor accepts gifts.

REFERENCES

Armstrong, D. 2004. "All Things to All Men: Philodemus' Model of Therapy and the Audience of De Morte." In *Philodemus and the New Testament World*, J. Fitzgerald, G. Holland, and D. Obbink, eds., pp. 15–54. Leiden: Brill.

Aronoff, P. 1997. "Lucretius and the Fears of Death." PhD dissertation, Cornell University.

Bradley, B. 2009. *Well-Being and Death*. Oxford: Oxford University Press.

Feldman, F. 1992. *Confrontations with the Reaper*. New York: Oxford University Press.

Feldman, F. 2004. *Pleasure and the Good Life*. Oxford: Oxford University Press.

Henry, W. B. 2009. "Philodemus, on Death" (*Writings from the Greco-Roman World*, v. 29). Atlanta: Society for Biblical Literature.

Konstan, D. 2008. *A Life Worthy of the Gods: The Materialist Psychology of Epicurus*. Las Vegas: Parmenides Publishing.

Long, A. A., and Sedley, D. N. 1987. *The Hellenistic Philosophers*. 2 vols. Cambridge: Cambridge University Press.

Luper, S. 2009. *The Philosophy of Death*. Cambridge: Cambridge University Press.

Nagel, T. 1970. "Death." *Noûs* 4: 73–80.

Parfit, D. 1984. *Reasons and Persons*. Oxford: Oxford University Press.

Rosenbaum, S. E. 1986. "How To Be Dead and Not Care: A Defense of Epicurus." *American Philosophical Quarterly* 23: 217–225.

Rosenbaum, S. E. 1989a. "Epicurus and Annihilation." *Philosophical Quarterly* 39: 81–90.

Rosenbaum, S. E. 1989b. "The Symmetry Argument: Lucretius against the Fear of Death." *Philosophy and Phenomenological Research* 50: 353–373.

Rosenbaum, S. E. 1990. "Epicurus and the Complete Life." *Monist* 73: 21–41.

Sanders, K. R. 2009. "Philodemus and the Fear of Premature Death." In *Epicurus and the Epicurean Tradition*, J. Fish, and K.R. Sanders, eds., pp. 211–234. Cambridge: Cambridge University Press.

Silverstein, H. 1980. "The Evil of Death." *Journal of Philosophy* 77: 401–424.

Striker, G. 1989. "Commentary on Mitsis." *Proceedings of the Boston Area Colloquium in Ancient Philosophy* 4: 323–330.

Velleman, J. D. 2000. "Well-Being and Time." In *The Possibility of Practical Reasoning*, Velleman, ed., pp. 56–84. Oxford: Oxford University Press.

Warren, J. 2004. *Facing Death: Epicurus and His Critics*. Oxford: Oxford University Press.

Williams, B. 1973. "The Makropulos Case: Reflections on the Tedium of Immortality." In *Problems of the Self*, Williams, ed., pp. 82–100. Cambridge: Cambridge University Press.

CHAPTER 9

THE BADNESS OF DEATH AND THE GOODNESS OF LIFE

JOHN BROOME

WHAT harm does death do you? To put the question differently: when you die, what do you lose by dying? To put it differently again: when you do not die, what do you gain by continuing to live? The question of what harm death does you is the same as the question of what good is done you by living. It is the question of the goodness of your life.

Two extreme answers can be given. One is "everything"; we might think that, for you, your life is everything, and by dying you lose everything. Another is "nothing"; we might think that you lose nothing by dying. I shall start by rejecting these extreme answers. Then I shall go on to the moderate, quantitative answer that I favor.

1. DO YOU LOSE NOTHING BY DYING?

I shall take the "nothing" answer first. Epicurus may be read as giving this answer. He says:

> Become accustomed to the belief that death is nothing to us. For all good and evil consists in sensation, but death is deprivation of sensation....So death, the most terrifying of ills, is nothing to us, since so long as we exist death is not with us; but when death comes, then we do not exist. It does not then concern either the living

or the dead, since for the former it is not, and the latter are no more. (Epicurus, 1926, pp. 30–31)

Epicurus seems to be saying that death does you no harm. If this is right, it follows that continuing to live does you no good.

Most of us find the "nothing" answer implausible because we take it for granted that dying would be a terrible thing to happen to us. Epicurus himself may not mean to give this answer. When he says "death is nothing to us," he may not mean that death does us no harm—I shall come to that. Nevertheless, his argument does supply materials that can be used to construct a case for the "nothing" answer. I shall lay out this case and try to make it persuasive despite its initial implausibility. But in the end I shall argue that it fails.

The beginning of the case is to recognize that the goodness of life has two dimensions: its quality and its quantity. It is quite easy to slip into thinking that the quantity of life does not matter at all; only its quality matters. This is exactly what most of us think about the goodness of life in another context. One way of adding to the quantity of life in the world is by having more babies; that way, more life is lived in total. But most of us do not favor increasing the quantity of life this way. We favor increasing the quality of life of the people who live, but we do not favor increasing the number of people who live. When the Chinese government instituted its one-child policy, its aim was to increase the quality of life of the Chinese. The policy also decreases the quantity of Chinese life: there are fewer Chinese now than there would have been without the policy. But the government did not think of this reduction in quantity as a bad thing, to be set against the increase in quality. Most of us would have agreed.

Moreover, this attitude we commonly have to the number of people can be supported by an argument. Suppose a couple are thinking of having a child, but eventually decide not to. As a result of their decision there is less life in the world than there would have been had they decided differently. Is this reduction in quantity a bad thing? Well, no one is harmed by it. No one is harmed by not being brought into existence. It is not as though there is some child who suffers the misfortune of not existing. There is simply no child, so no one is harmed. Consequently, we might plausibly think no harm is done. We might conclude it cannot be a bad thing to reduce the quantity of life in this way.

This argument needs to be qualified. Perhaps some people will be worse off as a result of the child's nonexistence. Perhaps her potential parents will come to regret having no child, and perhaps the child would have grown up to make a great contribution to civilization. So perhaps some people will be harmed by her nonexistence. But these are indirect effects, and to keep the argument sharp, let us assume them away. Let us assume there are no indirect effects of this sort, even though in practice there will almost certainly be some. Under this assumption, the argument has some force.

Now back to our context, which is extending life rather than creating life. Bringing more people into the world is one way of increasing the quantity of life. Another is to extend the lives of people who are already in the world. Epicurus shows us that we can take the same attitude to quantity in this context too, and there is a parallel argument for thinking that quantity has no value. We can ask a parallel question about the quantity of a single person's life. Previously we asked who is harmed by not being created; now let us ask at what time a person is harmed by not continuing to live. Suppose you might have lived longer, but you actually die now. Is that a bad thing for you? Well, there is no time when you are harmed by your early death. As Epicurus says, you are not harmed at any time before your death, since so long as you exist "death is not with [you]." And you are not harmed at any time after your death, since at no time after your death do you exist. Since there is no time when you are harmed by your death, we might conclude your death is not a bad thing for you. In the same way, the previous argument concluded that, since there is no one who is harmed when a couple declines to have a child, they do nothing bad in acting as they do.

In response, you may say there is indeed a time when death harms you: the time when you die. In saying this, you could be making either of two points. The first is that the process of dying is often dreadful. That is obviously true, and it does mean that your death harms you in one way. But it is not relevant to the question I am asking. I am asking what is the benefit to you of continuing to live. Conversely, what harm would be done you by not continuing to live? What harm would be done you by having your life cut short? I sometimes express this question in the form: what harm does your death do you? This is a graphic but not entirely accurate way of putting the question of what harm would be done you by having your life cut short. The terribleness of the process of dying is not a part of the answer to this question. Cutting your life short does not necessarily harm you in this way, because your dying may be dreadful whether it occurs at the end of a long life or a short one. So we can set aside this aspect of the badness of death.

The second point you might be making is this. If death harms you, it is obvious when the harm is done. It is done at the time of your death, since your death does the harm. This is true too, but it is also not relevant to the question I am asking. We must distinguish the time when a harm is caused from the time when it is suffered. If I drop a banana skin on the road, and you later slip on it and hurt yourself, we may say your harm is caused when I drop the banana skin. But it is suffered when you fall. Epicurus is interested in the time when the harm of death is suffered, not when it is caused. His conclusion is that it is not suffered at any time. If there were any harm, it would be caused at the time you die, but that is another matter. We can set aside this point too.

Once those two points are set aside, I think we should agree that there is no time when death harms you. That is a truth we should learn from Epicurus. Epicurus apparently draws the conclusion that, because there is no time when death harms you, it does not harm you at all. But to reach that conclusion, we have to make the further assumption that an event cannot harm you unless it harms you at some time. Is that a good assumption?

Once again, Epicurus supplies us with material that at first seems to support it. He says that "all good and evil consists in sensation." He means that the only sort of good that can come to us is a good sensation, and the only sort of bad is a bad sensation. This is a version of what is nowadays called "hedonism." It is highly contentious, and one way of responding to Epicurus is to deny it.[1] But denying hedonism is also contentious, and for my purposes I do not need to deny it. Instead, I shall show that, even if we grant Epicurus's hedonism, it does not truly support the claim that you cannot be harmed unless you are harmed at some particular time.

So let us assume like Epicurus that all good and evil consists in sensation. Since all sensations occur at particular times, we can quickly conclude that all goods and evils occur at particular times. So the goodness or badness of your life is made up of good and bad things, all of which occur at particular times in your life. This is a consequence of hedonism.

But the notions of *benefit* and *harm* are different from the notions of *good* and *bad*, and just because all goods and bads occur at particular times, it does not follow that all benefits and harms do. *Benefit* and *harm* are comparative notions. Normally, if something benefits you, it makes your life better than it would have been, and if something harms you it makes your life worse than it would have been. "Better" and "worse" are the comparatives of "good" and "bad," respectively. A comparison is between two things. To determine whether some event benefits or harms you, we have to compare the goodness of your life as it is, given the event, with the goodness it would otherwise have had. The comparison is between your whole life as it is and your whole life as it would have been. We do not have to make the comparison time by time, comparing each particular time in one life with the same time in the other life. So even if the goodness of your life is made up of good and bad things that all occur at particular times, there is no need for the comparison between lives to be made up of benefits and harms that can all be tied down to particular times.

Take an analogy. Suppose the text of a book is shortened before it is published: the last chapter is cut out. The book is shortened by six thousand words, but all the earlier chapters are left intact. Then six thousand words are cut from the book; yet no words are cut from any page in the book. This is so even though every word in the book appears on a particular page. Moreover, had the book been published in the longer, uncut version, every word in the longer book would have appeared on a particular page. The number of words cut from the book is determined by comparing the whole book as it is, with the whole book as it would have been had it not been shortened. It is not determined by comparing any particular page with that same page as it would have been.

Similarly, death may harm you by shortening your life, even though there is no time when it harms you. To determine whether it harms you, we compare the goodness of the shorter life you have, taken as a whole, with the goodness of the longer life you would have had, taken as a whole. If we believe Epicurus's hedonism, the goodness of the shorter life is made up of the good and bad sensations that occur within it. The goodness of the longer life includes all those sensations too, and it also includes all the good and bad sensations you would have had in later life had you not died. If your life is going well, presumably these extra sensations would have been predominantly good ones. So the longer life would have been better than the shorter one. You are therefore harmed by the shortening of your life. But there is no time when you suffer this harm, just as, when the book is shortened, no page in the book loses any words. Epicurus's hedonism actually implies that death normally harms you. Epicurus thinks it implies the opposite, but he is making a mistake.

Go back briefly to the analogous argument about the world's population. It fails for the same reason. The question is whether a couple's decision not to have a child is a bad thing. To answer, we must compare the goodness of the world without the child with the goodness it would have had if the child had existed. The world might be better without the child, or worse, or equally good. In particular, it might be worse, even though there is no one for whom it is worse. Again: a book can be shorter than it would have been, even though no page has any fewer words.

The argument I took from Epicurus fails. Epicurus is right that there is no time when death harms you. But even granted hedonism, it does not follow that death does not harm you. It may harm you, even though it harms you at no time.

2. SHOULD WE MIND ABOUT DYING?

I took the argument from Epicurus, but Epicurus may not mean to argue that death does not harm you. By "death is nothing to us," he may mean simply that you should not mind about dying. It is possible that you should not mind about dying even though your dying will harm you. Perhaps that is what Epicurus thinks.

How could it be so? If dying will harm you, surely you should mind about it. Not necessarily. It depends on what you should care about. Dying will harm you, but possibly you should not care about what happens to you, yourself. You are a person, with a life that extends from when you come into existence to when you go out of existence. Caring about what happens to you involves caring about the whole of that life. But why should you care about that? For instance, as an alternative, why should you not care just about what happens to you in the present? What you care about may change from time to time. Why should you not, at each particular time, care about just what happens to you at that particular time?

This needs to be put carefully. Probably you anyway care about what happens to other people besides yourself. But you probably care in a different way about what happens to you yourself. Call this sort of care "self-care." The suggestion is that you should attach your self-care, not to what happens to the person you are, with the whole of your life, but just to what happens to you in the present.

Wittgenstein uses the expression "living in the present," and I think this is what he means by it. He points out: "For life in the present there is no death. Death is not an event in life" (1961, p. 75). He is saying that, so long as you care only about what happens to you in the present, rather than about yourself as a whole, you will never encounter death among the things you care about. Your death does not occur during your life, so for you it is never in the present.

Possibly Epicurus is making a similar point. Since there is no time when death harms you, death does not harm you in the present, whatever time happens to be the present. So if you should care only about what happens to you in the present, you will never have any reason to mind about dying.

I am here not concerned with the correct interpretation of Epicurus. I am interested in how good it is for you to continue living. This is a question about the good of you, the person you are, who has a whole life. It is not about what you should care about at any particular time. The question is whether dying—ceasing to live—harms you. I asked whether we could find in Epicurus's remarks any reason for thinking it does not. His remarks provide the materials for an argument, but in the end the argument fails.

3. DO YOU LOSE EVERYTHING BY DYING?

Now I come to the opposite extreme answer to the question "what do you lose by dying?": the answer that you lose everything.

Here is an argument that supports this answer: after you die you will not have anything, so in dying you will lose everything. But this argument is invalid. Its premise is true: after you die, indeed you will not have anything. But it is true only in a peculiar way, and in this peculiar way it does not support the conclusion that in dying you will lose everything. I shall explain why not.

The sentence "you will not have anything" can be true in two different ways. One is when you exist and do not have anything. In this case, the negation contained in the sentence is often called "internal," because it negates the sentence's predicate. The sentence may be parsed "you will (not have anything)." The other way is when you do not exist. The negation is then "external" because it negates the sentence as a whole. The sentence can only be understood as meaning "it is not the case that you will have something." (A little point of English that may be confusing: in our context, "anything" replaces "something" under negation.)

The premise of the argument—that after you die you will not have anything— is true in this second way and not the first. This is what I called the "peculiar" way of being true. In the same peculiar way it is true that Pegasus—a winged horse— has no wings, because he does not exist. In the same way, too, it is true that Nelson now has no left arm; it is true because, being dead, Nelson now does not exist.

An external negation does not support the claim that something is lost. Think some more about Nelson's arms. Before he attacked Santa Cruz de Tenerife, Nelson had a right arm. Afterward he did not. The negation here is internal: after the attack, Nelson did (not have a right arm). Because the negation is internal, we may correctly draw the conclusion that Nelson lost his right arm in the attack. His loss consisted in the difference between two states of Nelson: the previous state in which he had a right arm and the subsequent state in which he did not. So an internal negation makes loss possible.

Compare what happened at the Battle of Trafalgar, when Nelson died. Before the battle, Nelson had a left arm. Afterward he did not. But in this case the negation is external. After the battle, it was not the case that Nelson had a left arm, but it is not correct to say that he did (not have a left arm), since he did not exist. Because the negation is external, we cannot correctly conclude that Nelson lost his left arm at Trafalgar. There is no comparison to be made between a previous state of Nelson in which he had a left arm and a subsequent state in which he did not, since subsequently there was no Nelson.

There were indeed two states of Nelson's body: a state previous to the battle and a state subsequent to it. This means the body could have lost its left arm. As it happens, it did not; the arm remained attached to the body. In any case, whatever happened to his body, Nelson himself did not lose an arm at Trafalgar.

In the same way, there is no comparison to be made between your state before you die and your state after you die. From the premise that after you die you will not have anything, with its external negation, we cannot correctly conclude that you lose everything by dying. The argument I have been discussing purports to make a temporal comparison between what you have before your death and what you have after it. The argument fails because there is no real temporal comparison to be made.

To determine what you lose as a result of a particular event, we do have to make a comparison. But there are two sorts of comparison we might make, and two corresponding sorts of loss. One comparison is temporal. We compare what you have after the event with what you had before it. If you have less afterward, you have suffered a temporal loss. We can only make a temporal comparison like this if you exist both before and after the event. When the event is your death, you do not exist afterward. Therefore, your death cannot cause you temporal loss.

I admit we say that, at your death, you lose your life, and this loss is plainly meant to be temporal. But this is a unique idiom; we do not commonly say that, at your death, you lose other things besides your life. When a husband dies, we say his wife loses her husband, but we do not say the husband loses his wife. We recognize that would be false. We should also recognize that, although idiomatic, it is strictly false to say that the husband loses his life.

The other sort of comparison we may make is atemporal, and yields an atemporal sort of loss. This sort of comparison does not require you to exist both before and after the event that causes the loss. When we ask what you lose by dying, we do not have to answer the question by comparing what you have after your death with what you have before it. We can instead compare what you have, given that you die at a particular time, with what you would have had if you had not died then. When we think this way, "what you have" does not refer to what you have at a particular time, but to what you have atemporally, taking your whole life together. What you lose by dying, understood this way, is not everything. It is just a part of the longer life you would have led, had you not died when you do. What you lose by dying is not your life, but only the rest of your life.

Our question is "what do you lose by dying?" The incorrect answer "everything" encourages the idea that living is infinitely good for you. But no one should believe that. No one's life is infinitely good. How could it be? Dying shortens your life by only a finite length of time. Our human lives are only finite in length, and during them we can experience and achieve only a finite number of things.

The only way to answer the question correctly is to understand it atemporally. What you lose by dying is the finite difference between a longer life and a shorter one. This answer lies between the extremes of "everything" and "nothing," or between "infinity" and "zero." It is "something."

4. How Much Do You Lose by Dying?
A Practical Question

But "something" is not a good enough answer; we need to know how much. Excluding the two extremes puts us in the domain of quantities. I have said that what you lose by dying is the rest of your life. I now turn to assessing what you lose in quantitative terms. More exactly, I turn to assessing the value to you of what you lose. How bad for you is your loss? I said that what you lose is the rest of your life; how bad is that? Put differently, how good for you is the rest of your life?

We should not expect all deaths to be equally bad; some people lose more by their deaths than others do. Indeed, some unfortunate people benefit from their deaths. I shall continue to write of the badness of death, but I mean to allow for the possibility that some deaths are good, which is to say that they have negative badness.

The badness for you of your death is the difference between the goodness of the longer life you would have led had you continued living and the goodness of the life you actually do lead. In general, the badness of death is the difference between the goodness of a longer life and the goodness of a shorter one. (In some cases this difference may be negative.) So, to assess the badness of a particular death, we need first to work out what life is led by the person who dies and what life she would have led had she continued living. Then, second, we need to judge the goodness of those two lives.

The first task is partly empirical and partly a matter of evaluating the counterfactual notion of "the life the person would have led." Some writers on death give space to evaluating this counterfactual,[2] but I shall not. One reason is that it is not particularly a problem for the philosophy of death; it is a problem of counterfactuals in general. Another reason is that the counterfactual is not important in practice, as I shall soon explain.

In the rest of this chapter, I shall therefore concentrate on the second task, of judging the goodness of lives. The task of judging the badness of death transmutes into this task of judging the goodness of lives. We have to compare the goodness of a longer life with the goodness of a shorter one.

I have described this difference as the goodness of the rest of your life. This is correct in one sense: it is the amount of good that the rest of your life would bring you if you lived it. But it is not necessarily the amount of good that you would enjoy during the rest of your life. The goodness of your life may be determined holistically, in a way that involves interactions among different parts of it. So the rest of your life may benefit you in some way that is not simply by being good in itself. It may add good to earlier parts of your life, or it may contribute in other ways to the goodness of your life as a whole. There will be examples in section 5.

Why do we need to do this quantitative work? Because in practice important decisions hang on it. Life and death decisions are constantly being made—I mean decisions that affect the lengths of people's lives. Some are on a small, individual scale; others on the scale of the whole world. On a small scale, all of us regularly make decisions that shorten or lengthen our lives. Statistically, each doughnut shortens your life. Is it worth it? That is probably something you do not want to think about. But in other cases, you will want to make the calculation. If you have a terminal illness, you will need to decide at what point to give up aggressive treatment aimed at prolonging your life, and accept only palliative care till you die. You may think carefully about that. Your decision may depend on your judgment of the goodness of extending your life—for instance, on whether you have a work of art to finish and on whether you expect to lose your capacities.

You will be weighing the quantity of your life against its quality. You may need to do this for yourself explicitly only in rare and tragic circumstances. But when the decision is for other people, you will need to be more careful. You can be cavalier about your own doughnuts, but not about other people's lives.

Governments in particular make decisions that lengthen or shorten many people's lives, so they need to judge the goodness of those lives. Governments often have to weigh some people's lives against others. They also often have to weigh the quantity of lives against the quality of lives. Take the provision of health care. Some treatments (such as hip replacements) improve the quality of people's lives without extending them. Some (such as heart replacements) extend lives. Many governments explicitly or implicitly set priorities among different sorts of treatment. To do so properly, they must weigh the quality of life against the quantity of life. They need to assess the goodness of people's lives.

On a much larger scale, we must decide what to do about global warming. One of the greatest harms that global warming will do is to kill huge numbers of people. It will kill them in floods and famines and in heat waves; it will kill them by extending the range of tropical diseases; and it will kill them in marginal areas of the world by making them poorer—poverty is a killer. By reducing our emissions of greenhouse gases, we can reduce the number of people who will be killed. But to do that we shall have to sacrifice some of the quality of our own lives. What sacrifices should we make? What reduction in the quality of our lives in the present is worthwhile for the sake of extending the quantity of people's lives in the future? Again, we need to assess the goodness of people's lives, and weigh quality against quantity.

So the practical need for judging the goodness of lives is as an input into decision making. I am not suggesting that goodness is the only input. Fairness in the distribution of goods also matters, particularly in making public decisions that influence which people die and which survive. But goodness is one input.

Decision making is a matter of choosing among a number of options. Each option will lead to a particular state of the world. But we never know exactly what state will result from the option we choose; the results are always uncertain to some degree. To judge the goodness of each option we therefore have to take account of its uncertainty. Expected utility theory tells us the correct way of doing so. In principle, we must assess the goodness of each state of the world that might result from the option, and calculate a weighted average of those goodnesses, in the way expected utility theory tells us to. The details of the method do not matter here.

For example, suppose you are deciding whether to reject or accept aggressive treatment for your terminal disease. If you reject it, you will die after some time, which is uncertain, and your life till that time will have some quality, which is also uncertain. If you accept aggressive treatment, you will die after some time that is probably longer, and your life till that time will have some quality that is probably less good. You should assess the goodness of each possible result of each option, and compare the weighted average goodness of the possible results of one option with the weighted average goodness of the possible results of the other.

None of this requires you to evaluate the counterfactual notion of "the life you would have led" had you decided differently. For practical purposes, you do not need to evaluate this counterfactual. You do not need to assess the badness of your death in a way that involves it. So it is not needed for practical purposes. That is the main reason why I do not give space to it.

5. Theories of the Goodness of Lives

The goodness of lives determines how bad it is to die; the question of how bad death is transmutes into the question of how good life is. So how good is a life? I am sorry to say this is too difficult a question for me to answer here. It is one of the topics of my book *Weighing Lives*, and even there I was able to offer only a "default theory" of the goodness of lives (2004, chs. 15–17). I meant a theory that it is reasonable to hold so long as there are no good arguments against it. A very large range of theories are available and, in the present state of discussion, choosing among them is generally more a matter of intuition than argument. Here, I shall survey part of the range, and provide a partial taxonomy of it. I shall give just a few examples of the theories that are available. I shall not try to adjudicate between them.

Two clarifications are needed at the start. One is about the tightness of the scale of goodness we should aim at. The simplest aim would be just to put lives in the order of their goodness—to determine which lives are better than which. That would be enough to answer the most basic question about the value of a person's death: is it good or bad? It is good if the shorter life the person leads is better than the longer one she would have led, and bad if the shorter life is worse.

But for practical decision making we need more than this. Because the results of a decision are always uncertain, we need to apply expected utility theory. That requires us to have a cardinal scale for goodness, including the goodness of lives. So in valuing lives, we need to aim for a cardinal scale.

I do not say we can expect to get one. Indeed, it seems unreasonable to expect even a determinate ordering of lives by their goodness. It seems likely that there is sometimes no determinate answer to the question of whether it would be a good or a bad thing to prolong a particular life, at some cost in its quality. We should surely expect a lot of incommensurability in assessing the goodness of lives. But I shall have to leave aside the question of how this incommensurability should be dealt with. The theories I shall mention ignore it. But this does not vitiate their value, because there may well be ways of extending them to take incommensurability into account.[3]

A second clarification is that I am dealing with the goodness of lives for the person who lives them; I call this their "personal goodness." The question is how good it is for a person to live a particular life. We could also ask how good it is simpliciter, rather than for the person, that a person lives a particular life. This is a question of "general goodness," as I call it. It is not the topic of this chapter. As it happens, I think personal goodness generates general goodness:[4] if one life A is better for the person who lives it than another B, it is better simpliciter that this person lives life A than that she lives life B. But that assumption plays no part in this chapter.

Theories of the goodness of lives range from very particular ones to ones that have a lot of formal structure. One example of a very particular theory is that the only thing that makes a life good for a person is the excellence she achieves, so the goodness of a life is the amount of excellence it contains. I shall concentrate on more structured theories.

5.1 Distributed Theories

More structured theories can be developed if we make what I shall call the assumption of "distribution." It is the assumption that the goodness of a life is distributed across times. Put another way, it is the assumption that the goodness of a life is made up of its goodness at all times. It is really a combination of two assumptions. First, that there is such a thing as the goodness of a life at particular times—I shall call this "temporal goodness" and contrast it with the "lifetime goodness" of a life as a whole. Second, that the goodness of the life supervenes on its goodness at times. In mathematical terms, it is a function of its goodnesses at times.

It will be helpful to express this assumption in symbols. For convenience, I shall imagine that times are discrete. The assumption of distribution is that life-time goodness G is given by the formula:

$$G = G(g_1, g_2, g_3, \ldots g_n).$$

The indices $1 \ldots n$ denote a sequence of times, and $g_1, g_2, g_3, \ldots g_n$ are the temporal goodnesses of the life at those times. I call $G()$ the "goodness function." Let us call a theory of goodness "distributed" if it satisfies the assumption of distribution. Different distributed theories disagree about the form of the goodness function.

The assumption of distribution does not specify the scale on which temporal goodness is measured. Different views about the goodness function require different scales, as will appear.

You might well reject the assumption of distribution. You might think there are good features of a life that cannot be assigned to particular times. I have already mentioned the theory of goodness as excellence. You might hold this theory and also think that the excellence of a life cannot always be assigned to particular times. For another example, there is the view that the lifetime goodness of a life depends on its degree of internal coherence in some way that is not reflected in its sequence of temporal goodnesses. Perhaps a life is better if it is directed toward one particular broad aim, rather than toward an eclectic mixture of aims. It might not be possible to allocate this good feature of the life to any particular times within the life.

Still, the assumption of distribution is not very restrictive. It leaves room for very many different distributed theories. It even allows a life to have temporal goodness at times outside the boundaries of the life; it does not rule out posthumous or antenatal goods and bads. However, for the sake of convenience in what follows, I shall assume that all the temporal goodness of a life occurs within its temporal boundaries. So in the formula above, I shall assume that the times indexed by $1 \ldots n$ constitute the sequence of successive times within the life. It would take only minor adjustments to remove this assumption.

The assumption of distribution leaves it open how temporal goodness is determined. The nature of well-being is a large and hotly debated subject, and much of this debate is about temporal goodness. Does your good at a time consist in your experiences at the time, as Epicurus assumed, or in the satisfaction of the preferences you have at the time, or in something else? All of this is left open by the assumption of distribution, and it is left open by all the distributed theories I shall mention in this section. These are theories about how a person's good at particular times comes together to determine her lifetime good. They are not theories about the nature of her good at particular times.

In particular, the assumption of distribution does not require temporal goodness at a time to be determined only by events that happen at that time. Indeed, it is implausible that it would be, unless events are construed very broadly. Suppose, say, that you work hard on a project, and the project is later successful. We might think that your later success adds to the goodness of the earlier times when you work hard on it; it might cause a change in the goodness of those earlier times. This would be a sort of backwards causation of goodness, and it is perfectly compatible with the assumption of distribution. I mentioned in section 4 that, were your life threatened at some time, but you survive, the rest of your life might benefit you by adding value to earlier parts of your life. If that is so, it is another example of backward causation of goodness, and it is compatible with the assumption of distribution.

5.2 Additively Separable Theories

A vast range of forms are possible for the goodness function. The one that may first spring to mind is simple addition, which makes a life's lifetime goodness the total of the goodness of its times. Call this the "total theory":

$$G = g_1 + g_2 + g_3 + \ldots + g_n.$$

It demands a tight scale for measuring temporal goodness: the scale must be cardinal. Furthermore, goodness at each time must be comparable with goodness at other times. Furthermore again, the scale must have a fixed zero, which means it is a ratio scale. This is because we need to compare the lifetime goodnesses of lives of different lengths. Take a life of some length, and imagine shortening it by removing the last time in it. Imagine the person dies one time earlier, that is to say. According to the total theory, the shorter life is worse than the longer one if and only if the goodness of that last time is above zero. So the level of the zero makes a difference to the ordering of lives.

The total theory belongs to a class of distributed theories that may be called "additively separable." The characteristic of additively separable theories is that they treat the goodness of a life as the sum of values, each of which is assigned to a particular time and is a function of the temporal goodness of that time. The value assigned to a time must be independent of the goodness of other times, and of the length n of the life. Put roughly, each time can be valued independently of other times. The general formula of an additively separable theory is:

$$G = v_1(g_1) + v_2(g_2) + v_3(g_3) + \ldots + v_n(g_n).$$

I shall call $v_1()$, $v_2()$ and so on the "temporal value functions." The form of these functions is independent of n and of temporal goodness at other times.

In the total theory, the temporal value functions are the identity function. Other additively separable theories have other functions. The "weighted total theory" departs from the total theory only by giving different weights to goodnesses at different times:

$$G = a_1 g_1 + a_2 g_2 + a_3 g_3 + \ldots + a_n g_n.$$

Here, a_1, a_2 are constants that specify the weights. If later weights are greater than earlier ones, later times in life count for more than earlier ones. One result is that a life that improves over time is better than one that deteriorates, if they both have the same total of temporal good. This is a consequence of the weighted total theory.[5] By contrast, some authors—generally economist or public health analysts— "discount" the goodness of later times in a life (e.g., Murray 1994). This means they give later times less weight than earlier ones.

Another additively separable formula is:

$$G = v(g_1) + v(g_2) + v(g_3) + \ldots + v(g_n).$$

Here all the temporal value functions are the same, $v()$. Take the case where $v()$ is an increasing, strictly concave function, which means its graph slopes upward but curves downward. Then we may call the theory "prioritarian." It gives priority to improving bad times over improving good ones. This has the indirect effect of assigning more goodness to a life that has an even tenor than to one that has extreme highs and lows, if they both have the same total of temporal good. It gives indirect value to evenness, that is to say.

5.3 Constant-Length Additively Separable Theories

A different type of theory is the "average theory," that the goodness of a life is the average of its temporal goodnesses. Its goodness function is:

$$G = g_1/n + g_2/n + g_3/n + \ldots + g_n/n.$$

This theory does not require temporal good to be measured on a ratio scale; a cardinal scale is enough. It is one formulation of the view, mentioned in section 1, that only the quality of life matters, and not its quantity.

The average theory is not additively separable by the definition I gave. It does treat the goodness of a life as the sum of values, each of which is assigned to a particular time and is a function of the temporal goodness of that time. However, the form of this function depends on the length of the life n.

When lengthening or shortening the life is not in question, the average theory is equivalent to the total theory. Among lives that are all the same length, it orders them just as the total theory does. So the average theory is additively separable among lives with the same length.

But think about extending a life by one time. If the temporal goodness of this time is above the average of the existing times, then the life is improved by extending it. If it is below, the life is made worse by extending it. So the value of adding an extra time depends on the temporal goodness of other times. In this sense the value of this extra time is not independent of other times. That is why I do not count the average theory as truly additively separable. Instead, I say it is "constant-length additively separable."

Another theory in the same class is:

$$G = g_1 + g_2 + b(g_2 - g_1) + g_3 + b(g_3 - g_2) + \ldots + g_n + b(g_n - g_{n-1}).$$

This theory gives value to improvements in temporal good, as the weighted total theory can do, but it does so more directly. b is the weight assigned to improvements. This goodness function may be rewritten in the form

$$G = (1 - b)g_1 + g_2 + g_3 + \ldots + (1 + b)g_n.$$

This makes it look superficially like an instance of the weighted total theory. But actually it is not additively separable because the weight given to any particular time depends on whether or not it is the last time. However, this theory is constant-length additively separable.

5.4 Nonadditively Separable Theories

Some theories are not additively separable at all. Some start out from the total theory, and modify it in one way or another, to take account of values it does not accommodate. One of these gives value directly to evenness:

$$G = g_1 + g_2 + g_3 + \ldots + g_n - cI(g_1, g_2, g_3, \ldots g_n).$$

$I()$ is some measure of unevenness in the life's temporal goodnesses; it is a measure of inequality among the temporal goodnesses in the life. Various measures could be used: the variance, the Gini coefficient, and so on, and c is a parameter that assigns a weight to evenness. This formula values evenness more directly than the prioritarian formula does.

Other theories of lifetime goodness are much more remote from the total theory, but nevertheless satisfy the assumption of distribution. One is the theory that the goodness of a life is given only by how good it is at its end:

$$G = g_n$$

Another is the theory that the goodness of a life is given by the best time in it:

$$G = \max\{g_1, g_2, g_3, \ldots g_n\}$$

Like the average theory, these theories are alternative expressions of the idea that only quality of life matters, and not quantity. They may be combined into the "peak and end rule."[6] Either of them is able to order lives by their goodness so long as temporal goodnesses are ordered and comparable between different times. To order lives, neither requires a cardinal scale of temporal goodness. However, if the overall goodness of lives is to be on a cardinal scale, temporal goodnesses must be on a cardinal scale too.

I hope I have given enough examples now to illustrate the range of choice available among theories of lifetime goodness.

6. Conclusion

When you die, what you lose is neither nothing nor everything. It is the rest of your life. The badness of this loss is, seen differently, the goodness of rest of your life. More accurately, it is the difference between the goodness of the longer life you would have led, had you survived, and the shorter life you do lead. So the question of how bad is death transmutes into the question of how good is life.

I have not tried to answer this latter question, but I have outlined and classified some of the answers that are available.

NOTES

1. This is the way adopted by Thomas Nagel, 1970.
2. For instance, Ben Bradley, 2009, pp. 47–60.
3. A valuable recent discussion of how this might be done is Wlodek Rabinowicz, 2009.
4. This view is formalized in something I call "the principle of personal good." See my 2004, p. 120.
5. The view that improvement is good is championed by David Velleman, 1991.
6. Kahneman, 1999. But note that Kahneman does not favor the peak and end rule as a formula for the value of a life.

REFERENCES

Bradley, Ben. 2009. *Well-Being and Death*. Oxford: Oxford University Press.

Broome, John. 2004. *Weighing Lives*. Oxford: Oxford University Press.

Epicurus. 1926. "Letter to Menoeceus." In *Epicurus: The Extant Remains*, Cyril Bailey, trans., pp. 83–93. Oxford: Oxford University Press.

Kahneman, Daniel. 1999. "Objective Happiness." In *The Foundations of Hedonic Psychology*, Daniel Kahneman, Ed Diener, and Norbert Schwarz, eds., pp. 3–25. New York: Russell Sage Foundation.

Murray, Christopher. 1994. "Quantifying the Burden of Disease: The Technical Basis for Disability-Adjusted Life Years." *Bulletin of the World Health Organization* 72: 429–45.

Nagel, Thomas. 1970. "Death." *Noûs* 4: 73–80.

Rabinowicz, Wlodek. 2009. "Incommensurability and Vagueness." Proceedings of the Aristotelian Society, Supplementary Volume 83: 71–94.

Velleman, David. 1991. "Well-being and Time." *Pacific Philosophical Quarterly* 72: 48–77.

Wittgenstein, Ludwig. 1961. *Notebooks 1914–16*. Oxford: Blackwell.

CHAPTER 10

THE SYMMETRY PROBLEM

ROY SORENSEN

JAMES Boswell trailed the ailing David Hume in the hope of chronicling a death-bed conversion. Chagrinned by the philosopher's buoyancy, Boswell asked Hume whether the thought of annihilation caused him any uneasiness. "He said not the least; no more than the thought that he had not been, as Lucretius observes." Hume was alluding to a poem by the Roman Epicurean Lucretius Carus (99–55 BC):

> Look back:
> Nothing to us was all fore-passed eld
> Of time the eternal, ere we had a birth.
> And Nature holds this like a mirror up
> Of time-to-be when we are dead and gone.
> And what is there so horrible appears?
> Now what is there so sad about it all?
> Is't not serener far than any sleep?

"De Rerum Natura" ("On the Nature of Things," translated by William Ellery Leonard)

When Boswell reported Hume's reply to Samuel Johnson, Johnson concluded that Hume was either mad or insincere. Yet philosophers such as A. J. Ayer continue to cite Lucretius as furnishing cogent consolation (1990, p. 185).

Contemporary philosophers picture Lucretius as rejecting the first member of the following trilemma:

Your posthumous nonexistence is bad for you.
Your prevital nonexistence is not bad for you.

> There is no relevant different between your posthumous nonexistence and
> your prevital nonexistence.

The first three sections of this essay correspond to the three possible resolutions of this inconsistent triad.

Maybe that exaggerates my tidiness. The trilemma will actually be drafted into service like the connected flower pots (see figure 10.1) used for collective irrigation.

In section 1, the reader expects to find the symmetry argument studied by contemporary philosophers. But historical scholarship, especially James Warren's *Facing Death*, shows that this compartment actually contains an ancestral syllogism (what I call "the symmetricized no-subject argument"). Steven Luper dismisses this precursor as having merely antiquarian interest (2009, p. 61). And Stephen Rosenbaum regards it as too shallow to be charitably attributed to Lucretius (1989). But the roots of this weed in Epicurus's garden point to a lost philosophical enterprise: the epistemology of death. This project is worth resurrecting in light of recent work on the perception of absences (Sorensen, 2008) and the continued role of Epicurean arguments as rational consolation.

Section 2 switches attention to the sterile second compartment. This should be occupied by those who embrace the negation of the second member of the trilemma. But here we find a counterexample to Cicero's principle that "there is no statement so absurd that no philosopher will make it." No philosopher laments his prevital nonexistence—despite the fact that the first and third members of the triad stand ready for incorporation into a syllogism for just this conclusion.

Section 3 has the flower—the true symmetry argument. I classify it as a "mondegreen." The word "mondegreen" originates from a 1954 *Atlantic* magazine article by Sylvia Wright in which she reports mishearing the folk lyric "Oh, they have slain the Earl o'Morray and laid him on the green" as "Oh, they have slain the Earl o'Morray and Lady Mondegreen." My hypothesis is that the symmetry argument

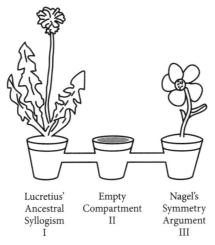

Lucretius'   Empty   Nagel's
Ancestral   Compartment   Symmetry
Syllogism   II   Argument
    I   III

Figure 10.1 Epicurean flower pots.

arose from a "slip of the ear" by Thomas Nagel. His mishearing was abetted by a uniquely confusing translation of the key line. (Nagel infers he used R. E. Latham's [Lucreitus, 1951] translation of poem because that's one in his library and it has Nagel's marginalia.)

The final section of this chapter is ahistorical. It is devoted to the hypothesis that we care about "personal time" rather than time. This resolution technically returns to a rejection of the first leg of the triad. However, the resolution does not follow Lucretius's line that death is harmless. It merely translates our objection to death into the more accurate medium of personal time.

1. THE SYMMETRICIZED NO-SUBJECT ARGUMENT

The Greek love of geometry is evident in their fondness for symmetry reasoning. For instance, Anaximander explains why the earth does not fall by pointing out that it has no more reason to fall in one direction rather than another.

Anaxagoras hints at a symmetry argument for death: "There are two lessons for death: the time before birth and sleep" (attributed by Stobaus). Yet no symmetry argument appears in any of Epicurus's surviving works. This suggests that symmetry reasoning was, at best, a minor consideration.

Epicurus's disciples agreed that he had solved the major philosophical problems of metaphysics (through atomism) and ethics (through hedonism). Just as the nineteenth-century physicists believed that the future belonged to engineers, the Epicureans believed that the future belonged to therapists.

Lucretius did not seek to outdo the Greeks by innovating at the theoretic level. As a practical Roman, he works with Epicurus's *On Nature* as his sole philosophical source (Sedley, 1998). Lucretius's originality lies in making poetry a therapeutic tool (rather like the French cellist Juliette Alvin innovated in the 1960s by making music medicine).

The ancient texts suggest that the Epicurean symmetry argument is an empirical variation of the a priori no-subject argument. The pure no-subject argument uses the metaphysical principle that harm is harm to some specific individual. I cannot be harmed by my death because I will not exist when this event occurs.

Epicurus propounds the no-subject argument with a geometer's certitude. But even a geometer is free to supplement his a priori reasoning with the audience's own experiences. This license to use looser forms of inference is in keeping with Epicurus's therapeutic agenda. Epicurus appeals to his audience's own experience with past nonexistence. You have already "been" through prevital nonexistence! How bad was it? Not bad at all. Could your future existence be any worse? There is no relevant difference. So you should not expect to suffer after death.

"A priori" means knowable without experience and so is compatible with being actually known through experience. Since Lucretius is trying to reach a wide Roman audience, he will use the easier concrete demonstrations rather than the abstract demonstrations favored by Greek purists.

Contemporary purists such as Luper and Rosenbaum are like mathematicians who dismiss empirical demonstrations of mathematical principles as second-rate. They underestimate the value of second-rate evidence. Even experts benefit from the fact that there are empirical paths to theorems that have already been demonstrated by a priori proofs. The eminent number theorist Paul Erdos was unpersuaded by an a priori proof (accessible to undergraduate mathematics students) of the correct solution to the Monty Hall problem (a cognitive illusion in probability theory). He was instead persuaded by the cumulative effect of hundreds of computer simulations (Hoffman, 1998, p. 239).

Erdos still laments that he did not understand the solution. This illustrates an important way in which empirical demonstrations tend to be second-rate.

Notice that the symmetricized no-subject argument merely concludes that your future nonexistence will not bad be for you. It does not make the present-tense claim that your future nonexistence is not now bad for you. After all, you now exist, and so can now suffer harm.

In his Tusculan Disputation, Cicero astutely objects that the symmetricized no-subject argument leaves a gap for the present tense:

> All right, I concede that those who are dead are not wretched, since you have forced me to admit that those who do not exist at all cannot even be wretched. But what of it? We who are alive, surely we are wretched since we have to die! What joy can there be in life when have to contemplate day and night the fact that inevitable death is imminent? (Tusc. 1.14, trans. Warren, 2004, p. 5)

Lucretius should reply that his arguments are designed to work together. The present-tense gap of the symmetricized no-subject argument is filled by Epicurus's timing argument: If some event harms you, then it harms you at some specific time. Death cannot harm you before it occurs (because that would be reverse causation) or while it occurs (because as soon as it occurs, you cease to exist) or after it occurs (because you are no longer around to be affected by it).

Lucretius's ambition for the symmetricized no-subject argument is modest. It merely provides a precedent to show your future nonexistence cannot harm you while you are dead. This is why he adds the precedent of sleep. Dreamless sleep involves an interruption of consciousness—perhaps even an interruption of existence. Since we are familiar with sleep, we are not frightened of it. Thus sleep reinforces the a priori metaphysical principle that harms require a subject.

Lucretius's target (fear that death is painful) is apparent from the ensuing assurance that the reader will not suffer the hell of Tantalus, Tityas, or Sisyphus. The target is also clear from the preceding psychological explanation of why there is so much fear of the oblivion that follows life: instead of consistently following out the supposition that we are dead, we picture ourselves as a little bit alive—indeed, as being sufficiently conscious to helplessly suffer in a state of impotent paralysis.

1.1 Swamped by Infinity?

Intuitions should receive less weight if they concern a subject matter for which they have proven unreliable. Human intuitions about infinity, nonexistence, and time have a poor record. Perhaps Lucretius believed our fear of our infinite future nonexistence is at the intersection of these three mazes. Toward the end of his poem, he argues that prolonging a life cannot make it better. He reasons that any finite improvements would be swamped by the infinite period of nonexistence.

The Greeks were more geometrical than arithmetical. Their metaphors for a good life are spatial: balance, symmetry, and proportion. Just as being longer does not make a story better, a life is not improved merely by lengthening it. Extra life is only good insofar as it completes your story.

By the time Jeremy Bentham was writing, Europeans were accustomed to Hindu-Arabic place notation. This promotes a quantitative outlook in social thinking—and the statistical tools to formulate utilitarianism.

Intellectual inheritors of Jeremy Bentham's hedonic calculus will be dismayed by Lucretius's transfinite arithmetic (Bradley, 2009). Given that life is pleasurable, the modern hedonist finds it obvious that life ought to be prolonged. How long? Forever!

Thomas Nagel reveres the nuanced rejection of utilitarianism in John Rawls's *A Theory of Justice*. Yet Nagel shares Bentham's conclusion that immortality is best. He tries to justify the preference with a recursive principle less redolent of the hedonic calculus:

> Given the simple choice between living for another week and dying in five minutes I would always choose to live for another week...I conclude that I would be glad to live forever. (1970, p. 224)

Adrian Moore objects that this is fallacious.

> I might be appalled at the thought that I shall live for ever, without at any particular time in the future, wanting these to be my last five minutes. (That is, I might never want to die without wanting never to die.). (Moore, 2001, p. 227)

To deflect Adrian Moore's logical point about desire, Nagel needs to cast his point normatively. Moore's agent is weak-willed or temporally biased in favor of the near future. He is like an apprehensive patient who wants his bandage ripped off: But not yet! Never now. Just at some time. Nagel can dismiss this inconsistent pattern of preferences as irrational.

This verdict of irrationality would also be supported by our willingness to paternalistically intervene against suicide attempts. If someone's life is going as well as Nagel assumes in his slippery-slope argument, then a decision to commit suicide need not be respected—and should be thwarted.

Others would put Nagel's point more strongly; it is never rational to want to die (given that one's life is going well), so it is rationally mandatory to want immortality.

Why stop here? Once you reflect on the symmetry between prevital non-existence and posthumous nonexistence, it becomes preferable to have an earlier start. Or better yet, to have always been around. The insatiability of this desire for life gives it the infinite scale needed to overcome Lucretius's swamping argument.

2. Reversing the Symmetry

How good a pessimist are you? From a logical point of view, you might conclude that the symmetry between prevital nonexistence and posthumous nonexistence shows that you should be horrified by your prevital nonexistence.

2.1 Fatalistic Symmetry

The ancients laugh off this pessimistic reaction. Seneca writes,

> Doesn't the person who wept because he had not been alive a thousand years ago seem to you an utter fool? Equally foolish is he who weeps because he will not be alive a thousand year's time. These two are the same: you will not be, nor were you. These times do not belong to you. (Ep. Mor. 77.11, trans. Warren, 2004)

Malcolm Schofield suggests that Seneca could have run a slippery-slope argument starting from the absurdity of weeping at not being alive a thousand years hence to the absurdity of weeping at not being alive tomorrow (Warren, 2004, 72 fn). This would reverse Nagel's slippery-slope argument for desiring immortality.

However, Seneca's actual argument seems to be an invitation to extend fatalism about the past (in other words, the commonsense platitude that the past cannot be changed) to fatalism about the future. We should serenely accept what is inevitable because resistance is futile. This wisdom about the unalterability of the past explains our tranquil resignation to prevital nonexistence. The fatalist goes on to infer it warrants comparable composure toward our posthumous nonexistence. Fatalism is symmetricized common sense.

According to the fatalist, we are necessary beings. Our existence could be neither longer nor shorter ("These times do not belong to you"). Nor could any nonexistent person become existent. Since deprivation requires the possibility of an alternative, there are no winners or losers in the "lottery" of existence. All individuals are necessary existents. All nonexistent "individuals" are necessarily nonexistent.

The fatalist is no gladder of his existence than he is glad of the existence of an even prime number. Both are necessary beings. The fatalist does not experience Jean Paul Sartre's sense of being thrown into existence. There is no vertigo of contingency. Only serenity.

2.2 Neglected Deprivations

If you could somehow be appalled by your prevital nonexistence, then other infinite deprivations should also be appalling. In principle, you could experience the infinitely many moments that lie between any two moments that you are aware of.

Indeed, if time is continuous, then there are more points of time than the denumerably many depicted in figure 10.2. This superdenumerable deprivation dwarfs the merely denumerable loss of posthumous discrete time.

Actual experience resembles the frames of a movie. Only a small number of experiences can be processed in a minute. This limit on how finely we experience time drastically reduces how much time is accessible to us.

Consider someone who prefers to live at an even coarser grain than normal. This person will have only half the experience. Acting on this preference would be semisuicide. Instead of cutting off the latter half of one's life, one would be spreading out the cuts.

We lament being limited in time. But we do not object to being limited by space. Thus, one strategy of consolation is to spatialize time.

But perhaps this consolation is fallacious. Extra space does not help because it cannot expand consciousness. Experience is sequential. It cannot spread out when given more room.

Although you are right not to lament your restricted occupation of space, you could still lament the sequential nature of your conscious experience. If you had parallel consciousness, you could experience twice as much in the same amount of time. Many of your unconscious processes run in parallel. Indeed, neuroscientists who study split brains conclude that people with a severed corpus callosum have periods of divided consciousness. Derek Parfit has given a consistent description of what such a divided mind is like from a first person perspective (1987, pp. 246–247).

Human beings have difficulty lamenting the absence of parallel consciousness or having dense experience or not starting life earlier. We may be like sufferers of Williams syndrome. Although intellectually challenged and very clumsy, they are cheerful, highly verbal, musical, and love to make friends. They have "cocktail party personalities." This happy demeanor is accentuated by an elfin facial appearance.

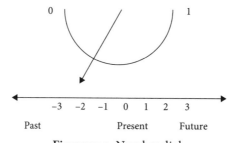

Figure 10.2 Number dial.

Figure 10.3 Giovanni Francesco Caroto's painting *A Boy with a Puppet*.

A hedonist may be tempted to side with those who define health in terms of traits conducive to happiness. Yet with Williams syndrome, happiness is a psychological symptom of a genetic disorder. The same goes for "happy puppet syndrome," first discovered in 1964 by Dr. Angelman upon viewing Giovanni Francesco Caroto's painting *A Boy with a Puppet* (see figure 10.3).

Perhaps pessimistic extraterrestrials would view homo sapiens as having emotional blind spots. The extraterrestrials marvel at the human inability to be disappointed by not starting life earlier. Naturally endowed with parallel consciousness, the extraterrestrial visitors pity our single-track minds. They are further astonished that human beings do not miss all the infinite experiences that could dwell between any pair of thoughts.

The extraterrestrials give us partial credit. We understand our deprivations. We just cannot be upset by them. The single exception to this macabre buoyancy is consternation at the infinite nothingness that will follow our lives.

The extraterrestrials can figure out why we (perversely) try to console ourselves with the symmetry of prevital nonexistence. But they wonder why we do not try analogous appeals, such as to our contentment with sequential consciousness or our contentment with coarse-grained consciousness.

Recall David Hume's explanation of why skeptics cannot carry their doubts outside the study: Commonsense beliefs are so important for our welfare that nature has made them compulsory. What applies for belief extends to desire. Human beings need to emotionalize the deprivation imposed by death just as they need to see the light in the "visible" band of the light spectrum. But we secure no advantage outside this narrow band—and may even be distracted by it (just as sensitivity to ultraviolet light secured by artificial lenses introduces glare).

3. THE NAGELIAN RENAISSANCE

Lucretius's poem was passed on partly for its philosophical content and partly for its merit as a poem. His literary influence had waned by the end of the first century. His poem was hardly read and passed out of circulation.

"De Rerum Natura" was recovered during the Renaissance. Epic poets such as Milton, Whitman, and Wordsworth revived the poem mainly as literature.

3.1 Criticisms of Epicurus's Main Arguments

Epicurus believes each harm must be experienced by a victim. But common sense implies a broader, externalist conception of harm. Consider the Spartan king Agis. In 413 BC, he had to leave his wife Timea to hold a fortified position in Decelea. While Agis lay in Decelea, his guest Alcibiades lay with Timea. The hedonist insists "what you don't know can't hurt you." He dates the harm to the time at which the victim, King Agis, discovers he has been cuckolded. But, an externalist dates the harm prior to the Agis's awareness of his wife's infidelity. After all, reasons the externalist, when Agis returned home to his unexpectedly pregnant queen, he discovered that Alcibiades had already harmed him.

Once Nagel pries open the range of harms, he is poised to challenge Epicurus's principle that each harm must have a date. A dead man is harmed if the terms of his will are ignored. His interests have been damaged even though he is no longer alive to experience frustration.

Our desires extend to matters beyond the scope of what we experience. So contrary to Epicurus, we can be painlessly harmed. There need be no specific time at which such harms occur. Thus Nagel denies any need to specify the time at which his death will harm him.

Recall that the timing argument plugged a hole in the symmetricized no-subject argument; the timing argument addresses the issue of why death cannot harm you while you are alive. By undermining the timing argument Nagel had inadvertently unplugged a hole in Lucretius's "symmetry argument."

But Nagel missed this side-victory. Possibly because of hypnotic fixation on the subjective point of view, Nagel misconstrued Lucretius's symmetricized no-subject argument as making a present-tense evaluative claim about one's future nonexistence. This spawns an argument that can stand on its own, unassisted by the timing argument.

Nagel correctly sees that this present tense argument is independent of Epicurus's internalism. He also appreciates that the argument is independent of Epicurus's corollary that each harm has a specific time of occurrence. Nagel realizes that he needs an entirely separate response to the symmetry argument.

3.2 The Asymmetry of Material Origin

Is it possible to begin existing earlier than you actually began existing? According to Saul Kripke, you could not have originated from any other sperm-egg combination than the actual combination. Therefore, reasons Nagel, you could not have been conceived significantly earlier than when you were actually conceived. (Nagel does not mention Kripke in "Death," but in e-mail correspondence (April 24, 2010) Nagel confirms he had Kripke in mind—and not the "psychological self," which will be discussed in the following section.) Nagel proposes a metaphysical asymmetry between prevital nonexistence and posthumous nonexistence. Only posthumous nonexistence is time that Nagel is deprived of.

In a footnote, Nagel discusses Robert Nozick's objection that there might be creatures for whom prevital nonexistence constitutes a deprivation (1970, p. 80). If we were like spores that can be activated early, then we might regard the failure to gain this extra time as a deprivation. Yet this deprivation does not have the horror of death.

Technological developments have vindicated Nozick's thought experiment. Human sperm and eggs are commonly frozen. Conception can be indefinitely delayed. Currently there are siblings whose birth order does not match their order of conception. Some of these shuffled children coherently lament their birth order.

If any of these delayed children are persuaded by John Leslie's *Doomsday*, they will intensify their laments. Given the exponential population growth, Leslie says we should attach a surprisingly high probability of looming human extinction (to ensure that we have an average location in history). So any person who believes he could have been born earlier has a reason to regret the delay.

This systematic reason for regretting any delay is hostage to Leslie's controversial Doomsday argument. The alternative is to stipulate a scenario in which astronomers discover that homo sapiens will be rendered extinct by a giant comet strike in 2030 (Belshaw, 2000, pp. 74–78). Those with delayed births will regret their shorter life spans.

This regret may result in some people who challenge the second horn of the trilemma. They would lament not being born earlier. But there is still the lack of proportionality (in their degree of regret) that bothered Nagel in his discussion of Nozick's spores.

3.3 The Asymmetry of Psychological Origin

Frederick Kaufman (1999) maintains the relevant asymmetry is psychological rather than material. Given a choice between dying immediately after a fall or a delayed death in a vegetative coma, people do not prefer the longer life. For this longer bodily life does not extend consciousness. What counts is the psychological self, not the bodily self.

If you had been born a century earlier, you would have a different upbringing, career, spouse, and children. According to Kaufman, this would suffice to make you a different person. Wishing to be born earlier is therefore tantamount to wishing for annihilation. Naturally, you lack this suicidal desire.

Kaufman's answer explains our reluctance to gain happier lives by overwriting our present memories and personalities with ones that make us easier to please. We prefer lives that conserve our past—especially our early past.

Some of the controversy surrounding Kaufman's proposal echoes the debate over personal identity. Those who identify people with their bodies (or brains) have thoroughly developed objections to the reality of the psychological self. They are impressed by our willingness to entertain counterfactuals involving radical psychological transformations. For instance, if you were told that you were nearly assigned to the wrong mother as an infant, then you would infer that you nearly had a very different life. You would not infer that you nearly perished.

Kaufman mounts thought experiments that reveal aversion to psychological transformations. We recoil from these metamorphoses despite the obvious survival of our bodies.

Glen Pettigrove complains that Kaufman's thought experiments contain distracting levels of violence and coercion (2002, p. 413). Perhaps our conservatism is actually a reaction to the assault.

We may not be as squeamish as Pettigrove fears—at least when people undergo improvements. Consider audience reaction to the movie *Regarding Henry* (1991). Henry Turner (played by Harrison Ford) is a Manhattan attorney. Professionally, Henry is conniving, haughty, and ruthless. At home, he is callous. At the zenith of his career, Henry is shot in the head during a convenience-store robbery. The brain damage results in almost total amnesia (and his ruin as a litigator). Henry also loses some inhibitions. He emerges as a more loving, empathic man. Henry's relationship with his wife and daughter flourishes.

When Henry learns of his past abuses, he is ashamed. He atones for his professional misconduct. When Henry Turner discovers that his wife had an affair before the shooting, he is angry. Henry storms off. Eventually he forgives her. These emotions presuppose that the gentle Henry is the same man as the ruthless Henry.

Historical cases of brain injuries are more nuanced. On September 13, 1848, 25-year-old work-crew foreman Phineas Gage had a damping iron (shaped like javelin) accidentally blast through his head. The brain injury left Gage impulsive, vulgar, and pugnacious. This decline led his disappointed friends to say Gage was no longer Gage. At first blush, this makes Phineas Gage a trophy for Kaufman. However, recent biographical research suggests that Gage recovered some social skills. He learned to live with his injury. Indeed, he partly made a living off of the injury, going on exhibition with the damping iron. When not posing with "his constant companion," Gage worked at a livery stable in Hanover, New Hampshire. Later, he served as a stagecoach driver in Chile. The interest of Gage's life accrues from the contrast between his life before and after the accident and a unifying thread of heroic buoyancy. Gage stitched the disparate halves of his life together, incorporating the psychological discontinuity into an amazing life.

3.4 Disappointment over Necessary Truths

Suppose Nagel or Kaufmann or someone else were able to prove that it is impossible for us to have begun life earlier than we actually started. Would that really explain why we do not regret being born earlier?

Derek Parfit answers no. We can regret necessary truths. His example is the Pythagoreans. They regretted that the square root of two is not a rational number because it spoiled their numerological metaphysics.

Some regrets do not aim at change or prudential improvement. John Keats's fiancée, Fanny Brawne, regretted that he died under the misapprehension that his poetry would soon be forgotten. (Keats's tombstone bears his epitaph: "Here lies one whose name was writ in water.") Her regret was not undermined by the fact that the past cannot be changed or that Keats's ignorance does not affect her own welfare.

Nagel and Kaufman could retreat to the claim that after the necessity of origin is learned, any distress ought to die down. In contrast, distress about your death date is robust under metaphysical enlightenment.

3.5 Future Bias

Although Derek Parfit believes that impossibility results cannot explain the patterns of our laments, he thinks evolutionary psychology succeeds (1987, pp.170–186). We prefer pains to be in the past and pleasures to be in the future. Suppose a nurse informs you that you are either the patient who had ten hours of excruciating surgery followed by amnesia or the patient who will have a single hour of this agonizing surgery (which will later be followed by amnesia to prevent trauma). While waiting for her to find out which patient you are, you hope that you are the patient who suffers more overall pain. For that pain is in the past. Parfit says this future bias explains why we are indifferent to our prevital nonexistence but dread our posthumous nonexistence.

Parfit notes that future bias is unaffected by inevitability. News that you will definitely be tortured does not make you serene. News that you might die in the next hour warrants distress; news that you will definitely die in the hour warrants even more distress!

Critics complain that future bias is not broad enough to explain the asymmetry between prevital and posthumous nonexistence. For instance, Walter Glannon concedes that future bias is plausible for pleasures and pains (1994). But he reminds us that death is not painful.

Once we become used to a pleasure, we are frustrated by its absence. Frustration is a bad experience, so the evil of these absences is easily explained. However, the dead cannot experience frustration.

Parfit himself grants that future bias does not extend to disgraces. He prefers to commit a faux pas tomorrow than to have made a fool of himself last night. Parfit also notes that future bias is limited to the first person.

Our preference for the near future is irrational because it leads to poor conduct. But Dan Moller denies that Parfit's future bias connects to any choices (2002). It is confined to hoping and other attitudinal states. Moller then appeals to the principle that attitudes can be irrational only insofar as they generate irrational actions.

Is future bias so hermetically sealed from action? The patient is acting on the bias when he asks the nurse to find out whether he has already undergone the procedure. Future bias makes you anxious and thereby curious—and those states lead to conduct.

We approve of attention flowing to where it does the most good. As Moller notes, if I must go through a painful operation tomorrow and then a much more painful operation ten years from now, then my distress will gravitate to the smaller, nearer pain. This does not strike us myopic. The preoccupation with "what's next?" is a corollary of an efficient policy for allocating concern.

Perhaps Moller can show that future bias is not irrational. The residual concern would be whether future bias is comprehensive enough. For it does not address our apathy toward comparable deprivations. Those who believe that split-brain patients have parallel streams of consciousness do not envy them. Nor do we pine for finer-grained experience. In three out of four cases (prevital nonexistence, lack of parallel consciousness, and the coarseness of experience), we understand massive deprivation without being alarmed. We are even less alarmed by these personal deprivations than we are alarmed by newspaper reports of mass starvations.

3.6 Fortifying Future Bias with a Theory of Time

Despite this incompleteness and the shaky grounds for characterizing future bias as rational, many philosophers treat future bias as a potential justification of our asymmetrical attitudes toward prevital nonexistence and posthumous nonexistence.

In principle, a theory of time could underwrite this optimism. For instance, if only the present and future exist, then the preference that pleasure be in the future and pain in the past is readily intelligible as a preference for nonexistent pain and existent pleasure.

But selective irrealism toward the past has trouble making sense of retrospective emotions such as pride and shame. There is considerable pressure to regard the past and future as equally real. When philosophers have treated one part of time as more real than the other, their order of preference is: present, past, then future coming in last. For instance, on C. D. Broad's "growing block" universe, the future becomes real by becoming the past. Making the past real and future unreal does yield a temporal asymmetry—but in the wrong direction! For now our preference for real pleasure puts them in past and favors locating pain in the future.

Parfit declines to fortify future bias with a congenial metaphysics of time. Indeed, his metaphysical preference is for an impartial perspective on time fostered by four-dimensionalism.

Parfit says it is irrational to care about pain only when it occurs on future Tuesday (1987, p. 123 ff). He vigorously and effectively criticizes temporal discounting in economics.

Parfit also suggests we would be better off if we were temporally neutral (1987, p. 175). For then we would be open to comfort offered by the symmetry argument.

One might be tempted to classify Parfit as an ally of Lucretius. This is not quite right because Parfit is pessimistic about the therapy promoted by Lucretius. Parfit thinks future bias is so deeply entrenched in our makeup that it cannot be removed.

Future bias evolved because only the future can be changed. The practical benefits of the bias prevent it from being a matter of choice. The bias ensures that the symmetry argument has no force for human beings. Or so says Parfit.

Parfit sets too high a standard for consolation. Patients with needle phobias make some progress by recognizing that the needles are nearly harmless. A periodontist who recommends a creepy procedure understands that the patient has a limited ability to control his fears and disgust. But recognition that these emotions are irrational helps us apply indirect methods of minimizing the discomfort. Patients who know the needle is harmless avert their eyes and distract themselves by talking during the injection. They do not fixate on their fear like children.

The symmetry argument is consoling even if its persuasiveness is diluted by our bias toward the future. Rational argument cannot do all we hope. But it does not need to do everything in order to do something significant.

4. THE HEGEMONY OF PERSONAL TIME

In this last section, I argue that we care about personal time rather than external time. Under this hypothesis, the first member of the triad is false:

1. Your posthumous nonexistence is bad for you.

Strictly speaking, we do not have future bias. We do not lament posthumous nonexistence more than prevital nonexistence. Nor are we guilty of temporal myopia. We do not have any practical concerns about time.

We instead care about personal time, a time-like relation that in ordinary circumstances coincides with external time. So we must turn to extraordinary circumstances to distinguish personal time from external time.

4.1 Time Travel

If a woman believes that she will time travel back to the excruciating ten-hour surgery described by Parfit, then she will dread the operation. She will acknowledge it is in the past. But she will not exclaim, "Thank goodness that is over!"

Relief tracks personal time—a time-like relation that is standardly used to straighten out apparent inconsistencies in time travel stories. Consider Donald Williams's charge that the epilogue of H. G. Wells's *The Time Machine* is inconsistent (1951, p. 463). Wells writes of the time traveler that "he may even now—if I may use the phrase—be wandering on some plesiosaurus-haunted oolitic coral reef, or beside the lonely saline seas of the Triassic Age." David Lewis says that the apparent contradiction turning on "now" can be avoided by relativizing it to a pseudo-chronology.

> If you take the stages of a common person, they manifest certain regularities with respect to external time. Properties change continuously as you go along, for the most part, and in familiar ways. First come infantile stages. Last come senile ones. Memories accumulate. Food digests. Hair grows. Wristwatch hands move. If you take the state of a time traveler instead, they do not manifest the common regularities with respect to external time. But there is one way to assign coordinates to the time traveler's stages, and one way only (apart from the arbitrary choice of a zero point), so that the regularities that hold with respect to this assignment match those that commonly hold with respect external time... The assignment of coordinates that yields this match is the time traveler's personal time. It isn't really time, but it plays the role in his life that time plays in the life of a common person. (Lewis, 1986, pp. 69–70)

Armed with personal time, Lewis revisits the sentence that Donald Williams regarded as inconsistent. According to Lewis, Wells is not relativizing "now" to objective time but rather to the time traveler's personal time.

The clarifying effects of personal time extend into the world of commerce. "Accelerated aging" is a technique for predicting the shelf life of products. The archivist W. Herzberg pioneered it in 1899. He wanted to predict how long books would last. Since Herzberg could not wait for the books to go through their natural stages of decomposition, he expedited deterioration by stressing the paper with light, heat, and humidity. There is a scientific basis for this enterprise. The Arrhenius equation from chemistry supports the conjecture that heating paper seventy-two hours at 100 degrees Celsius is equivalent to from eighteen to twenty-five years of natural aging. In the year 2000, the Library of Congress began a 100-year experiment to test such conjectures with natural aging.

"Personal time" is a double misnomer. In addition to misleading us into thinking it is time, it also misleads us into thinking that it a matter of personal experience (and so is something like "felt time"). Personal time can encompass inanimate objects such as books. It can encompass immense portions of the universe. Consider the scenario envisaged by Sydney Shoemaker (1969) in "Time without Change." World ABC is naturally divided into three regions: A, B, and C. Inhabitants migrate from one region to the other. Events from any region can be observed from any other. Each region undergoes a periodic freeze in which there is no motion, growth, or decay. The freeze lasts one year, and then everything resumes exactly as if there had been no freeze. Here is the schedule: A freezes every three years, B every four years, C every five years. The three cycles of local freezes are in phase. This implies a "total freeze" every sixty years. Shoemaker wished to show that there can be indirect evidence of time without change. But his thought experiment also shows how personal time can apply on a grand scale. For the practical purposes of growing crops, assigning pensions, and running races, each region of the universe would run by its local personal time. This would be no more inconvenient than our practice of relativizing time to regions on earth.

4.2 The Compatibility of Life and Death

David Lewis goes on to present a four-dimensionalist model of time travel. Whereas normal people are continuous space-time worms, time travelers have gaps in their objective histories. They disappear at one moment and reappear at a very different time. These scattered space-time worms look as jumbled as a mispaginated autobiography. Personal time repaginates the parts into a coherent story. Since Lewis permits backward causation and causal loops, he honors the intuition that time travel is genuine travel. Later stages of the time traveler cause changes in their previous stages.

Lewis's model solves several time travel paradoxes. Of special relevance is the self-visitation paradox. You travel back to your first day of kindergarten. You are standing as an adult and yet sitting as a child. But no one can sit and stand at the same time!

Normally, you cannot simultaneously sit and stand. But when two of your temporal parts meet, you can both sit and stand (in much the same way your left leg can be bent while your right leg is straight).

This resolution of the self-visitation paradox shows that death can coexist with life. Indeed, death can coexist with immortality. Consider Miss Paginate. She is born in 2000. In 2030 she time travels to a future funeral in 2050. She finds herself in the coffin as a fifty-year-old. Just as a distinction between temporal parts allows you to both sit and stand, it also allows Miss Paginate to be both dead and alive. Indeed, by slowing down her aging to an asymptotic rate from 31 to 39, Miss Paginate lives forever. At age 40, she finds herself back in 2040. She learns that she has been missing from 2031 to 2039. Miss Paginate also discovers that her normal rate of aging has resumed. She commences a memoir of her life, with special attention to the infinite portion that commences from 2050. She regrets her upcoming death in 2050. That will deprive her the time needed to complete her autobiography. But she takes comfort in knowing that she will live forever after her death (albeit as something akin to a partial amnesiac—since she will not remember her experiences from forty to fifty).

We have talked easily about memory in this time travel scenario because of a natural relativization to personal time. This relativization salvages Norman Malcolm's tense-based definition of memory: "A person B, remembers that p, if and only if B knows that p because he knew that p" (1963, p. 223). Since personal time incorporates causal connections, no adjustment is needed for causal theories of episodic memory. These primarily require a causal connection between the event and the memory of the event. Such tensed definitions only secondarily involve time.

4.3 Resurrecting the Epistemology of Death

Many people explain their fear of death as a fear of the unknown. Miss Paginate has endless experience of being dead. She resembles a man whose leg has fallen asleep. His representation of an absence of sensation in his leg is not an absence of representation. He needs to be awake to experience a limb that has fallen asleep. Similarly, Miss Paginate needs to be alive to perceive that her fifty-year-old body has a total absence of sensation.

Although non-time travelers cannot perceive their own death in this vivid fashion, we have the precedents cited by Anaxagoras. Take sleep, or better yet, a brief lapse of consciousness as one nods off during a lecture. The lapse is experienced as a discontinuity bordered by consciousness on both sides.

We also have a more lopsided experience of the absence of prevital experience. This retrospective experience of an absence strains the scruples of an empiricist. Our credentials would be stronger if we went in and out of existence with the frequency of a stroboscope.

Nevertheless, David Hume approvingly quotes Pliny the Elder:

> Everyone, from their last day will be in the same state as before their first and there will be no more sensation of body or soul than there was before birth.
>   But how much easier and more sure for everyone to believe in himself taking as an example of the tranquility to come what was undergone before birth?
> (*Natural History* 7.188, 190, trans. Warren, 2004, p. 70)

Hume concurs that "our insensibility before the composition of the body seems to natural reason a proof of a like state after dissolution" ("On the immortality of the soul," III.X.41).

This experience of our past absence of experience gives us an epistemic advantage over a dying man with an infinite past. Unlike you, this infinitely old man has not sampled prevital nonexistence.

Even less seasoned would be an infinitely old woman who has been continuously conscious. She is dying without any experience with nonbeing. She may regard you as a guru. She is heartened by your serene acceptance of prevital oblivion and intermittent unconsciousness.

Believers in an afterlife have an empirically straightforward epistemology of death: one somehow continues to have experiences after death. But I was assuming the secular model in which death is the absence of any further experience. The natural precedent for this model is the perception of absences: holes, shadows, and especially silence (Sorensen, 2008, pp. 272–274).

4.4 Veiled Immortality and Pseudo-Immortality

Personal time can be organized so as to preserve the harm characteristic of death while eliminating death itself (Sorensen, 2005). Suppose you are god who has "veiled immortality" (Moore, 2001, p. 228). Specifically, a demon rearranges your life to proceed in a staccato familiar from Zeno's paradox: You live half your life, followed by a trillion years of nothingness, then a quarter of your life followed by a trillion years of nothingness, then an eighth of your life followed by a trillion years of nothingness, and so on, ad infinitum. During the intermissions, everything stops. You will live forever. But you will not have a better life than a mortal. How good is your life? Since it is indiscernible from your actual life, you are in an excellent position to ascertain this. There are drawbacks, of course. Since nothing will come after you, none of your posthumous projects will succeed. On the other hand, there is no posthumous nonexistence to worry about. Notice that this makes little difference. The mere limit on your personal time suffices to inflict the catastrophic harm we are apt to think is unique to death.

Now consider Zeno-style pseudo-immortality. During the first minute, you live the first day of his life. During the next half-minute, you live the second day. During the following quarter minute, a third day passes. Since there are infinitely many junctures in this sequence, you enjoy infinitely many personal days. If you discover your veiled mortality, then you will realize that you will be dead in two minutes. But you will not be bothered by this future nonexistence.

What makes death bad is the limit on your personal experience. When limit is imposed, we are harmed even without death. When this limit is removed, death no longer harms us.

4.5 Incommensurable Times

The primacy of personal time can also be demonstrated with scenarios in which there are distinct, objective, temporal systems. The inspiration for this scenario is Anthony Quinton's "Two Space Myth" (1962). Suppose that a man in England goes to bed and wakes up in a tropical fishing village. A woman whom he somehow realizes to be his wife, tells him to catch fish. So he begins a day filled with the incidents typical for a lakeside fisherman. At the end of the day, he climbs into his hut and falls asleep. He awakes back in England and begins a typical British day. When he falls asleep the next day, he awakes back at the lakeside fishing village. He alternates back and forth in this fashion, never being able to trace a route between the two places. Since his English experiences and his lakeside experiences are equally coherent, he has no reason to say one set of experiences is a dream. And unlike dreams, there are robust causal effects. Physical events at the lakeside cause recollections in England. Quinton concludes that the Englishman would be reasonable in inferring that he dwells in two separate spaces.

Quinton amends this basic scenario to meet various objections. For example, the lack of intersubjectivity is remedied by stipulating that many British subjects have similar lakeside experiences. While in England they can make appointments to meet at landmarks around the lakeside. Richard Swinburne (1981) supplements Quinton's efforts. To avoid the absurdity of a body being in two (primary) places at once, Swinburne stipulates that the Englishman's body disappears when he falls asleep. Swinburne also strengthens the grounds for thinking that the spaces are separate by assigning different laws of nature. In England, gravity obeys an inverse square law. At the lakeside, gravity obeys an inverse cube law.

Having made his case for multiple spaces, Quinton turns to the question of multiple times. He denies that his two-space myth is also a two-time myth. Quinton's reasoning is that the Englishman's bi-spatial experiences form a single temporal series. After all, the Englishman lies down in his English bed before he awakes in his lakeside bed. So Quinton feels we must start our quest for a multitemporal myth from the beginning. Yet, he contends, "Such a search seems doomed from the start. How can these experiences be my experiences unless they constitute a single temporal series?" (Quinton, 1962, p. 145)

The answer is that personal time unifies my experiences. Read "the Englishman lays down in his English bed before waking in his lakeside bed" as a remark about the Englishman's personal time. Indeed, the whole narrative relating the Englishman's oscillations can be understood as benefiting from the organizing effect of Lewis's concept.

The recourse to personal time becomes more compelling as Peter King elaborates the two worlds so that they become objectively incommensurable:

> Imagine a team of historians of the distant future, working on the private journals of various people of their past. A strange pattern begins to emerge. In 1734 a woman in St Albans (call her Mabel) describes her alternating Quintonian Earth/Lakeside existence. In 1842 a man in Bolton (call him Sidney) describes a similar dual lives, as Mabel's neighbor dating the same Lakeside period. In 1895 a woman in Tokyo (call her Cho-Cho-San) describe her Earth/Lakeside lives; in Lakeside she was Mabel's mother—again, during the same Lakeside period. By ignoring the our-worldly chronology of these and many other similar writers, and concentrating purely on the content of what they wrote, the historian build from the journals a coherent account of the lives of the inhabitants of Lakeside. (King, 1995, p. 538)

The extant Lakeside journals describe many other Lakesiders who would have written journals on Earth. The historians can even predict the contents of these missing journals. But where are these missing links? Years go by. Then someone finds a journal written by Mabel's Lakeside sister that was written after the historians made their predictions (and in isolation from these predictions). They realize that they have the historical equivalent of a periodic table. They need only wait for the gaps to be filled in.

King further supposes that comparison of the journals shows that Lakeside is temporally unrelated to Earth (1995, p. 539). Lakeside does not exist in Earth's past, present, or future. Each world will have a period of objective time in which Mabel no longer exists. But Mabel will not be able to say, "In the other world, I no longer exist." For the two worlds are incommensurable. It isn't that she is living in two worlds simultaneously.

King's Two-Time myth undermines the notion of posthumous nonexistence by creating distinct objective temporal systems. The incommensurability of these two systems gives us new reason to doubt principles that link time with value. For instance, Epicurus assumes that each harm is at a time. But Mabel's death only has a definite date in one of the temporal systems, not both.

Nagel is committed to atemporal harms. Julian Lamont has objected that this should be rejected because it entails there are causes that have effects that obtain at no particular time (1998, p. 208). But this would be common in King's scenario involving incommensurable times.

As long as personal time remains familiar, objective time can vary without disturbing our practical concerns. What counts for practical rationality are causal relations. What appear to be irrational asymmetries in our attitudes toward time may be redeemed as rational distinctions at the level of causation.[1]

Notes

1. I thank Thomas Nagel for e-mail correspondence (April 24–25, 2010) about the history behind his "Death" article. I am also grateful for comments by Ben Bradley, Jens Johansson, Steven Luper, and James Warren.

References

Ayer, A. J. 1990. *The Meaning of Life*. New York: Scribner.
Belshaw, Christopher. 2000. "Later Death/Earlier Birth." *Midwest Studies in Philosophy* 24 (1): 69–83.
Bradley, Ben. 2009. *Well-Being and Death*. Oxford: Clarendon Press.
Glannon, Walter. 1994. "Temporal Asymmetry, Life, and Death." *American Philosophical Quarterly* 31: 235–244.
Hoffman, Paul. 1998. *The Man Who Loved Only Numbers*. New York: Hyperion.
Kaufman, Frederik. 1999. "Pre-Vital and Post-Mortem Non-Existence." *American Philosophical Quarterly* 36: 1–19.
King, Peter. 1995. "Other Times." *Australasian Journal of Philosophy* 73(4): 532–547.
Lamont, Julian. 1998. "A Solution to the Puzzle of When Death Harms Its Victims." *Australasian Journal of Philosophy* 76: 198–222.
Lewis, David. 1986. "The Paradoxes of Time Travel." In his *Philosophical Papers*, pp. 67–80. New York: Oxford University Press.
Luper, Steven. 2009. *The Philosophy of Death*. Cambridge: Cambridge University Press.
Lucretius. 1951. *On the Nature of the Universe*. Latham, reg. trans. New York: Penguin Classics.
Malcolm, Norman. 1963. *Knowledge and Certainty*. Englewood Cliffs, NJ: Prentice-Hall.
Moller, Dan. 2002. "Parfit on Pains, Pleasures and the Time of Their Occurrence." *Canadian Journal of Philosophy* 32: 67–82.
Moore, Adrian. 2001. *The Infinite*, 2nd edn. London/New York: Routledge.
Nagel Thomas. 1970. "Death." *Noûs* 41: 73–80. Reprinted in his *Mortal Questions*. Cambridge: Cambridge University Press, 1979.
Parfit, Derek. 1987. *Reasons and Persons*. New York: Oxford University Press.

Pettigrove, Glen. 2002. "Death, Asymmetry, and the Psychological Self." *Pacific Philosophical Quarterly* 83 (4): 407–423.

Quinton, Anthony. 1962. "Spaces and Times." *Philosophy* 37: 130–147.

Rosenbaum S. E. 1989. "The Symmetry Argument: Lucretius against the Fear of Death." *Philosophy and Phenomenological Research* 50: 353–373.

Sedley, D. N. 1998. *Lucretius and the Transformation of Greek Wisdom*. Cambridge: Cambridge University Press.

Shoemaker, Sydney. 1969. "Time without Change." *Journal of Philosophy* 66: 363–381.

Sorensen, Roy. 2005. "The Cheated God: Death and Personal Time." *Analysis* 65 (2): 119–125.

Sorensen, Roy. 2008. *Seeing Dark Things*. New York: Oxford University Press.

Swinburne, Richard. 1981. *Space and Time*, 2nd edn. New York: St. Martin's Press.

Warren, J. 2004. *Facing Death: Epicurus and His Critics*. New York: Oxford University Press.

Williams, Donald C. 1951. "The Myth of Passage." *Journal of Philosophy* 48: 457–472.

CHAPTER 11

....

THE TIMING PROBLEM

....

JENS JOHANSSON

1. INTRODUCTION

....

Epicurus wrote, in his letter to Menoeceus,

> Become accustomed to the belief that death is nothing to us. For all good and evil
> consists in sensation, but death is deprivation of sensation. So death, the most
> terrifying of ills, is nothing to us, since as long as we exist death is not with us; but
> when death comes, then we do not exist. (Epicurus, 1940, p. 31)

These words have been repeated so many times over the centuries that, if
Menoeceus to this day still hasn't become accustomed to the belief that death is
nothing to us, I suppose he never will. But perhaps he should. Epicurus's formulations suggest the following argument:

(1) Anything that is bad for a person is bad for her at a time.
(2) There is no time at which death is bad for the person who dies.
(3) Hence, death is not bad for the person who dies.

I'll call this "the Epicurean Argument," despite that it is not altogether clear
that Epicurus accepted it, and that several related arguments can be extracted from
the quoted passage.

The argument is valid, and the premises look fairly promising.[1] Reflection on
some ordinary bad things seems to support (1). Just an hour ago I decided to buy an
apple, instead of the orange I was also considering. The taste of the apple, however,
was appalling. Plausibly, my decision was bad for me; and, just as (1) dictates, there
also seem to be times at which it was bad for me: in particular, those at which I was
eating the terrible-tasting fruit. Or suppose you throw an apple at my head, putting
me in a coma for two months. Plausibly, your action was bad for me; and, just as

(1) dictates, there also seem to be times at which it was bad for me: in particular, those times during my comatose period when I would have been enjoying myself had I escaped your Golden Delicious. Indeed, it seems that any reason to doubt that there are times at which my well-being is affected negatively by these events—my decision to buy an apple and your throwing one at me—would also be a reason to doubt that they are bad for me at all.

But what about death? When is my death bad for me? Before I die, it seems, I am still alive and well, or at least no worse off than I would have been were it not for my death. And once I die, it seems, I am no longer there at all—and hence no longer there to be affected for the worse by anything. So premise (2) seems reasonable as well.

Yet common sense tells us that death, in lots of cases, is bad for the one who dies. Those who accept this commonsense view—"anti-Epicureans," as I shall call them (or us, rather)—need to explain where the Epicurean argument goes wrong. There are five main routes available. According to *atemporalism*, death is bad for the deceased, but not at any time. Atemporalism thus rejects premise (1). The remaining strategies all reject (2), but differ in their answers to the question of when death is bad for the subject. On *eternalism*, death is bad for her at all times; on *priorism*, before death (and only then); on *concurrentism*, at the time of death (and only then); on *subsequentism*, after death (and only then).[2] (Priorism does not entail, of course, that death is bad for the person at *all* times before death; similarly, subsequentism does not entail that death is bad for her at *all* times after death.)

My aim in this chapter is to clarify the Epicurean challenge and to point out some important merits and disadvantages of the various anti-Epicurean views. The currently most popular are probably priorism and subsequentism; my vote, however, is for atemporalism.

2. SIX CLARIFICATIONS

Six further introductory remarks are in order.

(a) *The Time of the Badness.* The Epicurean Argument does not concern the time *at which the bad thing happens*. That would render hopeless both the argument itself and all responses to it save concurrentism. Instead, the argument concerns the time *at which the bad thing (death) is bad*—if you like, the time at which the relation *x is bad for y* obtains between death and the one who dies. (This kind of distinction is easily blurred by the not uncommon talk of "the time of the *harm* of death." For if death harms its victim, death *is* a harm; and obviously enough, death occurs when death occurs.)

(b) *Death.* When we speak of someone's "death" in this context, we are referring to the particular, concrete event of her death, and not, for instance, to the fact that she dies at all.[3] Thus, if we ask what would have happened if a person's death hadn't taken place, we're not wondering about a scenario where she lives forever, but rather one in which she dies at some other, presumably later, time.

(c) *The Deprivation Approach.* And that question—about what would have happened if the person's death hadn't occurred—is a question that typical anti-Epicureans think we have good reason to ask. For, while they concede that death is not *intrinsically* bad—that is, bad in itself—for the deceased, they claim that her death is *overall* bad for her insofar as it makes her intrinsically worse off than she would otherwise have been. (Correspondingly, it is overall good for her insofar as it makes her intrinsically better off than she would otherwise have been.) This view, the so-called "deprivation approach," is often formulated in something like this way:

(DA)   The overall value of event E, for person S, at possible world w = the intrinsic value of w for S, minus the intrinsic value for S of the closest possible world to w, w*, where E does not occur.[4]

(You might find it unnatural to speak of the intrinsic value for someone of a possible world. But, as I see it, it is just a handy way of speaking of how intrinsically well-off the person would have been—that is, which well-being level she would have occupied—if such-and-such had been the case.) While anti-Epicureanism is compatible with other accounts of overall value, my focus in this chapter is on what friends of the deprivation approach, glossed as something like (DA), should say in response to the Epicurean Argument.

(d) *Well-Being.* Of course, how well-off a person is in a world depends on which theory of well-being is correct. Some philosophers have based their rejection of the Epicurean Argument on a denial of the straightforward form of hedonism that Epicurus apparently endorsed.[5] According to this "simple hedonism," as we might call it, someone's well-being level is solely determined by her receipt of pleasure (the more, the better) and pain (the less, the better). However, if an answer to the Epicurean Argument is incompatible with simple hedonism, I shall consider this a drawback of that answer. For one thing, simple hedonism can hardly be dismissed as implausible: though it has its problems, they are not obviously more serious than those faced by rival views. More importantly, since the Epicurean Argument seems stronger if simple hedonism is correct than if it is false, it is philosophically more interesting if we can answer Epicurus while granting him that axiological view. (And if it turns out that we can't, this might be considered useful evidence against simple hedonism.)

(e) *The Termination Thesis.* Epicurus subscribed to the "Termination Thesis," the view that we go out of existence when we die.[6] (That is: when we die, we cease to be *present.*) Similar remarks apply here as in (d): the Termination Thesis is not obviously implausible, and helps the Epicurean Argument. In this chapter I am simply going to assume that the thesis is true.[7] I don't think anyone will protest; so far as I know, no actual anti-Epicureans have based their view on a denial of the Termination Thesis.

(f) *The Subject.* More than once has it been suggested that the anti-Epicurean needs to tackle, not only the question. "When is death bad for the one who dies?"

but also the supposedly different, and supposedly challenging question "Who is the *subject* of death's badness?"[8] Candidate answers to the latter question, it is suggested, are "the antemortem person" and "the postmortem person." It is true that some anti-Epicurean views face problems to do with the fact that the subject fails to exist when death is, according to those views, bad for her. However, I can discern no problem in specifying *who* the subject is. If, for instance, Michael Jackson's death is bad for *him*, it seems clear that the subject is Michael Jackson. Who else? It is hard to see what we could mean by, for example, the expression "antemortem Michael Jackson" other than simply Michael Jackson as he was before his death. To say that death is bad for antemortem Michael Jackson, then, seems merely to be a poetic way of stating the priorist view that death was bad for him before he died (though it has its defects even when considered as a piece of poetry). Formulations such as "Who is the subject of death's badness?" should, I think, at most be regarded as misleading ways of putting the question, "When is death bad for the one who dies?"

3. ETERNALISM

We can further elucidate that question by considering Fred Feldman's view in some detail. Writers in this debate often start off by arguing that Feldman has somehow misconstrued the question, or based his answer on the wrong kind of consideration. Although, as we shall see, there is some truth in this charge, it also seems to me that *they* have misconstrued *his* position.

Here is Feldman's answer to the question of when his daughter Lindsay's death is bad for her:

> It seems clear to me that the answer to this question must be "eternally." For when we say that her death is bad for her, we are really expressing a complex fact about the relative values of two possible worlds. If these worlds stand in a certain value relation, then (given that they stand in this relation at any time) they stand in that relation not only when Lindsay exists, but at times when she doesn't. (Feldman, 1991, p. 221)

Feldman's main point is that we should focus on the value relation between (a person and) two entire possible worlds. For, on the deprivation approach—which Feldman espouses—the fact that a person's death is bad for her amounts to the fact that the closest world (in its entirety) where her death occurs, w, is intrinsically worse for her than the closest world (in its entirety) where it does not occur, w*. Given this approach, surely it is very natural to see the question, "*When* is S's death bad for S?" as equivalent to,

(Q1)   When is the intrinsic value for S of w (in its entirety) lower than the intrinsic value for S of w* (in its entirety)?

"Eternally"—that is, "at all times"—is a plausible answer to this question, because the total amounts of intrinsic goods and bads (e.g., pleasures and pains) received by the person in the two worlds can hardly vary over time. Compare with utilitarianism's account of moral wrongness. Someone might want to know, concerning some wrong action, "*When* is the action wrong?" Given utilitarianism, it is natural to regard that question as equivalent to, "*When* is the total consequence of the action intrinsically worse than the total consequence of some alternative action?" "Eternally" is a good answer. Feldman's view applies this kind of consideration to overall badness.

And that, I think, is a more reasonable sort of consideration than those ascribed to Feldman by various commentators. Let us look at four examples.

First, William Grey claims that Feldman endorses eternalism because he regards "[v]alues…as relations between abstract objects"—more specifically, as relations between possible worlds, which Feldman regards as abstract (Grey, 1999, p. 359). This interpretation strikes me as unfair, especially since Feldman surely realizes that abstract objects can stand in certain relations at certain times and yet fail to do so at others. For instance, the numbers 2 and 3 are abstract, but may well jointly exemplify a relation—for example, *x is more liked by me than y is*—today and fail to do so tomorrow (my mathematical taste is unstable). Moreover, it is hard to see how the view that possible worlds are concrete objects would jeopardize Feldman's answer to (Q1).

Second, Julian Lamont suggests that the "when" question Feldman addresses is "about the conditions under which a harm occurs—the conditions are such that a state of affairs is harmful 'when' the nearest relevant possible world in which the state of affairs does not obtain is a better world from the point of view of the agent" (Lamont, 1998, p. 200). As Lamont notes, "[T]his question is not really about time, even if you can tack on the end of the analysis that the relation between these two worlds is eternal" (1998, p. 200). This interpretation also is odd. Feldman addresses (Q1); and (Q1) is about time. If nothing else, this is shown by the fact that his answer provides times: indeed, all of them.

Third, Neil Feit, Steven Luper and others contend that Feldman understands the "when" question as, "When is it *true* that the person's death is bad for her?"[9] And, they think, he is then led to eternalism because he regards the proposition that the person's death is bad for her as true at all times. But, the critics point out, this view about truth fails to establish that death is bad for the deceased at all times (just as, for instance, the eternal truth of the proposition that Lindsay dies in 1987 fails to show that Lindsay dies at all times). As I see it, though, Feldman's suggestion does not appeal to any particular idea about truth. His main claim is that w (in its entirety) is *worse* at all times for the one who dies than w* (in its entirety). This is compatible with, for instance, the not unpopular view that all true propositions are only *timelessly* true (and thus very far from being true at all times). The reference to truth is simply a red herring in this context.

Fourth, Ben Bradley suggests that Feldman is drawn to eternalism in the following way (Bradley, 2009, p. 84). Suppose w has an intrinsic value of 100 for the subject; and w*, 120. According to Bradley, what Feldman asks himself is then, "when is the number 120 greater than the number 100?"—and his answer, supposedly, is "eternally." Bradley thus takes Feldman to be asking a "de re" question about the numbers themselves. However, Feldman's position is, rather, based on the observation that, in the case of overall badness, *what the relevant numbers are* does not change over time. And that a certain number never stops being greater than a certain other number holds regardless of that. Compare: sometimes my brother's income is higher than my sister's; sometimes it's lower. But this is not because a certain number ceases to be greater than a certain other number; it is because what the relevant numbers are—how much my brother and sister earn—changes over time. Bradley's interpretation neglects that Feldman's point is rather analogous to the claim that my sister's total lifetime income is eternally higher than my brother's.

Feldman's answer to (Q1) is, though plausible, not obviously true. A notable rival answer is atemporalist: "The relation does indeed obtain, but not at any time." The choice between these two rivals depends on thorny issues in the philosophy of time, and I cannot enter into this discussion here.[10] In any case, Feldman's approach seems to me less misguided than the above four interpretations suggest.

Nonetheless, I agree with the common complaint that the question Feldman addresses fails to bring out the Epicurean challenge in the most forceful way. Even though (Q1) is difficult to answer (eternalism or atemporalism?), the difficulty does not stem from any particular problem to do with death. It seems that, for any bad thing, the (Q1)-analogous question—for example, "When is the closest world (in its entirety) in which you did throw the apple at me intrinsically worse for me than the closest world (in its entirety) in which you didn't?"—must receive an eternalist or atemporalist answer, and for the same reason as in the case of death. So long as the Epicurean Argument is taken to be concerned with (Q1), we can be sure that one of the premises is radically mistaken (the first, given atemporalism; the second, given eternalism)—and this for reasons not specifically related to death.

Here is a more Epicurean-friendly reading of the "when" question:

(Q2)   When is S intrinsically worse off in w than S is at that time, or those times, in w*? (In other words: At which time, or times, is S's well-being level lower than it would have been then if S's death hadn't occurred?)[11]

It is (Q2), or something very much like it, that has troubled many anti-Epicureans. Unlike (Q1), (Q2) is challenging in a way that analogous questions about other evils are not. (Q2)-analogous questions about ordinary evils seem to have rather straightforward answers: as I indicated in section 1, my decision to buy an apple an hour ago made me worse off while I was eating it; your throwing one at me made me worse off while I was in a coma.[12] (It will make you worse off as well, when I wake up.) But the dead don't eat, and are not comatose.

Eternalism cannot be a correct answer to (Q2): it is false that I would have been intrinsically better off ten billion years ago were it not for my death. In order to answer (Q2), then—and that is what we will try to do in the remainder of this chapter—we have to look elsewhere.

4. CONCURRENTISM

But where? I think it is clear that concurrentism—the thesis that death is bad for the deceased when, and only when, death occurs—does not give anti-Epicureans what they need, not in all relevant cases. Perhaps death makes a few people worse off exactly when they die. Surely, though, if someone's continued life would have been fantastic if she hadn't died, her death is bad for her, even if the very moment she dies happens to be nice enough. As I've indicated (section 2), there is admittedly one question to which "at the time of death" is doubtless the correct answer: When does the bad thing—death—occur? As a general answer to (Q2), however, concurrentism is dead.

The finalists, therefore, are priorism (section 5), subsequentism (section 6), and atemporalism (section 7).

5. PRIORISM

Priorism is the view that death is bad for the deceased before it occurs (and only then). Priorists are usually not claiming that my death *causes* me to be worse off before I die than I would otherwise have been. The standard priorist strategy is instead to emphasize that death deprives me of the satisfaction of many of my desires, and that I have these desires while I am still alive. For example, I desire right now—Thursday 1 p.m., if you're interested—that I eat chocolate on Saturday; suppose I die tomorrow, and that I would otherwise have eaten chocolate on Saturday. In this case, according to typical priorists, my death—despite being in the future—affects my present well-being level negatively.

Note that priorism does not presuppose that I can occupy a well-being level when I don't exist. This seems to be an advantage over subsequentism and eternalism (and concurrentism, if I don't exist at the time I die—a controversial issue). Still, priorism faces a number of important objections. Here are three.

First, recall one desideratum mentioned in section 2: compatibility with simple hedonism. The standard priorist strategy—appealing to the times when I have the desires—evidently relies on a preferentialist axiology, and it is difficult to see any reasonable way to combine priorism with simple hedonism. Apparently, there is no time before my death such that my receipt of pleasure and pain at that time would have been any different if it were not for my future death. Granted, if I hadn't died tomorrow, it would *now* be the case *that I am going to feel pleasure on Saturday*. But this fact does not allow priorism to be married with simple hedonism: any simple hedonist would say that my current well-being solely depends on how much pleasure and pain I receive *now*.

Second, the standard priorist strategy does not seem to capture all relevant cases.[13] Suppose that my death does not deprive me of the satisfaction of any desire

I actually have, but that it does deprive me of the satisfaction of many desires that I would have acquired after tomorrow if I hadn't died tomorrow. (For simplicity, suppose also that there is no difference in desire frustrations between the two scenarios.) Plausibly, my death is bad for me in this case. But the standard priorist strategy is, of course, of no use here. It might be replied that priorism still works for more ordinary deaths, and that we can adopt one of the other views in this unusual kind of case: atemporalism, for example. But this would be no minor concession. Going atemporalist about this kind of case would require a rejection of premise (1) of the Epicurean Argument—that is, that anything that is bad for a person is bad for her at a time—and we would thus now have to tackle general worries about atemporalism. If these can indeed be dealt with satisfactorily, there's just no need for priorism.

Third,[14] priorism appears to conflict with the intuitively attractive, "internalist" view that a person's well-being level at a time solely depends on the intrinsic features of that time. Return to the chocolate example. According to the priorist, my present well-being level partly depends on what goes on in my mouth on Saturday. However, it does not seem intrinsic to the present time whether these future events will occur or not. (Some might want to say that my present desire to eat chocolate on Saturday is *already frustrated*—perhaps because it is already *true* that I am not going to not eat chocolate on Saturday. But this (objectionable) claim is irrelevant here. Even if my desire is already frustrated, its being so still depends on what happens on Saturday.)

As Ben Bradley notes in his recent book on death, internalism follows from the more general, "Moorean" view that something's intrinsic value only depends on its intrinsic features (2009, p. 19).[15] He also puts forward an interesting argument for the claim that any theory of well-being needs to respect the Moorean view.

> This is because...the value atoms [i.e., the states of affairs that are intrinsically good for us in the most fundamental way] should be *instantiations of the fundamental good- or bad-making properties*—the properties that are fundamentally and completely responsible for how well a world (or a life, or...) goes. Suppose [the Moorean view] were false. Then there could be two properties, F and G, such that the only intrinsically good states of affairs are those involving the instantiation of F alone, but whose values are determined by whether there are any instantiations of G. But if that were true, F would fail to be a *fundamentally* good- or bad-making property, for instantiations of F would fail to completely determine what value there is. The fundamental good- or bad-making property would involve both F and G, contrary to our assumption. (Bradley, 2009, p. 19)

This argument is problematic, however. It seems correct, for the reason Bradley gives, that the intrinsic value of the *value atoms* must depend only on their intrinsic features. Even if we are preferentialists, then, we ought not to say, for example, that the following state of affairs is a value atom that helps determine my present well-being: *I desire, at Thursday 1 p.m., that I eat chocolate on Saturday.* For it is also crucial whether the desire is satisfied; and that is extrinsic to this state of affairs. To avoid this problem, the preferentialist could instead say that the following, more

complex state is a relevant value atom: *I desire, at Thursday 1 p.m., that I eat choco-*
late on Saturday; and I do eat chocolate on Saturday. For it *is* intrinsic to *this* state
that my desire is satisfied. But none of this seems to imply that the intrinsic value
of a *time* for me must depend solely on *its* intrinsic features. On the contrary, if the
atoms that determine how intrinsically well-off I am at a time are of the complex
sort just exemplified, the intrinsic value for me of the time Thursday 1 p.m. does
depend in part on things other than the intrinsic features of Thursday 1 p.m.—
though, again, it solely depends on features that are intrinsic to the *atoms*.

Admittedly, given certain respectable views of the nature of times, it might
after all be intrinsic to a time that certain events are going to occur later: for
instance, the view that a time is just a conjunction of everything that is true at that
time, including propositions about future events. This would undermine my argument against Bradley. Fortunately for the priorist, though, it would also show that
internalism is compatible with priorism.

However, priorism is still incompatible with the following principle, which is
similar to but more narrow than internalism: a person's well-being at a time is not
at all determined by what goes on at other times. This narrow principle also seems
to me very attractive. Suppose your childhood and mine are exact duplicates of
each other (i.e., they consist of exactly similar events), but that only your childhood desires about the future—about the post-childhood times—are satisfied. (For
instance, each of us desired to eat chocolate on a certain Saturday in 2012, but only
you are actually going to do that.) Perhaps it would be reasonable for me to be envious, but it seems utterly unreasonable for me to be envious about your *childhood*.
Similarly, if God somehow gave us the chance to switch childhoods (but no later
parts of our lives), it seems I would have no reason at all to accept this offer. The
best explanation of these judgments, it seems, is that the narrow principle is true;
since our lives differ only in what happens to us after our childhoods, you and I
were equally intrinsically well-off during our childhoods.

It may be suggested that we must reject the narrow principle in order to accommodate the popular view that it is intrinsically good for a person to have a desire
satisfied even if the desire and its object are not simultaneous. For instance, suppose that, aside from the fact that your childhood desires about the future were
satisfied and mine weren't, our desire satisfactions and frustrations do not differ in
any relevant way. Many would say here that your overall well-being level is nonetheless higher than mine. Personally, I don't find this view particularly appealing.[16]
More importantly, it is fully compatible with the narrow principle. The most natural thing for proponents of the view to say is that the calculation of the intrinsic
value of a world for a person is not simply a matter of adding the well-being levels
she occupies at the different moments in that world.[17] Thus, even if, in the just
mentioned case, the actual world as a whole is intrinsically better for you than for
me, this does not entail that there is any moment at which you are better off than
I am.

"Before death" is probably the best answer to questions such as the following:
When do I have reason to fear death? When do I have reason to believe that my

death is bad for me? When is my worrying about death bad for me? Perhaps some people have been led to priorism—that is, priorism about (Q2)—because they have failed to clearly distinguish these questions from (Q2).

6. SUBSEQUENTISM

If I die on Friday, death deprives me of many goods: the pleasure of eating chocolate on Saturday, a holiday in Spain next month, and so on. Obviously, these nice events would have taken place after Friday. It is therefore a very natural thought that my death is bad for me after it occurs. Subsequentists embrace this natural thought. I'll focus here on Ben Bradley's view—by far the best version of subsequentism.[18]

According to Bradley, my well-being level after death is zero. My death is thus bad for me at all and only those times after it occurs at which I would have had a positive well-being level if I hadn't died. As Bradley is a hedonist, he identifies these times with those at which I would have had a surplus of pleasure over pain if my death hadn't occurred. However, his form of subsequentism could be combined with other axiological views as well.

It may be tempting to advance a very general argument against subsequentism, an argument that has nothing in particular to do with well-being. Recall that we are assuming that the Termination Thesis is true: we cease to exist when we die. But a claim of the type "x is F at t" (e.g., "Michael Jackson is alive in 2008," "Michael Jackson has zero well-being in 2012") is true only if the object has some property at the time in question. And an object has a property at a time only if it exists. These reasonable theses, someone might argue, are incompatible with subsequentism.

While the issues here are complex, a good response is one that Bradley provides to a closely related challenge.[19] The theses are indeed reasonable, but compatible with subsequentism. What the Termination Thesis says is that, when we die, we cease to exist in the sense that we cease to be *present*: we fail to be *located* at the times following death. In order to threaten subsequentism, the theses need to be supplemented with the view that purely past objects—objects that have gone out of existence in the just-mentioned sense—don't exist simpliciter. However, something can exist *simpliciter* without being located at the present time (just as something can exist *simpliciter* without being located *here*). And if an object exists *simpliciter*, it can have properties at a time even if it doesn't exist (isn't located) *at* that time.

Actually, it seems that even those who deny the existence *simpliciter* of purely past objects should resist the general argument against subsequentism.[20] For they will have to find some way of accommodating what seem to be undeniably true claims about purely past objects (e.g., "Michael Jackson is dead in 2012," "Michael Jackson is remembered in 2012"). One option is to hold that such a claim somehow manages to be true even though the object does not have any properties; another is to hold that objects that lack existence *simpliciter* do have properties after all. We cannot settle here which option is most promising. But we don't have to, for each option evidently involves denying one part or other of the general argument against subsequentism. Unless there is some special problem to do with well-being, the subsequentist could simply adopt either of these strategies for claims like "Michael Jackson has zero well-being in 2012."

If subsequentism fails, this seems to be because there *is* some special problem to do with well-being. The crucial issue, it seems, is whether I occupy a well-being level of zero after death or rather no well-being level at all. Here are two reasons to prefer the latter view.

First, consider a future time at which there are no longer any sentient individuals.[21] Given Bradley's view, all people (e.g., Menoeceus, Michael Jackson, and you) will occupy a well-being level of zero then. In terms of well-being, then, there will be perfect equality at that time. But even adherents of the egalitarian view that equality is intrinsically good should hesitate to say that there will be anything intrinsically good about that time. A possible reply is, of course, that the well-being level at a time of someone who does not exist then is irrelevant to the intrinsic value of that time. In that case, however, one may wonder why it should be used to account for the evil of death. Another possible reply is that, because we have strong reasons to accept subsequentism, the argument speaks against egalitarianism rather than subsequentism. As I see it, however, we have strong reasons to accept subsequentism only if it is needed to respond to the Epicurean Argument—and I'll suggest in the next section that it is not.

Second, some objects apparently fail to occupy any well-being level at any time at all—for instance, my shoe. But how can my shoe fail to have a well-being level now if even a dead person succeeds? Unlike Michael Jackson, the shoe is at least still with us. Bradley proposes that the difference might be this: there is no possible world and time at which the shoe has a positive or negative well-being level; whereas in the case of the dead person, there is such a world and time (e.g., a time in the actual world when Michael Jackson is alive and happy). However, this proposal seems to sit uneasily with simple hedonism. A simple hedonist should say that my present well-being level solely depends on the intrinsic features of my present mental states. Just as it does not depend on, for example, my reputation or whether I have true beliefs about the external world, so it should not depend on what goes on at other times in other possible worlds. However, this is precisely what it does on Bradley's proposal. It implies that Michael Jackson, unlike the shoe, has a well-being level now—despite the fact that there is no intrinsic difference between their current mental states: there are no such states.[22]

Bradley gives an argument for the view that we occupy a well-being level after death (2009, p. 109). In one of two possible futures, you die instantly. In the other, you instantly go comatose, never regain consciousness, and die in ten years. Prudentially speaking, it seems that you should be indifferent between these two futures. This seems to show that you are equally intrinsically well-off in them; consequently, you have a well-being level in each.

As David Hershenov has argued, however, this seems to prove too much (Hershenov, 2007, p. 174). Prudentially speaking, you should also be indifferent between two possible worlds in which you never exist. But never-existing people have no well-being level. Bradley replies that since you do exist, that latter claim seems irrelevant. As he suspects, however, Hershenov's idea must be that a person who does not exist *in a certain possible world* has no well-being level *in that world*. But this idea, Bradley submits, is unhelpful, as it is no more or less plausible than the very claim at issue: that a person who does not exist (i.e., is not located) at a *time* has no well-being level then. This objection is questionable, however. Arguably, having a well-being level in a world, or at a time, requires having properties there, or then. Arguably, you have properties in a world only if you exist there: if you had never existed, you would not have had any properties. But, as suggested above (in the reply to the general argument against subsequentism), the corresponding claim about time is doubtful: it is doubtful that you have properties at a time only if you exist then. As I said, Bradley himself denies that claim.

"After death" seems to be the correct answer to a question in the vicinity of (Q2): When does it hold both that (a) I would have been intrinsically well-off at that time if I hadn't died and (b) I am in fact not as intrinsically well-off then as I would have been if I hadn't died? Unlike this question, though, (Q2) is about being *worse* off.

Still, the problems with subsequentism strike me as less serious than those that afflict eternalism, concurrentism, and priorism. If atemporalism fails, subsequentism is probably the best answer to Epicurus. But that is a big "if."

7. ATEMPORALISM

According to atemporalism, death is bad for the deceased, but not at any time. There are some perhaps nearby views suggested in the literature—especially in connection with Thomas Nagel's discussion—which should not be confused with atemporalism. First, Nagel himself says that death's badness, unlike the subject, cannot be "easily located" in time (and space) (Nagel, 1970, p. 67). By contrast, atemporalism is incompatible with the idea that the time of death's badness can be located if we try hard. Second, William Grey suggests that Nagel's view is that there is no *precise* time—no time with sharp boundaries—at which death is bad for its victim (1999, p. 363). Atemporalism, on the other hand, says that there is *no* such time, precise or imprecise. Third, Steven Luper ascribes to Nagel "indefinitism," defined as the view that a person's death is bad for her "at an indeterminate time" (2007, p. 41). If an indeterminate time is a time, this view is inconsistent with atemporalism. Fourth, Harry Silverstein contends that the question of when someone's death is bad for her has (and needs) no answer.[23] The atemporalist, however, need not deny that "at no time" counts as an answer—a correct answer—to the question.

Even if "at no time" is in fact not an answer to the question, this fact does not seem to follow from atemporalism.

Here is what seems to me a good reason to look favorably upon atemporalism. Death is bad for the deceased; all rival responses to the Epicurean Argument have considerable costs; atemporalism does not.

However, that last claim is often disputed. According to a popular line of thought, atemporalism makes death objectionably different from other evils.[24] Other things that are bad for me seem to be bad for me at times: the apple incidents of section 1, for instance. And death's badness does not seem to be different in kind from other evils: like them, it deprives the victim of a better scenario. Atemporalism, however, implies that death—unlike the rest of the gang of evils— has a badness that, as Chris Belshaw puts it, slips "through the calendar" (2009, p. 80). This, it might be held, only serves to confirm the Epicurean charge that death is at most bad in some non-standard sense. (Of course, the critics need not deny that death's badness is different in *degree*: arguably, death is much worse than most other evils. If anything, this fact makes the critics' case stronger. For if the calendar has room for the badness of deciding to buy an apple, apparently death's much more serious evil shouldn't slip through either.)

I shall consider three different versions of this "uniformity objection," as we might call it. First, it may claimed that atemporalism gives us a disunified account of overall badness: death's badness will have to be explained in some special, unusual way.

Not so. A uniform account that covers both death and other evils has been with us since section 2. Here it is:

(DA)   The overall value of event E, for person S, at possible world w = the intrinsic value of w for S, minus the intrinsic value for S of the closest possible world to w, w*, where E does not occur.

Nothing prevents atemporalists from accepting (DA). It would, no doubt, be problematic to claim that what makes death bad is something else than what makes other things bad (e.g., that while death is bad for me by frustrating my desires, all other evils are bad for me by virtue of depriving me of pleasure). But atemporalism implies no such thing. What makes my death bad for me, the atemporalist should say, is exactly the same as what makes other events bad for me: namely, that the closest world where the event in question occurs is intrinsically worse for me than the closest world where it doesn't occur.

In drawing attention to this uniformity, I am not saying that other evils are atemporally bad as well. The point is rather that these evils are covered by exactly the same account of overall badness—(DA)—as death is.

On a second version of the uniformity objection, atemporalism implies that a single relation—namely, *x is bad for y*—obtains atemporally in the case of death but timefully in other cases. This implication seems as unsavory as the claim that, whereas I eat oranges and pears at certain times, I eat apples without doing this at any time.

However, atemporalism does not have the alleged implication. As before, we must distinguish between two interpretations of the question "when is S's death bad for S?":

(Q1)   When is the intrinsic value for S of w (in its entirety) lower than the intrinsic value for S of w* (in its entirety)?

(Q2)   When is S intrinsically worse off in w than S is at that time, or those times, in w*?

Assuming the deprivation approach, (Q1) is about the relation, *x is overall bad for y*. This relation obtains atemporally—or maybe eternally (see section 3)—not only in the case of death, but in all cases: the entire closest possible world where you didn't throw the apple at me is atemporally—or eternally—intrinsically better for me than the entire actual world. (Q2) concerns another relation: *x makes y intrinsically worse off now* (or, if you like, *y has a lower well-being level now than y would have had now if x had not occurred*). In the case of most evils, this relation does hold at certain times. For instance, in the case where I decided to buy an apple, the relation obtained (between my decision and me) at the time I was eating the apple. Given atemporalism, however, the relation does not obtain at all in the case of death: not at a time, and not atemporally (whatever that would mean). Thus, there does not seem to be any single badness relation that, according to atemporalism, obtains atemporally in the case of death and timefully in the case of other evils.

However, perhaps this response suggests a third version of the uniformity objection. Remember premise (1) of the Epicurean Argument: anything that is bad for a person is bad for her at a time. The atemporalist, it seems, must say that other evils satisfy (1)—provided that "is bad for her at a time" is understood on the lines of (Q2), that is, as "makes her intrinsically worse off at a time"—but that death is an exception. This special treatment, it may be held, is problematic.

In the end, I do not think it is. Consider four points the atemporalist could make in response.

First, one way to defuse the worry would be to give other examples, not involving death, of atemporally bad things. Some candidates in the literature are: never getting what one deserves; never seeing one's loved ones again; never having fallen in love.[25] However, this is not promising. For instance, suppose you never get what you deserve, and that this is bad for you. It may be that your never getting what you deserve does not obtain at a particular time. As noted in section 2, though, the relevant issue is not when the bad thing takes place, but when it is bad. Suppose that, if it weren't true that you never get what you deserve—that is, if there were a time at which you do get what you deserve—then you would have been intrinsically better off at 2 p.m. today than you actually are. Then even if the bad thing itself does not obtain at a particular time, it is bad for you at 2 p.m. today.[26]

Bradley considers another candidate of an atemporal evil (2009, pp. 76–77, p. 91). As a result of a head injury, you spend the remaining twenty years of your life with no good or bad experiences. If it hadn't been for the head injury, those twenty years would have contained either (a) ten years of extreme happiness followed by ten years of moderate unhappiness or (b) ten years of moderate unhappiness followed by ten years of extreme happiness. Assume, further, that there is no fact of the matter as to which of these two futures would have obtained had the injury not occurred. In this case, the head injury seems bad for you; yet there is apparently no time at which you would have been better off were it not for the head injury.

As Bradley says, this is also unpersuasive. His own response is that the head injury is bad for you at many *durations*—for example, the period of twenty years following the injury—though not at any *moment*. While I have no quarrel with the appeal to durations, Bradley's concession about moments seems uncalled for. It seems to me that there are many moments at which the head injury is bad for you; it's just that there is no fact of the matter as to *which* moments these are. For example, even if there is no fact of the matter whether the injury is bad for you at noon April 4, 2012, or instead at noon April 4, 2022, this does not prevent it from being determinately true that the injury is bad for you at one of these two moments.[27]

The first atemporalist response does not seem very tempting, then. But the atemporalist has more to offer. A second response notes that even the subsequentist—arguably the atemporalist's chief rival—should grant that some bad deaths might well be exceptions to (1). Maybe time—time itself, the whole of time—has an end. At any rate, a number of philosophers regard this as metaphysically possible. Suppose it is, and consider a possible world in which a certain creature dies at the last point in time. Suppose this individual would have been overall better off if she had instead continued to live (thus time itself would, in that counterfactual scenario, continue a bit longer). Here, friends of the deprivation approach should say that her death is bad for her. But, because there is no time after her death, there is no time after her death at which she is worse off than she would have been if her death hadn't occurred. Even subsequentists (i.e., subsequentists about ordinary deaths, like yours and mine), it seems, must be atemporalists about this case. In a way, then, subsequentists might have to accept a *less* uniform view than atemporalists. Of course, you might claim that the case is metaphysically impossible; but it does seem to be a cost to have to say this. And at any rate, so long as it is not an absurd idea that time could have an end, the case seems to show that it is not an absurd idea that something can be overall bad for a person without making her worse off at a time.

Third, since death makes the person's life shorter, it is unavoidable that there is *some* difference to do with time between death and most other evils. For example, the subsequentist seems to be committed to the following striking asymmetry between death and other evils. Most evils put the victim in a "deprived state": that is, there are times at which the person exists and would have been intrinsically better off if the bad thing hadn't occurred. For instance, in the apple incidents of section 1, I was in a deprived state when I ate the apple and when I was comatose. My death, by contrast, does not seem to put me in a deprived state. Perhaps this observation might inspire some Epicureans to advance the following argument:

(4) Anything that is bad for a person puts her in a deprived state.
(5) Death does not put the person who dies in a deprived state.
(6) Hence, death is not bad for the person who dies.

What should the subsequentist—that is, the subsequentist about (Q2)—say in response? She should grant that (5) is correct. And she should say that while (4) does hold for most evils, death is an exception. This asymmetry, she should insist, is not embarrassing: since death puts a stop to the person's existence, there simply must be some difference to do with time between death and most other evils. The crucial thing, the subsequentist should add, is that this difference does not prevent her from saying that death's badness is explained by exactly the same account— (DA)—as other evils. This reply is plausible. But it seems arbitrary not to allow the atemporalist the same kind of defense against premise (1) of the Epicurean Argument.

Fourth, a further reason for the atemporalist to be unabashed is that the Epicurean should also concede a noteworthy asymmetry. Consider this anti-Epicurean argument:

(7) Anything that satisfies (DA)'s condition of overall badness for a person is overall bad for her.
(8) In some cases, death satisfies (DA)'s condition of overall badness for the person who dies.
(9) Hence, in some cases, death is overall bad for the person who dies.

It is hardly reasonable to reject (8). Nor is it reasonable to deny that (7) holds for most deprivers. In order to resist the conclusion, then, the Epicurean should say that death is an exception to (7). The atemporalist's asymmetry between death and other evils seems no worse than the Epicurean's asymmetry between death and other deprivers.[28]

NOTES

1. For a recent defense of the argument, see Hershenov, 2007.
2. Atemporalism is endorsed in Broome, 2004, p. 237; Draper, 2004, p. 104; eternalism, in Feldman, 1991 and 1992, p. 154; priorism, in Feinberg, 1984; Li, 1999; Luper, 2007 and 2009b, ch. 6; and Pitcher, 1984; concurrentism, in Lamont, 1998; subsequentism, in Bradley, 2004, 2009, and 2010; Feit, 2002; and Grey, 1999. (However, Feldman seems to answer a different "when" question than the others: see sect. 3 below.) Except for "atemporalism," the labels are from Luper, 2009a. Naturally, there is room for other anti-Epicurean views than the five on the list, especially because of the "and only then" clauses. In the literature, it is admittedly sometimes unclear whether an "and only then" claim is intended or not. But I think it will facilitate the exposition if we take each view to be incompatible with each of the other four on the list. (For instance, without the "and only then" clauses, priorism, concurrentism, and subsequentism would be entailed by eternalism, and compatible with each other.)
3. This event-talk is convenient, but not crucial to our discussion. For instance, we could instead concentrate on the fact that the person dies at a certain time.
4. See especially Bradley, 2009, p. 50, and also Broome, 1993; Feit, 2002, p. 368; Feldman, 1991 and 1992, p. 138.
5. E.g., Nagel, 1970.

6. The label is from Feldman, 1992, p. 89.

7. In chapter 3 of my doctoral dissertation, I defended the following version of this thesis: human people cease to exist when they die. According to Chris Belshaw, I also *denied* that *non*human beings cease to exist when they die (Belshaw, 2009, p. 229n). However, what I said was only that the view I argued for only concerns human people, and entails nothing about, e.g., angels and computers (Johansson, 2005, pp. 45–46). Also, I think Belshaw misinterprets Fred Feldman in a similar way in the same footnote.

8. See e.g. Lamont, 1998; Luper, 2007.

9. Feit, 2002, pp. 372–373; Li, 1999, p. 350; Luper, 2007, p. 240, and 2009b, pp. 127–128. On Harry Silverstein's interpretation, as I understand it, Feldman is concerned with either this question about truth or something like (Q2) below (2000, p. 121). Silverstein thus neglects (Q1).

10. In fact, Feldman seems nowadays to lean toward atemporalism about (Q1): see Bradley, 2009, pp. 84–85n.

11. A similar distinction is drawn in Luper, 2009b, p. 124, as well as in Johansson, forthcoming (which also contains early versions of some of my arguments in the present paper).

12. It is sometimes suggested (e.g., in Lamont, 1998, p. 202) that the following question has the virtue I just ascribed to (Q2): When do the *truthmakers exist* for the proposition that S's death is overall bad for S? However, I don't see any asymmetry between death and other evils here. Truthmakers of a proposition make the proposition true, just by existing. For each overall evil—whether a death or something else—the main candidates seem to be (provided that the truths in questions have any truthmakers at all): (a) certain entire worlds; (b) a set of certain entire worlds; (c) a fusion of certain entire worlds; and (d) the state of affairs of a certain entire world being intrinsically worse for the person than a certain other entire world. And each such entity seems to exist eternally or atemporally (or not at all).

13. Cf. Luper, 2009b, p. 136.

14. Thanks to Chris Heathwood for helpful discussion of this third problem.

15. To be exact: it follows from the Moorean view together with the reasonable claim that my well-being level at a time only depends on that time's intrinsic value for me.

16. For a powerful attack on this and related views, see Bradley, 2009, pp. 18–30.

17. See e.g., Velleman, 1991 (though he speaks of lives rather than worlds).

18. Bradley, 2004, 2009, ch. 3, and 2010. The second-best version might be Neil Feit's. Feit himself concedes that Bradley's version seems, at least in many respects, preferable (Feit, 2002, p. 382n).

19. E.g., Bradley, 2004.

20. Bradley, 2009, pp. 82–83.

21. For a related argument against a different view, see Bykvist, 2007, pp. 344–345. My rejoinders to the counterarguments are also similar to his.

22. Bradley, 2009, p. 104n also suggests that it might in fact be acceptable to ascribe a well-being level of zero to a shoe; and in personal communication, he has reported that he has become increasingly sympathetic to that view. Personally, I regard it as at least a cost—a cost avoided by atemporalism, for instance.

23. Silverstein, 2010, p. 284.

24. E.g., Bradley, 2004; 2009, pp. 74–78; Feit, 2002, p. 361.

25. These suggestions are mentioned (but not endorsed) in Bradley, 2009, pp. 77–78 and Hershenov, 2007, p. 173.

26. It might be replied that there is no fact of the matter as to when you would have been better off. If so, the responses to the next suggestion—about the head injury—can be applied here as well.

27. Well, it does given so-called many-valued logic. But many-valued logic is dubious. My position works given more reasonable—and more popular—views of indeterminacy, for instance, supervaluationism.

28. Many thanks to Ben Bradley, Chris Heathwood, and Jason Raibley for very helpful comments on an earlier draft. I am also very grateful to audiences at the Philosophy Society Seminar at the University of Birmingham 2009; the Moral Philosophy Seminar at the University of Oxford 2009; and the Stockholm June Workshop in Philosophy at Stockholm University 2009.

References

Belshaw, Christopher. 2009. *Annihilation*. Stocksfield: Acumen Press.

Bradley, Ben. 2004. "When Is Death Bad for the One Who Dies?" *Noûs* 38: 1–28.

Bradley, Ben. 2009. *Well-Being and Death*. Oxford: Oxford University Press.

Bradley, Ben. 2010. "Eternalism and Death's Badness." In *Time and Identity*, M. O'Rourke, J. Campbell and H. Silverstein, eds., pp. 271–281. Cambridge, MA: MIT Press.

Broome, John. 1993. "Goodness Is Reducible to Betterness: The Evil of Death Is the Value of Life." In *The Good and the Economical: Ethical Choices in Economics and Management*, P. Koslowski and Y. Shionoya, eds., pp. 70–84. Berlin: Springer-Verlag.

Broome, John. 2004. *Weighing Lives*. Oxford: Oxford University Press.

Bykvist, Krister. 2007. "The Benefits of Coming into Existence." *Philosophical Studies* 135: 335–362.

Draper, Kai. 2004. "Epicurean Equanimity towards Death." *Philosophy and Phenomenological Research* 69: 92–114.

Epicurus. 1940. "Letter to Menoeceus." In *The Stoic and Epicurean Philosophers*, W. J. Oates, ed., trans. C. Bailey, pp. 30–34. New York: The Modern Library.

Feinberg, Joel. 1984. "Harm to Others." Relevant passage reprinted in *The Metaphysics of Death*, J. M. Fischer, ed., pp. 171–190. Palo Alto, CA: Stanford University Press.

Feit, Neil. 2002. "The Time of Death's Misfortune." *Noûs* 36: 359–383.

Feldman, Fred. 1991. "Some Puzzles about the Evil of Death." Reprinted in *The Metaphysics of Death*, J. M. Fischer, ed., pp. 307–326. Palo Alto, CA: Stanford University Press.

Feldman, Fred. 1992. *Confrontations with the Reaper*. New York & Oxford: Oxford University Press.

Grey, William. 1999. "Epicurus and the Harm of Death." *Australasian Journal of Philosophy* 77: 358–364.

Hershenov, David. 2007. "A More Palatable Epicureanism." *American Philosophical Quarterly* 44: 170–180.

Johansson, Jens. 2005. "Mortal Beings: On the Metaphysics and Value of Death." Doctoral dissertation. Stockholm University.

Johansson, Jens. Forthcoming. "The Time of Death's Badness." *Journal of Medicine and Philosophy*.

Lamont, Julian. 1998. "A Solution to the Puzzle of When Death Harms Its Victims."
    Australasian Journal of Philosophy 76: 198–212.

Li, Jack. 1999. "Commentary on Lamont's When Death Harms Its Victims."
    Australasian Journal of Philosophy 77: 349–357.

Luper, Steven. 2007. "Mortal Harm." *Philosophical Quarterly* 57: 239–251.

Luper, Steven. 2009a. "Death." *The Stanford Encyclopedia of Philosophy* (Summer
    2009 edition), Edward N. Zalta, ed. URL = <http://plato.stanford.edu/archives/
    sum2009/entries/death>.

Luper, Steven. 2009b. *The Philosophy of Death*. Cambridge: Cambridge University
    Press.

Nagel, Thomas. 1970. "Death." Reprinted in *The Metaphysics of Death*, J. M. Fischer,
    ed., pp. 61–69. Palo Alto, CA: Stanford University Press.

Pitcher, George. 1984. "The Misfortunes of the Dead." Reprinted in *The Metaphysics
    of Death*, J. M. Fischer, ed., pp. 159–168. Palo Alto, CA: Stanford University Press.

Silverstein, Harry. 2000. "The Evil of Death Revisited." *Midwest Studies in
    Philosophy* 24: 116–134.

Silverstein, Harry. 2010. "The Time of the Evil of Death." In *Time and Identity*, M.
    O'Rourke, J. Campbell, and H. Silverstein, eds., pp. 283–295. Cambridge, MA: MIT
    Press.

Velleman, David. 1991. "Well-Being and Time." Reprinted in *The Metaphysics of
    Death*, J. M. Fischer, ed., pp. 329–357. Palo Alto, CA: Stanford University Press.

CHAPTER 12

DEATH, VALUE, AND DESIRE

CHRISTOPHER BELSHAW

Most of us think that death is often bad. We think, too, that it is often bad for the one who dies. How does this badness in death relate to the value of life? A widespread thought is that death is bad only when the life it takes away would have been good. I'll assume this is about right, and say not much more about it here. And how does this badness relate to desire and the frustration of desire? Many people think there is some sort of connection, but doubt that it's straightforward. I agree. Still, it is in some respects more straightforward than is often supposed. I'll argue here, first, that having categorical desires is a necessary condition of death's being bad for those who die, and second, that the degree to which death is bad bears a close relation to the number and strength of those desires.

Some of this may well appear somewhat controversial. So much the worse, it might be thought. For how can new or exciting or controversial views on something as familiar as death have any hope of being right? I am sympathetic to such skepticism. And toward the end of the chapter much of the controversy will fall away.

1. SOME VIEWS ABOUT DESIRE

We want many different, and different sorts of, things. I want new shoes, and I want again to visit Venice. Bernard Williams, famously, contrasts conditional and categorical desires: though, of course, you need to be alive to want anything at all, the former are those that you want satisfied on the condition, or assuming, that you'll continue to be alive; while the latter stand independent of this, and so, often at least, give you a reason to go on living (Williams, 1973, p. 85). So, assuming I'll be alive next week, with places to go, then new shoes will be useful, whereas going to Venice isn't just a way of passing the time, but something for which I'll make time. I won't undergo a painful life-saving operation in order to get shoes, but will to see Venice. Though in the end related, the salient difference, of course, lies not in the objects themselves, but in our attitudes toward them. Given that he's alive Billy wants a bike to get to work. Jilly wants to cycle coast to coast in Africa. She wants a bike, and to stay alive, in order to do this.

There is, however, need in several respects for clarification here. Williams appears to suggest that his distinction is both sharp and exhaustive, with categorical desires just those that are unconditional. But that cannot be right. Another distinction is the one between self-regarding and other-regarding desires. Let's say that I want, as you want, that you should finish your book. This isn't something I want to happen only on the condition I'm alive, but nor does it give me, though it does give you, a reason to go on living. But there are mixed cases here. Suppose your finishing your book requires my help. Then I do now have reason to live on.

Yet, even when considering only the things I want for myself, the picture is more complex. I can want things to be true in the past. I want to have made a reasonable impression with my valedictory address last week. Suppose I wanted this beforehand, and in such a way that it was then properly thought of as a categorical desire. Looking back, I don't know what impression I actually made, but I still want it to have been good. This doesn't give me reason to go on living now. Nor should we overlook some future-directed and self-regarding desires, the satisfaction of which doesn't require my living on. I might want for myself posthumous fame or the glory of death in some current battle. And it may be that I think I've already done enough to achieve this fame or glory. So more life won't help. There are issues, too, about realism. I want to fly, unaided, to Jupiter. Or I want to be the first philosopher to land on Mars. The former desire is for something physically impossible, the latter for something extremely unlikely. Do I have reason to live on? If I were reasonable, I wouldn't have such desires at all. But given that I do, then consistency gives me reason to avoid death. A final complication: my desire to visit Venice isn't altogether unconditional. I don't want to go to that city under any condition, no matter what the price. Some operations would be just too painful to bear.[1] This suggests, perhaps, that the difference between the two sorts of desires is one of degree, rather than kind. Although much here deserves to be further explored, I'll proceed as if the notion of a categorical desire can be adequately grasped.

Talk of reasons needs considerably more unpacking. How strong are they? What Williams says at the outset of his discussion is perhaps right:

> To want something...is to that extent to have reason for resisting what excludes that thing: and death certainly does that, for a very large range of things that one wants. If that is right, then for any of those things, wanting something itself gives one a reason for avoiding death. Even though if I do not succeed, I will not know that, nor what I am missing, from the perspective of the wanting agent it is rational to aim for states of affairs in which his want is satisfied, and hence to

regard death as something to be avoided; that is, to regard it as an evil. (Williams, 1973, p. 85)

But it's right, if it is, because of the qualifications—thus, I have reason *to some extent*, and *from my perspective*, death will appear an evil. Other, later, things may be less right. Someone who has categorical desires "will have a reason, and a perfectly coherent reason, to regard death as a misfortune" and "we, looking at things from his point of view, would have reason to regard his actual death as a misfortune" (Williams, 1973, p. 88). Moreover, "granted categorical desires, death has a disutility for the agent" (Williams, 1973, p. 88). All of this perhaps implies that death is bad for such a person. But the implication is questionable. First, death might be good for me. Suppose my life is one of endless agony, with no chance of relief. It may be better for me, in my interests, to die, even though I want to live on. In this sort of case I will, as Williams suggests, regard my death as an evil. But I'll be wrong. Second, my desires themselves may be in conflict. Though I want to visit Venice, and so want to live, I want also no longer to be a burden to my relatives, and for my nephew to inherit before he is to marry. So, though I have some reason to live on, I have other reasons, and perhaps these will be, and will appear to me to be, stronger reasons, to die. Third, there are cases—and I've given examples concerning interplanetary travel—where one's desires are quite irrational. I shun death, but even if I have in some sense a reason, it isn't clear I have a coherent reason for doing so. Fourth, and closely related, even if my desires are wholly reasonable, and for things that might reasonably seem to be within my grasp—say I am an epidemiologist looking to understand, and then limit, the spread of some disease—it may be they just won't be satisfied. Even if death is bad, it isn't because it stands in my way.

So, even if those with categorical desires think death will be bad for them, believe it has a disutility, they may be wrong. Even if they have some reason to avoid death, it may not be overriding or fully coherent. Williams's position isn't altogether clear. But if he thinks that having categorical desires is sufficient for death's being bad then, again, he is surely mistaken. Nevertheless, the relation between such desires and death's badness remains close. For, or so I'll claim, the existence of such desires is a necessary condition for death's being bad. Absent such desires and, for the one who dies, death isn't bad at all. That is something of a bald claim, and there will be need for a couple of qualifications later on. But the bald claim can usefully stand for now.

2. FURTHER VIEWS

I've contrasted two views. In one, having categorical desires is sufficient for death's being bad. Williams may hold this, but it isn't certain. In another, having categorical desires is necessary for death's being bad. I hold this. In two further views such desires play a less critical role.

Nagel, as Williams observes, thinks death's badness can stand independently of desire (Williams, 1973, p. 88). Consider this puzzling passage:

> The situation is roughly this: There are elements that, if added to one's experience, make life better; there are other elements that, if added to one's experience, make life worse. But what remains when these are set aside is not merely *neutral*: it is emphatically positive. Therefore life is worth living even when the bad elements of experience are plentiful and the good ones too meagre to outweigh the bad ones on their own. The additional positive weight is supplied by experience itself, rather than any of its contents. (Nagel, 1979, p. 2)

The claim here isn't that death is always bad. There's no suggestion that it's bad for the irreversibly comatose. But it is bad for those having good experiences, and bad also for at least some of those whose experiences are overall bad. Having experiences is good, even when the experiences themselves aren't good. And whether or not these experiences are desired has, apparently, nothing to do with it.

Jeff McMahan also thinks that death's badness is more wide-ranging than Williams seems to allow:

> The idea that the badness of death can be fully explained by reference to the frustration of categorical desires is, I think, decisively undermined by two considerations.... One is that this idea cannot recognise that death can be bad for fetuses, infants and animals. The other is that the loss of future goods that are undesired at the time of death can contribute to the badness of death.[2] (McMahan, 2002, p. 182)

There are three points here, only the central one of which needs to be pursued at length. First, "fully explained" seems to overstate the case—Williams appears to claim, as I read him, that having categorical desires is sufficient for death's being bad. Suppose he also wants to claim, as do I, that such desires are also necessary. It's far from clear that he does think this. Even so, there might be a lot more to say about death's badness, say, about the Epicurean challenge, or again about the degree to which it is bad, before any full explanation is claimed. Second, McMahan's final point will take us into complex territory. I can put aside the detail for now. But it links with the middle point.

McMahan refers to infants. I can only suppose that he means by this what I mean by "baby," and thus a very young child. I'll refer simply to babies from here on. These, along with fetuses and most animals, lack categorical desires. Someone who thinks only that categorical desires are sufficient for death's badness is not thereby committed either way on animal, fetus, and baby deaths. But someone who thinks such desires are necessary is so committed. So if I'm persuaded that fetus, animal, or baby deaths are bad, then I'll have to give up on my view.

I'll say more about Nagel's and McMahan's positions below.

3. IMPLICATIONS

I claim that having future-directed categorical desires is a necessary condition of my death's being bad for me. But I should clarify one point. If at a certain time I lack categorical desires, then death isn't bad for me, at that time. I don't, of course, hold that lacking such desires at some time means that death isn't bad for me at any time. I'll call this the *Desire View*. It contrasts with claims that death can be bad even when such desires are absent. What then is present? Well, life, for a start. Perhaps also health, or experience, or good or pleasurable experience, or a desire, albeit conditional, for such experience. Any view of this kind I'll call a *Life View*. And the salient difference between these views, in broad terms, is roughly thus: on the Life View death is bad when it prevents there being more life or, in some sense or other, more good or worthwhile life, or some such. On the Desire View this isn't sufficient for badness. That life has to be something you want to live.

I say that the Desire View is true, while the Life View is false. This will need to be qualified—it is in several respects too blunt as it stands. But it has some fairly evident implications for when death isn't bad that I will stick by—the qualifications won't impinge on those.

If the Desire View is true, then death isn't bad for:

a) Plants. They have no mental life at all, and so have neither categorical no conditional desires. I take it that when we say that a plant wants some fertilizer we are speaking only metaphorically.

b) Animals. Even if they have desires, they are not of the right kind. Wanting a mate right now isn't the same as, or the same sort of thing as, wanting to settle down and raise a family. Of course, my claim that animals lack categorical desires will be challenged. So perhaps I should say lower animals—cows, rabbits, frogs, worms—though sentient, lack these desires. Or, insofar as animals lack these desires, then their deaths are not bad.

c) The PVS patient. The patient in a persistent vegetative state had such desires. But her mental life is over. She has no desires now and will have none in the future.[3]

d) The late-stage Alzheimer's patient. He had such desires in the past. And he has some desires now. But he doesn't have, and will never have again, categorical desires in the sense outlined. We might say his condition is similar to that of an animal whereas the PVS patient, as indeed "vegetative" suggests, can be likened to a plant.

e) The fetus. Though, assuming normal development, it will come to have categorical desires, it has no such desires at either the present or at previous times.

f) The baby. Its condition is, in the relevant respects, the same as that of the fetus.

My claim here, then, is that it isn't bad for things in any of these categories when that thing dies. I am not saying, of course, that it isn't bad at all when such things die—it can be bad for owners, viewers, bystanders, friends, relatives, and dependents. Maybe it can be bad, in some sense, for the universe. Nor am I saying that it isn't wrong to kill any such things. Abortion may be wrong, and killing a fetus may wrong it, even while its death isn't bad for it.[4] Nor, finally, am I denying that the manner of death might be bad. A painful death will usually be bad for the thing that dies.

My claim can be put in a different way. Using the term "person" as philosophers often use it, where it links to rationality, self-consciousness, and an awareness of time's passage, I might say that death isn't bad for nonpersons. Things in the above categories are not persons, even if in several cases they were or will be persons. This isn't to say, of course, that death is bad, ever, or always, for persons. But I'll simply assume what I think is a common sense view here. Death is sometimes, or in some circumstances, but by no means always, in all circumstances, bad for persons.

4. AN OBJECTION

The Desire View will be found objectionable. Consider the PVS and baby cases. There are some similarities. In both there are no categorical desires now, and in both there are such desires at a different time. But the location of these times will seem to many to be a relevant difference. Perhaps death isn't bad when all such desires are in the past. But when, as with the baby, there's a period still to come that will feature such desires, death is bad.

Of course I agree that if this baby—call him Baby—reaches, say, the age of seventeen, and has then desires for more life or for activities that require more life, then death at that time will be bad. But is it bad now? I say no. For I say that death is bad, for he who dies, only when it cuts off a life that he wants to live. Baby isn't living such a life. So death now isn't bad for Baby.

There might be offered some support for this view. Relatively few think it bad when a new life fails to start. So relatively few think that failing to conceive is bad, or that we should, other things equal, have as many children as possible, or that it would, other things equal, be better if deserts, jungles, and seas were all teeming with life. But many think it bad, other things equal, when a life already under way prematurely ends. I see no important difference here. Focus just on human life. If a fetus dies, then a particular individual, already alive, is prevented from being born, developing in many ways, and living out its life. If some conception that might have occurred doesn't occur, then a particular individual is prevented from coming into existence, being born, and living out its life. And this is so even if we don't know who that individual would be, what he or she would be like, whether it would be a he or a she. Suppose you agree, it isn't bad when conception fails to occur. Then you should agree that it's similarly not bad when, in effect, conception is reversed, and a fetus dies.[5]

It will be objected that there are salient differences. In the nonconception case, no life is ended, no one is harmed, there is no victim to consider. But is there an important contrast with the fetus case? Whether the fetus is harmed by death, whether it is in the ordinary sense a victim, is the point at issue. And certainly it isn't pained or distressed, its desires are not frustrated, its life plans not overturned. My suggestion, then, is that just as it isn't bad not to start a new life, so it isn't bad, in cases like these, to end a life.[6]

Again, the point can be put in terms of personhood. Baby will become a person. But as he isn't a person now, so death isn't bad for him now.

5. Disruptions

The objection considered above is that having categorical desires isn't necessary for death's badness. For Fetus and Baby lacks such desires. Here's another form of that objection: when I'm fast asleep, or under anesthetic, or flat on my back in a boxing ring, it seems I have no desires. But it would be bad for me to die in these circumstances. So much, then, for the Desire View.

My response is different. Though I deny that death is bad for either Fetus or Baby, I agree it's bad here. And this is because of a structural difference that needs to be noted. In sleep, coma, and similar cases, although there are no evident desires right now, there were previously and, without death and other serious mishaps, there will be again. Moreover, in most such cases seemingly the very same desires are recovered—I wake up and continue to want, as I wanted yesterday, to buy a Harley and drive it to Spain. We might say that while our desires are for some period not evident, they are present, latent, or tacit throughout that period. Death, in sleep, cuts off the life I want to live.

The examples merely sketched here involve relatively brief and clear-cut interruptions to an unfolding life. Elsewhere things are less straightforward:

> *The Teenager.* Beth, a teenager, is moping about the house. Some boyfriend has dumped her. She hates school. Her parents are so misunderstanding. She wants to die. Though she had plenty of categorical desires previously and will, if she lives, have plenty again, Beth has right now no categorical desires. But she has desires nevertheless. She wants, while she's alive, to be left alone, to listen to her music, to eat only what she wants to eat.

Would it be bad for Beth to die now? We mostly want to say yes. Suppose we are right to say this. She used to have desires to live, and to live beyond her teenage years. That she's had such desires is a part of the reason for thinking her mood a temporary aberration. It may be less tempting here to say that she has these desires, though latent, right now. Nevertheless, it's because this mood, though hardly fleeting, is still temporary, because similar desires will surface, and she'll pick up the threads of her life, because further (as we can assume) this life will be good, that Beth's death now would be bad for her.

Contrast her case with two of her friends. Zoe last had such desires when she was seven. Since then, she's been clinically depressed. And she'll never recover, never again sustain any categorical desires. There is no unfolding life. So death now isn't bad for Zoe. Lou is enjoying her life, and does have plans for the future. But she will soon suffer a brain hemorrhage that will leave her in PVS. Her life is unfolding but won't continue to do so. Death, as an alternative to PVS, isn't bad for her.

Consider now a minor variation of a related case, offered by Jeff McMahan, where again, I want to say, death isn't bad for the one who dies. His case runs thus:

> *The Cure.*   Imagine that you are twenty years old and are diagnosed with a
> disease that, if untreated, invariably causes death (though not pain or
> disability) within five years. There is a treatment that reliably cures the
> disease but also, as a side effect, causes total retrograde amnesia and
> radical personality change. Long-term studies of others who have had
> the treatment show that they almost always go on to have long and
> happy lives, though these lives are informed by desires and values that
> differ profoundly from those that the person had prior to treatment.
> You can therefore reasonably expect that, if you take the treatment,
> you will live for roughly sixty more years, though the life you will have
> will be utterly discontinuous with your life as it has been.[7]

We might say here that your psychology, your biographical life, has either zero or five years to run.[8] If you choose five, it will then be ended, without replacement. If zero it will be replaced now, with another, quite distinct, biographical life. McMahan thinks most of us would believe ourselves rational in refusing this cure. Your personality, memory, character could survive another five years. Choose the cure and they go out like a light, replaced by others altogether unknown to you. Why choose that? The patient here will undergo psychological rupture. He prefers five years of the life to which he is already committed, and which he can hope to pull into shape, rather than sixty years of something about which he knows little and cares less. Of course, just as some people will sacrifice themselves for their children, or their fellow soldiers, or a cause, so this patient might take the cure, in order to bring a long and worthwhile life into existence. But first, this isn't obviously a rational thing to do and second, though I'll need to come back to this point, it surely isn't in his interests, or best for him, to act in this way.

McMahan is suggesting only that most of us will prefer the shorter to the longer future. This doesn't itself imply that the longer future is of no value at all. But, of course, that is what I want to claim, of cases where psychological disruption is, as here, complete. So, my variation runs thus. You fall into a coma. Suppose well-meaning but, as I contend, poor-thinking doctors attempt to save your life, knowing that they can succeed only at the cost of such disruption. Would it have been bad for you if, while unconscious, you'd died? I say no. Death isn't bad when, if you live, a completely different biographical life unfolds. So even if it isn't worse, the longer life is no better than death. And some such view is at least suggested by McMahan's example. For, first, the difference between five years and sixty is already substantial, and second, since it's hard to believe the precise numbers here are critical, then perhaps even one year, or less, will also outweigh sixty, or more. So we are at least on the way to supposing the longer life is of just no value to the patient. As it isn't bad to die when there is no good life ahead, so also it isn't bad to die when that life, though good, isn't wanted.[9]

One thing should be noted here. Even if you agree that it isn't bad if someone with irreversible depression dies, you'll surely think it bad that someone should be in that condition. Similarly, even if it isn't bad that someone should die rather than live on but with a completely different personality, it is surely bad that they are in this no-win situation. These cases contrast, then, with some—but only with some—of those considered earlier. It isn't bad that a plant is only a plant, an animal merely an animal. It isn't bad for them that death isn't bad for them. But it is bad that someone should be depressed, or in PVS, or faced with no options preferable to death. It is bad for them that death isn't bad for them.

6. PERSONS, AND DEGREES

The concern so far has been with circumstances in which, as I've claimed, death isn't bad for the one who dies. Often it is bad. But how bad it is will vary from case to case, and from circumstance to circumstance. And there are, I've suggested, two broad brush factors to take into account. How bad it is to die depends, first, on the length and quality of the life ahead and, second, on how much you want to live that life. Again, the focus is on the second.

Death, I've said, isn't bad for the fetus or for the PVS patient. They have no categorical desires, and are not persons. But now personhood comes, and goes, by degrees. Baby grows into Child, and Woman begins to suffer from Alzheimer's. In these intermediate states they have, let us suppose, some categorical desires, but only a few, and with a very limited reach. Death, in general, is less bad for partial persons than it is for persons.

Lou, who is a person and has many such desires, is fated either to live in PVS or to die. It isn't bad to die, when the alternative is PVS, and the life of a nonperson.

Jan and Jen are just beginning their retirement. They anticipate a further twenty years of worthwhile life. But Jen will soon begin to develop Alzheimer's. Suppose they both die in ten years' time. Jen's death is less bad than is Jan's. For, in general, it's less bad to die when the alternative is the life of a partial person, someone unable to realize, or even fully comprehend, one's earlier categorical desires.

McMahan's man declines the treatment. He prefers a short life, as himself, to a long life as someone altogether different. And it isn't bad to die, I've said, when the alternative is to live on as a completely different person. Suppose the post-cure man is only partially different from the man pre-cure. He has the amnesia but not the personality change. It is, in general, less bad to die when the alternative is the life of a partially different person.[10]

This is all sketchy but, I believe, nevertheless correct. It is going to be worth-while, however, to look now at two cases, both less clear-cut than those outlined here, in some detail. So, first:

> *Child and Student.*   Is it worse to die at age three, or at twenty-three? Freddie
> isn't a baby any more. He talks, can already read a little,
> is wondering what school will be like. Ask him if he's
> a person and he won't understand. But he is. Derek is
> in graduate school, looking forward to finishing the
> dissertation, thinking about whether to put career or
> prospective family first, keeping an eye open for post-
> doc opportunities. Both have categorical desires, but the
> twenty-three-year-old has more of them, and they are
> longer ranging and more stable.[11]

As Baby becomes a child he becomes a person. Freddie is a person. Death is bad for him. And the partial person move won't explain why his death is less bad than Derek's. But appeal to the number and reach of his categorical desires will. Normally, we think the earlier death is worse. Assuming a life span of around eighty years, then it is worse to die at forty than at seventy. Similarly, it's worse to die at twenty than forty. But is the pattern here to be repeated, such that, again assuming they'd otherwise live to eighty, Freddie's is the worse death? I say no. Even though he has fewer years ahead of him, Derek has a greater sense of those years, stronger desires in relation to them, much more of a life plan. Freddie's loss, thought of just in terms of the number and quality of years ahead, far exceeds Derek's. Still, I say Derek's is the worse death. If this is right, then the Life View has to go.

Here's another case, again not altogether tidy:

> *Stars.*   In her fifties now, Sally has what many would think of as a good career
> acting in a long-running TV soap. And at Christmas she's usually in a
> pantomime. But through her twenties and just a little beyond she was
> at the top of her game—Hollywood, Oscars, Cannes. It's not a bad life
> now, but it's a long way short of what it was. Sometimes she thinks it
> wouldn't have been a bad thing, maybe would have even been better,
> if she'd exited the stage in some dramatic fashion at that earlier time,
> rather than continue with this muddling through.[12]

The idea here might be expressed in terms of narrative structure.[13] Sally's thought is that her life up to her early thirties had an elegance or shape or coherence that is now noticeably absent. Let's assume this is true, and she isn't simply deluded.

Let's assume, further, that on a year-by-year basis her life then was better than it is now. But it is still year-by-year a good life, and one worth living. And she has, and satisfies, some categorical desires. And, on any defensible account, she is the same person, and as much a person, as she was before. The hard question, then, is whether she might nevertheless be right that dying around age thirty would have been better for her than living on.

This case has some similarities with certain of the others. As with *The Cure* the question is whether choosing the shorter life might have been the better bet. But there two biographical lives, wholly or partially different, were involved— here there is just the one. That's true in *Child and Student* also. But in that case, there's no question the longer life is the better, such that it would clearly be good for Freddie to live on—the question is whether we can hold to that alongside believing that Freddie's death is less bad than Derek's. Here an emphasis on death, and death's bringing about the loss of further life, is perhaps misleading—Sally isn't so much thinking that the later death is worse as that the longer life is in one important sense less good for her than the shorter.

Though it's less clear than the others, I think she might be right. Certainly in many cases of broadly this form suspicions of romantic self-indulgence would be well-placed. But must they always be so? Sally is making no obvious mistake about the content or value of parts of her life, or about the way these parts relate to one another. It doesn't prevent her life from being worth living, doesn't even rule out a kind of happiness, but she does have around her always the regret that in comparison with what went before, her life now doesn't amount to much.

If this is right, then again, it counts against the Life View. It wouldn't straightforwardly have been very bad for Sally to have died in her early thirties just because, again straightforwardly, she would thereby have lost many worthwhile years. Though the longer life in some clear sense contains more value, it isn't so obviously of high value for her.

7. BRADLEY'S VIEW

I've argued that having categorical desires is necessary for death's being bad, and that the degree to which it is bad relates to the number, reach, strength, and realizability of these desires. From this, it follows, first, that it just isn't bad for many sorts of things—plants, people in PVS, fetuses—and second, that even when death is bad for some sort of thing—someone living a worthwhile life, and wanting, and able to have, more—there is no straightforward correspondence between death's timing and its value.

It seems that proponents of the Life View will oppose these claims. Ben Bradley is a committed advocate of this view. The view in general, and Bradley's particular stance in relation to it, needs now to be considered.

Start with the Deprivation Account of death's badness, the belief that death is bad, when it is, not in virtue of its intrinsic properties but because of what it takes from us, or prevents us from having.[14] One might think some version of this is surely right while doubting whether the particular refinements of the Life View should be maintained. Bradley puts the view thus:

> the overall value of an event for a person is equal to the difference between the value of her actual life and the value of the life she would have had if the event had not happened.[15] (Bradley, 2009, p. 113)

This is quite general. So if a life has an overall value, then the value of some event for that life is precisely what it adds to or subtracts from this overall value. Its value, then, is what it contributes to the whole. And so if a long life has a higher overall value than a short life then death is bad, and bad just to the extent that it costs in terms of value.

There are two assumptions and one minor mistake that should be noted here. The assumptions are, first, that we can assign values to lives and events, and second, that these values can in some sense be relativized—we are to consider the value of an event *for a person* and this event's impact on the value of life *for that person*. The minor mistake is the needless restriction here to persons. Bradley makes clear he thinks that animal lives also have value. And even if we were thinking only of human lives, the slipperiness of the notion of a person suggests that if we can easily avoid it, then perhaps we should. Perhaps, then, it is better to think of the value of lives and events for individuals. One advantage will emerge shortly.

This is, as Bradley observes, a simple view.[16] It implies the following. If all the periods in a thing's life are of positive value, then death is worse, the earlier it comes. If all the periods in a thing's life are of positive or neutral value, then, so long as there are some good periods ahead, death is bad. And, even supposing some periods of negative value, if the overall value of the final period of life is positive, then a death that deprives a thing of that period is bad for that thing.

This represents the bare bones of a Life View. But clearly there is already enough here to generate conflict with the Desire View. For I want to deny that the value of death is just the value of the life thereby lost and to deny, too, that the earlier the death, the worse it is.[17] Further conflict will depend just how this Life View is fleshed out. For the view is in itself compatible with a variety of positions on what gives a life, or a part of a life, some value, and compatible too with holding that some value contributor is either necessary for value or, more weakly, that while not necessary, it still adds to value. Now Bradley's is in fact a hedonist position—he holds that having good experiences is what makes life good, and so it can be good for animals as well as for human beings, but not for plants (Bradley, 2009, pp. 9–45). He appears to hold also that though self-conscious experience is especially valuable, contributing to the overall value of a life, it isn't necessary for value. Thus it is normally bad if healthy animals die, but normally worse if healthy human beings die. And various further positions on value are compatible with the Life View. One could hold that integration between moments adds to value, so that a fragmented life is of less value than a better integrated, more cohesive standard life. One could hold that desire satisfaction is relevant to value—other things equal the more desires are satisfied, the better it is. And now a potential confusion—one could also hold that having categorical desires is necessary for life to have value. But confusion can be dispelled. Suppose a life has to contain categorical desires at some point, in order for it to have value. Only if there are such desires to come, will it be bad if Baby dies. But on the Life View Baby's death can be bad, and bad for Baby, even if these desires are a long way off. Not so on the Desire View.

What is to be said for and against these rival views? Consider first Bradley's take on various of the cases discussed above. And start with *The Cure*. He thinks the patient should accept:

> The decision to refuse treatment is shortsighted and irrational. It seems in many ways similar to the decision of a child to ignore the consequences of his behaviour on his adult self, since he does not currently care about the things his adult self will care about. (Bradley, 2009, p. 117)

Many will find this puzzling. Why should this man sacrifice a medium-term future to which he is fully committed, for a longer and in some ways overall better future in which he has no interest? Issues about identity and personhood come up again here. Suppose that treatment affects identity—take the medicine and you cease to exist, being then replaced by someone else. Here Bradley thinks that refusal is appropriate (2009, p. 118). You can reasonably want to put your future before someone else's. But there are questions about what identity consists in. Perhaps we should adopt some sort of psychological account. Then very plausibly, given the details—"total retrograde amnesia and radical personality change"—you don't survive the operation. Perhaps, as many now believe, you are an animal. Then, as the same animal or biological life continues—only the mind is altered—you do survive. Should you take the cure? Bradley might appear to think that we really need to do some work in the metaphysics of identity before deciding on what to do. But this can't be right. For he thinks death can be bad for Baby, even before Baby is a person. And he thinks death can be bad for someone like Clive Wearing, where fragmentation subverts personhood as ordinarily understood (Bradley, 2009, p. 119).[18] Bradley seems, then, to be drawn toward an animalist account of identity and so thinks that one and the same individual exists both before and after the cure. But it remains unclear why that should settle anything. If I am not required to sacrifice my future for someone else's, why am I required to sacrifice the future I do want for one I don't?

An objection should be considered. Suppose our man decides to accept the treatment. It is highly plausible to suppose that the later person, enjoying his long life, will be pleased that the earlier person so decided. So he did have reason to accept. This objection is weak. I might be pleased that someone sacrificed their life on my behalf, but this doesn't show they had reason to make that sacrifice.[19] But suppose we agree that the very same individual survives the operation. Still, this pleasure settles nothing. For imagine the patient had a further option offering an even longer life but where the post-op psychology seemed even more alien to him. As our man's pleasure doesn't show the patient was right to refuse this second option, it doesn't show he was right to accept the first.

As we disagree about *The Cure*, so also will we disagree about *Child and Student*. Bradley doesn't, however, discuss this case explicitly, but focuses instead on *Baby and Student* (2009, p. 115). For, because he thinks Baby's death is bad for Baby, he can use the comparison here to make his point that the earlier death is worse. In denying this I needed an example in which I nevertheless allow that both deaths are bad.

Baby is just three weeks old. Unlike Child, he has no categorical desires. As, on Bradley's view, it is bad for an animal to die, so it is bad for Baby. But his death is considerably worse because of the rich future ahead, which threatens now to be lost. Bradley supposes that Baby and Student, assuming they don't die, live nearly identical lives. We can either think there are two people to consider, Freddie and Derek, of different ages, each of which might die now, or we can think about just the one unfolding life, that of Frederick, and consider different times at which it might be ended. Either way it seems that Baby loses just what Student loses—say sixty years of a good life—along with some more good years—say another twenty. So on the Life View his must be the worse death.

On my view, even if development and change are gradual, still the strength, number, and reach of desires is relevant to how bad it is for an individual to die. And certainly there is this seemingly salient difference in play—Student wants, now, to go on living, has, now, various realizable plans. Baby doesn't. So although Bradley can point out that Baby, should he live, will, when he is as old as Student, also want to go on living, and will also have hopes and plans for that life, it's hard to see how present and future desires are on an equal footing,[20] and how the difference here doesn't impact on the badness of their deaths. More precisely, it's hard to see how it fails to impact on how bad death is *for them*.

Finally, Bradley discusses also cases like Sally's. Unsurprisingly, he's against the shorter life, and earlier death. But again, some might think his position a little firmer than circumstances warrant. Using the example of a famous film star, he considers, and finds wanting, ways of improving on an alleged "inconsistent triad":

1. James Dean's actual life is better than the life he would have had if he had not died when he did.
2. James Dean's death was bad for him.
3. DMP is true. (Bradley, 2009, p. 159)

DMP—the Difference Making Principle—is in effect a statement of what I am calling the Life View.[21] Bradley insists that it, or some near equivalent is surely true, such that we have no option but to reject either 1 or 2 in order to be rid of inconsistency. And he thinks it plain enough that 2 is true while 1 is false. Now, clearly, I am far from wedded to the Life View or DMP, but I wonder anyway whether 2 is as obviously correct as Bradley supposes.[22] It obviously costs the actor, as we are supposing, future good years, but part of what is involved in this sort of appeal to narrative structure is a questioning of the alleged overall unambiguity of such claims. A little later, when asking whether such appeal is based on aesthetic intuitions, Bradley insists that "Dean's actual life makes for a better story than the imagined longer life, but clearly this has nothing to do with whether it is a better life *for him*" (2009, p. 160). Is this so clear? Interestingly, Bradley goes on to concede that some people really do want their lives to make a good story, and it may actually be better for them if they succeed. Still, "not everyone cares about such things, and it is not clear why they should if they do not" (2009, p. 161). But this case is different from those considered earlier. My claim is just that Sally might not irrationally think an earlier death would have been better, and not at all that she should think this.[23] Similarly for James Dean. And I might revisit now an earlier point. Someone sacrifices their life for their children. It is surely tempting to say both that death is bad for them, in costing them many good years, and good for them, in bringing about what they most value. I said earlier that it surely isn't in someone's interests to sacrifice themselves in this way. But my suggestion now is that this isn't obviously correct. And as you might, not irrationally, care more for your children than for living on yourself, so you might similarly care more that your life has a good shape. But I'll say more about these ambiguities in the next section.

As well as looking further into these cases, it's worth thinking, too, about some of the broader implications of Bradley's position. If we ought, as with *The Cure*, to be indifferent to the psychological details of parts of our lives, so too for the whole of our lives. We'll all die in ten years, when an asteroid hits the Earth. Jane will be only thirty years old. She could have been born earlier, since she was in fact born from an embryo that had been on ice for thirty years. So she could have lived to sixty. Should she wish she had been born earlier, even though virtually none of her current psychology would in that case have emerged? Bradley must think she should.[24] I will die in five years because of exposure to chemicals when I was one year old. My parents had been on the verge of emigrating. Had they done so, then even though my psychology would have been radically different—friends, interests, language, schooling—I'd have had a much longer life ahead. Should I wish they'd caught the plane? Bradley will think I should. But for many of us, it's very hard to see why this attachment to the kind of persons we are, to the kinds of lives we're living, should be so easily set aside.[25]

There is an issue, too, about the ordering of events within a life, or a period of life. As I've noted, life is worth living, on the Life View, if it is overall good. My cat will live for another three years, and good years, if I subject it to an extremely painful operation, with six months of bad side effects, right now. Many people think that future pleasure cannot straightforwardly compensate for present pain in an animal life. It can, of course, in a human life, and I might rationally choose some drawn-out painful procedures in order to secure some future benefit. But I think I can, as well, rationally decline this. Two years of pain, starting now, will give me ten years of pleasure still to come. Even if I agree that, should I endure the pain, I'll later be glad that I did, I don't think it is clearly irrational, or cowardly, to decide now not to endure it. This is a hard case, complicated by my being already in the middle of things, with presumably desires now for later times. Baby's case is, I think, less hard. We're in a car crash together, both now unconscious. A doctor might well, and reasonably, decide it is worth giving me some painful operation to save my life, because, as he believes, I would want this. Ought he to do the same for Baby? I think we should look upon a baby here much as we'd look upon a cat, and be most concerned with its present pain. [26]

8. *For* and *That*

I said at the outset that my position would, in the end, turn out to be less controversial than it might first appear. I'll deliver on that now. And so I'll offer some sort of reconciliation between Bradley's position and mine. This involves discussion of two sets of contrasts, one between *bad that* and *bad for*, the other between three sorts of value, or ways in which something might be bad.

Our question has been about whether, when, and to what degree death is bad *for the one who dies*. We might say, somewhat roughly, that our concern is with badness for the individual or person, or with individual or personal value.[27] But what is the contrast here? There are two, one firmer than the other. My death might be bad for me, but good for you, as you inherit; or good for society, as I am a terrorist, or a despot, or a carrier of some deadly virus. It might be instrumentally good that I die, even though bad for me. The other contrast is with intrinsic value—we might say it is a bad thing that someone died, or bad just in itself, or bad for the universe, or some such. Two things should be noted here. First, this is the less firm contrast, for while personal and instrumental values might be at odds with one another—it's bad for me but not for others, or vice versa—intrinsic value seems to imply personal value—if it's bad just in itself that I die, surely it's bad for me also. Second, "bad for the world" is ambiguous. This might on the one hand link with something's being bad for others, or bad for society, and thus imply instrumental value; or it might connect with badness in itself, or for the universe, and thus intrinsic value. Thus when Bradley signals his concern as with "how bad death is for its victim, not for the world" it might not be wholly clear just what contrast he has in mind (2009, p. 116).

There's more to say about *for* and *that*. Rust is bad for my car. What this surely means, though, is just that rust is indirectly bad for me. There is no clear sense, independent of our interest and concerns, in which something can be bad for an artifact.

It is different with living things. Supposing there are no gardeners, still, drought is bad for plants. It interferes with their well-being or flourishing. But now if drought, or greenfly, or frost is bad for plants, so too, surely, is death. It's hard to see how it can be bad for plants to undergo a decline in well-being, without its being bad that their well-being hits zero, and death comes. Some will object that plants are on a par with artifacts here—change can occur, and damage, but harm is only improperly spoken of. But I can sidestep this. *If* drought is bad for plants—and it is at least a familiar and not wholly implausible thought that it is—then death is bad for them also.

Things are somewhat similar with animals. "Somewhat" as there is sentience and experience to take into account. So consider the sudden and painless death. We might agree that it is bad for a cow, or a lamb to die, at least prematurely, as again flourishing is curtailed, and some seemingly natural process is prevented from running its course. And then, of course, similarly too for embryos, fetuses, babies—if death is bad for plants, it is bad also for human beings in the early stages of life.

This is to concede something to Bradley and the Life View, then. And I might concede more. In the sense in which it is bad also for a fetus to die—bad in that it is thereby prevented from growing, maturing, and living out its life—the earlier the death, in general the worse it is. It is in one clear sense worse for Baby to die as a baby, than to die later, as a student. His good moments are fewer.

This, however, is as far as the concessions go. I introduced above the rough idea of personal value. It can be made a little less rough. Consider some of the weird and far from wonderful things I happen to value—a stupid poem I wrote as a kid, my pink socks, a clapped out bike that it's no longer safe to ride. Evidently these things are of *merely* personal value, and it would be in no way bad, either for others, or in itself, should they be destroyed. Now the value of life is not to be understood in quite this sense. Nevertheless, we should distinguish two ways in which death might be bad for the thing that dies. From conceding that death is bad for the plant it doesn't at all follow that we should be exercised about plant death, regret its occurrence, or make any sacrifices to prevent it. Similarly for the animal, the embryo, the fetus or baby. We can agree that death is bad for these things while yet not agreeing it is bad that they die. Dissimilarly, however, elsewhere. Just as it's both bad for animals to be in pain and bad that they are in pain—this is something we should regret and in some circumstances try to prevent—so also it's both bad for Student to die and bad that he dies—this also is something we should regret, and want to prevent. When someone has worthwhile plans and projects, wants to live on, and—barring death—is likely to realize these plans and projects, then death is bad for that person, and in a way that makes demands on us. We might say that it's bad that he dies, or that his death is intrinsically bad, or that it's bad not only for him but also for the universe, or for the world.

When I suggest, then, that Baby's death isn't bad, and that Child's death is less bad than Student's, it's this sort of badness I have in mind. Baby's death isn't, for Baby's sake, something we should try to prevent, and Child's death, though normally we ought if possible to prevent it, should come lower in our priorities than Student's death. Now suppose a defender of the Life View objects here that her position has not been fully understood. Nagel, remember, suggests that experience itself is valuable. A hedonist thinks good experience is valuable. So even if we can forget about plants, still, the claim is, the preservation of animal lives and the lives of young and very young human beings should be among our concerns. Keep away death and there will be more of value in the world. As it's good, and intrinsically good, or good in itself, that this value is sustained, so it's good that we prevent death.

I've already outlined the response to this. If we should save lives already under way, just because of their future potential, then surely we should start extra lives when, if started, they will have similar potential. For if the thought is that, say, pleasure is intrinsically valuable, then the more of it the better. And if so maximizing overall value is to be my concern then I should take the cure whether or not the post-op person is still me. That is one consistent position. Another is to hold that even though there is some sense in which death is bad for the thing that dies, some sense in which individuals are replaceable by those leading longer or better lives, there is no requirement to prevent death from occurring, or to engage in such replacing. The middle position—we have obligations to actual but not to possible lives, and stronger obligations to this animal than to others—is one that is so far underexplained.[28]

9. CONVERGENCE

Where does Bradley stand in relation to this? Interestingly, there are a number of occasions on which he hints that he might be at least half willing to entertain a position somewhat closer to mine. First,

> There is one way in which it might be argued that Student's death is much worse than Baby's: Student has put a lot of work into his future, and thus deserves that future much more than Baby does. And we might think Student's death is more tragic for this reason. But this is not to say that Student's death is worse *for Student* than Baby's death is *for Baby*. Rather it is to say that even though Student's death is not as bad for Student as Baby's is for Baby, *the world* is made worse by Student's death than by Baby's death. (Bradley, 2009, p. 116)

Two points about this: first, though desert is not desire there is some relation. And desire is arguably the more important. Imagine he works hard for some future but then loses interest. He may still deserve that future, but if the desire is gone, then it won't obviously be tragic if he doesn't get it. Second, this is the claim about badness for the world that I drew attention to earlier. And, though it's impossible to be certain, I think Bradley is more likely to have intrinsic than instrumental value in mind here. But then, because it is unjust or unfair that Student rather than Baby dies, it might seem that Student's death is the one that we, as would-be moral agents, should be most concerned to prevent.

Bradley has, however, something to say about this: "We might make a distinction between the extent to which an event *harms an individual*, and the extent to which that harm *matters morally*" (2009, p. 124). This comment comes in the context of a more or less self-contained discussion about abortion, and it isn't clear what weight Bradley wants to put on it. But take a reasonably generous understanding of moral obligation, and it appears that at least a critical part of the distinction here is between the harms that matter, and that third parties should be concerned with, and those that don't.

A related distinction surfaces a little later. For Bradley notes that we do more highly value those goods that figure in periods where there are close psychological connections to the present, calling this the *bias toward psychological sameness* (2009, p. 147). He says, (though he doesn't explain the point) that this "seems irrational" but then insists that even if it is rational, nothing straightforwardly follows about overall values: "How rational it is to prefer a given event is not necessarily proportional to the overall value of that event" (2009, p. 146). But this is to grant rather a lot. If it might be rational for me to refuse the cure, then equally it might be rational also for my friends to urge such a refusal on me. I ought to opt for five years, and then death. And conversely—if I don't have reason to save the fetus's life, then it just doesn't matter, even if it is in some sense bad for it, that it dies. Unless he's prepared in the end for us to get along famously, Bradley needs to stick to his guns about this bias being irrational.

10. SUMMARY

It is sometimes bad to die. And, or so I've claimed, both there being a good life ahead and there being a desire to live this life are necessary conditions of death's being bad. The first claim finds widespread support, the second considerably less. The focus here has been on this latter claim. So neither the desire nor the good life ahead are sufficient conditions for death's being bad. The claims here follow, of course, from the necessity claims, but are, I believe, independently plausible. Nevertheless, there are qualifications and complexities attendant on both.

It isn't bad to die just when you desire to live on, for your desire might be unrealistic—you don't see that there is simply no chance of your doing what you hope to do, of living the life you want to live. But isn't there something bad about someone's not getting what they want? Wouldn't it be better if this man were reconciled to death? We can concede this. Nevertheless, it's far from clear that the badness here gives us reason to help this man live on.

It isn't bad to die just when there's a good life ahead, for you may have no interest in living this life, may, further, have a not irrational desire to die. But isn't there something bad about death, when life would otherwise be good? We can concede this also. Again, however, this sort of badness needn't engage us.

I promised a return to McMahan. Though we agree about a lot, we seem to disagree about fetuses and animals. He says, remember, that a problem with a desire-based account is that it fails to recognize that their deaths can be bad for them.

In *The Ethics of Killing*, he says this is a point he's discussed elsewhere. But that discussion isn't very full:

> What makes the death of a fetus, infant or animal bad is primarily that death deprives it of a range of future goods that its life would otherwise have contained. Because these entities lack self-consciousness they are incapable of foreseeing or contemplating most of these goods and hence are incapable of desiring them. But, because the good would occur within their own lives, it seems plausible to regard the loss or deprivation of these goods as a misfortune for them—not just an impersonal loss or loss of impersonal value but a loss that is against the interests of the fetus, infant or animal itself.[29] (McMahan, 1998, p. 477)

I've offered one sense in which premature death typically goes against the interests of a living thing. But in this sense, there is no direct reason for us to be exercised about death. If the claim here is to be made plausible in some other sense, one which will lead us to conclude it is a bad thing—something that should be prevented—that an animal or fetus dies, then more needs to be said.

Notes

1. See Broome, 1999, p. 234–237 for good discussion.
2. This follows on from explicit discussion of Williams's position, and it seems clear that it is indeed that position that is alleged to be "decisively undermined."
3. I am oversimplifying the position regarding the persistent or permanent vegetative state. There is considerable dispute, relating to and generating the different terms here, as to what is going on in the brains of those in such a condition. My assumptions are that such patients are unconscious, have nothing that we'd call a mental life, lack desires. It doesn't matter, for present purposes, whether these assumptions are true. See Belshaw, 2009, for more discussion.
4. I want to stress this point. A considerable number of writers, some of them advancing versions of the Desire View, have focused on questions about the permissibility or impermissibility of killing, often in context of the abortion debate. Though the concerns are clearly related, my emphasis is on value, and what we should want to occur, rather than on morality, and what we should do. And see footnote 28 following.
5. Imagine two test tubes. In the one, an egg and sperm have fused and form a zygote. In the other, the egg and sperm are kept apart by a divider. Both test tubes are accidentally dropped and break. It is surely strange to deeply regret this in the one case, and to believe that nothing important has happened in the other.
6. For discussion see Parfit, 1984, pp. 487–490; McMahan, 2002, pp. 306–308; and Rachels, 1998.
7. McMahan, 2002, p. 77.
8. For more on the distinction between the biological and the biographical life, see Rachels, 1986.
9. There are complications lurking here. With *The Cure* the future life isn't wanted—I say quite reasonably—because it is so different. Suppose it is wanted. Still I say death isn't bad. For this is a desire the satisfaction of which doesn't, in the relevant sense, benefit you. But I am hanging nothing on this more controversial claim.

10. Another complication. For it will be objected that we are always partially different from how we were before. That is clearly the case. What is less clear is whether we should therefore talk of our being a partially different person. So I am after something stronger than this. Whether what I am after involves a difference in kind or only in degree from everyday change is a harder question. I'm not going to worry about it, however, suspecting that if we achieved precision throughout this area something would have gone wrong.

11. See Belshaw, 2005, pp. 46–47, and 2009, pp. 118–122; McMahan, 1988, pp. 259–266 in Fischer, and 2002, pp. 164–172; Bradley, 2008 and 2009, pp. 115–129, for discussion of this and closely related cases.

12. There are ancestors in Bradley, 2009, pp. 157–163; McMahan, 2002, p. 175; and Belshaw, 2009, pp. 112–114.

13. For narrative structure or unity see, as well as those mentioned in note 14, especially MacIntyre, 1981.

14. See Fischer, 1993, pp. 18–27, and, as there suggested, Nagel, 1979.

15. The statement in Bradley, 2008, p. 292, is extremely similar.

16. Bradley, 2009, p. 51. And that simplicity is a virtue is point he insists on in the book's introduction.

17. It should be noted that my opponent needn't hold to quite this position. Suppose life begins with conception, but has no moment-by-moment value until some way into the fetal stage. Death at conception is as bad as, but not worse than, death a few months later.

18. See also McMahan, 2002, p. 76

19. Or, that it was reasonable to make the sacrifice. Someone might claim we always have some reason to do that which will please another person.

20. Again, there's an ambiguity. Some say that bias to the present is irrational. So my current desires (a) for now and (b) for the future are on an equal footing. This claim, true or false, differs from my claim here: current desires, for now and the future, are not on an equal footing with future desires, for then and the future.

21. Bradley uses this formulation throughout his book. In earlier work he refers to what is in effect the same notion as the *Life Comparative Account*, or LCA. This, in nonabbreviated form, is the term much used by McMahan in a range of similar contexts. See Bradley, 2009, pp. 50–51, and 2008; McMahan, 2002, pp. 105–106 and 168–187.

22. It should be noted, however, that a critic of the Life View can accept that this early death is bad for James Dean. The question is whether it might be better—less bad— than a later death.

23. A further point. Bradley thinks the friend of narrative structure is on stronger ground in cases, like that of Socrates, where someone chooses and prefers the earlier death, much less strong where the person prefers to live on. Sally and James Dean may well have preferred to live at the time they died. But surely this is in part because they would then have expected the good times still to roll. Hence my emphasis on someone's looking back and thinking, with some reflection, that the shorter life would have been better.

24. Someone could claim that psychology is very much genetically determined and so resistant to environmental impact. Clearly, Bradley's position rests on no such empirical claim.

25. See Belshaw, 2000a and 2000b.

26. Bradley's elaboration of his position involves his engagement with and criticism of Jeff McMahan's *Time Relative Interest Account*. Both McMahan's account

and Bradley's treatment of it are generously extended, and there isn't space for a worthwhile discussion here. I make only two comments. First, I'm not sure that Bradley entirely wins the argument with McMahan. Second, though they are not unrelated, there are nevertheless important differences between TRIA and the Desire View. So even if the one is beaten, the other still stands. But see Bradley, 2009, pp. 129–146; McMahan, 2002, pp. 105–106, 165–174, 194–195, and elsewhere.

27. My thinking here is influenced by—but not always consonant with—discussion in Dworkin, 1993.

28. I might make a broader point here. The debate between Bradley and me resembles in many ways the *future like ours* view advanced by Don Marquis and desire-centered opposition to that view mounted by, for example, Tooley and Boonin. Two observations about this: first, as noted earlier (fn 11) an important difference is that the earlier debate centers on the wrongness of killing (and of the fetus in particular) while the focus here is on the badness of death; second, a key move in that earlier debate—an appeal to the notion of idealized desires—isn't anywhere replicated here. See Marquis, 1989; Tooley, 1972; Boonin, 2003; and Bradley, 2009, pp. 128–129.

29. See, for more on animal death, McMahan, 2002, pp. 195–198, Bradley 2009, pp. 147–154.

References

Belshaw, Christopher. 2000a. "Later Death/Earlier Birth." In *Midwest Studies in Philosophy—Life and Death: Metaphysics and Ethics*, Peter A. French and Howard K. Wettstein, eds., pp. 69–83. Oxford: Blackwell.

Belshaw, Christopher. 2000b. "Identity and Disability." *Journal of Applied Philosophy* 17 (3): 263–276.

Belshaw, Christopher. 2005. *10 Good Questions about Life and Death*. Oxford: Blackwell.

Belshaw, Christopher. 2009. *Annihilation: The Sense and Significance of Death*. Stocksfield: Acumen.

Boonin, David. 2003. *A Defense of Abortion*. New York: Cambridge University Press.

Bradley, Ben. 2008. "The Worst Time to Die." *Ethics* 118: 291–314.

Bradley, Ben. 2009. *Well-Being and Death*. Oxford: Oxford University Press.

Broome, John. 1999. *Ethics Out of Economics*. Cambridge: Cambridge University Press.

Dworkin, Ronald, 1993. *Life's Dominion*. New York: Alfred A. Knopf.

Fischer, John M., ed. 1993. *The Metaphysics of Death*. Palo Alto, CA: Stanford University Press.

MacIntyre, Alistair. 1981. *After Virtue*. London: Duckworth.

Marquis, Don, 1989. "Why Abortion Is Immoral." *Journal of Philosophy* 86: 183–202.

McMahan, Jeff. 1988. "Death and the Value of Life." *Ethics* 99.1: 32–61. Reprinted in Fischer, 1993.

McMahan, Jeff. 1998. "Preferences, Death and the Ethics of Killing." In *Preferences*, Christoph Fehige and Ulla Westels, eds., pp. 471–502. Berlin: de Gruyter.

McMahan, Jeff. 2002. *The Ethics of Killing*. Oxford: Oxford University Press.

Nagel, Thomas. 1970. "Death." in his *Mortal Questions*. pp.1–10. Cambridge: Cambridge University Press. Reprinted in Fischer 1993, pp. 59–70.

Parfit, Derek. 1984. *Reasons and Persons*. Oxford: Clarendon Press.

Rachels, James. 1986. *The End of Life*. Oxford: Oxford University Press.

Rachels, Stuart. 1998. "Is It Good to Make Happy People?" *Bioethics* 12 (2): 93–110.

Tooley, Michael. 1972. "Abortion and Infanticide." *Philosophy and Public Affairs* 2 (1): 37–65

Williams, Bernard. 1973. "The Makropulos Case: Reflections on the Tedium of Immortality." In his *Problems of the Self*, pp. 82–100. Cambridge: Cambridge University Press.

CHAPTER 13

....

DEATH AND RATIONAL EMOTION

....

KAI DRAPER

1. The Central Question

....

Is it rational to be troubled by death? That is the central philosophical question about death and the emotions. To be recognizable as such, however, it must not be conflated with the question of whether it is advantageous to be troubled by death. Answering that question would require an empirical investigation into the psychological and behavioral effects of each of the various ways in which one can be troubled by death. Such an investigation would not be philosophical in nature, and its results would be of limited philosophical interest. Moreover, it would not address the concerns that for millennia have motivated contemplation of the value and significance of death.

The more important and philosophically interesting question is whether death can be a fitting object of fear or dread or disappointment or sadness, or some other form of emotional distress.[1] It is natural to express that question in terms of whether it can be rational to be troubled by death, because when an emotion is unfitting, we say that there is no reason to feel that emotion. A fear of spider webs, for example, is an irrational fear because there is no reason to be afraid of spider webs, which is to say that there is nothing in the innocuous nature of a spider web that merits fear.[2] A fear of spider webs is also irrational in the sense that there is good reason to avoid being afflicted by it if one can. Typically, the two sorts of irrationality go hand in hand, but at least in principle they can come apart. If I were offered a million dollars to become afraid of spider webs, for example, it might well be advantageous and so rational for me to develop a fear that would nevertheless be irrational in the sense of being unmerited by its object.

Properly understood, then, the question of whether it can be rational to be troubled by death is no different than the question of whether death (in virtue of its own nature or the nature of its consequences) can merit emotional distress.[3] That question needs to be refined, however, in the same ways that axiological questions about death are typically refined. First, "death" is to be understood not as the dying process which, because it can involve prolonged and intense suffering, obviously can merit dread and other negative emotions. Rather "death" is to be understood either as the event of annihilation (i.e., ceasing to exist) that follows the dying process, or as "being dead," the perpetual posthumous nonexistence that begins with annihilation.[4] Second, the specific question of interest is whether one's own death can be a fitting object of *self-interested* emotional distress. It is easy to see that if, for example, my death would cause my children to become impoverished, it would be rational for me to be altruistically troubled by its prospect or approach, but it is less clear whether I can rationally be troubled by the consequences that my death will have for me.

Now suppose that we do find that death can merit a particular species of (self-interested) emotional distress. Then the general question of whether it can be rational to be troubled by death receives an affirmative answer; but we may not want to end our investigation of death and the emotions there, for we may want to identify the full range of negative emotions that can be merited by death. Should we discover that death can merit disappointment, for example, we may also want to explore whether death can merit fear or dread or sadness or despair or some other sort of emotional distress. After all, we might find that one sort of death merits one set of negative emotional responses while another sort of death merits a different set of negative emotional responses. Moreover, we may want to determine whether certain common emotional responses to death are irrational. Partly because the fear of death is so common, for example, it would be interesting to discover that it cannot be rational to fear death.

2. THE RELEVANCE OF THE EMOTIONS

The question of whether one's own death can merit self-interested emotional distress has received little direct attention in the contemporary philosophical literature on death. At first blush, that might seem reasonable. The crucial questions, one might suppose, are the familiar axiological ones—whether, and under what circumstances, and to what degree, death can be bad for the one who dies. Whether it can be fitting to be troubled by one's own mortality might seem to be of secondary interest. Moreover, it is natural to assume that x merits self-interested distress on the part of y if and only if x is bad for y. On that assumption, the question of whether one's own death can merit self-interested distress can be answered simply by determining whether death can be bad for the one who dies.

No one doubts the philosophical importance of the axiological questions, of course, but a case can be made that the contemporary philosophical literature on the value and significance of death has focused too narrowly on those questions and so has failed to give due attention to the emotions. The first thing to notice in this regard is that the question of whether death can be bad for the one who dies is itself ambiguous. One can ask whether death can be bad in the comparative sense in which "bad" means "worse than the alternative," or, one can ask whether death can be bad in the noncomparative or absolute sense of "bad."[5] The majority of contemporary philosophers who argue that death can be bad employ the comparative notion. The contemporary literature on the value of death is dominated by "deprivationists" (e.g., Nagel, 1979; Feldman, 1992; Grey, 1999; and Bradley, 2004), those who argue that, because death can deprive the one who dies of the benefits of survival, death can be bad in the sense that it can be worse than survival. It has not gone unnoticed, however, that many things that are comparatively bad do not seem to merit any sort of emotional distress, nor do they seem to qualify as harms or misfortunes (Glannon, 1994; Draper, 1999). It is comparatively bad for me that I am not omnipotent, that I am not universally loved, and that I do not receive a relaxing massage whenever I would like one. I do not, however, count any of those deprivations among my misfortunes, nor do I regard them as harms, nor do I find anything troubling in their nature. Or, to use an example I use elsewhere (Draper, forthcoming), suppose that I am receiving a massage, a wonderful massage from Bjorn at Bjorn and Sven's House of Swedish Massage. Suppose further that were I not enjoying that massage, I would be enjoying an even better massage from Bjorn's even more talented partner, Sven. Then Bjorn's giving me a wonderful massage is comparatively bad—worse, because less good (in the absolute sense of "good") than the alternative. Nevertheless, I should scarcely be entitled to count my massage among my misfortunes, or to accuse poor Bjorn of having harmed me. Nor would it be fitting for me to be troubled by the fact that I received a wonderful massage from Bjorn.

It appears, then, that the mere conclusion that death can be comparatively bad is compatible with the Epicurean view that it is irrational to be troubled by one's own mortality. Perhaps this is why Epicurus ignored the question of whether death can be comparatively bad in favor of addressing the question of whether death can be bad in the absolute sense of "bad." In his letter to Menoeceus, he argued that because "everything good and bad [lies] in perception," and death is the "deprivation of perception," death is "nothing to us." Notice that although the absence of pain is comparatively good and the absence of pleasure is comparatively bad, such absences are not "in perception." Thus, it appears that, according to Epicurus, such absences are not to be included in "everything good and bad." That makes perfect sense if Epicurus was using "good" and "bad" in the absolute sense of those terms; for if hedonism is true, then, although the absence of pain and the absence of pleasure are (intrinsically) comparatively good and bad, respectively, such absences have neither absolute intrinsic value nor absolute intrinsic disvalue.

Using "bad" in its absolute sense, Epicurus argued that inasmuch as only pain is intrinsically bad, and neither death nor its consequences can be painful for the one who dies, neither death nor its consequences can be intrinsically bad for the one who dies. Granting Epicurus his hedonism, the argument is sound. Moreover, even if hedonism is false, the proposition that neither death nor its consequences can (in the absolute sense of "bad") be intrinsically bad for the one who dies is quite plausible. Not everyone accepts the truth of that proposition, but most contemporary deprivationists have left it uncontested, preferring instead to attack Epicurus for not recognizing that death can be comparatively bad. I have argued elsewhere (Draper, forthcoming) that there is no reason to suppose that Epicurus denied that death can be comparatively bad, but we needn't resolve that historical issue here. What is important in the present context is that there is no inconsistency in claiming that although death and its consequences can be comparatively bad, neither death nor its consequences can be absolutely bad.

Suppose, then, that Epicureans and deprivationists are both right: neither death nor its consequences can be absolutely bad for the one who dies, but death can be comparatively bad for the one who dies. Then the axiological debate on death reaches an odd sort of stalemate: one victory for those who do not find death troubling and one for those who, at least typically, do find death troubling. It would be unsatisfying, of course, to end the debate there; and one natural way to move forward is to address the question of whether it can be rational to be troubled by death.

Unlike most contemporary deprivationists, Epicurus did just that. From his conclusion that neither death nor its consequences can be absolutely bad for the one who dies, he inferred that it is unfitting to be troubled by one's own death. In what little remains of his work, however, one finds no attempt to justify that inference. Nor is it obvious that the inference is justified. The problem is that certain states of affairs that do not appear to be bad in the absolute sense seem nonetheless to merit emotional distress. Imagine, for example, that for economic or political reasons my loved ones must live in a foreign land, and that it is impossible for me to join them. I might be dismayed by their absence, and that dismay would be absolutely bad for me; but my dismay would, at least in part, be a rational response to my being deprived of the various ways in which my life would be enriched by their presence, a deprivation that would be comparatively, but not absolutely, bad for me. Or suppose that my doctor has good news and bad news for me. The good news is that a rare, nonfatal disease will affect my brain in such a way that, as of next week, I will never suffer again. The bad news, of course, is that the same disease will also prevent me from ever enjoying anything again. Surely it would be rational for me to be troubled by the (comparatively) bad news, even though being permanently deprived of enjoyment would not be absolutely bad for me. At the very least, Epicureans owe us an argument to the contrary.

It appears, then, that the conclusion that death cannot be absolutely bad for the one who dies, like the conclusion that death can be comparatively bad for the one who dies, does not resolve the issue of whether it can be rational to be troubled by one's own death. This means that both deprivationists and Epicureans need to go beyond their respective axiological conclusions to resolve that issue. Again, there has been little movement of the contemporary literature in that direction. Part of the explanation for this, I suspect, is that there are other questions that compete with the question of whether it can be rational to be troubled by death for the attention of those who want to move forward. One might, for example, want to address the question of whether death can merit avoidance. There may not be much to debate here, however, for it seems quite clear that if death can be comparatively bad, then it can merit avoidance. If a wonderful massage by Bjorn will prevent me from receiving an even better massage from Sven, then, odd as it may seem, a wonderful massage from Bjorn merits avoidance. The oddness is due to the fact that there is nothing intrinsic to the nature of a wonderful massage from Bjorn that merits avoidance. It is only because of its contingent consequences that it merits avoidance. Similarly, if the only thing that can be bad about death is that it can prevent its subject from receiving certain absolute goods, then there is nothing intrinsic to the nature of death that merits avoidance; but death can still merit avoidance in virtue of its contingent consequences. Of course, this conclusion should come as no surprise to anyone. Any position on the value and significance of death entailing that death cannot merit avoidance, that the likely benefits of survival cannot possibly provide a self-interested reason to step out of the path of the proverbial bus, would be absurd. Indeed, if we are to interpret Epicurus charitably, one reason to suppose that he did not deny that death can be comparatively bad is that to suppose otherwise is to saddle him with the absurd view that no one ever has any reason to avoid death.[6]

There are other, more challenging, questions to ask about death if one wants to avoid asking about the rationality of being troubled by death. One can ask whether death harms the one who dies, or whether it can be a misfortune or a personal tragedy for the one who dies. Some writers have chosen to address one or more of those questions. Ben Bradley, for example, has argued that, because the notion of harm is purely comparative, the premise that death can be comparatively bad does justify the conclusion that death can harm the one who dies (2009). Jeff McMahan has attempted to identify certain criteria for distinguishing deprivations that are properly regarded as misfortunes from those that are not, and he has argued on the basis of those criteria that various sorts of deaths can be a misfortune for the one who dies (2002, pp. 95–159). I see no reason to abandon such lines of inquiry, but is it wise to pursue them without also investigating whether it can be rational to be troubled by death? On the one hand, it may be impossible to disentangle the question of whether death can be a harm, or a misfortune, or a personal tragedy, from the question of whether it can be rational to be troubled by death. It may be a conceptual truth, for example, that all misfortunes merit emotional distress on the part of their victims. "I know you've suffered a misfortune here, but there's no reason to be troubled by it" certainly invites the reply, "I'm not sure you know what a misfortune is." If it is a conceptual truth that all misfortunes merit emotional distress, then it may be necessary to argue that it can be rational to be troubled by death in order to establish that death can be a misfortune. At the very least, those who argue that death can be a misfortune would do well to consider the question of whether a misfortune merits distress at least in part because it is a misfortune or a misfortune is a misfortune at least in part because it merits distress. On the other hand, if the notion of a harm, or a misfortune, or a tragedy is not logically tied to rational emotional distress, then the conclusion that death can be a harm, or a misfortune, or a tragedy, may not advance the discussion any further than the conclusion that death can be comparatively bad. On Bradley's comparative analysis of harm, for example, he may well reach the conclusion that death can harm the one who dies, but his analysis also yields the conclusion that I am harmed by Bjorn's wonderful massage. If our notion of harm is that broad, then even if we are convinced that death can harm the one who dies, we will still want to ask, "But is death something to be troubled by?"

3. Is It Rational to Fear Death?

Epicurus had his own reasons for being interested in the question of whether it can be rational to be troubled by death. He offered a set of teachings aimed at happiness, and he believed that troubled thoughts about death are a significant source of unhappiness. Thus, he sought to help people overcome their negative attitudes toward death by exposing the irrationality of those attitudes. His main target was fear, for he believed that many of his contemporaries were fearful of death because they believed that the dead suffer divine retribution or otherwise fare poorly in Hades. Understanding why there is nothing in death to fear, Epicurus believed, could help such persons overcome their fear of death and so lead happier lives.

We need to be cautious, however, in our use of the term "fear." "Fear" is the name of a specific emotion,[7] one that typically takes as an object something that is at least believed to be a menacing evil. Its physiological expressions include (among others) sweating, diminished blood flow to the extremities, and rapid heartbeat, and its primary psychological expression is an inclination to flee or otherwise avoid its object. Statements of the form, "X finds Y frightening" or "Y scares X," among others, typically refer to this emotion. It has been noticed, however, that especially in expressions of the form "X fears that Y," sometimes the word "fear" is not used to refer to the emotion that goes by that name (Gordon, 1980; Davis, 1987). So, for example, "I fear that I have overcooked the pasta" indicates that I am concerned that my interest in not overcooking the pasta might not be fulfilled, but it does not imply that I would ever turn pale, tremble, or in any way feel afraid in the face of bloated linguine.[8]

Epicurus was using "fear" to refer to the emotion of fear when he argued that there is nothing in death to fear. He was interested in ridding himself and his followers of the disposition to experience that emotion in response to the prospect or approach of death. To appreciate his position, one should first notice that annihilation is not intrinsically frightening. If I were certain that almost immediately after being annihilated, I would exist once again, then I would be quite fearless in the face of annihilation. It is only annihilation coupled with the absence of regeneration that tends to evoke fear. In other words, it is the temporal approach of permanent nonexistence that fills many of us with dread. (By "dread" I mean "anticipation with fear.") One oddity here, however, is that although there is a sense in which my permanent nonexistence draws nearer every day, there is also a sense in which it never actually reaches me because, as Epicurus reminded his follower Menoeceus, "when death is [present] we are not." At least in part, the suggestion seems to be that because permanent nonexistence never has any effect on the one who dies, it cannot harm the one who dies, and so one's own death cannot be a suitable object of (self-interested) fear.[9] Lucretius added the further consideration that inasmuch as there is nothing frightening in the thought that I never existed prior to my generation, how can there be something frightening in the thought that I will never exist after my annihilation? (I return to Lucretius's argument below.)

Furthermore, if Epicurus was correct to suppose that neither death nor its effects can be bad in the absolute sense of "bad," then the only possible (self-interested) disadvantage to being mortal is that death can deprive one of something absolutely good. But why should the mere deprivation of something absolutely good, unaccompanied by anything absolutely bad, frighten us? Consider two examples. Suppose I am approached by a big, snarling dog. Then fear on my part might well be rational, but not if that fear is directed entirely at the possibility that a dog bite will cost me a lot of money in medical bills, with the ultimate consequence that I will not be able to afford a fine wine that I had hoped to enjoy. Or suppose that I learn that an unexpected financial loss will prevent me from taking a long-awaited and much-deserved vacation in Barcelona. Then disappointment might well be reasonable, but being frightened by such a misfortune would be unfitting. To sincerely say, "Not living it up in Barcelona scares the hell out of me," would be an indication that I suffer from a rather unusual phobia.

Such examples suggest the following argument to the conclusion that it is irrational to fear death:

P1: If neither death nor its consequences can be absolutely bad for the one who dies, then one's own death cannot merit self-interested fear.

P2: Neither death nor its consequences can be absolutely bad for the one who dies.

C: Thus, one's own death cannot merit self-interested fear.

In principle, even the deprivationist who believes that it can be rational to be troubled by death might endorse this argument. Indeed, although contemporary deprivationists typically pit themselves against Epicurus, some of them at least implicitly endorse P2; for some of them (e.g., Nagel, 1979) claim not only that death can be bad for the one who dies in virtue of depriving her of the "positive goods" of survival, but also that the only thing that can be bad about death for the one who dies is that it deprives that person of those goods. If the latter claim is correct, then death is not bad in the absolute sense of "bad."

I know of no philosopher who has directly addressed the argument under discussion, but many have explicitly rejected its conclusion. Western literature in general is certainly no stranger to the thought that permanent nonexistence is a terrifying prospect, and this thought has been championed by more than one philosopher. Some appear to believe that P2 is false, that permanent nonexistence is an absolute evil of a sort that merits fear and even terror. That view is subject to a difficulty, however, that can be illustrated by the following pair of cases:[10]

Case 1:   Tomorrow I will be annihilated and never exist again.
Case 2:   Some very powerful entity will keep me alive forever. However, beginning tomorrow, I will receive daily doses of an anesthetic to ensure that I am forever in an unconscious state.

Surely the following reaction to this pair of cases would be extremely eccentric: "My future in each of these cases is comparatively bad because in each I am deprived of all of the usual benefits of survival. Nevertheless, inasmuch as I face permanent nonexistence only in the first case, and that is an absolute evil of a sort that merits fear, it is only in that case that my future merits fear." It is difficult to believe that my future merits fear in case 1, but does not merit fear, or merits less fear, in case 2. Indeed, I see no reason at all to prefer my fate in case 2 to my fate in case 1. Assuming, then, that my future merits no more fear in case 1 than in case 2, those who believe that permanent nonexistence is an absolute evil that merits fear must say that in case 2 no less than in case 1, I am the victim of an absolute evil that merits fear.

But what is that evil? One might suggest that even if it is unaccompanied by permanent nonexistence, the permanent absence of consciousness is itself an absolute evil and fear or terror can be a fitting response to the prospect or approach of that evil. Alternatively, one might deny that the second case is correctly described as a case of immortality, and so suggest that in case 2 as in case 1 I face the absolute evil of permanent nonexistence. If the suggestion here is that necessarily I cease to exist at the moment at which I permanently lose consciousness, then assuming that I continue to exist so long as I do not permanently lose consciousness, this response would have the odd implication that whether an individual exists at a given time can depend entirely on what happens at a later time. We can set that worry aside, however, for both possible responses can be undermined by appeal to a third case:

Case 3:   Some very powerful entity will keep me alive forever. However, beginning tomorrow, I will receive daily doses of an anesthetic so that each day I am conscious only at midnight and only for a single second. I will not find my brief moments of consciousness pleasant or unpleasant, nor will they provide me with the opportunity to accomplish anything of even the slightest significance. When awake, I will be in the condition of someone who, although conscious, has not yet gathered his wits about him and so cannot even recognize his circumstances.

It is difficult to believe that my future in case 3 merits less fear than my future in cases 1 and 2, and I see no reason at all to prefer my fate in case 3 to my fate in the first two cases. (On the contrary, I would prefer my fate in case 1 to my fate in case 3.) Moreover, it seems quite clear that in case 3, I am truly immortal. Thus, it appears that the proponent of the view that in case 1 my future merits fear must also claim that in case 3 my future merits fear even though I am neither annihilated nor permanently deprived of consciousness in that case. It seems implausible, however, to suggest that in case 3, I am the victim of some absolute evil that merits fear. There may be some absolute evil to be found in the indignity of the treatment I receive in that case, but an indignity is not the sort of absolute evil that merits fear. I suspect that most of us would say that the main problem with my future in case 3 is that it contains nothing that is of value for me. It is the deprivation of all the usual benefits of life that makes the prospect of immortality without enjoyment or significant activity seem so bleak. Thus, if only absolute evils can merit fear, then my future in case 3 does not merit fear, and consistency will then require the conclusion that my future in case 1 does not merit fear either.

Such considerations make me strongly suspect that if death can merit (self-interested) fear, it is not because there is some absolute evil to be found in annihilation or permanent nonexistence. I can find no absolute evil that merits fear in my future in case 3, and I doubt a case can be made that even though there is no such evil in my future in case 3, there is nevertheless such an evil in my future in case 1. Thus, I believe that if death can merit fear, it is because a mere deprivation, unaccompanied by any absolute evil, can merit fear. Perhaps a case can be made that although the examples of the snarling dog and the long-awaited vacation demonstrate that not all deprivations merit fear, the permanent removal of all of the benefits that usually attach to human life is worthy of fear or even terror. The construction of either a serious case in defense of that conclusion, or a decisive case to the contrary, would, I submit, be an immense contribution to the literature on the value and significance of death.

4. PREMATURE DEATH

Perhaps the easiest path to the conclusion that it can be rational to be troubled by death is suggested by the very phrase, "premature death." Presumably, if death can come too soon, then it can be reasonable to be disturbed by its doing so. Because there are a variety of possible bases for claiming that death can be premature, there are a variety of possible arguments in defense of the conclusion that it can be rational to be disturbed by a premature death. I have argued elsewhere that an unlikely death that dashes one's reasonable hopes or expectations for the future can merit disappointment (Draper, 1999). Not all disappointment is rational, of course, for one's hopes and expectations for the future can be unrealistic. The person who irrationally expects to eradicate world hunger, for example, may be disappointed by his inevitable failure to do so, but that disappointment would be no more rational than the expectation responsible for it. We are inclined to say of such a person that his misfortune is that he expected too much, not that he didn't receive what he expected. On the other hand, if one reasonably expects, for example, that one will soon be reunited with one's family, but then learns that an unexpected change in immigration policy will prevent that from happening, one can reasonably feel disappointed. Nor does substituting "death" for "change in immigration policy" seem to alter the truth-value of this claim.

Opposed to any such line of argument, however, is a surprisingly rich tradition of thought according to which positive anticipation and hope, and therefore disappointment as well, are in every case irrational. From Buddhism to Stoicism, one finds the notion that one should not expect or even hope for uncertain goods. Epictetus, for example, argued:

> Do your best to rein in your desire. For if you desire something that isn't within your own control, disappointment will surely follow; meanwhile you will be neglecting the very things that are within your control that are worthy of desire. (1995, p. 6)

Many of us would concede to Epictetus that moderating the desires to avoid unnecessary dissatisfaction and disappointment is a worthy ideal; however, some things that are not entirely within our control are worthy of desire, and so it can be rational to hope or otherwise yearn for something even if doing so may lead to disappointment. Epictetus himself argued that wisdom and virtue and happiness are difficult to achieve but worthy of desire. Thus, it is difficult to see how he can avoid the conclusion that disappointment could be a reasonable response to the discovery that an untimely death will prevent one from achieving one or more of those things.

Disappointment is not the only emotion that, at least arguably, can be merited by an untimely death. The discovery that one's death will be premature in virtue of arriving earlier than one reasonably expected can merit disappointment; but death can also be premature in virtue of arriving earlier than would be considered normal for a human being (or for some relevant subset of human beings, e.g., human beings in the twenty-first century). In some cases of that sort, disappointment is out of the question. The person who is born with a disease that will inevitably take his life before he reaches the age of thirty, for example, cannot be disappointed by his short lifespan if his condition is revealed to him at such an early age that he simply never regards living longer than he will in fact live as a real possibility. Nevertheless, it is arguable that his death before the age of thirty, in virtue of being early relative to what is normal for a human being, could still merit some sort of dissatisfaction on his part.[11]

There are still other ways in which death can be premature. Even if your life span exceeds your hopes and expectations, and even if your life span is unusually long, you might appropriately feel resentful should you learn that you will soon be deprived of your future by being murdered. Moreover, some sort of dissatisfaction might be a fitting response to the knowledge that one's death at a certain time, although not unexpected or unusually early, will nevertheless prevent your life from having been worth living. There are a variety of possibilities here, and no doubt there are many issues to explore with respect to each, but I will not investigate those possibilities here.

5. ANTICIPATING DEATH

Presumably, most of us escape premature death. Thus, if a death that is not premature cannot merit self-interested distress, then barring altruistic (or other non-self-interested) reasons for distress, most of us should respond to our mortality and the approach of death with equanimity. There are, however, various approaches to arguing that death even at a ripe old age can merit self-interested distress. Some of them aim at the conclusion that death can merit what I shall call "negative anticipation." By "negative anticipation" I mean "anticipation with emotional distress" or, more precisely, "being troubled or disturbed by the temporal approach of some state of affairs." Obvious examples of negative anticipation include being frightened by the fact that tomorrow one will undergo a painful medical procedure and being saddened by the recognition that one's child will soon be leaving home. There are various forms of emotional distress that can take as an object the approach of some future state of affairs, among them fear, sadness, despair, and anger. Thus, there are various forms of negative anticipation.

Negative anticipation is the opposite of positive anticipation. When we speak of the latter, we often speak of someone's "looking forward to" or "eagerly awaiting" something that lies in the future.[12] "Not looking forward to" can, of course, be used to indicate the mere absence of positive anticipation, but it can also be used to indicate negative anticipation, as in "I am not looking forward to my dental appointment tomorrow." Perhaps "dread" can be used to refer generally to negative anticipation, but its primary use is captured by Webster's definition of "dread" as "anticipation with great fear or apprehension." Fear and apprehension do not exhaust the ways in which one can be troubled in anticipation of a future state of affairs, and obviously not all fear or apprehension is great.

We have seen that a case can be made that a mere deprivation, unaccompanied by an absolute evil, cannot merit fear, and so one's own death cannot merit self-interested fear. One might wonder if a similar case can be made to reach the conclusion that one's own death cannot merit self-interested negative anticipation. At least typically, the mere absence of some absolute good in one's future does not merit negative anticipation. If an unexpected financial loss were to prevent me from taking a much-deserved and long-awaited vacation in August, for example, disappointment would be reasonable, but unless I would suffer some absolute evil in August (a boring month at home perhaps), I would have no reason to be troubled by the approach of August, or by the approach of my failure to be on vacation in August. Similarly, if I were to learn that an unexpected death would prevent me from taking such a vacation, once again it seems that disappointment, but not negative anticipation, would be reasonable. If we could generalize from this example, we could reach the conclusion that, unaccompanied by an absolute evil, the mere deprivation of life's benefits cannot possibly merit negative anticipation. Assuming that there is no absolute evil to be found in death, we would thereby also reach the conclusion that death cannot merit negative anticipation.

Unfortunately, we cannot generalize from examples of this sort because the loss of present benefits can merit negative anticipation even if no absolute evil accompanies that loss. Furthermore, because death can inflict such a loss, death can merit negative anticipation. A simple appeal to symmetry can be used to establish these conclusions. The argument begins with the premise that escaping from misery can be a fitting object of positive anticipation. The miserable person who says, "I look forward to the day when I am no longer in misery," may be guilty of understatement, but she is not guilty of irrationality. It appears, then, that we are free to reason as follows:

(1) If I am miserable (i.e., extremely unhappy), then permanently escaping from that misery merits positive anticipation.
(2) Thus, if I am miserable and my misery will continue until death brings it to a permanent end, then my being dead merits positive anticipation.

Furthermore, if the value of happiness is parallel to the disvalue of unhappiness, then because permanently escaping unhappiness merits positive anticipation, permanently losing happiness must merit negative anticipation. Thus, we have:

(3) If I am blissful (i.e., extremely happy), then permanently losing that bliss merits negative anticipation.
(4) Thus, if I am blissful and my bliss will continue until death brings it to a permanent end, then my being dead merits negative anticipation.

Notice that 1 through 4 refer to a permanent end to misery or bliss, and not merely an end. The restriction is crucial because, focusing on the case of misery, a mere temporal break in one's misery does not necessarily merit positive anticipation. Suppose that one were to have a miserable waking life punctuated by periods of dreamless sleep. Then the next temporal break in one's misery would not correspond to an experiential break in one's misery and so looking forward to the break would be irrational. A permanent end to one's misery, on the other hand, would merit positive anticipation. Similarly, in the case of a blissful or, more broadly, a happy life, it is not the mere fact that (for some of us) death brings to an end a period of time during which one is happy that makes it a suitable object of negative anticipation; rather, death merits negative anticipation (when it does) because it brings one's happiness to a permanent end.

This appeal to symmetry will fail to convince those who are unwilling to concede that the mere future absence of an absolute evil can be a suitable object of positive anticipation. They will insist that, odd as it may seem, escaping an irredeemably miserable life through death cannot merit positive anticipation. Some of them might embrace the view, suggested by the example of the canceled vacation plans, that the only rational object of negative anticipation is an absolute evil and, correspondingly, the only rational object of positive anticipation is an absolute good. Such a view, however, can be refuted by way of another example. Suppose that I am in intense agony, but a pain-reliever will soon take effect and reduce my agony to a much less severe level of discomfort. I take it to be obvious that I can rationally look forward to the pain-reliever's taking effect even if, because I am looking forward to a time at which I will still be suffering, I am not looking forward to any absolute good. In such a case, what I eagerly await is the mere absence of the intense agony that I am currently experiencing. It might be objected that in such circumstances I would inevitably take pleasure in the reduction of my suffering; but even if that is so, the primary object of my positive anticipation is not that pleasure—I may not even realize that I will feel any such pleasure at all.

Parallel remarks suggest that rational negative anticipation can have as its object the mere absence of an absolute good. Consider, for example, the apparent fact that at some point in his life Beethoven came to the realization that deafness would eventually deprive him of the benefits of listening to music. I take it that negative anticipation of that deprivation was rational on his part. Nor is this conclusion undermined if we suppose that the object of his negative anticipation was the mere absence of certain absolute goods (e.g., the joy of listening to music) and not the presence of some absolute evil (e.g., missing the joy of listening to music).

The Epicurean will be quick to point out that the example is a case in which the loss that was anticipated arrived at a time when its victim still existed. Thus, in that case negative anticipation took as an object a loss that, we may assume, made its subject worse off than he was prior to the loss. One cannot, however, be worse off at a time at which one does not exist. Thus, another possible basis for denying that death can merit negative anticipation is the view that a loss cannot merit negative anticipation unless one will be worse off in virtue of that loss. Notice, however, that such a view would commit one to also denying that positive anticipation of death can be rational, for one cannot be better-off in virtue of escaping one's misery through death. This should, I think, raise doubts about the objection; but setting that aside, there is simply no good reason to insist that only those goods and evils that will make one better or worse off merit positive or negative anticipation. Granted, the person who looks forward to escaping her misery through death does not look forward to being better-off. Nevertheless, she does look forward to something (namely, the future absence of her present misery) that is clearly to her advantage because it is comparatively good. Similarly, the person who anticipates with distress the loss of her happiness through death is troubled by something (namely, the future absence of her present happiness) that is clearly to her disadvantage because it is comparatively bad.[13]

Another possible objection is suggested by my example of the immortal person whose misery is punctuated (but never permanently ended) by periods of unconsciousness. It might be supposed that the reason this person's temporary escapes from misery do not merit positive anticipation is that he does not experience those escapes. If that is the reason, however, then because the person who permanently escapes his misery through death also fails to experience any escape from misery, his escape also fails to merit positive anticipation.[14]

This objection is a serious one, and I have no conclusive reply. Nevertheless, I find it unconvincing partly because I believe that there is an alternative and more compelling explanation of why positive anticipation is irrational in my example. For in that case it is not to the advantage of the miserable individual to have his misery punctuated by periods of unconsciousness. Granted, at any given point in time after his first period of unconsciousness he will have experienced less misery in virtue of having been unconscious at various times in the past; but as his future still holds unending misery in store, he gains nothing in virtue of slowing his accumulation of misery. For the person who permanently escapes misery through death, on the other hand, it is quite clearly to his advantage that his misery does come to a permanent end.

6. LUCRETIUS'S SYMMETRY ARGUMENT

Focusing on the emotions sheds light on Lucretius's famous appeal to the symmetry between prenatal and posthumous nonexistence:

> Look back again to see how the past ages of everlasting time, before we were born, were nothing to us. These, then, nature holds up to us as a mirror of the time that is to come, when we are dead and gone. Is there anything that looks terrible in this, anything that appears gloomy? Is it not more tranquil rest than any sleep? (Lucretius, 1965)

Many contemporary philosophers who address this argument begin by reconstructing it so that some standard axiological term—typically "bad"—replaces Lucretius's richer expressions. However, given that Lucretius's primary aim is to demonstrate that there is no reason to be troubled by death, it is perhaps more faithful to his intent to reconstruct the argument so that it explicitly addresses the emotions.[15] It is also useful to consider whether the claim that some specific kind of emotion can be a fitting response to posthumous nonexistence is undermined by considering whether that same emotion can be a fitting response to prenatal nonexistence. It turns out that Lucretius's argument is at its most compelling if it is used specifically to attack the claim that death merits fear. For there is simply nothing frightening about prenatal nonexistence. Granted, we tend to be afraid of future evils and not past evils, but, at least ordinarily, we are quite capable of recognizing a past state of affairs as a fitting object of fear if it is one. Moreover, something that will evoke terror if it is imminent and fear even if it is in the distant future will typically be unsettling even if it is safely in the past. As Lucretius suggests, however, when we look back at our prenatal nonexistence, there is nothing terrible or gloomy in what we see, and so there is no reason for us to be unsettled by it. Nor does anyone find it comforting that her prenatal nonexistence is safely in the past. It appears, then, that if death merits fear, there must be some asymmetry between prenatal and posthumous nonexistence; but is there any such asymmetry? Granted, what most people do find frightening about death is not nonexistence as such, nor even long periods of nonexistence, but rather permanent nonexistence; and prenatal nonexistence is not permanent. Nonexistence with no end point, however, is simply the mirror image of nonexistence with no beginning point, and I for one cannot see any difference between the two that would justify saying that while nonexistence with no endpoint merits fear, nonexistence with no beginning point does not.[16]

Lucretius was not exclusively concerned with fear, however, and his argument is much less compelling when certain other emotions are considered. Consider disappointment. Even if one can be deprived of benefits by coming into existence later rather than sooner, such a deprivation is never a fitting object of disappointment. The fact that prenatal deprivations do not merit disappointment does not, however, cast doubt on the suggestion that posthumous deprivations sometimes do merit disappointment. Posthumous deprivations and prenatal deprivations are asymmetrical with respect to whether disappointment is merited because rational disappointment is a response to the discovery that expectations or hopes or desires will not be fulfilled, and expectations and hopes and desires are almost always directed toward the future.

Nor will it help Lucretius to suggest that in principle rational disappointment can be directed toward a past deprivation. Perhaps it would be rational for someone to be disappointed, for example, to learn that her parents, now long-deceased, never loved her. Or perhaps an amnesiac might hope that her past was a good one and, upon recovering her memories, might be disappointed to learn that it was not. Indeed, an amnesiac who knows that she will die tomorrow might hope that her forgotten life was a long and happy one and so be disappointed to learn that she is much younger than she had guessed. In all these cases, disappointment is no less rational when directed at a past deprivation than it is when directed at a comparable future deprivation. Such cases do not help Lucretius, however, because they only demonstrate that whether a deprivation is prenatal or posthumous, if the usual requirements for being a fitting object of disappointment are satisfied, disappointment is merited. The fact that posthumous deprivations often evoke disappointment while prenatal deprivations rarely if ever do is not due to some irrational failure to respond emotionally to like cases in a like fashion; it is simply due to the fact that in the case of prenatal deprivations, the requirements for rational disappointment are seldom if ever satisfied.

Perhaps the most interesting case to consider is negative anticipation of the sort discussed above. Does Lucretius's appeal to the symmetry between posthumous nonexistence and prenatal nonexistence offer a basis for rejecting my suggestion that negative anticipation can be a rational response to the knowledge that death will bring one's good fortune to a permanent end? One might suppose that it does, for if it is unreasonable to be troubled by the fact that one's happiness does not extend farther into the past than it in fact does, then given the symmetry between past and future, it might seem that it must also be unreasonable to be troubled by the fact that one's happiness does not extend further into the future than it in fact does. Consider, however, the parallel case of unhappiness. Here there is a clear asymmetry between past and future. If I am miserable now, it is reasonable for me to look forward to the freedom from misery that the future holds in store; but no comparable attitude toward the freedom from misery that I enjoyed in the past is rational for the simple reason that, because time's arrow is not pointed in that direction, the past offers no escape from my current, unhappy condition. Even if, per impossible, I could somehow return to my past freedom from misery, it would not be rational for me to want to do so; for, given that the direction of time remains the same, that would entail having to go through my misery all over again! Assuming once again that happiness is parallel to unhappiness, if I am happy now, then even though being deprived of that happiness in the future merits negative anticipation, the direction of time's arrow precludes the rationality of any comparable attitude toward the absence of happiness in my past. Indeed, if my whole life has been happy, I might even wish that somehow my prenatal nonexistence could return, for that would provide the opportunity to enjoy my whole life all over again.[17]

To my knowledge, I am the first to propose this sort of response to Lucretius's symmetry argument. Some of those who argue for asymmetry claim that unlike one's annihilation, one's generation at a particular time cannot possibly deprive one of any benefits (e.g., Nagel, 1979; Kaufman, 1999). Others concede the possibility of being deprived of benefits by being born too late, but argue that such deprivations are less serious than the deprivations that death inflicts. Anthony L. Brueckner and John Martin Fischer (1986), for example, argue that because we care less about past deprivations than future ones, it is less bad to be deprived of benefits by a late birth than to be deprived of benefits by an early death. More recently, Jeff McMahan (2006) finds it relevant that, unlike dying later, being born earlier would involve having very different particular concerns (e.g., instead of wanting to marry my beloved Chris, I would have wanted to marry some other person). According to McMahan, it can be rational to prefer one's actual life to a longer and better possible life if one's particular concerns would have been substantially different had that possible life been actual. Unlike all these writers, I deny neither the possibility nor the relative gravity of prenatal deprivations. Rather, I deny that there is a rational analog to negative anticipation that takes as its object a past deprivation.

7. CONCLUDING REMARKS

A number of important issues have been ignored in this brief discussion of death and rational emotion. Some of those are foundational issues about the nature of rational emotion. The crucial notion of an emotion being merited by its object is both puzzling and problematic. Consider, for example, the fact that the emotions that we judge to be "fitting" or "merited" are judged by us to be so only because of certain contingent facts about human psychology. Rational beings who were not susceptible to the emotion of fear, for example, would not be able to discern in the nature of even prolonged and intense agony anything that merits fear. The skeptic might therefore object that there is simply no basis for saying that a state of affairs x merits a particular negative emotion y except that x is bad and x tends to evoke y in human beings. But then a comparatively bad death may turn out to be a fitting object of fear, for example, simply because such a death does in fact evoke that emotion in many human beings. A related skeptical argument is based on the suggestion that the only rational standard for measuring whether and to what degree a given state of affairs merits emotional distress is the axiological judgment about whether and to what degree that state of affairs is bad. If this suggestion is correct, then insofar as our ordinary "commonsense" judgments about whether and to what degree death merits emotional distress do not mirror our axiological judgments, they are simply mistaken.

It is clear, then, that much work remains to be done. A thorough investigation of the circumstances under which one's own death can merit self-interested emotional distress is apt to lead to an exploration of the nature of the emotions, an analysis of the very notion that an emotion can be merited, and an attempt to develop and defend a set of principles for determining whether and to what degree something (comparatively or absolutely) bad merits emotional distress. Because of the wide variety of emotions that are common responses to thoughts of death, there is also a wide variety of specific questions about death and rational emotion that merit thorough investigation. Among those, the question of whether death merits fear is, in my opinion, among the most significant questions about the human condition that remains unresolved.[18]

NOTES

1. The distinction between the question of whether being troubled by death is advantageous and the question of whether it is fitting to be troubled by death is drawn by Jeffrie Murphy, 1976. Murphy addresses the latter question. Rorty, 1983, addresses the former as well as the latter.
2. On certain theories of the nature of emotions, an unfitting emotional response is possible only if one misjudges the nature of the object of that emotion. On such theories, being afraid of spider webs, for example, would require irrationally, or at least mistakenly, thinking that spider webs are harmful. Other theories allow for

the possibility of an unfitting emotional response even in the absence of a cognitive mistake. On such theories I might know, for example, that spider webs are innocuous and yet still be irrationally afraid of them. Useful discussions of competing theories of the nature of emotions can be found in Baier, 1990, and Ben-Zeev, 1987.

3. The notion of an emotion's being "fitting" or "merited by its object" is more problematic than my brief remarks here might suggest. Although nothing I am saying presupposes a "fitting attitude analysis" of value terms, explorations of the "wrong-kind-of-reasons problem" for such analyses are relevant to the question of how precisely to define "fittingness" for purposes of exploring whether death can be a fitting object of emotional distress. Useful discussions of that problem can be found in D'Arms and Jacobson, 2000—they call it the "conflation problem"—and in Rabinowicz and Rønnow-Rasmussen, 2004.

4. I am not suggesting that "death," as ordinarily understood, refers either to annihilation or to posthumous nonexistence. As Feldman, 1992 has argued, it may well be that biological death precedes annihilation, and so after death one exists for a time as a corpse. Mostly for the sake of convenience, I prefer to work with the ontological rather than the biological sense of "death."

5. John Broome, 1999, pp. 162–174, has claimed that what I am calling the absolute sense of "bad" is reducible to a comparative notion meaning, roughly, "worse than nothing." Perhaps I am missing Broome's point, but inasmuch as "nothing" is neither good nor bad (in the absolute sense of those terms), it is hardly a surprise that something is bad if and only if it is worse than nothing. Be that as it may, we needn't assess Broome's view here; for even if it is correct, "bad" in the sense of "worse than nothing" is still distinct from "bad" in the sense of "worse than the alternative."

6. Some contemporary critics of Epicurus (e.g., Warren, 2004) attack his position on death on the grounds that it has this absurd implication.

7. The term "fear" is sometimes used to refer to the emotion itself and sometimes to refer to the disposition to experience the emotion.

8. Notice that if one is certain that one has overcooked the pasta, one cannot fear that one has overcooked it. In general, x can fear that y only if x is uncertain that y. Thus, as noticed by Davis, 1987, one cannot possibly fear that one will die (at some time or other) unless one is uncertain that one will die, and such uncertainty would itself be irrational. On the other hand, most of us are quite rationally uncertain about when death will arrive, and so it is quite possible to fear that one's death will arrive sooner rather than later.

9. Rorty, 1983, p. 175, agrees with Epicurus on this point. She insists that the fear of death is irrational because "a harm must be a harm-to-someone; but if the dead are by definition extinct, they cannot be harmed by not existing."

10. My discussion of the issue at hand resembles Frances Kamm's much more intricate discussion of related issues in Morality, Mortality (1993, pp. 39–55). Her interest there is not in the question of whether death merits fear, but rather in the related question of whether death is an intrinsic evil.

11. Although he does not explicitly address the emotions, Jeff McMahan, 2002, especially pp. 145–165, has explored this second sort of premature death in impressive detail. He arrives at the somewhat tentative conclusion that receiving fewer years of life than a normal human being can be a misfortune even if a longer life was never in the cards.

12. If I am right, not all positive anticipation can be captured by the expression "looking forward to," for one cannot look forward to the absence of an experience, but I want to say that such an absence can merit positive (or negative) anticipation.

13. That a person's failure to receive a good at a time t can be comparatively bad for s even if s does not exist at t has been demonstrated by more than one writer (e.g., Feldman, 1992; Grey, 1999; Bradley, 2004; and Draper, 2004).

14. I owe this objection to Sarah Stroud.

15. Rosenbaum, 1989, pp. 356–359, argues that Lucretius's symmetry argument is best understood to be aimed at the conclusion that it is not reasonable to fear one's death, and not at the conclusion that death is not bad. He also effectively rebuts a variety of objections to the argument so understood.

16. Of course, if time itself has a beginning, then prenatal nonexistence has a beginning; but the crucial point is that even if time has no beginning, there is nothing to fear in prenatal nonexistence.

17. Of course, stories of time travel typically involve going back in time without reliving one's past. If that is how it works, then it could be rational to "look forward to" traveling to the (objective) past because the past might offer a genuine escape from one's present unhappiness. Traveling to the past could also merit negative anticipation because one's happiness might thereby be lost.

18. I would like to thank Ben Bradley, Chris Heathwood, Jens Johansson, and Fred Schueler for their helpful comments on earlier versions of this chapter.

REFERENCES

Baier, Annette. 1990. "What Emotions Are About." *Philosophical Perspectives* 4: 1–29.

Ben-Zeev, Aaron. 1987. "The Nature of Emotions." *Philosophical Studies* 52: 393–409.

Bradley, Ben. 2004. "When Is Death Bad for the One Who Dies?" *Noûs* 38: 1–28.

Bradley, Ben. 2009. *Well-Being and Death*. Oxford: Clarendon Press.

Broome, John. 1999. *Ethics out of Economics*. Cambridge: Cambridge University Press.

Brueckner, Anthony, and John M. Fischer. 1986. "Why Is Death Bad?" *Philosophical Studies* 50: 213–221.

D'Arms, Justin, and Daniel Jacobson. 2000. "The Moralistic Fallacy: On the 'Appropriateness' of the Emotions." *Philosophy and Phenomenological Research* 61: 65–90.

Davis, Wayne A. 1987. "The Varieties of Fear." *Philosophical Studies* 51: 287–310.

Draper, Kai. 1999. "Disappointment, Sadness, and Death." *Philosophical Review* 108: 387–414.

Draper, Kai. 2004. "Epicurean Equanimity towards Death." *Philosophy and Phenomenological Research* 69: 92–114.

Draper, Kai. forthcoming. "Epicurus on Death." In *Death: Metaphysics and Ethics*, James S. Taylor, ed. New York: Oxford University Press, forthcoming.

Epictetus. 1995. *The Art of Living*. Translated by Sharon Lebell. New York: Harper Collins.

Feldman, Fred. 1992. *Confrontations with the Reaper*. New York: Oxford University Press.

Glannon, Walter. 1994. "Temporal Asymmetry, Life, and Death." *American Philosophical Quarterly* 31: 235–244.

Gordon, Robert M. 1980. "Fear." *Philosophical Review* 89: 560–578.

Grey, William. 1999. "Epicurus and the Harm of Death." *Australasian Journal of Philosophy* 77: 358–364.

Kamm, F. M. 1993. *Morality, Mortality*. Vol. 1. New York: Oxford University Press.

Kaufman, Frederick. 1999. "Pre-Vital and Post-Mortem Non-Existence." *American Philosophical Quarterly* 36: 69–83.

Lucretius. 1965. *On Nature*. Indianapolis: Bobbs-Merrill.

McMahan, Jeff. 2002. *The Ethics of Killing*. New York: Oxford University Press.

McMahan, Jeff. 2006. "The Lucretian Argument." In *The Good, the Right, Life and Death*, R. Feldman, J.R. Raibley, and M.J. Zimmerman, eds., pp. 213–226. Aldershot, UK: Ashgate Publishing.

Murphy, Jeffrie. 1976. "Rationality and the Fear of Death." *Monist* 59: 187–203.

Nagel, Thomas. 1979. "Death." In T. Nagel, *Mortal Questions*, pp. 1–10. New York: Cambridge University Press.

Rabinowicz, Wlodek, and Toni Rønnow-Rasmussen. 2004. "The Strike of the Demon: On Fitting Pro-Attitudes and Value." *Ethics* 114: 391–423.

Rorty, Amelie Oksenberg. 1983. "Fearing Death." *Philosophy* 58: 175–188.

Rosenbaum, Stephen E. 1989. "The Symmetry Argument: Lucretius against the Fear of Death." *Philosophy and Phenomenological Research* 50: 353–373.

Warren, James 2004. *Facing Death: Epicurus and His Critics*. New York: Oxford University Press.

CHAPTER 14

RETROACTIVE HARMS AND WRONGS

STEVEN LUPER

ACCORDING to the immunity thesis, nothing that happens after we are dead harms or benefits us. This seems defensible on the following basis:

1. If harmed (benefited) by something, we incur the harm (benefit) at some time.
2. So, if harmed (benefited) by a postmortem event, we incur the harm (benefit) while alive or at some other time.
3. But if we incur the harm (benefit) while alive, backward causation occurs.
4. And if we incur the harm (benefit) at any other time, we incur it at a time when we do not exist.
5. Yet nothing incurs harm (benefit) while nonexistent.
6. And nothing is causally affected at one time by events that occur at a later time.
7. So no postmortem event is ever bad (or good) for us (the immunity thesis).

Despite its plausibility, I mean to resist this argument. I will reject premise 1 on the grounds that dying may be atemporally bad for us. I will also reject premise 3. Some postmortem events are bad for some of us while we are alive. But I am not going to report some new exotic particle that makes backward causation possible. As far as I know, 6 is true. If an event is responsible for a harm that we incur before the event itself occurs, it might be said to harm us retroactively; if when or after it occurs, it might be said to harm us proactively. My view is that some postmortem events harm us retroactively, but without backward causation (Pitcher, 1984).

Premise 6 is not the only thing worth retaining. I will salvage other bits of the argument for the immunity thesis, too, and put them to use in support of the claim that postmortem events do not harm anyone proactively. As I see things, postmortem events harm us retroactively or not at all.

Is anything of significance at stake here? I think so. If the immunity thesis is true, our prudential horizon is limited to things that happen during the time we exist, and not a moment beyond. Once we die, it makes no sense for others to do anything, like carrying out our final wishes, out of concern for our interests. Meeting our final wishes may even be impossible, since, on one view which I will discuss, it is impossible to fulfill any of our desires after we die. Yet probate law requires that legally declared wishes be carried out. And it is standard practice in hospitals to honor the directives that competent patients create concerning the treatment they are to receive if they later become incompetent, say due to dementia or brain injury. Yet a severely demented patient will no longer have the desires she had while competent. These familiar practices make sense if people may be benefited, and their desires fulfilled, retroactively. And that is not insignificant. Some will say it is not very important, though, for the charges may be met without appeal to the idea of retroactive benefit. Even if we cannot be harmed by posthumous events we can be wronged by things people do after we are dead, and obviously people have good reason not to wrong us. But I do not think we can make such pronouncements about wronging the dead until we tell a clear story about the way such wrongs are wrought. I will attempt to clarify one way, but my story involves retroactivity.

My argument against premise 1 appears next. In the section that follows I develop a case against the existence of proactively harmful postmortem events. After that, I argue that postmortem events sometimes harm people retroactively. In the final section I defend the view that an action taken after people die may wrong them retroactively, by harming them, or interfering with their desires, while they are alive.

1. HARM

I reject premise 1 of the argument for the immunity thesis. To explain why, I need to make some points about the nature of harm.

First, something is intrinsically good (bad) for us if and only if it is good (bad) for us and its goodness (badness) is not derivative from or due to the goodness (badness) of anything beyond itself. Anything else that is good (bad) for us is extrinsically good (bad) for us. For example, other things being equal, a cut is extrinsically bad for us because it causes us to suffer, while the suffering itself is intrinsically bad for us. On this view, something may be intrinsically good for us even though its goodness depends on various relations it bears to (nonevaluative features of) other things, or on various conditions being met that concern (nonevaluative features of) other things. For example, the view is consistent with the claim that things are (intrinsically) good by virtue of being the objects of a suitable kind of rational desire (Korsgaard, 1983).

Second, some of the things that are extrinsically good for us in a limited context or time frame are not overall good for us: they are not good for us all things considered. Comparativism, the view I will assume here (and whose proponents include Nagel, 1970; Feldman, 1991 and 1992; and many others), says roughly that an event is overall good (bad) for us if and only if it makes life better (worse) for us than it would have been had the event not occurred. In what follows, I assume that something benefits (harms) us if and only if it is overall good (bad) for us.

We can state comparativism a bit more clearly if we measure how good our life is in terms of our lifetime welfare level, and our lifetime welfare level in terms of the intrinsic goods and evils included in our life. Our lifetime welfare level is the sum of the intrinsic goods we have during our life, which boost our welfare, and our intrinsic evils, which lower it. There are events that boost or reduce our goods or evils, events that preclude our having goods or evils, and events that do combinations of these things. Comparativism says that an event is overall good (bad) for us just in the case it makes our lifetime welfare level higher (lower) than it would have been had the event not occurred.

Using the same idea, we can measure how overall good or bad life is over a period of time in terms of our welfare level during that time, and our welfare level over a period of time in terms of the intrinsic goods and evils we have during that time. Then we can say that an event is overall good (bad) for us at a time, or during a period of time, if and only if it makes our welfare level during that time higher (lower) than it would have been had the event not occurred.

Back to premise 1 of the argument for the immunity thesis. Typically, when an event is overall bad for us simpliciter, it is also overall bad for us at some time or another. But this is not always the case. Consider the case of

> Cheerful Mary: Mary is a cheerful soul who does not concern herself about the future. On New Year's Eve, she is killed painlessly, in her sleep, by a previously undetected aneurysm; had she not died, she would have had many more years of good life.

Dying on New Year's Eve was bad for Mary simpliciter, as her life would have been much better had she not died. But at no time is she worse off as a result of dying. After she is dead she lacks any level of welfare at all. As this example illustrates, some things harm their victims (simpliciter) without harming them at any time. To be bad for us simpliciter is to be timelessly (or atemporally) bad for us. Hence premise 1 is false.

To make the case against 1 clearer, I need a bit of jargon. I will say that an event E is negative for us at time T if and only if E is responsible for our having, at T, intrinsic evils we would not otherwise have had at T, or for our failing to have, at T, intrinsic goods we would otherwise have had. E might be negative for us before it occurs or later. I will say that E is retroactively negative for us if and only if E is negative for us at some time prior to E's occurrence, and E is proactively negative for us if and only if E is negative for us at some time T at or after E's occurrence.

Comparativism implies that an event harms us simpliciter only if it is retroactively or proactively negative for us. Cheerful Mary's death was proactively negative for her—it deprived her of goods she would otherwise have had during the following year. But her death also made her nonexistent during that year; because of it she incurred no harm during that year.

This argument against 1 is not uncontroversial. It relies on the claim that when death harms its victims wholly by depriving them of goods they otherwise would have had, as Mary's did, then its victims do not incur harm at any time, as they are left without any welfare level. This claim has resourceful critics, such as Ben Bradley (2004, 2009) and Chris Belshaw (2009). But in rejecting this claim they pay a price: they also reject 5.

According to Bradley, if I die at time T, I may actually incur harm, for which my death is responsible, after T, in that I can be worse off after T than I otherwise would have been. His argument involves the following assumptions. Our welfare level in world W at time T equals the intrinsic value for us of time T in W. The latter value, in turn, equals the value of the intrinsic goods we attain in W at T together with the (dis)value of the intrinsic evils we attain in W at T. The overall value of event E for us in W at T equals the intrinsic value for us of T in W minus the intrinsic value of T in the nearest world in which E fails to occur. Thus E is good (bad) for us at T, and E makes us worse off at T, if and only if E's overall value for us at T is greater (less) than zero.

Suppose that, had I not died at T, my welfare level would have been on the whole positive for a period of time following T. Suppose also that my welfare level while I do not exist is 0. Then death is bad for me during that time: it leaves me worse off during that period of time, as it leaves me with a welfare level of 0 during that time, and a welfare level of 0 is not as good as a positive welfare level. So says Bradley.

Of course, Bradley's position presupposes that people have a welfare level while dead (namely 0). This I question (see Luper, 2007, 2009a, and 2009b). It is not plausible to attribute a welfare level to a subject at a time when that subject does not exist, or is for some other reason wholly incapable of attaining anything intrinsically good or evil. It is the capacity to attain intrinsic goods or evils that distinguishes subjects who have some welfare level from things that do not, such as shoes and shingles.

In support of his claim that the dead have a welfare level, Bradley points out that it is reasonable for a person, say Kris, to be (prudentially) indifferent as between two futures that might follow his being struck by an anvil: F1, being killed instantly, or F2, being made comatose for the ten years prior to death (2009, p. 108). Kris's indifference makes sense only if F1 and F2 have (the same) value for Kris, which in turn entails that Kris has a welfare level during F1—that is, at a time when he is dead.

As Bradley says, we can assess the intrinsic value of the times during which F1 and F2 unfold; during each, Kris attains neither intrinsic goods nor evils, and so it makes sense to say that the intrinsic value of these times for Kris is 0. But it does not follow that Kris has a welfare level during these times. That time T has a value for Kris, as assessed in terms of intrinsic goods and evils Kris attains during T, does not imply that Kris has a welfare level at T. After all, a shoe cannot have a welfare level, yet the value for a shoe of any time T, as assessed in terms of the intrinsic goods and evils the shoe attains at T, is always 0. There is an intimate relationship between our welfare level at a time and the value for us of that time as assessed in terms of the intrinsic goods and evils we attain then: as long as we exist, and have a welfare level at all, the two coincide. But we cannot equate our having a welfare level at time T with T's having a value for us as assessed in terms of the intrinsic goods and evils we attain at T.

Since we have a welfare level only when we exist, I doubt it makes sense to say that death leaves its victims worse off than they otherwise would be. So I accept 5.

2. PROACTIVE HARM

If asked whether a postmortem event harms anyone proactively, most people would respond in the negative, and draw on something like premise 5 to prove it, as follows: by the time a postmortem event occurs, we no longer exist; so if a postmortem event harms us proactively, we incur harm while we are nonexistent. But nothing incurs harm (benefit) while nonexistent (premise 5). So no postmortem event harms us proactively.

I have attempted to show (in the previous section) that reservations about 5 can be allayed. So I think the argument that deploys 5 against the existence of proactively harmful postmortem events is sound. However, for good measure, I will provide another argument, one which does not draw on premise 5.

I assume that an event E is responsible for our incurring harm at a time T only if E is overall bad for us at T. Given this assumption, an event E is responsible for our incurring harm proactively only if E is overall bad for us when E occurs or later. Now, if E is overall bad for us when E occurs or later, then E is proactively negative for us. So to show that no postmortem event is responsible for our incurring harm proactively, I need only show that no postmortem event is proactively negative for us. And this I can do by establishing that (a) no postmortem event is responsible for our having intrinsic evils we would not otherwise have had at or after E's occurrence, and that (b) no postmortem event is responsible for our failing to have intrinsic goods we would otherwise have had at or after E's occurrence.

It is easy to defend (a). We are not afflicted with intrinsic evils at times when we fail to exist. (Even death cannot make that happen.) So if an event is responsible for our having intrinsic evils we would otherwise not have had at a time T, then we exist at T. However, when a postmortem event occurs, and at all later times, we do not exist.

Now consider (b). Suppose Cheerful Mary dies at time T. It may be that, had she not died, she would have had various intrinsic goods after T. If so, death is responsible for her not having these goods. Whether or not it deprives her of goods she would otherwise have had, however, her death ensures that she will have no goods after T. Hence no event that occurs after she dies—that is, after T—is responsible for her failing to have goods she would otherwise have had after T.

I conclude that postmortem events never harm us proactively. However, I am not ready to declare them to be entirely innocuous, as I have yet to consider whether they harm some people retroactively. I will get to that next. First, a recap of the argument I just gave:

1. An event E is responsible for our incurring harm at a time T only if E is overall bad for us at T.
2. So E is responsible for our incurring harm proactively only if E is overall bad for us when E occurs or later.
3. E is overall bad for us when E occurs or later only if E is proactively negative for us.
4. E is proactively negative for us only if either (a) E is responsible for our having intrinsic evils we would not otherwise have had at some time T at or after E's occurrence, or (b) E is responsible for our failing to have intrinsic goods we would otherwise have had at some time T at or after E's occurrence.
5. If E is postmortem, neither (a) nor (b) hold.
6. So no postmortem event harms us proactively.

3. Retroactive Harm

What about it: does retroactive harm exist? Consider the following case:

The Achievement: Suppose I want to conduct research that will lead to a cure for amyotrophic lateral sclerosis, or ALS. Suppose, too, that my desire is essential to my life plan, and that my plan is rational (more about this later). Unfortunately, I will die before a cure is found, but I will still succeed if various events occur, and fail if some other events occur, after I am dead. For example, I will succeed if my research gives another scientist a critical clue that she develops into a cure she otherwise would not have found. And I will fail if all of the records of my research are destroyed in a fire before they prompt another scientist to devise a cure. Upon reflection, I dread the prospect of the fire destroying my files, even though I will be dead at the time it would occur; I judge that it would be against my interests. By contrast I welcome the prospect of my research inspiring a colleague; I judge that it would be in my interests.

I presume that people make these sorts of judgments, and that they are prima facie plausible. Many of us want to accomplish things we consider significant, and

our motives are not (entirely) altruistic. We devote our lives to bringing certain
things about, and we believe that succeeding bears heavily on how good for us our
lives will turn out to be. We consider things that help us succeed to be in our interests, and we regard things that make us fail as against our interests, other things
being equal.

Such judgments are true only if retroactive harm and retroactive benefit
occur, for they imply that certain postmortem events harm me while others
benefit me, and we have seen that postmortem events harm or benefit me, if
at all, only retroactively. Hence the plausibility of the judgments supports the
existence of retroactive harm. However, the support is defeasible; if we cannot
make good sense of retroactive harm, we must give up both the judgments as
well as the claim that retroactive harm exists. So let us see whether we can
make sense of it.

The existence of retroactive harm entails that some events are responsible for
our having intrinsic evils, or failing to have intrinsic goods, at a time that precedes
the events. To make good sense of retroactive harm, we will need to identify the
kind of intrinsic good or evil it involves and the sense in which future events are
"responsible for" our having or lacking such goods or evils.

Of course, retroactive harm is inconsistent with some accounts of value, such
as the following:

> Exclusive hedonism: for any subject S, S's experiencing pleasure at time T is
> the one and only thing that is intrinsically good for S at T; S's experiencing
> pain is the one and only thing that is intrinsically bad for S at T.

(This view is usually called hedonism; I call it *exclusive hedonism* because it
implies that pleasure is the only thing that is intrinsically good for us.) Paired with
comparativism, exclusive hedonism says that it is not bad for me if my research
records burn in a fire, and my life's work ends in failure. It says that no postmortem event whatever benefits or harms me. So why do people fret about such things?
For exclusive hedonists, the explanation must be that achieving things typically
is (extrinsically) good for us, as it is pleasant, so we mistakenly think that any
achievement will be good for us and that events that make us fail are bad for us.
But this explanation is unsatisfactory for two reasons. First, exclusive hedonism
is itself implausible. It faces well-known objections which I will not rehearse here
(for a resourceful defense of hedonism, see Feldman, 2004). Second, it forces us to
reject claims that are prima facie quite plausible, namely, judgments like those in
the achievement case. We should explain them away only if we cannot make sense
of their truth.

The following partial account of value (versions of which are defended by
Scanlon, 1998, and Keller, 2004) may point the way:

> Achievementism: for any subject S, it is intrinsically good for S at time T that,
> at T, S succeeds at something S set out to achieve; it is intrinsically bad for S at
> T that, at T, S fails at something S set out to achieve.

(Achievementism says that achievements are one of the things that are intrinsically good for us; we can use the term exclusive achievementism for the position that achievements are the only things that are intrinsically good for us.) As achievementists, we can explain the judgments in the achievement case this way: I have set out to do research that leads to a cure for ALS; whether or not I succeed depends on postmortem events; if a fellow scientist picks up where I left off, I will achieve what I set out to do; if a fire burns my files, I will fail. Achievements are intrinsically good for me, so the former event is in my interests, while the latter is against my interests.

It might appear that this explanation fails because what I do, what I achieve, depends only on what is directly under my control, and not, for example, on the actions of others. In the achievement case, all I really accomplish is some research; if it leads to a cure, that is the doing of others. However, this criticism seems misguided. It is not uncommon for the things we do to depend crucially on things that are not in our control. Having planned to bring about your death, my pulling the trigger of my gun can be all I need to do directly for my act to constitute killing you. Yet whether you die depends on many other things. I might obtain my objective even if I die well before you do (say because you kill me back). Similarly, my doing my research may be all I need to do directly for my act to constitute "doing research that will lead to a cure for cancer."

Though the preceding objection is unconvincing, achievementism faces others. It is not clear that succeeding at just anything I set out to do is intrinsically good for me. My aims might be irrational. They might also be of no real importance to me, but rather something I take on in order to pass the time. Simon Keller says that accomplishing even trivial and silly things is at least a little bit good in itself (2004). But those who disagree with Keller could easily revise achievementism.

However, even if we draw on an improved version of achievementism, we may be unable to show how retroactive harm is possible, since it is hard to see how something I achieve posthumously can be an intrinsic good I accrue. I accrue goods only while I exist; if I set out to do something, and I succeed with the help of postmortem events, I succeed after I am dead. We are left wondering how I can accrue a good whose existence does not begin until my own is over. (Should we say that my achievement is a good I can accrue before it (fully) exists? Do I take hold of the entire thing by accruing the first part of it, much as I might seize a snake by its tail?)

Perhaps we can tell a clearer story about retroactive harm if we draw on a different account of welfare, according to which it is intrinsically good for us that we get what we want. Assuming that the object of a desire can be expressed in the form of a proposition, we can formulate this view as follows:

> Simple Preferentialism: for any subject S, it is intrinsically good (bad) for S at time T that, at T, S desires P, and P is true (false). The stronger S's desire for P is, the better (worse) it is for S that P is true (false).

A bit of jargon will help me to clarify this account. Call the event that makes a proposition true its "truth maker." For example, the proposition I am now typing is made true by my typing now. This proposition is made true at the very same time as its truth maker occurs; but many propositions are made true at one time by events that occur at some other time. For example, it is true now that I will marry next week, and what makes this true is the marriage that takes place next week. According to simple preferentialism, it is good for me, now, that two things come together: I desire that I will be married next week, and I will be married next week. I accrue this good now, even though the relevant truth maker, my marriage, does not occur until next week. This good is retroactive in the sense that an event that happens after I incur the good is responsible for it. None of this involves backward causation; events that occur at some time make propositions true then or at other times without causing anything to happen.

On this approach, it is easy to make good sense of the judgments in the achievement case: I desire, now, that I will conduct research leading to a cure for ALS; if, in the future, my research causes a colleague to think of a cure, it follows that what I desire is true now, which is good for me now, and I am benefited, now, by an event in the future. If, on the other hand, the records of my research are burned before they prompt another scientist to devise a cure, then what I desire is false now, which is bad for me now, and I am harmed by a future event.

Unfortunately, simple preferentialism is overly simple. Some desires concern the welfare of others; getting what we want for others may be good for them rather than us (Parfit, 1984). Another problem is that, typically, the fact that something is desired has no bearing on whether it is desirable. Friendship is intrinsically good for me whether I desire it or not. A third worry is that it is not intrinsically good to have and meet irrational desires, such as the desire to wash one's hands ten thousand times a day.

It may be possible to close these holes by adopting a version of preferentialism that borrows a bit from achievementism. Let our life plan be our plan for how our life is to go, the shape it is to take. Let the term "achievement desire" refer to any desire to accomplish something. For example, the desire that I will build a rocket is an achievement desire. Finally, if an achievement desire is essential to (or plays a substantial role in) our life plan, let us say that it is one of our essential achievement desires. Now, pack all this into a formulation of preferentialism:

> Strategic Preferentialism: for any subject S, it is intrinsically good for S at time T that, at T, S desires P, S's desire for P is an achievement desire that is essential to S's life plan, and P is true; it is intrinsically bad for S at T that, at T, S desires P, S's desire for P is an achievement desire that is essential to S's life plan, and P is false. The larger the role S's desire plays in S's life plan, the better (worse) it is for S that P is true (false).

Strategic, like simple preferentialism, provides for the possibility of retroactive harm. In the achievement case, my desire to do research leading to a cure for ALS is an achievement desire, and, by hypothesis, it is essential to my life plan. What is more, some later events would determine that I fail, and that would be intrinsically bad for me now while I desire what I do.

How does the new account fare against the objections to simple preferentialism? It handles the worry about desires that only concern others, since it focuses on desires embedded in my plan for my own life. Although these desires might concern others, their being embedded in my life plan entails that they concern me as well, and that fulfilling them is in my interests. (Those who disagree can restrict the account to desires that solely concern the individual whose life plan is in question.)

The second criticism was that the desirableness of things does not hinge on their being desired. Some readers may well reject strategic preferentialism on the strength of this objection. However, in my view the objection is weak. There is no doubt that we may judge something to be valuable for its own sake, and set out to attain it for that reason. We desire it because we judge it to be desirable. But achievements have this peculiarity: their desirability, qua achievements, hinges on their being desired. To achieve is to reach a goal; a goal is a kind of desire (even though not all desires are goals; as Keller notes, having a goal entails intending to attain it); so if reaching some sort of goal is in itself good for us, fulfilling some sort of desire is in itself good for us.

In response to the third criticism, concerning irrational aims, we can emphasize that many frivolous desires (such as obsessive hand washing) are not essential to our life plan, and may even be irrational in that fulfilling them makes it more difficult for us to achieve our plan. Hence, fulfilling such disconnected desires is not intrinsically good. Individuals who occupy themselves with disconnected pursuits, and who take no interest in the shape of their lives as wholes, can be criticized on the grounds that they deny themselves the distinctive kind of intrinsic good envisioned by strategic preferentialism.

However, it is not obvious that this sort of response goes far enough. An entire life plan, as well as an individual desire, might be flawed in various ways. A person might plan her life around silly projects such as counting blades of grass, or eating marbles, and it is not clear that fulfilling such plans is good in itself. To meet this kind of worry, some theorists (such as Rawls, 1971; Brandt, 1979; and Railton, 1986) develop versions of critical preferentialism, according to which the only desires that bear on one's welfare are one's rational aims. Our aims are rational, on this view, if and only if we would retain them after rational scrutiny and under conditions of full information.

It is tempting to combine critical preferentialism with strategic preferentialism; doing so provides us with more resources for resisting criticisms that draw upon bizarre desires. To combine the two accounts, we need only specify that the desires whose fulfillment is intrinsically good for us are achievement desires that are essential to our rational life plan. However, there are good reasons not to replace strategic preferentialism with a critical variant. One is that critical preferentialism itself faces significant objections (see Sobel, 1994; Rosati, 1995; Loeb, 1995; and the replies by Murphy, 1999; some of these criticisms are directed at exclusive critical preferentialism, the view that the only thing that is good for us is the fulfillment of our rational aims). Another is that strategic preferentialism is not as vulnerable as it might at first appear to be. It does not say that the fulfillment of salient desires is the only thing that is intrinsically good for us. Preferentialists can be pluralists; they can say that various things, such as pleasure and friendship, are also intrinsically good for us. Accordingly, they can insist that it is a bad idea to plan one's life exclusively around counting grass blades, even though, for those with this plan, success is intrinsically good. It is good for grass-blade counters to succeed in the one thing they set out to do, but bad for them to limit themselves to such a narrow concern, since they will miss out on other things that are intrinsically good.

Strategic preferentialism also resists an objection, raised by Douglas Portmore, to accounts that imply that whether the fulfillment of a desire is bad for us depends on whether or not that desire is later given up (2007). Such accounts are implausible, Portmore says, since we might vacillate about giving up desires. Portmore also worries about the situation in which we would have given up a desire, but died first: it seems strange to say that fulfilling a desire is good for us if we do not live to give it up. Such worries are not serious. Strategic preferentialism says that fulfilling desires that are essential to our life plans is good for us, and although there is no doubt that, while forming our life plan, we might waffle, and revise as we go, such a plan is apt to be a fairly stable matter. It strikes me as quite plausible to say that if we adopt a goal as a tentative part of our plan, only to abandon that goal in the course of revising our plan, then failing to reach that goal is not bad for us. It is the life plan we ultimately would adopt that determines which achievement desires affect our interests.

Consider a further complication. Earlier, it was assumed that my desire for P is fulfilled at time T (at T I get what I want in desiring P) if I desire P at T and P is true at T. For example, in now desiring that I will marry next week, I now get what I want if it is now true that I will marry next week. There is, however, another view. Perhaps my desire for P is not fulfilled at T unless P's truth maker occurs at T. At issue is which of the following positions is correct:

> Conformist claim: Subject S's desire P is fulfilled at T only if, at T, S desires P and P holds.
> Effectivist claim: Subject S's desire P is fulfilled at T only if, at T, S desires P and P's truth maker occurs.

On the conformist claim, and not on the effectivist claim, it makes sense for the preferentialist to countenance retroactive benefit and harm: conformists can say that if what I desire right now is that I will marry next week, and it is true now that I will marry next week, I get what I want now, even though my marriage has yet to occur.

One problem with the effectivist claim is that not all desires have objects with temporally discrete truth makers (e.g., the desire that some law of nature or mathematical truth holds); for such desires, presumably the conformist claim is more plausible.

But conformism faces objections too. Recall that often the objects of desires are true before the occurrence of the events that make them true. The object of my desire that I will meet with Warren Buffett next week is made true, now, by the meeting which takes place next week. The conformist claim is consistent with the view that we can get what we want in desiring something before our desire's object's truth maker has occurred. However, when people desire something P, they typically just do not think they have gotten what they want until P's truth maker occurs. This suggests that effectivism is correct.

There are at least two good responses to this objection. One is that people who desire P are not satisfied until P's truth maker occurs only because they do not know whether P holds until P's truth maker occurs. Suppose we had a crystal ball that revealed the future, and we spent some time checking to see whether our desires would come true. In time, I suspect, we would come to regard our present desires as fulfilled now if the ball reveals that their objects are made true now by the relevant bits of the future. Now consider

> The Bucket List Wish: Hal has a crystal ball and a bucket list wish: He desires that, sometime before he dies, he will visit France. He consults his orb, and discovers that he will visit France in one year's time. Immediately upon seeing the future, he concludes that he now has what he now wanted.

I would say that Hal is correct, and so would we be in his place. Of course, we must be clear about what it is that we desire. In Hal's place, we desire that we will visit France sometime. In that case, we get what we want right now, before the trip takes place. But we may want other things which we do not get now. For example, we may desire that we are *now visiting* France, and maybe peering out from the top of the Eiffel Tower, or we may want to *have visited* France. We cannot fulfill the desire to *be* in France until we *are* in France. And we cannot fulfill the desire to *have* visited France until the visit is behind us.

A second response to the objection helps confirm the first. Consider the following case:

> The Contest: Today Bart becomes aware of a contest that took place last week. Not knowing who won, he comes to desire that he did. Later he discovers that he won, and concludes that he got what he wanted.

If effectivism were correct, Bart would be mistaken! Effectivism says we get what we want in desiring P only if two things coincide: our desiring P and the occurrence of P's truth maker. For Bart, these things never coincide: the events that make his desire's object true are over and done with long before he forms his desire. Effectivism implies that we cannot get what we want in cases like the Contest, which cannot be right.

By contrast, conformism seems to get things right. Not only can conformists say that Bart got what he wanted; they can tell a plausible story about when Bart got what he wanted. It wasn't when he won the contest, although winning was the event that made his desire's object true. Conformism and effectivism alike rule out that story, since Bart lacked the desire to win at the time he won. Both imply that a desire cannot be fulfilled at a time when it does not exist. According to conformism, he fulfilled his desire after he won; specifically, at the time he desired to have won. We can fulfill a desire concerning the past even though the truth maker of its object occurs in the past, prior to our forming the desire. It suffices that the desire and the truth of its object (and of any requirements on which it is conditional, as will be discussed later) hold simultaneously. Why should the same not be true of desires concerning the future, as in the Bucket List Wish case?

Are there any other grounds for preferring the effectivist claim? Perhaps; it seems to be supported by the fact that our desires are tentative (Luper, 2005); in desiring what we do, we defer to our own future competent judgment in the following way: suppose we desire P now, but later, before P's truth maker or falseness maker occurs, we voluntarily give up the desire. Then we never get what we want, even if P's truth maker eventually occurs. For example, if we now desire to go to Pakistan, but change our minds, we never get what we want in desiring to go to Pakistan—not now and not ever—even if we end up in Pakistan. Our desires are, in this sense, conditional on our not voluntarily giving them up before the truth makers (or falseness makers) of their objects hold. If mere conformity between the desire P and P's truth were what we wanted, dropping our desire in the future would not stop us from getting what we want now. Yet dropping a desire before its truth maker occurs does stop us from getting what we want, which suggests that what we really want is that the truth makers of our desires occur.

In order to meet this objection, I will need to say more about what it is for a desire to be conditional on something. Here is a rough account (which borrows heavily from McDaniel and Bradley, 2008). If I desire to eat at Joe's tonight on the condition that you will come, then my desire is conditional in this way: eating at Joe's gives me what I want, but only if you come, and not eating at Joe's gives me something I do not want, but again, only if you come. If the conformist claim is correct, then, we can adopt the following account of conditionality:

Subject S's desire P is conditional on C if and only if (a) P's truth gives S what S wants only if C holds, and (b) P's falseness gives S what S does not want only if C holds.

Effectivists will prefer the following account of conditionality:

Subject S's desire P is conditional on C if and only if (a) the occurrence of P's truth maker gives S what S wants only if C holds, and (b) the occurrence of P's falseness maker gives S what S does not want only if C holds.

We can now redraw the battle lines over what "getting what we want" entails. Let us stipulate that our desire P is fulfilled if and only if we get what we want in desiring P, and unfulfilled if and only if we get what we do not want in desiring P. On one hand, there is the following position concerning the fulfilling of a desire:

Conformism:
—Subject S's desire P is fulfilled at T if and only if: at T, S desires P, P holds, and, if S desires P on condition C, then C holds.

—S's desire P is unfulfilled at T if and only if: at T, S desires P, P does not hold, and, if S desires P on condition C, then C holds.

On the other hand, proponents of the effectivist claim will insist on the following account:

Effectivism:
—Subject S's desire P is fulfilled at T if and only if: at T, S desires P, P's truth maker occurs, and, if S desires P on condition C, then C's truth maker occurs.
—S's desire P is unfulfilled at T if and only if: at T, S desires P, P's falseness maker occurs, and, if S desires P on condition C, then C's truth maker occurs.

Back to the objection before us, which was that if, in desiring P, we got all we wanted when P holds, then dropping our desire before its truth (or falseness) maker occurred would not prevent us from getting what we want, yet it does, which supports effectivism and, in turn, effectivist conditionalism. We can now see that this objection overlooks the fact that most if not all of our desires are conditional on not being dropped. If, for example, my current desire to go to Pakistan one day is conditional on not being dropped before its truth (or falseness) maker occurs, and later it is dropped, then I never get what I want, not even while I still (conditionally) want to go to Pakistan. Hence, the tentativeness of our desires cannot be cited in favor of effectivism.

This response assumes that we can fulfill a desire now, even though it is conditional on some requirement concerning the future, as long as that requirement is met. But this does not strike me as odd. Consider a different case, where the object and the condition of a desire are made true at distinct times: say we desire to rise before dawn on condition that the fish will be biting later, or we desire to become an activist for some cause, but only on condition that we will not later decide that the cause is unjust. Clearly, we can fulfill these desires. Presumably, we fulfill them when their objects hold (assuming that the fish bite and the cause always seems just). Or, should we say that we do not fulfill a desire at T unless the truth maker of its object and of the requirement upon which it is conditional both occur at T? In that case, absurdly, we cannot get what we want in desiring to rise before dawn: our desire's object's truth maker occurs before dawn, but the truth maker of the requirement upon which it is conditional does not occur until later in the day, and by that time the first truth maker is no longer occurring.

This last point suggests a further response to effectivism: if, as it implies, a desire may be fulfilled only at the time its object's truth maker occurs, then presumably, it may be fulfilled only at the time the truth maker of the requirement upon which it is conditional occurs. But that would mean that we cannot fulfill desires whose objects and conditions have truth makers that never coincide in time. Yet we can. We can fulfill the desire to rise before dawn if the fish will be biting later, even though the object of our desire is made true before dawn, and our desire is conditional on a requirement whose truth maker occurs later. The view left standing is conformism.

(There are, of course, further alternatives to conformism and effectivism, but the ones that come to mind strike me as less plausible than the accounts I have considered. I will briefly comment on a few of these. Conformism and effectivism are consistent in that they focus on the truth of propositions or on the truth makers of propositions, and not both; each of the following alternatives lack such consistency:

> Conformist effectivism: if S's desire for P is conditional on C, then S's desire is fulfilled at T if and only if: at T, S desires P, P holds, and C's truth maker occurs.
> Effectivist conformism: if S's desire for P is conditional on C, then S's desire is fulfilled at T if and only if: at T, S desires P, P's truth maker occurs, and C holds.

Something else that conformism and effectivism take for granted is that the fulfillment of a desire hinges solely on things that are concurrent with that desire; the following account rejects this assumption:

> Antecedent effectivism: if S's desire for P is conditional on C, then S's desire is fulfilled at T if and only if: S desires P at T and, at T or earlier, but not necessarily simultaneously, P's and C's truth makers occur.

If we also abandon the assumption that a desire is fulfilled, if at all, only when it exists, we might consider a further account:

> Detached effectivism: if S's desire for P is conditional on C, then S's desire is fulfilled at T if and only if: P's truth maker occurs at T and, at some time or other, but not necessarily simultaneously, S desires P and C's truth maker occurs.

The first two accounts depart from conformism and effectivism in ways that seem arbitrary. The third, antecedent effectivism, has the implausible consequence that we cannot fulfill desires whose conditions' truth makers occur after the desires cease to exist [e.g., my desire that my money go to Alcoholics Anonymous (AA) after I die, on condition that AA use it wisely]. The last account, detached effectivism, has the strange consequence that a desire may be fulfilled before we form it or after it has ceased to exist.)

Let us apply these points about desire fulfillment to the analysis of welfare. Conformism and effectivism point advocates of preferentialism to different views concerning when desire fulfillment benefits us. For simplicity, I will formulate these views without the complication added by strategic preferentialism:

> Conformist preferentialism: for any subject S, it is intrinsically good for S at T that, at T, S desires P on condition C, C holds, and so does P; it is intrinsically bad for S at T that, at T, S desires P, C holds, and P does not hold.
> Effectivist preferentialism: for any subject S, it is intrinsically good for S at T that, at T, S desires P on condition C, and the truth makers of C and P occur; it is intrinsically bad for S at T that, at T, S desires P, the truth maker of C occurs, and P's falseness maker occurs.

Given that conformism is the better account of desire fulfillment, the preferentialist should prefer conformist preferentialism over effectivist preferentialism. This is important, as the former, unlike the latter, supports the existence of retroactive harm.

4. RETROACTIVE WRONGS

I have argued that retroactive harm exists. Some will say that if I am mistaken, little of consequence follows. We still would have good reason to act on behalf of the dead, for even if nothing we do after people die harms them, it can still wrong them. I think that this view needs more support than it has received. There are various reasons for saying that we may wrong the dead, but the most straightforward one is that we have a prima facie duty to respect, hence fulfill, the desires of self-determining beings, even ones who have died, in at least some matters concerning themselves, and to avoid acting against their interests, except perhaps when that is what they wish. Similarly, when people are alive but no longer competent, we must honor various decisions they reached while competent, such as their decision to forgo various forms of medical treatment (Buchanan and Brock, 1990; a different approach is taken by Barilan, 2010). Unless retroactive harm is possible, this way of defending the possibility of wronging the dead is easy to challenge. Against the claim that we must act in (or at least not against) the interests of someone who has died, there is a case that taps the immunity thesis:

1. If, at time T, nothing we do will further (impair) subject S's interests, then, at T, we are not obligated to further (avoid impairing) S's interests.
2. Nothing we do after S has died will further (impair) S's interests (immunity thesis).
3. So after S has died we are not obligated to further (avoid impairing) S's interests.

And against the claim that we must fulfill the desires of someone who is now demented or dead, there is the following, related, argument:

1. If, at time T, nothing we do will fulfill subject S's desire for P, then, at T, we are not obligated to fulfill S's desire for P.
2. Nothing we do after S has lost the capacity to desire P will fulfill S's desire for P.
3. So after S has lost the capacity to desire P we are not obligated to fulfill S's desire for P.

In this final section I will rebut these arguments, and then briefly argue for the existence of retroactive wrongs.

I doubt that anyone will question the first premises of either argument. Both follow from the truism that "ought" implies "can"—we need not do what we cannot do. Hence each argument is as good as its second premise.

We can immediately reject the first argument, however. It stands or falls on the strength of the immunity thesis, and earlier it was shown that the immunity thesis is false since interests may be furthered (or impaired) retroactively.

So we are down to the second argument. According to effectivism, a desire for P is fulfilled at time T only if two things come together at T: S desires P and P's truth maker occurs. Once S dies, or becomes demented, S's desire for P cannot be fulfilled, even if P's truth maker is made to occur. Hence, if effectivism were correct the second premise would be true. However, it was shown above that conformism is more plausible than effectivism. If conformism is correct, then some desires are fulfilled retroactively.

So much for rebutting the two arguments. Next, let us see if there is positive reason for saying that we wrong some of the people whom we harm retroactively, and that we wrong some of those whose desires we fail to fulfill retroactively.

I assume that, other things being equal, it is morally objectionable to harm anyone. Given this assumption, it is reasonable to conclude that harming others retroactively is prima facie wrong.

I also assume there is a prima facie duty to fulfill the desires of self-determining beings concerning at least some matters concerning themselves, such as the medical treatment they do not wish to receive. And given this assumption, we may infer that there is a duty to fulfill these desires even if it can be done only retroactively.

What we do when we wrong others by harming them, or by thwarting their desires, retroactively, seems well described as retroactive wrongdoing, since the people we wrong become victims before we act. They are wronged before we act, hence they are wronged retroactively. However, there is plenty of ambiguity in the way we use the term "wrong," and it is as natural to say that we wrong others at the time we act as it is to say that we wrong them at the time they incur harm. (Suppose I set up a bomb to injure you a week later: we are similarly torn between saying that I wrong you at the time I act, and at the time, a week later, when you are injured.) We can also speak of timeless wrongdoing. I see no grounds for insisting on one of these ways of speaking rather than the others. The salient point, on which I do insist, is that some of our acts are objectionable because they are responsible for the fact that their victims have unfulfilled desires or lower welfare before the acts are performed. We may as well call these acts *retroactive wrongs*.

An interesting question remains: if we wrong others retroactively, at what time is it appropriate to punish us? It can be tempting to reject the possibility of retroactive wrongdoing on the grounds that, if it exists, we may properly punish people before they perform their objectionable acts (an argument like this is given by Callahan, 1987). But that response is simplistic. The proper timing of punishment is a complicated topic, and it is entirely possible to acknowledge the existence of retroactive wrongdoing yet deny that it is ever appropriate to punish people before they act improperly (Taylor, 2008). For example, one might argue that punishment for any wrongful act is appropriate only after the act is performed since only then will it be known that someone has acted improperly. (But what if, per impossible, it were known that we will do something in the future that wrongfully harms someone now—or in the future?)[1]

NOTES

1. I thank Ben Bradley for helpful comments on a previous draft of this chapter.

REFERENCES

Barilan, Michael. 2010. "Ethics of Anatomy." In *The Encyclopedia of Applied Ethics.* 2nd ed. Ruth Chadwick, editor, pp. 116–126. Amsterdam: Elsevier Press.

Belshaw, Chris. 2009. *Annihilation: The Sense and Significance of Death.* Durham, NC: Acumen Press.

Bradley, Ben. 2004. "When Is Death Bad for the One Who Dies?" *Noûs* 38: 1–28.

Bradley, Ben. 2009. *Well-Being and Death.* Oxford: Oxford University Press.

Brandt, Richard. 1979. *A Theory of the Good and the Right.* Oxford: Clarendon Press.

Buchanan, A. E., and D. W. Brock. *Deciding for Others: The Ethics of Surrogate Decision-Making.* New York: Cambridge University Press.

Callahan, Joan. 1987. "On Harming the Dead." *Ethics* 97 (2): 341–352.

Feldman, Fred. 1991. "Some Puzzles about the Evil of Death." *Philosophical Review* 100 (2): 205–227. Reprinted in Fischer, 1993, pp. 307–326.

Feldman, Fred. 1992. *Confrontations with the Reaper.* New York: Oxford University Press.

Feldman, Fred. 2004. *Pleasure and the Good Life: Concerning the Nature, Varieties, and Plausibility of Hedonism.* New York: Oxford University Press.

Fischer, J. M., ed., 1993. *The Metaphysics of Death.* Palo Alto, CA: Stanford University Press.

Keller, Simon. 2004. "Welfare and the Achievement of Goals." *Philosophical Studies* 121: 27–41.

Korsgaard, Christine. 1983. "Two Distinctions in Goodness." *Philosophical Review* 92: 169–195.

Loeb, Don. 1995. "Full-Information Theories of Individual Good." *Social Theory and Practice* 21(1): 1–30.

Luper, Steven. 2005. "Past Desires and the Dead." *Philosophical Studies* 126 (3): 331–345.

Luper, Steven. 2007. "Mortal Harm." *Philosophical Quarterly* 57: 239–251.

Luper, Steven. 2009a. *The Philosophy of Death.* Cambridge: Cambridge University Press.

Luper, Steven. 2009b. Review of Ben Bradley, *Well-Being and Death.* Notre Dame Philosophical Reviews. URL = ndpr.nd.edu/news/24085-well-being-and-death/.

McDaniel, Kris, and Bradley, Ben. 2008. "Desires." *Mind* 117: 267–302.

Murphy, Mark. 1999. "The Simple Desire-Fulfillment Theory." *Noûs* 33(2): 247–272.

Nagel, Thomas. 1970. "Death." *Noûs* 4 (1): 73–80.

Parfit, Derek. 1984. *Reasons and Persons.* Oxford: Clarendon Press.

Pitcher, George. 1984. "The Misfortunes of the Dead." *American Philosophical Quarterly* 21 (2): 217–225. Reprinted in Fischer, 1993, pp. 119–134.

Portmore, Douglas. 2007. "Desire Fulfillment and Posthumous Harm." *American Philosophical Quarterly* 44: 27–38.

Railton, Peter. 1986. "Facts and Values." *Philosophical Topics* 14: 5–31.

Rawls, John. 1971. *A Theory of Justice.* Cambridge, MA: Harvard University Press.

Rosati, Connie. 1995. "Persons, Perspective, and Full Information Accounts of the Good." *Ethics* 105: 296–325.

Scanlon, Thomas. 1998. *What We Owe to Each Other.* Cambridge, MA: Harvard University Press.

Sobel, David. 1994. "Full Information Accounts of Well-Being." *Ethics* 104: 784–810.

Taylor, James. 2008. "Harming the Dead." *Journal of Philosophical Research* 33: 185–202.

CHAPTER 15

IMMORTALITY

JOHN MARTIN FISCHER

If one lives intensely, the time comes when sleep means bliss. If one loves intensely, the time comes when death seems bliss... The life I want is a life I could not endure in eternity. It is a life of love and intensity, suffering and creation that makes life worthwhile and death welcome.

—(Kaufman, 1963, p. 372)

No animal endowed with much power of memory ought to live forever, or could want to, I should maintain; for the longer it lives, the more that just balance between novelty and repetition, which is the basis of zest and satisfaction, must be upset in favor of repetition, hence of monotony and boredom. Old animals and old people, in principle (exceptions are in degrees only) are bored animals and bored people. This is not essentially a glandular or circulatory phenomenon. It is psychological: one has felt and done most of the things that must be felt and done so many times before.

As Jefferson wrote to a friend: "I am tired of putting my clothes on every morning and taking them off every evening." Thus, he concluded, the Creator prepares us for death. Thus indeed. That many old people are spry and eager only proves that their chronological age gives but a rough index of psychological age. Thus all complaint against death itself seems misguided. Death is needed for the solution of an aesthetic problem, how memory is to be reconciled with zest.

—(Hartshorne, 1958, p. 387)

1. INTRODUCTION

Since the inception of philosophy, we have been interested in questions about death and immortality. In this "overview" paper, I will begin by distinguishing various different notions of immortality. I will then present three challenges to the idea that any kind of immortality could be appealing to us. These challenges come in part from a classic article by Bernard Williams (1973, reprinted in Fischer, ed., 1993, pp. 71–92), but they are also raised by various other philosophers. In this discussion I will focus primarily on a certain salient kind of immortality; antecedently, this sort of immortality would seem to be most promising candidate to present itself as choiceworthy (were it feasible) or, at least, appealing to human beings. I shall then sketch various ways of responding to the challenges. I shall defend the contention that certain kinds of immortality could be appealing to human beings; that is, I shall argue against the view of the Immortality Curmudgeons that immortality (in any of its forms) is necessarily not of any positive value (or in any way appealing) to human beings.

2. VARIOUS KINDS OF IMMORTALITY

One might think that immortality is simply living forever. But, as usual in philosophy, the issues are a bit more complicated. First, one might distinguish between actually living forever (but with the possibility of dying) and necessarily living forever (that is, living forever without the possibility of dying). As far as I know, the first philosopher to make this distinction in print was H. Steele, who made the distinction between "contingent body-bound immortality" and "necessary body-bound immortality" (Steele, 1976; also, see Burley, 2009a). A second distinction has to do with the immortal individual's epistemic status, and it cuts across the first distinction. That is, it is possible that one be either contingently or necessarily immortal and not know it; it is also possible that one indeed knows that one is immortal (either contingently or necessarily). For the purposes of this paper, I will focus primarily on necessary immortality in which the individual knows that he is necessarily immortal; one might call this "robust immortality," although I will generally dispense with this term and simply use "immortality."

Many different kinds of immortality have been discussed in literature and philosophy. (For a taxonomy and discussion, see Fischer and Curl, 1996, reprinted in Fischer, ed., 2009, pp. 93–102.) Some conceptions of immortality are "nonatomistic"; they posit the fusion of the individual with another individual or individuals. In contrast, I shall fix on "atomistic" conceptions of immortality. Whereas some atomistic conceptions of immortality appear to involve "serial" lives (such as in certain Hindu and Buddhist conceptions of reincarnation), of greater interest to me in this piece will be atomistic, nonserial conceptions.

Even so, there are many different ways of conceptualizing such immortality. I shall assume that the immortality in question is bodily immortality. Additionally, I assume that the individual in question is biologically "frozen" at some age understood as the biological "prime of life." Bernard Williams took this to be age forty-two (which was his age when he delivered the lecture at Berkeley that was the basis for Williams, 1973). Williams says, "If one had to spend eternity at any age, that seems an admirable age to spend it at" (Williams, in Fischer, ed., 1993, p. 81). It is interesting that Todd May chooses a rather earlier age as relevant—early to mid-thirties (May, 2009). Indeed, May says, "For some, this might be too old: mid-twenties may capture the point of physical and intellectual peak" (May, 2009, p. 55). The point is to imagine that by some means or another one is in possession of one's biological features and capacities at a relatively healthy point, and although one of course ages chronologically, one does not "age" biologically. (This does not imply that one is not subject to the consequences of risky choices, which may indeed result in temporary or even permanent physical consequences. One might worry that if physical injury is possible, then, given an infinite period of time, it would be highly likely that one would become crippled to the point of incapacity. I don't have the space here to address such worries adequately; one could however imagine the possibility of regeneration of biological health after a certain period of diminished capacity.)

The fact that one would not be subject to biological aging and deterioration is obviously important. Although there are different versions of the myth, in the ancient Greek myth of Tithonus, the youth is granted eternal life but, lamentably, not eternal youth. Similarly, in *Gulliver's Travels*, Jonathan Swift depicts the struldbrugs as immortal but subject to biological aging. The struldbrugs begin their biological decay at around age thirty, and this eventually leads to blindness and other maladies of old age. Reflections on Tithonus and the struldbrugs should make it evident that an immortality that involves biological aging and deterioration would be anything but desirable.

In what follows I shall focus mainly on robust immortality of the atomistic, nonserial sort in which the individual somehow is ensured eternal "youth"; that is, the individual is biologically in the prime of life, is healthy, and does not deteriorate biologically over time. It is plausible that this sort of immortality is the best candidate for being of value to human beings. Also, I shall assume that the individual knows, not just that he will necessarily live forever, but also that his immortality is atomistic and that he will not be subject to biological aging.

3. THREE CHALLENGES TO THE APPEAL OF IMMORTALITY

It will be helpful to employ Bernard Williams's framework for analyzing the potential desirability or value to humans of immortality, supplemented by an additional challenge. More specifically, Williams can be interpreted as posing two challenges to the appeal or value of immortality for human beings. (Williams, 1973; for discussion, see Fischer, 1994; and Fischer and Curl, 1996) These two challenges might be taken to presuppose two conditions on the appeal to us of any proposed conception of immortal existence: the identity condition and the attractiveness condition. Williams's view is that any proposed story that purportedly presents (say) my immortal existence must fail to satisfy at least one of these conditions: either the story does not depict the life of an individual who is genuinely identical to me, or it does not depict an attractive life.

I believe that it is analytically helpful to introduce a third condition: the "recognizability" condition. That is, many philosophers object to certain depictions of immortality as not presenting the story of an individual who is leading a "recognizably human life." This sort of objection might be thought to fit under either Williams's identity challenge or his attractiveness challenge. For the purposes of this paper, I will break the challenges into three: identity, recognizability, and attractiveness. So the Immortality Curmudgeon is here interpreted as contending that any story purporting to present my immortal existence either does not tell my story, or it does not tell the story of any human being at all, or the life it depicts is not attractive to me (although arguably it is the story of a recognizably human being: me).

Let us begin with the challenge to the identity condition. With respect to what appears to be a version of this condition, Williams says:

> The state in which I survive should be one that, to me looking forward, will be adequately related, in the life it presents, to those aims I now have in wanting to survive at all. That is a vague formula, and necessarily so, for what exactly that relation will be must depend to some extent on what kind of aims and (as one might say) prospects for myself I now have. What we can say is that since I am propelled forward into longer life by categorical desires, what is promised must hold out some hopes for those desires…at least this seems demanded, that any image I have of those future desires should make it comprehensible to me how in terms of my character they could be my desires. (Williams in Fischer, ed., 1993, p. 85)

The concern then is that in an infinite life, it is plausible that one's "categorical desires"—desires that propel one forward and are not simply conditional on continuing to live (such as the desire to be wellnourished if one continues to live, and so forth)—will change substantially (and, presumably, entirely). If an individual depicted in a story of infinitely long life has substantially or completely different categorical desires from mine now, how can this be my story? Why would I care especially about this individual (in the way in which we care especially about ourselves?

The second challenge—or set of challenges—comes from the worry that any story of an individual who lives an infinitely long life would not be the story of an individual who is recognizably human—sufficiently similar to us that we can understand the life as "human." (Of course, a positive answer to the identity challenge would entail a positive answer to the recognizability challenge, but not vice versa.) Williams suggests a version of the recognizability worry when he contends that EM (Elina Makropulos, who has taken an elixir of eternal life and is "now" chronologically 342 years old) might lack any coherent character at all. (EM is a character in a story originally presented in a 1922 play by Karel Čapek, *The Makropulos Case*, and also told in a 1926 opera by Leos Janacek) That is, if the categorical desires are not allowed to change over time, her character is in danger of falling apart or disintegrating. If the categorical desires are allowed to change, then we are back to the identity problem sketched above.)

But there are various other worries that can arguably be considered versions of the recognizability challenge. Some have argued that aspects of the content of our lives depend precisely on the fact that our lives are finite; on this view, a life without borders would be "indeterminate" or "formless" (Heidegger, 1927; May, 2009) Perhaps a related worry is that our lives are structured essentially by anxieties (either conscious or unconscious) about death. One might say that our lives are in this way fraught (May, 2009). If the possibility of death is taken away, arguably this also changes the fundamental experiential nature of our lives—and perhaps our deepest values as well (Nussbaum, 1994, 1999, and forthcoming).

Similarly, some have contended that our lives are "narratives" and that narratives must have endings; these philosophers conclude that since the accounts of infinite lives could not have endings, these accounts would not be "narratives," strictly speaking (May, 2009, pp. 70–72). Finally, some philosophers have simply pointed out that infinity is fundamentally different from finite magnitudes, and thus we cannot extrapolate from features of finite lives to those of infinite lives (Burley, 2009a). They would point out that, even if certain features would obtain in very, very long finite lives, there is no guarantee that they would obtain in infinite lives. We might then worry that we cannot even get a grasp on infinite lives; we cannot understand them well enough even to judge whether they are recognizably human.

A final challenge puts aside all the "recognizability" worries and simply posits that an infinitely long life would necessarily be unattractive. Perhaps the most salient version of this worry comes from Williams, who suggests that even if EM can be understood to have a determinate and recognizably human character, she would inevitably become hopelessly bored and alienated over the course of time. He says about EM:

> Her trouble was, it seems, boredom: a boredom connected with the fact that everything that could happen and make sense to one particular human being of 42 had already happened to her. Or, rather, all the sorts of things that could make sense to one woman of a certain character. (Williams, in Fischer, ed., 1993, p. 82)

Williams's argument in defense of the necessary unattractiveness claim is (roughly) a trilemma. Over time in an immortal life, the individual will either change his or her character (and categorical desires), or not. If the former, then evidently the story will not meet the identity criterion. If the latter, there are two possibilities. If experience does not affect the individual, he or she will become alienated and completely disengaged from life. But if one is indeed affected by experience without the possibility of that experience changing one's basic character, one will inevitably become bored.

4. The Identity Challenge

On Williams's view, we are propelled into the future by "categorical desires"—such as the desire to raise a family, write a book, help the needy, save the planet from environmental destruction, make a fortune, find a true love, master the Goldberg Variations, and so forth. These are distinguished from "conditional desires," such as the desire to be healthy, if alive, and so forth. Williams claims that it is the thwarting of categorical desires that makes death a bad thing for an individual who dies; thus, he contends that a life without any categorical desires would not be worth living. But equally problematic, it might seem, would be a future in which the categorical desires have changed substantially or even completely. Williams contends that a story of an individual with substantially different categorical desires would not be a story of me in a sense relevant to my special concern for my own future.

But the issues here are complicated. Suppose I now like to "challenge" myself in lots of ways—in work as well as hobbies. For example, I undertake many challenging commitments to write, lecture, and travel all across the world, and in my spare time I pursue "extreme sports," such as rock climbing and skydiving as well as world travel to exotic destinations. (The reader will note that this is obviously an entirely hypothetical scenario!) Even so, I might recognize that over time my preferences will change, so that toward the end of my career and life I will wish to be much more "conservative," undertaking less travel, fewer challenging commitments, and so forth. This is entirely "normal," and it does not in any way etiolate my concern for my future, so envisaged. I can also entertain the possibilities that I will undergo significant and even radical changes in my ethical, political, and religious beliefs without diminishing my current concern for my future self. If this is the situation in a finite life, why not also in an immortal life (Fischer, 1994)?

Employing the terminology of Frederik Kaufman, we might distinguish between the "thick self" and the "thin self" (Kaufman, 1999 and 2000). The thick self includes the categorical desires, whereas the thin self does not. One might think of the thick self as similar to the "moral self" or "moral personality" in the literature on autonomy, whereas the thin self is more like the "metaphysical self" (a self that can persist through changes in personality). Kaufman argues that invoking the distinction between thick and thin selves can help us to explain the intuitive asymmetry in our attitudes toward prenatal and posthumous nonexistence. On his view, we care about living longer than we actually do because we can envisage the thick self continuing at least for some period; but we are indifferent to having been born significantly earlier because the thick self could not have come into existence significantly earlier. After all, any individual who came into existence significantly earlier than I did would not have been me, thickly construed. (Here I will not pause to evaluate the inference from the previous sentence to the clause just before it; but, as I (and my coauthor) have argued elsewhere, the second sentence—with the merely subjunctive "would not"—does not entail the first—with "could not": Fischer and Speak, 2000). And note that this approach to the asymmetry problem seems to apply nicely to the identity worry. If we care about our thick selves, and if immortal life would inevitably cause a substantial or total change in our thick selves, then we would not wish to be immortal—the focus of our care would neces- sarily be extinguished.

But elsewhere I have argued against the thesis that our commonsense asym- metry in attitudes between prenatal and posthumous nonexistence can be explained by reference to the contention that we care only about our thick selves (and that our thick selves could not have come into being significantly earlier) (Fischer and Speak, 2000; and Fischer, 2006b). Note, for instance, that an indi- vidual adopted as an infant might regret that he was not raised by his biological parents; but this regret cannot be accommodated on the view that we only care about our thick selves. Also, it does not seem fundamentally confused (in the way envisaged by the proponents of the thick self view) to regret not having lived in a different era entirely. In these cases it seems that we can coherently care about our thin selves; our regret is that our thin selves did not get "filled out" in certain ways.

And a similar point would seem to apply to the identity challenge. That is, if I am correct in supposing that I can indeed care about my future self, even when I envisage significant (or even total) changes in my categorical desires, then it seems, again, that I do not only care only about my thick self. Arguably, I care about my thin self—my metaphysical self—in that special way that I care about my own future. This would appear to diffuse the identity challenge, insofar as it is based on the notions that I only care about my thick self that over time my thick self (cat- egorical desires) will change significantly.

It might, however, be helpful to pause to make a distinction here. That is, we should distinguish between the special way in which I care about my own future and its being the case that that future is desirable. I suppose that a proponent of a version of the identity challenge could concede that it is possible to care in the special way about the thin self, but still not deem it desirable to continue as a mere thin or "bare" self through significant changes of categorical desires. (This then pushes the objection toward the "attractiveness challenge.") But, as I contended above, we do appear to identify with, care about, and also judge desirable futures in which our categorical desires change considerably. It may be that what mat- ters to us is that these changes take place "organically," as it were, or via certain processes, rather than others. For example, one might feel the challenge strongly if one envisages that the changes in categorical desires are brought about via unconsented-to brainwashing, subliminal advertising, and even direct manipula- tion of the brain. But the crucial point is that it would be dialectically infelicitous to extrapolate from these special cases to the general claim that we would not ever find it desirable that our thin self continue to live through significant thick-self changes. That is, it is does not follow from the undesirability of such scenarios that we could not judge it desirable to live infinitely long lives, where our categori- cal desires are envisaged as changing organically (or even via certain radical and abrupt conversion experiences).

5. The Recognizability Challenge

In a sense, the recognizability challenge is even more "basic" than the identity challenge, since it contends that no story of an immortal life could be the story of a recognizable human life (much less the story of me). So if a story fails to meet the recognizability challenge, then (simply in virtue of this failure) it could not meet the identity or attractiveness challenges. The recognizability worry comes in different forms, and it will be helpful to address them individually.

5.1 Borders and Content

Some would argue that, in various more specific ways, an infinitely long life would lack the borders that define human life as we know it. One version of this worry makes the point that in general a thing is what it is at least in part because of its borders. So a particular sculpture is what it is in part because of its borders, a particular carpet is what it is because of its borders, and so forth. If one expands the borders of the carpet, one presumably generates a different carpet; and it might be argued that at a certain point, the imaginative expansion yields no carpet at all. Similarly, many have thought that an infinitely long life simply could not have any determinate content—it would not be a life of an individual human being at all. Todd May gives particularly vivid expression to this worry:

> For humans, an immortal life would be shapeless. It would be without borders or contours. Its colour would fade, and we could anticipate the fading from the outset. An immortal life would be impossible to make my life, or your life. Because it would drag on endlessly, it would, sooner or later, just be a string of events lacking all form. It would become impossible to distinguish background from foreground. (May, 2009, pp. 68–69)

Not so fast, though! First, note that extending one dimension of an object or process to infinity does not imply extending all dimensions similarly. So, for example, one can presumably imagine an infinitely long electrocardiogram (Fischer, 2006a). From the fact that its "horizontal dimension" extends to infinity, it does not follow that at any particular time the electrocardiogram is amorphous. There are objects and processes that can have a determinate shape, even though (say) one dimension goes to infinity, and from the fact that we allow one dimension to extend to infinity, it does not follow that we must allow all the dimension to extend similarly.

Now, it may well be the case that, for some kinds of objects, a change in any ofthe borders of a particular object of that kind will imply that it is a different particular object. So, presumably a change in the borders of a particular sculpture—especially a change of a significant sort—will result in a different particular sculpture. Further, I doubt whether we would even have a sculpture (or, say, a carpet), if any of its spatial boundaries were allowed to extend infinitely. But it does not follow that all objects and processes are similar in this respect. For example, the set of positive integers has various determinate features, although it is infinitely large. So it would be a spurious transition to extrapolate from (say) carpets and sculptures to (for example) electrocardiograms and human lives.

Think of the dialectic this way. Arguably, at least, there are things and processes that can have determinate structure or content while having aspects or dimensions that are infinite. There are other objects that, by their very nature, arguably cannot have certain infinite aspects or dimensions while maintaining their integrity. The question then becomes whether life is in the first or second subclass. Given this way of conceptualizing matters, it would clearly be dialectically unfair to note that there are things such as sculptures and carpets that appear to fall into the second subclass and then precipitously to conclude that life could not have an infinitely long temporal dimension! That would indeed be too fast. Of course, this way of framing the dialectic presupposes that there might indeed be some things or processes that have at least one infinite dimension but still have determinate structure or content; my point is simply that does not follow from the existence of examples that appear to fall into the subclass that does not admit of infinity along one dimension that all cases must be similar in this respect. (For a similar analysis of the dialectic concerning whether death can be a bad thing for an individual despite not involving unpleasant experiences, see Fischer, 1997.)

5.2 Human Lives Are Fraught

This worry comes in various specific forms. Sometimes it is put in terms of the essential nature of human experience. The idea here is that it is essential to our experience of life (in any recognizably human life) that we are aware—either consciously or somehow unconsciously—of its finitude. The possibility of death "haunts" us—either explicitly or implicitly. In the absence of this quality of being "fraught," life would lose its preciousness—its urgency and its intense beauty (as well, perhaps, as its capacity for poignant tragedy.) Without this structural feature of human experience, it might seem that we would not have genuinely human experience. Todd May gives more concrete expression to this sort of worry as follows:

> We learn as we grow older that one cannot be everything one wants to be. One must make choices. I would have liked to be a novelist, and have even written a couple of manuscripts. However, I could not become a novelist and a philosopher, and circumstances led me towards the latter. All of us, at some point or another, let go of futures we have envisaged for ourselves...
>
> If we were immortal, we would not face those choices. Our lives would not be constrained by the choices we do make, because we would be able to make others. I could be a philosopher and then be a novelist. I could ride a bike from New York to Arizona, as I once hoped I would...In this sense, it would eliminate one of the great sadnesses of life: regret. It would not eliminate all regret, of course. I could still, for instance, do things to others that I would come to regret. However, there is a certain and devastating kind of regret that immortality would eliminate ...associated with who or what one tried to become or, better, allowed oneself to try to become. To fail to become something one works or trains or educates oneself

for is a disappointment. But it pales in comparison to the regret of wondering whether one could have been that if one had only taken one's chances.

If we were immortal, we would not be subject to those regrets.... There would always be time to try something.... Personal relationships would change as well. They would become less serious, since less would be at stake. The bonds between parents and children would probably slacken if children were no long dependent on their parents for survival.... The same would be true of friendships. The activities I perform with a friend, the confidences I share, the vulnerability I display, the competition we provide for each other: all these things could still happen, but their significance would be diminished by the limitations my immortality places on my ability to sacrifice for him. Moreover, given an infinite amount of time, there would always be the possibility of the same kind of friendship with someone else: if not sooner, then later. There would always be time. (May, 2009, pp. 60–63)

Similarly, Martha Nussbaum states:

[T]he intensity and dedication with which very many human activities are pursued cannot be explained without reference to the awareness that our opportunities are finite, that we cannot choose these activities indefinitely many times. In raising a child, in cherishing a lover, in performing a demanding task of work or thought or artistic creation, we are aware, at some level, of the thought that each of these efforts is structured and constrained by time. (Nussbaum, 1994, p. 229)

Nussbaum has also emphasized the importance of finitude and death for human values. In particular, certain virtues—such as courage—seem to be defined at least in part by the way in which the individual confronts the possibility of death (Nussbaum, 1994, 1999, and forthcoming).

But I am not entirely convinced that such considerations show that an immortal life could not be recognizably human in the relevant respects. Start with a virtue such as courage. Why exactly is death (or an awareness of the possibility of death) required for courage? Why couldn't one show courage in the face of a whole range of terrible dangers, such as pain, dismemberment and/or disability, separation, loneliness, depression, and so forth? Courage, it seems to me, involves persistence despite an awareness of significant danger; but I do not think the dangers in question need to include death. Of course, for an immortal being the precise ways in which courage would be instantiated might well not be the same ways in which courage actually is instantiated in our finite lives. But it does not follow that the relevant behavior would not be courage (that is, it would not follow that the behavior would not instantiate the crucial feature of persistence in light of danger). I could contend that similar considerations apply to the other virtues.

One might also ask why human life would inevitably lose its urgency and beauty if one were immortal. Certain tasks do not lose their difficulty in an immortal life—it would still be extraordinarily difficult to write a great novel or a lovely poem, to paint a beautiful picture, to establish decisively that causal determinism is compatible with moral responsibility, to master Bach's Two-Part Inventions, or to run a four-minute mile (to name just a few tasks). Merely having more time does not make any of these tasks easy; also, to accomplish any challenging task would still be rewarding, even in an immortal life. With respect to other tasks, the bar might well go up in an immortal life. Given higher expectations that come with the opportunity for more attempts or more experience and skill, challenges will certainly remain.

Now, as May contends, in an immortal life at least we can sincerely try everything we truly care about. (Of course, as Jens Johansson has pointed out to me, we must believe that the actions in question are available to us; so, for example, I cannot try to be the first to swim the English Channel, insofar as I know that someone else has already done so.) I certainly grant that immortality would not be just like our finite lives. In an infinite life perhaps we can indeed try everything (or everything that might matter to us). Butthere would still be many and robust opportunities for failure in implementing our attempts. It does seem that an immortal life could be filled with challenges that would render it on balance sufficiently similar to finite life that we would deem it recognizably human.

Various features of our personal relationships would not change, under the assumption of immortality. Imagine that one is deeply in love with someone. Although one can certainly try to have a close and rewarding relationship with her, it takes two to tango, as they say. Further, the mere addition of an infinite amount of time does not diminish the pain, frustration, and loneliness attendant upon rejection; nor, if my own past experience is any guide, does it make it very likely that the rejections will (even eventually) turn into embraces. More time might simply provide more opportunities for rejection, separation, and despair. Further, we human beings seem to be acutely sensitive to what is going on with us now; arguably, we also are keenly attuned to what we take will happen to us in the future. But the mere thought—even if I had it—that eventually (say, after four hundred thousand years or a million years) my beloved will accept me (for awhile) does not provide much comfort to me now. If one is in pain or depression now, it is hardly comforting to know that eventually and given enough time one will feel better. We human beings are, as it were, psychologically attuned to the present and relatively near future. (Of course, someone might contend that this attunement is an artifact of our mortality. A less sketchy defense of my suggestion here would require serious consideration of the possibility that our psychological attunements would change under very different conditions, such as immortality.)

Even in an infinite life, there could be very long stretches in which I don't have what I want—I am separated from someone I love, I have not accomplished something I have set out to accomplish, and so forth. And there is no guarantee that the mere addition of more time will rectify the situation (or do so without bringing new challenges). In these ways infinite life would be no different from finite life. Also, I do not see any reason to suppose that the mere fact of infinitely long life would imply that my choices and actions at a particular time (or during a stretch of time) would not rule out other choices or close off other possibilities (including possibilities of relationships) at that time or into the foreseeable future. Granted: immortal life would not be just like finite life. But it is a mistake to leap to the conclusion that it would not be sufficiently similar to finite life to count as recognizably human. Although the challenges would be different in certain ways, they would, no doubt, reemerge in new forms.

5.3 Our Lives Are Narratives

Some have claimed that human lives are—or correspond to—narratives, and, as such, they cannot be infinitely long. According to this view, an essential feature of a narrative is that it has an ending; indeed, the distinctive kind of illumination provided by a narrative involves a resolution or a holistic grasping of the totality of the relevant sequence of events. We might say that a narrative provides totalizing illumination, and there can be no such illumination of an endless sequence. Stories must have endings, and thus immortal lives cannot be stories (strictly speaking). If being—or corresponding to—a narrative is essential to human life, then an immortal life could not be recognizably human.

One might, however, distinguish various features of narratives; it might be that immortal lives have some but not all such features, and in virtue of possessing some features of narratives, immortal lives could be sufficiently similar to finite human lives (although, as noted above, not just like finite human lives). Since immortal lives extend infinitely, their depiction cannot have endings, and thus such lives will not have an important feature of narratives. But I contend that an immortal life can have another of the crucial features of narrativity—a distinctive kind of "meaning holism."

In a narrative, an event gets its meaning from its relationships to other events in certain distinctive ways. The meaning of an event is not fixed and immutable, but it can change as the narrative develops in virtue of its relationships to subsequent events in the sequence; similarly, the meaning of an event in a narrative is in part a function of the event's relationships to prior events. So, for example, a difficult period in a marriage might be a "deadweight loss" if nothing positive comes of it; alternatively, if one or both members of the couple learn from the difficult time, it can have quite a different meaning. In general, when one learns from or grows as a person as a result of a putative misfortune, the meaning of the "misfortune" is transformed. Also, flourishing as a result of one's own hard work might well have a different meaning from the same flourishing that occurs as a result of a windfall (such as winning the lottery.) Similarly, subsequent events can vindicate a risky decision (or course of action) or exhibit it to have been wrong (Velleman, 1991; and Fischer, 1999).

Infinitely long lives could then be conceptualized as similar to (say) a series of novels (sets of interlocking stories) (Fischer, 2005). For instance, consider your favorite series of detective novels or even J. K. Rowling's *Harry Potter* series. Also, think of television "soap operas," which are frequently referred to as "stories"; my grandmother used to excuse herself to go and watch she called "her story"—a TV soap opera. Nowadays, most successful (dare one say "good"?) television shows are essentially soap operas (in the sense that they feature a relatively stable set of characters who develop over time through an interlocking set of stories): *Six Feet Under, Curb Your Enthusiasm, The Sopranos, The Office, Arrested Development, Mad Men*, and so forth. A series of interlocking stories—short stories, novels, television shows—can exhibit the sort of meaning holism that is distinctive of narrativity. My contention is that an infinitely long life could exhibit exactly this sort of meaning holism, even in the absence of the possibility of totalizing illumination. Thus it might well be the case that immortal life could have enough similarity to finite human life to be recognizably human. Even though it would not have all the elements of narrativity, it could have an important and central feature of narrativity. Thus, granting (for the sake of this discussion) that narrativity is essential to human life, immortal life could still be sufficiently similar to finite human life, even if not just like our ordinary, finite human lives.

5.4 Infinity Is Fundamentally Different

Some have highlighted the fact—and it is indisputably a fact—that infinite magnitudes are in important ways different from finite magnitudes. They have concluded that immortality would be fundamentally different from even very long finite life. Perhaps their conclusion is epistemic: given that infinity is fundamentally different, we cannot know that immortal life would be sufficiently like finite life to render it recognizably human.

Various versions of this sort of worry can be distinguished. I shall begin by focusing on what I take to be a problematic version. Mikel Burley gives a clear expression of it here:

> It seems reasonable to suppose that a proper judgment about the desirability of a life requires, as a minimal condition, the possibility of conceiving of that life in its entirety, rather than just some portions of it. With the possible exception of some mathematical contexts, it seems to make no sense to speak of completed infinite series. As many philosophers, from Aristotle to Kant to Wittgenstein, have pointed out, while we can make sense of the notion of a potentially infinite series—and hence of a process that could, in principle, be continued without end—there is nothing that could count as an infinite series that has reached its completion, for an infinite series is, precisely, a series that never reaches a point of completion: it just goes on and on forever. So if one agrees that a necessary condition of being able to assess the desirability of a life is that the life be conceivable as a whole, then it looks as though such an assessment cannot be made in the case of a putative immortal life (2009a, p. 539).

Burley goes on to emphasize what he takes to be a crucial difference between our finite lives and purportedly immortal lives:

> [I]n the case of a finite life, even if we have only limited information available to us, we could in principle acquire a fully rounded picture of the life in question, and could thus reach a well-informed judgement about the desirability of that life. In the case of a purportedly infinite life, by contrast, we could not acquire such a picture even in principle, since there is nothing that could count as a "fully-rounded" picture of an endless life. (2009a, p. 540)

Here the "fundamental difference" between finite life and purportedly immortal life flows from our manifest inability to conceive of an immortal life as a whole. But I do not know why we would need to conceive of immortal life as a whole, in order to judge such life as recognizably human. It might be that Burley is pointing to the impossibility of totalizing illumination in an immortal life; whereas I am willing to concede this point, I argued above that it is not clear that the possibility of such illumination is required to render a life recognizably human.(After all, such a life could still be importantly like a narrative in possessing meaning-holism.) Note that, on my view, "totalizing illumination" need not involve complete knowledge of all details of a life; rather, it involves a certain distinctive kind of "resolution" that can only come from conceiving the life as a whole.

Further, note that at any point in an immortal life, the individual has not yet lived for an infinite number of years. The important insight here flows from a distinction that is implicit in Burley's formulation above; that is, it is illuminating to distinguish between a potentially infinite series and an actually infinite series. (This distinction is also important in the discussions of the Kalam Version of the Cosmological Argument.) With the distinction in hand, we should notice that at any given point in even an immortal life, the individual has not yet lived an infinitely long time. At any given point in time, the individual has the potential to live for an infinitely long time, but he has not yet actually lived an infinitely long time. So, if we wonder about how such a life is going, we can, as it were, "freeze it" in our imagination at any given, arbitrary time and evaluate it relative to that time; and, for any such time, the individual in question would not have lived for an infinitely long duration (and thus there should be no special bar to envisaging and evaluating the life thus far). Given that we can so evaluate an immortal life with respect to any given time, it seems to me perfectly reasonable to suppose that this is enough to defuse the worry.

Perhaps we could put the point this way. It is frankly mind-boggling to try to imagine an infinitely long life as a whole. Friedrich Schleiermacher could be interpreted as capturing this idea when he asked, "[W]ho can endure the effort to conceive an endless temporal existence?" (Schleiermacher, 1799/1958, p. 100). But it is a mistake, in my view, even to try to conceive an infinite temporal sequence. Rather, it seems to me enough that we are able to conceive of (and evaluate) the entire life up to any arbitrarily given time, even in a potentially infinite life.

But even so, I admit that there are deep mysteries lurking in the relationship between finitely and infinitely long lives. Todd May says:

> What we have not really grasped yet is the temporal aspect of immortality. We have not yet come to terms with how long immortality really lasts. It is, after all, an infinite amount of time. [An aspect of immortality] that may challenge us as human beings is that our lives keep going on and on. (May, 2009)

Right, and it is difficult to know exactly what to make of this. At the very least, it should make us circumspect in extrapolating from features of our ordinary finite lives (or even very long finite lives that we can imagine) to immortal lives. The situation here is a bit like the situation with respect to the Divine Attributes. Some argue that insofar as infinite magnitudes are fundamentally different from finite magnitudes (and thus God's infinite goodness is fundamentally different from the finite goodness of which human beings are capable, and God's infinite powers are fundamentally different from the finite powers possessed by human beings, and so forth), God's nature must remain mysterious and inaccessible to us. Others would argue that we can understand the Divine Attributes on analogy with our own finite properties; so, on this sort of view, God's goodness is to be understood as analogous to our (finite) goodness, and so forth. Thus, on this view, although God's attributes are not just like ours, they are sufficiently similar to ours to allow us to grasp them.

In summary, I have argued that immortal life could be "recognizably human." But perhaps I have conceded too much to Bernard Williams, who himself accepts the bodily identity criterion of personal identity, which would seem to imply that continuing to be human is a necessary condition of personal identity. In replying to Williams on immortality, it is helpful to accept as much as possible of his overall framework. But I do not see why we would need to accept that remaining human is a prerequisite for having a life recognizably like ours; and perhaps all that is required (with respect to this criterion for the appeal of immortality) is that the life in question be sufficiently like ours, not that it be recognizably human. As Nicholas Smith has pointed out, it is not obvious that the main character in the film *Avatar* makes a mistake in supposing that the lives of the Na/vi (the natives of the planet, Pandora), could be appealing (even from a human perspective). Also, the requirement that a life be "recognizably human" would seem to rule out, from the start, various Buddhist and Hindu conceptions of immortality. Whereas there are various difficulties with such conceptions, it is not clear to me they should be ruled out in virtue of embodying reincarnation, including the possibility of reincarnation as a member of another species.

6. THE ATTRACTIVENESS CHALLENGE

Let us suppose that the identity and recognizability challenges have been met. We still want to know whether immortality (envisaged as we have been thinking of it) could be attractive. The Immortality Curmudgeons—such as Heidegger, Charles Hartshorne, Walter Kaufman, and Bernard Williams—contend that no sort of immortality could be attractive to us human beings. Williams emphasized that, under circumstances in which the identity and recognizability conditions are met, one would eventually suffer from boredom in an immortal life—a boredom so thorough, relentless, and alienating that it would render such life unattractive.

Recently Todd May has joined the Parade of the Immortality Curmudgeons (or, better, the torrent of rain on the Immortality Parade):

> There is no reason to think that I couldn't [immerse myself far more in jazz saxophone]. I might have decided to throw myself into jazz, staying up late at night to go to clubs, listening over and over again to old jazz records, practicing with

possibilities the horn has to offer. But for how long? Even if I became dedicated to the music, could I do it for a thousand years? Five thousand? At some point, it begins to strain credulity to believe that one could stay immersed in a practice for an infinite amount of time.

Does it, though? Great musicians practice for hours a day, day after day. They never seem to get tired of it. However, musicians, like the rest of us, are mortal. They throw themselves into what they are doing because they want to be as accomplished as possible in the limited amount of time they have to play. And that time is very limited: seventy to eighty years at the outside. Multiply that amount of time by ten. Then by a hundred. Then by a thousand. That is an awfully long time to be playing an instrument. And it would only be the beginning. There would always be more time to practice (May, 2009, p. 61).

But I would suggest that the view of the Immortality Curmudgeons may be excessively bleak. I would concede that certain projects and activities—and the associated pleasurable experiences—might lose their force over time, perhaps becoming entirely extinguished at some point. I would however distinguish between what I have called "self-exhausting" pleasures and "repeatable pleasures." If we focus entirely on activities that produce self-exhausting pleasures, we can lose sight of the existence of activities that plausibly generate positive experiences that are "repeatable"; I have called the latter experiences, "repeatable pleasures" (Fischer, 1994). An immortal life with an appropriate mix (or distribution) of activities that generate repeatable pleasures would not necessarily be boring, and would seem to offer at least one model of an attractive immortality (for an interesting discussions, see Wisnewski, 2005; and Burley, 2009b).

I have contended that such activities as sex, eating fine meals, listening to music, experiencing beautiful works of art or nature, meditation, and prayer might provide repeatable pleasures (although perhaps "pleasures" was a slightly misleading term). It might have been better to put my pointas follows: such activities (and others) might well reliably (and repeatedly) generate experiences that are sufficiently compelling to render an immortal life attractive on balance. Unbeknownst to me, I was following a tradition (Lamont, 1965; Momeyer, 1988; see also the recent Chappell, 2009). Replying to Hartshorne's curmudgeonly attitude toward immortality (expressed in the epigraph to this paper), Corliss Lamont says:

> I deny that repetition as such leads necessarily to "monotony and boredom." Consider, for instance, the basic biological drives of thirst, hunger, and sex. Pure, cool water is the best drink in the world, and I have been drinking it for sixty-two years. If we follow through with Hartshorne, I ought to be so tired of water by this time that I seek to quench my thirst solely by wine, beer, and coca cola! Yet I still love water. By the same token, the average person does not fall into a state of ennui through the satisfaction of hunger or sexual desire.(Lamont, 1965, p. 33)

Although it is difficult to prove my contention, I am confident that a suitable mix or distribution of such activities could in fact reliably produce compelling experiences, even in an immortal life. Such a life could well be on balance attractive, even if it had periods of pain, suffering and boredom. After all, we do not suppose that a worthwhile finite life must never contain pain or boredom; why would we insist on a higher bar for an immoral life than a mortal life in this respect? Wouldn't that constitute a doublestandard?

One might ask why so many excellent philosophers have focused on certain activities that arguably generate self-exhausting pleasures and have thus ignored the activities that could plausibly generate repeatable pleasures. I would offer the speculative suggestion that philosophers are attracted (at least in their philosophizing) to activities that reflect the uniqueness of human beings, rather than those that we share with mere animals. Some of the salient suggestions for repeatable pleasures come from behavior we share with the brutes, such as eating and sex. It is hard for many philosophers to confront the notion that such animal pleasures (rather than the higher, distinctively human rational activities) might be a basis for the appeal of immortal life.

Note, however, that the animal pleasures are not the only pleasures (or compelling experiences) on my list; I also included those associated with confrontation with beauty in art or nature, meditation, and prayer. Presumably, some will find doing mathematics or philosophy similarly compelling. There is no magic to any particular list, and, I would argue, no shame in sharing the fun with the animals (as it were!). Further, note that my suggestion proposes one way of addressing the problem of boredom in an infinite life; I do not suppose that this is the only promising way of addressing this problem. I certainly do not seek to reduce all value to pleasures of a certain sort (or even experience). It is important to emphasize this last point: nothing in my view implies a reduction of all value in our finite lives to pleasures or experiences. Our finite human lives may well have a rich texture of valuable activities of various kinds, for all I have said about the potential appeal of a certain sort of immortality.

I have observed that the Immortality Curmudgeons tend to focus on "projects" and activities that require "discipline" (such as practicing a musical instrument). There is a sense of the word "project" that involves something that one undertakes just to keep busy or take up time; I think here of activities one does in the last few minutes of an elementary school class before the bell rings (or after school and before one's parents pick one up). And practicing a musical instrument can be a chore. Maybe the Immortality Curmudgeons are such spoilsports because they are operating too much within the framework of projects and activities that require effort and discipline. In some moods, I am tempted to think that they (or, at least some of them) just need to chill out a bit and allow themselves to be receptive to the magic and beauty of life as it unfolds. (This point evidently does not apply to Walter Kaufman, as quoted in the first epigraph to this paper.)

But even I must confess that it seems a bit reductionistic to fix even in part on (say) the pleasures of sex rather than the beauty of friendship and love, or the pleasures of eating good food rather than undertaking important and great accomplishments. If all other activities, including the development of relationships and striving for great accomplishments were to lose their power to engage us in an immortal life, this would, I confess, be significant and terrible. I am simply unsure about whether it is indeed true that in an immoral life, all "projects" involving activities that typically do not generate repeatable pleasures (or reliably compelling experiences) would become boring. But I wish to emphasize that nothing in my views requires taking a stand on this thesis. For all I know, one could still care about the development and enjoyment of deep relationships, even in an immortal life. (Sometimes I think that marriage requires an infinity of time to have a chance at getting it right!) All I am committed to is the notion that the activities associated with the repeatable pleasures could themselves be enough to warrant a positive attitude about immortality, quite apart from the difficult question about whether other activities would eventually and necessarily become boring. More needs to be said about these issues, but (lamentably!) I don't have forever (or unlimited space)...[1]

NOTES

1. I am very grateful to helpful and generous comments by Mikel Burley, Todd May, Jens Johansson, and Ben Bradley. I have given a version of this paper at the Lewis and Clark College; I have benefited from comments I received on that occasion, in particular from Nicholas Smith, Rebecca Copenhaver, and Joel Martinez. Also, I have given a version of this paper as the College of Humanities and Social Sciences Distinguished Research Lecture at the University of California, Riverside.

REFERENCES

Burley, Mikel. 2009a. "Immortality and Meaning: Reflections on the Makropulos Debate."*Philosophy* 84: 529–547.

Burley, Mikel. 2009b. "Immortality and Boredom: A Response to Wisnewski."*International Journal for Philosophy of Religion* 65: 77–85.

Chappell, Timothy. 2009. "Infinity Goes up on Trial: Must Immortality Be Meaningless?"*European Journal of Philosophy* 17: 30–44.

Feldman, Richard, Kris McDaniel, Jason R. Raibley, and Michael J. Zimmerman, eds. 2006. *The Good, the Right, Life and Death*. Aldershot, UK: Ashgate Publishing.

Fischer, John Martin, ed. 1993. *The Metaphysics of Death*. Palo Alto, CA: Stanford University Press.

Fischer, John Martin, ed.. 1994. "Why Immortality Is Not So Bad."*International Journal of Philosophical Studies* 2: 257–270. Reprinted in Fischer, ed., 2009, pp. 79–92.

Fischer, John Martin, and Ruth Curl. 1996. "Philosophical Models of Immortality in Science Fiction." In George Slusser, Gary Westfahl, and Eric S. Rabkin, eds., 1996, pp. 3–12. Reprinted in Fischer, ed., 2009, pp. 93–102.

Fischer, John Martin. 1997. "Death, Badness, and the Impossibility of Experience."*Journal of Ethics* 1: 341–353. Reprinted in Fischer, ed., 2009, pp. 37–50.

Fischer, John Martin. 1999. "Responsibility and Self-Expression."*Journal of Ethics* 3: 277–297.

Fischer, John Martin 2005. "Free Will, Death, and Immortality: The Role of Narrative."*Philosophical Papers* 34: 379–404.

Fischer, John Martin. 2006a. "Epicureanism about Death and Immortality."*Journal of Ethics* 10: 355–381.

Fischer, John Martin. 2006b. "Earlier and Later Birth: Symmetry through Thick and Thin." In R. Feldman, K. McDaniel, and J. R. Raibley, eds., 2006, pp. 189–192; reprinted in Fischer, ed., 2009, pp. 63–78.

Fischer, John Martin, ed. 2009. *Our Stories: Essays on Life, Death, and Free Will*. New York: Oxford University Press.

Fischer, John Martin, and Daniel Speak. 2000. "Death and the Psychological Conception of Personal Identity." In P. French and H. Wettstein, eds., 2000, pp. 84–93. Reprinted in Fischer, ed., 2009, pp. 51–62.

French, Peter A., and Howard Wettstein, eds. 2000. *Midwest Studies in Philosophy*. Vol. 24. Notre Dame: Notre Dame University Press.

Hartshorne, Charles. 1958. "Outlines of A Philosophy of Nature, Part II." *The Personalist* 39: 380–391.

Heidegger, Martin. 1927. *Being and Time*, trans. 1962 by J. Macquarrie and E. Robinson. New York: Harper and Row.

Kaufman, Frederick.1999. "Pre-Vital and Post-Mortem Non-Existence."*AmericanPhil osophical Quarterly* 36: 1–19.

Kaufman, Frederick. 2000. "Thick and Thin Selves: Reply to Fischer and Speak." In P. French and H. Wettstein, eds., 2000, pp. 94–97.

Kaufman, Walter. 1963. *The Faith of a Heretic*. New York: Anchor Books.

Lamont, Corliss. 1965. "Mistaken Attitudes toward Death."*Journal of Philosophy* 52: 29–36.

May, Todd. 2009. *Death*. Stocksfield, UK: Acumen Publishing.

Momeyer, R.W. 1988. *Confronting Death*. Bloomington: Indiana University Press.

Nussbaum, Martha. 1994. *The Therapy of Desire*. Princeton: Princeton University Press.

Nussbaum, Martha.1999. "Reply to Papers in Symposium on Nussbaum, The Therapy of Desire."*Philosophy and Phenomenological Research* 59: 811–819.

Nussbaum, Martha. Forthcoming. "The Damage of Death: Incomplete Agents and False Consolations." In James S. Taylor, ed., forthcoming.

Schleiermacher, Friedrich. 1799. *On Religion: Speeches to Its Cultured Despisers*, trans. 1958, J. Oman. New York: Harper and Row.

Slusser, George, Gary Westfahl, and Eric S. Rabkin, eds. 1996. *Immortal Engines: Life Extension and Immortality in Science Fiction and Fantasy*. Athens: University of Georgia Press.

Steele, Hunter. 1976. "Could Body-Bound Immortality Be Liveable?"*Mind* 85: 424–427.

Taylor, James. S., ed. Forthcoming. *Death: New Essays on Metaphysics and Bioethics*. New York: Oxford University Press.

Velleman, David. 1991. "Well-Being and Time."*Pacific Philosophical Quarterly* 72: 48–77. Reprinted in Fischer, ed., 1993, pp. 329–357.

Williams, Bernard. 1973. "The Makropulos Case: Reflections on the Tedium of Immortality."In his *Problems of the Self*, pp. 82–100.

Williams, Bernard, ed. 1973. *Problems of the Self*. Cambridge: Cambridge University Press.

Wisnewski. Jeremy. 2005. "Is Immortal Life Worth Living?"*International Journal for Philosophy of Religion* 58: 27–36.

CHAPTER 16

THE MAKROPULOS CASE REVISITED

REFLECTIONS ON IMMORTALITY AND AGENCY

CONNIE S. ROSATI

> We die like beasts. God, what comes after life, what is the immortality of the soul but a desperate cry against the shortness of our lives? Man has never accepted this animal span of life. We can't endure it, it's too unjust. Man is more than a tortoise or a raven. Man needs more time to live.[1]

IN Karel Čapek's play *The Makropulos Case*, Emilia Marty, an opera singer renowned for her talent and beauty, appears at an attorney's office to inquire about one of his cases. The litigation concerns an estate valued at 150 million, and it has dragged on over four generations of disputants and their sons, and lawyers and their sons. It seems Emilia knows of facts favorable to the attorney's client, Albert Gregor. In particular, she knows of the existence of a will supporting Gregor's claim to the estate, which is likely in an old chest in the possession of Jaroslav Prus, Gregor's adversary. All of the parties to the dispute initially express disbelief, then bewilderment as to how Emilia could know what she does, given that the testator of the newly recovered will had died nearly 100 years earlier. We discover in the fourth act that the apparently 30-odd year-old Emilia Marty—a.k.a. Elina Makropulos, a.k.a. Ellian MacGregor, a.k.a. Eugenia Montez—has lived to the ripe old age of 337.[2] As she recounts it, her father, personal physician to the Emperor Rudolph II, was ordered to test on her the elixir of life he had invented for the Emperor.[3] The serum extends life, allowing one to "stay young" for 300 years, and as we encounter the seeming effects of this extension on Emilia, we find a life of boredom, apathy, and emptiness.[4]

Why, then, has Emilia appeared? Gregor, it turns out, is her great great grandson, and he is about to lose the case. Emilia has not come, however, to aid him in his cause. In fact, she has only just learned of the dispute, and she arrives apparently unaware that the document supporting Gregor's claim remains hidden.[5] In any event, she is as indifferent to Gregor's lineage as she is to nearly everything else. What moves Emilia is not familial affection but apprehension of her own impending death: she seeks to recover the formula for the elixir, which she also believes to be in the old chest that is still, as she learns, in Prus's possession.[6] Once her story is revealed, a heated discussion ensues about what to do with the formula, and Čapek's characters debate the merits of immortal existence, teasing us with questions about meaning and value and the nature of a life worth living. In the end, all, including Emilia, decline to take the formula, and amidst some protest, the aging parchment on which it is written is destroyed.

It is uncertain what lessons, if any, Čapek intended us to draw from his tale. Bernard Williams, in a striking essay, takes Čapek's play to illustrate that immortality would be intolerable: an endless existence would be a dreary, meaningless existence, simply because of what it is to have a human character and to live a human life.[7] Perhaps Čapek meant to convey just this, but the play is more suggestive than conclusive. As will become clear, Williams's reasons for insisting that an endless life would be endlessly boring, that "in a sense, death gives the meaning to life," are ultimately unpersuasive.[8] His claims are, in any case, somewhat puzzling.

As Williams would surely acknowledge, his claims conflict with common intuitions about value, as well as with widespread fantasies, long reflected in art, religion, and literature, about magical potions extending our existence in this life or divine dispensation extending it in an "afterlife." The conflict runs yet deeper, however, for his claims collide not only with common beliefs and imaginings but with a most basic and irresistible force: the felt imperative *to live*.[9] We cling to life, ferociously at times, even the nihilists among us, and it seems, to most of us at least, that we are rational to do so. How, then, could too much life be a bad thing, and what would "too much" of it be? Our finite lives can, it seems, be both richly rewarding and profoundly meaningful. Why think, then, that a life without death would become deadeningly dull? Why think that a life without end would become a life without point?[10]

Whether or not Čapek intended any particular message, we are free to draw our own morals, and so we might as well draw ones that leave us well instructed. I am inclined to think that Williams misses the significance of the Makropulos case. His negative answer to the question of whether immortality would be desirable is, as I shall explain, an answer to no determinate question at all, and to the extent that his arguments bear on any clear question about the desirability of extending our lives, they fail to support his assessment. For pretty obvious reasons, then, we ought to view with skepticism any effort to appraise the desirability of an endless or substantially extended existence. I here revisit Williams's essay, then, not to defend an alternative assessment, but the better to reflect on our mortal lives. In my view, Williams's position rests on questionable ideas about desire, character, meaning, and human life. As a consequence, he leaves unexplained what seems critically in need of explanation, namely, *the widespread and seemingly rational longing for extended existence.*[11]

In what follows, I suggest that the rational appeal of extended existence rests on the fact that, although we are each humans with something like an individual human character, we are also autonomous agents with a distinctively agential character. The widespread longing for an extended existence is an expression of our agency, and contra Williams, satisfying that longing need not be practically at odds with satisfying the perhaps equally widespread longing for a meaningful existence. Whatever message it may impart about a limitless life, the deeper lessons of *The Makropulos Case* concern how to live the limited life each of us has. Absorbing those lessons may, in one sense, do more to burnish than to diminish the appeal of an "eternal life." For the lives we each do best to seek may be ones in which we find at least "intimations of immortality."[12]

1. IN SEARCH OF A QUESTION

Human lives, as we know them, have a characteristic cycle: an early stage of physiological and psychological development; a middle period of intense learning, social expansion, production, and reproduction; and a final phase of physical and mental decline and social contraction, ending in death. Of course, individual lives vary markedly, and development and decline of many sorts need not be limited to a single period. Psychological growth, thankfully, can occur throughout a life. Decline and decay, sadly, can occur far too early, due to injury or illness or owing to our own self-destructive choices. With social, economic, and technological advances, we have ever increasing flexibility in how we structure our lives, in our opportunities for charting a new course, and for correcting or overcoming defective or deficient conditions. Both the fact of something like a typical human life cycle and the fact of its malleability bear importantly on the possibilities for value and meaning in any life we could know.

A fundamental difficulty arises in efforts to assess the desirability of immortality, for our ordinary judgments about value and meaning are tied to our sense of a typical, if variable, finite human existence. When we try to imagine an *eternal* human existence, our judgments lose their natural mooring. The difficulty is not that we must assess a very different sort of human life; rather, unless we can carefully stipulate the terms of an endless existence, we must assess no particular sort of human life at all.[13]

Consider the difficulty of determining what we are to imagine. Would the person living an immortal life age as we do in our finite lives but very slowly? Would she repeatedly undergo cycles of development, decline, and renewal? Or would she live indefinitely at a particular age, and what age might that be?[14] If at a particular age, how would her development—physical, intellectual, and emotional—be affected? Would she have a body? If so, would her physique and psyche be in or out of sync? And what of her relations with others? Would she be alone in her immortality? A member of some small group? Or would all humans be immortal? And, finally, what other features of our world, if any, would remain fixed as those immortals among us carried on endlessly?

The terms of a person's existence make all the difference to its desirability.[15] No one, for instance, would rationally want to spend a life—mortal or immortal—trapped in early childhood or in decrepit old age. Too many goods become accessible to us only as our powers mature; too many escape us as those powers decline. No one would rationally want to live a life—mortal or immortal—in a state of physical and psychological mismatch.[16] Recall what Tithonus endured because of Eos's error in requesting eternal life for her lover without also requesting eternal youth.[17] Without a clear fix on the terms of immortal existence, we cannot reasonably guess what goods would enrich our lives or elude us, what ills we would escape or suffer; we cannot guess how our view of what is a good or ill or of what makes a life meaningful would change.[18]

One might be tempted to think we could avoid the foregoing complications simply by imagining eternal existence under "ideal conditions." Suppose, for example, that one were to carry on indefinitely in "one's prime."[19] That seems to be just the condition in which we find Emilia—at the height of her operatic powers and, as the swooning of the men who encounter her attests, at the height of her physical beauty and sexual allure. Perhaps, other things being equal, such a life would be highly desirable. But other things aren't equal, and in fact, once the familiar limits on a human life have been lifted, we no longer understand what it would be for other things to be "equal."

Whatever the attractions of living forever "at the top of one's game," no one would rationally want to do so if, like Emilia, they would be alone in this endlessness. I do not mean, of course, that Emilia has spent her 337 years alone. On the contrary, she has had many relationships—with parents, husbands, lovers, children—all of whom have predeceased her. The fact that she has outlived them all suggests a rather different problem for an extended life, at least of Emilia's sort, than the one Williams claims to find. For there may be a limit to how much loss any human being can bear before she loses the will or the ability to invest herself emotionally in ways required to create and secure value. Without such investment, a person is doomed to be cut off from the concerns that animate, and render desirable, human life as we know it.[20]

Our need for connection finds recurrent and striking expression in literary depictions of endless existence, including Čapek's. Despite her countless lovers and children, despite the adulation of her fans and the attentions of her many male admirers, Emilia's complaints concern not only her boredom but her solitude.[21] For all Čapek tells us, Emilia's shallowness and self-absorption—indeed, her callousness—may have been, at least to some degree, long-standing features of her character, but they may also reflect a narcissism induced by emotional isolation.[22]

2. THE ALLEGED PROBLEMS FOR EXTENDED EXISTENCE

Williams well recognizes the problem of what to imagine when we contemplate immortality. Moreover, he himself observes that Emilia occupies a unique position in that she "is in a world of people who do not share her condition"; as a consequence, he remarks, her personal relationships require a certain concealment, resulting in "a form of isolation that would disappear if her condition were generalized."[23] Still, he thinks he can argue that an endless life would involve the tedium Emilia endures—and *inevitably* so.[24] Of course, Emilia is not immortal; she has just gone on living for a very long time. Williams's concern would thus seem to lie not with immortality per se—with our living forever—but simply with our living for too long.[25]

For the remainder of this essay, then, I focus on the more modest, if only slightly less ill-defined, notion of "extended existence." We cannot clearly imagine immortality, but we can imagine average life expectancy extended by ten or twenty years, or perhaps even doubled; and were it doubled, those who lived extendedly would no doubt be able to imagine life extended yet again, even if we cannot.[26] Now, Williams would surely not find an additional ten or twenty years problematic. But if an extra twenty years would pose no difficulty, whereas an extra, say, approximately 257 years (as in Emilia's case) would, then this will require some explanation.[27] Williams arguments against the desirability of immortality, in effect, promise to provide an explanation.

Although I focus on the notion of extended existence, I shall have to leave unspecified, for now obvious reasons, the precise terms of such an existence. As for how much additional existence counts as "extended," choosing any particular end point would be hopelessly arbitrary. More important, as I hope to show, it would miss something critical to explaining the common longing for extended existence, namely, that insofar as we are autonomous agents, no natural stopping point presents itself.

Williams thinks that a natural stopping point does present itself—or at least that death, thankfully, provides a stopping point. He tells us that he will "pursue the idea that *from facts about human desire and happiness and what a human life is,* it follows both that immortality would be, where conceivable at all, intolerable, and that (other things being equal) death is reasonably regarded as an evil."[28] But what does he take these facts to be, and how is the intolerability of immortality supposed to follow from them?

As the passage just cited indicates, although Williams believes that immortality would be a bad thing, he nevertheless maintains, pace Lucretius, that other things being equal, death is reasonably regarded as an evil, and we rationally prefer a later to an earlier death. The thought that it is better to die later than earlier, he remarks, "will depend only on the idea, apparently sound, that if the praemia vitae and consciousness of them are good things, then longer consciousness of more praemia is better than shorter consciousness of fewer praemia."[29] A decent argument can be offered to support this idea, he thinks. Other things being equal, when a person desires something, he prefers a state of affairs in which that desire is satisfied, something that for most of his desires, death would prevent. To be sure, should he die, he will not know what he is missing, but "from the perspective of the wanting agent it is rational to aim for states of affairs in which his want is satisfied, and hence to regard death as something to be avoided; that is, to regard it as an evil."[30] Williams allows that many of the things we want we want "only on the assumption that [we are] going to be alive."[31] This accounts, he thinks, for the situation of some elderly persons who may continue to want things even though they are ready, and may even wish, to die. But with respect to other things, wanting them will itself give us a reason to avoid death, which necessarily precludes getting them.

Williams here draws a distinction between *conditional desires* and what he calls *"categorical desires."*[32] The distinction can be understood in terms of a difference in propositional content, and so a difference in what it would take to satisfy desires of each sort. The conditional desire, for example, to finish writing my book—to finish it, given that I'm alive—can be satisfied *either* by my completing the book (that is, by the truth of the consequent) or by my dying (the falsity of the antecedent). The categorical desire to finish writing my book, in contrast, can be satisfied only by my completing it, and for that I must live long enough.

If the distinction between conditional and categorical desires turns on a difference in propositional content and satisfaction conditions, its importance, turns on a supposed difference in motivational and rational implications: categorical desires, in contrast to conditional desires, both *motivate* a person to continue living and give her *reason* to live.[33] The categorical desire to finish my book, for example, motivates me, not only to secure time to write, to sit at my desk composing sentences, and so on, but to live; and it gives me reason to live, at least long enough to finish. The conditional desire to write my book likewise motivates me to do what it takes to write my book—it motivates me, we might say, relative to the desire's propositional content and my presumed existence. But it does not motivate me to live or give me reason to live, just reason to write so long as I am alive and not taking steps to alter the status quo. Call the difference in motivation a difference between being *life-motivating* and *content-motivating.* Call the difference in rational implication the difference between giving a *categorical reason* and giving a *conditional reason.*

The importance of categorical desires evidently derives, on Williams's view, not only from their being life-motivating but also, and more significantly, from their providing categorical reasons to live.[34]

Williams's interest in the normative role of desire, and its bearing on the desirability of extended existence, becomes clear when he rejects the suggestion that all desires are conditional. He invites us to consider the "idea of a rational forward-looking calculation of suicide."[35] The suicidal man is in doubt about whether to remain alive. If he nevertheless decides to undergo "what lay before him," the desire that propels him forward "is not one that operates conditionally on his being alive, since it itself resolves the question of whether he is going to be alive."[36] Williams evidently thinks that either conditional or categorical desires might, as a matter of fact, propel a person into the future, but that only categorical desires can do so while resolving the doubts of the man rationally calculating suicide, for only they provide reasons to seek that future. Happiness, he contends, "requires that some of one's desires should be fully categorical, and one's existence itself wanted as something necessary to them."[37]

Although Williams thinks that we can arrive at no interesting generalizations about what those categorical desires must be, he considers whether the bare desire to stay alive could be the categorical desire that propels the suicidal man forward. "The answer," he offers,

> is perhaps "no." In saying that, I do not want to deny the existence, the value, or the basic necessity of a sheer reactive drive to self-preservation: humanity would certainly wither if the drive to keep alive were not stronger than any perceived reasons for keeping alive. But if the question [whether to remain alive] is asked, and it is going to be answered calculatively, then the bare categorical desire to stay alive will not sustain the calculation—that desire itself, when things have got that far, has to be sustained or filled out by some desire for something else, even if it is only, at the margin, the desire that future desires of mine will be born and satisfied.[38]

When a person has reached the point of rationally considering suicide, a bare desire to live will not do, even if it is categorical and so reason-giving; something more will be needed to "sustain the calculation" in favor of life. According to Williams, the reasons any of us has for avoiding death derive from our (other) categorical desires. These desires not only give us reason to live but also to regard death as a misfortune.[39]

Williams's claims about categorical desires seem doubtful. Consider his claim that happiness requires that some of our desires be "fully categorical." Williams does not argue for this directly. Perhaps he thinks his "rational suicide" case shows that happiness requires that some desires be life-motivating and categorical reason-giving. But a person could, it seems, derive happiness just from the things that she desires given that she is alive.[40] She might not wish to die but might also not desire to live as something necessary to her desires; she might simply have conditional desires and an ordinary "reactive drive to self-preservation." Her outlook, moreover, need not preclude believing that an early death is a misfortune. She might think her life would be better *as a life* were her projects completed, perhaps because, as some might say, it would make for a better story. Even a preference for such a life need not be categorical or rest on categorical desires; it might rest simply on beliefs about the value of a life as a whole.

Williams's claim that categorical desires provide reasons to live also seems doubtful. Whether any desires provide or ground reasons is, of course, open to dispute.[41] Still, if categorical desires do not provide reasons, they might at least be (fallible) indicators of reasons. Our categorical desires might be for things that are, or could become, a part of our good or for things to which we are otherwise reflectively committed; and our good and our reflective commitments can, and ordinarily do, give us reasons to live. Yet Williams appears to recognize no limits on the objects of our categorical desires. Now, perhaps any desire, regardless of its object, can be life-motivating. But one can reasonably doubt, for familiar reasons, that a desire can be reason-giving, regardless of its object, simply because its propositional content is not conditional.[42] Insofar as desires ground or indicate reasons, one might argue, they must have as their objects things like participation in a seemingly valuable project or relationship. In fact, it is, most commonly, desires of this sort that we tend to experience as categorical when the threat of an early death would prevent the completion of a project or prematurely end a relationship. For example, a terminally ill father ordinarily wants to live as long as possible so he can continue to love and parent his children, for their sake and his. Some of our desires are for engagements with an internal shape or trajectory, and these in turn give our lives shape, putting us in a position to assess our lives as fulfilling or stunted, as meaningful or meaningless. Insofar as happiness requires that some of our desires be "fully categorical," it would seem to be because of what our categorical desires usually concern.

Let us grant for now, though, Williams's claims about the desire to live and the necessity of categorical desires. Why does he think it follows from these supposed facts about human desire and happiness that an extended existence would be intolerable? Why think it follows that Emilia's fate would be our own? Williams offers two distinct lines of reasoning against the desirability of immortality. The first argues from a certain claim as to why nothing would be gained, the second, from the necessity to any desirable human life of what would be lost.

2.1 Nothing Gained

Williams argues that "nothing would be gained" by living extendedly, because "[t]here is no desirable or significant property which life would have more of, or have more unqualifiedly, if we lasted for ever."[43] It follows that a person could not rationally desire a life that would have more of some such property or have it more unqualifiedly. A desire for a better life in *that* sense could not be among her categorical desires; it could neither give her a reason to live extendedly nor contribute to her happiness.

Williams's premise is, of course, open to dispute; surely hedonists and some proponents of desire and objective list theories would reject it. So long as we would continue to enjoy our activities and relationships, for example, pleasure seems an obvious candidate for a relevant desirable property. And if the value of a life were additive, then an interest in our own enjoyment and in having more rather than less valuable lives would seem to favor extended existence.[44] In any case, Williams does not explain why vindication of our attraction to extended existence would require that there be some property of the sort he describes.[45] Why wouldn't it be enough that life continue to have, only just as unqualifiedly and in roughly the same quantity, whatever desirable properties it now has? Why wouldn't it be enough that we continue to lead the happy, apparently meaningful lives we are already living?

2.2 Something Lost

Williams does not address the latter questions directly, evidently because he is convinced that extended lives would cease to have whatever desirable properties and meaningfulness our actual lives have. The supposed facts to which his more central, and more promising, "something would be lost" argument appeals concern not only human desire and happiness but human character.

According to Williams, Emilia lives an empty life for quite explicable reasons: she has ceased to have categorical desires and, thereby, anything that would give her an interest in life and a reason to live. Emilia's problem, which presents itself precisely because she has been living too long, is boredom—

> a boredom connected with the fact that everything that could happen and make sense to one particular human being of [her age] had already happened to her. Or, rather, *all the sort of things that could make sense to one woman of a certain character*; for EM has a certain character, and indeed, except for her accumulating memories of earlier times, and no doubt some changes of style to suit the passing centuries, seems always to have been much the same sort of person.[46]

Boredom, he seems to want to say, is the inevitable consequence of having a human character *and* too much time on one's hands.

Suppose we grant that boredom is the enemy—the real threat that must be warded off to vindicate the longing for extended existence.[47] Ordinary boredom, it's worth remembering, is not a problem at all, any more than ordinary ambivalence is. Both express a deep fact about us, one which I'll later suggest is important to explaining the rational appeal of extended existence. The problem, rather, is the sort of *enervating* boredom that apparently afflicts Emilia; only the latter could be any true threat to the desirability of extended existence. We have simple, familiar remedies for ordinary boredom and malaise: make a change, find something else to do. Why believe that extended existence would result in a boredom beyond the reach of our usual cures?

Emilia's existence, Williams observes, satisfies one of two conditions that must be met if a person's hope for an endless life is to be fulfilled, namely, that it be she who survives endlessly. Emilia's existence fails, however, to satisfy a second condition: that the person who continues to survive live in a state adequately related to the aims for the sake of which the person wants to survive.[48] Even supposing that a person was propelled into the future only by the categorical desire that "future desires of [hers] be born and satisfied," it must be intelligible to her, given her own character, how these future desires could be *her* desires.[49] Otherwise, presumably, neither this categorical desire nor "her" future categorical desires would give *her* reason or motivation to live.

Williams maintains that Emilia's difficulty was due not to her particular character but, rather, to the fact that she had a character, and so in virtue of our each having a character, extended existence would—for any of us—be incompatible with the second condition being met.[50] The source of the alleged incompatibility, however, remains obscure. The problem cannot be, say, that you, from your standpoint at the moment of being offered the elixir, would be unable to see your "survivor state" as adequately related to the aims you have in wanting to survive. You might easily—and accurately—picture your surviving self (that is, *you*) writing the novel you would now, looking forward, have yourself write, or embarking on those travels which you would now, looking forward, have yourself begin, or watching your grandchildren grow just as you now, looking forward, long to do. Williams gives us no compelling reason to doubt that at any particular point, as you look forward to the next year or two or ten, the surviving you would be in a state adequately related to the aims you had in wanting to continue.[51] It seems the second condition, like the first, would ordinarily be met.[52]

The problem must instead be that although all might look well at any particular point as we consider the next year or two or ten, we can see how grim things would be when we reflect and, so to speak, take the long view. Suppose that given what it is to have a character, everything that could happen and make sense to a person would, at some point during an extended existence, have already happened. At that point, then, perhaps there would be nothing more for her to desire—not even, per impossibile, that future desires of hers be born and satisfied. And so her future desires couldn't be adequately related to her aims in wanting to survive because there wouldn't be any.

One might think that the difficulty could be escaped so long as a person's categorical desires included desires for things that never lost their appeal. But Williams does not consider this a real possibility. In the process of living a human life, he claims, any individual will have acquired a character, with certain interests, likes, and dislikes. We cannot imagine any unending state or activity that wouldn't, in the end, become boring, at least if a person "remains conscious of himself." When it comes to eternity, Williams contends, "Nothing less will do...than something that makes boredom unthinkable. What could that be? Something that could be guaranteed to be at every moment utterly absorbing? But if a man has and retains a character, there is no reason to suppose that there is anything that could be that."[53] If Williams is right, a person would indeed be unable to conjure up an image of future categorical desires coming to be born that would be her desires. Given her character, nothing can endlessly interest her, and at some point, she will have desired and done everything it can make sense to someone like her to desire and do.[54] For these reasons, the boredom extended existence would induce could not be relieved by making a change or finding something new to do.

An extended life would thus be tedious. What's more, it would be *meaningless*.[55] Williams does not say what makes for a meaningful life, but he appears to think an important connection exists between categorical desires and both happiness and meaning. Perhaps he thinks that meaningfulness depends on happiness: a person's life is meaningful insofar as it is happy, which requires that she have life-motivating and categorical reason-giving desires. Or perhaps he thinks that happiness depends on meaningfulness; it requires just that a person have reasons for living, which only categorical desires can provide. Either way, "death gives the meaning to life" by ending it before categorical desire ceases and ceaseless boredom ensues.[56] Extended existence would exhaust categorical desire, something essential to happiness and meaningfulness, and so to any desirable human life.[57]

Williams's "something lost" argument seems to rest heavily on two basic claims about what supposedly follows from the fact of our each having a character: a person can find nothing that would perpetually interest her and so make boredom "unthinkable," and, given enough time, she would run out of things that could interest her at all and so serve as the object of a categorical desire. Williams may be right, but he has, so far as I can see, provided no substantial support for either claim.[58]

One difficulty for Williams's view is that he seems to suppose a near conceptual or necessary connection between having a character and, given enough time, the exhaustion of categorical desire. But he does not explain, at least within his critique of immortality, what he thinks a human character is and how, precisely, having one would necessarily create a problem for extended existence.[59] He seems to assume a view of character that treats it as rather strictly limiting, in scope and duration, an individual's desires and interests.[60] Yet, even if those who have argued against the existence of global character traits have sometimes overstated their case, we can reasonably ask whether, on a more conceptually nuanced and empirically adequate understanding of character, having a human character is as limiting of our futures as Williams seems to think.[61]

Williams is surely right that in virtue of having something like a human character, or at least a certain physiological and psychological makeup, we will each encounter some built in limits to the sorts of undertakings and lives that could hold any interest for us. Still, whether an extended existence would be problematic in the ways he describes would seem to be a purely contingent matter. It would depend, for starters, on the terms of an extended existence and the circumstances of an individual's existence, which may or may not be sufficiently varied and engaging. It would also seem to depend on individual character. We all know people, for example, who seem to find just about everything interesting, whose inquisitiveness and capacity for enjoyment seem nearly boundless. We all know people who are easily contented with what may seem to us meager offerings. Of course, some people do have a limited capacity for enjoyment and especially rigid aims and interests. But nothing necessarily stops even those of a more "unfortunate" character from continuing to enjoy their narrow interests. Perhaps the moral, then, is not that extended existence would be undesirable simply because of what it is to have a human character and live a human life, but that it would be undesirable for those whose circumstances will be seriously impoverished or for those who have, as a matter of their individual characters, both limited interests and a tendency to become easily and intolerably bored.[62]

As for meaning, whatever Williams's view about what makes for a meaningful human life, the clash between meaning and extended existence remains to be explained. It would seem to be enough not only for the desirability of extended existence but also for meaningfulness that a life continue to have, only just as unqualifiedly and in roughly the same quantity, whatever desirable properties it now has; there need be no desirable property that life has more of or has more unqualifiedly. And for all Williams says about character and desire, whether categorical desire would cease, and so whether an extended existence would be not only tedious but meaningless, seems to be a contingent matter.

Williams's discussion of meaning faces a deeper difficulty. If he says little about what he thinks makes for meaningfulness in a life, he says nothing about what he thinks meaningfulness is. Williams is not alone, of course, in making claims about meaning in life without offering an analysis of *what it is for a life to be meaningful*. Unfortunately, we lack an adequate account of what normative assessment is made of a life when we appraise it as meaningful, rather than as morally valuable, aesthetically pleasing, or personally good.[63] Assessments of meaningfulness certainly appear to be distinctive. When we appraise a life that is good for an individual as meaningful, we are surely not expressing the tautology that the life that is good for her is good for her.

Whatever Williams thinks is the precise relationship between categorical desires and meaningfulness, categorical desires would seem to figure neither in a plausible substantive account of a meaningful life nor in a plausible analysis of what it is for a life to be meaningful. As a substantive matter, if we treat common judgments as our guide, categorical desires, as Williams seems to describe them, are neither necessary nor sufficient for meaningfulness. Categorical desires are unnecessary, because we can imagine lives that people would regard as paradigmatically meaningful but that are animated wholly by conditional desires; or, if animated partly by categorical desires, then by ones that bear no important relationship to why we assess the life as meaningful.[64] Imagine, for example, a Mother Theresa who wants to serve God by aiding the poor of Calcutta, given that she is alive, but who has no particular desire to live on that account, perhaps because she views her life as in God's hands and desires only that "his will be done." Categorical desires are also insufficient. So long as there are no restrictions on their object, a person could have categorical desires to pursue utterly trivial ends. Not just any categorical desire can be reason-giving; likewise, not just any categorical desire can play a part in rendering a life meaningful. Consider how our assessment of Mother Theresa's life would change had the categorical desire that propelled her forward been the desire to spend all her days merely reciting the Hail Mary. As a matter of analysis, if lives can be meaningful without categorical desires or meaningless with them, then *being meaningful* is not itself a matter of having categorical desires.

In sum, Williams does not offer compelling reasons to think extended existence would be tedious or meaningless. The dismal outcome he predicts neither follows inevitably from the facts nor, so far as his arguments show, from any non-contingent considerations about human life and character.

3. EXPLAINING THE APPEAL OF EXTENDED EXISTENCE

Williams allows, as we have seen, that other things being equal, a later death is preferable, that "longer consciousness of more *praemia*" is better, that a rational person prefers (what death tends to preclude) that his desires be satisfied. These remarks aside, he does not attempt to explain why, if his verdict is so obviously correct, the idea of extended existence has long had broad and seemingly rational appeal. One might argue, of course, that people do not so much desire to continue living as fear dying. But not everyone fears death, and we have no reason to suppose that so many have mistaken aversion for desire. One might also argue, for different reasons, that the desire for extended existence is irrational or at least misguided, that Williams was right in his conclusion, if not in his reasoning. I briefly consider one such line of argument later. In the remainder of this essay, my interest will lie with explaining the rational appeal of extended existence.

As a starting point, consider that Williams's conclusion seems to depend most critically on two claims: the first concerns categorical desire as a source of reasons to live; the second concerns human character and the inevitable extinction of categorical desire. Williams makes no appeal to sources of reasons apart from desire or to features of our nature apart from our character. [65] Yet, this may be precisely what is needed if we are to account for the rational appeal of extended existence.

In what follows, I shall sketch an alternative framework, one that looks to another source of reasons and to a different aspect of our nature. My aim is not to defend this alternative so much as to shed light on what Williams's framework overlooks.[66] Of course, insofar as an alternative captures overlooked considerations, insofar as it might better explain the lure of extended existence, there is something to be said for it.

3.1 The Value of Simply Being

Let's set aside the rational suicide case and consider the more ordinary case of persons who are not actively contemplating ending their lives. What might give them (us) reason to live? Even if we allow that categorical desires, or the value of their objects, can provide reasons to live, our most fundamental reasons may have a different source. We need to understand what that might be if we want to understand the appeal of extended life—indeed, if we want to understand the central act that drives Čapek's play, namely, that Emilia seeks to extend even her own empty life, a life, if Williams is right, in which categorical desire has exhausted itself.[67]

In writing of a "bare desire to live" or a "reactive drive to self-preservation," Williams points to something we have in common with nonhuman animals. To explain their self-preserving behavior, we would presumably appeal to basic features of their motivational systems, and no doubt, a similar explanation could be invoked to explain our own drive to preserve ourselves. Yet, we experience something more than a mere reactive drive to self-preservation. For whatever we may have in common with the other animals, we humans are peculiarly *agential* animals.

The point I wish to make borrows from some of Karl Marx's observations in "Economic and Philosophic Manuscripts" of 1844. "It is obvious," Marx tells us, "that the *human* eye enjoys things in a way different from the crude, non-human eye; the human ear different from the crude *ear*, etc."[68] He elaborates:

> Only through the objectively unfolded richness of man's essential being is the richness of subjective *human* sensibility (a musical ear, an eye for beauty of form—in short, *senses* capable of human gratification, senses confirming themselves as essential powers of *man*) either cultivated or brought into being. For not only the five senses but also the so-called mental senses—the practical senses (will, love, etc.)—in a word, *human* sense—the humanness of the sense—comes to be by virtue of *its object*, by virtue of *humanised* nature. The *forming* of the five senses is a labour of the entire history of the world down to the present.[69]

As I would understand the phenomenon Marx describes, the history of the development of our human senses is the history of our development as beings with the capacity to transform nature and ourselves, and so to realize and experience apparent value.[70] Our nature and development is such that we create and experience not mere sounds but *music*, not mere forms but *beauty* of form, and so on, for our other physical and "mental" senses. As we exercise and develop our capacities for discrimination, we both refine what we create and alter what it takes to gratify us. We create a "humanized" nature and a rich human sensibility to match. Our history manifests our nature as agents, beings with the capacity for autonomy, who can deliberately act on the world and bring about what we can come to appreciate and apprehend as value.

For present purposes, it does not matter how the phenomenon just described is best explained. Perhaps the capacities that constitute us as agents—among them, our capacities for reason and higher-order reflection—equip us for tracking objective values and for creating and coming to appreciate what instantiates them. Or perhaps value, real or apparent, just is, in some sense, a product of the exercise of our agential capacities, which tends to bring about a rough match between our world and our critical sensibility as we act and shape them both. What does matter is the upshot, which is a world that we do not experience simply in terms of desire—bare, conditional, or categorical.

Suppose, then, that human senses and sensibility and human engagement with the world are distinctive in something like the way Marx suggests.[71] Then perhaps our experience is also distinctive when it comes to those drives or bare desires we may share with the other animals—including the "reactive drive to self-preservation." In the latter case, it certainly seems so. Although we tend to be moved automatically to preserve our lives, we can *rationally entertain* the possibility of ending them—a fact Williams's rational suicide case exploits. Moreover, we can *act* to end them or to allow them to be ended for us; we can choose extinction over life, not only directly, by suicide, but indirectly, by committing ourselves, with full cognizance, to a risky cause or endeavor. Even as we feel the grip of that drive, we can stand reflectively apart from it and reject it as normative—as giving any reason for choice or action. We do not experience the drive to self-preservation as utterly inexorable, then, either motivationally or rationally. But neither do we experience categorical desires merely as such. For just as we can stand back from our drives and bare desires, we can stand back from our categorical desires and judge them as not worth having, or their objects as not worth pursuing.

We need, then, to look for a more fundamental source of reasons. To locate it, we might start by considering, as Williams claims to do, "what it is to live a human life." But what it is, what it is *like*, involves something more than our experience of desire. Williams comes close to stumbling upon it when he quotes a passage from Miguel de Unamuno's *Tragic Sense of Life*. He aptly describes this work as giving "extreme expression" to the desire to be immortal.[72] Indeed. Unamuno writes, "I do not want to die—no, I neither want to die nor do I want to want to die; I want to live for ever and ever and ever." But the passage continues, "I want this 'I' to live— this poor 'I' that I am and that I feel myself to be here and now, and therefore the problem of the duration of my soul, of my own soul, tortures me."[73]

Unamuno writes not merely of wanting to live but also of wanting "this I" to live—*the I that he feels himself to be here and now*. If the first part of the passage emphasizes the desire to live, the second points to what gives it its insistence: the *felt desirability of just being, of persisting as the conscious being that you are*.[74] The felt desirability of just being should not be confused with another kind of felt desirability in living. The latter rests on the myriad mundane pleasures we experience. You awaken in the morning, aware of the morning light seeping into your room, the feel of the sheets against your skin, the warmth from the blankets. You hike through the woods awash with fall color, listening to the soft thud of your boots striking the ground and the snap of the twigs beneath your feet. You pause from your reading and take notice of your breathing, the expansion and contraction of your lungs as the air slides down your throat and slips back out again. As Joseph Raz expresses it, we experience the pleasure that comes with being "saturated with valued sensations": "the skin and one's muscles feel good, and one is full of the pleasure of living, even while just walking the street looking at familiar sights."[75] Raz reminds us that we commonly experience not only pleasurable but also painful sensations, not only pleasing but also heartrending thoughts and imaginings; and so, he concludes, the value of a life is determined by the value of its contents, and life itself is not unconditionally and intrinsically valuable.[76] But the felt desirability of just being is distinct from the pleasure of living, and so the fact that we have conscious moments of physical and emotional pain is inapposite. In any case, my point is not that *life itself* is unconditionally and intrinsically valuable, whatever that might mean.

The experience I have in mind need involve no conative state of the sort we ordinarily associate with pleasure; and yet, we certainly may find satisfying our awareness of our own conscious existence—of the "I" we each are, here and now. The experience of just being is deeply attractive, pleasing in that sense, and that it is shows up in our resistance to the extinction of our consciousness, even as we feel pain and even as we may rationally consider ending our lives.[77] These considerations bear on our interest in extended existence, for the longing we may feel to linger beyond a normal human life span is, at least in significant part, a longing that we continue simply to *be*. We care, of course, about the quality of our being here, about what we do while here, but except under quite dire circumstances, and often despite them, being here—that is, existing as the conscious being each of us is—has an attraction all its own.

How, though, might the felt desirability of existing bear on the *reasons* a person has to live? It might, if it were responsive to some value, and so an indicator of something inherently reason-giving. Just how it might be responsive to some value is a difficult question, but no more difficult than the question of how any of our experiences might be responsive to, and indicators of, value. In any case, to make sense of the appeal of extended existence we need only see how our experience might be *as if of something valuable*, and so of something more than a mere drive or want.[78]

Consider candidate experiences of something as having value: looking with wonder at a fine painting, joyfully listening to a symphony, loving our family and friends. These experiences exhibit a common structure: each, phenomenally, involves a seemingly fitting emotional engagement with some seemingly worthy object, activity, or being.[79] But why think that, in these cases, our experiences are as if of something with value, rather than merely of something we enjoy or desire? There are certain standard indicators that we treat something as a matter of value, chief among them, that we treat the thing itself or responses to it as appropriately subject to critical assessment. For example, we may judge that a particular sonata doesn't merit appreciation or that another is better and more deserving. If ever we have what is plausibly an experience of something as if it were valuable, our experiences of appreciative engagement with the arts and loving connection with others count as such. In the same way, we can have an experience of something as of value in appreciating our own existence.[80]

How might the structure of paradigmatic experiences as if of value exhibit itself in the experience of one's existing?[81] The object of seeming worth cannot be merely life or being alive, but *your* (or *my*) being alive, *your* (or *my*) existing as individual agent with a distinctive vantage point. How might this be thought an object of value? One possible answer might draw on broadly Kantian ideas.[82] Suppose that persons have what seems an unconditional value on account of special features they possess. These might include capacities to reason and assess, to explore and discover, to create and appreciate beauty of form and sound, to will and to love— in short, the agential capacities that enable us to realize and experience a world of seeming value. In virtue of our having such features—of our being valuers—we can also value our selves as beings with those very features.

A standard indicator of when we treat something as a value rather than as a mere object of desire operates with persons, much as it does with putative intrinsic values, though in ways particular to the unconditional, equal value persons seemingly have. We judge one person's treatment of another as just or unjust, respectful or degrading; we assess her treatment of herself as fair or unfair, self-respecting or self-destructive. Our reactive attitudes, from outrage at mistreatment of another to indignation at mistreatment of our selves, suggest that we regard persons as having a special status and standing.[83]

In our experience, then, of "this I" that we each are, here and now, we make direct contact with a seemingly valuable being. And just as with other experiences as if of value, there are modes of fitting emotional engagement with seemingly valuable beings, including oneself—most notably, respecting, caring for, and loving. Self-respect and self-love, appreciating and finding satisfying your existing, are appropriate responses to the worth you seem to have, much as having due regard for others' existing is an appropriate response to their apparent value. We ordinarily do appreciate our own existing, whether that engagement is enjoyment or mature self-love.[84]

Now, if to continue living as the conscious beings we each are is to remain in touch with something of seeming value, then we can explain not simply the appeal of remaining alive but why we might have reason to live, quite apart from our desires. We can also more deeply appreciate why Epicurus's famous counsel provides cold comfort. It does little good to tell us not to fear death on the grounds that "when death is present, then we do not exist," for that is precisely the problem— when death is come, *we* are not: "this I" that we each are and feel ourselves to be, here and now, ceases to exist, and so we can no longer be apprehended, whether by self or others, as the valuable beings we apparently are.[85] Our resistance to dying isn't due merely to a reactive drive to self-preservation, any more than is our attraction to life: it is at least partly a revulsion at the thought of our not being.[86]

In the ordinary case, and even in the rational suicide case, there would seem to be a thumb on the normative scale in favor of continued life. Yet, even if existing as the conscious beings we are has its own attraction, even if we are averse to the idea of our not being, more will be needed to account for the rational appeal of extended existence. For as already noted, we obviously care, and have reason to care, not merely about our existing but about the quality of our existence. This accounts for what force there may be in Williams's insistence on the need for categorical desires and his concern for their extinction. For reasons offered earlier, however, categorical desires just as such cannot explain the rational appeal of extended existence.

There is, to be sure, a place for categorical desires. But whereas on Williams's view, our categorical desires for things besides life itself give us reason to live, on the view I am exploring, what gives us reason to live gives us reason to have the sorts of projects and relationships that tend to be, and are capable of being (if they are to be categorical reason-giving), the objects of our categorical desires.[87] According to the latter view, we can explain how the felt desirability of our existing is an experience as if of value by appealing to our own seeming value, a value to which we respond appropriately with various forms of self-regarding engagement. Harry Frankfurt has remarked that a person expresses self-love by trying to find things that he can love, just as parents show love for their children by helping them to discover things that they can love.[88] That seems right, at least insofar as loving is a way of valuing as opposed to merely desiring. Because we are the sorts of creatures capable of realizing and experiencing seeming value, we are capable not only of valuing ourselves but, as we have already seen, a great many other things as well. Part of how we show proper self-regard is by filling our lives with activities and pursuits that we can love and see as worthwhile, that express and answer to our agential capacities. Part of how we show proper self-regard is, in short, by giving ourselves a good.[89] Among the most critical of the engagements that make up our good will be those that I earlier suggested tend to be the objects of our categorical desires, those that have an internal shape or trajectory, that give our lives shape and put us in a position to assess them as fulfilling or stunted, as meaningful or meaningless. Happiness may indeed require, as Williams contends, that some of our desires be "fully categorical" in the sense that we want to continue to exist in part because of those very desires. But insofar as that is true, that is because we are creatures with capacities that enable us to value and find reasons to live, and in particular, to value ourselves on account of those very capacities.[90]

We can now understand what Williams's framework overlooks. We can also appreciate why his example of the rational suicide, which he employs to argue for the necessity of categorical desires, may mislead us. Suicide does not typically involve rational calculation, and where it does, the calculation may favor suicide only instrumentally in the service of a cause or, more sadly, in the interest of escaping recalcitrant and debilitating depression. Unsurprisingly, various adverse conditions can dull our ability to appreciate what ordinarily seems of value—including our own existence. People who suffer from depression commonly report a diminished capacity to enjoy or care about the things that would ordinarily excite their interest.[91] But their problem isn't merely the loss of categorical desire. More fundamentally, as common reports of feelings of worthlessness would indicate, they have lost the satisfying appreciation of their own being.

Suicide is, no doubt, a complex phenomenon with multiple causes. In some cases, external rather than internal conditions may rob life of its appeal. Sadly, a person's circumstances may sometimes be so adverse that she faces a life of overwhelming horror. Consideration of both the adverse internal and external conditions a person may confront in leading a life brings into stark relief the normative burden that accompanies the choice of parenthood. We bring into the world a conscious being, someone who will occupy a distinctive point of view. Our own experience may support a reasonable prediction that our child's existence will be for her, on balance, a good thing. But we cannot know for certain that the person we create will not be someone for whom the genetic lottery or calamitous circumstances renders existence a nightmare.

3.2 Agential Character and Alternate Possibilities

Emilia's life has become, if not quite a nightmare, then at least a long, dull dream. Although what drives Čapek's narrative is Emilia's quest to extend her life again, she does, in the end, forego the formula for the elixir, and so we can suppose that she regards any felt desirability in just being as outweighed—or better, as overwhelmed—by the negative features of her condition. Whatever else it might teach us, Emilia's case does illustrate how the desirability of extended existence depends on what it would be like. But as Williams correctly insists, what *it* would be like depends, in part, on what *we* are (and would be) like.

What we are like, however, is not simply a matter of our character. Our psychological and physiological makeup sets limits on what undertakings and lives could appeal to us. But the capacities that render us autonomous agents—that equip us to think creatively and act effectively within the parameters of the natural world— also enable us to think creatively and act effectively within the parameters of our own makeup and circumstances. We can reflect, reason, discover, imagine, and evaluate, and we can guide ourselves in accordance with our values, choices, and plans. In exercising these capacities, at least under favorable conditions, each of us decides what sort of life to lead. We also decide what sort of person to be or become, for the different lives we might lead will draw on and develop different facets of our makeup and lead us to have, in significant ways, different desires and interests.[92] We can also reevaluate and reimagine, altering our plans, our lives, and our selves. Most often, we do so seeking improvement and personal growth, but sometimes we change our lives and selves, not to make them better, but to make them different. Given our capacities, it is unsurprising that the rational appeal of extended existence survives awareness of the limits of our human character. Our agential character leads us, in effect, to reject the suggestion that we would, in an extended existence, run out of things to desire and do.

My point is not merely that human agents happen to be particularly adept at imagining other possibilities and finding new interests. Rather, the capacity to imagine other possibilities is necessary to our *being* agents in the first place. Debates in the literature on free will and moral responsibility have often centered on what has been called the "principle of alternate possibilities," or "PAP." According to that principle, a person is morally responsible for what she has done only if she could have done otherwise. Philosophers have argued about what is required for it to be true that a person could have done otherwise, as well as about whether PAP, or some variant of it, is true.[93] Whatever we might conclude, the latter principle rests on a prior principle, what we might call the "principle of imaginative possibilities." As a rough statement of the principle, we might say this: an individual could not *be* an agent, a being with the capacity for self-governance, unless she had the capacity to imagine otherwise. It must be possible for her to deliberate and decide what she shall do, but she cannot deliberate and choose except as between at least apparent possibilities. Whereas PAP concerns the conditions for morally responsible action, the principle of imaginative possibilities concerns the conditions for being an agent and a practical reasoner in the first place.

As with many of the capacities that have been thought to be necessary to or constitutive of autonomous agency, the capacity to imagine possibilities admits of degrees. Presumably, the most minimal exercise of that capacity, say, imagining one alternative on one occasion, is insufficient for self-governance. I cannot here address the difficult question of how generally the capacity must operate, but it's plausible to think that autonomous agency requires meeting some threshold and that beyond that threshold, individuals can be more or less autonomous.[94] As it happens, despite wide variation, human agents tend to have a fairly robust capacity to imagine possibilities. Otherwise, we would not find ourselves contemplating the desirability of extended existence so variously conceived. Of course, what matters to explaining our being agents and practical reasoners is not mere imaginative capacity but the capacity to imagine other seemingly *desirable* possibilities, and more precisely for present purposes, the ability to imagine other desirable lives we might live and the selves we would be living them. In the full exercise of our agency, with not only our imagination but our motivational and critical faculties engaged, we have just that capacity.

Now I want to suggest that, even if there is no perpetual activity that could make boredom "unthinkable," our agency might—at least, unthinkable enough to make sense of the appeal of extended existence. As we live our lives and exercise our capacities, we will find ourselves in countless situations in which we imagine and entertain various options, more than one of which might appeal to us. We might be drawn, for example, to a career in law and in the arts, to a life of public service and a quiet life in the country. We will envision differing things we might do, differing lives we might live, and the differing selves we would become in living those lives. From our standpoint as agents, our futures seem open, albeit not unrestricted, and our features seem flexible, albeit not entirely malleable. To be sure, it does not follow from the fact that we can imagine other possibilities for ourselves that we would be able successfully to realize those possibilities; it does not follow from the fact that we can imagine other selves we might become that we would be able successfully to become those others selves. It does not follow, then, that we would not, in fact, run out of things to desire or do. But these considerations bear on the actual—and, as I have stressed, contingent—desirability of extended existence.

It is worth noticing that our attraction to the idea of extended existence is rooted in the same capacities that make us susceptible to regret.[95] We are subject to regret because we are able to reflect on our lives and our selves and to imagine other lives we might have had and other selves we might have become. But we live our lives under conditions of material and temporal scarcity—we have just one life to live, and a limited one at that; we must therefore choose among the possibilities if we are to succeed in leading satisfying lives at all. The options we forego, however, may lose none of their appeal, and so we are prone to experience the loss of our other lives and selves, not only at the time of choosing but also later in reflecting on our lives and choices.

Because of our nature, our imagining persists, of course, and appealing options continue to present themselves. As a consequence, even if our hearts must be whole enough to live happily the lives we choose, even if we must resolve our inner conflicts and be unified enough to act and live, we can reasonably expect that we will often be less than wholehearted, that we will often experience some ambivalence, that we will, in sum, find ourselves *less* than fully unified agents. The capacities that consti-tute us as agents are thus a continuing source of disunity, even as they enable us to constitute ourselves as cohesive individuals. Some may find this worrisome.[96] But I am inclined to put in a plug for the (in my view) healthy ambivalence and disunity to which our agency inclines us—to put in a plug for being less than wholehearted and fully unified. There is, after all, an upside to imaginative straying, to keeping a bit of one's heart in reserve. For it helps to increase the odds that when the lives and selves we have chosen fail us or cease to fit us, we will be able to find someone else to be and something else to do. It thus helps to ensure that the emotional engagement with our lives necessary to support categorical desire does not give out.

The appeal of extended existence, then, should come as no surprise. For insofar as the options we forego present themselves as desirable, as alternate opportunities for realizing value in our lives, insofar as our imaginings persist, alerting us to options that we must or will forgo, extended existence seems to hold out the tantalizing pros-pect of recouping some of our losses. But also of preventing loss, for it also holds out the prospect of continuing to live the lives we have chosen and still love, whatever the temptations of our imaginings. Either way, our agency would make not only bore-dom but regret almost unthinkable.[97] Whether or not an extended existence would be desirable, then, its rational appeal, it seems to me, is undeniable.

3.3 On the Need for an Ending

And yet, one might well deny it. As noted earlier, one might argue that the wide-spread desire for extended existence is misguided, that such an existence would, as Williams concludes, be problematic, but for reasons other than those Williams offers. I here consider briefly just one such line of argument, and this one in partic-ular because like my efforts to explain the rational appeal of extended existence, it rests, in part, on considerations about our agency.

According to this line of argument, the desire for extended existence reflects a mis-understanding about the nature of personal good and the requirements of a meaning-ful life. Suppose, as David Velleman has suggested, that because later events can alter the meaning or significance of earlier events and thereby alter the welfare value of a life, an individual's welfare depends not simply on good moments, or benefit at a time, but on the "narrative relations" that hold among events in her life over time. Personal good thus has a diachronic as well as a synchronic dimension, and along its diachronic dimension, the welfare value of a life is a matter of its shape and, more specifically, its "narrative structure."[98] Whether a person successfully completes a project or fails, for example, affects the welfare value of her life by determining whether her earlier efforts were vindicated or wasted. Whether she overcomes adversity or is overcome by her own recklessness likewise affects the welfare value of her life by determining whether her life's narrative is ultimately a story of personal triumph or a cautionary tale. Because narrative relations affect the relative welfare value of lives, even lives equal in their momentary welfare value may be better or worse for the persons living them. Personal good arguably could have this diachronic dimension only because, as agents, we have capacities that enable us to step back from our momentary experience and to reflect on and assess extended periods of our lives or even our lives as a whole.[99] Our good is, as it were, the good of creatures who are natural storytellers and who, in living and choosing, each constructs his or her own life story.

The "narrativity thesis" about welfare might seem to require that a life, like a good story, come to an end.[100] If a life is to be good for the person living it, it must play out and conclude a successful narrative arc, thereby resolving in a satisfying way what to think and feel about that life, considered as a whole. I have much sympathy for the idea that the narrative shape of our lives matters and that our capacity for storytelling has an impact not only on our welfare but even, as some have suggested, on the meaningfulness of our lives.[101] But I do not believe such considerations help Williams's case.

Even as we respect the insights of the narrativity thesis, we must be careful not to confuse the need for endings with the need for an end or the need for shape in a life with the need for the shape of a single, completed narrative.[102] Many successful human lives, even with our limited temporal and material resources, successfully complete one "story line" only to change course and open up a new one; and some successful lives become successful only after abandoning a failed story line. A life that takes the form of a single narrative, whatever that might require, is not obviously superior from the standpoint of welfare value or meaning to a life of "second acts," short stories, and sequels.[103] As for completion, we certainly have some need for *endings* and, in particular, for endings that mark the successful completion of a project or endeavor. This is particularly true of those projects and endeavors that I have suggested tend to be the objects of our categorical desires, that give shape to our lives and lend them meaning. It doesn't follow, however, that we have need for an end. Even if we did, an extended existence would have *some* end. And, as Williams's rational suicide case reminds us, we can choose our own end.

4. CONCLUSION

Let's return, at last, to Emilia's predicament and to the question of what morals we might draw for the mortal lives we lead. Emilia's life, we learn, is not only one of utter boredom but also of intolerable isolation. She does not appear to categorically desire anything, but more important, she does not feel; she lacks emotional responsiveness and, it appears, the capacity to find value in anything.

Čapek offers scant evidence that Emilia ever imaginatively engaged with her life or cared for anyone or anything.[104] When asked whether she had had any children besides Ferdy, Gregor's great grandfather, she reports, "Twenty or so. I can't keep track of everything." When asked why she hadn't told Ferdy about the will, she replies, "I never cared much about my offspring."[105] She appears beautiful from a distance, but hideous up close, and her sometimes shocking indifference leads Gregor to exclaim in horror, "You're evil, Emilia, you're wicked and terrible. An animal, without human feelings....Nothing matters to you. You're cold, like a knife, like a corpse risen from the grave."[106]

Her coldness and detachment elicit reactions that only seal her isolation. Repeatedly, the men in her thrall express their desire to kill her or to kill themselves over her, and in the fourth act, Prus's eighteen-year-old son, Janek, does kill himself. When Emilia learns of his suicide, she casually responds, "Ah, well, so many have killed themselves," and goes about fixing her hair and ordering breakfast.[107] Earlier, she responds with equal indifference when Gregor threatens to kill her. "So he wants to kill me. See this scar here on my neck? That was another man who wanted to kill me. Shall I take my clothes off and show you all my other little love mementoes?"[108] She has become for others, in Gregor words, something "wild" and "terrible," something "wonderful," "provoking," "maddening." The tendency of men thus to objectify her expresses a certain sexism, but it is also a natural reaction to her emotional detachment. For our recognizing another as a human agent, our responding to her as such, partly depends on her exhibiting not only the relevant cognitive capacities but also the emotional capacities that equip us for human and inter-agential engagement.

According to Emilia, her extended existence has induced her nihilism, for what one sees when life goes on too long is that "nothing changes," "nothing matters," nothing merits our belief, "nothing exists"—not love or art.[109] She expresses envy of those with short lives who are "still close to things," for whom "everything means something," "everything has value."[110] And yet Emilia points to nothing that would rationally connect a life's going on for too long with the claimed epistemic insight. What would one see in going on for 337 years about the value of a Picasso or the value of one's child that one couldn't see in living a currently normal lifespan? Why would everything mean something for eighty years, say, but not for 300? Surely the problem is not that if a person were to live an extended existence, she would see that nothing matters, but that she may reach a point at which, as it happens, nothing matters or could matter *to her.*

That is the point Emilia has reached, and for all that I have argued herein, were we to live long enough, each of us would meet a similar fate.[111] And yet it is hard to separate Emilia's fate from the peculiarities of her situation. What would one expect, after all, for someone whose father would follow so outrageous an order, thereby cutting his own child loose from human life as we know it and leaving her to drift alone through time? What would *that* do to a person? In the end, I'm inclined to think that the real worry Emilia's story presents is that our lives might be extended in a way that eliminates what strikes me as truly indispensable, and that is not categorical desire so much as hope and the capacity to love. Without hope, we will not see our lives as holding out something to look forward to. Without the capacity to love—to connect—nothing our lives might hold out will seem to us to matter.

Is it a good thing, then, that we are not immortal? As I have explained, unlike Williams, I think the question too ill-formed to admit of a determinate answer. As for a merely "extended existence," we can only guess at how our psychologies and our ideas about how to build and shape a life would change were our temporal resources doubled or quadrupled. Of more interest, I think, is the question of why the idea of extended existence might reasonably have a hold on us. The answer I have sketched appeals to our peculiarly agential character. As agents, I have suggested, we are able to experience a seeming value in our being and in other things besides that makes us self-propelling into the future; we have, moreover, capacities that incline us to be hopeful by inclining us to imagine worthwhile possibilities, perhaps most important among them, possibilities for engagement with others. These things are related, obviously, but more to the point, they are related in a way that makes explicable why it has seemed to many that "man needs more time to live." In seeing ourselves, our own existence, as valuable, we see it as we do any seemingly unconditioned or intrinsic value, as fit for valuing *timelessly*. And we respond appropriately to our own (seeming) value, as well as that of others, by seizing possibilities for connecting and for creating and securing value in our lives.[112]

NOTES

1. Čapek, 1999, p. 248, spoken by Vitek, assistant to the lawyer, Dr. Kolenaty.
2. She had many other aliases besides: "I was Ekaterina Myshkina and Elsa Müller too, and God knows who else. One can't live with you people for three hundred years with the same name" (Čapek, 1999, p. 239).
3. Ibid., 1999, p. 242.
4. I say "seeming effects of this extension" because despite Emilia's claims about herself in the fourth act, it's unclear what is cause and what is effect of her sad condition.
5. Emilia is also unaware that the testator is deceased. Her surprise upon learning of Josef ("Peppy") Prus's death is initially puzzling, but as the story unfolds, we learn that she had revealed her secret and given him the formula, which apparently killed him.
6. Emilia thus does not arrive in order to reveal the existence of the will but ends up revealing it simply in the course of inquiring about the case. The story does not make this clear, but insofar as her disclosure is deliberate, it is in the form of a quid pro quo: Gregor and his lawyer will get the will, she will get the rest of "the Greek papers" (Čapek, 1999, p. 188).
7. Williams, 1973. Williams mentions that Čapek's play was made into an opera. I have not seen the opera and do not know how closely it follows the play, but Williams's recounting of the story omits some important details. For instance, he describes Emilia as refusing to take the elixir again, and, she does, in the end decline to take it, but only after going to some lengths to obtain the formula.

8. Williams,1973, p. 82.
9. Williams seems to acknowledge this imperative when he tells us that he does not mean to deny "the existence, the value, or the basic necessity of a sheer reactive drive to self-preservation: humanity would certainly whither were the drive to keep alive not stronger than any perceived reasons for keeping alive" (1973, p. 86; see also p. 98).
10. For a survey of competing views about the relevance of immorality to life's meaning, see Metz, 2003.
11. Of course, not all people long for an extended life, let alone for an immortal life, yet it's undeniable that a great many do. Perhaps most commonly, the desire for extended existence finds expression in religious beliefs about an afterlife, but contemporary efforts by doctors and scientists to discover ways of extending average human life expectancy offer further testimony. See Temkin, 2008, pp. 194–195, for a brief discussion of research on longevity. Consider also, as Sarah Payne has reminded me, the "transhumanist" and cryogenics movements. When I talk in terms of the "desire" or "longing" for an extended existence, this should be understood to include a range of stances from genuine longing to mere standing readiness to continue living, other things equal, for as long as one can.
12. Wordsworth, 1807.
13. Temkin, 2008, pp. 195–196, assumes, when he undertakes to engage with the question of whether "living longer is living better," that each of us will be able to choose the biological stage of development at which we will live extendedly, perhaps indefinitely, and that living longer does not mean undergoing physiological or psychological decline. It should be clear why I do not think this is enough specificity to enable reasonable assessment of extended existence. In any case, even if we could carefully stipulate the terms of an endless existence, more than one stipulation would be available to us, and so more than one answer to the question of whether an endless life would be desirable.
14. Williams, 1973, p. 90, also briefly poses this question, and considers as well other contingencies, such as deterioration with old age, that may in fact make death desirable.
15. As I shall explain, though, this seems to be just what Williams, in effect, denies.
16. I'm inclined to add that no one would want to live endlessly in a world of deprivation or devastation, but I acknowledge that this introduces serious complications. The will to live is remarkably resilient even under quite horrifying circumstances, though perhaps it would disappear if one knew those circumstances would never improve.
17. Thanks to Judith Ferster, who reminded me of the Tithonus myth, and to Gil Chesbro, who directed me to Lord Alfred Tennyson's poem, "Tithonus," which takes a few liberties with the original story. Tennyson captures wonderfully the imagined point of view of Tithonus:

The woods decay, the woods decay and fall,
The vapours weep their burthen to the ground,
Man comes and tills the field and lies beneath,
And after many a summer dies the swan.
Me only cruel immortality
Consumes: I wither slowly in thine arms,
Here at the quiet limit of the world,
A white-hair'd shadow roaming like a dream
The ever-silent spaces of the East,
Far-folded mists, and gleaming halls of morn...
Poetry Foundation. http://www.poetryfoundation.org/poem/174656, June 28, 2012.

18. Temkin, 2008, pp. 203–204, observes that, were we to live forever, changes in our psychologies might enable us to envision new, and presumably appealing, life
    . plans. But he confesses to sharing Williams's doubts about whether he would have much reason to be interested in an immortal life in which he would develop a psychology and pursuits so unlike those that make him value and take an interest in prolonging his actual life. Of course, Temkin's musings point to further ambiguity in the question of whether it would be desirable to be immortal. The question might concern whether it would desirable for we actual humans—just as we now are—to live forever, or whether it would be desirable for some humans at some time. It may well be a good thing that we are not immortal, but that hardly entails that immortality would not be desirable for any humans. Presumably, any realistic extensions of human life expectancy would occur over time, and for persons other than us. I have already expressed skepticism about our ability to clearly imagine immortality or to predict how immortal persons would think about what it is to live a human life. Given Temkin's observations, noted above, I assume he would agree.

19. Even the idea of living forever in one's "prime" is insufficiently determinate. Some additional practical complications are explored in Lenman, 2004. One could, in any case, rationally doubt the desirability of foregoing future experiences of learning and mastering a craft in favor of pursuing an already mastered craft. Michael Jordan's much-ridiculed experiment with a second career in baseball was not about nothing. Of course, he couldn't have carried on at his peak in basketball for more than a few additional years. Still, people often deliberately change track, giving up for a new undertaking an activity in which they could have excelled for the remainder of their active lives.

20. For a picture of endless existence that seems to combine the worst imaginable conditions, see Swift, 1726/2010, part 3, ch. 10. Among the many regrettable features of the condition of the Struldbruggs, they were "uncapable of any Friendship, and dead to all natural Affection, which never descended below their Grand-children," and owing not only to this but to various other features of their condition, they were "cut off from all possibility of Pleasure." Thanks to Kent Mullikan for the reference.

21. Čapek, 1999, p. 256

22. Perhaps the most striking example of her callousness occurs when news arrives that Prus's son, Janek, who believes himself to be in love with Emilia, has committed suicide. Emilia, seeking to secure the Greek papers, agrees to have sex with Prus. Janek sees his father enter her hotel, waits outside for two hours, then shoots himself in despair. Upon receiving the news, Emilia evinces no feeling, no sympathy for Prus (Čapek, 1999, p. 223). I discuss these distortions in Emilia's affect and her relations with others briefly toward the end of this essay.

23. Williams, 1973, p. 90

24. Ibid., 1973, p. 83, emphasis added: "EM's state suggests at least this, that death is not necessarily an evil, and not just in the sense in which almost everybody would agree to that, where death provides an end to great suffering, but in the more intimate sense that it can be a good thing not to live too long. It suggests more than that, for it suggests that it was not a peculiarity of EM's that an endless life was meaningless."

25. See the quotation in note 24. This is important, because it means that Williams's arguments, if successful, would bear more generally on things like longevity research and the ambitions of some transhumanists.

26. Allen Buchanan has observed, in conversation, that average life expectancy has increased and that people seem to have had no difficulty adjusting to the extension.

My framing of the issue in terms of "extended existence" draws on this thought. I leave claims about actual increases in life expectancy aside, however. As I understand it, such claims may be misleading, because the increase is due largely to such factors as a decrease in the infant morality rate.

27. If we assume, as I have in the text, an average life expectancy of 80, then given her current age, Emilia will have lived an extra 257 years.

28. Williams, 1973, p. 82, emphasis added

29. Ibid., p. 85. For a different take on why death is bad, see Fischer, 2005, p. 390.

30. Ibid. p. 85.

31. Ibid.

32. Fischer, 2009 uses the label "conditional desire." Thanks to David Velleman for helpful suggestions regarding how to clarify and sharpen Williams's distinction.

33. The latter, I take it, is supposed to be a conceptual point. On the motivational role of categorical desires, see Williams, 1973, p. 100.

34. See, e.g., Williams, 1973, pp. 87–88. A person can, of course, have categorical reason to do something without having overriding reason to do it.

35. Ibid., p. 85.

36. Ibid., p. 86.

37. Ibid., p. 86.

38. Ibid., pp. 86–87.

39. Ibid., p. 88.

40. Thanks to David Velleman for suggesting that I develop this point.

41. See Williams, 1973, p. 87, describing reasons for avoiding death as "grounded" in categorical desires. For criticism of desire-based accounts of reasons, see, e.g., Darwall, 1983 and Scanlon, 1998. I talk in terms of the desire providing a reason, but, presumably, it is not the desire itself but (in part) the fact that one has that desire that would provide a reason.

42. Just apply, in this context, common examples—the person with a desire to count blades of grass or to exact revenge for trivial slights. Contra Williams, some interesting generalizations likely can be made about categorical desires. Fischer, 2009, p. 89, suggests that desires for "repeatable pleasures" might have the propelling force of categorical desires, though that doesn't quite address whether they are reason-giving.

43. Williams,1973, p. 88. Presumably, when Williams says that there is no desirable property "life" would have, he means to be talking about an individual person's life. That is to say, "life" should be read as a count noun rather than a mass noun. Thanks to David Velleman for suggesting the need for clarification of this ambiguity in the passage from Williams.

44. Fischer, 2009, pp. 85–90, distinguishes between self-exhausting and repeatable pleasures, where the former include things like the pleasure of climbing Mt. Whitney; and the latter, the pleasures of sex, fine food, and beautiful music. Insofar as pleasures are repeatable, and insofar as the value of a life is additive, a longer life might well be a life with a higher total of pleasure; and in this respect, a better life. For competing views as to whether the value of a life is additive, see Velleman, 1991; and Feldman, 2006, ch. 6.

45. See Fischer, 2009 for extended criticism of Williams's apparent assumption that an immortal existence must answer to a different set of standards than mortal existence.

46. Williams, 1973, p. 90, emphasis added.

47. For discussion of the effects of boredom in an ordinary life, see Frankfurt, 1999a, pp. 88–89. By "vindicating" our longing for extended existence, I do not mean showing that such longing is correct but, rather, that it is not irrational or without reason.

48. Williams, 1973, p. 91.
49. Ibid., pp. 91–92.
50. Ibid., p. 91.
51. David Velleman has suggested that perhaps Williams means to say the following: if happiness and meaningfulness in an extended future depend upon a person's future categorical desires, then her rational interest now in having that extended future requires that she have a categorical desire now that those desires be fulfilled. But those future desires would be unrelated to the categorical desires she has now, and so she wouldn't be able to recognize them as hers, and it would make no sense for her to have a categorical desire now that they be fulfilled. The reply, Velleman observed, is that even if there is no moment at which a person has reason to want an infinite future, for each moment, she will have had reason to want the finite period up to and including it. I take it that the suggested reply essentially expresses in different terms the point I am making in the text, though I may read Williams a bit differently. There is, however, more we can say in response to Velleman's suggested interpretation. For in fact, we can't assume that a person's future categorical desires would be unrelated to the categorical desires she has now; we simply don't know. Consider how things work in our actual lives. I don't know what my desires might be twenty years from now, anymore than I knew two years ago what my desires would be today. The shifts in our desires are typically, though not always, incremental, and even when our new desires surprise us, only rarely do we regard them as utterly alien. Unless a person has reason to believe she is likely to come to have desires so alien to what she can make sense of valuing, it seems entirely rational to assume that her future desires will be hers and adequate to the aims she has in wanting to survive. See also note 52.
52. Of course, one might then suspect that even if a person's aims, at any particular time, will be adequately related to those she had in wanting so survive at an immediately prior time, cumulative changes in character will cause a failure of the first condition. But as Williams sees it, Emilia meets the first condition, so this cannot be the problem he means to raise. Even if it were, as both Fischer, 2009, pp. 89–90, and Temkin, 2008, pp. 200–201, observe, an appropriate relationship between a person and her future desires can obtain even if her character and aims change over time. Fischer emphasizes that how a person would view her changed self and her new aims depends upon how and why these changes came about; in this respect, immortal existence need be no different from mortal existence. Temkin argues that on Williams's own desire-based view of reasons, what matters isn't that a person's character and commitments remain constant over time but that she have, within her current motivational set, "an unconditional desire that [she] have, a future flourishing self...even if it is radically different than [her] current self." In any case, he argues, Williams ignores the fact that a future self that may now seem vastly different from a person's present self usually gets that way through a process of gradual change, with significant continuity between any one stage and the next. "As long as there is significant continuity of character from period to period, that is enough for us to be self-interestedly concerned about the preservation and wellbeing of our evolving self. Thus...there could well be reason to seek immortality, even if there would not be constancy of one's deepest projects, commitment and character over time" (p. 201). On Temkin's own view, as he explains, there are also value-based reasons, and a person may have such reasons to seek immortality, if that would be better for her, even if her character, projects, and commitments were to change over time (p. 201).

53. Williams, 1973, p. 95. See Fisher (2009: 82–84) for criticism of what he takes to be Williams's suggestion that there must be some *single* activity that is endlessly fascinating and that any activity must be *endlessly* fascinating.
54. Ibid., p. 100.
55. Ibid, p. 100.
56. Williams might seem to have in mind something like what Frankfurt, 1999a, has described in writing about the necessity or usefulness of "final ends." His emphasis on categorical desires, however, falls short of Frankfurt's suggestion that for our lives to be meaningful, we must engage in activity that seems to us to serve some point, that is "devoted to something [we care] about," for caring about is a more complex attitude than desiring, and one can categorically desire things that serve no particular point at all (Williams, 1973, p. 85). For commentary and reply, see Wolf, 2002; and Frankfurt, 2002.
57. Williams, 1973, p. 89.
58. For a different reply to the worry about boredom than the one I shall offer, see Fischer, 2009, pp. 84–88. Fischer's reply draws on his distinction between self-exhausting and repeatable pleasures. Given an adequate mix and distribution of repeatable pleasures, he contends, an endless life need not be a one of abject boredom. Temkin, 2008, pp. 202–204, expresses some sympathy for Williams's worry about boredom but also stresses as a key difference between their views that he thinks even a very boring life might well be worth living.
59. Of course, he does offer an account of character elsewhere, most notably in Williams, 1981b. Elijah Millgram has suggested that Williams's essay must be read, not only in conjunction with his essay, "Internal and External Reasons," but also in connection which much of the rest of his corpus. I'm less certain than Millgram about the propriety of this interpretive strategy because of doubts as to when we may fairly read into earlier work views that may not have been developed until later. But even if we suppose that Williams's later views about character ought to be read into his exploration of *The Makropulos Case*, I doubt it helps his case. On the contrary, it seems to create additional difficulties for him. Williams treats a person's character as constituted by her desires and projects. He is free, of course, to stipulate a meaning for the term, but his isn't the ordinary notion of character. It would seem to have the result, for example, that a person's character changes continuously, in smaller and larger ways, over the course of a lifetime, whereas the more common, and more intuitive view, would be that a person's character might remain relatively stable even as her desires and projects change. In any case, it seems implausible that unless a person's future self is executing her current projects, she will be unable to see that future self's aims as adequately related to her own. If that were so, we might expect to be as alienated from our adult selves or elderly selves as from our extended selves. Temkin, 2008, pp. 200–201, considers Williams's view of character and likewise concludes that so long as there is continuity from one period of life to the next, it would be enough to provide reason to continue living. The more common view of character that I suppose Williams to hold in his essay on the Makropulos case is, I believe, both more plausible than his view of character elsewhere and more consistent with the arguments in his essay.
60. For remarks suggesting such a view, see Williams, 1973, pp. 90–91.
61. For a recent and especially thoughtful treatment of issues about the stability of character traits and virtue, see Railton (2011).
62. Nagel, 1986, p. 224, writes that "given the simple choice between living for another week and dying in five minutes I would always choose to live for another week; and

by a version of mathematical induction I conclude that I would be glad to live forever. Perhaps I shall eventually tire of life, but at the moment, I can't imagine it, nor can I understand those many distinguished and otherwise reasonable persons who sincerely assert that they don't regard their own mortality as a misfortune." He cites Williams as an example of the latter sort of person, asking, "Can it be that he is more easily bored than I?" (p. 224, n. 3).

63. For a couple of rare efforts to unpack the concept of a meaningful life (or of meaning in life), see Metz, 2001; and Wolf, 2010.

64. But see Wolf, 1997. Perhaps meaning in life arises, as Wolf has argued, when "subjective attraction meets objective attractiveness"—when an individual is happy and engaged in objectively worthwhile pursuits. But if that is true, it is not because a life's being meaningful just is its being happy and engaged with worthwhile pursuits; such a view would fail to distinguish a life's being meaningful from it's being good for the person living it. For further development of her view about meaning in life, see Wolf, 2010.

65. The framing perhaps already hints at his own later view of "internal reasons." See Williams,1981a. A great deal of ink has been spilt trying to interpret Williams's view. For extensive discussion, and a novel take on Williams, see e.g., Finlay, p. 2009. Williams, 1973, p. 88 does acknowledge that there may be other reasons for regarding death as a misfortune than the sort he explores (those that are grounded in categorical desires).

66. Defending this framework would be quite an undertaking, much as would be defending the framework Williams himself deploys.

67. My interest lies not with understanding the psychological or biological basis of our desire to remain alive, but with understanding how the widespread longing to continue—and Emilia's—might be rational, or more precisely, might be supported by reasons. Consequently, I am also not concerned with Emilia's own explanations of her actions or her expressions of a fear of death.

68. See Marx, 1978, p. 88.

69. Ibid., pp. 88–89.

70. Throughout, I talk chiefly in terms of apparent value rather than value, because the alternative framework I sketch can be understood and elaborated in either realist or irrealist terms. I take the expressions "apparent value," "seeming value," and so on, to be neutral on the question of whether what we see as valuable really is as we see it.

71. We would need to take care, of course, to avoid any too-crude distinction between human and nonhuman animal.

72. Williams, 1973, p. 98.

73. Unamuno, 1954, p. 45.

74. My claim is not, I should stress, that people would report their experiences in just this way, that they would claim to have an experience as if of something with value, though people do talk all too commonly about the value of life, about how "good it is to be alive," about valuing their own lives and those of the people near and dear to them.

75. See Raz, 2001, p. 116.

76. Compare Nagel, 1979, p. 2: "We need not give an account of these goods [that life contains] here, except to observe that some of them, like perception, desire, activity, and thought, are so general as to be constitutive of human life. They are widely regarded as formidable benefits in themselves, despite the fact that they are conditions of misery as well as happiness, and that a sufficient quantity of more particular evils can perhaps outweigh them. That is what is meant, I think, by the allegation that it is

good simply to be alive, even if one is undergoing terrible experiences. The situation is roughly this: There are elements which, if added to one's experience, make life better; there are other elements which, if added to one's experience, make life worse. But what remains when these are set aside is not merely neutral: it is emphatically positive. Therefore, life is worth living even when the bad elements of experience are plentiful, and the good ones too meager to outweigh the bad ones on their own. The additional positive weight is supplied by experience itself, rather than by any of its contents." Although I agree with much of what Nagel says, as will become clear, it does not yet capture what I have in mind.

77. What about sleep? Sleep is not, of course, the extinction of our consciousness, both because the mind is active, often consciously, while we sleep, and because our consciousness does not literally go out of existence when we sleep.

78. See Marx, 1978, p. 88.

79. Variations on this rough idea can be found, e.g., in Moore, 1993/1903; and Darwall, 2002. For an extremely helpful explication of Moore's view, see Hurka, 1998.

80. Again, I describe the experience "as if" of something valuable, because there may be no real values. This is, obviously, consistent with our having experiences that seem to us as of something that genuinely matters, and these experiences are quite different from our experiences of merely wanting or enjoying something.

81. For a different model of how our experience of someone might be an experience as if of value, see Darwall, 2002, p. 70. According to Darwall, in feeling sympathetic concern—toward other or ourselves—we experience a person's plight as mattering because we experience her as mattering.

82. See Kant, 1959, but I stress Kantian, to make room for any number of ways of attempting to make out the special normative status of persons. For criticism of extant views about the value of rational nature, see Regan, 2002. For a reply to Regan, see Sussman, 2003. I draw on Kantian ideas herein for illustrative purposes.

83. For a recent well-developed view about the nature of this special standing, see Darwall, 2006.

84. For illuminating discussion of the significance of self-love, see Frankfurt, 2000.

85. Epicurus, 1994, p. 29.

86. For related thoughts, see Nagel, 1986, pp. 223–232. Our trepidation might arise from a confused "fear of the unknown," but it needn't; the nonbelievers among us may dread death while denying there is anything to know, and so any unknown to fear.

87. See supra text accompanying note 29.

88. Frankfurt, 2000, p. 10. For related discussion, see Rosati, 2006b.

89. See Rosati, 2006a and 2007. Of course, under particularly dire conditions, we may express a regard for our own seeming value by choosing to forego continued life. For some discussion in the context of questions about the justification of physician-assisted suicide, see Velleman, 1999.

90. These remarks about agency should not be confused with the thought that we are autonomous agents insofar as we pursue the good. For all I have said, agents can reflect and act against what they judge to be of value. For differing views about whether agents necessarily act "under the guise of the good," see Stampe, 1987; Stocker, 1979; and Velleman, 1992.

91. See, e.g., Casey, 2001.

92. When I talk about deciding what sort of person to be or become, about altering or changing our selves, and as I do later, about our "other selves," I obviously do not mean to suggest that we could each literally become a different person.

93. For a classic challenge to the principle of alternate possibilities, see Frankfurt, 1969.

94. Thanks to David Sobel for raising the question of how much exercise of imaginative capacity is enough.

95. The claims about regret in this paragraph draw on Rosati, 2007.

96. Frankfurt, 1999a, for example, suggests that a kind of dissolution of the active self may result from boredom, which according to Frankfurt, consists in the absence of any compelling cares or interests. And he describes ambivalence as another threat to the active self, because when a person is ambivalent, some aspect of her self will be sacrificed when she chooses. See Frankfurt, 1999b, p. 139, n. 9. But it isn't clear how strictly Frankfurt means for us to take claims like these. The wholeheartedness he thinks essential to the self involves her being, not wholly undivided, but unequivocal as regards her most central concerns. For critical discussion of Frankfurt, see Velleman, 2002.

97. I emphasize almost, for at least two reasons. First, there would be no real "do-overs" in an extended existence, and so we would certainly still be subject to regret. And whether we would experience problematic boredom would remain a contingent matter. So we need not be concerned that extended existence would make choice seem less significant. Thanks to Valerie Tiberius for raising this concern and also for observing that our choices would still involve some loss and so occasion for regret.

98. See Velleman, 1991. (For discussion of the kind of understanding narrative peculiarly provides, see Velleman, 2003.) For related ideas about how narrative structure bears on a life's welfare value, see, e.g., McMahan, 2002, pp. 175–180; and Brännmark, 2003.

99. See Velleman, 1991, pp. 69–71, explaining why the welfare of nonhuman animals does not have the diachronic dimension that he has described.

100. Although David Velleman has, in conversation, expressed some sympathy for Williams's view about extended existence based on considerations about the narrative structure of a life, I do not mean to attribute the argument I consider to Velleman or to any other proponent of the idea that the welfare value of a life partly depends on its narrative structure.

101. On the latter point, see, e.g., McMahan, 2002, p. 178, and, more generally, pp. 175–180; and Brännmark, 2003, p. 337.

102. Fischer, 2005, likewise rejects the need for a life to have an end or to take the shape of a single narrative, and like me, he rejects the idea that considerations about narrative structure count against the desirability of an extended (he says "immortal") existence. Fischer's take, however, rests on ideas that I am inclined to reject. Fischer observes that on the view of narrative explanation developed by Velleman, 2003, narratives must have endings, so it would follow that if our lives are narratives, they must have endings, and so an immortal human life would lack narrative value or meaning. Fischer evidently accepts that if narratives must have an ending, then "this is correct." But he thinks an immortal life could have "something very much like narrative meaning." Each part of an immortal life might be considered as a narrative even if that life as a whole could not be. Such a life would be like a "collection of shorts stories" or a "series of novels" rather than a novel. Fischer tries to salvage narrative value and meaning by suggesting that we can consider parts of a life as narratives. In my view, what we ought to do instead is remind ourselves that our lives are not narratives or stories, even if they can be recounted as stories, and we should reject Fischer's idea that there is a distinct narrative value or meaning (which is not quite the view that

Velleman, who Fischer in large part follows, himself defends). I attempt to make sense
of the narrativity thesis and of how storytelling might affect welfare value in Rosati,
manuscript.

103. There are, to be sure, complicated questions about how to individuate narratives and
how to distinguish narrative continuity from narrative change. But any adequate answer to these questions should not affect what I have said about lives. A life of successive narratives might, in short, have whatever in the way of value conferring structure
a good life requires.

104. She seems to show some genuine emotion on learning that Peppy Prus, the testator,
is dead and remarks that she loved him best of all. Life, she says, "was sweet" with
Maxie, too (Čapek, 1999, p. 240).

105. Ibid., p. 240, and see p. 241.

106. Ibid., p. 215.

107. Ibid., p. 223.

108. Ibid., p. 216.

109. Ibid., pp. 255–256.

110. Ibid., p. 255.

111. Temkin, 2008, while criticizing Williams's argument, offer various reasons—some
pertaining to the quality of an individual's life, some to the negative social, political, practical, and moral effects—for thinking that Williams may be right after
all about the merits of an immortal existence. See especially pp. 202–207. For a
recent literary depiction of the practical complications of extended existences, see
Saramago, 2008.

112. This chapter was first drafted in the fall of 2006, during a year in which I had the good
fortune to be supported by the John E. Sawyer Fellowship at the National Humanities Center. Warm thanks to Geoffrey Harpham, Kent Mullikan, and the Center for
creating an ideal work environment. I presented the first version on two occasions
to two very different audiences. In the spring of 2009, I benefited from a stimulating
discussion with members of the philosophy department at the University of Vermont.
But earlier, just after drafting the paper, I presented it at the Osher Lifelong Learning
Institute, through Duke University Continuing Studies. The rather skeptical audience,
consisting of retired persons mostly in their seventies and beyond, asked just the
sorts of insightful questions one would expect, quickly impressing on me the down-
side of aging. But when I asked, "what if you could have had an extra ten years in the
middle?" nearly everyone responded, without skipping a beat, "that would be great."
This is, in microcosm, the phenomenon that interests me herein. Besides the opportunity to learn from both audiences, I have benefited from conversations with Allen
Buchanan, Cheshire Calhoun, Gil Chesbro, Chris Maloney, and Susan Wolf. David
Velleman provided extremely helpful comments on the initial draft, and David Sobel,
Valerie Tiberius, and the editors of this volume, on a later draft. Elijah Millgram offered helpful comments on the final draft, which I was unable to address in time with
the care they deserved.Some twenty-odd years ago, I first read and was captivated
by Bernard Williams's essay, "The Makropulos Case: Reflections on the Tedium of
Immortality." I sent my mother, Elaine Rosati, a copy of the essay, and over the years
we have revisited it any number of times in our wide-ranging conversations. In talking with her, I have benefited not only from the wisdom she has acquired over years
of working with geriatric clients, first as a social worker, and later as lawyer, but also
from her willingness to engage in shared reflection, from our different vantage points,
on what it is like to live a human life. This essay is for her.

References

Brännmark, Johan. 2003. "Leading Lives: On Happiness and Narrative Meaning." *Philosophical Papers* 32: 321–343.

Čapek, Karel. 1999. "The Makropulos Case." In *Four Plays*, Peter Majer and Cathy Porter, trans. London: Methuen World Classics.

Casey, Nell, ed. 2001. *Unholy Ghost: Writers on Depression*. New York: William Morrow.

Darwall, Stephen. 1983. *Impartial Reason*. Ithaca, NY: Cornell University Press.

———. 2002. *Welfare and Rational Care*. Princeton: Princeton University Press.

———. 2006. *The Second-Person Standpoint*. Cambridge, MA: Harvard University Press.

De Unanumo, Miguel. 1954. *Tragic Sense of Life*, trans. J. E. Crawford Fitch. New York: Dover Publications.

Epicurus. 1994. "Letter to Menoeceus." In *The Epicurus Reader: Selected Writings and Testimonia*, Brad Inwood and L. P. Gerson, trans. and ed., pp. 26–31, Text 4. Indianapolis, IN: Hackett.

Feldman, Fred. 2006. *Pleasure and the Good Life*. Oxford: Oxford University Press.

Finlay, Stephen. 2009. "The Obscurity of Internal Reasons." *Philosophers' Imprint* 9: 1–22.

Fischer, John Martin. 2005. "Free Will, Death, and Immortality: The Role of Narrative." *Philosophical Papers* 34: 379–403.

———. 2009. "Why Immortality is Not So Bad." In *Our Stories: Essays on Life, Death, and Free Will*, pp. 79–93. New York: Oxford University Press.

Frankfurt, Harry G. 1969. "Alternate Possibilities and Moral Responsibility." *Journal of Philosophy* 66 (23): 829–839.

———. 1999a. "On the Usefulness of Final Ends." In *Necessity, Volition, and Love*, pp. 84–86. Cambridge: Cambridge University Press.

———. 1999b. "Autonomy, Necessity and Love." In *Necessity, Volition, and Love*, pp. 129–141. Cambridge: Cambridge University Press.

———. 2000. "The Dear Self." *Philosophers' Imprint* 1: 1–14.

———. 2002. "Reply to Susan Wolf." In *Contours of Agency*, Sarah Buss and Lee Overton, ed., pp. 245–252. Cambridge, MA: MIT Press.

Hurka, Thomas. 1998. "Two Kinds of Organic Unity." *Journal of Ethics* 2: 299–320.

Kant, Immanuel. 1959. *Foundations of the Metaphysics of Morals*, trans. L.W. Beck. Indianapolis, IN: Bobbs-Merrill Co.

Lenman, James. 2004. "Immortality: A Letter." In *Life, Death, and Meaning*, David Benatar, ed., pp. 323–330. Oxford: Rowman & Littlefield Publishers.

Marx, Karl. 1978. "Economic and Philosophic Manuscripts of 1844." In *The Marx-Engels Reader*, Robert C. Tucker, ed. New York: W. W. Norton, pp. 66–125.

McMahan, Jeff. 2002. *The Ethics of Killing*. Oxford: Oxford University Press.

Metz, Thaddeus. 2001. "The Concept of a Meaningful Life." *American Philosophical Quarterly* 38: 137–153.

———. 2003. "The Immortality Requirement for Life's Meaning." *Ratio* (new series) 16: 161–177.

Moore, G. E. 1993/1903. *Principia Ethica*, revised edition. Cambridge: Cambridge University Press.

Nagel, Thomas. 1979. "Death." In his *Mortal Questions*, pp. 1–10. Cambridge: Cambridge University Press.

———. 1986. *The View from Nowhere*. New York: Oxford University Press.

Railton, Peter. 2011. "Three Cheers for Virtue: or, Might Virtue Be Habit Forming?" *Oxford Studies in Normative Ethics*. Oxford: Oxford University Press, pp. 295–329.

Raz, Joseph. 2001. "The Value of Staying Alive." In *Value, Respect, and Attachment*, pp. 77–123. Cambridge: Cambridge University Press.

Regan, Donald. 2002. "The Value of Rational Nature." *Ethics* 112: 267–291.

Rosati, Connie. 2006a. "Personal Good," In *Metaethics after Moore*, Terry Horgan and Mark Timmons, eds., pp. 107–132. Oxford: Oxford University Press.

———. 2006b. "Preference-Formation and Personal Good." *Royal Institute of Philosophy Supplements* 81, Supp. 59: 33–64.

———. 2007. "Mortality, Agency, and Regret," In *Moral Psychology* (Poznan Studies in the Philosophy of the Sciences and the Humanities, vol. 94), Sergio Tenenbaum ed., pp. 231–259. Amsterdam/New York, NY: Rodopi.

———. Unpublished manuscript. "The Story of a Life."

Saramago, José. 2008. *Death with Interruptions*, trans. Margaret Jull Costa. New York: Harcourt.

Scanlon, T. M. 1998. *What We Owe to Each Other*. Cambridge: Harvard University Press.

Stampe, Dennis. 1987. "The Authority of Desire." *Philosophical Review* 96: 355–381.

Stocker, Michael. 1979. "Desiring the Bad: An Essay in Moral Psychology." *Journal of Philosophy* 76: 738–753.

Sussman, David. 2003. "The Authority of Humanity." *Ethics* 113: 350–366.

Swift, Jonathan. 1726/2010. *Gulliver's Travels*, Part 3, Ch. 10. Calgary: Qualitas Publishing.

Temkin, Larry S. 2008. "Is Living Longer Living Better?" *Journal of Applied Philosophy* 25: 193–210.

Tennyson, Lord Alfred. 1859. "Tithonus." Poetry Foundation. http://www.poetryfoundation.org/archive/poem.html?id=174656, accessed June 28, 2012.

Velleman, J. David. 1991. "Well-Being and Time." *Pacific Philosophical Quarterly* 72 (1991): 48–77.

———. 1992. "The Guise of the Good." *Noûs* 26: 3–26.

———. 1999. "A Right of Self-Termination?" *Ethics* 109: 606–620.

———. 2002. "Identification and Identity," In *Contours of Agency*, Sarah Buss and Lee Overton, eds., pp. 91–123. Cambridge, MA: MIT Press.

———. 2003). "Narrative Explanation." *Philosophical Review* 112: 1–25.

Williams, Bernard. 1981b. "Persons, Character, and Morality." In *Moral Luck*, pp. 1–19. Cambridge: Cambridge University Press.

———. 1973. "The Makropulos Case: Reflections on the Tedium of Immortality." In his *Problems of the Self*, pp. 82–100. Cambridge: Cambridge University Press.

———. 1981a. "Internal and External Reasons." In *Moral Luck*, pp. 101–113. Cambridge: Cambridge University Press.

Wolf, Susan. 1997. "Happiness and Meaning: Two Aspects of the Good Life." *Social Philosophy and Policy* 14: 207–225.

———. 2002. "The True, the Good, and the Loveable: Frankfurt's Avoidance of Objectivity." In *Contours of Agency*, Sarah Buss and Lee Overton, eds., pp. 227–244. Cambridge: MIT Press.

———. 2010. *Meaning in Life and Why It Matters*. Princeton: Princeton University Press.

Wordsworth, William. 1807. 536 Ode, "Intimations of Immortality from Recollections of Early Childhood." Poetry Foundation. http://www. poetryfoundation.org/archive/poem.html?id=174805, accessed June 28, 2012.

CHAPTER 17

THE WRONGNESS OF KILLING AND THE BADNESS OF DEATH

MATTHEW HANSER

1. THE EQUAL WRONGNESS THESIS AND A PUZZLING ASYMMETRY

It is natural to think that the reason killing people is typically wrong is that dying is typically such a bad thing for the victim.[1] Yet there are grounds for doubting that this is the whole story, or even the most important part of the story.

For the purposes of this chapter I shall assume that an event is on balance bad for someone if and only if his life would have been on balance better had that event not occurred. (From here on I shall usually omit the qualifier "on balance.") A person's actual death, then, is bad for him if and only if his life would have gone better had that death not brought it to an end.[2] Of course, if the person hadn't died that death, he would have died some other death instead—none of us is immortal. But if his life would have gone better had he died that other death instead of his actual one, then his actual death is bad for him.

I shall also assume, for simplicity, that how well a person's life goes is determined by his lifetime well-being. Not every death is bad for its subject. If someone's life would have gone worse—if his lifetime well-being would have been lower—had he not died his actual death, then that death is good for him. Nor are all bad deaths equally bad. Suppose a young person and an old person are both killed in an accident. Had the accident not occurred the young person would have lived another sixty happy years; the old person, another twenty. While dying in the accident is bad for both, it is worse for the young person: his death makes a greater difference to his lifetime well-being. Nor is age the only variable that affects death's degree of badness. Those who are naturally cheerful tend to derive more happiness from life than those who are naturally melancholy, so other things being equal, death is worse for the former than for the latter—the cheerful lose more well-being with each lost year of life than do the melancholy. Likewise, those in comfortable social and economic circumstances may lose more with each lost year than do those in severely disadvantaged circumstances. But while such factors make a difference to how bad a person's death is for him, we do not generally think they affect the wrongness of killing the person. Jeff McMahan calls this the Equal Wrongness [of Killing] Thesis and formulates it thus:

> [T]he wrongness of killing persons does not vary with such factors as...the age, intelligence, temperament, or social circumstances of the victim, whether the victim is well liked or generally despised, and so on.[3] (2002, p. 235)

So stated, the thesis requires clarification. Wrongness is arguably not the sort of thing that comes in degrees. For an action to be wrong is simply for it to be impermissible, and one action cannot be more impermissible than another. Some actions are worse than others, but not more impermissible or more wrong. When McMahan writes of actions varying in their degree of wrongness, he means that the pro tanto moral objections to the actions differ in strength. The stronger the pro tanto moral objection to an action, the harder it is to justify its performance. Killing someone and kicking him in the shin, for example, are both pro tanto wrong, but the moral objection to the former is stronger than the moral objection to the latter. It is much harder to justify killing someone than it is to justify kicking him in the shin. McMahan would express this by saying that killing and shin kicking are not equally wrong.[4]

McMahan's formulation of the Equal Wrongness of Killing Thesis contains an open-ended list of factors said to be irrelevant to the strength of the pro tanto objection to killing. Not every imaginable factor belongs on this list. Perhaps some people's past actions make it easier to justify killing them; perhaps killing is less objectionable when the victim has given his consent; perhaps the duty not to kill one's own children is stronger than the duty not to kill strangers; and so on. The thesis consequently does not entail that all killings of persons are equally objectionable. But it does entail that the strength of the pro tanto objection to killing persons does not vary with how bad death is for the victim—for as noted above, death's badness does vary with such factors as the victim's age, temperament, popularity, social circumstances, and so on.[5]

McMahan argues that if the strength of the pro tanto objection to killing a person is unaffected by how bad death is for him, then the reason killing him is pro tanto wrong cannot be that his death would be bad for him. For if the badness of the death were what made the killing wrong, one would expect the strength of the moral objection to vary with the badness of the death. The less bad the death, the more easily justified the killing (McMahan, 2002, pp. 237–238).[6] McMahan concludes that if we wish to accept the Equal Wrongness of Killing Thesis, we must find some other account of what makes killing people wrong—an account that is consistent with, and that explains the truth of, the Equal Wrongness of Killing Thesis. And he proposes just such an account: killing people is wrong because it is a failure properly to respect them. All persons have a special value or worth in virtue of which they are owed respect, and since all persons are of equal value, all are owed equal respect. The old are no less valuable than the young, the melancholy no less valuable than the cheerful. They all thus have equally strong claims not to be killed (McMahan, 2002, p. 242).[7]

Not every creature has this special sort of value. Persons have it precisely because they are persons—because they are self-conscious, or because they are autonomous agents, or because they possess whatever else it might be that makes one a person. Since nonpersons lack this special value, we have no duties of respect towards them; but nonpersons do still have interests, and we are still morally required to take their interests into account when choosing what to do. McMahan thus distinguishes two aspects or parts of morality. The "morality of interests" concerns how others' interests (and perhaps our own) constrain what we may do, while the "morality of respect" concerns what we owe to persons in virtue of their special status.[8] Both parts of morality generate pro tanto objections to killing. The morality of interests generates a pro tanto objection whenever death would be bad for the victim, while the morality of respect generates a pro tanto objection whenever the victim is a person. The strength of the respect-based objection does not vary with the degree to which death would be bad for the victim, but, according to McMahan, the strength of the interest-based objection does. The killing of nonpersons is governed solely by the morality of interests. This is why killing a young dog is more objectionable than killing an old one, other things being equal. When it comes to our treatment of persons, however, both the morality of interests and the morality of respect apply. There may be cases in which killing a person would not be disrespectful (perhaps because he freely consented to it) but in which it would be objectionable because dying would be bad for him; and there may be cases in which dying would not be bad for the person but in which killing him would be objectionable because it would be disrespectful (perhaps because he didn't consent to it). But when killing someone would be both disrespectful and against his interests, McMahan thinks that the morality of respect takes precedence. In such cases the overall strength of the pro tanto moral objection to killing the person is unaffected by the degree to which death is bad for him. The strengths of the respect- and interest-based pro tanto objections to killing do not combine (McMahan, 2002, pp. 244–247).[9]

When killing is not disrespectful, the strength of the pro tanto objection to it depends upon how bad death is for the victim. The Equal Wrongness of Killing Thesis, then, is meant to hold only of those cases where the respect-based pro tanto objection arises. I shall not here consider whether McMahan is right that when objections of both sorts arise, the morality of respect takes precedence. I shall instead ask whether we should accept

The Equal Respect-Based Wrongness of Killing Thesis: The strength of the
respect-based pro tanto objection to killing persons does not vary with such
factors as the age, intelligence, temperament, or social circumstances of the
victim, whether the victim is well liked or generally despised, and so on.

If McMahan's precedence claim is correct, this narrower version of the thesis arguably entails his original version, which for clarity we may now rename the Equal
Overall Wrongness of Killing Thesis.

An important aspect of the distinction between the morality of respect and
the morality of interests, already hinted at, is that duties arising within the morality of respect are owed to those who are proper objects of respect. It's not just that
we have a duty not to kill persons; we owe it to persons not to kill them. Looked at
from another direction, the morality of respect concerns rights or claims that others have against us. The duties we owe people and the rights they have against us
are correlative: B has a right against A that A not φ if and only if A owes it as a duty
to B not to φ.[10] When one person violates another's right, or fails in a duty he owes
him, he doesn't merely do wrong, he wrongs that person, or does him a wrong. In
claiming that the strength of the respect-based pro tanto objection to killing a person does not vary with such factors as his age, temperament, popularity, social and
economic circumstances, and so on, then, McMahan is saying that the seriousness
of the wrong one does a person by killing him does not vary with such factors.

We were looking for an account of the respect-based pro tanto objection to
killing persons that can explain why the strength of this objection doesn't vary
with the factors just listed. McMahan's account is designed to meet this condition. The respect-based pro tanto objections to killing the young and the old, the
cheerful and the melancholy, and so on, are equally strong, McMahan suggests,
because all persons are of equal value. But as McMahan himself acknowledges, this
explanation is not satisfactory as it stands.[11] To see why, it helps to consider nonlethal attacks upon persons. Each person a general right that others not inflict
injuries upon him. Yet not all infringements of this right are equally objectionable,
or equally hard to justify. An attack that inflicts a minor injury wrongs the victim
less seriously than one that inflicts a major injury. Suppose that in order to rescue
another person I must shove a bystander out of the way. If shoving him would
cause him only a minor injury—a scraped arm, perhaps, or a sprained ankle—then
I might well be justified in proceeding. But if the shove would injure him more
severely—if it would cause him to lose a limb, say, or to become paraplegic—then
proceeding would most likely be impermissible. Again, each of us has a general
right not to be gassed into a state of unconsciousness.[12] Yet it clearly makes a difference how long the effects of the gas will last. Suppose that the police can rescue
a group of hostages only by pumping knockout gas into the building in which they
are being held. Doing this would knock out everyone in the building: hostages,
captors, and bystanders. If the gas would cause these people to lose consciousness
for just an hour or two, using it would no doubt be morally justified. But it would
clearly be wrong to use the gas if those exposed to it would remain unconscious for

several years. We could, if we liked, postulate a continuum of more specific rights here—a right not to be knocked unconsciousness for a period of length L_1, a right not to be knocked unconsciousness for a period of length L_2, and so on—and say that these rights differ in strength. We could likewise distinguish a variety of rights against being physically injured, some of which would differ in strength. But we needn't do this. It's enough to acknowledge that not all infringements of a given general right are equally objectionable.

Now suppose that A and B are persons of equal value, possessed of equal rights, and that among these are the rights that others not injure them or knock them unconsciousness. It does not follow from the equal value of A and B, or from their equal possession of these rights, that the respect-based pro tanto objection to inflicting a minor injury upon A is just as strong as the respect-based pro tanto objection to inflicting a major injury upon B, or that the respect-based pro tanto objection to knocking A unconscious for a short period is just as strong as the respect-based pro tanto objection to knocking B unconscious for a long period. Why, then, should the equal value of all persons, and their equal possession of the right not to be killed, be thought to support the Equal Respect-Based Wrongness of Killing Thesis? If the seriousness of the wrong one does someone by injuring him or knocking him unconscious can vary, why shouldn't the seriousness of the wrong one does someone by killing him likewise vary? Proponents of the Equal Respect-Based Wrongness of Killing Thesis must explain this prima facie puzzling asymmetry.

Before one can explain this asymmetry one must understand it correctly. On perhaps the most natural understanding, the problem is that the seriousness of the wrong one does someone by injuring him or knocking him unconscious varies with how bad the resulting injury or episode of unconsciousness is for him. It is, after all, worse, other things being equal, to suffer a more severe injury, or to be knocked unconscious for a longer period of time. But then why shouldn't the seriousness of the wrong one does a person by killing him likewise vary with how bad the resulting death is for him? The following two theses are clearly in tension:

(1) The strength of the respect-based pro tanto objection to killing a person does not vary with how bad the person's death is for him.

(2) The strength of the respect-based pro tanto objection to inflicting a nonlethal injury upon a person, or to knocking him unconscious, does vary with how bad the injury or period of unconsciousness is for him.

Anyone wishing to accept both theses consequently has some explaining to do. The respect-based objection to killing seems unique among respect-based objections to harmful actions in not having its strength depend upon how bad the resulting harm is for the victim. Why should killing be special in this respect?[13]

There are certainly moral views that make the Equal Respect-Based Wrongness of Killing Thesis appear mysterious, unmotivated, even absurd. My aim in this chapter is to describe, in rough outline, an attractive alternative outlook within which the thesis loses its air of mysteriousness. Whether this outlook should be preferred to its rivals is another matter, one that I shall not attempt to settle here. At best, then, I offer only a partial, qualified defense of the thesis.[14]

2. Killing versus Knocking Unconscious

I just said that two theses—(1) and (2) above—are in tension, and that anyone wishing to accept both has some explaining to do. But perhaps this understates the problem. Kasper Lippert-Rasmussen observes that we cannot consistently hold both (1) and (2) if we also accept what he calls the Equivalence Thesis:

> (3) Other things being equal, the respect-based pro tanto objection to killing a person, thereby depriving him of a certain period of conscious experience, and the respect-based pro tanto objection to rendering a person unconscious for an equal period of time, are equally strong.

And he argues that we should indeed accept (3). Given what he takes to be the obvious truth of (2), we have no choice but to reject (1) (Lippert-Rasmussen, 2007).[15]

It is easy to see that (1), (2), and (3) are jointly inconsistent. The "other things being equal" clause in (3) ensures that we are comparing cases where the value of the conscious experience lost is the same whether it is lost through being killed or through being rendered unconscious. Now consider two pairs of cases. In the first pair, one person is killed a year before he would otherwise have died, while another is knocked unconscious for a year. The lost year would have had equal value for both.[16] The second pair of cases is exactly the same, save that this time the victims are each deprived of ten years of consciousness experience. According to (3), in each pair of cases the respect-based objections to the acts are equally strong. And according to (1), the respect-based objections to the two killings are equally strong, even though one of the victims is deprived of ten years of life; the other, of only one. It follows that the respect-based objections to the two renderings unconscious are also equally strong, despite the fact that one of the victims is rendered unconscious for ten years; the other, for only one. But this contradicts (2), since being unconscious for ten years is worse for a person than being unconscious for just one, other things being equal.

I agree that we cannot accept both the Equal Respect-Based Wrongness of Killing Thesis and the Equivalence Thesis. Let us look, then, at Lippert-Rasmussen's defense of the Equivalence Thesis. He asks us to consider a case in which an agent can achieve some personal ambition either by killing a person or by knocking him unconscious for a period equal to the time he has left to live, after which he will die of natural causes without regaining consciousness. Lippert-Rasmussen claims that barring extraneous factors, no one would prefer, for the sake of the victim, that the agent choose one of these options rather than the other. (We are to assume it really is certain that the subject will never regain consciousness if he's knocked out.) Lippert-Rasmussen concludes that the respect-based pro tanto objections to choosing these options are equally strong (2007, p. 722).[17] But the datum Lippert-Rasmussen cites is adequately explained simply by the fact that the losses produced by the two options are equally bad for the victim. Which potential loss we would prefer for a victim's sake generally depends only upon which we think would be better for him, not upon how objectionable we think the acts producing those losses would be. We do not, for example, prefer for a victim's sake that he be killed accidentally rather than intentionally, or that he be struck by lightning rather than by an assailant's bullet. All we can directly infer from Lippert-Rasmussen's datum, then, is that other things being equal, being killing and being knocked unconscious for the rest of one's life involve suffering equally bad losses. And that's not much progress, since we had already stipulated that actions whose equivalence is asserted by the Equivalence Thesis produce equally bad losses.

It is only because Lippert-Rasmussen assumes that actions producing equally bad harms are equally objectionable that he draws the further conclusion that the respect-based objections to killing people and to knocking them unconscious for the rest of their lives are equally strong. But this is not an assumption those attracted to the Equal Respect-Based Wrongness of Killing Thesis will accept. They take the (supposed) equal strength of the respect-based objections to killing the young and the old, the cheerful and the melancholy, to show that the strength of the respect-based pro tanto objection to a harmful action does not always correlate with how bad the resulting harm is for the victim. If the respect-based objections to harmful actions can be equally strong even though the resulting harms are not equally bad, why shouldn't the respect-based objections to actions sometimes differ in strength even though the actions produce equally bad harms? Lippert-Rasmussen acknowledges that "on some views one act may be more wrong than another even if they involve equally serious harms," but he maintains that "in the absence of an account of what special factors make this the case, the fact that both cases involve an equally serious harm supports the Equivalence Thesis" (2007, p. 722).[18] In other words, our default position should be that, quite generally, the strength of the respect-based pro tanto objection to a harmful action correlates with how bad the resulting harm is for the victim. Other things being equal, the worse the harm, the stronger the respect-based objection to the action producing it; and if two harms are equally bad, the respect-based objections to actions producing them are equally strong. We should accept a view inconsistent with this position only if we can provide a satisfactory theoretical rationale for that view.

Suppose Lippert-Rasmussen is right about where the burden of proof lies here. We already acknowledged that proponents of the Equal Respect-Based Wrongness of Killing Thesis need to explain why the strength of the respect-based pro tanto objection to killing a person shouldn't vary with how bad death is for the victim. But if they can provide such an explanation, Lippert-Rasmussen's defense of the Equivalence Thesis loses its force. That the Equal Respect-Based Wrongness of Killing Thesis is inconsistent with the Equivalence Thesis thus provides no additional reason for doubting the truth of the former, beyond that identified at the end of section 1.

3. RIGHTS AND WELL-BEING

In fact, I think there is little reason to accept either the Equivalence Thesis or the broader thesis that, quite generally, the strength of the respect-based pro tanto objection to a harmful action correlates with how bad the resulting harm is for the victim. The morality of respect does not directly concern what's good or bad for those to whom respect is owed.

First, note that not every action whose effects are bad for someone infringes his rights. A person's rights jointly define a presumptively protected sphere within which he is free to pursue his innocent ends as he sees fit. It would certainly be advantageous to have a general right against others that they not perform actions that are bad for us; but if everyone else had such a right against us, our protected spheres would be small indeed. It is simply too easy for one person's actions to affect negatively the well-being of another. Perhaps seeing others succeed always makes me dwell upon my own failures, which in turn depresses me. It would surely be a mistake to conclude that other people infringe my rights whenever they succeed in doing impressive things. Our rights, then, do not bar others from doing things that are bad for us; rather, they bar others from interfering with us in certain rather particular ways. Recall also that objectionable infringements of our rights needn't be on balance bad for us. Respecting rights means not interfering with people even when they'd be better off if we did. Possessing rights and having those rights recognized and respected by others arguably contribute to our well-being, but the point of our rights is not to prevent the performance of all and only those acts that are detrimental to our well-being. The point of our rights is to create a space within which the determinations of our wills are presumptively authoritative and efficacious.[19]

Now, I take it for granted that we have rights against others that they not injure us, knock us unconscious, or kill us. So let us look more closely at these three forms of objectionable interference.

Injuries are usually painful, sometimes disfiguring, but their primary ill effect is that they impair our proper functioning. Insofar as an element of proper functioning is in itself good for us, having it impaired is bad for us (in a respect, if not on balance). Impairments often also diminish other abilities, or impede their successful exercise. Some injuries undermine our strength or stamina, thereby limiting our ability to engage in strenuous or prolonged activities. Others impair our perception, making certain actions difficult or impossible. Still others rob us of the ability to move our bodies in particular ways. Any diminution of our practical abilities is bad for us (in a respect, if not on balance). So impairments to proper functioning can be bad for us in multiple respects. Still, not every action that results in our suffering an injury infringes our rights. If, at my request, someone removes an obstacle to my performing a certain action (perhaps by lending me his skateboard), and if, as a result of my performing that action, I predictably suffer an injury (perhaps by falling off his skateboard), it does not follow that the remover of the obstacle infringes my rights. My right against him is that he not inflict an injury upon me. It would be no easy task explaining what exactly it is to inflict an injury. Direct contact with the victim is not required: one can injure someone by means of a projectile, or by poisoning his food. Nor need the causal connection be especially immediate: one can injure him using a complicated, Rube Goldberg device. But every way of inflicting an injury upon someone might reasonably be described as involving an attack upon his person.[20]

The next sort of interference to consider is knocking someone unconscious. Unconsciousness does not so much impair a person's practical and perceptual abilities as remove a necessary condition for their exercise. Does it follow that unconsciousness is in some respect bad for us? We don't ordinarily think that time spent sleeping is time spent in a bad state, but perhaps that's because sleep's restorative effects render it on balance good. Perhaps, that is, sleep should be regarded as a necessary evil. But then we don't ordinarily think that dropping into an unneeded slumber, say while sitting in a comfortable chair reading a book, is bad for us either, simply insofar as it deprives us of consciousness for some period. (Dozing off might of course be bad for us insofar as it prevents us from doing something we particularly wanted or needed to do during that period.) So perhaps only sleep far in excess of what we need for our physical and mental health is bad for us. However that may be, a person wrongs us if, without our consent, he inflicts any period of unconsciousness upon us—no matter how brief the period and no matter how much we need the rest. Furthermore, as was the case with injuring, not just any way of causing someone to lose consciousness infringes his rights. I do not infringe a person's rights if my lecture puts him to sleep, but I do infringe them if I achieve the same result by gassing him, slipping him a drug, or hitting him on the head. As was the case with injuring, "rendering a person unconscious" (to use Lippert-Rasmussen's phrase) infringes his rights only when it is achieved via some sort of attack upon his person.

Finally, there is killing, which "inflicts" death upon its victim. Death consists not in an impairment of abilities, but in the complete and permanent cessation of certain life-sustaining (or perhaps life-constituting) bodily operations. Someone who has been injured or knocked unconscious continues on in an impaired state; someone who has been killed does not continue on at all.[21]

Although acts of all three types are typically bad for their victims, they interfere with their victims in very different ways, and there is no reason to assume that when interferences of different types are equally bad for their victims, they therefore infringe equally strong rights. Suppose, for example, that one agent knocks A unconscious (without his consent) for a period of length L_1, while another injures B (without his consent) in a way that leaves him walking with a limp for a period of length L_2.[22] Let us stipulate that in each case the impact upon the victim's lifetime well-being is the same. It does not follow that the wrongs committed against A and B are equally serious. Being knocked unconscious is arguably a much graver assault on one's autonomy than being caused to walk with a limp, so one's right against being knocked unconscious might well be more stringent than one's right against being caused to walk with a limp, other things being equal.[23] We get the same result when we compare killing people with knocking them unconscious, the act types that Lippert-Rasmussen's Equivalence Thesis concerns. Actions of these types arguably affect their victims' lifetime well-being in exactly the same way: in each case the badness for the victim consists in his being deprived of a period of valuable consciousness that would otherwise have been his. Yet killing and knocking unconscious remain two very different forms of interference: the former causes the complete and permanent cessation of the victim's basic life-sustaining (or life-constituting) bodily operations; the latter leaves the victim alive but, for a time, unable to exercise a variety of his practical and perceptual capacities. An agent arguably interferes with someone in a much more fundamental way by killing him than he does by knocking him unconscious. It would thus not be surprising if a person's right against being killed were more stringent, other things being equal, than his right against being knocked unconscious.

But even if this is right, it provides no positive support for the Equal Respect-Based Wrongness of Killing Thesis. It might still be that among interferences of a single type, the strength of the respect-based objection correlates with the degree to which the action is bad for its victim. And indeed this appears to be case with the act-types *injuring* and *knocking unconscious*: it appears that the worse the injury or episode of unconsciousness, the stronger the respect-based objection to the act of injuring or knocking unconscious. So why shouldn't the same be true of killing? Why shouldn't we also say: the worse the death, the stronger the respect-based objection to the act of killing? Proponents of the Equal Respect-Based Wrongness of Killing Thesis must still confront the puzzle posed at the end of section 1.

4. THE ASYMMETRY EXPLAINED

I argued in section 1 that if the Equal Respect-Based Wrongness of Killing Thesis is correct, then there is a prima facie puzzling asymmetry between the respect-based objections to killing people and to injuring them or knocking them unconscious. And I said that on perhaps its most natural interpretation, this asymmetry concerns the relationship between the strength of the respect-based objection to the act and the badness of the resulting harm. So interpreted, what's puzzling is how to resolve the tension between the following two claims:

(1) The strength of the respect-based pro tanto objection to killing a person does not vary with how bad the person's death is for him.

(2) The strength of the respect-based pro tanto objection to inflicting a nonlethal injury upon a person, or to knocking him unconscious, does vary with how bad the injury or period of unconsciousness is for him.

It is certainly difficult to see how this tension might be resolved. But we should reject this interpretation of the asymmetry. Proponents of the Equal Respect-Based Wrongness of Killing Thesis needn't resolve the tension between (1) and (2) because they needn't accept (2).

The asymmetry whose interpretation is at issue arises because the respect-based objection to inflicting a major injury upon someone is stronger than the respect-based objection to inflicting a minor injury upon him, and because the respect-based objection to knocking someone unconscious for a longer period is stronger than the respect-based objection to knocking him unconscious for a shorter period. It does not follow, however, that the strength of these respect-based objections depends upon how bad the injuries or episodes of unconsciousness are for the victims. Indeed, there is good reason to deny that the strength of the respect-based objections so depends. Consider an injury of a given severity—say one that leaves its victim unable to walk for a month. Not everyone suffering such an injury has his lifetime well-being affected to the same degree. Some people derive much of their happiness from activities requiring the use of their legs, while others prefer more sedentary pursuits. Some people have great difficulty adapting to physical impairments, while others are able to do so with ease. Any number of differences among people can affect how bad injuries of a given severity are for them, but we do not generally think that these differences affect the strength of the respect-based objection to inflicting such injuries upon them. Those who lead active lives and those who are more contemplative, those who are cheerful and those who are melancholy, those who are set in their ways and those who are adaptable, those who are young and those who are old, all have equally strong rights not to have injuries of a given severity inflicted upon them. Similar remarks apply to the strength of people's rights not to be knocked unconscious. A melancholy person and a cheerful one have equally strong rights not to be knocked unconscious for a month, even though spending a month unconscious deprives the melancholy person of less happiness.[24] The seriousness of a rights-infringement depends not upon how bad it is for the victim, but upon the nature and magnitude of the action's interference with the victim's functioning; and if an agent injures two people, leaving each of them unable to walk for a month, then he interferes with their functioning to the same extent. Both have the same fundamental capacity impaired, to the same degree, for the same period of time.[25]

According to the Equal Respect-Based Wrongness of Killing Thesis, the strength of the respect-based pro tanto objection to killing people does not vary with such factors as the victim's age, intelligence, temperament, social circumstances, and so on. But we can with equal justice say the same about the strength of the respect-based pro tanto objections to injuring people and to knocking them unconscious. The parallel "equal wrongness" claims are supported by egalitarian considerations of the very same sort.[26] If those considerations lead us to accept that

> (1) the strength of the respect-based pro tanto objection to killing a person does not vary with how bad the person's death is for him,

they should likewise lead us to accept that

> (2') the strength of the respect-based pro tanto objection to inflicting a nonlethal injury upon a person, or to knocking him unconscious, does not vary with how bad the injury or period of unconsciousness is for him.

This is not to say that respect-based objections to inflicting injuries upon people, or to knocking them unconscious, are always equal in strength. On the contrary, their strength varies with the severity of the injury or duration of the episode of unconsciousness.[27] This suggests another way of interpreting the asymmetry. For simplicity, let us say that longer episodes of unconsciousness are more "severe" than shorter episodes. The asymmetry might then be this: while the strength of the respect-based objection to injuring a person, or to knocking him unconscious, varies with the severity of the resulting injury or episode of unconsciousness, the strength of the respect-based objection to killing a person does not vary with the severity of the resulting death.

So interpreted, the asymmetry would be every bit as puzzling as it was on the previous interpretation. Why should severity of harm be relevant only in nonlethal cases? But I do not think proponents of the Equal Respect-Based Wrongness of Killing Thesis should accept this way of understanding the asymmetry either. Their view should be, not that the strength of the respect-based objection to killing does not vary with the severity of the resulting death, but rather that deaths do not vary in severity. Respect-based objections to harmful actions are always sensitive to the severity of the resulting harm. The respect-based objection to injuring a person, or to knocking him unconscious, varies in strength because injuries and episodes of unconsciousness vary in severity. The respect-based objection to killing does not vary in strength because deaths do not vary in severity.

Why should we think that injuries and episodes of unconsciousness differ in severity, but deaths do not? Let us begin with injuries. The severity of an injury depends upon three variables: (i) the nature and importance of the impaired capacity, (ii) the degree to which that capacity is impaired, and (iii) the duration of the impairment. Next, consider episodes of unconsciousness. When someone is knocked unconscious, he loses a precondition for the exercise of numerous practical and perceptual capacities; and he (typically) passes from being fully consciousness to being completely unconscious. When it comes to episodes of unconsciousness, then, the analogues of the first two variables just mentioned remain constant: everyone who loses consciousness loses the same thing, to the same degree. (I set aside cases in which the person knocked out was only semiconscious to begin with.) It is true that not everyone who is knocked unconscious possesses to the same degree the various capacities whose exercise unconsciousness prevents. While this might affect the value that the lost period of consciousness would have had for him, and hence how bad the episode of unconsciousness is for him, it does not affect the nature or magnitude of the loss in which his loss of consciousness consists. It consequently does not affect the severity of the inflicted episode of unconsciousness. The only variable affecting the episode's severity is its duration.

Finally, consider death. When a person dies, his basic life-sustaining (or life-constituting) operations cease entirely, with the result that he passes from being fully alive to not being alive at all. The loss in which death consists is thus the same for all, both in nature and in magnitude. Of course when a person dies, he loses all his non-life-sustaining (or non-life-constituting) capacities as well, in the sense that it ceases being true that he has them—it ceases being true that he can see, hear, walk, and so on. And since people possess these other capacities to varying degrees, the losses they suffer in losing them through death differ in magnitude. But these differences affect only the value of the lives they lose through dying, and hence the degree to which death is bad for them. These differences do not affect the nature or magnitude of the loss in which death consists, and so they do not affect death's severity.

What of the third variable? Episodes of unconsciousness differ in severity only because they differ in duration. But death does not have duration. Being knocked unconscious leaves the victim in an impaired condition, and the interfering effects of impaired conditions are cumulative over time. Being dead, however, is not an impaired condition that might last for a longer or shorter period of time. Some people have indeed been dead longer than others, but this just means that their deaths occurred further in the past. Those who have been dead longer have not so far undergone lengthier periods of interference. And as for the event of ceasing to be alive, it is for everyone pretty much instantaneous. No temporal variable, then, affects death's severity, and so death is equally severe for all.

It might seem that I've overlooked the way in which time really matters here. It would of course be absurd to suppose that the length of time a victim will spend dead bears upon the strength of the respect-based objection to killing him. But this is not the temporal variable those who reject the Equal Respect-Based Wrongness of Killing Thesis think is relevant. They think that, other things being equal, the strength of the respect-based objection to killing varies with how much longer the victim would have lived had the action not been performed. Notice, however, that the analogous temporal variable in cases of injuring people or knocking them unconscious is not the duration of the resulting impairment, but the amount of extra time the victim would have spent in an unimpaired (or less impaired) condition had the action not been performed. The alternative to the view I've been defending, then, is one according to which, other things being equal, the strength of the respect-based objection to killing a person depends upon the difference the action makes to how much time he spends alive, and the strength of the respect-based objection to injuring a person or knocking him unconscious depends upon the difference the action makes to how much time he spends in an unimpaired (or less impaired) condition.

This view and the one I've been defending differ in what they entail about the respect-based objections to injuring people or knocking them unconscious. This is so because the amount of extra time a victim would have spent in an unimpaired (or less impaired) condition had an action not been performed needn't be the same as the duration of the injury or episode of unconsciousness the action inflicts upon him. This is most obvious in cases of knocking people unconscious. If an agent slips someone a drug that knocks him out for twenty-four hours, then the duration of the episode of unconsciousness the agent inflicts upon him is twenty-four hours. But we may assume that the victim would have spent some of that time sleeping anyway; had the action not been performed he would have spent perhaps only sixteen more hours in a conscious state. Indeed, an agent might knock someone out who was going to fall sleep moments later anyway, with the result that the victim would have spent no more time in a conscious state had the action not been performed. Alternatively, the agent might knock the victim out moments before another agent was going to do the same. Here, too, the duration of the episode of unconsciousness the agent inflicts upon the victim differs from the amount of extra time the victim would have spent conscious had the action not been performed. And, of course, the same sort of thing can happen in cases of injuring people: it could be that if the agent hadn't injured him, the victim would have suffered another injury instead, either at the hands of a different agent or as a result of some other cause. According to the view I've been defending, the strength of the respect-based objection to injuring someone or knocking him unconscious does not depend upon whether the action preempts an alternative cause of injury or unconsciousness. The strength of the respect-based objection depends upon the duration of the injury or episode of unconsciousness that the agent inflicts upon the victim, not upon how much more time the victim would have spent in an unimpaired (or less impaired) state had the action not been performed.[28]

Killing a person, of course, always preempts some alternative cause of death. Sometimes the alternative cause would have killed the victim almost immediately thereafter, while in other cases it would not have done so for many years. According to the view I've been defending, the question how much longer the victim would have lived had he not been killed is no more relevant to the strength of the respect-based objection to killing him than the question how much more time he would have spent in an unimpaired (or less impaired) condition is to the strength of the respect-based objection to injuring him or knocking him unconscious. In neither case does the strength of the respect-based objection depend upon how much more time the victim would have spent in a better state had the action not been performed. This temporal variable arguably affects how bad the death, injury, or episode of unconsciousness is for the victim, but it does not affect the severity of the death, injury, or episode of unconsciousness.

I believe that the view I've been describing yields more attractive results than its rival, but my primary aim has not been to determine which view is better. My aim has been to show how the plausibility of the Equal Respect-Based Wrongness of Killing Thesis depends upon which view we adopt. I have thus offered only a partial, qualified defense of the Equal Respect-Based Wrongness of Killing Thesis. Also, I have not addressed the question how respect- and interest-based objections to killing interact when both arise. According to McMahan, the strength of the interest-based objection to killing varies with how bad death is for the victim. If the strengths of the two objections combine, the strength of the overall objection to killing also varies with how bad death is for the victim. This may not be of great practical significance. If the respect-based objection makes by far the greater contribution to the overall objection, variations in the strength of the overall objection will be relatively slight. McMahan, of course, thinks that respect- and interest-based objections do not combine: he thinks that the morality of respect takes precedence over the morality of interests. Whether he is right about this is another topic.[29]

NOTES

1. Some say instead that killing a person is wrong when and because it harms him. See, for example, James Rachels, 1986, p. 6. But many who say this also hold that an action harms someone if and only if it is on balance bad for him; their view about what makes killing wrong is thus meant to be equivalent to the one stated in the text. I defend a rival account of harm in my 2008, and Seana Shiffrin defends yet another alternative in her 1999. My topic here is the relationship between the wrongness of killing and the badness of death.
2. This is roughly the account Fred Feldman defends in his 1991.
3. Another factor McMahan takes to be irrelevant is the degree of harm caused to the victim. I omit this from his list because I do not share his understanding of harm.
4. It would be a mistake, however, to assume that pro tanto objections can be ranked along a single scale according to strength. Acts of type A might be easily justified by considerations of one sort but not by considerations of another, while with acts of type B it might be the other way around. Which type of action would in that case be more objectionable, or harder to justify, simpliciter? For elaboration and defense of the idea that pro tanto objections may rule out justification by considerations of some sorts but not others, see Joseph Raz's work on exclusionary reasons, e.g. Raz, 1975.
5. For discussion of necessary qualifications to the Equal Wrongness of Killing Thesis, see McMahan, 2002, pp. 235-237. One qualification is especially worth noting. Suppose that in order to achieve a certain end an agent would be justified in killing a suitably situated person, but that as it happens he could achieve this end by killing any one of several people. Given this choice, it might be wrong for him to kill anyone other than the person who would lose the least in dying. The Equal Wrongness of Killing Thesis is meant to be consistent with this possibility. Had there been only one potential victim, the permissibility of killing him would not have depended upon how bad his death would be for him.
6. By the time he advances this argument McMahan has argued that we should reject the view that killing persons is pro tanto wrong when and because death is bad for them in

favor of a somewhat more complicated view; he thus directs his argument against the more complicated view. But the argument works just as well against the simpler view. It is possible to resist McMahan's argument: one can consistently hold (a) that killing people is pro tanto wrong when and because death is bad for them, while nonetheless insisting (b) that the strength of the pro tanto objection does not depend upon how bad the death is for the victim. But such a view would face serious difficulties. Anyone holding it would presumably also hold that inflicting nonlethal injuries upon people is wrong when and because such injuries are bad for them. The objection to inflicting nonlethal injuries upon people, however, is generally weaker than the objection to killing them, and the objection to inflicting lesser nonlethal injuries upon people is generally weaker than the objection to inflicting greater nonlethal injuries upon them. How is the proponent of the view just described to explain these facts, if not by appealing to differences in how bad the actions' effects are for the victims? But then why shouldn't the strength of the objection to killing people also vary with how bad the action's effects are for the victim? (As we shall see shortly, McMahan's alternative account of the pro tanto objection to killing people appears to face a similar difficulty.)

7. I should stress that McMahan's proposal is not that killing persons is wrong because it involves the destruction of entities possessing special value. His point is not that something of special value is lost when a person is killed, but rather that in virtue of persons' special value, we owe it to them not to kill them.

8. For more on the significance of status, see F. M. Kamm, 1996 and 2007.

9. Even if we reject the Equal Wrongness of Killing Thesis, we have good reason to agree that killing persons can be objectionable on respect-based, and not just on interest-based, grounds: this view best explains why killing a person against his will is pro tanto objectionable even when death would be good for him. In developing the idea that pro tanto objections to killing can have two different sources, McMahan draws on the work of Warren Quinn, who distinguishes the morality of respect from the morality of humanity. See section IV of Quinn, 1984. This distinction mirrors that between the spheres governed, respectively, by the virtues of justice and charity (benevolence). For the view that killing a person can be contrary either to justice or to charity, see Philippa Foot, 1977.

10. For the classic statement of the correlativity of claim-rights and directed duties, see Wesley Newcomb Hohfeld, 1919, p. 38. Some rights are held against a single individual—an example would be the right that a promisee holds against a promisor. Other rights are held against every member of a certain class.

11. See McMahan, 2002, p. 247.

12. When specifying the contents of rights we often omit the relational element—we speak simply of a person's right not to be knocked unconscious, for example, rather than of his right against others that they not knock him unconscious.

13. This is how McMahan himself understands the problem. For McMahan, the magnitude of a harm is determined by how bad it is for its subject. And he asks: "If the gravity of the violation varies with the extent of the harm in nonlethal instances, why should it not do so in cases of killing as well?" (2002, p. 247). Later I shall argue against this way of understanding the problem.

14. McMahan raises another problem for his view. If we restrict the scope of the Equal Wrongness of Killing Thesis to the killing of persons—if we agree that the pro tanto objection to killing nonpersons does vary with the age, etc., of the victim—then we must explain why the distinction between persons and nonpersons should be

so morally momentous. This will be no easy task if possession of the features that distinguish persons from nonpersons is a matter of degree. See McMahan, 2002, pp. 248–265. I shall not discuss this problem here.

15. I have altered the wording of the Equivalence Thesis to better match my formulations of (1) and (2), which differ somewhat from Lippert-Rasmussen's. The differences are unimportant for present purposes.

16. Lippert-Rasmussen argues that since the lost year of consciousness would have had the same value for both victims, it doesn't matter when during the second victim's life the year of unconsciousness occurs (2007, pp. 726–727).

17. Lippert-Rasmussen offers another argument: whatever cost we may permissibly impose upon the agent to prevent him from choosing the one option, we may permissibly impose upon him to prevent him from choosing the other; and a plausible explanation of this is that the two options are equally objectionable (2007, p. 723). I doubt that anyone not already convinced of the options' moral equivalence would accept the premise of this argument.

18. It is clear that for Lippert-Rasmussen, the seriousness of a harm is determined by the degree to which it is bad for its subject.

19. I shall not enter into familiar and long-standing debates about the ultimate source of people's rights. For a summary of these debates, see Kramer, Simmonds, and Steiner, 1998. What I say about the contents of people's rights should be compatible with a variety of plausible views about more foundational matters.

20. I shall not address the question whether an agent who, for example, hires another to attack his rival thereby infringes the same right the hired attacker infringes, or whether he should be thought of as infringing a distinct right.

21. Some hold that we are our bodies, and that consequently many of us survive our deaths, at least for a time, as corpses. See Fred Feldman, 1992, chapter 6. But even if this view is correct, it would still be a mistake (one, I hasten to add, that Feldman does not make) to think that when death is bad for someone, this is because it causes him to spend his post mortem existence in a bad state. Death would then be bad only for those whose bodies are not destroyed the moment they die, and the extent of its badness would depend upon how rapidly their bodies decompose.

22. A right is not infringed if it has been waived, and on some views any right can be waived. On these views, your right that I not φ gives you authority to determine whether I will wrong you by φing. I will wrong you unless you consent to my φing by waiving your right that I not do so. But perhaps some rights cannot be waived— perhaps I would wrong you by φing even were I to φ with your competent consent.

23. Similar variations in strength might be found among rights against having different sorts of injuries inflicted upon one.

24. The degree to which a given injury or period of unconsciousness is bad for a person might nonetheless legitimately play a "tie-breaking" role when the agent has a choice of victim. Suppose that in order to achieve a certain morally worthy end an agent would be justified in inflicting an injury of a certain severity upon a properly situated person. If he could inflict this injury upon either of two potential victims, it might be that he ought to inflict it upon the one who would lose less well-being in suffering it. Granting this is consistent with holding that the potential victims have equally stringent rights not to be injured in this way. For the parallel point about killing see note 5 above. The cases are symmetrical.

25. I leave it an open question whether a capacity can be of fundamental importance for one person but of merely peripheral importance for another, and whether in that

case the former person would have the stronger right against having the capacity impaired.

26. Not everyone gives weight to such considerations, or is moved by them to accept the Equal Respect-Based Wrongness of Killing Thesis. My point is that those who are drawn to the Equal Respect-Based Wrongness of Killing Thesis should also be drawn to parallel theses regarding the objections to injuring people and to knocking them unconscious.

27. No doubt there is a rough correlation between the severity of an injury, or the length of an episode of unconsciousness, and the degree to which it is bad for its victim. But the strength of the respect-based objection to an act is not sensitive to the badness of the resulting injury or episode of unconsciousness.

28. If the action prevents the victim from suffering an even worse injury, and if the agent performs it for that reason, then the action might be justified. But it is still pro tanto objectionable. Any act that inflicts an injury upon someone stands in need of justification.

29. I am grateful to Ben Bradley and Jens Johansson for their helpful comments on an earlier version of this chapter.

REFERENCES

Feldman, Fred. 1991. "Some Puzzles about the Evil of Death." *Philosophical Review* 100: 205–227.

Feldman, Fred. 1992. *Confrontations with the Reaper.* Oxford: Oxford University Press.

Foot, Philippa. 1977. "Euthanasia." *Philosophy and Public Affairs* 6: 85–112.

Hanser, Matthew. 2008. "The Metaphysics of Harm." *Philosophy and Phenomenological Research* 77: 421–450.

Hohfeld, Wesley Newcomb. 1919. *Fundamental Legal Conceptions.* New Haven: Yale University Press.

Kamm, F. M. 1996. *Morality, Mortality.* Vol. 2. Oxford: Oxford University Press.

Kamm, F. M. 2007. *Intricate Ethics.* Oxford: Oxford University Press.

Kramer, Matthew H., N. E. Simmonds, and Hillel Steiner. 1998. *A Debate over Rights.* Oxford: Oxford University Press.

Lippert-Rasmussen, Kasper. 2007. "Why Killing Some People Is More Seriously Wrong Than Killing Others." *Ethics* 117: 716–738.

McMahan, Jeff. 2002. *The Ethics of Killing.* Oxford: Oxford University Press.

Quinn, Warren. 1984. "Abortion: Identity and Loss." *Philosophy and Public Affairs* 13: 24–54.

Rachels, James. 1986. *The End of Life.* Oxford: Oxford University Press.

Raz, Joseph. 1975. *Practical Reason and Norms.* Hutchinson & Co. (reissued with a new postscript, Princeton University Press, 1990).

Shiffrin, Seana. 1999. "Wrongful Life, Procreative Responsibility, and the Significance of Harm." *Legal Theory* 5: 117–148.

CHAPTER 18

ABORTION AND DEATH

DON MARQUIS

HERE is a view concerning abortion and death. It has the following parts:

1. Abortion causes the death of a fetus.
2. If your mother had had an abortion when she believed she was pregnant with you, but before that fetus became sentient, then she would have caused your death.
3. Because bringing about your death when you were a fetus would have deprived you of all of the valuable experiences of your past, present, and future life, bringing about that death would have greatly harmed you.
4. Causing such harm to a fetus presumptively severely wrongs it.

These claims are controversial. In what follows I shall discuss some reasons for thinking these claims are true, some important objections to them, and some responses to those objections.

1. DOES ABORTION CAUSE THE DEATH OF A FETUS?

Some famous views concerning abortion are incompatible with the view that we know that abortion causes the death of a fetus. According to Harry Blackmun's majority opinion in *Roe v. Wade*,

We need not resolve the difficult question of when life begins. When those trained
in the respective disciplines of medicine, philosophy, and theology are unable to
arrive at any consensus, the judiciary, at this point in the development of man's
knowledge, is not in a position to speculate as to the answer. (1973, p. 30)

Blackmun's view might be understood in two ways: a narrower way and a wider
way. On the narrow version, he might be understood as claiming, not that fetuses
may not be alive, but that we do not know at what point very early in pregnancy
fetal life begins. However, this understanding of Blackmun's view is not plausible, given the remainder of his opinion. Presumably, he is attempting for forestall
the objection that even if women have a full-blown right to privacy, that right is
trumped by a fetal right to life. This narrow understanding of Blackmun's view
would not support that argument strategy.

This suggests that Blackmun's claim should be understood in a wider version.
On a wider version of his claim, he is stating that whether fetuses are alive or not is
not known. An entity is dead only if it was once alive. Therefore, an abortion will
cause the death of a fetus only if that fetus was once alive. If it is not known whether
any fetus is alive, then it is not known that an abortion would cause its death.

Is Blackmun's view a candidate for the truth? Fetuses grow. Their cells metabolize and divide. They exhibit a unity of metabolic function in virtue of which we
can say that they are biological organisms. Biological organisms are by definition
living. (Corpses are not biological organisms.) The wider version of Blackmun's
claim seems utterly incompatible with our knowledge of biology.

Perhaps Blackmun's claim should not be taken quite so literally. Perhaps he
should be understood as claiming that, even though we may know that fetuses are
alive, we do not know whether a human life has yet begun. Therefore, we don't
know that abortion involves taking a human life.

If Blackmun's claim is understood in this way, could it be true? A fetus is a
biological organism. Biological organisms are categorized in terms of species and
genus and family and kingdom, and so on. It is hard to know how a fetus that is
produced by humans could be characterized other than in terms of being a member of the species *Homo sapiens*. It is not a mouse or an oak tree or a mosquito.
You are a member of the species *Homo sapiens*. If you are a member of the species
Homo sapiens, then there was a fetus that was an earlier phase of you. If a fetus is an
earlier phase of the same individual you are, then it is just as much a member of the
species as you are. Notice that these claims are not about morality; they are claims
in elementary biology. If the claim "a fetus is a living human being" is assigned its
plain meaning, then it is not a moral or a legal or a theological or a philosophical
claim at all. Therefore, whether theologians or philosophers are uncertain about
whether or not it is true is irrelevant.

This analysis suggests that Blackmun's claim should be given another interpretation. How might it be understood? No doubt many would understand Blackmun's
claim that there is a lack of consensus concerning when life begins as the claim that
there is a lack of consensus concerning whether fetuses have full human rights or
whether they have moral status. Perhaps we can take Blackmun to be claiming

that because there is lack of consensus concerning the moral status of fetuses, it is impossible to say whether fetuses should have the same protection under the law as human beings who have already been born.

This understanding of Blackmun's view—and, to be fair, the view is held by many—still makes the view untenable. In the not-so-distant past there was lack of consensus in some parts of the world concerning whether or not women had full human rights—that is, the same rights as men—or whether African Americans had full human rights or whether Jews had full human rights. Surely no decent person believes that because of these failures of consensus the Supreme Court of the United States should have ruled that any state law that prohibited others from severely harming women, or African Americans, or Jews was unconstitutional. Nevertheless, this belief is a one that is analogous to the majority holding in Roe, for the holding of Roe is that no state may prohibit bringing about the death of a fetus—when a pregnant woman chooses to terminate a pregnancy—at least, through the second trimester of pregnancy.

It is important to note that the argument of the above paragraph is only that lack-of-consensus considerations are plainly insufficient to show that bringing about the death of a young member of our species is morally or legally permissible. It is entirely compatible with anything said so far that fetuses lack moral standing, or the right to life, or the right not to be killed. Ending the life of a fetus may be permissible on grounds other than the lack of consensus concerning whether or not ending the life of a fetus is wrong. It is entirely compatible with the analysis thus far that ending the life of a fetus may be permissible on grounds that fetuses lack moral standing or that they are not persons or some such view.

I suspect, however, that getting into such matters will shed no light whatsoever on the analysis of Roe. My very strong suspicion is that Blackmun took for granted the commonly held view—and the view that, even now, one finds in the law—that all innocent human beings have the right to life, and even the right to ordinary care to sustain their lives, unless they waive that right. I surmise that Blackmun, when thinking about the Holocaust, and if he were asked to think about syllogisms, would have endorsed the syllogism:

1. All human beings have the right to life.
2. Jews are human beings.
Therefore, Jews have the right to life.

He would also, when thinking about race relations, have endorsed the syllogism:

1. All human beings have the right to life
2. African Americans are human beings.
Therefore, African Americans have the right to life.

However, Blackmun (like, I'm sure, many others) did not want to endorse the following syllogism:

1. All human beings have the right to life.
2. Fetuses are human beings.
Therefore, fetuses have the right to life.

He wanted, without thinking clearly about syllogisms at all, to reject the truth of the conclusion of this syllogism. However, to reject the major premise of this syllogism would have been to reject also to reject those earlier syllogisms, which was out of the question. Therefore, he had to find some way of rejecting the inference from the major promise to the conclusion of this syllogism. That accounts for his comments about when life begins and (I am sure) the comments of many others about when life begins. That analysis of Blackmun's comments suggests that they are deeply confused does not cast doubt on the compelling motives that can account for his making them.

It is worth noting at this point in the analysis that there is a clear explanation of the truth of Blackmun's assertion that there is no consensus concerning when life begins. There is bound to be no consensus concerning the answer to a question when, upon analysis, there is no consensus concerning what the question is, or, indeed, when it is doubtful that the question has an intelligible meaning. Such is the basis for a part of American law that is regarded by many as so settled that it would be wrong even to consider changing it.

Nevertheless, whatever our complaints about Roe, it seems reasonable to believe that abortion causes the death of a fetus. On the one hand, there are good reasons for believing that fetuses are living, even if very young, immature, and underdeveloped, human organisms. On the other hand, the difficulties with the alternatives to that view are overwhelming.

2. WERE YOU EVER A NONSENTIENT FETUS?

To assume that we are members of the species *Homo sapiens* (as most people do) is to assume that we are biological organisms. If so, then it seems reasonable to believe that if my mother had had an abortion when she believed she was pregnant with me, then she would have caused the death of an individual who was an early phase of me. A friend of mine who is a thoughtful person once told me that he is opposed to abortion because, when his mother was pregnant with him, she considered having an abortion. Whether or not his reason for being opposed to abortion is a good reason, plainly he was supposing that if she had had an abortion at that time, then she would have caused his death.

Some philosophers have rejected this view, at least in its unqualified form. They say we are essentially mental entities. This view has interesting consequences. Since an essential property of a thing is a property the absence of which is incompatible with the existence of that thing, if we are essentially mental entities, then we did not exist before we acquired the capacity for sentience, that is, before we acquired the capacity for awareness. Fetuses do not become sentient until they reach a gestational age of twenty weeks. Therefore, we did not exist when our mothers first thought they became pregnant with us. We began to exist only later. Therefore, if your mother had had an abortion when believed she was pregnant with you and the gestational age of that fetus was less than twenty weeks, she would not have caused your death.[1] If my friend's mother had had the early abortion that concerned him, then my friend would have been wrong to think that his life would have been ended.

Although this mental essentialist view may seem like the idle chatter of metaphysicians, it has profound implications for thinking about whether abortion during the first half of pregnancy is wrong. On this mental essentialist view, such an early abortion cannot have ended the existence of an early phase one of us. Instead, the early abortion would have ended the existence of a predecessor of one of us. Therefore, on this mental essentialist view, early abortion is like contraception. Contraception prevents the existence of a successor of a sperm and ovum; early abortion prevents a successor of a less than twenty-week-old fetus from coming into existence. Neither ends the existence of an early phase of one of us. If your mother had had an early abortion when she believed that she was pregnant with you, then she would have prevented you from ever coming into existence. Since you would not yet have existed, you could have been neither harmed, nor wronged by the abortion. She would have brought about the death of a fetus, of course, but that fetus would not have been you.

Plainly the view that we are essentially mental entities has important implications for the ethics of abortion. Jeff McMahan is a leading proponent of this mental essentialist view. He has offered two arguments for it. We can name them, following McMahan, "Brain Transplant" and "Dicephaly." In Brain Transplant you are invited to imagine that Kobe Bryant has suffered a terrible accident, is brain dead, is on life support, and has not been injured below his chin. You want to be a great basketball player, so you arrange to have your brain transplanted into Kobe's body (McMahan, 2002, pp. 31–35).[2] Psychological continuity considerations, that is, considerations involving memories, beliefs, plans, desires, and so on, make it plain, not that Kobe would have a new brain, but that you would now inhabit Kobe's body. Thus your brain with the capacity for mental function, not your (former) body, is the basis for your continuing identity. Because you cannot be in two places at once, your former body, even if maintained on life supports, is not you. Brain Transplant renders transparent our conviction that we are, continue to be, and have been essentially mental entities. We are essentially functional brains. We are not biological organisms.

You might wonder whether the claim that we are essentially brains yields, all by itself, McMahan's conclusion that we are not biological organisms. Why couldn't we be essentially (functional) brains and also biological organisms, even if we are not essentially biological organisms? The trouble with this supposition is that if we are biological organisms at all, then we came into existence when that biological organism with which we are so intimately associated came into existence. According to mental essentialism, we did not exist then. No individual can both exist and not exist. Therefore, if mental essentialism is true, then, not only am I not essentially a biological organism, I am not a biological organism at all.

Notice that the opposite is not true. Suppose I am essentially a biological organism. I can still be a mental entity, even though I am not essentially a mental entity. Being a mental entity is possible because my entire career as a mental entity is only a phase in my career as a biological organism. The beginning of my existence as a mental entity occurred later than the beginning of my existence as a biological organism, and the time at which I will be no longer a mental entity may not mark the end of my existence as a biological organism. (Think of Terri Schiavo.) My existence as a mental entity is, in this respect, like my existence as an adolescent. If I am essentially a biological organism, then my existence as a mental entity, like my existence as an adolescent, is a phase of my life. However, if I am essentially a mental entity, then my existence as a biological organism cannot be a phase of my existence. Therefore, if mental essentialism is true, then I am one individual, and the human biological organism with which I am so intimately associated is another individual. Mental essentialism leads to a kind of dualism.

McMahan offers another argument for the same kind of dualism that he calls "Dicephaly" (McMahan, 2002, pp. 35–39). Abigail and Brittany Hensel are twins. They actually exist. The head of each emerges from the same body. Abigail and Brittany Hensel communicate with others independently. They have different personalities. Plainly they are different individuals. Because identity is transitive, if they were identical to the one biological organism they share, then they would be identical to each other. Plainly they are not. There is no reason to think that one of them is identical to their biological organism and the other is not. Therefore, neither of them is identical to their biological organism. Each is some other thing. McMahan believes that this argument also establishes dualism.

Are Brain Transplant and Dicephaly considerations that compel us to adopt the mental essentialism that underwrites McMahan's view concerning when we began to exist? Consider first the Hensel twins. Are they two persons who share one body? They are indubitably two persons. But do they share one body? Actually, there is some duplication of organs above their waist. Along with other duplications, they have two spinal cords and two vertebral columns above the waist. It seems apt to think of their biological organism as a case of incomplete twinning. What would we say in other cases of incomplete twinning?

Consider an amoeba in the process of fission. There will be phases of that process at which whether there is one amoeba or two is indeterminate. The Hensel twins' body seems analogous. Accordingly, they are not clear counterexamples to the claim that we are biological organisms.

Dicephaly is subject to another problem. Even if we neglect issues that concern the anatomies of the Hensel twins below their necks, their "twoness" involves much more than cerebra. They are, in addition, two heads and necks within which there are separate veins and arteries, separate boney structures, separate sets of cranial and cervical nerves and, for that matter, separate brain stems. These could be thought of as separate, although most unusual, biological organisms with substantial common physiological support mechanisms. Accordingly, Dicephaly does not compel us to accept a dualism between the mental (as embodied in cerebra) and the physical.

Now consider Brain Transplant. The case that McMahan calls "Division" complicates its analysis (2002, pp. 39–43). In Division your cerebrum will be divided and each hemisphere transplanted into a different body. Psychological continuity obtains between you prior to the transplant and each transplanted hemisphere. On the one hand, Division seems to be a great deal for you. Suppose you are deeply conflicted over whether to pursue a career as a full-time professional basketball player or as a full-time philosopher. You might think you could go through Division and not have to choose! You could be both—or at least you could if we don't think carefully about the hurdles involved in getting into the NBA and getting tenure! On the other hand, if, after Division, each cerebral hemisphere were a later stage of you, then, since identity is transitive, each hemisphere would be identical to the other. That is false. Because there is nothing to choose between them, neither hemisphere would be identical to you. To undergo Division is to cease to exist. So much the worse for your two careers!

Here is the difficulty. Mental essentialism is based on the claim that our psychological continuity is the basis for our continuing identity as individuals. If it were, then we could undergo division and continue to exist. We cannot. It follows that the doctrine on which mental essentialism is based is false. Can McMahan get around this difficulty?

McMahan's strategy is to say that, if I were to undergo Division in the future, even though I (now) would not be the same individual as each of my hemispheres after Division, I would have egoistic concern for each. However, this cannot be quite right. The best candidate in ordinary English for what we would mean by "egoistic concern" is the concern we have for our later future selves. However, after the time of my division, my later self does not exist. McMahan recognizes that his view, taken literally, will not do. So McMahan stipulates that "egoistic concern" as he uses the term means "special egoistic-like concern." Special egoistic-like concern is, he says, concern that is "phenomenologically indistinguishable from concern for oneself" but need not be concern for oneself (McMahan, 2002, p. 42).[3]

Now suppose that the operation I am about to undergo is not Division, but merely standard, run-of-the-mill, everyday brain transplant. (Suppose your local neurosurgeon is advertising a special.) Plainly, I will have "special egoistic-like concern" for what seems to be my future self. Furthermore, others will think that considerations involving psychological continuity show that I continue to exist in a new body. But why should I assume that what seems to be my future self actually will be I? Why should others infer that what seems to be my future self actually is I? McMahan's analysis of Division shows that I am not entitled to that inference. The trouble is that the inference to which I am not entitled is the basis for McMahan's conclusion in Brain Transplant. The existence of the psychological unity relation, even in a first person case, is not a sufficient condition for our continuing identity.[4] This is because, as Division shows, psychological continuity is one thing; identity is another. Psychological continuity is compatible with fission; identity is not.

This being the case, McMahan's arguments for mental essentialism fail. Unless relevant arguments are lurking around other than McMahan's, we do not have good reasons for rejecting the standard view that we are biological organisms. Therefore, McMahan has not provided us with good reasons for rejecting the view that we existed earlier than a gestational age of twenty weeks. It follows that he has not provided good reasons for rejecting the view that if the early fetus that was my precursor had been aborted, then that abortion would have caused my death.

3. Does Bringing about the Death of a Fetus Greatly Harm It?

So far I have offered reasons for rejecting the claim that abortion may not cause the death of a fetus. I have also offered reasons for rejecting the claim that even if early abortion does cause the death of a fetus, it could not have caused the death of an early phase of one of us. Given this, one might hold that, just as bringing about the death of a postnatal human being greatly harms that human being, bringing about the death of a fetus harms that prenatal human being at least as much.

Why might we think this? We all believe that our premature deaths, whether brought about by human agency, or disease, or natural catastrophe are harmful, indeed, very harmful, to us. We believe this because we believe that our premature deaths deprive us of all of the goods of our futures that we would have experienced in the absence of those premature deaths. Our premature deaths make our lives considered as a whole worse, and that is because our premature deaths make our lives shorter. A shorter life is, in general, worse than a longer life, because a shorter life contains fewer of life's goods than a longer life. Therefore, our premature deaths harm us.

If this is true, then it would seem that bringing about the death of a fetus harms it. Indeed, it would seem that bringing about the death of a not-yet-sentient fetus greatly harms that fetus, for it deprives that fetus of all of the experiential goods of life that it would have experienced in its whole lifetime had it not been aborted. Let us call this view of the harm of death, following McMahan, "the whole lifetime perspective."

David DeGrazia and Jeff McMahan have rejected this view. They have claimed that abortions do not greatly harm fetuses.[5] Their claim is based on what they have called "the time-relative interest account of the harm of death." Let's call this "the TR interest account."

Both DeGrazia and McMahan have tried to make TR interest account plausible in the following way. They have pointed out that if we evaluate the harm of death in terms of the whole lifetime perspective, then, ceteris paribus, the younger the victim, the more she is harmed by death. A presentient fetus is harmed more by death than an infant; an infant is harmed more by death than a ten-year-old; a ten-year-old is harmed more by death than a twenty-five-year-old. McMahan and DeGrazia note that most of us would reject these judgments. Indeed, we would affirm the opposite judgments.[6] According to DeGrazia, we would regard the death of a presentient fetus as, perhaps, unfortunate. We would consider an infant's death a major misfortune for him. We would think that the death of a ten-year-old or a twenty-five-year-old was utterly tragic for either of them (DeGrazia, 2007, pp. 63–64).

How can these judgments be explained? According to DeGrazia,

> Our reflections on the harm of death suggest that it is a function not only of lost opportunities for valuable life, as understood from a whole-lifetime perspective, but of another factor as well. Stated simply, the second factor according to the TRIA [TR interest account] is the way one is psychologically "invested" in, or connected with, one's possible future life. (2007, p. 65)

According to DeGrazia, this second factor "discounts the importance of death to the victim, at the time of death, for any weakness in the psychological unity that would have connected the victim at that time with himself in the future." What are the constituents of this psychological unity? According to DeGrazia,

> The degree of psychological unity in a life, or over a stretch of time, is a function of (1) the richness of the subject's mental life, (2) the proportion of the mental life that is sustained over the stretch of time in question, and (3) the degree of internal reference between earlier and later mental states. Example of internal reference include memories of past experiences (ranging from dim to highly detailed), anticipation of future experiences (ranging from simple anticipation implicit in the most primitive fear to intricate expectations for the distant future), and intentions to perform certain actions (ranging from simple intentions for the immediate future to elaborate life plans). (2007, pp. 65–66)

DeGrazia concludes that "the utter lack of psychological unity between the presentient fetus and the later minded being it could become justifies a very substantial discounting of the harm of the fetus' death" (2007, p. 72).

Both McMahan and DeGrazia believe that the TR interest account is the best explanation of these standard judgments. A whole-lifetime perspective account of the harm of death is incompatible with these standard judgments. Therefore, we should accept the TR interest account of the harm of death. Let's call this argument "the standard judgment argument" (DeGrazia, 2007, p. 67). McMahan claims that this argument is "one of the strongest reasons for accepting" the TR interest account (2002, p.67).

Is McMahan correct? On the one hand, there is, of course, no doubt that many people possess the discounted view of fetal harm that McMahan and DeGrazia endorse. On the other hand, the whole-lifetime perspective is based on a plausible account of the harm of killing. Why, then, should we accept the TR interest account? According to McMahan the TR interest account and the intuition that fetal harm should be discounted are mutually supportive. Each is justified on the ground that each coheres with the other.

McMahan admits that this standard judgment argument "invites a charge of circularity" (2002, p. 78). Why then should we accept it? Consider a racist who does not think that a jury should convict a white person who kills a black person of a felony. You ask him to defend his view. He says that everyone he knows believes that blacks aren't harmed as much by death as white persons, and so killing a black person should be no more than a misdemeanor. When you ask for a theory to account for such a claim, he says that he holds a race-relative interest account of the harm of death for black folks. When you ask him to defend that account of the harm of death, he says that the account explains the standard judgment of everyone he knows concerning the harm of death for black folks. (He doesn't say "black folks.") Although he knows that this leaves him open to the charge of circularity, mutual coherence considerations support his views. I leave it to you, reader, to construct the analogous account for the virulent anti-Semite. I am quite certain that neither McMahan nor DeGrazia are racists or anti-Semites. Nevertheless, it is difficult to see how the form of their standard judgment argument is different from the analogous standard judgment argument that could be constructed for the racist or anti-Semite. Since the racist and anti-Semitic versions of a standard judgment argument should be rejected out of hand, it seems that the standard judgment argument for the TR interest account should be rejected as well.

Of course, this critique of the standard judgment argument would be weakened if the judgments on which the standard judgment argument is based could be explained only by appeal to the TR interest account. However, two other explanations are quite plausible. One is that presentient fetuses are not part of the universe to which we pay much attention. They have not yet emerged into our social world. They do not interact with the rest of us. We tend to discount death's harm in such cases. Fetuses appear, to many Americans at least, like Iraqis killed in that stupid war, or like all of the Vietnamese killed in that other stupid war, or like people starving in Darfur. Nevertheless, in our better moments, we believe that discounting the harm of death in these cases is incorrect.

A second reason why the harm of fetal death is easily discounted appeals to our very limited sense of how a nonsentient fetus's life might have developed if it had not ended. Therefore, we lack knowledge of what particular opportunities were foreclosed to a fetus by her death. Our sense of what these particular opportunities are in the case of the deaths of young humans grows as the young human being gets older. Because of this we have a better sense of how death harms them. As a consequence, it is easier to believe that young human beings are harmed more by death as they grow older. However, this belief is due to our ignorance of the particular ways in which they are harmed, not how much they really are harmed.

Therefore, we have at least two reasons to reject the standard judgment argument for the TR interest account of the harm of death. Further analysis of the McMahan-DeGrazia standard judgment argument opens the door to a metaethical issue of the very last importance. I don't think that people who believe it is presumptively seriously wrong to end the lives of fetuses have that belief because they have some intuition that fetuses are harmed by being killed at least as much, and perhaps even more, than adults. Their belief that fetuses are seriously harmed by being killed is based on what they believe to be an appeal to reason—on an appeal to syllogism with such premises as (1) it is wrong intentionally to kill innocent human beings, and fetuses are innocent human beings; or (2) it is generally wrong to kill individuals who would otherwise have an opportunity to experience the goods of living that a person experiences, and fetuses, if not aborted, would have an opportunity to experience such goods of living; or (unfortunately) (3) whatever my preacher says is true and my preacher says that abortion is wrong. Such syllogisms are intended to overcome any casual judgments people may make about fetuses, just as arguments for racial equality appeal to reason and are meant to overcome any judgments one may make because one was raised in a society in which racism was taken for granted, or just as arguments about equality for gays and lesbians appeal to reason and are meant to overcome any judgments heterosexuals may make because they have the intuition gay sex is disgusting. Those who would hold that standard judgments in these latter cases do not provide a basis for trumping the relevant syllogisms should also hold that standard judgments in the cases of fetuses do not constitute a basis for trumping the relevant syllogisms.[7] If there is something wrong with the relevant syllogism, that error cannot be based on a conflict with such standard judgments. The basic strategy of the standard judgment argument is unacceptable.

4. THE INTERMEDIATE JUDGMENT ARGUMENT

Both McMahan and DeGrazia also have offered what I shall call "the intermediate judgment argument" in favor of the TR interest account of the harm of death. They have claimed that a virtue of the TR interest account of the harm of death is that it explains why "the badness of death for an infant is intermediate between the badness of death for a person [that is, a standard adult] and the badness of a person's failing to come into existence at all."[8] According to McMahan, the following judgments concerning the harm of death are reasonable: when a person dies, there is a great loss of future good and a victim who is related in ways that matter to the victim. In the case of nonconception, there is a loss of future good, but no victim. In the intermediate case of the death of an infant, there is a victim, but the victim is only weakly related, in ways that matter, to the good that is lost. When McMahan speaks of ways that matter, he is thinking of those relations that are constitutive of psychological unity.

McMahan believes that the TR interest account of the harm of death is preferable to the whole-lifetime perspective on the harm of death because the TR account

better explains how this judgment regarding the harm of death to a fetus is intermediate between the other two judgments. Here is his argument:

> If identity were what matters, the worst death, involving the most significant
> loss, would be the death of an individual immediately after the beginning of his
> existence. But the loss that would have occurred if that individual had simply
> been prevented from beginning to exist would not have been significant at all.
> This is hard to believe. It suggests that it is profoundly important to prevent the
> existence of an individual who would die within seconds of beginning to exist.
> This might make sense if we came in to existence fully formed psychologically, as
> Athena emerged from the head of Zeus. But given the way we in fact develop, this
> view is very hard to accept. (2002, p. 171)

McMahan's view that the whole-lifetime perspective implies that it is important to prevent the existence of an individual who would soon die is questionable.
What does it mean to say that "it is important"? Presumably McMahan means that
if the whole-lifetime perspective were correct, we would have a moral obligation to
prevent the existence of such an individual.

How can this be? Presumably one can have a moral obligation only if it is possible to fulfill that obligation. How is it possible to fulfill a moral obligation to an
individual who never did exist, does not now exist, and never will exist? To have
a moral obligation to someone is to stand in a moral relation to her. A necessary
condition for the truth of a sentence containing a relational predicate is that there
are two things that stand in the relation to which the relational predicate refers.
Thus, a necessary condition for the truth of "a is to the left of b" is that a exists and
b exists and that they stand in the relation of to the left of. It follows that one cannot have the obligation to prevent someone from coming into existence because
there is no one to have the obligation to. This is not a claim that turns on when the
individual to whom one has the obligation exists. I stand in the relation of being
the great grandson of to a number of people none of whom exist now. Similarly,
I can have obligations to future generations and I can have obligations to persons
who no longer exist. There are excellent reasons, therefore, to deny that someone
who holds the whole-lifetime perspective is committed to the view that we have
an obligation to prevent someone from coming into existence. Therefore, we may
conclude that the considerations that McMahan offers in favor of the intermediate
judgment argument are unsound.

5. THE UNEQUAL HARM OF DEATH JUDGMENT

DeGrazia (but not McMahan) also has offered what I shall call "the unequal harm
of death argument" for the TR interest account of the harm of death. This argument is based upon what DeGrazia calls "the Unequal Harm of Death Judgment."
Following DeGrazia I shall refer to this as "the UHDJ." The UHDJ is our belief

that humans are harmed more by death than animals. What explains this judgment? DeGrazia claims that the TR interest account of the harm of death is a better account of the harm of death than the whole-lifetime account because it better explains UDHJ. Because the lives of humans—after early childhood, at least—are psychologically more unified than the lives of other animals, and because, according to the TR interest account, the relative lack of psychological unity in animals implies that the harm of death should be discounted in their cases, the TR interest account can explain the UHDJ. DeGrazia realizes that it does not follow that the TR interest account is correct because it is the best explanation of UHDJ. Perhaps human life's qualitative superiority to animal life could explain UHDJ just as well. DeGrazia rejects the qualitative superiority explanation: "Suffice it to say here that no one has provided arguments of such a high quality in support of this strategy for vindicating the UHDJ. It would not be unreasonable to suspect that this approach...is on the wrong track" (2007, p. 62).

Will this do? His characterization of his conclusion is ambiguous. Sometimes he claims only "that the Time-Relative Interest Account furnishes adequate support for the UHDJ independently of any assumption of human life's prudential superiority" (2007, p. 63n). Even if there is something to be said for his claim, this claim plainly does not, by itself, support the TR interest account on the basis of an inference to best explanation. Sometimes DeGrazia claims that

> I don't preclude the possibility of an adequate defense for the assertion of human life's prudential superiority [the qualitatively superiority claim]. My intention is to cast doubt on defenses that have been offered thus far and to argue...that the Time-Relative Interest Account furnishes adequate support for the UHDJ independently of any assumption of human life's prudential superiority. (2007, p. 63)

Although I don't agree, let us suppose that DeGrazia is correct about the claim that adequate defenses of life's qualitative superiority have not yet been offered. Would we have adequate support for DeGrazia's view that the TR interest account offers the best explanation for UHDJ?

The problem with DeGrazia's argument is that human life's qualitative superiority to the lives of animals seems obvious and does not need elaborate defense. Think the ways in which the lives of persons seem superior to those of animals. The lives of persons involve autonomy. They involve significant human accomplishments. They involve aesthetic delights. They involve important personal relationships. Virtually all of us believe that it is obvious that these features of the lives of humans make those lives qualitatively superior to the lives of animals. McMahan has explicitly endorsed the qualitative superiority claim on the basis of such cursory considerations, which is, no doubt, why he does not use the UDHJ argument to defend the TR interest account (2002, p. 192).

I shall buttress these considerations by referring to a well-known discussion of this matter in the history of ethical theory. Mill famously argued that the pleasures of persons are greater than those of swine because they are qualitatively superior. There is no evidence that it occurred either to Mill, or to the critics of the hedonistic utilitarianism to whom Mill was replying, that the lives of persons might not be vastly qualitatively superior to the lives of swine.[9] Both Mill and his critics took this for granted. Both Mill and his critics were concerned with whether the (obvious) qualitative superiority of the lives of persons was compatible with hedonistic utilitarianism. The reason for the absence of argument for the qualitative superiority of the lives of persons is that most people, like Mill, like his critics, and like the readers of all of them, have assumed that the qualitative superiority claim is too obvious to argue for! Accordingly, the absence of extensive argument for this claim would not cast doubt on its truth. Accordingly, DeGrazia's UHDJ argument for the TR interest account of the harm of death is unconvincing.

6. The Cure

Let's consider one final argument for the TR interest account of the harm of death. This argument is based on a hypothetical case described by McMahan.

> The Cure. Imagine that you are twenty years old and are diagnosed with a disease that, if untreated, invariably causes death…within five years. There is a treatment that reliably cures the disease but also, as a side effect, causes total retrograde amnesia and radical personality change. Long-term studies of others who have had the treatment show that they almost always go on to have long and happy lives, though these lives are informed by desires and values that differ profoundly from those that the person had prior to treatment. (2002, p. 77)

McMahan claims that "most of us would at least be skeptical of the wisdom of taking the treatment and many would be deeply opposed to it" (2002, p. 77). He claims this is best explained by the TR interest account of the harm of death.

Why would we have such reservations about the treatment? According to McMahan,

> the future offered by the treatment is too much like someone else's future. In that future you would be a complete stranger to yourself as you are now. The psychological distance between you now and yourself as you would be after the treatment is too great for you to think of the goods in that future as fully yours…[Y]ou now would not be sufficiently related to yourself in the future in the ways that matter to make it rational for you to care about them in the normal way. It may seem rational instead to opt for the lesser good (five more years only) which would more clearly be your good or to which you would be more strongly related in the ways that matter. (2002, p. 78)

I think that McMahan is plainly right to suggest that most of us initially would be skeptical about taking The Cure. However, McMahan needs a stronger claim than this to make his case. He needs this claim: Not choosing The Cure would be rational, all things considered. I think that it would not be rational. However, that fact that my intuition differs from McMahan's hardly settles the matter. Let's reflect on a real situation very much like McMahan's Cure. Suppose a young man is wondering whether to begin smoking. He realizes that, in all probability, once he starts, he will become habituated to cigarettes, and will be unable to stop. There are data that support the claim that his median life expectancy will be reduced by thirteen to fourteen years.[10] Most of us, if asked, believe it would not be rational for him to begin smoking and would advise him against it.

Consider the argument he might offer for rejecting our advice. "The thirteen years of life I would lose by smoking is life mostly in my seventies. My life then will be too much like someone else's life. At that time I would be a complete stranger to the person I am now. The psychological distance between me now and myself so far in the future is too great for me to think of the goods of that future as fully mine." We would reject this argument and we would suggest that the young man reject it also. But this looks like the argument for rejecting The Cure (because I set it out that way). Therefore, we should reject McMahan's argument for rejecting the cure.

Can McMahan find a different, but related, argument such that the decision to smoke is not rational but the decision not to take The Cure is? Here is a possibility. McMahan might argue that the potential smoker cares about his life after ten more years, since he will not then be so different from the person he is now. The person he is after ten more years will care about his life after twenty more years, since the person ten years older will not be substantially different from the person ten years younger. Such considerations should result in the judgment that it is not rational to begin smoking. Call this "the transitivity of caring argument."

The trouble with this transitivity of caring strategy is that it essentially involves an appeal (unlike in the case of McMahan's original argument) to what one would care about at other stages of one's life. However, if it is reasonable to appeal to what one would care about at other stages of one's life, then one wonders why it would be unreasonable to appeal to whether one would care about five years or more after having taken The Cure? Plainly, at those times one would regard it as rational to have taken The Cure. Indeed, this is merely one example of a standard strategy that we use to convince people to choose a particular course of action. This strategy has a name: "Try it, you'll like it!" I see no nonarbitrary reason why McMahan should reject the "try it; you'll like it" strategy, which is a standard rational choice strategy in favor of a "transitivity of caring" strategy, which is a good deal less than intuitively obvious. I conclude that McMahan's example and analysis of The Cure does not provide us with good reasons for preferring the TR interest account of the harm of death to the whole-lifetime perspective. To summarize, none of the arguments in favor of the TR interest account of the harm of death are successful. As a result we should retain the intuitively plausible whole-lifetime perspective on the harm of death. Therefore, it seems reasonable to conclude that ending the life of a fetus greatly harms it.

7. THE HARM-WRONG GAP

Should we infer from the fact that ending the life of a fetus greatly harms it that ending the life of a fetus greatly wrongs it? Many would make this inference. However, the great harm to a fetus that is a result of a human agent causing its death does not entail that it was wronged. Furthermore, the missing premise needed to convert the above inference to a valid inference is false. Someone who destroys a forest may harm each of the trees in the forest and so may inflict very great harm on the forest. Nevertheless, this does not give us reason for thinking that any of the trees or all of the trees have been wronged by the destruction. Great harm to the forest is compatible with no wrong at all to the forest or to the trees in it (although, of course, the destruction of a forest can be a great wrong to people). In short, "A is greatly harmed" does not entail "A is wronged." The obvious premise "everything that is greatly harmed is wronged," required to generate a valid argument is false.[11]

Plainly, what we can call "a harm-wrong gap" exists. Is there a way of bridging it in the case of fetuses without appealing to a premise that is plainly false? Here is a possibility. Call the future lives of which premature death deprives persons like us, "futures-like-ours." I shall henceforth call them, "FLOs."[12] I shall stipulate that FLOs are the kinds of things possessed by those human beings we all agree it is presumptively seriously wrong to kill, but not by (nonhuman) animals or plants. Now the following argument becomes available: All individuals deprived of FLOs by human agency are presumptively greatly wronged. Fetuses have FLOs. Therefore, fetuses are presumptively greatly wronged by being deprived of FLOs by human agency. This argument is an improvement over the previous argument because it does not rest on a premise that is known to be false.

Improvement or not, this move does not solve the problem of the harm-wrong gap. That the premise used in the reformulated argument is not obviously false certainly does not entail that it is true. Therefore, the harm-wrong gap is still with us.

Of course, the problem of the harm-wrong gap is general. It applies to the deaths of postnatal humans as well as to fetuses. What bridges the harm-wrong gap in the case of postnatal human beings? One standard answer to this question is that postnatal human beings have moral status; fetuses lack moral status. Therefore, fetuses are subject to the harm-wrong gap, while postnatal human beings are not.

Not just any arbitrary account of moral status will serve our purposes. If any arbitrary account will do, then a Nazi can find an account of moral status that will serve his purposes. This shows that a defensible account of moral status is needed that will plug the harm-wrong gap in the cases of postnatal human beings. Furthermore, most people would agree that animals have some moral status. Having some moral status is compatible with the existence of the harm-wrong gap, at least as far as ending the lives of animals is concerned. Therefore, what we need is an account of full moral status. The account of full moral status that is supposed to fill the gap is typically given in terms of being a person. Someone who adopts this account will claim that being a person confers full moral status on an individual. Because fetuses are not persons, they lack full moral status. Being a person is understood, for the purposes of an analysis of this kind, as having the immediately exercisable capacity to exhibit the kinds of mental functions typical of postnatal human beings.[13]

So far we have a proposal, not a convincing analysis. What is needed is an account of what a person is that explains how the harm-wrong gap is bridged in a way that permits reproductive choice. Put another way, we need an account of how and why being a person is morally significant. I consider three candidates.

According to a well-entrenched philosophical view, an individual is a person if and only if she is a rational agent.[14] Therefore, no matter how much death harms a fetus, harming it does not wrong it because it is not a rational agent. Because postnatal human beings are rational agents, the harm-wrong gap is bridged in their cases, and so killing them is wrong.

The problem with this account is that it does not sort clear cases correctly. Young children are not rational agents. Therefore, the rational agent account of moral status renders killing young children morally permissible. Plainly this won't do. Notice that if we try to fix this problem by allowing individuals with the potential to become rational agents to be persons and therefore to have moral status, then fetuses will be persons and the harm-wrong gap will be filled in their cases. This view is incompatible with reproductive choice.

Here is another candidate. It has been argued that being a person is morally significant because only persons can have a concept of self as a continuing subject of experience. Only individuals with the concept of self as a continuing subject of experience can desire, hope for, value, care about, or plan for their futures. A person with a future life in prospect is wronged because we fail to respect her pro-attitude toward her future life. Fetuses lack such pro-attitudes. Therefore, ending their lives does not wrong them.[15]

This account also does not sort clear cases correctly. If it were correct, then it would be morally permissible to kill suicidal individuals with untreated bipolar disorder. We all agree that it is not permissible. Plainly such an account also won't do.

Finally, someone might argue that being a person is morally important because it accounts for the comparative moral judgments we make concerning postnatal humans and other animals. We believe that killing postnatal humans wrongs them. We don't believe killing animals wrongs them. What accounts for the difference in judgment? Mere biology is not morally significant; therefore, one's species, all by itself, is morally irrelevant. Therefore, what must account for the moral difference is that postnatal humans are persons and animals are not. Being a person gives one the requisite moral status in order to bridge the harm-wrong gap. Since fetuses are not persons, the harm-wrong gap is not bridged in their cases.

Will this do? The above argument is an inference to best explanation. We can account for the moral difference between postnatal humans and animals in a different way. A FLO is a life that has the quality of an adult human life. Persons have FLOs. Animals do not. Fetuses are like persons in this respect, because they also have FLOs. Therefore, the moral difference between animals and persons can be accounted for in virtue of the fact that members of one group have FLOs and members of the other do not. Accordingly the "best explanation" defense of an account of full moral status in terms of present personhood fails, although it leaves the door open to an account of an individual's full moral status in terms of personhood at some time, and opens the door to an account of moral status in terms of an individual's present potential for future personhood.

Another strategy that one finds in the literature on abortion is concerned less with bridging the harm-wrong gap in the case of individuals we all believe it is wrong to kill than with reinforcing the harm-wrong gap in the case of nonsentient fetuses. Some people have held the view that inflicting great harm on an individual is wrong only if the individual in question has at least minimal moral status and one has at least minimal moral status only in virtue of being a sentient being, or a being capable of awareness.[16] Therefore, nonsentient fetuses cannot be wronged, whereas postnatal human beings can be. One might defend this view on the grounds that it preserves the harm-wrong gap in the case of comparing members of the animal kingdom to members of the vegetable kingdom, but fills the harm-wrong gap, at least partially, in the case of animals. After all, most of us believe that to inflict pain and suffering on an animal is to wrong the animal.

This strategy does not apply to our present issue quite as unambiguously as some might like. Nonsentient fetuses are merely phases in the lives of human beings and human beings are, when considered as a whole, sentient beings. Trees are not. Therefore, we might ask: Should the sentience criterion for moral status apply to phases in the life of a biological organism or to the biological organism as a whole?

There is reason for preferring the latter. People who are nonsentient in the present phase of their lives, such as patients under anesthesia for surgery or patients who are in a medically induced coma for other reasons, plainly have moral status. Consequently, we have a reason for preferring the biological-organism-as-a-whole version of the sentience criterion to the phase version of the criterion. It follows that the sentience criterion for at least minimal moral status does not supply us with a reason to deny moral status to nonsentient fetuses. The reasonable claim that sentience confers (at least some) moral status on individuals does not, apparently paradoxically, entail that nonsentient fetuses lack moral status.

Another kind of sentience strategy for denying moral status to nonsentient fetuses exists. It has been argued that sentience is a necessary condition for having interests and therefore for having an interest in living. Morality is concerned with respecting the interests of others. Therefore, nonsentient fetuses fall outside the scope of morality, but animals and sentient humans are included within morality's scope, or so goes the argument.[17]

Will this do? The claim that sentience is a necessary condition for having interests seems reasonable. After all, animals have interests; no plant has interests. Nevertheless, the notion of "having an interest" has more than one meaning. One can have an interest in something in virtue of taking an interest in it. One cannot take an interest in something in the absence of mental activity, since taking an interest in something involves having a mental attitude. It follows that non-sentient fetuses cannot take an interest in anything and therefore, cannot have interests at all if a necessary condition of having an interest is taking an interest in something.

The trouble with this line of thought is that something can be in one's (best) interest even if one is, at present, not taking an interest in that thing. It follows that something can be in one's interest even if one is presently nonsentient. Patients who have been anesthetized for surgery and other patients who are in a medically induced coma have interests even though they are presently nonsentient, and even if they were put in the medically induced coma as the result of an accident that occurred because they were suicidal and, therefore, did not take an interest in living. Such patients as well as nonsentient fetuses will (we hope) later become sentient. Even though they are presently not able to take an interest in anything, they can have interests in the other sense of "interest." Nonsentient phases of sentient beings can have interests, even if they cannot at present take an interest in anything. Therefore, the claim that sentience is a necessary condition of having interests and having interests is a necessary condition of having moral status does not entail that nonsentient fetuses lack moral status. Because nonsentient human fetuses are phases in the life span of sentient beings they can have, and, indeed, do have, interests.

The analysis of this section has supported the view that standard accounts of moral status that imply that fetuses lack moral status are inadequate. It is tempting to conclude that there is no adequate account of moral status that underwrites the inference from "this fetus is greatly harmed" to "this fetus is greatly wronged." Those who support reproductive choice should not rejoice. Consider all of the individuals we all believe it is wrong to kill. We have found no adequate account of moral status that applies to them either. The difficulty in filling the harm-wrong gap is perfectly general. If that failure is a defect in the views of critics of abortion, then it is a failure in the views of critics of the Holocaust. This suggests that our difficulty is not fatal.

So what should we do? The only acceptable view seems to be to ground the inference from harm to wrong on the kind of deprivation that the death of a human produced by human agency causes. A standard human being who is killed is deprived of a FLO. Standard animals and plants are not. Therefore, it seems that the deprivation of a FLO is the kind of harm such that to bring about that kind of harm is to wrong someone. If this view is correct, then fetuses are not only harmed by being killed; they are wronged as well.

This move in ethics has a precedent. Consider animals. We believe that inflicting pain and suffering on animals harms them. We believe (apparently) that because inflicting pain and suffering on animals harms them, for us to inflict it on them is to wrong them. If someone challenges us to defend that conclusion by producing a defensible account of moral status that underwrites it, we cannot. On the contrary, we believe that suffering is bad for animals because we are sure that it is bad for us. We attribute (weak) moral status to the animals simply on this basis.[18]

I am simply proposing that we treat humans in the same way. We believe that the loss of a FLO is bad for others because we believe that it is bad for us. We conclude that we have full moral status on this basis. The matter of moral status (at least with respect to the ethics of killing) turns out to be just that simple. This being the case, the fact that ending the life of a fetus greatly harms it supports the view that ending the life of a fetus greatly wrongs it.

8. The Issue of Equality

Jeff McMahan has defended a different version of the harm-wrong gap. He rightly notes that the whole-lifetime account of the harm of death implies that, as a rule, young people will be harmed by death more than older people. This is because the young have more future life to lose than the old. If death's harm to a person were the primary source of the wrongness of bringing about the death of a person, then killing the young would be a worse crime than killing the old. McMahan argues that, "this implication profoundly offends our sense of the moral equality of persons" (2002. p. 34).[19] The doctrine of the moral equality of persons supports what he calls the "the equal wrongness principle." Different killings of persons are equally wrong. Therefore, what makes killing a person wrong is not even partially a matter of the harm inflicted on that person. If it were, then when two people are killed, they would usually not be wronged equally. This would violate the equal wrongness thesis. Notice how different McMahan's respect objection is from the moral status objection.

Because, for McMahan, the wrongness of killing persons has nothing to do with death's harm, whether death's harm is understood from the whole-lifetime perspective or the TR interest view, McMahan needs a harm-independent account of the wrongness of killing. He says that killing a person is wrong because the killing conflicts with that person's autonomous will to live (2002, pp. 240–256).

Is this account correct? In the first place, McMahan's view that the harm of death and the wrongness of death are totally independent considerations is (to use a favorite McMahan expression) hard to believe. In the second place, the view that killing a person is wrong because the killing conflicts with that person's autonomous will to live is subject to counterexamples. It does not account for the wrongness of killing those who lack the will to live because of psychiatric disease. Furthermore, it does not lead to a satisfactory account for why is it wrong to kill children. In many dimensions of living we do not respect the autonomy of children. Surely there is something odd about basing a certain wrong, such as the killing of children, on a consideration which, in other contexts, we do not regard as important.

In the third place, it is most unclear that the doctrine of the equal respect for persons has the implications that McMahan thinks it does. Surely some plausible version of the doctrine of the equal respect for persons is true. McMahan's view is correct only if there is no reasonable version of the doctrine of the equal respect for persons that is compatible with the view that killing a person is wrong because of the great harm to that individual caused by the killing. Is there a reasonable version of the equal respect doctrine compatible with the apparently obvious view that killing people is wrong because it harms them and that the harm of death is, as a rule, greater for the young rather than the old? Here is a candidate: Each human individual has the equal right to the opportunity to live a flourishing human life. I should have no less opportunity (at least, relative to my natural capacities) than you, and conversely. To kill someone infringes on that opportunity. Nevertheless, ceteris paribus, killing the young infringes on that opportunity more than killing the old, for the old have had already a greater opportunity to flourish in their lifetimes. To kill someone who is twenty years old infringes on his opportunity to flourish over the course of his lifetime far more than killing someone who is eighty years old. Although this claim is incompatible with the thesis of the equal wrongness of killing it is not incompatible with the equal right of all persons to have the opportunity to flourish. This conception of human equality looks at flourishing over the whole lifetime of each individual, not at an individual at a particular age. This is entirely compatible with, and fits in well with, understanding the harm of death from a whole-lifetime perspective. McMahan's claim that a whole-lifetime account (or any other harm-based account) of the wrongness of causing death is incompatible with a doctrine of the equal respect for persons is false.

9. Conclusion

In this chapter I have defended a view about abortion and death by defending four theses concerning abortion and death. I have not replied to all published criticisms of these theses. I have not replied to all possible objections to these theses. In particular, I have not replied to the sorts of criticisms famously offered by Judy Thomson (1971). My reason for not discussing the matters raised by Professor Thomson is that there are adequate critiques of her views elsewhere in the literature and that discussion of her views would draw me away from the related topics discussed in this essay.[20] In this essay I have discussed the objections to the views I have defended that I believe have the most force.[21]

Notes

1. Jeff McMahan has defended this view in his 2002. Michael Tooley has also defended this view in Tooley, Wolf-Devine, Devine, and Jaggar, 2009.
2. The above version of Brain Transplant is mine, but it is not different in any important philosophical way from McMahan's version.

3. I shall refrain from commenting on how misleading McMahan's labels are.
4. This problem also emerges in teletransportation cases.
5. DeGrazia's most recent defense of his view is his 2007. His earlier defenses of his view can be found in DeGrazia, 2006, 2005, and 2003. Page numbers in parentheses will refer to DeGrazia's most recent Philosophical Forum views. For Jeff McMahan's views, see his 2002.
6. See DeGrazia, 2007, p. 63, and McMahan, 2002, p. 172.
7. Notice that this argument does not take for granted the soundness or lack of it of any of the appeals to reason.
8. McMahan has offered this argument in 2002, p. 170. DeGrazia offered this argument in 2006, p. 55, and 2005, p. 287, but not in his most recent defense of the TR interest account.
9. See John Stuart Mill, 1979. Mill's discussion is early in chapter 2, pp. 8–10.
10. See Centers for Disease Control and Prevention, Smoking and Tobacco Use, Fast Facts.
11. Elizabeth Harman has pressed this objection in conversation and in her 2003.
12. This is pronounced flow.
13. There are problems about this definition which would divert us from the task at hand, so I shall waive them. Such accounts of being a person famously are found in Peter Singer, 1979; Mary Anne Warren, 1973; and elsewhere.
14. The view that personhood, rational agency, and moral status are all of a piece is, of course, due to Kant. See Kant, 1998. Kant would not agree, of course, with some of what I have said about this view.
15. The two best known proponents of this view are Michael Tooley, 1972, and Peter Singer, 1979.
16. Bonnie Steinbock is the best known proponent of this view. See her 1992.
17. One can find arguments of this kind in Steinbock, 1992; and in Ronald Dworkin, 1993.
18. This line of argument can be found in Peter Singer, 1979.
19. This objection has also been set out clearly by Dean Stretton, 2004.
20. The essays in Pojman and Beckwith, 1998, are particularly interesting.
21. I thank Ben Bradley and Jens Johansson for their very helpful comments on an earlier draft of this chapter.

References

Blackmun, Harry. 1973. "Majority Opinion in *Roe v. Wade*." Reprinted in *The Abortion Controversy: 25 Years after* Roe v. Wade: *A Reader*, Louis P. Pojman and Francis J. Beckwith, eds., pp. 19–32. Belmont: Wadsworth.

Centers for Disease Control and Prevention. *Smoking and Tobacco Use, Fast Facts.* Accessed January 3, 2011. URL = http://www.cdc.gov/tobacco/data_statistics/fact_sheets/fast_facts/index.htm.

DeGrazia, David. 2003. "Identity, Killing and the Boundaries of Our Existence." *Philosophy and Public Affairs* 31: 413–442.

DeGrazia, David. 2005. *Human Identity and Bioethics.* Cambridge: Cambridge University Press.

DeGrazia, David. 2006. "Moral Status, Human Identity, and Early Embryos: A Critique of the President's Approach." *Journal of Law, Medicine and Ethics* 34 (1): 49–57.

DeGrazia, David. 2007. "The Harm of Death, Time-Relative Interests, and Abortion." *Philosophical Forum* 38: 57–80.

Dworkin, Ronald. 1993. *Life's Dominion*. New York: Alfred A. Knopf.

Harman, Elizabeth. 2003. "The Potentiality Problem." *Philosophical Studies* 114: 173–198.

Kant, Immanuel. 1998. *Groundwork of the Metaphysics of Morals*. Translated by Mary Gregor. Cambridge: Cambridge University Press.

McMahan, Jeff. 2002. *The Ethics of Killing: Problems at the Margins of Life*. Oxford: Oxford University Press.

Mill, John Stuart. 1979. *Utilitarianism*. George Sher, ed. Indianapolis, IN: Hackett Publishing Co.

Pojman, L., and F. Beckwith 1998. *The Abortion Controversy: A Reader*. 2nd ed. Belmont: Wadsworth.

Singer, Peter. 1979. *Practical Ethics*. Cambridge: Cambridge University Press.

Steinbock, Bonnie. 1992. *Life before Birth: The Moral and Legal Status of Embryos and Fetuses*. New York: Oxford University Press.

Stretton, Dean. 2004. "The Deprivation Argument against Abortion." *Bioethics* 18: 144–180.

Thomson, Judith Jarvis. 1971. "A Defense of Abortion." *Philosophy and Public Affairs* 1: 67–95.

Tooley, Michael. 1972. "Abortion and Infanticide." *Philosophy and Public Affairs* 2: 37–56

Tooley, Michael, Celia Wolf-Devine, Philip E. Devine, and Alison M. Jaggar. 2009. *Abortion: Three Perspectives*. Oxford: Oxford University Press.

Warren, Mary Anne. "On the Moral and Legal Status of Abortion." *Monist* 57: 43–61.

CHAPTER 19

THE MORALITY OF KILLING IN WAR

SOME TRADITIONAL AND NONTRADITIONAL VIEWS

F. M. KAMM

THIS chapter is about killing in war from a moral (not a legal) perspective. It aims to give an overview of some "classic" views and some recent alternatives to these on selected issues. These views are derivative of deeper nonconsequentialist perspectives in ethics. The chapter seeks to raise questions, often without providing answers.

1. SOME ASPECTS OF STANDARD JUST WAR THEORY

1.1 Jus Ad Bellum versus Jus In Bello

a. Standard just war theory's first stage is jus ad bellum, or justice in starting a war. This includes having a just cause and also meeting conditions of necessity (no other way to achieve the just cause) and proportionality (the costs of war in terms of harm to people would be proportional to the achievement of the just cause). Failure to meet these conditions and others can result in failing jus ad bellum. Standard just war theory is concerned with war between nation states. But the question may arise whether a nonstate agent can satisfy the conditions of jus ad bellum and so be a legitimate agent for war. Similarly, the question may arise whether a nonstate entity may be the target of war.

b. According to the standard theory, questions of jus ad bellum are separate from the questions of jus in bello (justice in war) that are the primary concern of this chapter. On this view, a nation can fail the first and still satisfy the second because its combatants fight properly even if their side should not be fighting at all. Alternatively, on this view, an agent can satisfy jus ad bellum and fail jus in bello because its combatants fight improperly. Furthermore, according to the standard theory, the same conditions on justice in fighting apply to both just combatants (those on the just side) and unjust combatants (those on the unjust side); so what counts as a violation of jus in bello will be the same for all sides. This is referred to as the moral equality of combatants (which I shall abbreviate as the Equality Thesis).

1.2 What Does Jus In Bello Prescribe according to Standard Just War Theory?

a. The discrimination condition distinguishes what combatants (Cs) may do on the basis of to whom they do it, to other Cs or to noncombatants (NCs). There is also a distinction between what may be done: roughly, Cs on the opposing side(s) may be deliberately attacked and killed to achieve a military goal as well as killed as side effects, but NCs may not be deliberately attacked and killed. However, NCs may sometimes be killed as a side effect, even foreseen to certainly occur, of a deliberate action undertaken for military purposes. This is referred to as collateral damage. These elements are enumerated in figure 19.1 and discussed in what follows.

(i) Who are Cs? Standardly, they are thought to be members of a recognized fighting force who deliberately present a current threat to the physical well-being of opposing Cs or NCs. Cs are considered "noninnocent" in the sense that they are threats, not in the sense that they are at fault or to blame. Cs at t1 who are not threats (e.g., they are sleeping before an attack) may be attacked "preemptively" to stop their forthcoming attack. This suggests that "noninnocent" is used in standard theory more broadly than "currently presenting a threat" and closer to "part of a military operation," thereby also including commanders who only send Cs into battle.

Object of Harm	C		NC
Type of Harm	Deliberate	Side effect	Side effect

Figure 19.1 Types and objects of harm.

As many opponent Cs may be killed as is necessary to achieve a military mission or save one's own people. Hence, it is not out of proportion to kill many opponent Cs to save one of one's own Cs. One way of understanding this is to see the determination of proportionality as involving a form of pair-wise comparison between a victim and each of those who threaten him: If one opponent C is liable to be killed to save one's own C, then so is each opponent C. There is no aggregation of all the deaths of opponent Cs to determine the proportionality of one's response.[1]

If there is no restriction on numbers of opponent Cs permissibly harmed when necessary to achieve military ends, there may still be restrictions on how they are harmed. Thomas Nagel has argued that within jus in bello, Cs may be attacked only in a way that directly responds to the threat they do or will present, not in any way at all that furthers the defeat of their side. This implies, Nagel claims, that one may not starve them, deny them medical care, or use weapons that disfigure. These methods attack Cs simply as human beings, not as threats, even if attacking them as human beings is a means to stop them from being threats. But the complaint one has is not with their humanity but with their being a threat, and so he thinks one's response should be directed at their threat itself.[2]

(ii) Who are NCs? They are thought to include all those who are innocent in the sense that they do not present current threats or they are not part of a military operation. In addition to civilian NCs, there might be noncivilian NCs (e.g., members of the military not part of a current military operation). However, civilians who take up arms and become threats to Cs do not thereby achieve combatant status if they are not part of a recognized fighting force. NCs may be, to varying degrees, morally responsible for the existence of threats that Cs present (e.g., by voting to start and continue the war) and yet not be subject to deliberate attacks. It is said that even those who help to make others into threats by making munitions may not be targeted while they do their work but only collaterally harmed by attacks on munitions plants. Those who supply food to Cs and so keep the threat going are not subject to deliberate attack. (Nagel, however, distinguishes between deliberately attacking NCs whose activities support Cs as threats when they are engaged in these activities [e.g., making munitions] and attacking NCs who support Cs when they are simply acting as human beings [e.g., asleep], even though surviving as a human being is a necessary condition for being able to help a threat.)

(iii) What is the deliberate/side effect distinction in standard jus in bello? Some (e.g., Michael Walzer, 1977) think it is based on the Doctrine of Double Effect (DDE), which says that (1) it is morally impermissible to intend evil as an end or even as means to a greater good; but (2) if we are seeking a good end, (3) we may deliberately (including intentionally) use means that (a) are not evil in themselves and (b) are necessary to achieve the good, and then (4) the foreseen bad side effects (of the means or the achievement of the end) need not stand in the way of action if and only if the bad side effects are proportional to the good to be achieved. Conditions (3b) and (4) are the necessity and proportionality conditions of jus in bello. So, sometimes causing the very same harm that was ruled out as a means to a good need not rule out achieving the good when the harm is a side effect. (It should be noted that the necessity condition does not refer to the necessity of pursuing the good. It may seem odd that the DDE nowhere requires one to consider whether pursuing some other, perhaps lesser good the means to which would cause no harm, might be a substitute for the good one is actually pursuing.[3])

For the DDE, foreseen bad side effects to be considered in determining proportionality are primarily those that are direct effects of what is done to achieve some end in war and the effects of the achievement of these ends within war. (For example, the direct effects of a bomb used to blow up munitions and the effect of the munitions blowing up.) Such bad effects do not necessarily include those foreseen to come about but through the intervening agency of an opponent. For example, suppose one side drops bombs on a military facility that causes no harm to NCs. However, it is foreseen that the opponent will respond to the destruction of their munitions by engaging in activities that cause collateral deaths among its own NCs. Though these deaths are foreseen, they do not have the same role in a proportionality calculation done by the side that would drop the bombs as would collateral harms from the bombs themselves. This is because they are most directly due to the opponent's acts.[4] The bad effects also seem to be limited to rights violations, such as physical harm and property harm. Making people unhappy may be a bad effect but not one they have a right to avoid, and so it is not counted in a proportionality calculation.[5]

Strictly speaking, the DDE can also be applied when dealing with Cs. So, Aquinas says that, even though it is permissible to stop an attacker foreseeing his death, one may not intend his death as a means to stopping his attack (1947). Yet, standard jus in bello permits intentionally killing Cs if this is necessary to stop their attacks and, in this way, does not conform to the DDE.

The DDE implies that it is wrong to intentionally kill NCs in terror bombing where some NCs would be deliberately killed in order to demoralize other NCs into pressuring their government to surrender. By contrast, the DDE implies that it may be permissible to bomb a munitions plant when either the bombs or the destruction of the plant foreseeably cause the same harm and terror to NCs as terror bombing, only as a side effect.

Walzer suggests what he sees as an addition to the DDE:[6] not only must one not intend to harm NCs, one must intend not to harm NCs (short of not fighting the war at all). So one should accomplish a military aim by intentionally killing more enemy Cs (or running greater risks to one's own Cs) instead of doing what would cause even a proportional number of deaths of NCs collaterally. Note, however, if there are such alternative ways to accomplish one's aim that harm only Cs, this may imply that one has not met the necessity condition of the DDE, and so doing what causes even proportionate NC collateral harm may not be justified, even according to the DDE. Intending not to harm NCs, however, may require one to also think about changing one's goal (e.g., to pursue a lesser good). In this respect, Walzer's proposal for a second intention may indeed modify the DDE.

Some think intended effects can be distinguished from side effects by the Counterfactual Test: suppose, counter to fact, that harm to NCs would not occur. If we would then not proceed with our mission, this is said to be a sign that we intend the harm. There are well-known line drawing problems involved in using the DDE. For example, perhaps one need not intend the death of a C when one rams a blade into his heart, but only intend to incapacitate him until victory is won. Of course, one foresees with certainty that the C will die but one can also foresee with certainty the deaths of victims in collateral damage. A revision to the DDE aims to deal with this problem by prohibiting intended involvement of someone without his consent even when one only foresees harm to him (by contrast to merely foreseen involvement leading to harm.)[7]

To avoid the line-drawing problems raised by the intention/foresight distinction, Nagel instead distinguishes "what we do to someone" from "what happens to someone as a result of what we do."[8] He thinks the moral constraints on doing harm to someone are stronger than those on doing what will result in harm. He argues that bombing an area where we know there are opponent Cs and NCs in order to get the Cs (without intending the involvement of NCs) still involves "doing something to" the NCs and should be ruled out on this ground.[9]

It is important to see that one cannot justify the intended/foreseen harm distinction (or something like it) on grounds that it leads to fewer NC deaths overall. For it is possible that terror bombing a few NCs could end a war that will cause many more NC collateral deaths if it continues. This is one indication that we are dealing with a nonconsequentialist distinction (i.e., one not based solely on producing the best consequences, though perhaps required by respect for the worth of the person).[10]

b. Standard jus in bello has been interpreted to allow deliberate harming of NCs in a "supreme emergency."[11] Permitting such exceptions might be part of what is known as "threshold deontology" (or threshold nonconsequentialism): the prohibitions are not absolute but have thresholds and so may permissibly be overridden even if this involves infringing rights of NCs. Nagel, however, calls deliberately killing NCs in a supreme emergency a "dilemmatic situation," by which he means that we do wrong if we kill the NCs and we do wrong if we do not kill them. Hence, he thinks this is not just a situation in which we wrong someone (by infringing his right) in the course of doing what is overall not a wrong act.

2. SOME ALTERNATIVES TO STANDARD JUS IN BELLO

Now consider some alternatives to the above claims. First, consider issues connected to killing Cs (in [1] and [2]) and then to killing NCs (in [3] and [4]).

2.1 Rejecting the Equality Thesis

a. Jeff McMahan has argued[12] that it is impossible morally to separate jus ad bellum from jus in bello and because of this, unjust Cs are not morally permitted to do whatever just Cs are permitted to do. McMahan attacks the Equality Thesis by rejecting the standard view of what makes someone noninnocent (and so liable to being intentionally attacked). That is, he denies that just Cs are noninnocent merely because they are threats to their opponents. On his view, what is crucial for being liable to attack is not presenting a threat but being morally responsible for an objectively wrong (impermissible) threat. (McMahan denies that objective wrongdoing is sufficient for being liable to attack in the absence of an agent's being morally responsible for such wrongdoing, and he does not require that an agent be engaged in the wrongdoing to be liable to attack so long as she is morally responsible for it, for example, by making someone else act wrongly.)[13] An objective wrong is what would be known to be morally wrong in a perfect epistemic state. Its opposite is objective right, including objective permissibility and, when there is a positive reason to act, objective justifiability. Emphasizing objectively permissible and impermissible (wrong) threats contrasts with, for example, holding that presenting a threat can be morally permissible when it is the result of beliefs that it is reasonable for a threatening agent to have even if the beliefs are in error. I shall call this alternative "the nonobjective view of permissibility."[14]

Just Cs who have a just cause and act in accordance with discrimination, proportionality, and necessity conditions in war (and any other conditions of jus in bello) are not morally responsible for objectively wrong threats. Hence, McMahan believes that they are not liable to be attacked by unjust Cs who attack them even if they do so in self-defense. (He uses the analogy of a policeman who justifiably attacks a criminal but does not, he thinks, thereby become liable to any attacks on him by the criminal or others.)[15] McMahan thinks unjust Cs cannot satisfy the discrimination condition when they attack such just Cs because they then deliberately attack the innocent, which standard just war theory rules out. This is so even if unjust Cs reasonably believe the just Cs are unjustly attacking them. However, if unjust Cs are morally responsible for objective wrongdoing (in pursuing an unjust war), they themselves are noninnocent and liable to attack by just Cs. This is so even if it is reasonable for unjust Cs to believe they are just (and perhaps unreasonable for just Cs to believe they are themselves just). In attacking such unjust Cs, just Cs can satisfy the discrimination condition.[16]

McMahan further claims that unjust Cs also cannot satisfy the proportionality condition of jus in bello because (1) the deaths of those who are liable to be killed (unjust Cs) do not count as bad effects in a proportionality calculation but the deaths of innocents, including just Cs, do; and (2) many just Cs are killed intentionally by unjust Cs, not merely killed as side effects. McMahan believes that a higher degree of good is needed to compensate for intentional killing rather than for side effect killing of the innocent. (He is not an absolutist about the DDE.) Hence, more good is needed to make these killings not be out of proportion to one's aim;[17] but (3) unjust Cs have no just cause whose achievement can be a good weighed against harms they cause, and saving unjust Cs who are liable to be killed is not a good that can be weighed against the killing of just Cs or NCs. Saving (4) NCs from improper treatment by misbehaving Cs on the just side is a good that can be counted when achieved by unjust Cs. However, killing such Cs on the just side who violate jus in bello must also meet the necessity condition, and if the improper killing of NCs could also be prevented by unjust Cs' ceasing to wage war, killing misbehaving Cs on the just side is not necessary to stop the wrongs they do.

b. Consider possible objections to, and implications of, these arguments reject-ing the Equality Thesis.

(i) In explaining the impermissibility of unjust Cs attacking just Cs, McMahan emphasizes that in rightfully defending themselves or pursuing some other just cause, just Cs have done nothing to make themselves liable to attack. However, he also considers the possibility that this is consistent with its sometimes being objectively permissible to kill them deliberately. For example, he supposes that NCs would have their rights infringed if they die as a side effect of a C attack on a munitions plant that is justified despite collateral damage. He thinks these NCs might be permitted to target the just C (even when they know he is justified in his act) in order to stop his bombing and save themselves (2009, pp. 45–47).[18] This case suggests that it is not sufficient for the impermissibility of killing someone, and even for his not being liable to be killed, that he bears no moral responsi-bility for a wrongful threat. What may be crucial is whether the victim of his threat was liable to that attack or instead would have his rights at least infringed if he were permissibly attacked. (Though I will later suggest that this, too, may not be crucial.) If the rights of unjust Cs responsibly involved in an unjust war would not be infringed if just Cs attack them, then it is this factor that should be emphasized in an argument for the impermissibility of unjust Cs' attacks on threatening just Cs.

(ii) One reason McMahan reaches his conclusions that unjust Cs may not (ordinarily) attack just Cs seems to be that he accepts the "objective account" of wrong, permissible, and justified. It might be argued that we need not reject many elements of the Equality Thesis if we accept the nonobjective account (as described above). Then, at least when unjust Cs are epistemically justified (even if wrong) in believing that their war is just and that actual just Cs are engaged in an unjust war, unjust Cs could permissibly attack just Cs. (McMahan, by contrast, would say that such unjust Cs may be excused but are still doing impermissible acts.) However, unjust Cs acting permissibly on the nonobjective view would not imply that it was (objectively or nonobjectively) impermissible for others (such as actual just Cs) to stop unjust Cs' attacks by killing them.[19] (The Equality Thesis speaks to whether opponents may do the same acts; this is consistent with it being permissible for third parties who know who truly has a just cause to attack only unjust Cs, not just Cs.) Hence, on the nonobjective account of permissibility, the unjust Cs and just Cs could both satisfy at least nonobjective proportionality and discrimination requirements.[20]

To better understand the role of the objective account of permissibility in McMahan's rejection of the Equality Thesis, consider the following Debate Analogy: suppose two people are debating an important issue to which no one yet knows the correct answer; they take opposite positions and one and only one of the positions is correct though no one yet knows who is correct. Are these debaters moral equals entitled to do the same things in the debate? We know that one of them must be defending an untruth (though he is not lying), and he may influence other people to believe in an untruth on an important matter. We would ordinarily think these debaters are moral equals and that it is permissible for each to do what the other does to defend his view and defeat his opponent in the debate. This is so even though an omniscient being (not us) might be correct in interfering with the debater who is in the wrong as he speaks but not interfering with the other. But it seems that on McMahan's view, the mere fact that one debater is objectively wrong makes him not be an equal in the debate.

Of course, there may be cases where a debater may not have good grounds for holding his position. But it is important to realize that on the objective view that McMahan seems to employ, this is not necessary in order for one of the opponents to not be a moral equal. For that, it is sufficient that he is wrong even if he has good grounds for holding his position. (Not being reasonable in one's beliefs is a different ground [that McMahan may also accept] for not being a moral equal to someone who holds a correct position [even if his reasons for holding the correct position do not definitively prove the position is correct].)

(iii) If jus in bello were dependent on jus ad bellum, it is possible that most unjust Cs would not satisfy even the nonobjective account of permissible action in war. This is because they do not act on reasonable beliefs about the justice of their cause. Indeed, they may themselves recognize either that their side has no just cause or that they have only weak grounds for believing it has a just cause. It might be suggested that they are nevertheless the moral equals of just Cs with respect to being permitted to attack just Cs since just Cs may attack them. The argument for this might be that it is (even objectively) morally permissible (and perhaps obligatory) for Cs to carry out the directives of legitimate government officials. This could be true even if those officials mistakenly conclude that the war satisfies jus ad bellum. Indeed, especially in a democracy, Cs may have no right to interfere (by military inaction) with the democratic decision to go to war even though Cs will be the ones who do the killing. Similarly, a clerk who must carry out a legitimate democratic policy may have no right to disobey orders to carry out the policy even though it is the wrong policy and he will be the one who ultimately affects people by carrying it out. This is not to deny that someone might, on occasion, have the right to refuse to remain a C if he disagrees with the decision to go to war. However, remaining a C and then refusing to carry out orders, or undermining them, does not seem to be a right Cs should have, at least when it is not a matter of their refusing to violate requirements of jus in bello.

Suppose it is permissible (objectively or nonobjectively) to accept the role of a C who acts on orders in a system of government that is legitimate (judged objectively or nonobjectively). Then it might be permissible for people as Cs to do acts that it would be impermissible for them to do were they not in such a role (e.g., killing when it is not reasonable for them as individuals to think that their cause is just). And again, it being permissible for them to accept and act in the role need not imply that it is impermissible for others to try to stop their action. Similarly, an adversary system of law might be justified, and in it a lawyer might be permitted to defend someone she knows to be guilty, even though it might be wrong for her to engage in such a defense outside of the adversary system. Furthermore, another lawyer is also permitted to try to stop the success of her defense.

(iv) Suppose McMahan were correct that unjust Cs would act unjustly in intentionally killing just Cs, because the latter are innocent. McMahan believes that it is harder to justify intentionally killing the innocent than to justify killing them as a side effect. If unjust Cs will do wrong whether they intentionally kill just Cs or kill them and NCs collaterally, should not those who believe they are unjust Cs, but for some reason will not stop fighting entirely, choose to do the less serious rather than the more serious wrong? If so, then McMahan's views seem to imply that such unjust Cs who continue any war should at least minimize intentional killing of just Cs (as well as just NCs). This may mean carrying out a war by targeting only munitions and infrastructure sites and causing increased side effect harm to NCs on the just side. Since just Cs are no more liable to harm than just NCs on McMahan's view, there might also be no reason to bomb military sites causing just C collateral damage rather than NC collateral damage. (At a certain point, the constraint on intentional killing of innocents might be overridden, on McMahan's view, in order to minimize killing overall.) In principle, this would be a moral argument for waging war that involved no intentional killing of just Cs, but only intentional killing of unjust Cs and targeting munitions and infrastructure with collateral harm to just Cs and NCs.[21]

These points bear on the following argument that McMahan gives for a convention permitting equal rules of jus in bello for Cs on all sides in the absence of moral equality of all Cs:[22] (1) each side will think it is the just side and there is now no definitive way to alter this; (2) the just side might, in fact, be objectively morally permitted to do even more to the unjust side than the content of current jus in bello permits either side to do to the other; (3) however, given (1), it would be dangerous to allow the just side to do more than current jus in bello rules permit because then the unjust side would do it too; (4) so, (a) there should be (what could be called) a conventional equality of combatants (b) at a level that is actually lower than what morality would permit only to the just side (c) but that makes it at least possible for the just side to wage a winning war; and (5) these considerations imply (roughly) the rules of standard jus in bello that we have now.

However, recall McMahan's view that intentionally targeting just Cs is a more serious wrong than collaterally harming just Cs and also NCs, and combine it with the assumption that it is at least possible for the just side to win a war by a strategy that involves targeting munitions and other facilities despite collateral harm to Cs and NCs. This, in conjunction with accepting considerations (1) through (4), seems to imply a convention of equality that is very different from current rules that allow the targeting of Cs. It would imply, at least, a convention with no intentional killing of any persons, C or NC (subject to any threshold that would apply to intentionally killing NCs), to eliminate the possibility of intentionally killing just Cs whom McMahan treats as innocents.[23]

2.2 What May Be Done to Enemy Cs Assuming Either Moral Equality or Conventional Equality?

a. The usual concern is with what may be done to enemy Cs by opponent Cs. First, consider possible revisions to the limits that some, like Nagel, would put on what may be done to enemy Cs even if targeting enemy Cs is sometimes permissible.

(i) As noted earlier, Nagel objects to attacking enemy Cs as human beings per se rather than as Cs per se. The examples he gives of attacking Cs as human beings, however, arguably involve treating Cs worse than if their attacks were stopped directly, even by killing them. But there could be cases in which attacking a person as a human being in order to undermine his military effectiveness treats him much better than an attack on his combatant activities. For example, suppose we could win a war either by killing 1000 troops as they attack or by putting a diarrhea-inducing substance in their food (or using a diarrhea-inducing spray on the battlefield instead of bullets), thus making them unable to fight. In the case I am imagining, it is certain that we will win the war by killing the 1000, and we consider substituting less harmful means to victory directed at the same forces for the same end. At least in such cases, I find it hard to believe that we should kill rather than induce the incapacitating condition.

What if it is not clear who would win with conventional means? If enemy Cs were ordinary wrongdoers, or even fully excused wrongdoers, the diarrhea spray would seem a morally acceptable means by which to win what could not otherwise be won. But suppose unjust enemy Cs are appropriately viewed as engaged in something like a legitimate action as either moral or conventional equals to just Cs. This might make it wrong to undermine their capacity as human beings to use conventional means to try to win the war. (This assumes that from their point of view it is better to risk death and win the war than to suffer less personal harm but lose.) Hence, another reason Nagel may reach his conclusion about ways of fighting is that he takes such a view of Cs and only considers cases in which it is not known that one side is certain to win by conventional harming and killing.

(ii) Suppose that in order to win the war, we must destroy a munitions plant. However, we lack the bombs to attack the plant directly (with collateral deaths of enemy Cs). We can only destroy it by toppling enemy Cs onto it. The very same Cs would be killed by toppling as would have been killed collaterally had we been able to bomb the plant. Might it be permissible to make use of the Cs for this purpose? Similarly, suppose some NCs are about to be killed by enemy Cs coming from the right whom we cannot stop. However, we could drive in enemy Cs from the left, using them as a protective human wall between the enemy right flank and the NCs. Given that it is dark and the enemy cannot make out who will be harmed, they will kill their own Cs, not our NCs. Are these uses of Cs morally permissible even though they involve instrumentalizing some Cs, and do not involve our attacking those Cs to eliminate any threat they do (or will) present?

(iii) Killing NCs for the purpose of creating terror in order to win a war is ruled out by standard jus in bello. But is it permissible to kill Cs for the purpose of creating terror either in NCs or in other Cs, thereby getting the enemy to surrender? This is an example of what I have called "nonstandard terror bombing."[24] Consider the Rear Combatant Case: Our Cs are fighting an enemy attack and they cannot win simply by defeating the attacking forces. The rear of the force is near a village. Our Cs can kill some enemy Cs at the rear who actually present no threat to our Cs (and even in the future will not present a threat, as they are retiring after this engagement). Attacking them will terrorize the villagers, who fear they will die collaterally and the villagers will stop their Cs from attacking.[25] It seems permissible to kill the rear Cs as a means to create this terror. Alternately, we could suppose that killing the same enemy Cs at the rear of the force would be effective in stopping the attack only because it terrorizes other enemy troops into think our capabilities are much greater than they actually are. (In this variant, no terror is created in NCs). This, too, seems morally permissible.

One way to characterize standard ways of killing enemy Cs, by contrast with the examples in 2.2a[ii] and [iii]), is as "eliminative agency," a term that Warren Quinn introduced (1994). Such agency could involve killing Cs to eliminate the threat they do or will shortly present that would harm us. By contrast, Quinn applied the term "opportunistic agency" to using people so that we thereby improve our prospects (perhaps by preventing ourselves being harmed by others), even though the people used do not (and even will not) present a threat that would harm us. Examples (ii) and (iii) seem to involve opportunistic agency on certain enemy Cs, using these Cs in order to stop the threat that other Cs present. Yet, I suggest, such action may be morally permissible.

Suppose that only eliminative agency were permitted in dealing with enemy Cs. This would make the standard account of when we may target Cs and NCs more uniform to some degree. This is because if NCs do not (and will not) present threats, we can explain why we may not target them if only eliminative agency is permitted.[26] Further, prohibitions on opportunistic use of NCs (as in terror bombing them) would not be unique to them, as the prohibitions would apply to enemy Cs (as in 2.2 a.[iii]) as well.[27] However, suppose eliminative agency includes killing Cs who may be threats in the future. Then being restricted to eliminative agency should not alone rule out undermining Cs simply as human beings (e.g., by contaminating their food supply) for this too eliminates their future threat.

b. Related to deciding what types of acts may be done to Cs by other Cs is the question of how many enemy Cs may be killed to preserve one's own Cs or to pursue a military mission. This is an instance of what I have referred to as "violability ratios" among classes of people.[28] As Thomas Hurka points out, how many enemy

Cs it is permissible to kill to achieve a military mission or to spare our own Cs bears on whether our conduct satisfies the proportionality condition of jus in bello.[29]

Hurka accepts close to what I have described as the traditional view, that there is "virtually" no limit on the number of enemy Cs (at least volunteers) that may be killed (as targets or side effects) if this is necessary to save even one of one's own Cs or to pursue a militarily necessary mission.[30] He bases this conclusion on the view, also described above, that in ordinary self-defense a person under attack by many aggressors may kill any number of them if this is necessary to save himself, and a bystander is permitted to do the same in defense of another. (As noted earlier, I think the concept of pairwise comparison is a useful way of characterizing the view that killing so many is permissible.) However, also thinking of ordinary self-defense, McMahan considers cases in which our just Cs are merely defending their own lives and achievement of the just cause is not put in jeopardy. He argues (contrary to traditional jus in bello) that if enemy Cs have reduced moral responsibility for their actions due to duress and to epistemic limitations on knowing what cause is just, our Cs may have to absorb some costs to avoid killing those enemy Cs merely to save themselves. This implies that sometimes our Cs should bear more costs for the achievement of the just cause in order to spare enemy Cs whose behavior is to some degree excused.[31]

My own concern in the discussion of this topic is to emphasize a distinction between (1) what should be done to avoid exposing one's Cs to risk of death and (2) what should be done to prevent one's Cs' certain death.[32] Suppose one could achieve a military mission that would end a war in either of two ways. The first would present a 0.01 risk of dying to each of one's 5000 Cs, and a 0.8 risk of dying to each of the enemy's 5000 Cs. This is the same as the certainty that 50 of our Cs will die and 4000 enemy Cs will die. The second way would present a 0.012 risk of dying to each of our 5000 Cs and a 0.4 risk of dying to each of 5000 enemy Cs. Even if we are certain there will be ten additional deaths on our side with the second way, at the time we decide on the way (ex ante), there would be only a very small increase in the risk to each C of being one of the dead. This increased risk means that in choosing the second way, 2000 fewer enemy Cs will die and each will have a much reduced ex ante risk of dying. Some might argue we should use the second way. My concern here is not to argue that this choice is correct, but only to suggest that this choice could be consistent with killing more than 4000 enemy Cs if this were necessary to save ten of our Cs, each of whom would otherwise certainly (i.e., with a probability of 1) be killed by those enemy Cs. (There is a difference between it being certain ex ante that ten more Cs will die and it being true of ten particular Cs that they will certainly die. It is the latter scenario that most clearly compares to killing in self- and other-defense.) Put another way, the permissibility of saving ten of our Cs from certainly being killed if we can, by killing an enormous number of enemy Cs, need not be inconsistent with it being morally right to increase slightly the risk to each of our Cs to avoid killing an enormous number of enemy Cs. This is so even when increasing the risk will certainly lead to ten more of our Cs dying when we will not be in a position to save them from the death each will then certainly face.[33]

Suppose there were a requirement to reduce risks to one's opponent by having one's own combatants assume risks. This requirement need not apply if opponent soldiers would shortly be killed anyway, nor if reducing this risk to them in one operation actually increased their risk overall.

c. It is also important to consider what a given side in a war may permissibly do to its own Cs.[34] Assume that it is sometimes permissible to use enemy Cs opportunistically (not just eliminatively) for military purposes or to save one's own NCs. Is it also permissible to do something like this to one's own Cs? Consider analogs to cases in 2.2 (a. [i]and [ii]). Suppose one may send one's Cs to destroy a munitions plant knowing that 100 of them will either be killed by enemy Cs or die from exertion. Would it also be permissible to fatally topple 100 of one's Cs onto the munitions plant (or topple more, knowing that 100 of them will die), if only this would destroy the plant? If enemy Cs were moving to kill our NCs and there was no way to protect them but station one's own unarmed Cs around them to take the hits, would this be permissible? Also, if one way to bomb the enemy munitions plant near our own border would result in collateral deaths to our NCs while another way would result in collateral deaths to our Cs, should we use the second way? (The Equality Thesis, which concerns the equality of Cs on opposing sides, is consistent with either side deciding what to do to its own Cs as a function of their status relative to NC co-citizens.)[35]

On what I call the Bodyguard Model of one's own Cs, they can be assigned to take a hit headed for an NC and, assuming there is no shortage of Cs to achieve the just cause, Cs should be the preferred victims of our bombing the munitions plant.[36] An objection may be raised to the Bodyguard Model: Our Cs are trained and have duties to defend our NCs and to further their countrymen's goals only by fighting. They are not resources to be used in just any way for military aims and for the defense of NC co-citizens. On this view, lives of our Cs are not available for absorbing (rather than fighting off) enemy attacks or collateral damage.

Suppose that the permissibility of using enemy Cs opportunistically as mere resources would have to be argued for independently of the Cs being (presumed to be) on the unjust side. (The Equality Thesis [moral or conventional] implies that it would not be wrong of an opponent to use our Cs in comparable ways. This suggests that permissible opportunistic use of enemy Cs is independent of whether one is a C on the just or unjust side.) Then the grounds of our not treating our own Cs opportunistically for the sake of our NCs will have to be their status relative to fellow citizens rather than their status as just Cs who may not be used in the way unjust Cs may be used.

2.3 Deliberately Killing Noncombatants

Standard jus in bello rules out (most) deliberate killing of NCs. However, it permits some military operations foreseen to kill NCs collaterally. The permissibility of such killings is not usually thought to rest on NCs' past acts having made them liable to being killed collaterally. (A possible exception is their choosing to remain near a military target when they could, at no great cost, have left.) [37]

a. An alternative view suggests that many NCs are liable to varying degrees of deliberate harm when a war is being fought. One ground of such liability is some degree of moral responsibility for having a role in causing an unjust war (as judged from an objective or nonobjective view). On this alternative view, heads of state, politicians, or journalists who are fully morally responsible for having a large role in producing an unjust war are liable to be targeted and may permissibly be targeted if this is useful in ending a war (either militarily or by causing terror).[38] Indeed, sometimes Cs may be excused for actively presenting threats whereas NCs are fully morally responsible for sending those Cs into combat. Then, some argue, those with high moral responsibility for the existence of a threatening military force are liable to be deliberately killed rather than those Cs with weak moral responsibility for actually posing a threat. This is so even though Cs' act of posing a threat intervenes between NC behavior and the actual harm in war. McMahan provides the following analogy: a corrupt sheriff deputizes an uneducated local and misleads him into thinking that an innocent person is a criminal. The sheriff further puts great pressure on the deputy to kill the innocent. The innocent can defend himself by either shooting at the deputy (as the deputy shoots at him) or shooting at the unarmed sheriff (who watches the deputy and the innocent from behind a tree). The sheriff's death will lead the deputy to drop his gun. McMahan thinks it is morally permissible and preferable to shoot the liable sheriff (2009, ch. 5).

Many NCs, however, will have only minimal moral responsibility for their role in an unjust war (because, for example, they are nonnegligently ignorant of either the injustice of the war or that what they do supports it). Or they may play only a small causal role in generating a threat (e.g., by voting). Many NCs will have no moral responsibility or causal role (e.g., children). McMahan concludes that deliberate killing of NCs is rarely morally permissible due to facts such as these,[39] combined with the further facts that deliberate killing of NCs would (usually) involve opportunistic rather than eliminative agency, NCs who are liable are not isolated from those who are not liable, and killing NCs has low effectiveness in ending a war.

However, McMahan also argues (in discussing other issues) that when there is no way to avoid someone's life being lost, even slight moral responsibility in one party for a threat can imply that he should be the one to die (2009, ch. 5).[40] Further, it is not clear that McMahan should think that opportunistic agency used on NCs who are not innocent is worse than eliminative agency. (In his case of the guilty sheriff, he himself says it would be permissible to make opportunistic use of the sheriff. For example, the sheriff can be made to fall on the deputy when it is foreseen this would kill the sheriff and stop the deputy's gun from going off (2009, pp. 226–227).) Hence, if big funders of war were separated from others at a political gathering and bombing a few of them would be effective in stopping the war, it seems McMahan should think it morally preferable to kill them rather than many conscripts, though the latter actually pose the threat of harm.

To support the conclusion that having a small causal role in bringing about the threat does not rule out NCs being deliberately killed, Helen Frowe imagines a case in which each of many people eagerly contributes a small sum to hire someone to kill an innocent person. She argues that any one of the contributors is liable to being killed and doing so would be permissible if it were necessary and useful to save the innocent person's life from the killer.[41] From this, she concludes that NCs who knowingly accept even small roles in war efforts are equally liable to be deliberately killed and that it may be permissible to kill them.

But notice that, ordinarily, it would be permissible for an innocent person threatened by thousands of evil attackers to kill all of them, even if they only threatened him with significant paralysis, not death. This suggests that if those responsible for hiring the killer in Frowe's case are liable to attack, they all may be killed even if this were necessary only to prevent significant paralysis in the innocent person. Suppose that NCs being morally responsible for small causal contributions to an unjust war (e.g., by knowingly voting for war or by buying war bonds) made them similarly liable to deliberate opportunistic attack. Then, could targeting large numbers of such NCs be morally permissible, even if this were not effective in winning a war or saving lives but only in saving a few Cs or NCs on the other side from significant paralysis? This is a radical implication that casts doubt on Frowe's argument.

(Liability to being deliberately killed as a result of one's acts is not the only sort of liability. McMahan notes that in virtue of having voted for war, NCs might become liable to the risk of death collateral to tactical bombing [2009, pp. 219–221].)

b. An objector to these nonstandard views on deliberately killing NCs might try to derive liability to deliberate attack from moral responsibility for posing a threat (or simply posing a threat) rather than from moral responsibility for starting or supporting war. For example, suppose it is permissible for A members of country X to have agreements with B co-members that Bs will fight on behalf of As' policies. Could it then be wrong for country Y, with whom X is at war, not to honor that internal (supposedly permissible) relation between As and Bs by targeting As rather than Bs, on grounds of As' moral responsibility? Ordinarily, it is not impermissible to attack a Mafia boss who employs a bodyguard rather than to attack his bodyguard, even if the relation between the two calls for the bodyguard to bear all costs. However, not all agents who make decisions to go to war, even incorrect ones, are criminals like the Mafia boss.

Perhaps whether outside parties should honor the agreement between As and Bs depends on whether there are morally good reasons to insulate As from bearing certain costs even if they are to some degree morally and causally responsible for the war. For example, this might be true if As would be less likely to decide to go to war on the basis of only factors that make that decision right were they subject to personal attack for that decision. It is also possible that when members of a community are obligated to make certain decisions as best they can, moral responsibility for bearing the costs (what Scanlon calls "substantive responsibility")[42] need not affix to them. To illustrate this point, we might reimagine

McMahan's sheriff as an administrator not licensed to shoot but who, to the best of her ability, carries out her obligation to stop criminals. She sends out her uneducated, pressured deputy to stop what the sheriff believes is a true criminal attack. Unfortunately, she was mistaken and the deputy is about to shoot an innocent person who is defending himself against the deputy. Is it still true that the sheriff sitting in her office, who bears moral responsibility to a high degree for the conflict between her deputy and the innocent person, may be killed by the innocent if this would be as effective in stopping the deputy's attack as directly attacking the deputy?

c. Let us now consider NCs on the opponent's side who have not acted in a way that would give them any moral or causal responsibility for starting or maintaining a war. Is deliberately killing these NCs always impermissible, as standard jus in bello claims (excluding only supreme emergencies)? Here are some reasons to think not.

(i) Suppose such deliberate killing is not the only way to stop a supreme emergency. However, the number of collateral NC deaths that would be caused by a permissible alternative means could be so great that a threshold is reached on the prohibition of deliberate killing.

(ii) Now consider a case in which this is not so. Suppose that 1000 NCs will be killed and terrorized as a proportionate side effect of our bombing a munitions plant to achieve a military goal. The only alternative way to achieve our goal is to terror bomb ten of the very same people who would otherwise have died collaterally. It might be permissible to terror bomb in this case, in part because those killed and terrorized would have been killed and terrorized anyway at the same time and 990 other lives are saved. Such terror bombing could be permissible even if it would have been impermissible to terror bomb ten people who would not otherwise have died collaterally. Secondary to the expected deaths and terror of some people collaterally, terror bombing them that would otherwise have been impermissible becomes permissible. Indeed, it may become the only permissible harmful act. Being constrained by someone's right not to be treated in a certain way (e.g., terror killed rather than collaterally killed) may not have the same moral significance when it will not make a difference to whether he is harmed or terrorized as it has when it makes such a difference. This as an instance of what I call the Principle of Secondary Permissibility (PSP).[43]

(iii) Now suppose that while it is permissible for us to bomb the plant, causing 1000 NC collateral deaths, we would supererogatorily refrain from killing so many. Then we learn that if we terror bomb ten of the NCs who would die collaterally if we did bomb the plant—as it is still permissible and possible for us to do—we can also achieve our goal. In this case, the NCs we would kill would not otherwise have been killed by us, and there are no additional NCs who would have otherwise died who will be saved. It may nevertheless be permissible to terror bomb in this case because we can still, though we will not, kill the people (plus others) in the initially permissible way and we would kill ten in the initially permissible way if this were possible.[44] This is an extension of the PSP (EPSP).

(iv) What if criminals within our opponent country were about to wrongfully kill NCs and we could not stop them? Would it be impermissible to deliberately kill a few of these NCs if this would somehow achieve an important military mission (e.g., their being killed confuses opponent troops) when this also scares the criminals away and so saves many NCs who would otherwise have been killed?[45] This seems permissible even though we rather than others will kill. The constraint on our harming NCs in certain ways, I believe, stems less from a concern with whether we or someone else acts than from a concern that the potential victim be protected from mistreatment and retain authority over himself.

d. Assuming that it is often wrong to terror bomb or otherwise deliberately kill NCs, let us consider traditional and alternative views about what makes this so.

(i) As noted, some proponents of the DDE argue that intending to kill NCs makes an act that kills them impermissible. It is important to see that even this traditional view need not imply that it is impermissible to bomb some military facility only because NCs will be killed. That is, there is a conceptual difference between intending to kill NCs and acting only because (or on condition that) we will kill them. Consider what I call the Munitions Grief Case:[46] we need to bomb a munitions plant for military purposes, and we know this will unavoidably cause collateral deaths of children next door. Their deaths would be proportionate if the destruction of the plant were permanent. However, we know the community would quickly rebuild it better than ever—thus making bombing pointless and the collateral damage disproportionate—if not for the fact that they will be depressed by the deaths of their children. Hence, it is only because (we know) the children will die that we bomb the munitions plant; we would not bomb if they did not die as an effect of the bombing. I think bombing in this case is permissible and not inconsistent with the DDE, even though we would act because the deaths help sustain the destruction of the plant. We here take advantage of an unavoidable side effect of bombing the plant; we do nothing extra that is not necessary to bomb the munitions plant merely to make it the case that the bombing does cause the deaths of children.

This case helps, I think, show that we can distinguish conceptually among effects that are intended, merely foreseen, and because of which we act. I have referred to a view that takes account of these three distinctions as the Doctrine of Triple Effect (DTE).[47] Suppose it is possible to act only because we will produce a certain effect and refrain from acting if we would not produce it, without thereby intending the effect. This would show that the Counterfactual Test (discussed earlier) for the presence of intention is inadequate (Kamm, 2000 and 2007, ch. 4).

(ii) Contrary to what the DDE claims, some have argued that acting with a wrong intention need not make an act morally impermissible, and so it does not matter that our acts in war be consistent with the DDE. Consider Judith Thomson's example:[48] we need to bomb a munitions plant, for its military effects and the collateral deaths of NCs are proportionate. However, the bombardier who will carry out the bombing has always wanted to kill NCs, and he drops the bombs on the munitions plant only in order to kill the NCs (Bad Bombardier Case). If this morally bad bombardier behaves no differently in all respects from a good bombardier, who only intends to bomb the munitions plant for its military effects despite the side-effect deaths, is his act of bombing morally impermissible when the good bombardier's act is permissible? Thomson thinks not.

It might be said that the bad bombardier acts permissibly because he at least intends to bomb the munitions plant and this is a permissible intention, even if he only has this intention as a means to killing NCs. But the bad bombardier need not intend to bomb the munitions plant; he may only intend to drop the bombs as his means to kill the NCs. He foresees that the bombs will also destroy the munitions plant, and he would not act if they did not, for he needs a pretext for his actions. But this need not mean that he intends that further effect. Even with this revision, it seems that his dropping the bombs is permissible, if a good bombardier's dropping the bombs would be permissible. This revised case shows that the DDE is also wrong if it claims that only a good we are seeking (i.e., intending) can compensate for bad side effects. The unintended destruction of the munitions plant (and its further good military effect) can also compensate for the NCs' deaths, at least if the intended destruction could so compensate.

(iii) Thomas Scanlon argues that deliberately killing NCs is impermissible because it serves no military purpose. He argues that "military purpose" involves reducing munitions and forces, not causing terror to NCs as a means to surrender.[49] But even if we have such a narrow understanding of military purpose, we can imagine cases where bombing NCs would serve that purpose: In the Stampede Case, we bomb some NCs so as to terrorize other NCs, leading them to stampede and destroy a military facility. In the Human Tinder Case, we bomb NCs who live near a munitions plant in order to set the plant on fire.[50] Alternatively, killing NCs who are the relatives of Cs could demoralize Cs, leading them to stop fighting. It seems to me that deliberately killing NCs in these cases (when the NCs do not have characteristics discussed in 3.3c.[ii]) is wrong despite its usefulness in narrow military terms. (It is important to note, however, that as a matter of historical fact, such bombings of NCs may not have been ruled out in past wars and indeed may not have been considered "terror bombings.")[51]

(iv) A different account of the impermissibility of deliberately killing NCs in most circumstances claims that it is wrong to cause harm to NCs as a necessary means to produce effects, if the harm results from processes whose other effects do not themselves justify the harm. To understand this proposal, consider a version of the Bad Bombardier Case. It might be that the intended harm and terror to NCs is what actually causes the country to surrender before the elimination of the munitions can have this effect, as Thomson notes. Yet this would not affect the permissibility of bombing because in this case the harm and terror are not necessary to produce surrender. Another effect of the bombardier's act, destroying the munitions, would have done this too and so would have justified the deaths of some NCs as a side effect. By comparison, in terror bombing cases standardly contrasted with strategic bombing, NCs are either directly bombed or some facility is bombed whose destruction will kill NCs, but neither type of bombing will have any other useful military effect, produced without a necessary causal role for NC deaths, that is sufficient to justify NC harm as a side effect.

How do cases in which harm to NCs is causally required for any good effect differ from the Munitions Grief Case (discussed earlier)? In that case a necessary causal role for NC deaths in sustaining destruction of the plant did not, I claimed, make bombing impermissible. In Munitions Grief, unlike standard terror bombing cases, the deaths are caused by and sustain the very outcome (the factory destroyed) that could justify the deaths if it were sustained. It may be that the permissibility of bombing can be affected by what causes the NC deaths and whether these deaths are necessary to "sustain" a sufficiently good effect already produced rather than to "produce" such a new effect.[52]

2.4 Collateral Harm to Noncombatants

a. Let us first deal with NCs who would not otherwise shortly die or be seriously harmed anyway and who would in no way reap benefits from the loss of their lives.

(i) As noted, a prominent traditional justification of some collateral killing in war is the DDE. However, it has long been thought by many nonconsequentialists that in nonwar contexts, the DDE incorrectly licenses collateral harm that is morally impermissible.[53] For example, suppose you and four other people are unjustly attacked by a villain. The only way to stop the villain is to throw a bomb at him. However, fragments of the bomb will also penetrate and kill an innocent bystander (Domestic Villain Case). It is ordinarily thought that it is impermissible for you, or any outsider helping you, to use the bomb.[54] This is so even though the bystander's involvement and death would be unintended side effects and a greater number of people would be saved. In a variant, setting the bomb to defeat the villain requires you to drive over a road where a person is immovably located. His involvement and death are foreseen but unintended effects and a greater number of people would be saved, yet it seems impermissible to drive on. However, the DDE seems to permit acting in both these cases. The problem is that the DDE allows side-effect harm to some to be outweighed by greater good to others, as in any consequentialist calculation.

As noted earlier, Thomas Nagel tries to account for the permissibility of some collateral killing of NCs by distinguishing between what we do to someone and what happens to someone as a result of what we do. This distinction would, I think, rule out driving over someone in the case above. However, it would not prohibit using the bomb whose fragments kill the bystander.

(ii) Another general principle for determining when harming innocent bystanders is permissible for the sake of a greater good for others distinguishes (roughly) between (1) side effects of achieving a greater good, (2) side effects of causal means that we introduce into a context in order to achieve a greater good, and (3) side effects that depend on interaction between causal means that we introduce into a context in order to achieve a greater good and what is independently present in the context.[55] This Principle of Permissible Harm (PPH) claims that it may be permissible to cause bad side effects in manners (1) and (3) but not in manner (2). Hence, condition (1) implies, in a further variant of the Domestic Villain Case, that it is permissible for the five people to escape the villain even if their moving into a safe spot pushes a bystander into a deadly ravine. Condition (3) implies that it could be permissible to attack the villain with the bomb even when it is foreseen that vibrations from it will cause a house in the area to collapse, killing a bystander.[56] In the Domestic Villain Case, condition (2) rules out both driving over the person to get to the bomb and using the bomb whose fragments kill a bystander.

The question is whether it is plausible to think that there are comparable moral distinctions among the ways we produce collateral deaths in war. For example, is it impermissible to bomb a munitions factory when side-effect deaths result from fragments of our bomb but permissible when the deaths result from the munitions factory itself blowing up? If both are permitted (which seems likely), supporters of the PPH I have described will have to explain why side-effect harms are permitted in war that are ruled out elsewhere by the principle.[57]

(iii) Another problem with applying any general moral principle concerning side effect harm (such as the DDE or the PPH) to innocents in war contexts is that such principles treat all innocent bystanders as equals. Hence, they tell us to select among permissible means to a greater good that are equally effective and otherwise the same on the basis of reducing deaths of innocent bystanders. However, suppose we must bomb a munitions factory that lies near the border between our country, the enemy, and a neutral country. We can bomb from any of three directions with the following collateral NC deaths: (1) direction 1 will kill 100 enemy NCs; (2) direction 2 will kill fifty of our own NCs; and (3) direction 3 will kill twenty-five neutral NCs.[58] A general moral principle, such as the DDE, would say that (3) is less bad than (2) which is less bad than (1). Yet, I believe, in war the reverse is true, that is, (1) is less bad than (2), which is less bad than (3) (at least, when remaining neutral is a morally permissible option). This reverse ordering suggests that there are violability ratios between neutral NCs, our NCs, and enemy NCs, with the enemy NCs having highest violability. This could affect the proportionality calculation for wartime acts, as a given mission may satisfy proportionality if it collaterally kills enemy NCs but not if it kills the same number of neutral or our own NCs. And even if deaths of both our NCs and enemy NCs were proportional to the mission, it could still be morally preferable to choose the route that killed more enemy NCs rather than fewer of our own NCs.

(The ratios need not imply lexical priority among different groups. Suppose taking one route killed one of our NCs and taking another route killed a thousand enemy NCs. Even if both routes satisfied proportionality relative to achieving the military mission, it could be morally correct to choose the first route if the ratio of enemy NC deaths to our NC deaths exceeds the morally permitted violability ratio between these groups.)

It might be argued that direction (1) should be preferred to direction (2) because a government has a special duty of care for its own NCs. However, even if this

is correct, a different explanation is needed for why direction (2) should be preferred to (3). Concern about making a neutral country into an enemy by harming
its NCs is inadequate, as the order might apply even when the neutral is militarily
insignificant.[59]

(iv) A form of "group liability," where liability does not depend on any actions
of NCs, may explain both the higher violability of enemy NCs and the expanded
range of ways it is permissible to harm enemy NCs (by contrast to what a general principle for harming bystanders in nonwar contexts implies [as discussed
in 2.4.a[ii]). To consider this possibility, suppose our country has unjustly sent a
missile to another country where it will collaterally kill NCs. We realize the moral
error of our ways but the only thing that can be done is send another missile to
destroy the first one. Unfortunately, the second missile will backfire and collaterally kill some of our NCs (Backfiring Missile Case). I believe we are obligated to
stop our unjust attack and that NCs of our country must be prepared to have certain costs (and the risk of certain costs) imposed on them in this way in order to
stop the unjust behavior of their country. This is so even if they have done nothing
to bring about the injustice. (Hence, this form of liability to bear costs has nothing
to do with liability grounded in prior acts.) They are members of a community
ordered for mutual benefit; as potential beneficiaries, they should also bear costs,
not only to achieve benefits for the country but also to make it not be an unjust
country. (It being permissible to impose such costs [and risk of costs] on them is
not the same as their having a duty to volunteer for such costs.[60])

When our country fights a war it considers (reasonably, let us suppose) just, it
considers its enemy to have been unjust (e.g., in firing missiles at us). As the enemy
is not stopping its own injustice (and there is no international policeman to stop
it), we try to stop it. If enemy NCs who are not responsible for having started or
supported the unjust war are still liable to bear costs in order to stop their country from being unjust, perhaps we may impose the costs when their government
should but fails to do so.[61] (In this case, neither their government nor the enemy
NCs may believe they are unjust, unlike what is true in the Backfiring Missile Case.
This does not, I believe, affect the acceptability of the argument.)

(v) Does this group liability proposal bear on the relative violability of NCs and
the opponent Cs who would harm them collaterally? For example, does it bear on
whether NCs may stop collateral harm to themselves by attacking the opponent Cs
who would be justified in doing what causes them such harm?

In a domestic villain case, suppose it is permissible (objectively or nonobjectively) to redirect a villainous threat away from five people in a direction where one
other person will be killed as a side effect. This need not imply, I believe, that the
one person may not try to stop the threat to himself, even if this requires harming
the person who permissibly redirected the threat and also results in the originally
threatened five being killed by the threat. Now consider a war case in which an
innocent NC of an unjust country wishes to prevent himself from being collaterally killed by a just C's permissible attack on munitions.[62] Suppose that if he kills
the just C, this will interfere with the just C's mission (to whose achievement NC

deaths were proportionate). Such defense by the NC seems permissible. This is so even if innocent NCs are liable (in virtue of group liability) to costs being imposed on them to stop the injustice of their country, and so they will not even have their rights infringed if the just C does what harms them collaterally. (By contrast, in the domestic case the person in whose direction the threat is redirected arguably has his rights infringed.) The permissibility of imposing collateral death on NCs need not imply that NCs must volunteer to let themselves be harmed or not resist being harmed just so that their unjust country will be defeated. (This is true even if they know it is unjust.) This case suggests that having one's rights (at least) infringed is not necessary for permission to attack defensively, due to the compatibility of someone being liable (via group liability) to having harms imposed on her and her permissibly resisting that imposition.[63] Yet it may also be permissible for the just C to defend himself to ensure the completion of his mission. Indeed, it seems that he might now permissibly target the NC (not just harm him collaterally) to stop the NC's attack on him. (In [vi], we shall consider cases where he would act only to defend himself rather than pursue his mission).

(vi) More broadly, the question of the relative violability of Cs and the NCs whom they would collaterally harm concerns how much risk of harm Cs must take on themselves to achieve their mission in order to not collaterally harm innocent enemy NCs. (This question arises even when harm to NCs would satisfy proportionality and be permissible were there no other way to achieve the mission). Suppose an enormous number of Cs would be morally obligated to accept certain death to achieve a mission rather than impose some risk of death on enemy NCs by using alternative means to achieve the mission. This would imply that Cs are highly violable relative to enemy NCs that they would harm (and the NCs would be highly inviolable relative to these Cs, at least when it is a matter of the Cs not harming them).

Thomas Hurka argues that the fact that certain Cs "are one's own" (even if they are not irreplaceable for winning our war) counts in favor of their inviolability. (Similarly, "one's own" NCs may have greater inviolability than enemy NCs.) However, he also claims that the fact that they are Cs, who have accepted exposure to risks as part of their C role, counts in favor of their violability by contrast to enemy NCs. Balancing these two factors, he concludes that from a country's point of view, its C lives have equal weight to enemy NC lives.[64]

An alternative to Hurka's view emphasizes that turning some of our citizens into Cs who threaten others might eliminate our right to count "one's own" in their favor, at least relative to the NCs they threaten. (This is a form of "silencing" the "one's own" factor. This means we cannot weigh it in the balance against "C" as we weigh "not ours" against "NC" when comparing enemy NCs with our NCs.) This is an example of "contextual interaction" wherein a factor that matters in one context does not matter in another. In another case, suppose a member of our family is a firefighter (who does not himself threaten others), and we have to decide how much risk he should take by comparison to the victims of a fire who are not related to us. We should not balance "our relative" against his role and conclude the victims and our related firefighter should bear equal risks. However, there might be some reason, such as group liability or liability through acts, to believe that enemy NCs are susceptible to having costs imposed on them so that their country is not unjust to others. It could be this factor, not Cs being ours, that would allow our Cs to impose some risks on enemy NCs rather than assume more risks themselves.

What would this alternative to Hurka's view imply for the following case? Our C will certainly kill the 100 NCs near a military target as (proportionate) collateral damage to his military mission. During the course of the mission, it becomes clear that he can take another route to the military target and so harm no NCs. However, this will cost him his life after he hits the target (either because he will lose control of his plane or because he will be attacked by enemy Cs). Is he morally required to take the second route when there are no further bad effects of his dying?[65] Suppose these options had been known to our leaders initially. Would they have had to give up on sending the pilot on the first route and either command the second route or abandon the mission entirely because it would be wrong to require a "suicide" mission?

At the least, I think it is wrong to conclude that C must volunteer his own life when he pursues a just cause (objectively or nonobjectively) rather than impose a cost on enemy NCs that is (independently determined to be) proportional to the military goal. It is not correct to say that in imposing the cost on the NCs, he is requiring the NCs to volunteer their lives in the way he refuses to volunteer his own. A loss may permissibly be imposed on someone (including on oneself by other parties) without this implying that a person must impose the loss on himself or not resist its imposition. If this is true, an argument for the permissibility of NCs killing the pilot in resistance to losses he would impose on them cannot always rely on the fact that they are only imposing a loss on him that he should have imposed on himself had he been able to.[66]

(vii) A complete discussion of the relative violability of NCs and Cs, when the issue is collateral harm to NCs, should consider how many of one's own Cs should die fighting to defend one's own NCs from death. Figure 19.2, which lays out in graphic form some of the topics we have discussed, makes clear that even if we just consider four types of persons—C_{our}, C_{enemy}, NC_{our}, NC_{enemy}, there are six possible relations between them. [67] If there are limits on the ways in which we may treat our Cs (by contrast to enemy Cs),[68] "sacrificing" Cs to spare our NCs would not typically involve our deciding to kill our Cs to spare our NCs (or vice versa). Rather, it could involve deciding how many NCs should be allowed to be killed by enemy Cs rather than risk our Cs being killed by enemy Cs in order to save our NCs, holding constant achieving military missions. Or, it could involve deciding whether to pursue a military mission in a way that reduces risks of death to our Cs but increases threats to our NCs (e.g., sending a very large force on a mission, leaving fewer Cs to protect NCs from attack by the enemy, holding constant achieving military missions).

Might the violability relation that should hold between our Cs and NCs in this context bear on whether enemy Cs should properly decide to wage war in a

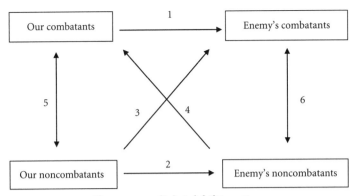

Figure 19.2 (In)violability ratios.

way that kills our NCs collaterally rather than target our Cs? For example, suppose we should not risk a large number of C deaths in fending off threats to a few of NC co-citizens. Does this bear on whether enemy Cs should decide to achieve a military goal by (1) attacking a munitions plant, collaterally killing a few of our NCs, rather than by (2) attacking and killing a large number of our Cs (other things being equal)? Probably not, for it may make a moral difference that enemy Cs would be killing NCs or Cs. By contrast, we would be deciding to allow enemy Cs to kill our NCs (by not protecting them) rather than allow the enemy to kill our Cs (by putting them in harm's way). In addition, the ratio between our C and NC lives may be perspective-relative. From our perspective, their violability may be closer both because we consider our Cs to be just and because we deny that they may be used in every way for NC benefit. From our opponent's perspective, our C's violability may be much greater than our NCs because Cs are taken to actively pursue an unjust cause and so can be used more liberally. This also implies that from our perspective, the violability of enemy Cs is much higher than the violability of enemy NCs.[69]

To summarize what has been said about the permissibility of both deliberate and side-effect killings, we can rank inviolability in decreasing order (or violability in increasing order) as follows, assuming we are not (or reasonably believe we are not) unjust:

$$NC_{our} < NC_{enemy} < C_{our} < C_{enemy}[70]$$

We might try to express the relative violability of enemy NCs and Cs in increasing order from our perspective as follows, assuming we are not (or reasonably believe we are not) unjust:

$$NC_{our} < NC_{enemy} < C_{our} <<< C_{enemy}[71]$$

The addition of "<<<" is meant to express how much more violable enemy Cs are relative to enemy NCs than our Cs are relative to our NCs (from our perspective). However, this does not yet capture the fact that while in a pair-wise comparison, our NCs are less violable than our Cs, relative to enemy Cs they are equal (from our perspective). That is, from our perspective, as many enemy Cs may be killed to save each (and, possibly, also to save enemy NCs). This relative violability in increasing order, from our perspective, may be represented as follows:

$$NC_{our} < NC_{enemy} < C_{our}$$
$$\wedge \qquad\qquad \wedge \qquad\qquad \wedge$$
$$\wedge \qquad\qquad \wedge \qquad\qquad \wedge$$
$$\wedge \qquad\qquad \wedge \qquad\qquad \wedge$$
$$C_{enemy}$$

b.   Now let us consider the collateral killing of enemy NCs who would die shortly anyway and/or who will benefit in some way by being exposed to a risk of death (or even by death itself).[72]

Intuitively, it seems that harm to such enemy NCs should weigh less in any proportionality calculation to determine whether one may proceed with a military mission. For example, consider the Scare the Criminals Case. We need to bomb a munitions factory but this will cause 100 enemy NC side-effect deaths, which would ordinarily be out of proportion to the good to be achieved. However, we learn that these NCs, along with many others, will shortly be killed by criminals. If we bomb the munitions plant, this will scare the criminals away. The NCs who die because of our bombing are no worse off than they would have been, and the lives of many others are saved. The bombing now seems permissible. This case shows us that what seems like unproportional collateral NC harm when considered on its own is no longer unproportional harm when we consider what would have happened to the very people we harm had we not bombed.

In another type of case, those who will be killed would not in fact have otherwise died. However, the ex ante risk of their dying was higher (e.g., due to criminals in their neighborhood) than it is if we engage in a military mission (and scare the criminals away). So it seems reasonable to think that it was better, even for each of those who die, that we engaged in the military mission, since it lowered their risk of death. Once again, NC deaths that on their own seem out of proportion to a military mission can be seen to be proportional once we compare the probabilities of these very people being killed at the same time if we bomb and if do not bomb.

Finally, there may be cases in which those NCs who die are themselves compensated for the risk of death, and their deaths that ensue, that our military mission imposes. The good to the very people who die can be weighed against the risk of harm and the actual harm to them so as to make deaths that would otherwise be out of proportion for a military mission be in proportion for it. For example, consider the Parents Case: suppose parents would be willing (and even have a duty) to take risks of deaths to prevent the deaths of their children. There has been an avalanche in the area near the munitions plant we would destroy. The avalanche has buried the children of the people who we would risk killing collateral to bombing the munitions plant. It will be a further good effect of bombing the munitions plant that the rocks will be moved, freeing the children who would otherwise shortly die. The risk of death to each parent from our bombing is no more than he or she should take to save the life of his or her child. This could mean that even though the actual number of parents who die is out of proportion on its own to the military mission, it is not out of proportion once the good to the very people who die of their children being saved is taken into account.[73, 74]

Notes

1. The idea of pairwise comparison is commonly used as a nonutilitarian decision procedure in deciding on the justice of outcomes and in allocating resources. I am suggesting its use can be extended to explain certain aspects of self- and other-defense against aggressors. Notice that there is also no use of the method of "balancing"; that is, the death of a victim is not simply balanced against the death of an attacker, the former thus having its moral weight used up and leaving the potential deaths of other aggressors to rule out the permissibility of responding. For more on these decision procedures, see Thomas Nagel, 1979; and my 1993.
2. See Nagel, 1972.
3. Jeff McMahan discusses the implications for the permissibility of action of having to consider the possibility of different goods and what it would cost to pursue them in his "Proportionality," manuscript.
4. Some theorists seem to deny the significance of an intervening agent's act. For example, Jeff McMahan has argued that if one foresees that a bad effect will occur if one does an act, it should be irrelevant to deciding to do the act that the bad effect would not occur but for another agent's intervening act. He argued in this way in his Appignani Lecture, at University of Miami, April 10, 2009, and in his 2010, criticizing my views in Intricate Ethics. More recently, in his "Proportionality," his view seems to have changed somewhat.
5. In "Jus Post Bellum, Proportionality, and Compensation" chapter 7 in my forthcoming (a), I discuss these characteristics of foreseen harms.
6. Indeed, he doubts that the distinction between intention and foresight that the DDE draws would be of moral significance in itself. See Walzer, 1977, p. 155.
7. Such a suggestion is made by Warren Quinn, 1994.
8. In "War and Massacre." He is more favorably inclined toward the DDE in his 1986.
9. Note that this distinction might also rule out bombing a munitions plant when this kills NCs working in it if they were to be treated like ordinary NCs.
10. For one discussion of the relation between certain sorts of permissibility and the worth of the person see my 1996, ch. 5.
11. For example, see Walzer, 1977, ch. 16.
12. For example, in his 2009.
13. McMahan distinguishes being liable (in his sense) to attack from permissibility of an attack, as possibly some who are not responsible for wrongdoing may sometimes be permissibly attacked. Neither of these notions implies that a person deserves to be attacked rather than that he may be attacked only if this is necessary to achieve an end. Unlike McMahan, some think that even a completely nonresponsible person (e.g., someone who has been turned into a human missile or someone who acts out of a drug-induced psychosis) may be liable to being killed (and this is also permissible),

if killing that person is necessary to stop the lethal threat he presents to an innocent victim. See, for example, Judith Thomson, 1991; along with my 1987 and 1992.

14. The objective view is defended by Judith Thomson in her 1992. What I call the nonobjective view is defended by Thomas Scanlon in chapter 2 of his 2008. Scanlon notes that this view is not merely subjective, since it is not enough that if what someone actually believes were true, his act would be permissible. Someone must satisfy an objective standard of what it would be reasonable for him to believe.

15. Note, however, that McMahan also believes that if one does an act that is otherwise objectively permissible for evil reasons, one does not act permissibly. Given this view, a C who satisfies conditions of jus in bello such as proportionality and necessity still does not act permissibly and is not innocent in achieving an objectively just cause, if he actually intends to do something unjust. Is such a C liable to be killed because he acts impermissibly? I doubt that McMahan would want to conclude this. If this is correct, then on his view not all Cs who kill impermissibly are liable to be attacked. Henceforth, I shall put to one side such cases.

16. Doubts have been raised, however, about whether unjust Cs are morally responsible agents. Many of them may be under duress to become Cs and to carry out attacks, and they may have limited access to information about the justice of their cause. If someone who does something wrong is fully or partially excused on these grounds, and if these excuses eliminate or reduce the attacks to which they are liable, would it be impermissible for just Cs to kill unjust Cs? McMahan argues that if unjust Cs' excuses are strong, just Cs might have to absorb some costs in battle rather than place all costs on unjust Cs, but they should not do so if it jeopardizes the just cause (2009, pp. 192–198). Furthermore, he thinks that given any moral responsibility at all on the part of unjust Cs for their objectively wrong conduct, they become liable to being killed if this is necessary to prevent the death of just Cs they attack. In support of this, he considers an analogy: Suppose a resident believes completely reasonably that the innocent identical twin of a mass murderer is the mass murderer who is about to kill the resident. The resident may himself be killed, if this is necessary to prevent his killing the innocent twin (see p. 164 and pp. 175–182).

17. McMahan holds a nonabsolutist version of how evil intentions can make acts impermissible. In particular, he thinks evil intentions have negative moral weight that needs to be overridden. Independently of disagreeing that evil intentions make acts impermissible, one might think this is too consequentialist an interpretation, even of a nonabsolute, nonconsequentialist side constraint. It does not capture the idea of a side constraint by contrast to something of negative value that weighs against other factors.

18. A possible explanation of this, which he attributes to me, is that the just C should have been willing to do what would cost him his life in order to attack the munitions without causing collateral damage to NCs. When there is no way he can do this on his own, the NCs may impose the cost on him to stop the collateral damage (at least when this does not interfere with the military success of the mission). However, this explanation (which I suggested but do not necessarily support) would be inconsistent with McMahan's view that the just C may defend himself by firing on the NCs to stop their attack on him. For if the NCs are only imposing a cost on the just C that he should have imposed on himself had he been able to do so, it does not seem that he should be permitted to defend himself against their attack.

19. This corresponds to McMahan's view that fully excused but mistaken attackers may be killed if this is necessary to save their innocent victims.

20. There is an additional element that can be added to this nonobjective account: Each warring side could not just be reasonable in thinking it is just and the other side is unjust, but each side can (and perhaps should) realize this about the other side. McMahan suggests that it is reasonable for each side, after it has done its best to determine the justice of its cause and has concluded that it is just, to doubt that it is correct, given knowledge of the history of errors made by others (2009, p. 152). I think this is too "external" and skeptical a view for an agent to take of his own thought processes and conclusions. Once he concludes, for the best reasons he can find taking account of the history of past errors, that his cause is just, it is inappropriate for him to act as if his conclusion is more likely than not to be false. In commenting on this point, Johann Frick says: "The possibility of error evinced by the past errors of ourselves and others may (and should) feature internally, as a pro tanto reason against believing that our cause is just. But it isn't also a reason for "externally" calling into question one's all-things-considered judgment about the justice of our cause, into which the possibility of error has already been factored."

21. Notice that this is not like the view that intentional harming, even if it is a more serious wrong, is to be balanced against the fact that it is a C who will die, which diminishes the seriousness of the wrong. On McMahan's view, killing just Cs is not a fact that diminishes wrongness of killing by comparison to killing NCs, except possibly because it involves eliminative versus opportunistic agency. (This distinction is discussed in the text. Notice also that the view that while it is prima facie wrong to intentionally kill, it is not wrong at all to kill a C is not a "balancing" view.)

22. See McMahan, 2009, pp. 108–109.

23. McMahan's argument could be extended to further reduce what jus in bello as a matter of convention permits, if one weighed the avoidance of wrong acts (such as unjust Cs collaterally killing just Cs or NCs) more than the promotion of right acts by just Cs without totally eliminating the possibility of achieving the just cause. Once one limits what acts are conventionally permissible for fear the unjust side will do them, it is no longer clear what the content of jus in bello should be.

24. I first used this term in my 2006.

25. I first discussed this case in my 2004.

26. This need not imply that all eliminative agency is permissible. For example, Noam Zohar has considered cases in which an NC stands in the way of our killing someone who threatens to kill us (or an NC blocks our escape from such a threat). Zohar argues that this NC is an indirect threat to us and killing him would also involve only eliminative agency, yet it is still impermissible. If this is correct, then eliminative agency would not be a sufficient condition for permissibly killing a threat to one's life. See his 1993.

27. This way of distinguishing what may be done to Cs and NCs does not rely on the distinction between intentional and nonintentional killing because intentional opportunistic killing of both Cs and NCs would be ruled out. It also does not rely on the idea that military advantage in a narrow sense (e.g., reducing military supplies or fighters) is to be achieved only by attacking Cs and not NCs. For it is physically possible to achieve narrow military advantage by opportunistic use of Cs (in the first case of 2.2a[ii]), yet this would be ruled out.

28. I introduced this term in my 2004. For a representation of some possible entities between which violability ratios could hold, see Figure 19.2. Contexts in which saving our own Cs could arise include preserving them from an attack by enemy Cs, rescuing them from being held captive by enemy Cs, rescuing them from a natural

disaster by means that kill enemy Cs, and using a military plan that kills fewer of our Cs and more enemy Cs than other possible plans.

29. See Thomas Hurka, 2005.

30. Hurka, 2005, p. 58.

31. See McMahan, 2009, pp. 192–198.

32. I first made reference to this distinction in my 2004.

33. Comparable issues arise in nonwar contexts. I discuss some of those that arise when allocating scarce funds or scarce medical resources in my 2007, p. 35. For example, I argue that each of many people may chose to bear a small risk of dying of a rare fatal disease in order to invest in a medicine for commonly occurring headaches. But it is not inconsistent with this that if someone were dying of the rare disease and only all of the headache medicine could save him, that it be given to him. I discuss these issues more generally in my 2008a, and in a longer, unpublished version of that essay. More recently, Johann Frick has argued for morally distinguishing (a) risk that will certainly lead to some deaths and (b) some particular individuals facing certain death. See his "Contractualism and the Ethics of Risk," manuscript. He argues against Alex Voorhoeve and Marc Fleurbaey, who deny the moral significance of the distinction in their "On the Evaluation of Expectedly Beneficial Treatments That Will Disadvantage the Worse Off," manuscript.

34. I first raised this issue in "Failures of Just War Theory" when I considered violability ratios between one's own Cs and NCs, by which I meant how many of one's own Cs should be sacrificed to save a given number of our NCs from attacks by enemy Cs.

35. It is a different question whether Cs should fight for or otherwise be sacrificed for enemy or neutral NCs.

36. I assumed something like the Bodyguard Model, without naming it this, when discussing violability ratios between Cs and NCs on one side in my 2004. The objection to this model described in what follows was raised by Craig Neuman. Even if one rejects the Bodyguard Model of Cs, the issue of violability ratios between Cs and NCs on one's own side can still arise when deciding how many Cs can be required to lose their lives in fighting to save co-citizen NCs. I discuss this issue in 4f.

37. See Walzer, 1977.

38. Helen Frowe argues that liability is not sufficient for permissibility if usefulness and necessity are not present. See her "Noncombatant Liability," manuscript. By contrast, McMahan argues that there is no liability at all to harm if it is not useful. (This is part of his view that liability has a proportionality condition involving consideration of what good can be achieved internal to it.) See his 2009.

39. However, Helen Frowe argues that McMahan does not distinguish minimal moral responsibility from minimal causal responsibility (McMahan, 2009, ch. 5).

40. For example, in his discussion of a driver of an out-of-control car.

41. See Helen Frowe, "Noncombatant Liability," manuscipt.

42. See his 1999.

43. I first discussed the PSP in my 1996. This case was first presented in my 2004.

44. I first presented this case and the EPSP in my 2004.

45. This case is modeled on my Scare the Criminals Case (which involved only collateral harm to NCs) presented in my 2011, ch. 3.

46. I discuss this case in my 1996 and 2007, ch. 4, among other places.

47. See my 2000a; and 2007, ch 4, among other places.

48. See her 1999.

49. See Scanlon, 2008, ch. 1.

50. I introduced the Stampede Case, which I described as nonstandard terror bombing, and the Human Tinder Case in my 2006. Notice that the permissibility of deliberately bombing NCs would not eliminate all distinctions between Cs and NCs, as we might still be required to harm Cs before harming NCs or require that more good be done in order to justify harming NCs than Cs. Note also that even if it were permissible to deliberately kill only Cs as a means of producing terror in NCs (as in the Rear Combatant Case), this would imply that deliberately terrorizing NCs (even if not terror bombing them) could be a permissible means to winning war. If such terrorizing of NCs were permissible, it is not clear how NC terror leading to surrender not being a "narrow" military advantage could explain the impermissibility of deliberately killing NCs, contrary to what Scanlon says. In this regard, see also the Trees Case in my 2006, and in my 2008b, a revised version of which is chapter 2 in my 2011.

51. I owe this information to Professor John Lewis, Ashland University (in conversation). For more on this issue, see my 2010.

52. For more on these distinctions and their possible significance, see my 2007, ch. 5.

53. Philippa Foot pointed this out in her 1967.

54. Judith Thomson uses this example in her 1991. However, Thomas Hurka seems to think it is permissible to save one's own child by doing what will harm bystanders in the domestic case. See his 2005.

55. I propose a general principle of permissible harm that makes these distinctions in my 2007, among other places.

56. Furthermore, there are means that have what I call a "noncausal" (by contrast to a causal) relation to producing the greater good. For example, suppose we turn a threat that a villain has sent toward killing five people away from them though it will kill a bystander instead. The five being saved (the greater good) is just the noncausal flip side of turning the threat from them, not a further effect caused by turning it. So turning the threat is a noncausal means to the greater good. In such cases, I believe, the harm caused to the bystander by redirecting the threat is as permissible as harm caused by the greater good itself (option [1]). For more on this, see my 2007, ch. 5.

57. I first discussed this issue in detail in my 2000b, and then again in my 2004.Thomas Hurka raised the issue in his 2005. Note that the factor that could account for the permission in war may be present in some nonwar contexts as well.

58. I first introduced cases of this form in my 2004. I am here discussing certain individuals who will certainly die, not just the imposition of risk on them or trade-offs between, for example, the risk of killing neutral NCs and the certainty of killing other NCs.

59. McMahan suggests it is relevant that our NCs, not neutrals, would benefit by reduced risk of harm from out winning the war. See his 2010a.

60. I believe that one problem with Judith Thomson's argument for the impermissibility of a bystander turning a trolley headed toward five when it will then kill one person on another track is that she does not allow for a distinction between imposing costs on the one person and his volunteering for them. See her 2008. I discuss this briefly in my forthcoming (b).

61. I first proposed such an account in my 2004. Such group liability may apply outside war to groups whose members are incorporated in ways similar to members of a nation state.

62. McMahan discusses such a case in his 2009.

63. This contrasts with the view proposed earlier. (2.1.bi).

64. See Hurka, 2005. Johann Frick has pointed out that one's own Cs have accepted risk to defend their countrymen. That alone does not imply that they have agreed to bear risks for enemy NCs. A more extreme view than Hurka's, that Cs being our citizens implies that they should accept few risks rather than impose harm on enemy NCs, is presented in Asa Kasher and Amos Yadlin, 2005.

65. This case is reminiscent of discussions of self-other choices by Peter Unger in his 1996, and Judith Thomson in her 2008. I respond to Unger in my 2007, ch. 6 (among other places) and to Thomson briefly in my forthcoming (b).

66. By contrast to the suggestion above in note 18.

67. Hurka fails to consider the relative violability of Cs and NCs on one side and the implications this has for proportionality in his 2005.

68. We considered this issue in 2.2, including whether we should redirect an enemy threat headed to our NCs to our Cs instead even if we should redirect it to enemy Cs.

69. I pointed this out in Kamm, 2004, p. 678. Hence, Hurka's claim that "our" should be balanced against "C" may be true when comparing our Cs with our NCs from our perspective, even if not when comparing our Cs with enemy NCs they would kill. This is another example of "contextual interaction"; a factor can matter in some contexts and not in others.

70. I provided this ordering in my 2004. If we know we are unjust, as in the Backfiring Missile Case, the order of increasing violability from our perspective could be $NC_{enemy} < C_{enemy} < NC_{our} < C_{our}$.

71. I am indebted to Beatrice Franklin for suggesting the addition of "<<<."

72. I discuss such cases (including the ones following in text) as well as cases in which collateral harm to some only benefits others in "Reasons for Starting War: Goals, Conditions and Proportionality," which is chapter 3 of my 2011.

73. For further discussion of such cases see my 2011, ch. 3. Suppose neutral NCs or Cs would similarly have reduced harm or risk of harm as a result of our actions (for a just cause) that results in their collateral harm. Then some harm to them could become permissible.

74. I am grateful to Johann Frick, Shelly Kagan, Jeff McMahan, Jens Johansson, and Larry Temkin for comments on earlier versions of this chapter.

References

Aquinas, Thomas. 1947. *Summa Theologica*. Translated by Fathers of the English Dominican Province. New York: Benziger Bros.

Foot, Philippa. 1967. "The Problem of Abortion and the Doctrine of Double Effect." Oxford Review 5: 5–15.

Frick, Johann. Manuscript. "Contractualism and the Ethics of Risk."

Frowe, Helen. Manuscript. "Noncombatant Liability."

Hurka, Thomas. 2005, "Proportionality in the Morality of War." *Philosophy & Public Affairs* 33: 34–66.

Kamm, F. M. 1987. "The Insanity Defense, Innocent Treats, and Limited Alternatives." *Criminal Justice Ethics* 6: 61–76.

Kamm, F. M. 1992. *Creation and Abortion*. New York: Oxford University Press.

Kamm, F. M. 1993. *Morality, Mortality*. Vol. 1. New York: Oxford University Press.

Kamm, F. M. 1996. *Morality, Mortality*. Vol 2. New York: Oxford University Press.

Kamm, F.M. 2000a. "The Doctrine of Triple Effect and Why a Rational Agent Need Not Intend the Means to His End," supplement, *Proceedings of the Aristotelian Society* 74 (1): 21–39.

Kamm, F. M. 2000b. "Justifications for Killing Noncombatants in War." *Midwest Studies in Philosophy* 24: 219–238.

Kamm, F. M. 2004. "Failures of Just War Theory." *Ethics* 114 (4):650–692.

Kamm, F. M. 2007. *Intricate Ethics*. New York: Oxford University Press.

Kamm, F. M. 2006. "Terrorism and Several Moral Distinctions." *Legal Theory* 12: 19–69.

Kamm, F. M. 2008a. "Should You Save This Child? Gibbard on Intuitions, Contractualism, and Strains of Commitment." In *Reconciling Our Aims: In Search of Bases for Ethics*, Alan Gibbard, ed., pp. 120–144. New York: Oxford University Press.

Kamm, F. M. 2008b. "Terrorism and Intending Evil." *Philosophy & Public Affairs* 36: 157–186.

Kamm, F. M. 2011. *Ethics for Enemies: Terror, Torture, and War*. New York: Oxford University Press.

Kamm, F. M. forthcoming (a). *The Moral Target: Aiming at Right Conduct in War and Other Conflicts*. New York: Oxford University Press.

Kamm, F. M. forthcoming (b). "The Trolley Problem." In *International Encyclopedia of Ethics*, Hugh LaFollette, ed. Wiley-Blackwell, forthcoming.

Kamm, F. M.2010. "Types of Terror Bombing and Shifting Responsibility." In *Action, Ethics, Responsibility*, J. Campbell, M. O'Rourke, and H. Silverstein, eds., pp. 281–294. Cambridge, MA: MIT Press.

Kasher, Asa, and Yadlin, Amos. 2005. "Assassination and Preventive Killing." *SAIS Review* 25: 41–57.

McMahan, Jeff. 2009a. *Killing in War*. New York: Oxford University Press.

McMahan, Jeff. 2010b. "Just Distribution of Harm between Combatants and Noncombatants." *Philosophy & Public Affairs* 38: 342–379.

McMahan, Jeff. 2010. "Responsibility, Permissibility and Vicarious Agency." *Philosophy and Phenomenological Research* 80: 673–680.

McMahan, Jeff. Manuscript. "Proportionality."

Nagel, Thomas. 1972. "War and Massacre." *Philosophy & Public Affairs* 1: 123–144.

Nagel, Thomas. 1979. "Equality." In his *Mortal Questions*. New York: Cambridge University Press, pp. 106–127.

Nagel, Thomas. 1986. *The View from Nowhere*. New York: Oxford University Press.

Quinn, Warren. 1994. "Action, Intention, and Consequences: The Doctrine of Double Effect." In his *Morality and Action*, pp. 175–193. New York: Cambridge University Press.

Scanlon, Thomas. 1999. *What We Owe to Each Other*. Cambridge, MA: Harvard University Press.

Scanlon, Thomas. 2008. *Moral Dimensions*. Cambridge, MA: Harvard University Press.

Thomson, Judith Jarvis. 1991. "Self-Defense." *Philosophy & Public Affairs* 20 (4):283–310.

Thomson, Judith Jarvis. 1992. *The Realm of Rights*. Cambridge, MA: Harvard University Press.

Thomson, Judith Jarvis. 1999. "Physician-Assisted Suicide: Two Moral Arguments." *Ethics* 109: 497–518.

Thomson, Judith Jarvis. 2008. "Turning the Trolley." *Philosophy & Public Affairs* 36 (4): 359–74.

Unger, Peter. 1996. *Living High and Letting Die*. New York: Oxford University Press.

Voorhoeve, Alex, and Marc Fleurbaey. Manuscript. "On the Evaluation of Expectedly Beneficial Treatments That Will Disadvantage the Worse Off."

Walzer, Michael. 1977. *Just and Unjust Wars*. New York: Basic Books.

Zohar, Noam. 1993. "Collective War and Individualistic Ethics: Against the Conscription of Self-Defense." *Political Theory* 21: 606–622.

CHAPTER 20

THE SIGNIFICANCE OF DEATH FOR ANIMALS

ALASTAIR NORCROSS

To address the question of the significance of death for animals, we first need to consider the significance of death for people. On the assumption that death is, at least usually, bad for people, what makes it bad? To get at least a rough idea, let's contrast a paradigm case of death that appears to be bad for the subject with one that, at least plausibly, isn't bad. First, consider Yorick. Yorick is twenty-two years old, has just graduated from a prestigious college with high honors, has several promising careers open to him, and is in a fulfilling romantic relationship. While Yorick is out walking one day, a drunk driver swerves onto the sidewalk and kills him. Now, consider Oliver. Oliver is ninety-one, and has lived a rich, fulfilling life. But now Oliver has an incurable terminal illness. As the illness progresses, Oliver is in increasing amounts of pain. There are no available treatments that significantly reduce the pain, without also rendering Oliver unconscious. He has no loose ends in his work or personal life. Oliver judges, and his doctors and family agree, that his remaining life is of such a low quality that it is not worth living. Luckily for him, he lives in a state that permits doctor-assisted suicide. Surrounded by loved ones, Oliver dies a peaceful, painless death.

Yorick's death is clearly bad for him. If any death can be good for the subject, Oliver's death appears to be. So, what is the most obvious difference between the two deaths? Yorick's death deprives him of well-being, but Oliver's death doesn't deprive him of well-being. On any remotely plausible account of well-being, Yorick's life would have had more of it, if he hadn't died when he did. He would have had more pleasurable experiences, more satisfied desires, more exercise of autonomy, more of whatever might appear on an objective list of what makes life go well. Oliver's life, on the other hand, would not have contained more of any of this.

The most obvious answer, then, to the question of what makes death bad, when it is bad, is that death negatively affects well-being. Yorick's life would have contained more well-being, if he hadn't died when he did. Notice that this way of describing the relevant effect of death on well-being sidesteps a puzzlingly popular, but pointless, discussion about the level of well-being associated with nonexistence. It might be tempting to say that Yorick's death is bad for him, because, if he hadn't died when he did, he would subsequently have experienced more well-being while alive than he actually did while dead. If Yorick had lived even a few more years, he would have been experiencing a positive level of well-being for those years. As it happened, he experienced a zero level of well-being for those years, so, as a result of his death, he was subsequently worse off than he would have been if he hadn't died at age twenty-two. Some philosophers, however, claim that it makes no sense to attribute *any* level of well-being, even zero, to someone who doesn't exist. Consequently, they say, we can't say that a particular death makes someone worse off than they would otherwise have been. As a result of their death, they have *no* level of well-being, not zero. The positive level of well-being they would have had cannot be compared with no level. While I think it makes perfect sense to attribute a zero level of well-being to someone after they die, or at least to treat them as if they have zero well-being for the purposes of comparison, we really don't need to get into this discussion. If Yorick would have experienced an overall positive level of well-being during the time he would have been alive, his actual shorter life contains less well-being than his counterfactual longer life. And that is all we need for it to be clear that his premature death at twenty-two negatively affects his overall well-being.

If the significance of death for humans consists in its effect on well-being, can we say the same of the significance of death for animals? Given that animals clearly experience well-being (we don't need to get into any neo-Cartesian silliness here), death can have an effect on their well-being in the same way that it can have an effect on human well-being. Consider two dogs, Spot and Rover. Spot is one, barely out of puppyhood, full of boundless energy and enjoying a happy life with his (human) family. While in the park one day, Spot is killed by a drunken hunter, who thinks he is shooting a bear in the wilderness. Rover is fifteen, barely able to move, beset by many crippling diseases, and in constant pain. Rover's loving family calls the vet, who euthanizes him painlessly. Just as with Yorick and Oliver, it is clear that Spot's death is bad for him but that Rover's death is not bad for Rover. As a result of the hunter's action, Spot's life contains less well-being than it would have had he lived considerably longer. Rover's life, on the other hand, wouldn't have contained more well-being, if he had lived longer.

It appears, then, that the answer to the question of the significance of death for animals is both fairly simple and the same as the answer for humans:

> **WB** Death is bad for an animal to the extent that it results in the animal's life containing less well-being than it would otherwise have contained.

Of course, if an animal hadn't died in the manner and at the time that it did, there are any number of different deaths it could have died instead, some of which may have resulted in more overall well-being in its life, and some in less. Strictly speaking, then, we should say that a particular death is worse for an animal than another one to the extent that the animal's life contains less well-being than it would have contained had it died the other death. The same, of course, goes for human deaths. The context in which we make claims about death being either good or bad for the subject usually makes clear which alternative, or range of alternatives, we are comparing with the death in question. So I will continue to talk of death being good or bad for a subject without the complicating factor of a specific comparison.

The foregoing account of the significance of death for animals doesn't rely on any particular moral theory. All that is required to apply the account to animals is a theory of well-being. However, it would seem that the account is particularly amenable to a consequentialist approach. It is, perhaps somewhat surprising, then, to find two prominent utilitarian proponents of animal welfare downplaying the significance of death for at least some animals. Jeremy Bentham is often quoted in support of the significance of animal welfare: "The question is not, Can they *reason?*, nor, Can they *talk?* but, Can they *suffer?*" Earlier in the same passage, though, we find the following:

> If the being eaten were all, there is very good reason why we should be suffered to eat such of them as we like to eat: we are the better for it, and they are never the worse. They have none of those long-protracted anticipations of future misery which we have. The death they suffer in our hands commonly is, and always may be, a speedier, and by that means a less painful one, than that which would await them in the inevitable course of nature. If the being killed were all, there is very good reason why we should be suffered to kill such as molest us: we should be the worse for their living, and they are never the worse for being dead. (Bentham, 2010, ch. 19)

Why does Bentham say that animals are "never the worse for being dead"? He does point out that their death at the hands of humans often involves less suffering than their death "in the inevitable course of nature." But this could hardly justify the claim that animals are *never* the worse for being dead. Is the natural death that otherwise awaits an animal *always* so painful as to render its life as a whole worse than if it had died a less painful death at the hands of humans? This hardly seems plausible.

Peter Singer, the foremost contemporary utilitarian advocate of animal welfare, draws a distinction between animals who are self-conscious and those who aren't.

> Some nonhuman animals appear to be rational and self-conscious beings, conceiving themselves as distinct beings with a past and a future. When this is so, or to the best of our knowledge may be so, the case against killing is strong, as strong as the case against killing permanently defective human beings at a similar mental level.... When we come to animals who, as far as we can tell, are not rational and self-conscious beings, the case against killing is weaker. When we are not dealing with beings aware of themselves as distinct entities, the wrongness

of killing amounts to no more than the reduction of pleasure it involves. (Singer, 1979, pp. 103–104)

The crucial distinction has to do with the possession of desires for continued existence.

> But what of a being which, though alive, cannot aspire to longer life, because it lacks the conception of itself as a living being with a future? This kind of being is, in a sense, "impersonal." Perhaps, therefore, in killing it, one does it no personal wrong, although one does reduce the quantity of happiness in the universe. (Singer, 1979, p. 102)

Grant, for the sake of argument, that some animals have a preference for future existence and some do not. Why should this matter to a utilitarian, or any consequentialist? The answer is to be found in Singer's preference utilitarianism.

> For preference utilitarians, taking the life of a person will normally be worse than taking the life of some other being, since a being which cannot see itself as an entity with a future cannot have a preference about its own future existence. (Singer, 1979, p. 81)

Killing a self-conscious being frustrates a preference for future existence. Killing a non-self-conscious being does not. Although Singer is here talking about the deontic status of killing, as opposed to the personal significance of death, the two must be closely related, as his talk of killing doing no "personal wrong" to a non-self-conscious being demonstrates. It would be strange indeed to claim that it is, ceteris paribus, worse to kill a self-conscious being than to kill a non-self-conscious being, but not also to claim that the significance of death for these two types of being is different.

On Singer's preference utilitarian approach, it appears that the significance of death is different for different animals, depending on whether they have desires for continued existence. For a self-conscious being, death (usually) frustrates a desire for continued existence. A non-self-conscious being doesn't have a desire for continued existence, so death can't frustrate *that* desire. But this difference doesn't get us very far, certainly not as far as Singer seems to want. Even for a preference utilitarian, the significance of an event can't be exhausted by what contemporary desires are satisfied or frustrated by the event. In fact, that would seem to be, at most, a small part of the story. Consider a familiar example, a trip to the dentist. Franny Forethoughtful realizes that she needs a filling in order to prevent future pain. She really doesn't want to experience pain now or in the future. When the dentist's massive needle pierces her gum to inject novocaine, her desire not to experience present pain is frustrated. Of course, among the effects of the injection are future preventions of frustration of her desire not to experience pain. She knows this, and consequently desires to have the injection and the subsequent dental work. Clearly, the overall significance of this event for Franny is positive. Thelma Thoughtless is also at the dentist to have her tooth filled. She also desires not to experience pain now. However, she doesn't currently have any desires concerning future pain, because she simply never considers the future. She doesn't desire to have the injection or the subsequent dental work, even though their effects on future desire satisfactions are the same as the corresponding events for Franny. If contemporary desire satisfaction or frustration were all that mattered for assessing the significance of events for subjects, Thelma's dental procedures would be negative for her, even though the same procedures would be positive for Franny. But clearly, Thelma's dental procedures are positive for her, as they are for Franny. The most we could say is that Thelma's procedures are not quite *as* positive for her as they are for Thelma, because she lacks the current desire to undergo the procedures. However, the fact that the dental procedures prevent so much future desire frustration is more than enough to outweigh the current desire frustration. It is irrelevant that Thelma currently lacks future-oriented desires. She *will* have desires in the future not to experience pain. If she doesn't have the dental procedure now, many of those desires *will* be frustrated. That is what matters.

So, how could Singer's position that the significance of death is affected by self-consciousness fit into WB? Presumably, we would have to say that an animal with a self-conscious desire for continued future existence has more to lose from a premature death than an animal without such a desire. But why is that? Let's consider two cases. Charles the chimp is self-conscious. Charles desires, among others things (like bananas), to continue to exist in the future. Harold the hamster is not self-conscious. Harold has plenty of desires. He desires to run on a wheel, to eat pellets of food, to drink from an upside-down bottle, to sleep. But he has no conception of himself as an independently and continually existing creature, so he has no desire for future continued existence. Now, suppose both Charles and Harold die prematurely (they are struck by the same tornado). Is Charles's death worse for Charles than Harold's death is for Harold? Does Charles lose out on more well-being? Well, chimps usually live longer than hamsters, so he would lose out on more time. But suppose that Charles is fairly old, and only has the same remaining life expectancy as Harold. In this case, how does the fact that Charles, while alive, had a desire for continued future existence affect the magnitude of his loss, compared with Harold's loss? Suppose they both would have lived for a further two years, if they hadn't been killed by the tornado. Suppose further that, had they lived, the vast majority of their desires would have been satisfied. Harold's various bodily desires would have been satisfied. So would Charles's bodily desires. In addition, Charles's desire for continued future existence would have been satisfied (for another two years). So, there's at least one desire that Charles would have had satisfied that Harold would not even have had, let alone have had satisfied. But is this enough to say that their losses are *qualitatively* distinct, as Singer certainly seems to think? How do we compare the contribution to well-being of the satisfaction of the various desires of Charles and Harold? We clearly can't count *instances* of desire satisfaction. Many desires, such as the desire not to be in pain, and the desire for continued existence, are satisfied continuously over a period of time, rather than discretely. Besides, even if the contribution to well-being of the satisfaction of Charles's desire for continued existence could somehow be compared with the contribution to well-being of the satisfaction of Harold's desire for, say, food, why think that the former would be greater in any way than the latter? Suppose that Harold has really intense desires for food, but Charles has much less intense desires for food and for continued existence. What could it be about the desire for continued existence that would render its satisfaction a greater and/or qualitatively distinct contribution to well-being?

Perhaps the desire for continued existence is significant because it connects with other desires. A creature who desires continued existence is likely also to have desires concerning that future existence. Most people, for example, don't simply desire to continue living into the future, but also want to do and/or experience things during their future existence. In fact, it's hard to imagine the desire for continued future existence unaccompanied by other desires concerning that future existence. It certainly seems irrational to desire mere existence, without also desiring *something* concerning that existence. Self-conscious creatures, who conceive of themselves as "distinct beings with a past and a future," desire continued existence, but also desire specific things for their futures. They make plans for the future, structuring much of their current behavior around these future plans. The ability to conceive of oneself as a distinct being with a past and a future makes possible a far more complex and rich structure of desires and intentions than is available to a non-self-conscious creature. This gives much greater scope for desire satisfaction, but also for desire frustration. On a desire-satisfaction account of well-being, then, self-consciousness provides the potential for greater value, but also for greater disvalue. There certainly seems to be no guarantee, or even presumption, that the life of a self-conscious being would contain more net well-being than that of a non-self-conscious being. So, once again, self-consciousness does not seem to affect the significance of death in the way Singer suggests.

The preference-satisfaction approach to well-being has proved unable to justify a distinction in the significance of death for self-conscious versus non-self-conscious beings. Do any other approaches fare better? Perhaps we could appeal to the value of autonomy. Perhaps only self-conscious beings exercise autonomy. Furthermore, perhaps the exercise of autonomy is particularly valuable. Death, then, deprives a self-conscious being of the opportunity to exercise autonomy. Whatever else it may deprive a non-self-conscious being of, it cannot deprive it of that. Is this enough to justify the distinction we find in Singer? Only if the value of autonomy were somehow so much greater than the value of all other elements of well-being as to swamp them in every instance. But how plausible is this?

Suppose that I am dying slowly and painfully, with no prospect of cure or even of pain relief, apart from death. As things stand, I have a couple of months of agony to endure before the disease will finish me off. Despite the pain, I am still able to exercise autonomy, and do so. I autonomously choose which television program to watch. I autonomously choose which political candidates to support. I autonomously choose to write scathing letters to the newspapers decrying the irrational refusal of state lawmakers to support legal, voluntary, active euthanasia. I want to die, and judge my present, and future prospective, existence to be not worth living. A freak accident in my hospital room kills me painlessly in my sleep. This (or something like it) is something that I, and all those who love me, had hoped for. The significance of my death is clearly positive for me. As a result of my accidental death, my life contains significantly less suffering than it would otherwise have contained. If the accident hadn't occurred, I would have endured two more months of progressively worse agony. But I would also have had more opportunities to exercise my autonomy. As the pain increased, these would have become fewer and further between. Intense pain can interfere with the exercise of autonomy. Nonetheless, my accidental death clearly deprives me of at least *some* opportunities to exercise autonomy. If the value of autonomy were so great as to swamp the value (or disvalue) of other elements of well-being, such as pleasure and pain, my life would be better if I continued to live for another two months in agony, wishing I were dead. The pernicious absurdity of this conclusion is self-evident. The failure of this appeal to autonomy is similar, for obvious reasons, to the failure of the familiar free-will defense against the problem of evil. Even if free will is highly valuable, its value can be outweighed by the prevention of suffering. A truly benevolent (and omnipotent and omniscient) god would interfere with the exercise of free will on at least those occasions when its exercise would lead to tremendous suffering. Only the most self-deluded of theists could deny this. Likewise, only the most dogmatic and simple-minded Kantian could maintain that the value of autonomy is so much greater than other values as to render the significance of the death of a self-conscious being thereby greater than the significance of the death of a sentient but non self-conscious being.

Where does this leave us? Must we conclude, contra Singer, that the significance of the death of all sentient beings, both self-conscious and non-self-conscious, is the same? Not necessarily. Perhaps there is a different route to something like Singer's position. Imagine that you are dying and are offered the following two treatment options:[1] (i) procedure A will extend your life by two years and relieve any pain associated with the disease; (ii) procedure B will extend "your" life by twenty years, but will permanently sever all psychological connections between you now and whoever inhabits your body when "you" wake up after the procedure. Whoever that is will have a valuable twenty years at roughly the same level of momentary well-being as you would have for two years if you choose procedure A. I think it is intuitively obvious that it is in your self-interest to choose A over B. Whether you still exist after B is, I think, irrelevant. It makes no difference whether we say that you exist but your future self has no psychological connection to your present self, or that you don't exist, because the psychological connections are necessary for personal identity. Either way, it would be rational for you now to choose A (though, if you choose B, future "you" will be glad you did). From your perspective, B is no different from your death combined with the creation of a physically similar, but psychologically unconnected, adult. From the perspective of objective value, B is the better choice. But from the perspective of what it makes sense for *you* to care about when thinking purely selfishly, A is the better choice. Perhaps this shows that the psychological connections are necessary to personal identity, as opposed to the identity of the organism. If so, it shows that what is significant about our deaths to us, and the deaths of other creatures who maintain personal identity over time, is the effect of the death on the well-being of the person, as opposed to the well-being of the organism.

This has obvious implications for approaches to the morality of abortion that focus on the putative wrong done to the fetus by depriving it of a valuable future. For example, Don Marquis claims that the wrong done to an adult human victim in a standard case of killing is the wrong of being deprived of a valuable future (Marquis, 1989). He then argues that most abortions similarly deprive the fetus of a valuable future, and thus that they wrong the fetus in the same way that murder wrongs an adult. But if, as seems likely, a fetus does not have significant psychological connections with the later person, the significance of death to the fetus is more like the significance to you of the failure of procedure B as opposed to the failure of procedure A. If you opt for procedure A, you will hope for your own sake that it succeeds. But if you opt for procedure B, its success or failure doesn't affect you personally. Suppose that there is no procedure A. There is only B. Furthermore, B has a 50 percent chance of success, with the results described above, and a 50 percent chance of failure, resulting in physical death. When faced with procedure B, it might make sense to hope it succeeds, rather than fails. But it makes sense in the same way it makes sense to hope that your organs will be successfully transplanted into another's body after you die, resulting in continued life for that other person. To the extent that you care about others, you want your organs to help others live. But it will make no difference to *your* well-being whether your organs help others live after you die. (I know there are those who claim that the posthumous satisfaction or frustration of your desires can positively or negatively affect your well-being, even though you no longer exist at the time. I don't know what to say about this position, except that I find it inordinately silly.) Likewise, an abortion may have an effect on the total amount of well-being in the world, but it doesn't personally deprive the fetus of well-being in the same way that murder personally deprives an adult victim of well-being. If you hear of a friend contemplating abortion, it might make sense to hope they don't go through with it, but only in the same way it might make sense to hope that another friend forgets to use contraception, or that their contraception fails. Marquis's mistake (one of them at least) is to assume that he doesn't need to explore the question of the personhood of the fetus. The significance of the deprivation of a future to a victim clearly differs between persons and nonpersons.

The comparison with abortion has clear implications for the claim that the significance of death is different for different animals. Recall Singer's emphasis on a self-conscious animal's ability to conceive of itself as a continually existing being with a past and a future. Such animals, including most humans, are persons. Non-self-conscious animals, including some humans, are, as he puts it, "in a sense, 'impersonal.'" Now compare Tom Regan's well-known criterion for the possession of what he calls "inherent value." In Regan's seminal work *The Case for Animal Rights*, and elsewhere, he appeals to what he calls the "subject of a life" criterion for possessing inherent value. Here is his account of subjecthood:

To be the subject-of-a-life... involves more than merely being alive and more than merely being conscious... [I]ndividuals are subjects-of-a-life if they have beliefs and desires; perception, memory, and a sense of the future, including their own future; an emotional life together with feelings of pleasure and pain; preference- and welfare-interests; the ability to initiate action in pursuit of their desires and goals; a psychophysical identity over time; and an individual welfare in the sense that their experiential life fares well or ill for them. (Regan, 1983, p. 243)

It is in virtue of being subjects-of-a-life that, for example, all mammals aged one or more have inherent value, and have it equally. Inherent value is distinguished from intrinsic value, and cannot be weighed against it. All creatures who possess inherent value have rights, in particular the Kantian-style right not to be used as mere means for the benefit of others. I don't wish to delve into the serpent-windings of rights theory here. It is Regan's subject-of-a-life status that interests me. Sentience, in particular the ability to experience pleasure and pain, is both necessary and sufficient for moral considerability. Singer is clearly right about that. He also seems to be right that sentience is *not* sufficient for personhood. His account of what self-consciousness adds to sentience seems quite similar to Regan's account of being the subject-of-a-life. Consider both the criterion of sentience and the criterion of subjecthood. What does the latter add to the former? Most significantly, what is added is a form of cross-temporal psychophysical identity. Merely sentient creatures can suffer and enjoy, and such sufferings and enjoyments are clearly significant. Subjects-of-a-life also have lives that are important to them. It is possible for more to matter to them than merely avoiding pain and experiencing pleasure. Their *lives* matter to them.

A merely sentient animal's life contains well-being. Its enjoyments contribute positively and its sufferings negatively to its well-being. The death of such an animal may prevent future enjoyments or future suffering. It may thus make a negative or positive difference to the net amount of well-being in the world. In this sense, the death of any merely sentient animal has significance. But it's not clear that it has significance *to the animal*. Whether a merely sentient animal lives or dies has, *to the animal*, the same kind of significance as whether procedure B succeeds or fails has *to me*. If a merely sentient animal continues to live, there will be more of whatever well-being that animal experiences, but there won't be personally significant connections between the animal now and the animal later. Likewise, if procedure B succeeds, there will be more of whatever well-being that later person experiences, but there won't be any personally significant connections between me and that person.

Notice that the kinds of psychological connections involved in Regan's account of subjecthood or Singer's account of self-consciousness could well come in degrees. If so, it is implausible to suggest that there is a sharp cutoff point at which subjecthood, or personhood, is fully acquired. It seems far more likely that personhood is a matter of degree. Suppose we add to the choice between procedures A and B a third procedure, C. C will extend "your" life by five years but will also sever most, but not all, of the psychological connections between you now and the person who exists after the procedure. That person will have some vague memories, that are similar to some of yours. She will also share a few of your personality traits. I suggest that, with this third choice added to the original two, it is much less clear what it makes sense for you to choose if you are only concerned with your own well-being. If personhood really can come in degrees, that is exactly what we would expect. This topic clearly deserves a much fuller investigation than I can give it here.

My suggestion, then, is that Singer is at least partly right. The significance of death to a self-conscious animal is different from the significance of death to a merely sentient animal. The death of a merely sentient animal may prevent the existence of well-being, and is thus morally significant. The death of a self-conscious animal is, in addition, *personally* significant.

NOTE

1. I was first introduced to a version of this example by Michael Tooley, who has been using it for many years. A version of it also appears in McMahan, 2003.

REFERENCES

Bentham, Jeremy. 2010. *The Principles of Morals and Legislation*. Nabu Press.

Marquis, Don. 1989. "Why Abortion Is Immoral." *Journal of Philosophy* 86: 183–202.

McMahan, Jeff. 2003. *The Ethics of Killing: Problems at the Margins of Life*. New York: Oxford University Press.

Regan, Tom. 1983. *The Case for Animal Rights*. Berkeley: University of California Press.

Singer, Peter. 1979. *Practical Ethics*. New York: Cambridge University Press.

CHAPTER 21

CAPITAL
PUNISHMENT

TORBJÖRN TÄNNSJÖ

1. Introduction

In this chapter I will discuss the following question. Think of a state, such as one of the Scandinavian countries, with a relatively low incidence of murder: would it be a good idea to introduce into such a state a system of capital punishment in which murderers are sentenced to death and executed once their guilt has been established beyond reasonable doubt?

The reason to focus on a society with a low incidence of murder is that this steers us clear of a lot of distracting facts. If we find good arguments for the death penalty in such circumstances, we need not bother with the question of whether other kinds of preventive measures, such as the introduction of a welfare state, should be resorted to instead of resorting to the death penalty. It also avoids a discussion about the death penalty in war or in relation to crimes against humanity. This is, once again, to avoid problems that can turn our attention away from the more basic aspects of the question. Furthermore, I will not discuss whether the death penalty should be resorted to when it comes to other crimes than homicide. This, however, is more a matter of space than of principle.

The problem of whether we should have a death-penalty system as a reaction to murder in countries with a relatively low incidence of murder is a problem of applied ethics. The proper way of dealing with such problems is as follows: we should search for a sound moral principle, give an account of all the nonmoral facts that, in light of the principle, are relevant to the solution of the problem at hand, and then deduce an answer to our practical question.

(1) Moral principle
(2) Relevant nonmoral facts

----

(3) Practical conclusion

By applying this model, we get, not only an answer to the question of what to do, but also a moral explanation of why it should be done. We can also use the model to test moral theories. We can see what we think of the conclusion of the various different theories, and we can consider our reflected intuitions about the case at hand as evidence. We then make an inference to the best explanation of the content of our intuitions, and we may treat our intuitions as evidence for the theory. When we use this method, we enhance the coherence among our beliefs and approach what John Rawls has called a "reflective equilibrium."

I will not attempt to argue conclusively in defense of one principle in particular, but rather will try to see what happens if we apply three promising moral principles to the case at hand, namely, the death penalty. These principles are, first, a deontological idea of retributive justice, second, a strict moral rights theory based on the notion of self-ownership, and finally, utilitarianism.

It will become clear that, according to the most plausible version of retributive thinking, there are indeed good reasons to adopt a death-penalty system for homicide. From the point of view of the moral rights theory, we must conclude that there exists no principled defense of death penalty. Finally, when attempting to assess the matter from the point of view of utilitarianism, which is a theory that is extremely demanding of empirical information, it seems as though no categorical answer to the question can, as yet, be arrived at. However, it is interesting to speculate about what a utilitarian would say about the death penalty if it could be established that, by executing a few murderers each year, one could avoid a significant number of homicides. Such speculation will be undertaken.

Some may feel uncomfortable with this speculation, since it points in the direction that utilitarians should favor the death penalty, if the death penalty could be suspected to be superior to long prison terms, when it comes to deterrent and incapacitating effects. It might therefore be of interest to query whether there is no way of avoiding this conclusion, by resorting, not to any principled stance to the question at all, but with reference to commonsense intuitions about a difference between acts and omissions. I will discuss and reject that possibility.

2. Retributivism

According to the retributive and deontological idea I will first focus on, as a putative principle to apply to our practical problem at hand, there are certain kinds of actions such that instances of them are proscribed or prescribed, simpliciter. Any rational individual should be able to grasp this, it is claimed. A way of finding out what is proscribed and what is prescribed is to consult one's rational capacities. Immanuel Kant is, of course, the main proponent of such a view. And the Categorical Imperative in its first version gives us guidance, he claims, when we ponder what we ought, and what we ought not, to do (Kant, 1997, p. 31). Kant finds one prohibition and one prescription obvious. The prohibition is against killing: no one is allowed to kill an innocent rational being, not even himself, not even to save lives, and not even at request from the person who is killed. The prescription is with regard to punishment. When a person is guilty of murder, he or she should be executed.

Perhaps Kant is too strict in his prohibition on killing. Perhaps Kant is wrong when he claims that it is wrong to commit suicide or when he claims that it is wrong to kill when an individual asks you to do so (as in euthanasia). Still, I will take for granted in this section his idea that "murder," at least what we usually classify as "murder" is wrong. And I will ponder whether it is a congenial part of a deontological theory like this to accept that those who have committed murder should be executed.

Kant's defense of capital punishment is part of his general idea of crime and punishment. This is how he writes about this in his *Rechtslehre*:

> Judicial punishment can never be used merely as a means to promote some other good for the criminal himself or for civil society, but instead it must in all cases be imposed on him only on the ground that he has committed a crime. (1797, p. 138)

This is, literally speaking, compatible with an interpretation along lines suggested by John Rawls to the effect that, while the punitive institutions should be designed to have the best overall effects, the individual sentence should never be decided on consequentialist grounds (1955, pp. 3–32). The criminal should only receive a sentence because of what he has done. However, I do not think this is true to the spirit of Kant's thinking. His deontological point is that we ought to punish the criminal for his own sake, to see to it that justice is done. We treat him merely as a means, not as an end in himself, if our system of punishment is designed to obtain good consequences either for him or for society. We are not doing him (retributive) justice, unless we punish him for what he has done. To see this point more clearly, one can draw a parallel with distributive justice here. Just as we are not doing justice to women if we pay them lower wages than we pay men for the same job, we are not doing justice to the criminal, if we do not punish him.

Could we not argue with reference to the version of the categorical imperative in which it is urged that you should use humanity, whether in your own person or in the person of any other, always and at the same time, as an end, never merely as a means, to argue that if the culprit himself accepts a more lenient punishment than he deserves, and if this more lenient punishment has good consequences for society, we can give it to the culprit without treating him as a mere means, provided he himself assents to this aberration from justice?[1]

No, this won't do. Consent is neither a necessary nor a sufficient condition for not treating someone as a mere means to our purposes. There are concessions a person is not allowed to make. And if he still makes them, they are, from a moral point of view, null and void. And, of course, we need not seek the culprit's consent before we punish him.

This is, I think, how Kant himself would answer the objection. We are not morally permitted to accept less punishment than we deserve (in the same manner that we are not allowed to have our physician euthanize us). If yet we do, our acceptance should not be taken for an answer. And irrespective of how Kant is best understood, this is the idea I want to discuss here. Given that idea, what are we to say about capital punishment? This is Kant's own answer to the question:

> Even if a civil society were to dissolve itself by common agreement of all its members (for example, if the people inhabiting an island decided to separate and disperse themselves around the world), the last murderer remaining in prison must first be executed, so that everyone will duly receive what his actions are worth and so that the bloodguilt thereof will not be fixed on the people because they failed to insist on carrying out the punishment; for if they fail to do so, they may be regarded as accomplices in this public violation of legal justice. (1797, p. 140)

Is Kant right about this? Is this the conclusion a retributivist should draw about the death penalty? Should he or she, as a matter of principle, defend the death penalty?

There is a strong presumption in favor of Kant's answer. It is congenial with the retributive idea that the criminal should get what he deserves. This is an idea of proportionality in punishing. But it is not just any theory about proportionality, but a very special one.

Many thinkers have argued that there should be some proportionality between crime and punishment. Not least utilitarians, such as Beccaria and Bentham, have held that view.[2] But at least one of them, Beccaria, was an abolitionist with regard to the death penalty. How is this possible?

The explanation is that utilitarians typically adhere only to a weak idea of proportionality. They claim that ordinal rankings of both crimes (with regard to how serious they are) and punishments (with regard to severity) can be made, at least roughly. They then go on to argue that a system in which a more serious crime receives a less severe sanction than a less serious one, would be counterproductive from the point of view they are interested in, to wit, the point of view of deterrence. As Bentham puts it:

> Where two offences come in competition, the punishment for the greater offence must be sufficient to induce a man to prefer the less. (1970, p. 168)

Both Bentham and Beccaria see punishment as a necessary evil. If we can fulfill the purpose of punishment without having recourse to the most serious kinds of punishment, we should avoid them. They disagree on an empirical matter, not a basic moral one. Bentham believes we need capital punishment, Beccaria thinks differently. To state their case (and their difference), they need only a weak notion of proportionality. However, this weak notion of proportionality sits ill with the kind of retributive thinking Kant advocates. Here one should have a stronger notion of proportionality in mind, where comparisons are made also between the seriousness of a crime and the severity of the punishment. Here there should be a rough balance.

Of course, such a proportionate system of crime and punishment is difficult to work out in all details,[3] but when it comes to premeditated murder it should not be too difficult to see what, according to this view, the relevant kind of punishment should look like. Here something like the lex talionis is at work. The murderer has intentionally killed his victim. He has acted upon a maxim, according to which it is in order to kill. But then, out of respect for the murderer as an autonomous individual, he should himself be killed.

In the contemporary discussion about crime and punishment, there are many less straightforwardly retributive theories, in which the punishment is seen as an expression of a message to the criminal or the general public,[4] and so forth, where this conclusion may not follow as easily as it does from the standard theory. However, here the interest is precisely in the hard-core standard retributive view. As a matter of fact, I think this view is superior to the more watered-down modern versions, but this is not the place to try to show this. Here it should suffice that the standard version of the view is the one being discussed.

Now, is this a plausible view? This question cannot be answered in the present context. Let me just indicate my own main reason for rejecting it. The problem with the view is that it is not sensitive to certain facts. Even if it should turn out that the death penalty is inferior to some other kind of punishment for murder, we would have to stick to it, according to this view. But this strikes me as wrong. We cannot make the world a better place by inflicting unnecessary pain and death. But I suppose Kant would just retort that we are not here speaking of unnecessary pain and death, but of morally necessary pain and death.

One standard objection, with roots in retributive thinking, has been that, even if, in a just world, murder should be punished with death, in the real world, there is no way to construct a system of capital punishment that is not biased against certain discriminated-against groups in society. So even if the death penalty is the ideal, in a nonideal world we have to stick to long prison times as a reaction to murder. The focus on the bias against perpetrators from the minority group (and in favor of perpetrators from the majority group) is typical of retributivist thinking. Utilitarians have been more concerned with the fact that crimes against the members of the minority group are punished less severely than crimes against the members of the majority group. Here I focus on the former line of argument.[5]

This argument is not convincing. First of all, the most obvious reaction to this argument is to call for social reform. The discrimination should be abolished, not the capital punishment. And, while we wait for this to happen, we should try to see to it that legal practices, at least, are not discriminatory in this way. The main objective, then, is not to stop sentencing people from the discriminated group to death, but to do so as well with murderers from the privileged group. Strictly speaking, moreover, when people in the privileged group escape execution, this means that, according to retributive thinking, they are not given their due. They are not treated in the way they deserve to be treated. So they are the ones the system discriminates against![6]

A final worry may be that, even if all precautions are taken, it may sometimes happen that innocent people will be executed. Does this possibility mean that a retributivist must reject a system of capital punishment? I think not.

On one line of argument, the killing of an innocent is right, provided it is done in good faith. This may have been Martin Luther's view. In his Large Catechism he comments that the fifth commandment does not apply to government:

> God and government are not included in this commandment, nor is the power to kill, which they have, taken away. For God has delegated His authority to punish evil-doers to the government instead of parents, who aforetime (as we read in Moses) were required to bring their own children to judgment and sentence them to death. Therefore, what is here forbidden is forbidden to the individual in his relation to any one else, and not to the government. (1529a)

And in his Small Catechism he urges us with reference to Rom. 13:1–4 to trust the government, whatever its decisions:

> Let every soul be subject unto the higher powers. For the power which exists anywhere is ordained of God. Whosoever resisteth the power resisteth the ordinance of God; and they that resist shall receive to themselves damnation. For he beareth not the sword in vain; for he is the minister of God, a revenger to execute wrath upon him that doeth evil. (1529b).

At least one way of making sense of this would be to take Luther to hold that whatever the authorities do in good faith is right.[7] How else could he believe the authorities to be morally infallible?

If this were correct, the problem of innocent victims would be no problem at all. But it is not a plausible view. It is more plausible to say that, even if the execution of an innocent is not a blameworthy action—provided that it happens in good faith—it is still wrong. But the retributivist can still claim that the establishment of a system of capital punishment is still right, even if it means that now and then a wrong, but not blameworthy action will take place. If the only option is never to give the murderer what he deserves, it seems to be sound retributive policy to have a system of capital punishment in place. Even if we can foresee that some innocent people will be executed, this is not an intended effect of the system. If, when we construct the system, we have done what we can to strike a reasonable balance between the number of false positives (innocent people who are executed) and false negatives (murderers who escape the death penalty), then we have done the right thing.

But why bother with an old thinker like Kant, one may ask. Why not turn to modern and more up-to-date versions of retributivism, where capital punishment is not accepted? Well, even in our times we find retributivists arguing in defense of capital punishment, in a way similar to the one adopted by Kant. See for example Robert Nozick, who claims that he does "believe that some deserve to die, to be killed, in punishment for their actions,"[8] even though he holds no definite position with regard to an institution of capital punishment, and see J. Angelo Corlett, who argues that "capital punishment is a proportional punishment deserving of harmful wrongdoings that take the lives of others," and who defends also the institution as such (2009, p. 133). And more importantly, the crucial question is not whether a doctrine is new or old, but whether it is plausible. And it seems to me that the version of retributivism here discussed makes the most sense of the core deontological idea. It is congenial to it in its insistence on respect for the murderer, in its way of handling the notion of moral guilt, and in its handling of the very idea of lex talionis.

I suppose we must leave it at that and conclude that, if Kant and his present-day followers are right, then a system of capital punishment should be in place, even in states with a low murder rate, and irrespective of whether it would mean that less, the same, or even more homicides would result. We owe the system to the murderers themselves.

3. THE MORAL RIGHTS THEORY

Each individual subject or person has a right to, or owns, him- or herself. This is the hard- core of the moral rights tradition elaborated upon by John Locke in his *Two Treatises on Government* and most famously defended in our time by Robert Nozick in his *Anarchy, State, and Utopia*. But the tradition does not stop at self-ownership. According to this (libertarian) moral rights tradition, we can also acquire rights to individual property. The right way to acquire property is to be the first to get hold of it or to receive or purchase it from someone who already owns it. There is also a right to restitution. If something that belongs to you has been taken away from you, your right to it has been violated, and you have a right to take it back. Furthermore, you have a right to defend what you own. And since you own yourself, this includes a right to self-defense. No one is allowed to kill you, at least not unless you have hired him to do so or have consented to it for one reason or the other. So you are allowed violently, if necessary, to resist any attempt at your life.

There are many problems with this theory; here are some of them: what does it mean to be a subject or a person who can have moral rights? How, more exactly, can we, even assuming that we own ourselves, acquire property in the first place? Locke has a famous proviso, stating the conditions under which this is possible. In modern times, Robert Nozick has his own (narrow) interpretation of this proviso. I will glance over all these problems, since they are irrelevant in the present context. Here only the hard-core of the theory matters: the idea of self-ownership. We can focus on the killing of individuals who obviously satisfy the requirement for being a person and on perpetrators who, equally, are clear examples of moral subjects (mentally sound adult human beings).

According to the moral rights theory, what punishment would be appropriate for a murderer? What kind of theory of punishment in general is dictated by the moral rights theory? The answers to these questions do not seem to depend on what exact version of the theory we opt for. Irrespective of this, we can raise and answer these questions. And here are the answers to them.

While the deontological theory, as conceived of here, focuses exclusively on the criminal in order to give him the punishment he deserves, the moral rights theory here described focuses exclusively on the victim. This aspect of the theory of moral rights is rarely discussed, and many of its adherents, including both Locke and Nozick (as we have seen), tend to combine it with a deontological theory of retributive justice. However, the theory of moral rights should also be taken seriously as such as a theory about crime and punishment. If taken seriously, and if rid of all retributive ideas, it would say something like the following.

The victim has a right to what he or she has been deprived of, or else is due fair compensation. And the compensation should include not only what has been removed, but also the costs of regaining it. This is easy to understand when applied to crimes such as theft, but what are the adherents of the moral rights theory to say of murder? Is it possible for murderers to compensate their victims?

This is in one obvious way impossible. And it means that if we want to abide by a strict version of the moral rights theory, then we must accept that there is no room for the punishment of murder. It is certainly true that when we want to guard ourselves against murder, we may resort to all kinds of means, according to the theory. In order to protect my life, I may kill the person who attacks me. However, if I fail, and he kills me, then there is no further room for any just action against the murderer. As a matter of fact, this is true of the thief as well. Suppose he cannot compensate his victim. This does not mean that we have a right to put him in prison. Strictly speaking, there is no room for punishment in the moral rights tradition. If he can pay me, on the other hand, he has to do so. And if he tries to hide away what he has stolen from me, we may keep him in prison until he surrenders and gives it back to me.

Could we not say that our murderer should pay compensation to our relatives? No, this argument sits ill with the moral rights theory. Our relatives do not possess us. The murderer has not deprived them of any property of theirs.

Could we say that the murderer, by committing his crime, has alienated his own right to life? That may be a way of finding a version of the theory compatible with capital punishment.[9] It does not strike me as plausible, however. Alienation of particular rights is something we can do on a voluntary basis, according to the standard version of the theory. It is not something that can just happen to us like this. Even a murderer is a person and hence possesses the rights of a person, including the right to life.

We noted that deontological retributivism is not interested in crime prevention. The punishment is there for the sake of the perpetrator, not for the sake of society. If the punishment has a preventive effect, then this is a second, and not sought for, effect. This explains why, sometimes, retributivists want less-harsh punishments than utilitarians. In a similar vein, the theory of moral rights, if taken seriously, is not interested primarily in crime prevention through punishment. According to the moral rights view, the state ought not to use the criminal as a means of deterring future crime. In this respect, it is similar to deontological ethics. Yet, in another respect it is very different from the deontological view. While the theory of moral rights makes plenty of room for police, locks, and security vaults; for violent resistance whenever someone tries to thwart the rights of someone else; and, if necessary, for restitution, it makes no room whatever for what we can genuinely call "punishment."

If this analysis is correct, then the theory of moral rights must reject, for principled reasons, capital punishment. For even if we want very much to do so, there is no way for us to compensate a victim of murder. If the murderer poses an immediate threat to others, we may detain him in self-defense, but there is no room for punishment, according to this tradition. There is no way we can argue that he should be executed because he deserves to die. Still, there is a way for an adherent of the theory who wants to defend a system of capital punishment to do so. Capital punishment can be defended if it is voluntary! We can imagine a society in which each member has become a member by making a free and voluntary decision to do so. Such a society can have any legal and other practices it sees fit. It can execute murderers; it can harvest organs for transplant purposes via a lottery, where those who draw the "winning" ticket must give up their vital organs to those who need them, and so forth.

Would it be a good idea for freely consenting libertarians, to establish a community where murder is punished with death? Paradoxically enough, this question leads us to the next section. For it seems as though it would be a good idea to do so if, and only if, capital punishment has a superior deterrent effect. And this question is at the heart of the utilitarian query about the death penalty.

4. Utilitarianism

Utilitarianism is the view that we ought to maximize the sum-total of well-being in the universe. What does that mean? As with deontology and moral rights theories, I will not go into detail. Instead I will take as my point of departure a classical hedonistic version of the utilitarian doctrine, according to which subjective, felt well-being (happiness) is what matters. Only when there are reasons to discuss other versions of utilitarianism (once) will I do so.

According to utilitarianism there are no conventional types of action, such as breaking promises, stealing, or lying, that are wrong as such. This is true also of murder. An act of murder is right, if and only if it maximizes the sum-total of well-being in the universe. This is probably true of some murders. Think of the killing of a murderer who is at large, who lives a poor life himself, and who is about to commit further violent crimes when he gets killed. Moreover, it is probably true of many of us that we should sometimes have committed a murder we did in fact not commit. I think in particular of situations where it was possible for us to kill a very nasty person and get away with it! This does not mean that we should all kill but, given that most people don't, each of us faces this kind of heavy utilitarian obligation.

Does all this mean that utilitarianism is complacent with regard to murder? No, it does not. Even if some murders are morally right actions, all acts of murder should be criminalized, according to utilitarianism. And the reason is that only if murder is made illegal will it be possible for us to be and feel secure in society. We do not want to trust the legal system to try to find out whether a particular act of murder produced good or bad consequences. We want a more general and reliable solution to the problem. If a murder is committed, and this is found out, there should exist a strict legal rule to the effect that the murderer should be punished, irrespective of whether his action was, morally speaking, right or wrong. Contrary to what is sometimes said, this is a strong defense of making murder illegal. It is strong because security, and the sense of it, is a public good. We all stand to gain from such a legal system. It is also a subtle view, as compared to retributivism, in that it allows for the intuition that some murders are indeed morally right.

Since the utilitarian is interested in security, and our sense of it, it is clear that, to a utilitarian, it is of crucial importance to know whether capital punishment has a deterrent effect on murder. If it has, it may mean not only that some wrong actions (murders) are avoided, but also that we can all feel more secure in society. There will be less need to fear that we ourselves, or people for whom we care, such as our children, shall become victims of murder—or murderers.

Does the extensive use of capital punishment for murder mean fewer homicides and violent crime in general? Many thinkers have found this self-evident. First of all, they have thought, capital punishment is superior to long terms in prison with regard to its deterrent effect. This is partly due to irrationality among us human beings. We fear death more than anything else. James Fitzjames Stephen has made the point about deterrence in the following words:

> No other punishment deters men so effectually from committing crimes as the punishment of death. This is one of those propositions which it is difficult to prove simply because they are in themselves more obvious than any proof can make them…Was there ever yet a criminal who, when sentenced to death and

brought out to die, would refuse the offer of a commutation of his sentence for the severest secondary punishment? Surely not.[10]

Furthermore, when a murderer is executed, he or she is definitely incapacitated. Finally, the execution of a murderer sends a clear message to society. Murder is not tolerated. How could any other sanction compete successfully with this?

And if it is true that the use of capital punishment means fewer homicides, there exists a strong utilitarian presumption in its favor. How could a utilitarian, convinced of the deterrent effect of capital punishment, argue against such a system?

One idea would be to argue that capital punishment is cruel and unusual. It inflicts more harm than it avoids. The idea must be then, that the murderer suffers (much) more than his victims, when he is killed. This seems to be a nonstarter, however. The execution of the murderer can be painless and similar to euthanasia. It then means that the murderer gets a better death than most of us. Is the very fact that you will be killed by others, at a certain moment, terrible as such? No, it seems to me. Death may be unwelcome as such, but the fact that it takes place at a certain time, which you know of before it happens, and painlessly, should rather be a source of comfort than despair. It makes room for preparation, a review of your life, and a closing of relationships. Some people get the message from their doctor that they will soon die. It means that they have the same possibility to finalise their lives. This is usually seen as something positive. Some people think, when the doctor tells them that their illness is fatal and that an untimely death is what awaits them, 'Why did this happen to me?" The murderer has an advantage over them. He knows the answer to this question.

Jonathan Glover thinks differently about this. He assumes that most people would "...rather die suddenly than linger for weeks or months knowing we were fatally ill..." and Woody Allen is said to have claimed something similar: "I have no objection to dying, if only I need not be present when it happens." This may be true of many people. However, it strikes me as an egoistic view. Even if, for your own sake, you want to leave without saying good-bye, this is not nice to those who are close to you.

But, the fact that your death is known beforehand to you, is not the only thing that is bad with an execution, according to Glover:

> He has the additional horror of knowing exactly when he will die, and of knowing that his death will be in a ritualized killing by other people, symbolizing his ultimate rejection by the members of his community. The whole of his life may seem to have a different and horrible meaning when he sees it leading up to this end. (1977, p. 232)

What about the claim that the execution is "...symbolizing his ultimate rejection by the members of his community..."? Well, if he believes in a retributivist theory of crime and punishment, as many people seem to do, there is no ground for this claim. As a matter of fact, his execution can on that theory, as we have seen, be understood as an act of respect. He is given what he deserves. What if he believes in the theory of rights? Well, then he has himself agreed to what is about to happen to him. This is so in a real sense in the US, where he could have chosen to murder in a state not practicing the death penalty. Finally, if he is a utilitarian he can comfort himself with the thought that he doesn't die in vain. His death is lifesaving. It will deter several murders.

There is still a difference between ordinary death and execution. In the execution we know that death is not necessary. It should not happen, if the authorities changed their mind. Does this render death from execution worse than "ordinary" death? Perhaps it does, perhaps it does for some people. And yet, in this execution is similar, not different from, death caused by a murderer when he murders. He too could change his mind.

Perhaps this argument is too myopic. Utilitarians count what we could call the entertainment value of practices. For example, according to hedonistic utilitarianism, it can be right to arrange public killings of people in order to entertain a public (as happened with the Roman Gladiator Games). If only the public is large enough, and pleased enough, the sacrifice of the victims on the arena may be worth its hedonic price. This has sometimes been taken as a reductio of hedonistic utilitarianism, but some of its adherents, the present writer included, are prepared to bite this bullet (I would not like to be the victim, of course, but I think it would lack a sound rationale if I were to complain). Could this kind of argument be turned upside down when applied to capital punishment? Could we argue that, in a civilised society, the knowledge that some people get executed, is so painful to the public at large, that, in order to spare them their pain, we should allow a certain number of murders, that could have been avoided, to take place?

Since I am prepared to bite the bullet in the first case, I see this as a promising utilitarian argument against the death penalty, even if it deters from murder. However, in both cases, I have my doubts about the calculus. What happens to the victims (on the arena, or to those innocent people who get murdered when we abstain from capital punishment) is indeed terrible, and the joy or agony respectively among the public, is ephemeral. I doubt that the argument has the bite it is supposed to have.

Moreover, those who are not prepared to rely on it in the first instance (the Gladiator Games) should not rely on in the second case (capital punishment). If they object to hedonism and claim that entertainment value should be discounted, they should discount it consistently. Or, they may argue, perhaps, that there is an important difference. While sadistic pleasure is bad, sympathetic suffering is a good thing. This would certainly tip the balance in the Gladiator case. But then the sympathetic suffering, when a murderer is executed, would count in favor of the system of capital punishment! What happened to the person executed would be bad for him, no doubt, but there is compensation for this in the fact that fewer people are killed. And it is a comforting fact that people suffer with him, when he dies.

If all this is correct, it seems as though a utilitarian who is convinced that the use of the death penalty deters from murder must be in favor of the death penalty. So we should ponder the question of whether it does indeed deter from murder.

This is not the place to settle this issue, of course. But we should not accept views such as the one put forward by James Fitzjames Stephen at face value. It is not self-evident that the death penalty is superior to long terms in prison if we want to obviate homicides. It has sometimes been claimed that the use of the death penalty has a brutalising effect on criminals. In order to avoid the death penalty, a murderer is prepared to resort to further murder. However, even long terms in prison may have a brutalising effect on murderers. After all, once you have received a sentence for life in prison, you are invulnerable. You may kill as you see fit, and there is no way of sentencing you to any stricter punishment, if the death penalty is not available.

It has been claimed that at least murderers who are irrational when they commit their crimes, murderers who kill in the heat of some emotion, will not be deterred by the threat of capital punishment. But this claim has been questioned.[11] Furthermore, even if a criminal is rational, it is not only the severity of the punishment he has to take into account when contemplating whether to kill or not, but also how likely it is that he will be caught, found guilty and executed. If the death penalty is practiced, it is likely that fewer false positives are accepted, and hence he may be tempted to take the chance and kill. On the other hand, it has also been pointed out that, if the criminal's rationality is "bounded," he may well misinterpret some very salient executions as a sign of the risk of getting executed being very high.

This is not the place to try to settle these empirical questions. In the final analysis, they should be solved through empirical studies, and not through speculation. There is indeed some recent US statistics indicating the death penalty may be effective. A review of these findings by Cass R. Sunstein and Adrian Vermeule points to results such that one execution deters from something between 5 and 18 murders (2006, pp. 703–750). These findings are questioned, of course. Not all arguments brought forward against them are convincing, however, as is clearly shown by Sunstein and Vermeule. It has sometimes been claimed that the statistical material does not show a deterrent effect in all cases. As a matter of fact, the deterrent effect is visible only in a few (six) states. This is not a good argument against the reliability of these studies, however. For, as it has often been pointed out, and as the authors note, the correct interpretation of this finding may be that only if there are enough executions, will the system work. In those states where the deterrent effect has been said to surface, there are indeed enough executions (at least nine, as a matter of fact). So what we may have to reckon with here may be a kind of threshold effect. Interestingly enough, it seems, according to the authors, as though the capital punishment, when it does deter, deters less rational people, killing in the heat of some emotion, alike with more rational ones.

Since I have no expertise in this area it is impossible for me to assess these recent and highly controversial studies, so I will abstain from any attempt to do so. It should be noted, however, that even if they would turn out to be reliable when it comes to the situation in those states where the system seems to work, the reason that it works need not be only that here the number of executions is above a certain threshold. It may also be a result of the high incidence of murder in these states. So even if the death penalty has a deterrent effect when murder is a usual way of solving personal conflicts, it need not work in a state, where murder seldom happens. If this is so, the utilitarian lesson to be drawn from the US experience is rather to introduce a welfare state, if that is a way of lowering the incidence of murder, than to resort to capital punishment. At least the good (capital punishment) should not be allowed to stand in way of the best (the introduction of a welfare state).

From this it does not follow that capital punishment would not have any deterrent effect in a state with low incidence of murder, of course. We know next to nothing about this. So, what conclusion should the utilitarian draw from this? One might despair and conclude that the model cannot be applied. We ought to introduce capital punishment in such states if it maximises the sum-total of happiness, but since we do know whether it does, we cannot reach any principled conclusion.

It is tempting to argue along the following lines, however. If we do not know if the introduction of the death penalty in a state with a low incidence of murder would mean fewer murders, we should try to find out. A problem with utilitarianism is that it is so demanding of factual information that we can never know for sure whether an act is right or wrong. Some have suggested that, in order to have criterion of rightness that can guide our actions, we should rather think therefore that what makes an action right is the fact that it maximises expected, rather than actual happiness.[12]

I have argued repeatedly that a probabilistic criterion is at variance with our moral phenomenology. It is strange with a criterion, which allows us to know, ever, that we have performed the right action.[13]Instead we should distinguish between the criterion of right action (cast in actualist, nonprobabilistic terms) and a method of decision-making, which has as at least as one important tenet that one should attempt to maximise expected rather than actual happiness.[14] And one should perhaps add that, if we have no knowledge of probabilities, we had better adhere to some kind of precautionary principle.

Where does this lead us with regard to the death penalty? It would not be too far-fetched to argue that, to err on the safe side, we should introduce the death penalty at least in some states with a low incidence of murder, partly as a matter of erring on the safe side given the present state of knowledge, but also, and more importantly, in order to gain the relevant knowledge. We should experiment with the death penalty.

Would anything like that be possible? Would such a suggestion gain public support? I have arranged with surveys where Swedes, Germans, and Norwegians have stated their views on capital punishment. 42 percent of the Swedes, 43 percent of the Germans, but only 26 percent of the Norwegians say that they would be in favor of capital punishment, if its introduction meant fewer murders. If we should experiment at all, it might be a good idea to make the experiment in a small country and in a country where the public opinion is not too negative to the idea. So perhaps one should make the experiment in Sweden.

5. ACTS AND OMISSIONS—A COMMON SENSE LINE OF ARGUMENT

We have seen that retributivists, if they stick to the most plausible version of their favored doctrine, should be in favor of the death penalty. Moral rights theorists should oppose the death penalty in principle, but if they want the practice to be adopted in a free association of consenting people, they may well accept it. And I suppose their decision for or against adopting it would depend on utilitarian calculation. Utilitarians finally have a hard time defending any other conclusion than the one that, at least for experimental reasons, we should try to find out whether capital punishment, with executions above a threshold, where the practice becomes salient to presumptive murderers, would deter from murder even in states with a low incidence of murder. We here seem to face an overlapping consensus. So one may wonder how it comes that so many people (a majority) in states, where the death penalty has been abolished, object to it. How do these people think about the problem?

A conjecture made by Cass R. Sunstein and Adrian Vermeule is that they rely on a common sense moral belief that there exists an important distinction between acts and omissions (2006). This allows them to say that, even if the state could save lives by executing a few murderers, the state is not compelled to do so. When it does not resort to the death penalty, this means that innocent people will get killed, but they are not killed by the state. We here face a situation very like the one each affluent member of a developed society faces with regard to global poverty. We do not aid people who die in distant poor countries, at least we do not make enough efforts to do so, but this is morally permissible, according to this common sense view since, by not aiding these people, even though we could easily do it, we do not actively kill them, we merely allow them to die.

Sunstein and Vermeule doubt that the acts and omission doctrine makes any sense when applied to states. They claim that "…there is no way to speak or think coherently about government "actions" as opposed to government "omissions," because government cannot help but act, in some way or another, when choosing how individuals are to be regulated" (2006, p. 720). They are wrong about this. It is true that no concrete and particular action is either an act or an omission as such, and this is true also of state actions, of course, but, given a relevant action type, we can often classify the particular action as active or passive with regard to this type. This is true in particular when it comes to killing (or allowing death to come). Our linguistic intuitions are here clear enough, at least for the present purposes, to settle such issues. We can tell if someone has killed another individual or just allowed his death to come.[15] And it is possible not only for an individual, but also for a state, either to kill actively or just to allow death to come.

The distinction is clear in the individual case. Typically the murderer kills actively.[16] I allow death to come if I do not stop him from killing, even if I could easily do so. The same distinction makes sense when it comes to the state (the government). It can kill actively (as it is done in executions) or just allow death to come (as is done when it does not practice capital punishment hence allowing a certain number for murders to happen, murders that would have been obviated by the use of the death penalty). And yet, the argument is not sound as it stands. A state has special responsibilities with regard to its citizens—something also noted by Sunstein and Vermeule. It would be objectionable if the government were to claim that it did not bother to establish safe traffic conditions since, by not doing so, it does not kill any one, it only allows that people get killed in traffic accidents.

Could one then, instead, argue in the following manner? To the extent that the person who is executed really is guilty, then it is no problem that he or she is executed. But no matter how cautious we are, if we practice a system of capital punishment, it is highly likely that, some time, an innocent person will get killed. And, given that the death penalty is irreversible, this is not morally acceptable.

The observation that this is likely to happen is of course correct. But note that if we do not practice a system with capital punishment, we will instead send the putative murderer to a long term in prison. In case she is innocent, it may well happen that this will never be found out. This means that, in this case, even the prison sentence was irreversible. We can safely conclude that it was, once the person sentenced to life in prison has deceased.

Note furthermore that, if we practice capital punishment, this may well lead to more severe requirements on the evidence for the guilt of the person sentenced for murder and hence to a system with fewer "false positives." If we abolish capital punishment, or do not adopt it, we are likely to tolerate more false positives. We may even be forced to do so, if we want to retain enough deterrent effects of the practice. So perhaps we are allowed to conclude that capital punishment has the property of leading more seldom to the situations where innocent people are convicted of murder, while it still is superior with regard to deterrence of future violent crimes. If this is so capital punishment seems again to have gained the upper hand in the discussion.

It may be objected, of course, that, if you are innocent of the crime for which you have been convicted, it is still worse for you to be executed than kept for life in prison. Here we should bear in mind, however, an observation made by J.S. Mill to the effect that this might be a misperception.[17] Not only may the time you spend in prison be filled with nasty experiences, the very fact that you know that you are innocent will add insult to injury. When the innocent person is executed, he is spared both of further nasty experiences and resentment. So the balance may well tip in the direction of capital punishment, even when it comes to the punishment of innocents.

6. CONCLUSION

My gut feeling tells me that there is something inherently wrong with the death penalty. It is difficult to find a sound rationale behind this gut feeling, however. At least this seems to be the lesson to draw from the argument here put forward.

Let me just add one more consideration, which renders even more difficult the resistance to capital punishment. When people get executed, society can also harvest their organs for transplant purposes. This conclusion seems inescapable, if the matter is assessed from a utilitarian point of view. Perhaps a retributivist would argue, that this means that the murderer doesn't really get what he deserves. No part of him should survive the execution. No such argument is available to the utilitarian, however. And I suppose most retributivists would accept such a practice too. After all, when the organs are used, the executed person is already gone.

It may be objected that the harvesting of the organs would implicate medicine in the criminal system in a way we should avoid. I have much sympathy for this argument, and I am prepared to accept it, at least when it comes to a situation where the organs are taken without consent from the person to be executed. However, would the person to be executed him- or herself give consent to donation, I think this last will should be respected. And now the operating physician can operate, not in order to kill the patient (this is merely a side-effect of what he does when he takes out the organs) but in order to respond properly to the wish from the patient, who should anyway die.

Would this tempt us to keep the death penalty even if it was found out that it did not deter from murder and other violent crimes? I find that far-fetched. But if it did indeed deter from murder, it would not only spare some lives of otherwise innocent victims of murder, it would not only spare some people from becoming murderers, it would also save lives of patients in vital need of organs.

So the case for at least trying out a system of capital punishment in states with a low incidence of murder seems to be stronger than many, including the present author, had at first though.

Let me just add one last caveat. In this chapter I have adopted the traditional comparison between capital punishment and long terms in prison. Are there no other alternatives? One idea, for those who feel uncomfortable with the idea that we should introduce capital punishment in welfare states, at least to see if it works, would be to resort to a more literal reading of "capital" punishment. After all, it is possible to take the head off a person, at least partly, without killing him. Would this be a good idea? Should perhaps the convict be offered a choice between the death penalty, and instead being incapacitated through some up to date form of lobotomy? If the lobotomy was performed at the prisoner's request, as a means to saving his life, it might prove possible also for physicians who want to adhere to standard principles of medical ethics to assist. Would such "soft" decapitation be a decent alternative to the death penalty? Would it be deterrent enough? I leave this question for some other occasion.

NOTES

1. I owe this objection to an anonymous reviewer of this chapter.
2. Bentham's view on punishment is developed in many places but it exists already in its basic form in his 1970, and for Becceria, see Cesare Beccaria Bonesara, 1764.

3. See Jesper Ryberg, 2005.
4. See for example Hampton, 1992.
5. For an early distinction between these two lines of argument, and a discussion of each of them, see Kennedy, 1988.
6. I owe this observation to Jens Johansson.
7. There exists another, Hobbsian, way of understanding Luther, however. Perhaps he does not think that the actions the government takes are always right (just because they are ordained by God); he only wants us to believe that this is the case, and hence obey, in order to keep social peace.
8. See his 1981, p. 377.
9. I owe this comment to Björn Eriksson.
10. I have the quotation from Glover, 1977. Glover gives as the source of the quotation *Fraser's Magazine*, 1864.
11. See Sunstein and Vermeule, 2006, p. 712 for references.
12. J. J. C. Smart oscilates between these two ideas in his seminal contribution to Smart and Williams, 1973.
13. Most recently in my 2010.
14. The first clear suggestion of this idea was in Bales, 1982. It is debatable, but beyond the scope of this paper to discuss, whether this move really meets the argument that utilitarianism cannot guide our choices. For a critique see Feldman, 2006.
15. I discuss this in my 2004.
16. In some rare cases in the United States people have been convicted of murder by omission. I owe this observation to an anonymous reviewer of this chapter.
17. In his famous speech before the British Parliament on April 21, 1868.

REFERENCES

Bales, R. Eugene. 1982. "Act Utilitarianism: Account of Right-Making Characteristics or Decision-Making Procedure?" *American Philosophical Quarterly* 8: 257–265.

Beccaria Bonesara, Cesare. 1764. Dei delitti e delle pene. Leghorn: false imprint Haarlem. First English edition, *An Essay on Crimes and Punishments*, translated from the French, London, 1767.

Bentham, Jeremy. 1970. *An Introduction to the Principles of Morals and Legislation*, ed. J. H. Burns and H. L. A. Hart. London: Methuen.

Corlett, Angelo, J. 2009. *Responsibility and Punishment*. Dordrecht: Springer.

Feldman, Fred. 2006. "Actual Utility, the Objection from Impracticality, and the Move from Expected Utility." *Philosophical Studies* 101: 49–79.

Glover, Jonathan (1977). *Causing Death and Saving Lives*. London: Penguin.

Hampton, Jean. 1992. "An Expressive Theory of Retribution." In *Retributivism and Its Critics*, W. Cragg, ed., pp. 1–25. Stuttgart: Fritz Steiner Verlag.

Kant, Immanuel. 1797. *Metaphysical Elements of Justice*. Reprinted by Hackett, 1999.

Kant, Immanuel. 1997. *Groundwork of the Metaphysics of Morals*. Mary Gregor, ed. Cambridge: Cambridge University Press.

Kennedy, Randall L. 1988. "*McCleskey v. Kemp:* Race, Capital Punishment, and the Supreme Court." *Harvard Law Review* 101: 1388–1443.

Luther, Martin. 1529a. "Large Catechism." In *The Book of Concord*. http://bookofconcord.org/lc-3-tencommandments.php, accessed July 4, 2010.

Luther, Martin. 1529b. "Small Catechism." In *The Book of Concord*. http://
    bookofconcord.org/smallcatechism.php, accessed July 4, 2010.
Mill, John Stuart. 1868. "Use of the Death Penalty." http://www.mnstate.edu/gracyk/
    courses/web%20publishing/Mill_supports_death_penalty.htm. Accessed July 4,
    2010.
Nozick, Robert. 1981. *Philosophical Explanations*. Cambridge, MA: Belknap.
Rawls, John. 1955. "Two Concepts of Rules." *Philosophical Review* 64: 3–32.
Ryberg, Jesper. 2005. *The Ethics of Proportionate Punishment: A Critical
    Investigation*. Dordrecht: Kluwer.
Smart, J. J. C., and Bernard Williams. 1973. *Utilitarianism: For and Against*.
    Cambridge: Cambridge University Press.
Sunstein, Cass R., and Adrian Vermeule. 2006. "Is Capital Punishment Morally
    Required? Acts, Omissions, and Life-Life Tradeoffs." *Stanford Law Review* 58 (3):
    703.
Tännsjö, Torbjörn, ed. 2004. *Terminal Sedation. Euthanasia in Disguise?* Dordrecht:
    Kluwer.
Tännsjö, Torbjörn, ed. 2010. *From Reasons to Norms. On the Basic Question in Ethics*.
    Dordrecht: Springer.

INDEX

....